Frommer's®

Vermont, New Hampshire & Maine

7th Edition

by Paul Karr

WILEY
Wiley Publishing, Inc.

Published by:

WILEY PUBLISHING, INC.

111 River St.
Hoboken, NJ 07030-5774

ISBN 978-0-470-60224-9 (paper); ISBN 978-0-470-88098-2 (ebk)

Editor: Jennifer Moore, with Kathleen Warnock
Production Editor: Katie Robinson
Cartographer: Andrew Dolan
Photo Editor: Richard Fox,
Production by Wiley Indianapolis Composition Services
Front cover photo: Grafton County, New Hampshire: Flume Covered Bridge in Franconia Notch State Park ©John and Lisa Merrill / Corbis
Back cover photo: Man kayaking in front of Pemaquid Point light house, Maine ©David McLain / Aurora / Getty Images

For information on our other products and services or to obtain technical support, please contact our Customer Care Department within the U.S. at 877/762-2974, outside the U.S. at 317/572-3993 or fax 317/572-4002.

Wiley also publishes its books in a variety of electronic formats. Some content that appears in print may not be available in electronic formats.

Manufactured in the United States of America

5 4 3 2

CONTENTS

3 PLANNING YOUR TRIP TO NORTHERN NEW ENGLAND 39

4 SUGGESTED NORTHERN NEW ENGLAND ITINERARIES 69

5 SOUTHERN & CENTRAL VERMONT 78

6 NORTHERN VERMONT 149

7 SOUTHERN & CENTRAL NEW HAMPSHIRE 199

8 THE WHITE MOUNTAINS & NORTHERN NEW HAMPSHIRE 242

9 COASTAL MAINE 275

10 NORTHERN & WESTERN MAINE 363

11 FAST FACTS, TOLL-FREE NUMBERS & WEBSITES 388

INDEX 395

LIST OF MAPS

HOW TO CONTACT US

In researching this book, we discovered many wonderful places—hotels, restaurants, shops, and more. We're sure you'll find others. Please tell us about them, so we can share the information with your fellow travelers in upcoming editions. If you were disappointed with a recommendation, we'd love to know that, too. Please write to:

Frommer's Vermont, New Hampshire & Maine, 7th Edition
Wiley Publishing, Inc. • 111 River St. • Hoboken, NJ 07030-5774

AN ADDITIONAL NOTE

Please be advised that travel information is subject to change at any time—and this is especially true of prices. We therefore suggest that you write or call ahead for confirmation when making your travel plans. The authors, editors, and publisher cannot be held responsible for the experiences of readers while traveling. Your safety is important to us, however, so we encourage you to stay alert and be aware of your surroundings. Keep a close eye on cameras, purses, and wallets, all favorite targets of thieves and pickpockets.

ABOUT THE AUTHOR

Paul Karr is an award-winning writer and editor and avid traveler. In addition to covering New England, he is the author of *Frommer's Nova Scotia, New Brunswick & Prince Edward Island; Frommer's Maine Coast;* and *Vancouver & Victoria For Dummies,* as well as a co-author of *Frommer's New England* and *Frommer's Canada.* He has also edited Frommer's guides to The Bahamas, Jamaica, London, Paris, San Antonio, and San Francisco; edited and updated *Irreverent Guides* to Rome, Vancouver, and Seattle; and written for *The New York Times, Sierra, Sports Illustrated* and *Insight Guides* to Austria, Montreal, Switzerland, and Vienna, among other places. He divides him between New York, New England, and Asia.

FROMMER'S STAR RATINGS, ICONS & ABBREVIATIONS

Every hotel, restaurant, and attraction listing in this guide has been ranked for quality, value, service, amenities, and special features using a **star-rating system.** In country, state, and regional guides, we also rate towns and regions to help you narrow down your choices and budget your time accordingly. Hotels and restaurants are rated on a scale of zero (recommended) to three stars (exceptional). Attractions, shopping, nightlife, towns, and regions are rated according to the following scale: zero stars (recommended), one star (highly recommended), two stars (very highly recommended), and three stars (must-see).

In addition to the star-rating system, we also use **seven feature icons** that point you to the great deals, in-the-know advice, and unique experiences that separate travelers from tourists. Throughout the book, look for:

Finds	Special finds—those places only insiders know about
Fun Facts	Fun facts—details that make travelers more informed and their trips more fun
Kids	Best bets for kids, and advice for the whole family
Moments	Special moments—those experiences that memories are made of
Overrated	Places or experiences not worth your time or money
Tips	Insider tips—great ways to save time and money
Value	Great values—where to get the best deals

The following **abbreviations** are used for credit cards:

AE American Express **DISC** Discover **V** Visa
DC Diners Club **MC** MasterCard

TRAVEL RESOURCES AT FROMMERS.COM

Frommer's travel resources don't end with this guide. Frommer's website, **www.frommers.com**, has travel information on more than 4,000 destinations. We update features regularly, giving you access to the most current trip-planning information and the best airfare, lodging, and car-rental bargains. You can also listen to podcasts, connect with other Frommers.com members through our active-reader forums, share your travel photos, read blogs from guidebook editors and fellow travelers, and much more.

1

The Best of Vermont, New Hampshire & Maine

One of the greatest challenges of planning a vacation in northern New England is narrowing down the options. Where to start? Here's an entirely biased list of top destinations, the places I enjoy returning to time and again. Over years of traveling through the region, I've discovered these places to be worth more than just a quick stop; they're worth a major detour.

1 THE 7 WONDERS OF NORTHERN NEW ENGLAND

- **The Appalachian Trail:** This 2,100-mile trail from Georgia to Maine has some of the most spectacular scenery in northern New England. The trail enters the region in southwest Vermont, winding through the southern Green Mountains before angling toward the White Mountains of New Hampshire. From here, it passes by remote Maine lakes and through hilly timberlands before finishing up on the summit of Mount Katahdin. See chapters 5, 8, and 10.
- **Lake Champlain** (Vermont): "New England's West Coast" is lapped by the waves of Lake Champlain, that vast, shimmering sheet of water between Vermont and New York. You can't help but enjoy good views when you're on this lake—to the west are the stern Adirondacks; to the east are the distant, rolling ridges of the Green Mountains. Sign up for a lake cruise, or just hop the ferry from Burlington for a low-budget excursion across the lake and back. See chapter 6.
- **Connecticut River** (Vermont and New Hampshire): The broad, lazy Connecticut River forms the border between New Hampshire and Vermont, and it's a joy to travel along. You'll find wonderful vistas, peaceful villages, and evidence of the region's rich past, when the river served as a highway for northern New England. Today it's a hidden gem of a destination. See chapters 5 and 7.
- **Franconia Notch** (New Hampshire): This rocky pass through the craggiest part of the White Mountains is spectacular to drive through, but it's even more wondrous to stop and explore on foot or bike. Hike the flanking ridges, bike the pathway along the valley floor, or just lounge in the sun at the edge of Echo Lake. See chapter 8.
- **Tuckerman Ravine** (New Hampshire): This glacial cirque high on the flanks of Mount Washington (New England's highest peak) seems part medieval, part alpine, and entirely otherworldly. Snow blown across the upper lip throughout the winter accumulates to depths of 70 feet or more. In spring, skiers from across the U.S. come to challenge its sheer face, and hikers find snow in its vast bowl during summer. See chapter 8.
- **Acadia National Park** (Maine): New England's only national park is also one of the most popular in the U.S. The

rocky, surf-pounded coastline is the main attraction, but don't overlook the quiet boreal forests and open summits of low mountains with spectacular coastal views. See chapter 9.

- **Mount Katahdin** (Maine): Rising abruptly from a thick blanket of North Woods forest, the nearly mile-high Mount Katahdin has an ineffable spiritual quality. It's the centerpiece of equally inspiring Baxter State Park, one of the last, best wilderness areas of the eastern states. See chapter 10.

2 THE BEST SMALL TOWNS

- **Grafton** (Vermont): Just a few decades ago, Grafton was a down-at-the-heels mountain town slowly being reclaimed by termites and the elements. A wealthy family took on the town as a pet project, lovingly restoring it to the way it once was—even burying electric lines to reclaim the landscape. It doesn't feel like a living history museum; it just feels *right*. See "Brattleboro & the Southern Green Mountains," in chapter 5.
- **Woodstock** (Vermont): Woodstock has a stunning village green, a range of 19th-century homes, woodland walks just outside town, and a settled, old-money air. This is a good place to explore by foot or bike, or to just sit on a porch and watch summer unfold. See "Woodstock & Environs," in chapter 5.
- **Montpelier** (Vermont): This is the way all state capitals should be—slow-paced, small enough that you can walk everywhere, and home to lots of shops selling wrenches and strapping tape. Montpelier also has a more sophisticated edge, with its culinary institute, a theater showing art-house films, and several fine bookshops. However, at heart, it's a small town where you could run into the governor buying duct tape at a corner store. See "Montpelier, Barre & Waterbury," in chapter 6.
- **Hancock** (New Hampshire): This quiet hamlet—a satellite of the commercial center of Peterborough—has a historic and settled, white-clapboard grace and has been utterly unperturbed since it was founded in the 18th century. See "The Monadnock Region & the Connecticut River Valley," in chapter 7.
- **Camden** (Maine): This seaside town has everything—a beautiful harbor, great old architecture, and even its own tiny mountain range affording great hikes and sweeping ocean views. With lots of elegant bed-and-breakfasts, it's a perfect base for explorations farther afield. See "Penobscot Bay," in chapter 9.

3 THE BEST PLACES TO SEE FALL FOLIAGE

- **Route 100** (Vermont): Winding the length of Vermont from Readsboro to Newport, Route 100 is the major north-south route through the center of the Green Mountains, yet it's surprisingly undeveloped for the most part. It can be crowded along the southern stretches on autumn weekends, but head farther north and you'll leave the crowds behind. See chapters 5 and 6.
- **I-91** (Vermont): An interstate? Yes, really. If you like your foliage viewing big and fast, cruise I-91 from White River Junction to Newport. You'll be overwhelmed with gorgeous terrain, from the Connecticut River Valley to

Northern New England

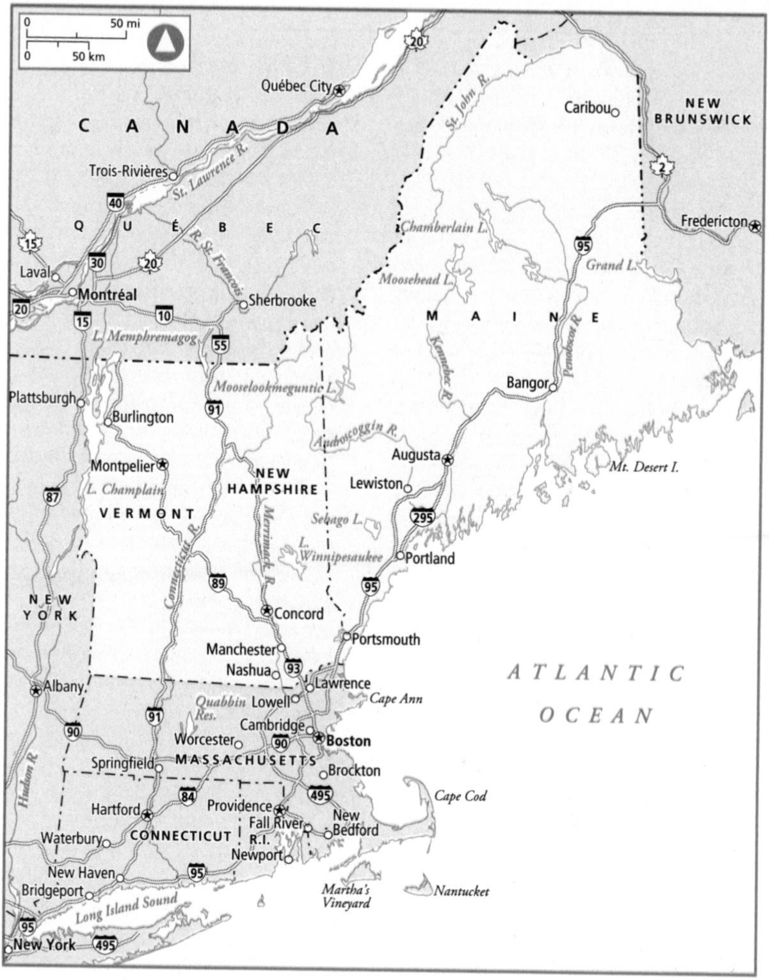

the rolling hills of the Northeast Kingdom. The traffic isn't as bad as on state roads, either. See chapters 5 and 6.

- **Aboard the MS *Mount Washington*** (New Hampshire): One of the more majestic views of the White Mountains is from Lake Winnipesaukee to the south. It's especially appealing from the deck of the *Mount Washington,* a handsome 230-foot-long vessel that takes tours on the lake through mid-October. The fringe of fall colors on the shoreline is a bonus. See "The Lake Winnipesaukee Region," in chapter 7.
- **Crawford Notch** (New Hampshire): Route 302 passes through this scenic valley, where you can see the brilliant red maples and yellow birches high on

the hillsides. Mount Washington stands guard in the background and, in fall, is likely to be dusted with an early snow. See "Crawford Notch," in chapter 8.

4 THE BEST COASTAL VIEWS

- **Bicycling Route 1A, Hampton Beach to Portsmouth** (New Hampshire): For a broad sampling of scenery on New Hampshire's minuscule coastline, you begin with sandy beaches, then pass rocky headlands and handsome mansions before coasting into Portsmouth, the region's most scenic seaside city. See "Enjoying the Great Outdoors" in chapter 7.
- **Driving the Park Loop Road at Acadia National Park** (Maine): The region's premier ocean drive starts along a ridge with views of Frenchman Bay and the Porcupine Islands, then dips down along the rocky shores where surf crashes against the dark rocks. Plan to do this 20-mile loop at least twice to get the most out of it. See "Mount Desert Island & Acadia National Park," in chapter 9.
- **Cruising on a windjammer** (Maine): See Maine as seafarers saw it for centuries—from the ocean, looking inland. Sailing ships depart from various harbors along the coast, particularly Rockland and Camden. Spend a night or a week exploring the dramatic shoreline. See "Penobscot Bay," in chapter 9.
- **Sitting in a rocking chair** (Maine): Views are often better when you're caught unaware—looking up from an engrossing book on the front porch of an oceanside inn, for instance. In chapters 9 and 10, I describe plenty of hotels and inns that are situated right on the water. Some of those with great views include the Beachmere Inn (in Ogunquit), the grand Samoset Resort (just north of Rockland), the Inn on the Harbor (in Stonington), and the Claremont (in Southwest Harbor, on Mount Desert Isle).

5 THE BEST ACTIVE VACATIONS

- **Biking from inn to inn** (Vermont): Vermont is a biker's paradise. Serpentine roads wind through verdant hills and along tumbling streams. Several organizations will ferry your baggage from inn to inn; you provide the pedal power to get from one point to the next. See "Enjoying the Great Outdoors," in chapter 5.
- **Skiing in the Green Mountains** (Vermont): Vermont has nearly two dozen ski areas, with everything from the cozy friendliness of Bolton Valley to the high-impact skiing of sprawling Killington. The state has long been New England's ski capital, and the resorts have learned how to do it right. My favorite? The village of Stowe, where great skiing is combined with fine lodging and dining. See "Downhill Skiing," under "Brattleboro & the Southern Green Mountains," in chapter 5.
- **Hiking the White Mountains** (New Hampshire): These rugged peaks draw hikers from all over the globe, attracted by the history, exceptional landscapes, and beautiful views from the craggy ridgelines. You can take day hikes and retreat to comfortable inns at night, or stay in the hills at the Appalachian Mountain Club's historic high huts. See chapter 8.

- **Mountain biking at Acadia** (Maine): John D. Rockefeller, Jr., built the carriage roads of Mount Desert Island so the gentry could enjoy rambles in the woods with their horses—away from pesky cars. Today this extensive network allows for some of the most enjoyable, aesthetically pleasing mountain biking anywhere. See "Mount Desert Island & Acadia National Park," in chapter 9.
- **Kayaking the coast** (Maine): With its massive, serpentine coastline and thousands of islands, mostly uninhabited, Maine is a world-class destination for those who like to snoop around by kayak. The Stonington area is considered the best spot for kayaking in Maine, but it's hard to go wrong anywhere north and east of Portland. Beware of dangers in the form of tides and weather—kayak with a guide if you're a novice. See "Enjoying the Great Outdoors" in chapter 9.
- **Canoeing the North Woods** (Maine): Maine has thousands of miles of flowing rivers and streams, and hundreds of miles of shoreline along remote ponds and lakes. Bring your tent, sleeping bag, and cooking gear, and come prepared to spend a night under the stars listening to the loons. See chapter 10.

6 THE BEST DESTINATIONS FOR FAMILIES

- **Montshire Museum of Science** (Norwich, Vermont): This children's museum, on the border of Vermont and New Hampshire, has wonderful interactive exhibits on the inside and nature trails along the Connecticut River on the outside. See p. 134.
- **Cog Railway** (Crawford Notch, New Hampshire): It's fun. It's terrifying. It's a great glimpse into history. Kids love this ratchety climb to the top of New England's highest peak (Mount Washington) aboard trains specially designed in 1869 to scale the mountain. As a technological marvel, the railway attracted tourists by the thousands a century ago. They still come to marvel at its sheer audacity. See "Crawford Notch" in chapter 8.
- **Weirs Beach** (New Hampshire): Cheesy? Yes. Scenic? No. Kid-friendly? You bet. Weirs Beach on Lake Winnipesaukee offers passive amusements like train and boat rides, plus some more active adventures for young teens, such as go-kart racing, water slides, and video arcades. Parents can recuperate on a small lakeside beach. See "Funspot: Video Geek Heaven" on p. 239 to learn about the area's most famous diversion.

7 THE MOST INTRIGUING HISTORIC HOMES

- **Hildene** (Manchester, Vermont): This lavish summer home was built by Abraham and Mary Todd Lincoln's son, Robert. A prosperous businessman, the younger Lincoln built this summer retreat complete with a 1,000-pipe organ and extensive formal gardens. If you're curious about how the other half lived late in America's Gilded Age, this is your destination. See p. 93.
- **Drisco House** (Portsmouth, New Hampshire): The Drisco House is the most fascinating of any at Strawbery Banke, the region's premier historic attraction. Half of this house was restored to its 1790s grandeur, and half was left as it appeared in the 1950s. You'll learn plenty about how a house adapts to the technology and culture of each era. See p. 209.

- **Saint-Gaudens National Historic Site** (Cornish, New Hampshire): Sculptor Augustus Saint-Gaudens has been overshadowed somewhat by Daniel Chester French, his contemporary, but Saint-Gaudens's work was extraordinary and prolific. Learn about the man, and the artistic culture of the late 19th and early 20th centuries, while touring his studio and house. See p. 233.
- **Zimmerman House** (Manchester, New Hampshire): Designed in 1950 by Frank Lloyd Wright, the Zimmerman house is so, well, *20th century* (mid-century modern, to be specific). A great example of a Wright Usonian home, it offers lessons in how to live right in any age. See p. 219.
- **Victoria Mansion** (Portland, Maine): Donald Trump has nothing on the Victorians when it comes to material excess. You'll see Victorian decorative arts at their zenith in this elaborate Italianate mansion, built during the Civil War. It's open for tours throughout the summer. See p. 305.
- **Parson Fisher House** (Blue Hill, Maine): Parson Jonathan Fisher, who served as minister to the quiet town of Blue Hill in the late 18th century, was a man of extraordinary talents, from designing his own house and building his own clocks to preaching sermons in five languages (including Aramaic). As if that weren't enough, his primitive landscapes of the region are widely regarded as among the best from the area. See p. 337.

8 THE BEST PLACES TO REDISCOVER AMERICA'S PAST

- **Plymouth** (Vermont): President Calvin Coolidge was born in this high, upland valley, and the state has done a superb job preserving his hometown village. You not only get a good sense of the president's roots, but also gain a greater understanding of how a New England village once worked. Don't miss the excellent cheese shop, owned until recently by the Coolidge family. See "Killington & Rutland," in chapter 5.
- **Shelburne Museum** (Shelburne, Vermont): Think of this sprawling museum as New England's attic. Located on 45 acres on the shores of Lake Champlain, the Shelburne Museum not only has the usual exhibits of quilts and early glass, but also entire buildings preserved like specimens in formaldehyde. Be sure to take in the lighthouse, railroad station, and stagecoach inn. This is one of northern New England's "don't-miss" destinations. See p. 183.
- **Portsmouth** (New Hampshire): Portsmouth is a salty coastal city that has some of the most impressive historic homes in New England. Start at Strawbery Banke, a 10-acre compound of 42 historic buildings. Then visit many other grand homes in nearby neighborhoods, including the house where John Paul Jones lived while building his warship during the Revolution. See "Portsmouth" under "The Seacoast" in chapter 7.
- **Mount Desert Island & Bar Harbor** (Maine): In the mid-1800s, America launched a love affair with nature and never looked back. See where it started, in a setting of surf-wracked rocks, where some of the nation's most affluent families ventured to erect vacation "cottages" with bedrooms by the dozen. The area still imparts lessons on how to design with nature as an accomplice rather than an adversary. See "Mount Desert Island & Acadia National Park" in chapter 9.

9 THE BEST RESORTS

- **Woodstock Inn & Resort** (Woodstock, Vermont; ✆ **800/448-7900** or 802/457-1100): The 140-room inn was built in the 1960s with a strong Colonial Revival accent. Right on the green in picturesque Woodstock, the inn allows easy access to the village, along with plenty of activities, including golf on a course designed by Robert Trent Jones, Sr., indoor and outdoor pools, hiking, and skiing (downhill and cross-country) in winter. See p. 130.
- **Basin Harbor Club** (Vergennes, Vermont; ✆ **800/622-4000** or 802/475-2311): This classic lakeside resort on 700 acres was founded in 1886 and is run by descendants of the original family owners. Fittingly, the resort's icon is an Adirondack chair, dozens of which are arrayed for enjoying views across the lake to New York. Most guests occupy cottages, which are simple rather than swank. See p. 185.
- **Mount Washington Resort** (Bretton Woods, New Hampshire; ✆ **800/314-1752** or 603/278-1000): The last of the grand Edwardian resorts, the Mount Washington has come back from the brink of bankruptcy with its famed flair intact. This is the place to golf, climb Mount Washington, or just sit on the broad porch and feel important. See p. 260.
- **The Colony Hotel** (Kennebunkport, Maine; ✆ **800/552-2363** or 207/967-3331): This rambling and gleaming white resort dates back to 1914 and has been upgraded over the years without losing any of its charm. You can play shuffleboard, putt on the greens, or lounge in the oceanview pool. More vigorous souls cross the street to brave the cold Atlantic waters. See p. 297.
- **Quisisana** (Center Lovell, Maine; ✆ **207/925-3500** or 914/833-0293 in winter): It's a rustic Maine vacation with a musical twist. The waiters, chambermaids, and other staff are recruited from conservatories around the nation, and they perform everything from light opera to chamber music for guests at this pine-filled lakeside resort. Between performances, there's ample opportunity for canoeing and hiking. See p. 368.

10 THE BEST COUNTRY INNS

- **The Inn at Manchester** (Manchester Village, Vermont; ✆ **800/273-1793** or 802/362-1793) sits on 4 acres of lawns and gardens just a half-mile from the budget shopping that draws so many visitors to Manchester. Rooms are in the main inn and a carriage house—both on the National Register of Historic Places—and are fresh and nicely furnished. Innkeepers Frank and Julie Hanes couldn't be friendlier or more helpful. See p. 97.
- **The Reluctant Panther** (Manchester Village, Vermont; ✆ **800/822-2331** or 802/362-2568): This is one of my favorite inns in all of New England, never mind Vermont. Completely renovated after a devastating fire, it's the perfect hybrid of upscale luxury inn and old Vermont: a gorgeous setting right at the foot of Mt. Equinox; a thoroughly professional staff; and modernized suites complete with Jacuzzis, fireplaces, flatscreen TVs, and the like. The inn restaurant is excellent, too. See p. 98.

- **Windham Hill Inn** (West Townshend, Vermont; ✆ **800/944-4080** or 802/874-4080): New innkeepers have skillfully upgraded this historic inn, adding amenities such as soaking tubs, while still preserving the antique charm of this 1823 farmhouse. It's at the end of a remote dirt road in a high upland valley, and guests are welcome to explore 160 private acres on a network of walking trails. See p. 107.
- **Blueberry Hill Inn** (Goshen, Vermont; ✆ **800/448-0707** or 802/247-6735): This remote, casual inn on a quiet byway surrounded by national forest is a great retreat. You can enjoy hiking and swimming in summer, skiing in the winter. See p. 141.
- **The Pitcher Inn** (Warren, Vermont; ✆ **802/496-6350**): Innkeepers who try to meld whimsy with class often end up with disaster, but that's not the case here. This New England–village inn feels more historic than many old places. The dining room is top-notch. See p. 160.
- **The Claremont** (Southwest Harbor, Maine; ✆ **800/244-5036** or 207/244-5036): The 1884 Claremont is a Maine classic. This waterside lodge has everything a Victorian resort should, including sparely decorated rooms, creaky floorboards in the halls, great views of the water and mountains, and a croquet pitch. The dining room is only so-so, but Southwest Harbor has other dining options. See p. 356.
- **White Barn Inn** (Kennebunk Beach, Maine; ✆ **207/967-2321**): Much of the White Barn staff hails from Europe, and they treat guests graciously. The rooms are a delight, and the meals (served in a gloriously restored barn) may be the best in Maine. See p. 298.

11 THE BEST BED & BREAKFASTS

- **The Woodstocker Inn B&B** (Woodstock, Vermont; ✆ **802/457-3896**): English owners possessed of a sense of humor, buckets of bright paint, a genteel dog, and an organic-product ethos add to a great place to stay just a stone's throw from both Woodstock's central green and Mount Tom. See p. 130.
- **Inn at the Round Barn Farm** (Waitsfield, Vermont; ✆ **802/496-2276**): The beautiful lap pool, hidden beneath the monumental former barn, is only one of the secrets of this charming inn. The rooms are romantic, the surrounding hillsides frame a picture of pastoral Vermont, and small touches everywhere make guests feel welcome. See p. 160.
- **Pomegranate Inn** (Portland, Maine; ✆ **800/356-0408** or 207/772-1006): Whimsy and history combine with good effect at this fine B&B in one of Portland's most stately neighborhoods. The Italianate mansion is stern on the outside, yet alive on the inside with creative paintings and an eclectic collection of unusual antiques. See p. 308.

12 THE BEST MODERATELY PRICED ACCOMMODATIONS

- **Inn at the Mad River Barn** (Waitsfield, Vermont; ✆ **800/631-0466** or 802/496-3310): It takes a few minutes to adapt to the spartan rooms and no-frills accommodations, but you'll soon discover that the real action takes place in the living and dining rooms, where skiers relax and chat after a day on the slopes and share heaping helpings at mealtime. See p. 160.

- **Birchwood Inn** (Temple, New Hampshire; ✆ **603/878-3285**): Simple comfort is the watchword at this quiet village inn, once visited by Henry David Thoreau. See p. 228.
- **Maine Idyll Motor Court** (Freeport, Maine; ✆ **207/865-4201**): The 1932 Maine Idyll Motor Court is a classic—a cluster of 20 cottages scattered about a grove of beech and oak trees. Each cottage has a tiny porch, wood-burning fireplace (birch logs provided), TV, modest kitchen facilities (no ovens), and timeworn furniture. The downside? Highway noise. See p. 318.

13 THE BEST ALTERNATIVE ACCOMMODATIONS

- **Camping in the Green Mountains** (Vermont): Whether your preferred mode of travel is by foot, car, canoe, or bike, you'll find plenty of good campsites in the verdant hills of Vermont. The state parks are well regarded, with many dating from the Civilian Conservation Corps days (1930s and early 1940s). The National Forest Service, aided by the Green Mountain Club, maintains dozens of backcountry sites and lean-tos as secluded getaways far from the noise of everyday life. See chapters 5 and 6.
- **Appalachian Mountain Club huts** (New Hampshire): For more than a century, the AMC has been putting up weary hikers at its huts high in the White Mountains. Today the club still manages eight of them (each about a day's hike apart), providing filling, family-style meals and sturdy bunks stacked three high in rustic bunkrooms. See chapter 8.
- **Windjammers** (Maine): Maine has the East Coast's largest fleet of windjammers, providing adventures on the high seas throughout the summer. You can explore offshore islands and inland estuaries, and learn how sailors once made the best of the wind. Accommodations in private cabins are typically spartan, but you'll spend most of your time on deck luxuriating in the stunning views. See "Penobscot Bay," in chapter 9.
- **Maine Island Trail:** About 70 remote islands along the Maine coast are open to camping, and from these remote, salty wildernesses, you'll see some of the best sunsets imaginable. See "Enjoying the Great Outdoors" in chapter 9.

14 THE BEST RESTAURANTS

- **Chantecleer** (East Dorset, Vermont; ✆ **802/362-1616**): Swiss chef Michel Baumann has been turning out dazzling dinners since 1981, and the kitchen hasn't gotten stale in the least. The dining room in an old barn is magical, and the waitstaff is helpful and friendly. It's a great spot for those who want top-notch Continental fare, but don't like the fuss of a fancy restaurant. See p. 100.

- **Hemingway's** (Killington, Vermont; ✆ **802/422-3886**): Killington seems an unlikely place for serious culinary adventures, yet Hemingway's meets the loftiest expectations. The menu changes frequently to ensure the freshest of ingredients. Be sure to order the wild mushroom and truffle soup, if it's available. See p. 144.
- **Arrows** (Ogunquit, Maine; ✆ **207/361-1100**): The emphasis at this elegant spot is on local products—often many ingredients from nearby organic vegetable gardens. Prices are not for the fainthearted (it's expensive even by New York City standards), but the experience is top-rate, from the cordial service to the silver and linens. Expect New American fare informed by an Asian sensibility. See p. 293.
- **White Barn Inn** (Kennebunkport, Maine; ✆ **207/967-2321**): The setting in an ancient, rustic barn is magical. The tables are draped with floor-length tablecloths, and the chairs have Italian upholstery. The food is to die for. Enjoy entrees such as grilled duckling breast with ginger and sun-dried cherry sauce, or rack of lamb with pecans and homemade barbecue sauce. See p. 298.
- **Fore Street** (Portland, Maine; ✆ **207/775-2717**): Fore Street is one of New England's most celebrated restaurants—listed as one of *Gourmet* magazine's 100 best restaurants in 2001—and the chef has been getting lots of press elsewhere. His secret? Simplicity, and lots of it. Some of the most memorable meals are prepared over an applewood grill. See p. 310.

15 THE BEST LOCAL DINING EXPERIENCES

- **Blue Benn Diner** (Bennington, Vermont; ✆ **802/442-5140**): This favorite, housed in a classic 1945 Silk City diner, has a barrel ceiling, acres of stainless steel, and a vast menu. Make sure not to overlook the specials scrawled on paper and taped all over the walls. Do leave room for a slice of delicious pie, including blackberry, pumpkin, and chocolate cream. See p. 90.
- **Curtis' BBQ** (Putney, Vermont; ✆ **802/387-5474**): Who gave the South and Midwest permission to claim the best barbecue? This classic roadside open-air joint is next to a gas station and has a heap of rustic charm and great food. Place your order at the blue school bus for a slab or smaller serving, grab a seat, dig in, and enjoy. See p. 116.
- **Bove's** (Burlington, Vermont; ✆ **802/864-6651**): A Burlington landmark since 1941, Bove's is a classic red-sauce-on-spaghetti joint that's a throwback to a lost era. The red sauce is rich and tangy, and the garlic sauce packs enough garlic to knock you clear out of your booth. See p. 188.
- **Lou's** (Hanover, New Hampshire; ✆ **603/643-3321**): Huge crowds flock to Lou's, just down the block from the Dartmouth campus in Hanover, for breakfast on weekends. Fortunately, breakfast is served all day. The sandwiches, served on fresh-baked bread, are huge and delicious. See p. 236.
- **Silly's** (Portland, Maine; ✆ **207/772-0360**): Hectic and fun, this tiny, informal, kitschy restaurant serves up delicious finger food such as pita wraps, hamburgers, and pizza. The milkshakes alone are worth the detour. See p. 313.

16 THE BEST DESTINATIONS FOR SERIOUS SHOPPERS

- **Manchester** (Vermont): The dozens of outlet stores clustered in this village include the usual high-fashion suspects and some notable individual shops. Head to Orvis, the maker of noted fly-fishing equipment, for outdoor gear and clothing. See "Bennington, Manchester & Southwestern Vermont," in chapter 5.
- **Portsmouth** (New Hampshire): Downtown Portsmouth has a grab bag of small, manageable, eclectic shops, ranging from funky shoe stores to classy art galleries. The downtown district is small enough to browse leisurely on foot, but you'll find a broad assortment of stuff for sale that will appeal to almost any taste. See "The Seacoast," in chapter 7.
- **North Conway** (New Hampshire): Combine outdoor adventure with serious shopping on a 3-mile stretch of discount outlet stores that makes up most of North Conway. Look for Anne Klein, American Tourister, Izod, Polo/Ralph Lauren, Donna Karan, Reebok/Rockport, and Eddie Bauer, along with dozens of others. See "North Conway & Environs," in chapter 8.
- **Freeport** (Maine): L.L.Bean is the anchor store for this thriving town of outlets, but you'll also find Patagonia, J. Crew, Dansk, Brooks Brothers, Levi's, and about 100 others. This is the most aesthetically pleasing of the several outlet centers in northern New England. See "Freeport to Midcoast Maine," in chapter 9.

2 Northern New England in Depth

Most of the rest of this book is intended to lead you toward the best or most interesting historical attractions, museums, eating and drinking places, shops, and lodgings in the three northern New England states. But this chapter is different: In these pages, I try to capture something of the elusive character of northern New England and its famously short-spoken, resourceful residents. I tell you how the region came to be formed geologically, how it was populated by people and animals, what kind of foods are most popular and distinctive here today, and how to recognize when you've moved from one imagined region across some invisible divide into another area. And I tell you about some of the best books, music, and films written in or about these three states. Ready? Buckle up: Here comes your crash course.

1 THE REGIONS IN BRIEF

On a map, northern New England might look like one big patch of scrubby woods, bordered by a single coastline. Yet it's anything but homogenous. The various states (and parts of states) here have carved out distinct identities, shaped by human history, geology, weather, fish, the quality of trees or soils in the area—you name it. Here are the key micro-regions to keep in mind as you travel through the region. Remember them; they're how northern New England talks about itself.

THE GREEN MOUNTAINS Extending the entire length of Vermont, this bony spine of mountains and forested foothills stretches almost due north from Massachusetts up to Canada. The mountains have been developed with great hiking trails and ski hills, scenic back-road drives, and wonderful inns. You can't go wrong with a drive up through one of the passes through these mountains: Every one of them is a Kodak mountain, from scenic Smuggler's Notch (squeezing between boulders as it tops the mountain) to Robert Frost's old haunt at Bread Loaf to Plymouth Notch, former home to a U.S. president and still a fine working demonstration of what Vermont life used to be like (and sometimes still is).

The nation's smallest state capital is located here, at Montpelier (pop. 8,000), but it feels like a small town—an arty small town with a great culinary school, okay—but still a small town where you see the same people every morning at the same bagel and coffee shops. The apples and maple syrup around here taste good, too; be sure and stock up at places like the Cold Hollow Cider Mill in Waterbury (try Sept) and one of the numerous sugar shacks dotting the hills. (***Hint:*** Early March is prime time for sugaring.) This is also the part of the state in which you'll find the world-famous Ben & Jerry's ice-cream factory. Tours and a tasting? Yes, please.

LAKE CHAMPLAIN Named for a widely traveled explorer (Samuel de Champlain), this is one of the most beautiful lakes in New England. It's also the second-biggest, *way* ahead of the rest (though far behind the winner and still heavyweight champ, Moosehead).

The basin containing the lake was scoured out by a huge, mile-high sheet of ice moving south from present-day Canada during the last ice age; when it retreated back in the same direction, it left this broad, flat sheet of land in its wake, and runoff from the surrounding hills and mountains eventually created a watery paradise. Today the Vermont (eastern) shores of this lake are extremely pastoral and scenic, filled with idyllic drives, little hilltops, thousands of boats, cute towns, and a sense of gracious openness—not to mention plenty of dairy cows and stunning views of the big, sharp Adirondacks.

It's also the place where you get the single strongest dose of urban culture you can get in little Vermont. That's because the state's biggest city, Burlington, is located here, right beside the lake. Burlington regularly wins best-quality-of-life-in-the-nation awards for its combination of fresh air, lake views, bike trails, a compact walkable downtown, a technology-and-manufacturing-driven economy (which remains healthy, thank you very much)—*plus* an unusually eclectic mixture of bookstores, bars, and restaurants brought here by the state's largest university and only medical school. And it's just a half-hour from those Green Mountains I mentioned earlier.

Even without factoring in Burlington, the Champlain Valley is arguably the part of Vermont with the best food options, from organic dairies to the Inn at Shelburne Farms' amazing dining (the inn has a culinary school tie-in) to the ever-changing roster of little gourmet bakeries, breweries, and quality New American eateries popping up in former market towns like Middlebury and Vergennes. If you're an eater or a boater, come here.

THE NORTHEAST KINGDOM The Northeast Kingdom isn't exactly a kingdom—if it is, then black flies, cows, and stones are its rulers. This is Vermont at its primeval and lost in time. There are very few emerald meadows or fancy inns here; these counties are rugged, hilly, and unpolished. Yet there are improbable grace notes, such as the little hilltop town of Craftsbury Common (with its outstanding outdoor center) and the little riverside city of St. Johnsbury, which possesses not one but *two* excellent museums. You can also buy great cheddar cheese here—practically right from the cows.

COASTAL NEW HAMPSHIRE Yes, New Hampshire *does* have a coastline—okay, there are only 18 miles of it, but this is a complete guide, so I'm giving you the straight dope. And packed into this tiny strip you'll find a surprising quantity of sand, sea, sea-tossed boulders, surf, honky-tonk boardwalks, beer cans, and sailboat views.

As a bonus, there's also the very historic and entertaining little city of Portsmouth: a smaller (possibly better) version of Boston. It's a flat-out great place to shop, snap photos of brick buildings and boats, or just hang out like a local drinking a microbrew or a cup of free-trade, fresh-ground coffee.

It's hard to believe this was once a string of poor (and then rich) fishing villages. There are still fishing boats in Portsmouth Harbor, alright, but the rest of this coastline sold its soul long ago to tourists and second-home owners. Here's a very quick primer to what this area looks like. New Castle: Rich people and really, really old homes. Rye Beach: Richer people. Hampton Beach: Bikers and working stiffs. Seabrook: Nuclear power plant. (No, I'm not kidding.)

Portsmouth, on the other hand, is an odd amalgam of pierced baristas, antique homes and inns and preservationists, fishermen, lobstermen, gardeners, folk musicians, and gourmet chefs. To tell the truth, I don't know *what* to call the funky mix here, exactly. But I like it a lot.

THE UPPER VALLEY The Connecticut River, in case you haven't glanced at a map yet, is the one that divides Vermont and New Hampshire into two reverse-image triangles (or pork chops, or blocks of cheese). This river and its valley, narrow in places but impressively wide and flat in others, are a world unto themselves. There are villages, rolling hills, rapids, and mud flats here; bright leaves, oodles of covered bridges, and canoes; and it's even got smarts. The Ivy League's Dartmouth College is located in Hanover, New Hampshire, and so is Colby-Sawyer College in the nearby, attractive town of New London.

Veer east a bit into New Hampshire and you get true slices of New England life: the historic mill town of Newport, lovely Lake Sunapee (some of the cleanest water in North America, they say), and plenty of back-road drives through good views and landscapes.

On the western flanks of the river, the Vermont side of the valley turns out to be a magical mystery tour stopping off at places like the King Arthur Flour Company ("Never bleached—never bromated") Baker's Store, Curtis' Bar-B-Q (one of the best in New England), and the Woodstock Covered Bridge. This valley isn't postcard-perfect at *every* turn of the road, but I really like it. And the geology here is mighty impressive.

THE LAKES REGION Lake Winnipesaukee is the crown jewel of New Hampshire's Lakes Region, though its charms are variable. Some of the roads circling this huge, oddly shaped lake are as charming as anything in New England. Others run through honky-tonk strips, past the likes of B.J.'s and water parks. Meredith and Wolfeboro are the de facto tourist capitals of the region, and I've concentrated on them in this guidebook in lieu of several other, more workaday (or flat-out corny) towns and attractions ringing the lake.

And Winnipesaukee isn't the only game in town. Countless smaller lakes and ponds scattered throughout the area supply in *charm* what they lack in *size.* The film *On Golden Pond* was filmed on one of these, although the region's fame and beauty long predate Hollywood's discovery of them: No less an observer than Henry David Thoreau remarked on the splendid views of Winnipesaukee and the White Mountains from one local hill in 1858. Note that Maine has its own Lakes Region, too, in the west-central part of the state, not far from this one. Glaciers will do that to a place.

THE WHITE MOUNTAINS Since the mid-1800s, New Hampshire's towering White Mountains have magnetically drawn travelers, with their rugged, windswept peaks, forests dotted with glacial boulders, and clear, rushing streams. You can find New England's best backcountry hiking and camping here, and also its wildest weather (really—it has been documented).

There are numerous resort towns in these hills, each abounding with inns old and new, towns with austere names like Jefferson, Bartlett, Lincoln, and Woodstock. Bretton Woods is world-famous not only for the sprawling, red-roofed resort that sits at the foot of Mount Washington, but also for a series of economic conferences *at* the resort in 1944 that established the U.S. dollar as the planet's effective monetary benchmark, replacing gold bars. The Old Man of the Mountain doesn't live here in the mountains anymore (sadly), but you can still take home his visage on a million different souvenirs.

Who should come? Leaf-peepers and serious photographers, by all means. And hardbodies will *absolutely* want to visit the Whites, with a full contingent of bikes, climbing gear, swim trunks, hiking boots, and bandages in tow—but be sure to also bring radios, GPS devices, and good cellphones or satellite phones, too. The weather can change in an instant here, and rescues of the unprepared are all too common in these mountains, all four seasons of the year.

Not quite in shape for a mountain ski or hike just now? That's okay. You can also drive to the summit of Mount Washington, though I recommend driving the Kancamagus Highway—a bit of a white-knuckle ride, but with unparalleled views—through these mountains instead.

WESTERN MAINE This oft-overlooked region, centered around the pretty prep-school/ski-resort town of Bethel but also taking in a wide swath of territory north and south from there, is as different from nearby North Conway as could be. Whereas the Conways teem with shopping and shoppers, this is the real Maine, home to brawny hills, wide fast rivers and flumes, extremely scenic lakes—I noted Maine's Lakes Region above—spectacular foliage, and endless opportunities for quiet hiking, skiing, golfing, canoeing, antiquing, and the like. You might hear a loon crying on a pond at night; spy a moose walking a road at dusk; or even spot author Stephen King (also walking a road at dusk).

COASTAL MAINE Maine's rocky coast is the stuff of legend, art, and poetry. Boiled down to simplest terms, the Maine coast consists of two regions: southern Maine—"down there," also sometimes derisively referred to as "Vacationland" or "not Maine"—and Downeast—"up there" or "the real Maine."

The two regions are as different as night and day; broadly speaking, the gourmet cuisine, fine cars, and luxury inns of the south coast gradually (and then quickly) give way to cottages, used cars tacked together with baling wire, and fried fish, though that distinction is blurring somewhat of late. The southern coast has the best beaches; to the north, the Downeast region offers rocky headlands and Acadia National Park. And the lobsters are everywhere.

THE NORTH WOODS OF MAINE The mostly uninhabited North Woods of Maine are almost entirely owned by timber companies, but there are still some spectacular places here. Two of Maine's hidden jewels are well worth a visit: big, wild Baxter State Park, home to the state's largest peak (impressive Mount Katahdin); and giant Moosehead Lake, the province of fishing camps and luxury inns. Numerous smaller lakes and ponds, accessible only by seaplane, shine like coins in the woods, and the Allagash River is a once-in-a-lifetime paddling adventure. You come here to canoe, hike, fly-fish, and commune with nature, because that's about all you *can* do.

This region also extends west to the skinny northern tip of New Hampshire, a place of tiny one-stoplight-and-diner towns like Colebrook and Pittsburg (potential marketing slogan: "Lose the H and find a life!"). There's not much in the way of gourmet foods or resorts up here. Instead, Christmas trees—and their fragrant tips, used to make wreaths (climbing trees to snag them is known as *tipping*)—are what passes for big business here.

2 NORTHERN NEW ENGLAND TODAY

As recently as a few decades ago, people in northern New England often lived off the land. They might have fished for cod, harvested timber in the back 40, managed gravel pits, worked in general stores, or worked in New England's many mills. Of course, some still do these things.

But hardscrabble work is no longer the only economic engine in the region. Today a New Englander might be a displaced editor from Boston or New York; a farmer who grows organic produce for gourmet restaurants in the big city; a banking or PR consultant who handles business in her slippers by fax and e-mail. You'll also find *lots* of folks whose livelihood is dependent on tourism—the tour guide, the family selling honey and maple syrup by the side of a Vermont highway, the math teacher moonlighting as a motel owner; the high school kid working summers in the T-shirt shop, the repair-shop guy fixing sports cars when they break down on mountain roads. (Not that that's ever happened to me. No way. Never.)

There's a slow change happening in the economy here in northern New England, from one that was strictly blue collar to something that's much more diverse, if still unclear. This is no longer the province of dairy farms and woolen mills, though those places still exist in pockets. It's a place of light industry, technology, arts and crafts, world-class cuisine—still all informed by a self-sufficiency, flexibility, and creativity rarely seen elsewhere. (People tend to double up on jobs around here.) And they *all* manage to deal with the awful weather.

As a region of humble means, the place's new value as a tourist drive-through and a place to buy a second home has ruffled some feathers. That process has also begun homogenizing a place that had been somewhat of a cultural holdout from the mall-ification of America. Once a region of distinctive villages, green commons, and prim courthouse squares, New England's landscape in certain places has begun to resemble suburbs anywhere else—strip malls dotted with fast-food chains, big-box discount stores, and home-improvement emporia. While undeniably convenient to locals, they aren't doing much for tourism.

Yes, strip malls have arrived in Portland, Burlington, Kittery, Freeport, North Conway, and along Maine's Route 1. Elsewhere, too. Some locals love 'em, and some hate 'em; it's a mixed blessing, because this region has always taken pride in its low-key, practical approach to life. In many smaller communities, town meetings are still the preferred form of government. Residents gather in public spaces to speak out—sometimes rather forcefully—on the issues of the day: funding for local schools, road repairs, firetrucks, and declarations of their towns as pro-America or anti-nuclear. "Use it up, wear it out, make do, or do without" still works here, but it's the polar opposite of the outlet-shopping ethos gradually filtering into the region. And therein lies the rub: This region is trying to have it both ways, Norman Rockwell *and* Relais & Chateaux.

Development is a related issue, even if tough economic times have cooled it off for the moment. Many old-timers (and some blow-ins) believe development shouldn't be ushered in regardless of the cultural cost. Others feel that the natural landscape isn't sacred, though, and the region has seen a surge of new town houses of late, covering ski slopes and hillsides throughout the three states. *Nobody's* happy about the rising property taxes and land prices here—except those already holding land in prime locations, that is.

No, development hasn't exploded here. Not yet. But if it ever *does,* many of the characteristics that make northern New England so unique—and attract those tourist dollars—could disappear. The brick mills, brick churches, cow pastures, big old maple trees, and whitewashed homes might slowly be replaced by a grayish blanket of condo associations, Banana Republics, outlet malls, and upscale B&Bs. Would the Green Mountains and the Maine coast still draw tourists if they began to look like any other place in America? Yes, of course, but maybe not as many; people like novelty. So it's a tricky balance to maintain.

Then there's the question of those new arrivals I mentioned earlier. The rise of the information age is drawing telecommuters and entrepreneurs to these pristine villages, because they can run entire businesses and move equities around the world wirelessly in a flash. These folks bring big-city sophistication (and appetites for gourmet dining) with them. So how will these affluent newcomers adapt to the ticky-tacky lawn ornaments on their neighbors' property; clear-cutting and moose hunting in the countryside nearby; and increasing numbers of tour buses cruising their village greens? Nobody knows.

Change has never come quickly in New England, and this one, too, will take time to play itself out. The question won't be resolved anytime in the near future. Residents' kids and grandkids will still be hashing out the exact same issues, years later.

But you're just visiting, right? So here's what to expect when you get here. Some say New England's character is still informed by its Calvinist history, which decrees that nothing can change one's fate and hard work is practically the only true virtue. That is partly true: Just take a walk down the main streets of towns like Bellows Falls, Rockland, Westbrook, and Newport.

On the other hand, look again: It's not *all* rock-hard mattresses, tasteless meals, and hunting licenses. There might even be art galleries and microbreweries in that old canning factory or shoe mill. Be sure to visit these places: They're great. But then also set aside time to spend an afternoon rocking and reading on the broad porch of an older inn or general store (if you can find one), or to wander around on some abandoned county road with no particular destination in mind.

Because if you crave great homemade pie; some of the best foliage in the world; quiet two-lanes; and lovely 19th-century inns and bed-and-breakfasts, this is *the* place for you to visit, one of my very favorite places in North America. Yes, it's becoming modern—you can now sleep in luxury inns (a pretty recent development) and dine on gourmet fare that wouldn't have had a chance of being accepted here a generation ago, food that's the equal of anything in Manhattan or San Francisco. The mix of new and old is *working,* so far, and that's why I love coming here—and you will, too.

Finally, Mother Nature has the last word: This is a sparsely populated place, enduringly quiet and lovely no matter whether it's sparkling with white powdery snow, brilliant autumn leaves, or reflections from a quiet New Hampshire pond at the dead center of summer. The chief export products here are indolence and self-reflection—increasingly rare commodities these days. Take time to savor them.

3 LOOKING BACK AT NORTHERN NEW ENGLAND

Viewed from a distance, northern New England's history largely mirrors that of its progenitor (Old England). This region rose from humble beginnings and hardscrabble obscurity—a place of long, cold winters and bad farmlands—to tremendous historical prominence. It captured a significant portion of the world's sea trade and became an industrial and marine powerhouse and center for creative thought, all in a pretty short span of time. And then what? The party ended almost as abruptly; the commerce and culture moved west, to the fertile farmlands and big mountains and opposite coast. Eventually it moved overseas.

To this day, the region refuses to be divorced from its past. As you walk through Portland, for instance, the layers of history are evident at every turn: the church steeples of Colonial times, parklands, and elaborate residences overlooking the Atlantic Ocean that speak to the wealth and refined sensibilities of the late Victorian era.

History is even more inescapable once you get *off* the beaten track. Travelers will find hints of what the Maine poet Henry Wadsworth Longfellow called "the irrevocable past" every way they turn, from stone walls running through old woods to Federal-style homes still standing proudly on the green central common that marks many a small town in northern New England.

Here's a brief overview of some historical episodes and trends that shaped northern New England.

INDIGENOUS PEOPLES

So far as we know, Native Americans have inhabited northern New England more or less continuously for the past 9,000 years. (Waves of migratory peoples undoubtedly also lived here before and after the last ice age; we just don't have any hard evidence.) At the time of about 7000 B.C., the region was inhabited chiefly by Algonquin and Abenaki peoples, who lived a nomadic life of fishing, trapping, and hunting. They changed camp locations several times per year to take advantage of the seasonal fish runs and wildlife movements. These peoples eventually fractured into local tribes, chief among them the Micmac, Maliseet, Penobscot, and Passaquamoddy.

Interestingly, these native peoples are still here, though in greatly diminished numbers and barely visible. After the arrival of Europeans (see below), Catholic missionaries succeeded in converting many local Native Americans, and tribes here sided with the French in the French and Indian Wars of the 18th century. Afterward these native people fared poorly at the hands of the British and were quickly pushed to the margins. Today they are found in greatest concentration on two tiny reservations in Downeast Maine. Their names have been taken by many towns and natural features in Maine, as well—but they're largely absent from the museums and subsequent histories of Vermont and New Hampshire. (Some natives married into the Anglo culture, and native tongues and folkways have largely disappeared, save a few arts such as canoe-making.)

Maine's native peoples actually won an $81-million cash settlement from the federal government in 1980 to buy land, yet they have little to show for it today. And there are *no* reservations in New Hampshire or Vermont, which is astounding considering the long indigenous history here. Visit the Abbe Museum in Bar Harbor, Maine (p. 349), or the archives of the University of Maine in Orono if you're interested in learning more about New England's native peoples.

FISHERMEN & COLONISTS

The England, Scottish, Irish, and French-coast colonists who came to North America were all well suited for the task of fishing these waters; they'd had plenty of practice back home, after all.

The French made the first significant attempts at establishing a new colony here. In 1604 some 80 colonists spent a winter on a small island on what today is the Maine–New Brunswick border. They didn't care for the harsh winter, and left in spring for Nova Scotia. Three years later, a few months after another colony was founded at Jamestown, Virginia, a group of 100 English settlers sailed into port at present-day Popham Beach, Maine. The Maine winter demoralized these would-be

Local Wisdom: Maine

As Maine goes, so goes the nation.

—Political folk wisdom

pioneers, too, and they returned to England with their proverbial tails (rudders?) between their legs the following year.

The colonization of the region was inevitable, however. The arrival of the Pilgrims at Plymouth Rock in 1620 proved to be the one that stuck. The Pilgrims—a religious group that had split from the Church of England—were a tough lot. Half of them perished during that first Massachusetts winter. But the colony hung on, in part thanks to helpful Native Americans, and their success soon lured more boats from England to what is now the Boston area. Throughout the 17th century, these colonists slowly pushed northward into what are now coastal New Hampshire and Maine (but were still part of Massachusetts at the time). The very first areas to be settled were lands near protected harbors along the coast, such as York, Maine.

Native Americans raided many of these towns and settlements, both independently and in concert with French forces pressing down from Québec, but these only proved temporary setbacks; the British naval forces were simply too stout. And so northern New England continued to gradually fill in more empty spaces on the map with villages and small towns throughout the 17th and into the 18th centuries.

But there was another threat to these new British colonies, as well: internal dissent. And the British brought it on themselves, the way empires often do: through unfettered greed.

TALKING 'BOUT A REVOLUTION

Beginning in or around 1765, Great Britain's king launched a series of ham-handed economic policies to reign in the increasingly feisty American colonies. These included a direct tax—infamous ever after as the Stamp Act—to pay for a standing army. The colonists were not amused. They could make no decisions about the ways the colonies were being run, and the further exacting of a pound of economic flesh by the king was something of a last straw.

The British crackdown provoked a surprisingly angry response. Under the banner of "No taxation without representation," the disgruntled colonists began engaging in a series of riots, one of which resulted in the Boston Massacre of 1770, when five protesting colonists were fired upon and killed by British soldiers. The pot continued boiling. In 1773 the most famous protest took place in Boston Harbor. The British had imposed yet another tax, the Tea Act (the right to collect duties on tea imports), and that prompted a group of colonists dressed like Indians to board three British ships and dump 342 chests of valuable tea into the harbor.

This incident is known down through history as the Boston Tea Party, and it hastened the flashpoint of conflict. A contingent of British soldiers was sent to Lexington, Massachusetts, to seize military supplies and arrest two high-profile rebels—John Hancock and Samuel Adams. But the colonists had by then formed a

Local Wisdom: Robert Frost

Two roads diverged in a wood, and I / I took the one less traveled by, / And that has made all the difference.

—Robert Frost, "The Road Not Taken"

volunteer militia, and they fired their hunting muskets back at the British, thereby igniting the American Revolution. (Those first ragtag shots are known as "the shot heard 'round the world.")

To the world's surprise, probably, the colonists not only held their own for a period of time, but also eventually wore out the British under the leadership of General George Washington.

THE GREEN MOUNTAIN BOYS

Meanwhile there was a fascinating side plot going on in the place now known as Vermont. New York state and New Hampshire (two British territories) were dickering over who should control it; New Hampshire, in fact, sold a number of land grants to farmers and other colonists, until the British stepped in and decided New York would control the grants. That didn't please those who had already bought in, and one Ethan Allen (his family held some of those grants) went to court to try to right the wrong.

The king's kangaroo court ruled against Allen's family; he refused a bribe to bow out of the process and headed back to Bennington to assemble the Green Mountain Boys—another volunteer militia. Beginning in 1771, the Boys drove off repeated incursions by settlers attempting to settle Vermont. Allen formed a company and made big profits selling land in the area that would become Burlington.

When the Revolutionary War broke, the Boys simply turned their ire from local settlers to Great Britain in general. Allen was replaced by Seth Warner as commander, but the squad continued to do yeoman's duty battling the king's soldiers, capturing Fort Ticonderoga and pitching in at the Battle of Bennington. They only finally succumbed when they became over-ambitious and staged a ridiculous march north in an effort to capture the French city of Montréal. They failed, of course, and were imprisoned in Montreal for several years.

The Boys weren't entirely through, though. Released, they would later declare Vermont a sovereign republic, and the new United States government actually recognized it as such for 14 long years until 1791, when Vermont joined the Union. (Some here still say it never *really* joined the nation, though.)

A NEW ENGLAND, BUILT ON FISH & FUR

The colonists' feud with the British had formally ended in 1783, when Great Britain blinked and recognized the United States as a sovereign nation. Surprisingly, only one significant battle of the entire Revolutionary War ever took place in or near northern New England: the Battle of Bennington, which took place a few miles west of the Vermont state line in 1777. (Result? A big rout in favor of the crafty Americans over England's surprised German commanders.)

On the other hand, an impressive number of forts were built or shored up throughout the three northern New England states at strategic points on river bends, hilltops, and along the coast during the War of Independence. Some had originally been built for the purpose of defending the British from the French, while others were built for (or repurposed with) the task of defending the new America from the British. Many of them still remain well preserved today, as state parks.

The war's aftermath significantly affected the region's northern neighbor. Huge waves of fearful British loyalists and their families began fleeing New England by horse, foot, and boot for places like Nova Scotia and Prince Edward Island. Eastern Canada is still largely a British place today, and this characteristic mostly dates from that surprising moment in 1783 when the upstart colonists triumphed over the repressive Brits.

So America was a new nation—and northern New England, in a sense, was also just getting started. The following decades saw an explosion in the fishing and whaling trades, and in trade per se. Along the coast, boatyards sprang up anyplace there was a good protected anchorage. Huge, Maine-built and ported windjammers sailed out of ports like Camden, Portsmouth, and Searsport and traveled around the globe, while nervous captains' wives walked widow's walks on the roofs of their opulent Victorian homes, praying for their husbands' safe return from the roiling seas.

More often than not, they did return—with huge holds of cod in tow, or goods like rum or sugar acquired in foreign lands in trade for New England's fish, lumber, and furs. It was the first phase of a two-step golden age in the region. The second was just about to come.

MILK & MACHINES: AN INDUSTRIAL AGE

The second half of the 19th century was a moment of incredible growth and excitement for New England. No longer were the towns here isolated fishing posts; railroads and ships (and soon, steamships) could bring local fish, milk, apples, and shoes to New York and Boston faster than ever.

As the new republic matured, economic growth swiftly followed. Residents of inland communities survived by farming, trading in furs, cutting trees, or building mills on the many rushing rivers that thread through this region. The machination of factory processes had brought some of the nation's first and largest textile, shoe, paper, and clothing mills to New England. Now Maine, New Hampshire, and Vermont were perfectly situated to take advantage of this new economy: Locals didn't mind hard work, and it could be done year-round, even in snowy weather. A burgeoning industry in machine-tool manufacture also popped up in the Connecticut River Valley.

Company towns and grand main-street architecture suddenly sprouted on the landscape in the unlikeliest of places. Old, cut-over Vermont hayfields suddenly became valuable for the dairy farming that could be done on them. The vast woodlots

Local Wisdom: Thoreau

We are in great haste to construct a magnetic telegraph from Maine to Texas; but Maine and Texas, it may be, have nothing important to communicate.

—Henry David Thoreau, *Walden*

of northern Maine—considered virtually useless, except for the occasional ship's mast—were suddenly worth their weight in gold as the world's population began reading more books and newspapers, and printers scrambled for reliable sources of pulpwood.

Times were heady indeed.

MODERN TIMES: TREES, TOURISM & SLOW FOOD

But this golden age did not last long in northern New England. Why? The world was changing too rapidly, and locals simply couldn't keep pace.

Everything from transport methods to agricultural research to world wars, development patterns, consumer tastes, and fashions were changing almost minute to minute. Local freight trains were swiftly replaced by trucks on interstate highways as the cheapest way to move goods cross-country—and that meant a woodlot, potato field, or mill in Oregon, Idaho, or Georgia, became more attractive than one in New England. While the railways had helped Maine to thrive in the mid–19th century, they now played an equally central role in undermining its prosperity.

The driving of the Golden Spike in 1869 in Utah, linking America's Atlantic and Pacific coasts by rail, was heard loud and clear in Maine; the coastal shipping trade was dealt a fatal blow. The bulk of the manufacturing first moved south and west, and then overseas. Working families began walking away from their farmhouses (there was no market for reselling them anyway) and setting off for regions with more promising opportunities. Vast tracts of farmland were reclaimed by forest.

The Great Depression played a hand, too, by bankrupting some local businesses. One good thing did come out of the worst depths of the Depression, however: Rather than cutting down all the remaining trees in northern New England, President Franklin D. Roosevelt used federal money to build parks and roads to those parks instead. And tourism blossomed as a result. The Hudson River Valley School of painters had helped, too, their idealistic, lovely paintings of the region drawing waves of curious city dwellers north. It became fashionable for the gentry and eventually the working class to set out for excursions to the mountains and shore. The grand resort hotels of the region, many built during this period, still testify to what was truly a golden moment of tourism, even if the rise of the automobile forced others to close their doors as less expensive motels siphoned off most of their business.

During the 70 or so years since, tourism has become the second twin engine of the rebuilt regional economy. Natural resources—timber, paper, lobsters, and fish—remained and probably always *will* remain the mainstays of the economy here. But tourism income is a rapidly growing, hugely important piece of the puzzle, whether all the locals like it or not.

Travelers to more remote regions might discover that some towns never experienced a renaissance at all; those places are still waiting to rebound from the economic malaise that hit last century. Small towns in coastal Maine and rural New Hampshire and Vermont, where many residents still depend on local resources—lobsters, fish, farmland, maybe a bed-and-breakfast or crafts business on the side—are still trying to eke out a living their own way.

Who do you see in the towns and cities today? Three people: Brits, the French, and out-of-towners. This British influence is most obvious in fishing towns (Portland, Portsmouth) and the dozens of little market and farm villages of Vermont and New Hampshire, places with names like Chelsea and Vershire and Tunbridge and Peterborough. The architecture tends toward either the solid (wood-frame homes that wouldn't look out of place near Plymouth Rock) or the spectacularly overblown:

Victorian homes and inns can be found in nearly every town in the region.

The French? They're here, too, throughout the three states (just flip through any phone book). That's because waves of French settlers from France and Québec steadily settled the region for several centuries once the French stopped warring with the British. The French strongly influenced this region's farmways and local foods: Baked beans came from recipes brought over by French sailors (adapted with local maple syrup), and New England fish chowder also likely came from the fish-and-cream stews originating in sailors' home towns in Brittany.

New England's mill towns, in particular, saw a flood tide of Québeckers migrating south during the Industrial Revolution of the late 19th century as farm kids flooded south, seeking escape from their province's crushing poverty in the new company towns; the mills were all too happy to accept this new pool of cheap labor. Most of the heaviest Franco-centric areas in northern New England today are still former mill towns—places such as Manchester, New Hampshire; Bangor, Sanford, Westbrook, South Portland, and Biddeford-Saco, Maine; and any part of Vermont tilting in the general direction of the Canada border. That includes the Northeast Kingdom, the Upper Valley, and the northern part of the Champlain Valley, where family names become nearly 100 percent French as you approach the Québec line. Look for the big spires of Catholic cathedrals: That's where you'll find a pocket of resident French culture.

It's the blow-ins, though, who may end up with final say over where this region is headed. They're the ones demanding stricter zoning and land-protection laws, building or dining in five-star restaurants, demanding *slow foods* (artisanal goat cheese, micro-greens, and the like), and hunting down organic baby clothes. These are *not* the sorts of things you normally associate with New England, and especially not with northern New England; yet there is absolutely no doubt in my mind that those things will continue to occupy a larger slice of the New England experience. Indeed, it could probably more accurately be called "new New England"—except that would be a mouthful.

4 NORTHERN NEW ENGLAND'S ART & ARCHITECTURE

You can often trace the evolution of a place by its architecture, as styles evolve from basic structures into elaborate mansions. Here's a primer to help you identify some of the key architecture types you'll spot in northern New England:

- **Colonial** (1600–1700): The New England house of the 17th century was a simple, boxy affair, often covered in shingles or rough clapboards. Don't look for ornamentation; these homes were designed for basic shelter from the elements, and are often marked by prominent stone chimneys.
- **Georgian** (1700–1800): Ornamentation comes into play in the Georgian style, which draws heavily on classical symmetry. Georgian buildings were in vogue in England at the time, and were embraced by affluent colonists. Look for Palladian windows, formal pilasters, and elaborate projecting pediments. Portsmouth, New Hampshire, has lots of great examples of later Georgian styles.
- **Federal** (1780–1820): Federal homes (sometimes called Adams homes) might best represent the New England ideal.

Spacious yet austere, they are often rectangular or square, with low-pitched roofs and little ornament on the front, although carved swags or other embellishments are frequently seen near the roofline. Look for fan windows and chimneys bracketing the building. Federal-style homes are best found in coastal Maine towns like Kennebunkport, Bath, and Brunswick.

- **Greek Revival** (1820–60): The most easy-to-identify Greek Revival homes feature a projecting portico with massive columns, like a part of the Parthenon grafted onto an existing home. The less dramatic homes may simply be oriented such that the gable faces the street, accenting the triangular pediment. Greek Revival didn't really catch on in New England the way it did in the South, however.
- **Carpenter Gothic** and **Gothic Revival** (1840–80): The second half of the 19th century brought a wave of Gothic Revival homes, which borrowed their aesthetic from the English country home.
- **Victorian** (1860–1900): This is a catchall term for the jumble of mid- to late-19th-century styles that emphasized complexity and opulence. Perhaps the best-known Victorian style—almost a caricature—is the tall and narrow Addams Family–style house, with mansard roof and prickly roof cresting. You'll find these scattered throughout the region; Portland, Maine, is one hot spot. The Victorian style also includes squarish **Italianate** homes with wide eaves and unusual flourishes, such as the outstanding Victoria Mansion in Portland. Stretching the definition a bit, Victorian could also include the **Richardsonian Romanesque** style, which was popular for railroad stations and public buildings of the day.
- **Shingle** (1880–1900): This uniquely New England style quickly became preferred for vacation homes in the region, especially in wealthy enclaves of coastal Maine (Cape Elizabeth, Mount Desert Isle). They're marked by a profusion of gables, roofs, and porches, and are typically covered with shingles from roofline to foundation.
- **Modern** (1900–present): Maine has produced very little in the way of notable modern architecture; you won't find a Fallingwater, but you *might* spy a minimalist, modernist masterpiece somewhere on a Vermont back road or ski slope if you look hard.

Beyond architectural styles, the visual arts are well represented in northern New England. Even the smallest town seems to have an arts organization, art gallery, or at least a regular series of exhibitions of local artwork at the town library.

The best art museums are sometimes, but not always, located in the biggest cities. The cities of Portland, Maine, and Manchester, New Hampshire, hold two of the top museums in the region. But two of the best half-dozen are in small- to medium-size Maine coastal communities: the Ogunquit Museum of American Art in Ogunquit and the Farnsworth Art Museum in Rockland. See chapter 9. Another top museum is improbably located in out-of-the-way St. Johnsbury, Vermont. See chapter 6.

Also check local colleges and universities such as Dartmouth College in Hanover, New Hampshire; its Hood Museum's art collection is especially good—and usually fully open to the public.

There are plenty of local undiscovered jewelers, potters, and other artists here in the towns and cities, too. Explore the compact downtowns of places like Burlington and Portland for a taste. And check the local daily and free weekly papers for listings of art exhibits, festivals, and crafts shows—you'll be rewarded not only with good art, but also the satisfaction that comes with meeting an artist on the rise face to face. New Hampshire's annual summertime Craftsmen's Fair is especially good.

5 THE LAY OF THE LAND

The human history of northern New England is usually thought of as beginning at a fixed point: in 1492, when Columbus sailed the ocean blue. But the clock actually winds *much* further back than that—beginning thousands of years ago, when Native American tribes fished Atlantic shores and hunted these hills. And even they were here for only a sliver of the long period of time required to create this place; situations like this call for the word *eons.* The rocks upon which you climb, sun yourself, and picnic are old—staggeringly old.

Before arriving, then, it's a good idea to acquaint yourself with the natural history of the place. Armed with a little respect and appreciation for the landscape before you, you just might treat it more reverently while you're here—and help ensure that it remains for future generations to behold for many years.

ROCKY ROAD: GEOLOGY SETS THE TABLE

The beginnings of New England are perhaps a half-billion years old. That's right: *billion,* with a B.

Deep wells of liquid rock known as magma were moving upward through the earth's mantle, exploding in underground volcanoes, then hardening—still underground, mind you—into granite-like rocks. Much later, natural forces such as wind and water wore away and exposed the upper layers of these rocks. Their punishment was only beginning, however; soon enough (geologically speaking, that is), what is now eastern North America and most of Europe began to shove up against each other, slowly but inexorably.

This "collision" (which was more like an *extremely* slow-motion car wreck) heated, squeezed, transformed, and thrust up the rocks that now form the backbone of the coastline. Ice ages came and went, but the rocks remained; the successive waves of glaciation and retreat scratched up the rocks like old vinyl records, and the thick tongues of pressing ice cut deep notches out of them. Huge boulders were swept up and deposited by the ice in odd places.

When the glaciers finally retreated for the last time, tens of thousands of years ago, the water melting from the huge ice sheet covering North America swelled the level of the Atlantic high enough to submerge formerly free-flowing river valleys and bays, giving the Maine coastline and places like Acadia National Park and Vermont's Smuggler's Notch their distinctively rocky, knuckled faces. The melting ice sheets also laid down tons of silt and sand in their wake, leaving the sandy barrens and gentle hills of western Maine and central New Hampshire.

Once the bones of this landscape were established, next came the flesh: plants and animals. After each ice age, conifers such as spruce and fir trees—alongside countless grasses and weeds—began to reform, then decompose and form soils. It was tough work: Most of northern New England is a rocky, acidic place, inhospitable to farming. Yet a few plants persevered (as plants tend to do), and spruces, firs, and hemlocks soon formed an impenetrable thicket covering much of the bedrock. When those evergreen trees died of old age, were struck by lightning and caught on fire, or were cut down by settlers (or beavers), different kinds of trees—beeches, birches, brilliant sugar maples—rushed in to replace them.

As the trees and flowers and fruits became reestablished, animals wandered back here, too—some now extinct, but some still thriving today in the fields, hills, and woods of the region. As temperatures warmed, deer and songbirds eventually followed, and polar bears and caribou were no longer regular features of New England—though caribou and moose still wander the northern stretches of all three states.

New England's unique position, near the warm Gulf Stream without quite touching it, has also bequeathed the region with an amazing variety of marine life. The warm offshore Gulf current passes over a high, shallow undersea plateau known as the Georges Bank, then collides with the much colder waters of the North Atlantic. This collision creates swirls and upwelling currents from the sea floor, bringing loads of microscopic food particles up toward the surface—food that sustains an astonishingly complex variety of microorganisms, the bottom rungs in a ladder of marine life.

The food chain culminates in migrating whales, which make for a wonderful spectacle off the Maine coast twice per year. Seabirds make similar passages, lighting upon the rocks, fields, and lakes of New England in spring and fall. The Maine coast also teems (though not as much as it once did) with codfish, lobsters, crabs, and other sea creatures.

The coastal tide pools of Maine are also worth exploring. This precarious zone, where land and rock meet ocean, is an ever-changing world of seaweed, snails, barnacles, darting water bugs, clams, shellfish, mud-burrowing worms, and other creatures. Interestingly, creatures live in distinct, well-marked "bands" as you get closer to the water: Rocks that are always submerged contain one mixture of seaweed, shellfish, and marine organisms, while rocks that are exposed and then re-submerged each day by the tides have a different mix. It's fascinating to discover how each particular organism has found its own narrow niche. Move it up or down a foot? It would perish.

What follows is a sketch of some of the nature life you'll find in northern New England. For a real look at it, though, get outside and see it for yourself. Whether you explore this region on foot, by bicycle, by kayak, by horse-drawn carriage, or by charter boat, you're certain to see something you've never quite seen before. Be attentive, and you'll come away with a deeper respect for nature—not only here, but everywhere.

TREES AND SHRUBS

Native plants and trees in the region include the following:

BALSAM FIR The best-smelling tree in the provinces must be the mighty balsam fir, whose tips are sometimes harvested to fabricate aromatic Christmas-tree wreaths. It's sometimes hard to tell a fir from a spruce or hemlock, though the balsam's flat paddlelike needles (white underneath) are unique—only a hemlock's are similar. Pull one off the twig to be sure; a fir's needle comes off clean, a hemlock's ragged. Still not sure you've got a fir

Balsam Fir

tree on your hands? The long, glossy, almost purplish cones are absolutely distinctive. Tree farms remain a distinctive part of the natural and cultural landscape in the northern one-third of Maine, New Hampshire, and Vermont.

RED AND WHITE PINES These pines grow in sandy soils and like some (or a lot of) sunlight. The **eastern white pine** is the familiar "King's pine" once prevalent throughout the northeast portions of North America; you can recognize it by its very long, strong needles that are always arranged five to a clump, like a hand's fingers. Its trunk was prized for the masts of ships of war in the 16th to 19th centuries, and countless huge pines were floated down Maine's big rivers by loggers. Sadly, old-growth white pines are virtually nonexistent today, but you can still find the tree throughout northern New England. The **red pine,** not so common, can be distinguished by its pairs of needles and pitchy trunk; it grows in sandy areas.

Red Pine

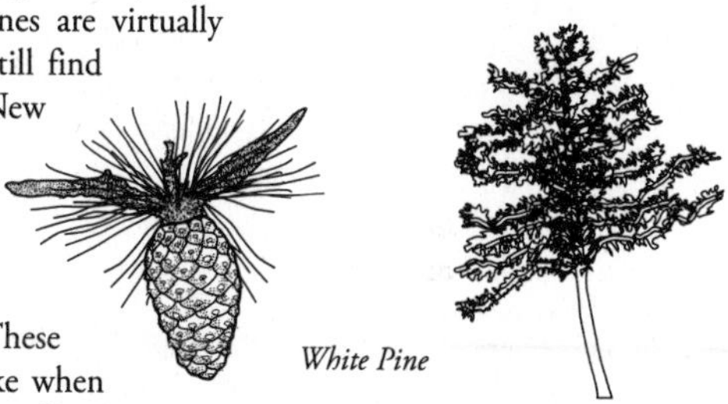

White Pine

RED AND SUGAR MAPLES These two maple trees look vaguely alike when turning color in fall, but they're actually quite different, from the shapes of their leaves to the habitats they prefer. **Red maples** have skinny, gray trunks and like a swampy or wet area; often, several of the slim trunks grow together into a clump, and in fall the red maples' pointy leaves turn a brilliant scarlet color almost at once.

Sugar maples, on the other hand, are stout-trunked trees with lovely, substantial leaves (marked with distinctive *U*-shaped notches), which autumn's cold nights transform magically into red and flame-orange colors. Vermont is world-famous for its stands of these trees and their October foliage. Sugar maples tend to grow in or at the edges of mixed forests, often in combination with birch trees, oak trees, beech trees, and hemlocks; they can also be found marking out lines on old farm properties. Sugar maples' sap is collected and boiled down in temporary *sugar houses* (huts in the woods, usually with wood-fired boilers) to make delicious maple syrup every March—a big business in the hills of Vermont and New Hampshire, and something you can also find in parts of Maine as well.

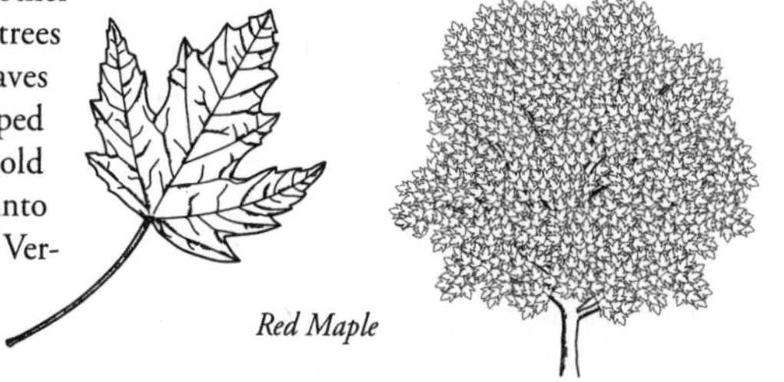

Red Maple

LOWBUSH BLUEBERRY Maine is one of the world's largest producers of wild blueberries, officially known as lowbush blueberries. With shrubby, tealike leaves and thick twigs, the plants lie low on exposed rocks on sunny hillsides, or sometimes crop up in shady woods; most of the year, the berries are inconspicuous and trail harmlessly underfoot. Come late summer, however, they're suddenly very popular—for bears as well as people. The wild berries ripen slowly in the sun (look behind and beneath leaves for the best bunches) and make for great eating off the bush, pancake baking, or jam making.

LAND MAMMALS

Beaver

BLACK BEAR Black bears still roam northern New England, though in small numbers (still, you may want to keep a cover on that campfire food). The bears are mostly—emphasis on *mostly*—plant eaters and docile; they're the smallest of the North American bears and don't want trouble. Though they'll eat just about anything, these bears prefer easily reached foods on the woodland floor such as berries, mushrooms, nuts . . . and campers' leftovers. (Suspend leftovers in a "bear bag" away from your tent if you're camping in bear territory.) Black bears fatten up in fall for a long winter hibernation that averages 6 months.

Black Bear

MOOSE Nothing says Maine like a moose, and the huge, skinny-legged, vegetarian moose is more than occasionally seen in the deep woods of northern and western Maine and northern New Hampshire. (They're less common in Vermont, because that steep, cleared-off dairy-farming state has far fewer deep woods, flat lakes, and ponds, which are the moose's preferred habitat.) The Maine moose population is about 30,000 today—enough that the moose hunt is big business in Maine. (The state holds an annual lottery dispensing moose permits, resulting in more than 2,000 moose kills per year in Oct and Nov; three out of four hunters bag one during the season.) The rack of antlers on the male, broad lineman-like shoulders, spindly but quick legs, and sheer bulk (it's as big as a truck) ensure you won't mistake a moose for anything else. Be careful driving on highways through remote wooded areas late at night: A collision with a moose is often fatal for the *driver.*

Moose

WHALES, DOLPHINS, PORPOISES & SEALS

FINBACK WHALE A seasonal visitor to the coast of Maine twice a year while migrating between polar and equatorial waters, the finback is one of the biggest whales—also one of the most collegial and most commonly found—in New England. It often travels in pairs or groups of a half-dozen or more (most whales are relatively solitary), though it does not travel close to shore or in shallow waters; you'll need a whale-watching boat

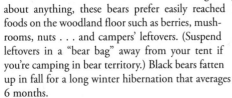

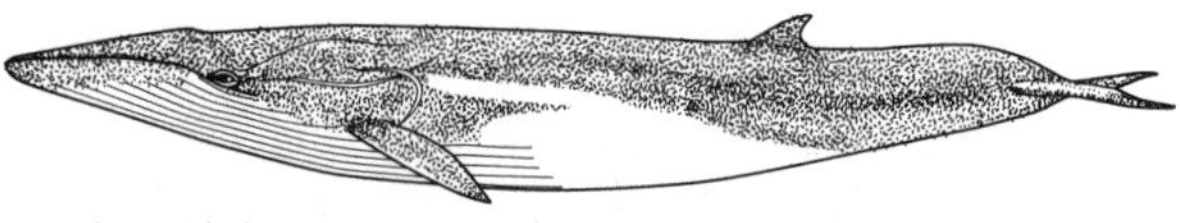

Finback Whale

to spot it. Find it by its rather triangular head and a fin that sweeps backward (like a dolphin's) rather than straight up like many other whales'. The whale's population is now believed to be on the rise off New England's coast, after a long decline precipitated by whaling.

HUMPBACK WHALE Though this whale's Latin name roughly translates to "large-winged New England resident," the gentle, gigantic humpback isn't often seen from shore in Maine. (That's mostly because they were easy targets in the heyday of whaling.) But whale-watching tours from Bar Harbor and coastal towns like Boothbay often pass by humpbacks, and if you see them, you'll never forget the sight: They are huge, jet-black, blow tremendous amounts of water when surfacing, and perform amazingly playful acrobatics above water. The males also sing haunting songs, sometimes for as long as 2 days at a time. The world population has shrunk to perhaps 20,000 whales.

MINKE WHALE The smallest (and most human-friendly) of the whales, the minke swims off the coast of Maine, usually moving in groups of two or three whales—but much larger groups collect in feeding areas and during certain seasons. It has a unique habit of approaching and congregating around boats and ships, making this a whale you're quite likely to see while on a whale-watch tour. The minke is dark gray on top, the throat has grooves, and each black flipper fin is marked with a conspicuous white band.

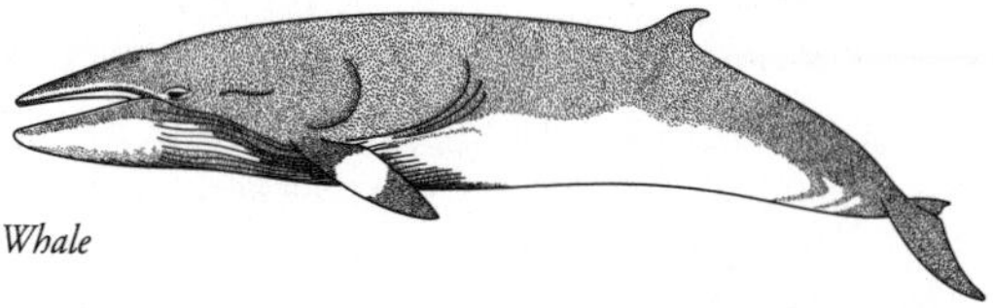

Minke Whale

PILOT WHALE A smallish whale, the pilot is sometimes seen off the coast of Maine by whale-watching boats, but it's still poorly understood: Its habits, true population, and diet are mostly unknown. It *is* known to congregate in large groups, sometimes numbering up to several hundred, and even to swim with other species of whale at sea. Nearly unique among whales in this part of the world, the pilot has teeth; its roundish fin is swept back like a dolphin's.

Pilot Whale

DOLPHINS Two very similar-looking species of dolphin—the **Atlantic white-sided dolphin** and the **white-beaked dolphin**—swim by the coast of Maine twice a year, but you won't see them from the beach; book a whale-watching tour to catch a glimpse. Cute and athletic, these dolphins also occasionally turn up on beaches, for the same reason as pilot whales: Large groups are occasionally stranded by the tides, then perish when they cannot get back to sea in time.

Atlantic White-Sided Dolphin

White-Beaked Dolphin

HARBOR PORPOISE Quiet in behavior and habit, the porpoise is not the same thing as the dolphin; in fact, it's darker, much less athletic, and has a blunter, triangular fin. (The dolphin jumps out of the water and has a sharper fin that sweeps backward.)

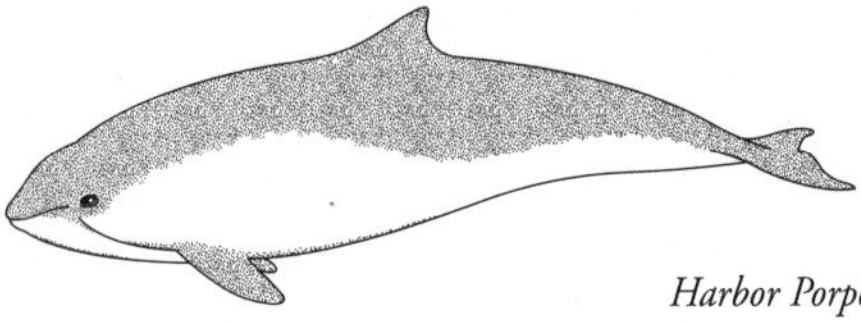

Harbor Porpoise

HARBOR SEAL The shy, bewhiskered harbor seal can be seen in rocky parts of the Downeast coast of Maine. It's best seen by using a charter-boat service, as you'll often find it basking in the sun on rocks offshore. You'll easily recognize it: The seal's flippers have five claws, almost like a human hand; its neck is stocky and strong (as are its teeth); and then there is its fur, and those whiskers.

INVERTEBRATES

AMERICAN LOBSTER The lobster is the single image that leaps to mind first when you say the word "Maine." Everyone knows the lobster by sight and taste; what few know is that it was once considered ugly, tasteless, and unfit to eat. There was a time not long ago when prisoners were served lobster and lobster stew three times a day. Today the situation is quite different: This is one of Maine's biggest export products. Lobsters are related to crabs, shrimp—even spiders and insects (sorry, diners). They feed by slowly scouring the ocean bottom in shallow, dark waters, locating food by smell (because they see very, very poorly). The hard shell, which is periodically shed in order to grow larger, is the lobster's skeleton; a greenish-black or (rarely) blue color when alive, the shell turns bright red only after the lobster is cooked.

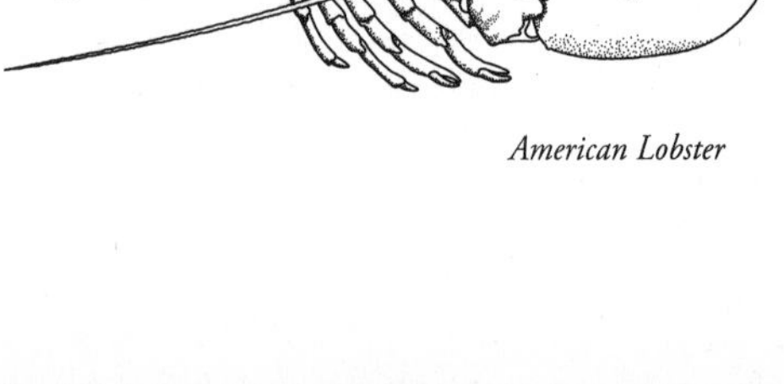

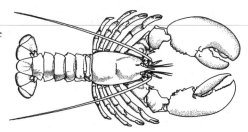

American Lobster

BIRDS

Waterfowl

Red-Breasted Merganser

DUCKS Between one and two dozen species of ducks and ducklike geese, brant, and teal seasonally visit the lakes, ponds, and tidal coves of Maine and New Hampshire every year, including—though hardly limited to—the **red-breasted merganser** and the **common eider.** Mergansers, characterized by very white sides and very red bills (in males) or reddish crests (in females), flock year-round but are more common in winter months. So is the eider, which inhabits offshore islands and coastal waters rather than provincial freshwater lakes; in winter these islands transform into huge rafts of birds. Male eiders are marked with a sharp black-and-white pattern.

Common Eider

GREAT BLUE HERON Everyone knows a great blue at once, by its prehistoric flapping wings, comb of feathers, and spindly legs. These magnificent hunters wade through tidal rivers, fishing with lightning strikes beneath the surface, from May through around October. The smaller, stealthier green heron and yellow-crowned night heron are rarely seen.

Great Blue Heron

LOONS Two species of loon visit the region's lakes and tidal inlets, fishing for dinner. The **red-throated loon,** grayish with a red neck, is a spring passer-through and very rare in summer or winter. The **common loon** is, indeed, much more common—it can be distinguished by a black band around the neck, as well as black-and-white stripes and dots—and can be found on the quieter lakes of Maine and New Hampshire year-round, though it's most easily spotted in late spring and late fall. It summers on lakes and winters on open patches of ocean inlets, giving a distinctively mournful, almost laughing call. Both loon populations have been decimated by environmental changes such as oil spills, acid rain, and airborne mercury.

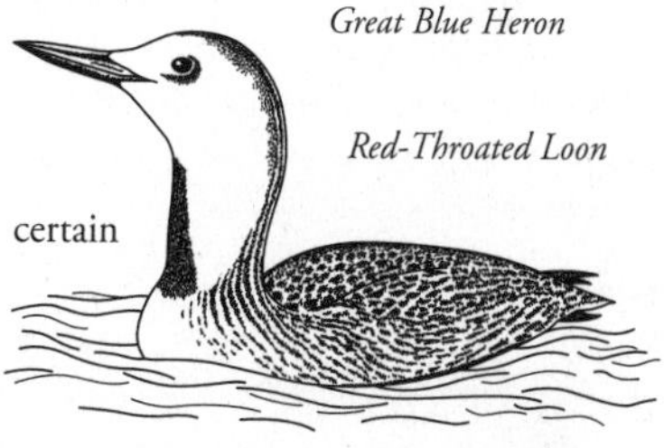

Red-Throated Loon

PLOVERS Plovers inhabit and breed in certain muddy tidal flats, and their habitat is precarious; a single human step can crush an entire generation of eggs. Four species of plover visit the Midcoast of Maine in a few spots (such as Phippsburg's Popham Beach), and they're here only for a relatively short time. The **lesser golden-plover** flocks in considerable numbers in September while passing through, and the **greater golden-plover** occasionally lands in Newfoundland during migration. The **semipalmated plover,** with its quite different brownish body and white breast,

Common Loon

has a similar life cycle and is also usually seen only in spring, passing through.

Semipalmated Plover

SEAGULLS No bird is as closely associated with Maine and the sea as the seagull. But, in fact, there's more than one kind of gull here. Some species live here year-round, while others visit seasonally, and a few more pop up only occasionally. Most common is the grayish **herring gull,** which is also the gull least afraid of humans. It's found in prevalence every month of the year. The **great black-backed gull** is similarly common, and is nearly all white (except for that black back and wings). This aggressive bird will even eat the eggs of another gull but in general avoids humans. You might also see **glaucous, ring-billed,** and even **laughing** and **Bonaparte's gulls** (rarely, and usually only in summer), not to mention the related **black-legged kittiwake.**

Herring Gull

Great Black-Backed Gull

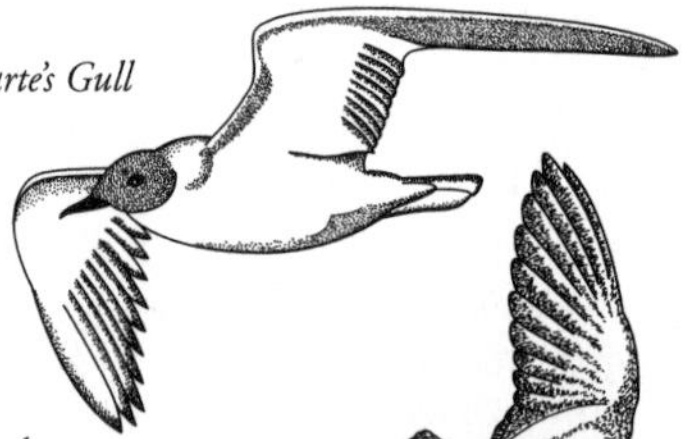

Bonaparte's Gull

STORM PETRELS The tiny storm petrel is a fascinating creature. These plucky little birds fly astonishing distances in winter, eating insects on the wing, only to return to the coast each spring like clockwork, usually in May. They spend an amazing 4 months incubating, hatching, and tending to their single, white eggs in nests eked out of rocks. **Wilson's storm petrels** sometimes follow behind offshore boats; the much less common **Leach's storm petrel** restricts its visits and nests solely to far-offshore rocks and islands and is also mostly nocturnal, which further reduces the chances of seeing it. Both breed in summer, then head south for winter.

Wilson's Storm Petrel

Land Birds

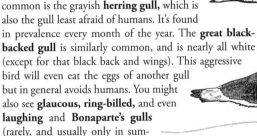

Bald Eagle

BALD EAGLE Yes, they're here in northern New England—year-round—and even breed here, though they're difficult to find and hardly conspicuous. (Their endangered status means you shouldn't really seek them out anyway.) The bald eagle's black body, white head, and yellow bill make it almost impossible to confuse with any other bird. It was nearly wiped out in the 1970s, mainly due to environmental poisons such as DDT-based pesticides, which caused female eagles to lay eggs that were too weak to sustain growing baby chicks. However, the bird is beginning

Landscape Is Not Just Scenery

Rural New England is not just scenery—it's home to millennia of natural history (bears, whales, and caribou, oh my!), as well as human history (Native Americans; fishermen and hunters who predate the earliest European settler; modern-day fisherman and lobstermen). And the story this history tells continues today, creating the place we call northern New England, replete with its gourmet chefs, antiques shop owners, marketing gurus, and IT professionals. Once you get to know this fuller history, and the creatures and landscapes you see, you'll have a better trip—and become a more ecologically aware traveler with a deeper respect for what you're experiencing.

For information about the whales you'll be glimpsing (and how to respect them), visit the web site of the **Whale and Dolphin Conservation Society** at **www.wdcs.org**. For info on traveling lightly in general, see **Tread Lightly** (www.treadlightly.org) online.

to make a comeback. They're most commonly found on lakes in remote areas such as those in northern Maine, Vermont, and New Hampshire.

SONGBIRDS Dozens of species of songbirds roost in New England's open fields, forests, abandoned (and still-operating) farm fields, and dead trees—plus in the rafters of homes and barns, inside fence posts, and in helpful bird boxes. They're not as common in remote, rocky places like the islands of Maine as they are in suburbia (greater Portland, for instance) and the farmlands of Vermont. Songbirds normally thrive on human company, so look for them near the settled areas.

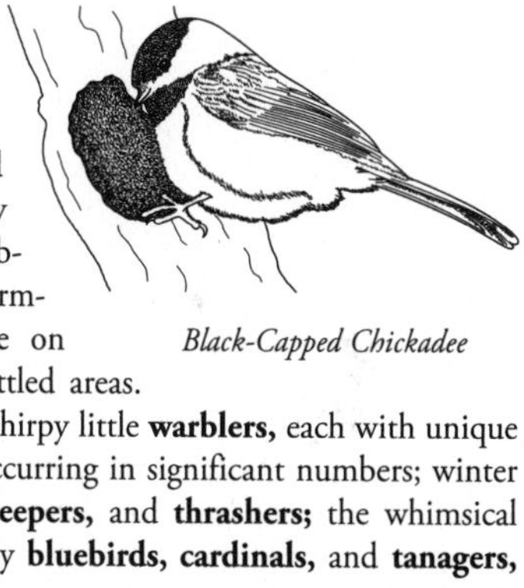

Black-Capped Chickadee

The region hosts a dozen or so distinct types of chirpy little **warblers,** each with unique and often liquid songs; a half-dozen **thrushes** occurring in significant numbers; winter **wrens, swallows, sparrows, vireos, finches, creepers,** and **thrashers;** the whimsical **black-capped chickadee;** and occasionally lovely **bluebirds, cardinals,** and **tanagers,** among many other species.

6 NORTHERN NEW ENGLAND'S POPULAR CULTURE

Northern New England may be sparsely populated, but it's got more than its per-capita share of writers, artists, and musicians. Here's a little "starter kit" of films, CDs, and literature to prepare you for a more rewarding visit to the region.

BOOKS

New Englanders have generated whole libraries, from the earliest days of hellfire-and-brimstone Puritan sermons to Stephen King's horror novels set in fictional Maine villages. Here are a few of them:

- ***In the Memory House,*** by Howard Mansfield (1993). This finely written book by a New Hampshire author provides a penetrating look at New England's sometimes estranged relationship with its own past.
- ***Inventing New England,*** by Dona Brown (1995). A University of Vermont professor tells the epic tale of the rise of 19th-century tourism in New England in this uncommonly well-written study.
- ***Lobster Gangs of Maine,*** by James M. Acheson (1988). This exhaustively researched book answers every question you'll have about the lobsterman's life.
- ***Northern Borders,*** by Howard Frank Mosher (1994). This magical novel is ostensibly about a young boy living with his taciturn grandparents in northern Vermont, but the book's central character is really Vermont's Northeast Kingdom.
- ***One Man's Meat,*** by E. B. White (1944). White was a writer's writer, a part-time resident of a saltwater farm on the Maine coast and a frequent contributor to *The New Yorker.* His essays, from the late 1930s and early 1940s, are only incidentally about Maine, but you get a superb sense of place by observing the shadows. Still in paperback.
- ***Serious Pig,*** by John Thorne with Matt Lewis Thorne (1996). One quick way to any region's character is directly through its stomach. The Thornes' finely crafted essays on Maine regional cooking are exhaustive in their coverage of chowder, beans, pie, and more.
- ***Vermont Traditions,*** by Dorothy Canfield Fisher (1953). Written in that somewhat overwrought style popular in the 1950s, this still remains the best survey of the Vermont character.
- ***The Maine Woods,*** by Henry David Thoreau (1848). The classic nature writer's take on the state's big rivers, mountains, and woods from a series of journeys taken only a quarter-century after Maine became a state.

Famous writers are legion in these parts, too. **Henry Wadsworth Longfellow** (1807–82), a Portland poet who later settled in Cambridge, caught the attention of the public with evocative narrative poems focusing on distinctly American subjects. His popular works included "The Courtship of Miles Standish," "Paul Revere's Ride," and "Hiawatha." Poetry in the mid–19th century was the equivalent of Hollywood movies today—and Longfellow could be considered his generation's Steven Spielberg (apologies to literary scholars).

Among other regional writers who left a lasting mark on American literature were **Edna St. Vincent Millay** (1892–1950), a poet from Camden, Maine, and **Sarah Orne Jewett** (1849–1909), who wrote the indelible *The Country of the Pointed Firs.* The bestselling *Uncle Tom's Cabin,* the book Abraham Lincoln half-jokingly accused of starting the Civil War, was written by **Harriet Beecher Stowe** (1811–86) in Brunswick, Maine. The former *New Yorker* editor **E. B. White** (1899–1985) wrote fine, wide-ranging essays and books (including the classic children's book *Charlotte's Web*) from his perch near Blue Hill, Maine, where he moved to a saltwater farm in 1939.

New England's later role in America's literary tradition is probably best symbolized by the poems of **Robert Frost** (1874–1963). Though born in California, he lived most of his life on farms in New Hampshire and Vermont. He found a certain peace in this region, and rich metaphors for his writing. Among his most famous lines: "Two roads diverged in a wood, and I— / I took the one less traveled by, / And that has made all the difference." He also wrote the line "good fences make good neighbors" (in the poem "Mending Wall")—as fitting a slogan for New England as I can think of.

The region continues to attract writers drawn to its fine educational institutions and the privacy of rural life. Prominent contemporary writers and poets who still live in the region part- or full-time include poet **Galway Kinnell,** fiction writer **Nicholson Baker,** nonfiction essayist **Bill Bryson,** and novelist **John Irving**. (The late novelist **John Updike,** poet **Donald Hall,** and nature writer **John Hay** also spent significant time here.)

Finally, Maine is the lifetime home of writer **Stephen King**—no longer just a horror novelist with a uniquely twisted take on everyday life in his home region, but more of a leading economic export at this point.

FILM & TV

Northern New England is captured through the lens of Hollywood from time to time, thanks in equal parts to its natural beauty; its Calvinist, slightly spooky history; and the star actors, actresses, and directors who were raised here or live here now and continue to push projects incorporating local storylines or landscapes.

Lillian Gish's 1920 silent film *Way Down East* was perhaps the first movie to bring cinematic attention to the region, and ever since films have periodically depicted both the bright and dark sides of living in New England. Still, it's somewhat surprising Hollywood script writers haven't written more films set in this region: Its overabundance of local characters and stories would seem to make it a natural set piece.

There have been a few attempts to bring Hollywood here, however.

Diane Keaton starred in the limp 1987 comedy ***Baby Boom,*** in which city-dweller J.C. Wiatt flees the big city for a Vermont cottage, only to discover mud season and the joys of motherhood, self-employment . . . and applesauce. Not a very good film, but it's good on visuals—and Harold Ramis is in it (as a Wall Street guy!). The film was shot in Manchester and Weston, among other locations in the state.

The forgettable 1996 film ***The Preacher's Wife*** is still touted by Portlanders for the filming it did on an ice rink in the city's Deering Oaks Park. The film features Denzel plus Whitney, but skip it. The 1999 Kevin Costner vehicle ***Message in a Bottle*** and 1993 Mel Gibson film ***The Man Without a Face*** (one of his better efforts) were both shot partly along the Maine coast, though they were not specifically set in the state.

Some films shot here are considered outstanding. The 2000 horror thriller ***What Lies Beneath,*** starring Harrison Ford and Michelle Pfeiffer, was partly filmed in a Vermont state park on lower Lake Champlain; it grossed hundreds of millions of dollars worldwide. Director Todd Field's 2001 film ***In the Bedroom,*** based on an Andre Dubus short story, was nominated for a half-dozen Academy Awards. The story (of a small-town doctor who avenges his son's death) takes place in Midcoast Maine, and the film was indeed mostly shot in the Camden-Rockland area.

And John Irving's novels (see "Books," above) ***The World According to Garp*** (1982) and ***The Hotel New Hampshire*** (1984) were each adapted and made into effective films set in northern New England starring Hollywood heavyweights like Jodie Foster, Rob Lowe, and Robin Williams.

But the benchmark of all feel-good New England films might be 1981's ***On Golden Pond,*** an epic tearjerker in which two dowagers—Henry Fonda and Kate Hepburn—heal their connections with family (Jane Fonda plays Henry's daughter, naturally) on a beautiful New England pond. Yes, it's a real pond in New Hampshire, and it's still just as beautiful today. It was a smash hit.

Then there's the not-so-nice. A host of horror films written by Maine's Stephen

King—from ***Carrie, Cujo,*** and ***The Dead Zone*** down through to a welter of TV miniseries—make it sometimes seem like the only inhabitants of these small New England towns are supernatural forces. However, King also penned the short story upon which the lovely film ***The Shawshank Redemption*** (a fictional story that takes place in Maine) was based.

Several television series have also been based in New England, most notably this wildly popular duo: ***Newhart*** (1982–90), in which actor Bob Newhart comically attempted to run a rural Vermont bed-and-breakfast inn; and ***Murder, She Wrote*** (1984–96), which saw crime novelist Angela Lansbury stumbling across and solving real-life crimes with seeming ease from her perch in the fictional fishing village of Cabot Cove, Maine. To tell the truth, neither series did a good job of representing the real New England experience (though most TV viewers probably didn't notice): These days most New Englanders don't walk around with unbearable accents and wearing flannel, even if their great-grandparents probably did.

MUSIC

New England musicians have contributed mightily to the American music scene. An exhaustive list of stars is impossible here, but a few of the notable local lights include:

- The rock band **Aerosmith,** which first assembled in New Hampshire
- Crooner **Rudy Vallee,** born in Vermont and raised in Maine
- Jam-band **Phish,** formed in Burlington, Vermont, by a bunch of college friends
- Country-folk musician **Slaid Cleaves,** now an Austin, Texas, fixture but originally from Maine
- Nashville singer-songwriters **Cindy Bullens** and **Patty Griffin,** also born and raised in Maine

7 EATING IN NORTHERN NEW ENGLAND

Northern New England got a late start in the food game—for a while, it was basically fish, vegetables, simple soup, and whatever was dragged home from a hunt, and updated versions of that—but it has caught up, in spades. Today you can eat really well in this region thanks to some unusually crafty producers, importers, and chefs.

Along the Maine and New Hampshire coasts, live lobsters can be bought off the boat at lobster pounds. The setting is usually as rustic it gets—maybe a couple of picnic tables on a slab of concrete, plus a shed where huge vats of water are kept at a low boil. But you come for the freshly steamed lobsters and the great water views. You can also buy fried fish and fried clams (by the bucket!) at divey shacks anywhere on the coast. More upscale seafood eateries in sea towns like Portland, Portsmouth, Freeport, Northeast Harbor, and Robinhood serve the local catch of the day grilled or sautéed with an array of sauces.

Inland, take time to sample local farm products such as the sweet maple syrup, sold throughout northern New Hampshire and Vermont; it's the best in the world. Look also for Vermont's famous apple cider and Maine's tiny, tasty wild blueberries.

Every summer, small farmers across the region set up stands at the ends of driveways selling fresh produce straight from the garden. You can find berries, fruits, and sometimes home-baked breads here. These stands are rarely tended; just leave your money in the coffee can, and maybe a bit of a tip. Also watch for the appearance of "U-pick" farms in summertime. For a fee that's much less than what you pay in a store for the packaged fruit, you fill up bags of strawberries or blueberries and take 'em home. Kids love this.

Restaurateurs haven't overlooked New England's bounty, either. Big-city chefs are flocking here every year to hang up new shingles and test themselves with the local ingredients; some restaurants maintain their own herb and vegetable gardens. Some of these places stretch the budget a bit. But plenty of others fall squarely into the "road food" category. Here's an abbreviated field guide to northern New England's distinctively local eats:

- **Apples:** Both Maine and Vermont are well-known for their fall apple harvests. Look for orchards in foothills, such as those in central and western Maine near Bridgton and Augusta or those in the Champlain Valley. Cold Hollow Cider Mill in **Waterbury** (near **Stowe**) is probably the most famous cider seller in the U.S.
- **Baked beans:** Boston will be forever linked with baked beans (hence the nickname "Beantown"), but the dish remains extremely popular in pockets of Maine, too. Saturday-night church dinners (also known as "bean hole" suppers) usually consist of baked beans and brown bread, plus pasta salads and the like. There's also a famous B&M baked-bean plant still operating in **Portland.**
- **Blueberries:** One sometimes gets the feeling that Downeast Maine's economy would collapse without the humble blueberry. To taste it, look for roadside stands and diners from the midcoast north, selling pies made with fresh berries from mid- until late summer. These tiny blueberries (which grow on low shrubs and wind-swept rocks or hilltops) are much tastier than the bigger, commercial variety. You can even pick your own pail of berries, for free, high on the slopes of certain hills like **Blue Hill** and **Pleasant Mountain.** Look for the bush's oval, leathery, tealike leaves.
- **Cheese:** Cheese is a Vermont specialty: Cheddar is the most common variety (you can buy a huge "wheel" of cheddar at any country store worth its salt), but goat cheeses are starting to make a serious run, too. The Northeast Kingdom and Connecticut Valley are especially rich in cheese. Take a cheese-factory tour in **Cabot, Grafton,** or **Plymouth Notch** to see what goes into your cheddar, or scour the local natural-foods store (often called a "co-op" in Vermont) for the most local version of cow and goat cheese.
- **Fish chowder:** My favorite coastal dish is also the simplest one: fish chowder, which in its purest form consists simply of the day's catch of chopped-up whitefish (cod, haddock), enough milk to satisfy a small animal, peeled potatoes, and a nice big chunk of butter. No thickener, cornstarch, or flour—*please.* This dish is best enjoyed with an ocean view, a square of blueberry cake, and a cup of bad coffee. And in the fishing villages of coastal Maine, that's exactly how it's still served to legions of tired and hungry local fisherman as they trundle in after long, cold days out on the water hauling nets or traps.
- **Lobster:** You can buy freshly steamed lobsters at pounds in most Maine fishing towns, usually from a shack right on the main fishing pier. Lobster *rolls* consist of lobster meat plucked from the shell, mixed with just enough mayonnaise to hold it all together, then served on a buttered hot-dog roll. (No celery, please!) You'll find them everywhere along the Maine coast; expect to pay $9 to $15 per roll, more in lean lobster-harvest years. One of the meatiest is served at Red's Eats, a stand by the side of the highway in **Wiscasset.**
- **Maple syrup:** Nothing says New England like maple syrup. You can buy the stuff in any of the New England states,

but the best is made in New Hampshire and Vermont. Visit in late spring (the first week of March is recommended) to get a close look at the process at the local sap houses. Sugarmakers boil up the sweet stuff and ladle it onto pancakes, ice cream, or snow to let you sample before you buy. And you *will* buy.

- **Moxie:** Early in the 20th century, the Maine soda known as Moxie actually outsold Coca-Cola. Part of its allure was the fanciful story behind its 1885 creation: A traveler named Moxie was said to have observed South American Indians consuming the sap of a native plant, which gave them extraordinary strength. The drink was then "re-created" by Maine native Dr. Augustin Thompson. Okay, that's a bunch of malarkey. But it's still quite popular in Maine, even if some outsiders liken the taste to a combination of cough medicine and dirt. I happen to like it a lot.
- **Shellfish:** Mussels, oysters, clams, and scallops can all be bought at fish markets up and down the Maine coast—or at restaurants in said towns and cities—raw (if you're renting a cottage), steamed, or fried. Take your pick. Be sure to know how to choose fresh bivalves at the market if you're cooking for yourself; a single bad one can make a person mighty sick.
- **Smoked fish:** Fish-smoking isn't a huge industry in New England, but it does exist, especially in Downeast Maine. That's not really surprising, given the huge supply of smokeable fish living just offshore.

Finally, no survey of food and drink in northern New England would be complete without serious mention of the **beer.** New England has more microbreweries than any other region outside the Pacific Northwest; in fact, it might outrank that region by now in quality (and maybe quantity).

The beers of Vermont and Maine, especially, are legion—and they're often in the places you'd least expect to find them: little towns like dour **Middlebury** (Otter Creek Brewing) and **Morrisville,** Vermont (Rock Art Brewing); august **Kennebunkport,** Maine (Federal Jack's); and the former mill town of **Topsham** (Sea Dog Brewing Co.), also in Maine. Once you get to the city, the situation gets even better.

The concentration of minibreweries in both **Burlington,** Vermont, and **Portland,** Maine, actually staggers the mind: There are a half-dozen distinct brewing operations in both of those small cities, all making great beer and all (so far) making profits. For a closer look at some of these craft brewers, pick up my *Frommer's Coastal Maine: Day by Day;* I have organized a special tour of Portland's area breweries for hopheads like me.

3

Planning Your Trip to Northern New England

Traveling in northern New England is a snap, mostly: The region is clean, scenic, crime-free, and (for the most part) blissfully traffic-free. The roads are well marked, and tourist services are plentiful. About the only truly dangerous situation you might have to cope with is driving in winter weather; sharks, water-borne illnesses, poisonous snakes, and the like simply don't come into play here.

In this chapter, I give you most of the nuts-and-bolts travel information you will need before setting off for this unique region. Browse through the section before hitting the road to make sure you've touched all the bases, and refer back to the regional map in chapter 1 when needed. For even more help planning your trip (and more listings of on-the-ground resources), see chapter 11, "Fast Facts, Toll-Free Numbers & Websites."

1 WHEN TO GO

THE SEASONS

One old joke about the climate in northern New England is that it has only three seasons: winter, "mud" season . . . and August. Though this saying might have originated as a ploy to keep outsiders from moving up here (and it works, partly), there's also a kernel of truth to it. But that's okay. The ever-shifting seasons here are precisely what make northern New England so distinctive, and three of the four are genuinely enjoyable so long as you're dressed properly. And the other one (not the one you might guess) is tolerable.

SUMMER The peak summer season in northern New England runs from around the Fourth of July weekend until Labor Day weekend. That's a pretty slim stretch, only about 8½ weeks. But, wow, does the population of each of these states ever swell between summer's starting line and its checkered flag. Vast crowds surge into northern New England on each of these two holiday weekends, and a constant stream also moves northward daily in between them.

It's no wonder. Summers here are exquisite. The daylight lasts very long—until 9 or 9:30pm in late June and early July. Forests are verdant and lush; the sky is a deep blue, the cumulus clouds puffy and almost painfully bright white. In the mountains, warm days are the rule, followed by cool nights. On the coast, ocean breezes keep temperatures down even when it's triple-digit steaming in the big cities. (Of course, these sea breezes sometimes also produce thick, soupy fogs that linger for days.) In general, expect moderation: In Portland the thermometer tops 90°F (32°C) for only 4 or 5 days each year, if that.

Instead, the weather in this region is largely determined by the direction of the wind. Summer's southwesterly winds bring haze, heat, and humidity to everywhere except the seashore; then northwesterly winds bring cooler, brighter weather and knife-sharp views. These systems tend to alternate throughout summer, the heat and humidity building slowly and stealthily for a few days—then swiftly getting kicked out on its ear by stiff winds pressing down from Canada. Rain is rarely far away—sometimes it's an afternoon thunderstorm, sometimes a steady drizzle of 3 or 4 days. On average about 1 day in 3 here will bring some rain. But hey, that's what keeps the Green Mountains green, right?

For most of this region (we'll get to Vermont in a moment), midsummer is prime time. Expect to pay premium prices at the hotels and restaurants. (The exception is in and around the empty ski resorts, where you can often find deep summer discounts.) Be aware that early summer brings out scads of biting black flies and mosquitoes; come prepared.

What to do in summer? Play golf. Go hiking in the woods. Swim in the ocean. Catch a minor-league ballgame. Or just rock in a chair on a screened porch and read a book, play your guitar, or listen intently to the sounds of loons and crickets and watch the night sky for stars.

AUTUMN Fall is my favorite season here. Don't be surprised to feel the tang of fall approaching even as early as mid-August, when you'll begin to notice a few leaves turning blaze-orange on the maples at the edges of wetlands or highways. Fall comes early to northern New England, and hangs on for awhile. The foliage season begins in earnest in the northern part of the region by the third week in September; in the southern portions, it reaches its peak by mid-October. And it's beautiful everywhere.

Fall in New England is one of the great natural spectacles of North America. As the rolling hills dress up in brilliant reds and stunning oranges, grown men pull to the sides of roads and fall to their knees weeping (well, snapping and Handycamming, at least). The best part? This spectacle is nearly as regular as clockwork, with only a few years in every decade that are "bad" for foliage (due to oddly warm or wet weather).

This means, of course, that fall is the most popular time of year for others to visit northern New England—bus tours flock like migrating geese to the region from late September onward. As a result, hotels are invariably booked solid. Reservations are essential. Don't be surprised if you're faced with a sudden rate spike of $50 to $100 per night at your inn or hotel. Deal with it; you can't buy scenery like this back home.

Helpfully, all three states maintain seasonal **foliage hotlines** and/or **websites** to let you know when the leaves are at their peak: **Vermont** (✆ **800/VERMONT** [837-6668]; www.travel-vermont.com/seasons/report.asp), **Maine** (✆ **888/624-6345;** www.mainefoliage.com), and **New Hampshire** (✆ **800/258-3608**). The **U.S. Forest Service** also maintains a foliage hotline at ✆ **800/354-4595,** updating conditions within the White Mountain National Forest in New Hampshire.

WINTER New England winters are like wine—some years are good, some lousy. During a "good" winter, mounds of light, fluffy snow blanket the deep woods and fill the ski slopes. There's a profound peace and tranquillity as the fresh snow muffles the noise and brings such a huge silence to the entire region—it's so quiet that the companionable hiss and pop of a wood fire at a country inn can seem noisy. During these sorts of winters, exploring the forest on snowshoes or cross-country skis is an experience bordering on the magical.

During the *other* winters, though—the yucky ones—the weather could bring a nasty mélange of rain, freezing rain, and sleet (in other words, frozen rain). The woods become filled not with powder but with crusty snow; the cold is damp and bone-numbing; and it can stay can for weeks beneath low, gunpowder-gray clouds.

There are some possible solutions for a bad winter. The higher you go into the mountains, or the farther north you travel (to such places as Jay, Vermont), the better your odds of finding snow and powder. Southern stretches are more vulnerable to the rain/sleet combo.

As for the coast in winter, it's a crapshoot at best, more likely to yield rain (or sticky, heavy "snowball" snow) than powder. Yes, winter vacations on the ocean can be spectacular—Winslow Homerian waves crashing onto and obliterating the beach—but after a day or two of trying to navigate around big, gray-slush snowbanks, you too will soon be heading for Stowe (or Hawaii).

Naturally, ski areas get crowded during the winter months. Some of them get *very* crowded. Expect maximum pricing, so-so food, and a herd mentality; that's the price you pay for enjoying great in-season skiing in the region. The resorts get especially packed during school vacations, when many resorts jack up rates at hotels and on the slopes.

But there are other pleasures besides skiing here in winter: public ice skating and ice hockey, to name two. You'll find locals skating on town greens, lakes, ponds, rivers, community rinks—anyplace that will hold a little water. How do you find these spots? Easy. Look for a clump of cars beside a little warming hut with a wood- or oil-burning stove inside, sending up smoke puffs like a signal.

SPRING I'm not going to lie to you: After the long winters, spring in northern New England isn't much of a payoff. Yes, it's pretty finery (see the delicate purple lilacs, which blossom for only a week). But in many years, spring only lasts for a week (I'm not kidding), often around mid-May but sometimes as late as June. There's a reason northern New Englanders hardly ever use the word "spring" in conversation. They just call this time of year "mud season."

It happens pretty quickly. One morning the ground is muddier than muddy, the trees barren, and gritty snow is collected in shady hollows. The next day, it's in the 80s and humid, maple trees are blooming with little red cloverlike buds, kids are swimming in the lakes where the docks have just been put in, and somewhere in New Hampshire, as we speak, a blue cover is being ripped off an aboveground pool. Then summer's here.

Travelers need to be awfully crafty to experience spring in northern New England—and once they get here, they often have trouble finding a room. That's because a good number of innkeepers and restaurateurs close up for a few weeks to a few months for repairs (or to venture someplace warmer). The upside? Rates are never cheaper than they are in spring. It's amazing how little you can pay in March for the exact same room that would cost 3 to 10 times more in the middle of summer or in October.

Burlington, Vermont, Average Temperatures

	Jan	Feb	Mar	Apr	May	June	July	Aug	Sept	Oct	Nov	Dec
Temp. (°F)	25	27	38	53	66	76	80	78	69	57	44	30
Temp. (°C)	–4	–3	3	12	19	24	27	26	21	14	7	–1
Rainfall (in.)	2.2	1.7	2.3	2.9	3.3	3.4	4.0	4.0	3.8	3.1	3.1	2.2

Portland, Maine, Average Temperatures

	Jan	Feb	Mar	Apr	May	June	July	Aug	Sept	Oct	Nov	Dec
Temp. (°F)	31	32	40	50	61	72	76	74	68	58	45	34
Temp. (°C)	–1	0	4	10	16	22	24	23	20	14	7	1
Rainfall (in.)	4.1	3.1	4.1	4.3	3.8	3.3	3.3	3.1	3.4	4.4	4.7	4.2

NORTHERN NEW ENGLAND CALENDAR OF EVENTS

For an even more exhaustive list of events in this region *beyond* those listed here, check **http://events.frommers.com**, where you'll find a searchable, up-to-the-minute roster of what's happening in cities all over the world.

January

New Year's and First Night Celebrations, region-wide. Portland, Portsmouth, and Burlington, among other cities, celebrate the New Year with family activities at venues across the city. Inevitably, there are fireworks at midnight. Ask local tourist offices for details. December 31 to January 1.

February

U.S. National Toboggan Championships, Camden, Maine. Raucous and lively athletic event where being overweight is an advantage. Held at the Camden Snow Bowl's toboggan chute. Call ✆ **207/236-3438.** Early February.

Dartmouth Winter Carnival, Hanover, New Hampshire. Huge, elaborate ice sculptures grace the green during this festive celebration of winter, which includes numerous sporting events and other winter-related activities. Call ✆ **603/646-3399.** Mid-February.

Stowe Derby, Stowe, Vermont. The oldest downhill/cross-country ski race in the nation pits racers who scramble from the wintry summit of Mount Mansfield into the village on the Stowe Rec Path. Call ✆ **802/253-7704.** Late February.

March

Maine Boatbuilders Show, Portland. Several hundred exhibitors and thousands of boat aficionados gather as winter fades to make plans for the coming summer. It's a great place to meet boatbuilders and get ideas for your dream craft. The venue is on upper Fore Street (free shuttles from Commercial St.). Call ✆ **207/774-1067.** Mid-March.

May

Annual Basketry Festival, Stowe, Vermont. A weeklong event with displays and workshops by talented artisans. Call ✆ **802/253-7223.** Mid-May.

Spring Shearing, Woodstock, Vermont. A celebration of spring and an educational event. Learn all about what happens on a traditional farm, from sowing to shearing. Events take place at the **Billings Farm Museum,** ✆ **802/457-2355.** Late May.

June

Old Port Festival, Portland, Maine. A daylong block party in the heart of Portland's historic district with live music, food vendors, and activities for kids. Call ✆ **207/772-6828.** Early June.

Market Square Day, Portsmouth, New Hampshire. This lively street fair attracts crowds of New Englanders here to dance, listen to music, sample food, and just enjoy summer's arrival. Call ✆ **603/433-4398.** Mid-June.

Marlboro Music Festival, Marlboro, Vermont. This popular 6-week series of classical concerts has talented student musicians performing in the hills outside Brattleboro. Call ✆ **802/254-2394** or 215/569-4690. Weekends from mid-June through mid-August.

Annual Windjammer Days, Boothbay Harbor, Maine. For nearly 4 decades, windjammers have gathered in Boothbay Harbor to kick off the summer sailing season. Expect music, food, and a parade of magnificent sailboats. Call ✆ **207/633-2353.** Late June.

Vermont Quilt Festival, Essex and Colchester. Displays are only part of the allure of New England's largest quilt festival. Attend classes and have your heirlooms appraised. Class and event descriptions at **www.vqf.org** or call ✆ **802/872-0034.** Late June through early July.

July

Independence Day, region-wide. Communities throughout all three states celebrate with parades, greased-pole climbs, cakewalks, cookouts, road races, and fireworks. The bigger the town, the bigger the fireworks. Contact chambers of commerce for details. July 4th.

Maine Lobster Festival, Rockland, Maine. Fill up on the local harvest at this event marking the importance and delectability of Maine's favorite crustacean. Enjoy a boiled lobster or two and take in the entertainment during this informal waterfront gala. Call ✆ **800/LOB-CLAW** (562-2529) or 207/596-0376. Late July through first week of August.

August

Southern Vermont Art & Craft Fair, Manchester, Vermont. Over 200 artisans show off their fine work at this popular festival that also has creative food and good music. Held at Hildene. Call ✆ **802/425-3399.** Early August.

Craftsman's Fair, Sunapee, New Hampshire. Quality crafts from several hundred New Hampshire artisans are displayed and sold at this weeklong festival in Sunapee State Park. Call ✆ **603/763-2416.** First Saturday of August.

Wild Blueberry Festival, Machias, Maine. Marks the harvest of the region's wild blueberries. Eat to your heart's content. Call ✆ **207/255-4402** or 207/255-6665. Mid-August.

September

Blue Hill Fair, Blue Hill, Maine. This classic country fair is held outside one of Maine's cutest little villages on Labor Day weekend. Call ✆ **207/374-3701.** Early September.

Windjammer Weekend, Camden, Maine. Visit Maine's impressive fleet of old-time sailing ships during "open houses" held each year in Camden's scenic harbor over Labor Day weekend. Call ✆ **207/236-4404.** Early September.

Vermont State Fair, Rutland. All of Vermont seems to show up for this grand annual event, a 10-day fest with a midway, live music, and plenty of agricultural exhibits. The fair has been going strong since 1846. Call ✆ **802/775-5200.** Early to mid-September.

Common Ground Country Fair, Unity, Maine. An old-time state fair with a twist: Emphasis is on organic foods, recycling, and wholesome living. Call ✆ **207/568-4142.** Late September.

October

Harvest Days, Canterbury, New Hampshire. A 2-day celebration of the harvest season, Shaker-style. Lots of autumnal exhibits and children's games. Call ✆ **603/783-9511.** Early October.

Fryeburg Fair, Fryeburg, Maine. Cotton candy, tractor pulls, live music, huge vegetables, and barnyard animals are just some of the fun events at Maine's largest agricultural fair, a weeklong affair. There's harness racing in the evening. Call ✆ **207/935-3268.** Early to mid-October.

November

Bed Races, Bar Harbor, Maine. Fun stuff gets awfully thin in the ground in this region during November, but Bar Harbor comes to the rescue. Yes, they really do race beds through the streets—but not until the morning early-bird sale and "bed parade" are finished. Call ✆ **800/288-5103** or 207/288-5103. Late November.

Chester Greenwood Day, Farmington, Maine. Help this Maine town celebrate local boy Chester Greenwood (1858–1937) . . . inventor of the earmuff! (Who knew?) His day-long festival includes a parade and earmuff-related fun. Really. Call ✆ **207/778-4215.** Early December.

Christmas Prelude, Kennebunkport, Maine. This scenic coastal village greets Santa's arrival in a lobster boat, and marks the coming of Christmas with 3 days and nights of shows, pancake breakfasts, tree lightings, caroling events, and tours of the town's inns. Call ✆ **207/967-0857.** Early December.

Candlelight Stroll, Portsmouth, New Hampshire. Historic Strawbery Banke gets in the Christmas spirit on 3 consecutive weekends with old-time decorations and hundreds of candles lighting up its 10-acre grounds. Many of the fine historic homes in the complex are opened to the public during this time. Call ✆ **603/433-1100.** First 3 weekends of December.

2 ENTRY REQUIREMENTS

PASSPORTS

Virtually every air traveler entering the U.S. is required to show a passport. Anyone, including U.S. citizens, traveling by air between the United States and Canada, Mexico, Central and South America, the Caribbean, and Bermuda is required to present a valid passport. U.S. and Canadian citizens entering the U.S. at land and sea ports of entry from within the Western Hemisphere will need to present government-issued proof of citizenship, such as a birth certificate, along with a government-issued photo ID, such as a driver's license. A passport is not required for U.S. or Canadian citizens entering by land or sea, but it is highly encouraged to carry one.

For information on how to obtain a passport, see "Passports" under "Fast Facts: Northern New England," in chapter 11.

VISAS

The U.S. State Department has a **Visa Waiver Program (VWP)** allowing citizens of the following countries to enter the United States without a visa for stays of up to 90 days: Andorra, Australia, Austria, Belgium, Brunei, Denmark, Finland, France, Germany, Iceland, Ireland, Italy, Japan, Liechtenstein, Luxembourg, Monaco, the Netherlands, New Zealand, Norway, Portugal, San Marino, Singapore, Slovenia, Spain, Sweden, Switzerland, and the United Kingdom. Citizens of Czech Republic, Estonia, Hungary, Latvia, Lithuania, Malta, Republic of Korea, and Slovakia are soon to be admitted to the VWP. (***Note:*** This list was accurate at press time; for the most up-to-date list of countries in the VWP, consult **http://travel.state.gov/visa**.) Even though a visa isn't necessary, in an effort to help U.S. officials check travelers against terror watch lists before they arrive at U.S. borders, visitors from VWP countries must register online through the Electronic System for Travel Authorization (ESTA) before boarding a plane or a boat to the U.S. Travelers will complete an electronic application providing basic personal and travel eligibility information. The Department of Homeland Security recommends filling out the form at least 3 days before traveling. Authorizations will be valid for up to 2 years or until the traveler's passport expires, whichever comes first. Currently, there is no fee for the online application. ***Note:*** Any passport issued on or after October 26, 2006, by a VWP country must be an **e-Passport** for VWP travelers to be eligible to enter the U.S. without a visa. Citizens of these nations also need to present a round-trip air or cruise ticket upon arrival. E-Passports contain computer chips capable of storing biometric information, such as the required digital photograph of the holder. If your passport doesn't have this feature, you can still travel without a visa if it is a valid passport issued before October 26, 2005, and includes a machine-readable zone; or between October 26, 2005, and October 25, 2006, and includes a digital photograph. For more information, go to **http://travel.state.gov/visa**. Canadian citizens may enter the United States without visas; they will need to show passports (if traveling by air) and proof of residence, however.

Citizens of all other countries must have (1) a valid passport that expires at least 6 months later than the scheduled end of their visit to the U.S., and (2) a tourist visa.

For information on obtaining a visa, see "Visas" under "Fast Facts: Northern New England," in chapter 11.

CUSTOMS

What You Can Bring into the U.S.

Every visitor who is 21 years of age or older may bring in, free of duty, the following: (1) 1 liter of wine or hard liquor; (2) 200 cigarettes, 100 cigars (but not from Cuba), or 3 pounds of smoking tobacco; and (3) $100 worth of gifts. These exemptions are offered to travelers who spend at least 72 hours in the United States and who have not claimed them within the preceding 6 months. It is forbidden to bring into the country almost any meat products (including canned, fresh, and dried meat products such as bouillon, soup mixes, and so on). Generally, condiments including vinegars, oils, spices, coffee, tea, and some cheeses and baked goods are permitted. Avoid rice products, as rice can often harbor insects. Bringing fruits and vegetables is not advised, though not prohibited. Customs will allow produce depending on where you got it and where you're going after you arrive in the U.S. International visitors may carry in or out up to $10,000 in U.S. or foreign currency with no formalities; larger sums must be declared to U.S. Customs on entering or leaving, which includes filing form CM 4790. For details regarding U.S. Customs and Border Protection, consult your nearest U.S. embassy or consulate, or **U.S. Customs** (www.customs.gov).

What You Can Take Home from the U.S.:

For information on what you're allowed to bring home, contact one of the following agencies:

Canadian Citizens: Canada Border Services Agency (© **800/461-9999** in Canada, or 204/983-3500; **www.cbsa-asfc.gc.ca**).

U.K. Citizens: HM Revenue & Customs at © **0845/010-9000** (from outside the U.K., 020/8929-0152), or consult their website at **www.hmce.gov.uk**.

Australian Citizens: Australian Customs Service at © **1300/363-263,** or log on to **www.customs.gov.au**.

New Zealand Citizens: New Zealand Customs, The Customhouse, 17–21 Whitmore St., Box 2218, Wellington (© **04/473-6099** or 0800/428-786; **www.customs.govt.nz**).

MEDICAL REQUIREMENTS

Unless you're arriving from an area known to be suffering from an epidemic (particularly cholera or yellow fever), inoculations or vaccinations are not required for entry into the United States.

Northern New England: A Travel Checklist

- Did you make sure to book advance reservations for popular tours (such as Frank Lloyd Wright's Zimmerman House in Manchester, New Hampshire) and restaurants that you don't want to miss?
- Did you make sure your favorite attractions are open? Especially if you're traveling early or late in the season, it's best to call ahead for opening and closing hours if you have your heart set on seeing certain places. (I have also listed open seasons of attractions, restaurants, and hotels in this book.)
- Do you have a safe, accessible place to store money?
- Did you bring identification that could entitle you to discounts, such as AAA and AARP cards, student IDs, and so forth?
- Did you bring emergency drug prescriptions and extra glasses and/or contact lenses?
- Do you know all your credit card and bank-card PINs?
- If you have an e-ticket for a flight, did you bring additional documentation?
- Did you leave a copy of your itinerary with someone at home?
- If you will rent a car, have you checked your auto insurance and credit card policies ahead of time to find out if they cover liabilities arising from rentals? You might be able to save money by declining the extra insurance (collision damage waiver) that will be offered by the rental agency.

3 GETTING THERE & GETTING AROUND

GETTING TO NORTHERN NEW ENGLAND

By Plane

Getting to northern New England by plane is a lot easier than it used to be. The three main hubs for major commercial carriers here are **Burlington,** Vermont (airport code: BTV); **Manchester,** New Hampshire (code: MHT); and **Portland,** Maine (code: PWM). Airlines most commonly fly to these airports from New York or Boston, although direct connections from other cities, such as Chicago, Cincinnati, and Philadelphia, are also possible.

Remember that many of the commuter flights into northern New England from Boston are short hops aboard smaller **turboprop** (propeller-driven) planes; ask the airline or your travel agent before booking if this type of travel makes you nervous.

A web of smaller airports in the region are lesser-known but also served by feeder airlines or charter companies, especially in summer, including airports in **Rutland,** Vermont (airport code: RUT); **West Lebanon** (code: LEB) and **Portsmouth** (code: PSM), in New Hampshire; and **Rockport** (code: RKD) and **Trenton** (near Bar Harbor; code: BHB) in Maine. These are generally much more expensive to fly into than the main hubs, but if price is not an object and you're looking to save time, ask your travel agent to check tickets for these airports as well.

Some visitors to northern New England fly into Boston's **Logan Airport** (code: BOS), then rent a car or catch a connection by bus to their final destination. Boston is about a 2-hour drive from Portland, less than 3 hours' driving from New

Hampshire's White Mountains, and about 3¼ hours to Stowe, Vermont.

Travelers who want to try this, however, should know that Boston's airport can become very congested. Delayed flights are endemic and traffic can be nightmarish. (Taking Rte. 1A north toward Maine is one good Logan escape route, if you're headed that way.) Increased security has also led to periodic long delays during check-in and screening.

But the regional airports have not seen these large-scale check-in delays, and traffic is never a problem around any of them. So you might find the increased expense of using these airports is more than offset by the less stressful experience of speedier check-ins, departures, and arrivals.

Discount airfares aren't easy to find in northern New England, but progress has been made. Over the past decade, for instance, the airport in Manchester, New Hampshire, has grown by leaps and bounds thanks largely to the arrival of **Southwest Airlines** (✆ **800/435-9792;** www.southwest.com), which has brought competitive, low-cost airfares and improved service. Manchester has gone from a sleepy backwater airport to a bustling destination. Travelers looking for good deals to this region do well to check with the airline first before pricing bigger gateways.

Discount airline **JetBlue** also offers direct service from Burlington, Vermont, to New York City's LaGuardia Airport with onward connections. For more information, call ✆ **800/538-2583,** or check online at **www.jetblue.com**.

(Also see the section "Getting There" at the beginning of each chapter in this book for the latest details on local airports, and "Flying into Northern New England: The Skinny," below.)

Overseas visitors may want to take advantage of the APEX (Advance Purchase Excursion) reductions offered by all major U.S. and European carriers. In addition, some large airlines offer transatlantic or transpacific passengers special discount tickets under the name **Visit USA,** which allows mostly one-way travel from one U.S. destination to another at very low prices. Unavailable in the U.S., these discount tickets must be purchased abroad in conjunction with your international fare. This system is the easiest, fastest, cheapest way to see the country.

Flying for Less

Here are some more tips to help you find the best airfares to northern New England:

- Passengers who book their tickets either **well in advance or at the last minute,** or who **fly midweek** or **at less-trafficked hours,** may pay a fraction of the full fare. If your schedule is flexible, say so, and ask if you can secure a cheaper fare by changing your flight plans.
- Search **the Internet** for cheap fares. This almost goes without saying. Of the many, many search engines, I find **kayak.com** and **orbitz.com** to be two of the most useful.
- Watch you local big-city newspaper for **promotional specials** or **fare wars,** when airlines lower prices on their most popular routes. Also keep an eye on price fluctuations and deals at websites that track fares closely, such as **airfare watchdog.com**.
- **Consolidators,** also known as bucket shops, are wholesale brokers in the airline-ticket game. Consolidators advertise in Sunday newspaper travel sections (often in small ads with tiny type), in both the U.S. and the U.K. They can be great sources for cheap international tickets. On the down side, bucket shop tickets are often rigged with restrictions, such as stiff cancellation penalties (as high as 50%–75% of the ticket price). And keep in mind that most of what you see advertised is of limited availability.
- Join **frequent-flier clubs.** Frequent-flier membership doesn't cost a cent, but it does entitle you to free tickets or

Tips Flying into Northern New England: The Skinny

Here's a breakdown of which airlines fly into this region's amalgam of airstrips, airfields, and larger airports:

- **Cape Air** flies Cessnas from Boston to Rutland, Vermont.
- **Continental** flies into Bangor and Portland, Maine, and Manchester, New Hampshire, from Newark Liberty International Airport outside New York City.
- **Delta** flies into Portland, Manchester, Bangor, and Burlington, Vermont.
- **JetBlue** flies into Portland and Burlington from New York City's John F. Kennedy International Airport.
- **Southwest** flies nonstop into Manchester from numerous faraway destinations, including even California and Hawaii.
- **United** flies into Burlington, Portland, and Manchester.
- **US Airways** and its commuter subsidiaries fly from Boston, Philadelphia, and New York's LaGuardia to Burlington, Manchester, and Portland, as well as some smaller airports in Maine such as Bar Harbor and Presque Isle.

upgrades when you amass the airline's required number of frequent-flier points. You don't even have to fly to earn points; **frequent-flier credit cards** can earn you thousands of miles for doing your everyday shopping. But keep in mind that award seats are limited, seats on popular routes are hard to snag, and more and more major airlines are cutting their expiration periods for mileage points—so check your airline's frequent-flier program so you don't lose your miles before you use them. (Remember, award seats are created almost a year in advance of travel dates, but seats *also* open up at the last minute, so if your travel plans are flexible, you might strike gold. Check out community bulletin boards at websites such as **FlyerTalk** [www.flyertalk.com] and **Inside Flyer** [www.insideflyer.com] for more information on the latest frequent-flyer policies and trends.)

By Car

From Boston, New York, and beyond, two interstate highways bring you to northern New England swiftly and efficiently.

One of these highways, **I-91,** heads due north from Hartford, Connecticut, up through the heart of Massachusetts, then right alongside the river that forms the Vermont–New Hampshire border, all the way to Quebec. It's your best choice for reaching such places as Brattleboro, Vermont; the Monadnock region of New Hampshire; and the Mount Snow ski resort.

The other highway, **I-95,** begins way down in Miami and strikes northeast from New York City through Boston, shaving off a thin (but expensive, thanks to the toll highway) slice of New Hampshire and then sailing on through the southern Maine coast. You'll need to exit from I-95 onto Route 1 to reach Midcoast or Downeast portions of Maine. Finally, the great highway turns north through the heart of the Maine Woods and on to the Canadian border.

You have several other options, too, depending on where you're headed. Take **I-93** to visit New Hampshire and the White Mountains. In Concord, New Hampshire, **I-89** splits off from I-93 and arrows northwest to Burlington, Vermont—grazing

Flying with Film & Video

Never pack **film**—exposed or unexposed—in checked bags, because the scanners in U.S. airports can damage the film. The film you carry with you can be damaged by scanners, as well. X-ray damage is cumulative; the faster the film, and the more times you put it through a scanner, the more likely the damage. Film under 800 ASA is usually safe for up to five scans. If you're taking your film through more than five gates, U.S. regulations permit you to demand a hand inspection. Highly trafficked attractions are X-raying visitors' bags with increasing frequency.

Most photo supply stores sell protective pouches designed to block X-rays. The pouches fit both film and loaded cameras. They should protect your film in checked baggage, but they also may raise alarms and result in a longer delay during your search.

You'll have little to worry about if you are traveling with **digital cameras.** Unlike film, which is sensitive to light, digital cameras and storage cards are *not* affected by airport X-rays.

Carry-on scanners don't damage **videotape** in video cameras, either, but the magnetic fields emitted by walk-through security gateways and handheld inspection wands *can* damage it. Always place your loaded camcorder on the screening conveyor belt, or have it hand-inspected. Keep batteries inside it, too, in case the security officers ask you to turn the camera on.

Hanover, Montpelier, and Waterbury along the way. This route is best for getting to Burlington, Stowe, or the Mad River Valley.

If scenery is your priority, however, the most *picturesque* way to enter northern New England from New York City is probably from the west. Drive north on the **New York State Thruway** through the scenic Adirondack Mountains to Port Kent, New York, on Lake Champlain, and catch a car ferry across the lake to Burlington. Need a quicker, but still scenic, route? Take the Thruway north as far as Albany; exit for Troy; then roll east into Bennington and southern Vermont. This is the best way to get from the Big Apple to towns like Manchester and Arlington.

By Train

Train service into northern New England is limited to just three **Amtrak** (✆ **800/USA-RAIL** [872-7245]; www.amtrak.com) trains: two to Vermont and one to Maine.

Amtrak's **Vermonter** service departs from Washington, D.C., once a day (currently at 8:10am weekdays, 40 min. earlier weekends), with stops in Baltimore, Philadelphia, and New York City (at 11:30am) before following the Connecticut River northward, mostly through Vermont. The train calls at Brattleboro, Bellows Falls, Claremont (in New Hampshire), White River Junction, Randolph, Montpelier, Waterbury, and Essex Junction (near Burlington), finally arriving in St. Albans some 10 hours after leaving Manhattan.

The **Ethan Allen Express** departs New York's Penn Station once daily at 3:15pm (except Fri, when it leaves at 5:45pm) and travels somewhat more quickly, moving north along the Hudson River before veering northeast into Vermont, stopping at

Fair Haven (near Castleton), and terminating in Rutland after about 5½ hours.

Amtrak relaunched rail service to Maine in late 2001, restoring a line that had been idle since the 1960s. The **Downeaster** service operates five times daily between North Station in Boston and Portland, Maine; if you're coming from elsewhere on the East Coast, you will need to change train stations in Boston—a slightly frustrating exercise requiring either a taxi ride through congested streets or a ride and transfer on Boston's aging subway system. The Downeaster makes stops in Haverhill, Massachusetts; Exeter, Durham, and Dover, New Hampshire; and Wells, Saco, and Old Orchard Beach, Maine. Travel time is about 2 hours and 25 minutes between Boston and Portland. Bikes are allowed to be on- or off-loaded at Boston, Wells, and Portland. The one-way fare from Boston to Portland is $24.

International visitors might want to buy a **USA Rail Pass,** good for 15, 30, or 45 days of unlimited travel on **Amtrak** (✆ **800/USA-RAIL** [872-7245]; www.amtrak.com). The pass is available online or through many overseas travel agents. See the Amtrak website for the cost of travel within the western, eastern, or northwestern United States. Reservations are generally required and should be made as early as possible. Regional rail passes are also available.

Also note that all **AAA members** get a 10% discount on Amtrak tickets if they're booked at least 3 days in advance. Bring your membership card to the station or train when you ride.

By Bus

Coming from anywhere outside New England, you'll probably need to take a **Greyhound** (✆ **800/231-2222;** www.greyhound.com) bus to Boston's big depot at South Station first, then switch to a local carrier. International visitors can obtain information about the **Greyhound North American Discovery Pass.** The pass can be obtained from foreign travel agents or at **www.discoverypass.com** for unlimited travel and stopovers in the U.S. and Canada.

For more information on the local carriers that can get you from Boston to your local destination, or from point to point, see "By Bus" under "Getting Around Northern New England," below.

GETTING AROUND NORTHERN NEW ENGLAND

I wish I could travel northern New England without a car, just once, the way my great-great-grandparents did. It's amazing to think that, barely 100 years ago, people traveled inland from the sea by *trolley.* I'd love to head for the White Mountains, Mount Desert Isle, or Lake Champlain in a carriage, a fancy train compartment, a steamship cabin, or even just Thoreau-style: on foot. But that's not really practical these days—I tried hitchhiking once, as a compromise, and it worked out miserably. People here enjoy their privacy, and that includes when they're inside their cars.

In northern New England, in fact, the best way—often the *only* way—to get around is by car. Don't expect to get point-to-point within the region by plane (except from Boston), bus, or train; it's next to impossible.

By Car

New Englanders are famously caricatured saying, "You can't get there from here," but you may conclude it's no joke when you actually try to navigate through the region yourself. Travel can be confusing, and it's a good idea to have someone skilled at map reading in the co-pilot's seat.

North-and-south travel is relatively straightforward, thanks to the **four major interstates** crisscrossing the region. But traveling east to west (or vice versa) across northern New England is a different proposition, usually involving a byzantine route stitching together various state, federal, and county roads.

On the other hand, northern New England is small enough that touring by car can usually be done pretty comfortably. You can drive from Portland to Hanover (or even Burlington) in a long summer day. **Maine is a lot bigger** than the other two states, however; when making travel plans, beware of road maps that don't fully convey the state's size. (By driving time, Portland is closer to New York City than it is to Baxter State Park.)

Also jot down the **Vermont road conditions hotline** for news about winter weather and other road conditions: ✆ **800/ICY-ROAD** (429-7623). Or, from your cell phone in Vermont, you can dial ✆ ***511.**

Here are some representative distances between points in northern New England:

Boston to:	
Bar Harbor, Maine	281 miles
Portland, Maine	107 miles
North Conway, New Hampshire	138 miles
Burlington, Vermont	214 miles
Portland, Maine, to:	
Bar Harbor, Maine	174 miles
Greenville, Maine	153 miles
Rangeley, Maine	118 miles
Manchester, New Hampshire	95 miles
Burlington, Vermont, to:	
Brattleboro, Vermont	148 miles
Killington, Vermont	92 miles
Stowe, Vermont	37 miles
Portland, Maine	232 miles
North Conway, New Hampshire, to:	
Concord, New Hampshire	80 miles
Bar Harbor, Maine	216 miles
Portland, Maine	65 miles
Burlington, Vermont	141 miles

Traffic here is generally light compared with that in urban and suburban areas along the East Coast, though there are exceptions; traffic on the interstates coming north from Boston can be heavy or even stopped still on Friday afternoons and evenings in summer, for instance. A few choke points, such as on Route 1 on the Maine coast, can back up for a mile or three as tourists jockey to cross two-lane bridges. North Conway, New Hampshire, is famed for its congested traffic, especially during foliage season, but "congested" is a relative term—this isn't midtown Manhattan.

To avoid the worst of the tourist traffic, **travel smart.** Try to avoid being on the road during big summer holidays or foliage weekends; if your schedule allows it, travel on weekdays rather than on weekends, and hit the road early or late in the day to avoid the midday crunch.

The major airports in northern New England (see "Getting to Northern New England," earlier in this chapter) all host national car-rental chains, and renting a car is also easy at any smaller airport in this region; the quaint small towns, however, usually have *no* rental options at all. Book before you arrive, online or by phone.

International visitors should note that insurance and taxes are almost never included in quoted rental car rates in the U.S. Be sure to ask your rental agency about additional fees for these. They can add a significant cost to your car rental. Also keep in mind that foreign driver's licenses are usually recognized in the U.S., but you may want to consider obtaining an **international driver's license.**

If you're a connoisseur of back roads and off-the-beaten-track exploring, you'll definitely want to pick up a **DeLorme atlas** of the region (p. 105) at a local gas station or bookstore.

By Bus

Once you're here in northern New England, express **bus service can be spotty**—though it's gotten somewhat better lately. You'll be able to reach the major cities by bus, but few of the smaller towns or villages. Tickets range from about $25, one-way for Boston to Portland, to $45 for Boston to Burlington. Buses require no advance planning or reservations, though buses can fill up on Fridays, Sundays, and around major holidays or holiday travel times.

Several bus lines serve the region. **Greyhound** (✆ **800/231-2222;** www.greyhound.com) operates to all three states—though mostly just along the interstate highways—with frequent departures from Boston.

Concord Coach Lines (✆ **800/639-3317** or 603/228-3300; www.concordcoachlines.com) serves Maine and New Hampshire, including Midcoast Maine and some smaller towns in the Lake Winnipesaukee, Upper Valley, and White Mountains areas. Buses on the Maine routes play (PG-13 rated or below) movies en route.

Tips Moose X-ing Ahead: Watch Out!

Driving across the northern tiers of Maine, New Hampshire, and Vermont, you'll often see MOOSE CROSSING signs, complete with silhouettes of the shaggy, gangly beasts. These are not here for frat boys to steal or tourists to photograph: It's a real danger. In Maine, collisions between moose and cars are increasingly common, and there have been more than 30,000 such accidents documented since the state began keeping statistics.

Though they're big, moose are hard to see at night. Their big eyes don't reflect in your headlights the way deer's eyes do, so you come upon them suddenly—sometimes in the middle of the road. A moose can weigh up to 1,000 pounds, with almost all of that weight placed high atop skinny legs. When a car strikes a moose, it knocks those out from under the load and sends a half-ton of moose right down through the windshield. Bad things ensue.

Let's just take one year randomly: 1998, when Maine recorded 859 car crashes involving moose, causing 247 injuries and five fatalities. Yikes. And that was just *one year,* on the most remote back roads in the state. So when you see those signs, snicker if you want; but drive slowly and carefully, especially at night and in fall.

C&J Trailways (✆ **800/258-7111** or 603/430-1100; www.ridecj.com) connects Boston with Portsmouth, Durham, and Dover, New Hampshire, on buses that promise Wi-Fi access.

By Train

Amtrak (✆ **800/872-7245;** www.amtrak.com) provides limited rail travel within the region, confined to a few stops in Vermont, New Hampshire, and southern Maine. It's not really a valid option for getting around, only for getting here and then leaving. See "By Train" under "Getting to Northern New England," earlier in this chapter, for full details about the three train lines that service northern New England and the stations at which they stop.

It's not a good deal for New England, since train service is to limited, but you can buy a **USA Rail Pass** good for 15, 30, or 45 days of unlimited travel on Amtrak. The pass is available online or through overseas travel agents. Reservations are generally required and should be made as early as possible.

4 MONEY & COSTS

The Value of U.S. Dollar vs. Other Popular Currencies

US$	C$	UK£	Euro €	A$	NZ$
1.00	1.07	.63	.72	1.13	1.42

Here's a scene I've seen repeated many times in Maine, New Hampshire, and Vermont. A couple has driven up from the city, just for the day, in great weather to sightsee and grab dinner before returning. But something magical has happened. They've fallen in love with each other all over again, and with the quaint lovely New England-ness of (insert town name or beach here). They've decided to sleep for the night in a feather bed, eat a nice meal, and maybe watch the sun set over the (ocean/mountains/lake), then head home in the morning.

Except that here they stand, in front of a tourist information center staff member (or hanging off a pay phone), looking despondent.

"Isn't there *anything* cheaper?" pleads one of the lovebirds. "No, and that's a good price," comes back the answer, as nicely as possible. "You won't find anything better this time of year."

It's true. Travelers are in for a little **sticker shock** in northern New England during peak travel season. From June through August, there's simply no such thing as a cheap motel room in places like Lake Winnipesaukee, Portland, Portsmouth, southwestern Vermont, Camden, or Bar Harbor. Even no-frills mom-and-pop motels can (and do) happily charge $100 a night or more for a bed that might rate just a notch above camping in a tent. Bland business hotels at the mall or airport, miles from sights or good restaurants, charge even more. A *lot* more.

To be fair, innkeepers here need to charge more in summer: Most of their annual income comes during a 2- or 3-month stretch. (Peak foliage season in Oct and holiday weekends are their only other chances to make money, and many places close down for the season from Oct through early May.)

So if you're coming to this region in summer, fall, or ski season (and I'll bet that you probably are), **lodging** will occupy a bigger chunk of your budget than you expected.

Luckily, however, the cost of meals, gas, and day-to-day expenses is generally **more**

affordable here than you'd pay in a major city elsewhere in the country. You can find excellent entrees at upscale, creative restaurants for around $20, comparing favorably with similar dishes at big-city restaurants that would top $30.

CASH & ATMS

How to pay? Well, it's always a good idea to bring money in a variety of forms on a vacation: a mix of cash, credit cards, and traveler's checks. You should also exchange enough petty cash to cover airport incidentals, tipping, and transportation to your hotel before you leave home, or withdraw money at an airport ATM (automated teller machine) upon arrival.

(Throughout this guide, I have listed exact prices in U.S. dollars. The currency conversions at the beginning of this section were correct at press time. However, rates fluctuate constantly, so if you're coming from outside the U.S., please consult a currency exchange website, such as **www.oanda.com/convert/classic** or **www.xe.com/ucc**, to get the up-to-the-minute rates.)

The easiest and best way to get cash away from home is from an **ATM.** ATMs are easy to find in New England's populated areas and regions that cater to tourists. Machines are also making their way into the smallest villages, but don't count on finding them in every last town; stock up on cash when you can.

The **Cirrus** (© **800/424-7787;** www.mastercard.com) and **PLUS** (© **800/843-7587;** www.visa.com) networks span the country; you can find them even in remote regions. Go to your bank card's website to find ATM locations at your destination. Be sure you know your daily withdrawal limit before you depart.

Many banks impose a fee every time you use a card at another bank's ATM; the fee is often higher for international transactions (up to $5 or more) than for domestic ones (rarely more than $2). In addition, the bank from which you withdraw cash may also charge its own fee. To compare banks' ATM fees within the U.S., use **www.bankrate.com**. Visitors from outside the U.S. should also find out whether their bank assesses a 1% to 3% fee on charges incurred abroad.

CREDIT CARDS & DEBIT CARDS

Credit cards are the most widely used form of payment in the United States: **Visa** (Barclaycard in Britain), **MasterCard** (EuroCard in Europe, Access in Britain, Chargex in Canada), **American Express, Diners Club,** and **Discover.** They also provide a convenient record of all your expenses, and offer relatively good exchange rates. You can withdraw cash advances from your credit cards at banks or ATMs, but high fees make credit card cash advances a pricey way to get cash.

It's highly recommended that you travel with at least one major credit card. You must have a credit card to rent a car, and hotels and airlines usually require a credit card imprint as a deposit against expenses.

ATM cards with major credit card backing, known as **"debit cards,"** are now a commonly acceptable form of payment in most stores and restaurants. Debit cards draw money directly from your checking account. Some stores enable you to receive cash back on your debit-card purchases as well. The same is true at most U.S. post offices.

TRAVELER'S CHECKS

Though credit cards and debit cards are most commonly used, traveler's checks are still widely accepted in the U.S. Foreign visitors should make sure their traveler's checks are denominated in U.S. dollars; foreign-currency checks are usually difficult or impossible to exchange in northern New England.

You can buy traveler's checks at most banks. Most are offered in denominations of $20, $50, $100, $500, and sometimes

What Things Cost in Northern New England	US$
Small cup of coffee at Capitol Grounds, Montpelier, VT	1.40
Bus ride into city from Burlington (VT) International Airport	1.25
Weekend admission to the Vermont State Fair in Rutland	10.00
Adult admission to the Portland (ME) Museum of Art	10.00
Lobster roll at Red's Eats, Wiscasset, ME	15.00
3-course dinner (no alcohol) at The Terrace at the Hanover Inn, NH	57.00
Double room at Hampton Inn Portland (ME) Airport, plus tax	145.00

$1,000. Generally, you'll pay a service charge ranging from 1% to 4%.

Be sure to keep a copy of the traveler's checks serial numbers separate from your checks in the event that they are stolen or lost. You'll get a refund faster if you know the numbers.

5 HEALTH

STAYING HEALTHY

New Englanders, by and large, consider themselves **a healthy bunch,** which they ascribe to clean living, brisk northern air, vigorous exercise (leaf raking, snow shoveling, and so on), and few excesses other than the stresses and strains of being a Red Sox fan (now greatly alleviated, thank goodness). Other than picking up a stray cold or flu, you shouldn't face any serious health risks when traveling in the region.

Exceptions? Well, yes—you may find yourself at higher risk when exploring the outdoors, particularly in the backcountry. If you're planning a long hike into the backcountry, bring a small first-aid kit of basic medicines and bandages. Towns and villages in all three states are well stocked with pharmacies, chain grocery stores, and Wal-Mart–type stores where you can stock up on common medicines (such as calamine lotion, aspirin, and painkillers) to cope with minor ailments along the way.

A few things to watch for when venturing off the beaten track:

POISON IVY This shiny, three-leafed plant is common throughout the region. If you touch it, you could develop a nasty, itchy rash that might seriously affect your vacation. Some people even experience a dangerous allergic reaction, though others are barely affected; it's best to simply just avoid the plant. If you're unfamiliar with what poison ivy looks like, ask at a ranger station or visitor information booth. Many have posters or books to help you with identification.

GIARDIA That crystal-clear stream in the woods might look pure, but it could be contaminated with animal feces. Disgusting, yes, and also dangerous. When ingested by humans, Giardia cysts can cause serious diarrhea and loss of weight. (The symptoms might not even surface until you're back home.) How to avoid it? Carry your own water in for day trips, or bring a small filter (available at any camping or sporting-goods store) to treat the local water. Failing that, at least boil your water and/or treat it with iodine pills before using it—even for cooking, drinking, or washing. If you feel diarrhea coming on, seek out a doctor as soon as you can.

LYME DISEASE Lyme disease has been a growing problem in New England since 1975, when it was identified in Connecticut; thousands of cases are reported nationwide annually. Left untreated, Lyme disease can damage the heart. The disease is transmitted by tiny deer ticks, which are difficult to see—but check your socks and body daily anyway with a partner. If you spot a bull's-eye-shaped rash, 3 to 8 inches in diameter (the rash may feel warm but usually doesn't itch), see a doctor right away. Lyme disease is more easily treated in early phases. Other symptoms include muscle and joint pain, fever, or fatigue.

RABIES Since 1989 rabies has increasingly been spreading northward into New England. The disease is transmitted through animal saliva and is especially prevalent in skunks, raccoons, bats, and foxes. **It is always fatal if left untreated** in humans. Infected animals tend to display erratic and aggressive behavior; keep a safe distance between yourself and wild animals, for starters. If you're bitten, wash the wound as soon as you can and immediately get to a hospital or clinic. Treatment is no longer as painful as it used to be, but it still involves a series of shots.

WHAT TO DO IF YOU GET SICK AWAY FROM HOME

Hospitals are easy to find in the cities of northern New England; rurally, however, you might need to depend on regional health centers or walk-in clinics. Check the phone book or ask your hotel concierge upon check-in to learn what the best, nearest option is.

If you suffer from a chronic illness, consult your doctor before your departure. Pack **prescription medications** in your carry-on luggage, and carry them in their original containers, with pharmacy labels—otherwise they won't make it through airport security.

Visitors from outside the U.S. should carry the generic names of their prescription drugs. Foreign visitors may also need to pay all medical costs upfront in an emergency and seek reimbursement later. For U.S. travelers, most healthcare plans provide coverage if you get sick away from home—but check. If yours doesn't, try to buy a temporary **travel insurance policy** for in-country travel from a reliable company such as **Travel Guard** (**© 800/826-4919;** www.travelguard.com).

For additional **emergency numbers,** see section 1, "Fast Facts: Northern New England," in chapter 11 (p. 389).

6 SAFETY

New England—with the exception of Boston—boasts some of the lowest crime rates in the entire country. Northern New England is even safer; the odds of anything really bad happening during your visit here are extremely slim. But travelers should still take all the usual precautions against theft, robbery, and assault when on the road.

Avoid any unnecessary public displays of wealth, for instance. Don't bring out fat wads of cash from your pocket, and save your best jewelry for private occasions. If you are approached by someone who demands money, jewelry, or anything else, hand it over. Don't argue or negotiate. Just comply. Afterward contact police right away by dialing **© 911.**

The crime you're statistically most likely to encounter here (as with anywhere in the U.S.) is the theft of items from your car. Don't leave anything of value in plain view, and lock valuables out of sight in your trunk. If you have an electronic security system, use it.

Also take the usual precautions against leaving cash, laptops, or valuables in your hotel room (or at least lying around in the open) whenever you're out of your room. Many hotels have safe-deposit boxes; use them. Smaller inns and hotels often do not offer any kind of safe, but it can't hurt to check.

Finally, when traveling late at night, look for a well-lighted area if you need to gas up or step out of your car for any reason.

7 SPECIALIZED TRAVEL RESOURCES

TRAVELERS WITH DISABILITIES

Most disabilities shouldn't stop anyone from traveling to northern New England. There are more options and resources out there than ever before—even if some older parks and small inns still have ancient stairs that can prove difficult for the mobility-challenged. Check ahead if this is an issue for you.

The free **America the Beautiful** national parks pass (formerly known as **Golden Access Passport**) gives visually impaired persons and those with permanent disabilities (regardless of age) **free lifetime entrance to federal recreation sites** administered by the National Park Service (which includes the Fish and Wildlife Service, Forest Service, Bureau of Land Management, and Bureau of Reclamation). It's especially useful in northern New England because the bearer gains entry into **Acadia National Park,** the **White Mountain National Forest,** and the **Green Mountain National Forest.** Other monuments, historic sites, recreation areas, and national wildlife refuges are also covered by the pass.

The pass can be obtained only in person, at any Park Service facility that charges an entrance fee. You need to show proof of a medically determined disability. Besides free entry, the pass also offers a 50% discount on some federal-use fees charged for such facilities as camping, swimming, parking, boat launching, and tours. For more information, go to the Park Service website at **www.nps.gov/fees_passes.htm**, or call ✆ **888/467-2757.**

GAY & LESBIAN TRAVELERS

Northern New England isn't yet the hotbed of gay culture that, say, Provincetown, Massachusetts, has become. But plenty of gays and lesbians live here and visit here, and find these three states mostly accepting of and welcoming to gay culture. (Urban communities are a lot more welcoming than small, rural ones, of course.)

Vermont has traditionally been the most open-minded of the three states on this issue. It's a major destination for gays and lesbians ever since state law acknowledged civil unions in 2000. A local backlash (marked by TAKE BACK VERMONT signs) has arisen in response to passage of the law, but opponents have so far failed to get the law repealed.

For information on Vermont civil unions, consult the state-run website **http://www.sec.state.vt.us/municipal/civil_mar.htm**.

A number of hotels and inns in the region, ranging from small B&Bs to the larger resorts, welcome gay and lesbian travelers and their friends for civil unions, and a growing number of these inns are actually owned by gay or lesbian couples. Check online ads and advertisements in gay and lesbian community newspapers and magazines for more information.

Ogunquit, on the southern Maine coast, is a hugely popular destination among gay travelers and features a lively beach and bar scene in the summer. In winter it's mellower. One place to learn more about the local and tourist community is at the website **www.gayogunquit.com**, which has good information on gay-owned inns, restaurants, and nightclubs around town.

For a more detailed directory of gay-oriented enterprises in New England, including coverage of northern New England, check out the ***Pink Pages*** (www.pinkweb.com), a useful website based in Boston.

SENIOR TRAVEL

Northern New England is well suited to older travelers, with a wide array of activities for seniors and very low crime rates. Mention the fact that you're a senior whenever you make your travel reservations. Throughout the region, travelers over the age of 60 qualify for reduced or free admission to theaters, museums, ski resorts, and other attractions, as well as discounted fares on public transportation.

The U.S. National Park Service offers an **America the Beautiful Senior Pass** (formerly the **Golden Age Passport**), which gives seniors 62 years or older lifetime entrance to all properties administered by the National Park Service—including Acadia National Park, the White Mountain and Green Mountain national forests, monuments, historic sites, recreation areas, and national wildlife refuges—for a one-time processing fee of $10. The pass must be purchased in person at any NPS facility that charges an entrance fee. Besides free entry, the American the Beautiful Senior Pass also offers a 50% discount on some federal-use fees charged for such facilities as camping, swimming, parking, boat launching, and tours. For more information, go to **www.nps.gov/fees_passes.htm**, or call ✆ **888/467-2757.**

Members of **AARP,** 601 E St. NW, Washington, DC 20049 (✆ **888/687-2277;** www.aarp.org), get discounts on hotels, airfares, and car rentals. AARP offers members a wide range of benefits, including *AARP The Magazine* and a monthly newsletter. Anyone 50 or older can join.

FAMILY TRAVEL

Families have little trouble finding fun, low-key things to do with kids in northern New England. The natural world seems to hold tremendous wonder for the younger set—an afternoon exploring mossy banks and rocky streambeds can be a huge adventure. Older kids may like the challenge of climbing a mountain peak or learning to paddle a canoe in a straight line, and the beach is always good for hours of afternoon diversion.

Be sure to ask about **family discounts** when visiting attractions. Many places offer a flat family rate that costs less than paying for each ticket individually. Some parks and beaches charge by the car rather than the head.

Also, when planning your trip, be aware that certain small inns cater only to couples and prefer that families not stay there, or at least prefer that children be over a certain **minimum age.** This guidebook notes the recommended age for children where restrictions apply, but it's always best to ask first, just to be safe. At any rate, if you mention that you're traveling with kids when making reservations, often you'll get accommodations nearer the game room or the pool, making everyone's life a bit easier.

To locate accommodations, restaurants, and attractions that are particularly kid-friendly, refer to the "Kids" icon throughout this guide.

Recommended destinations in northern New England for families include **Lake Winnipesaukee** and **Lake Sunapee** in New Hampshire (for splashing around and kid-friendly attractions), **York Beach** and **Acadia National Park** in Maine (ditto), and **Waterbury,** Vermont, for its famous ice-cream factory. **North Conway,** New Hampshire, also makes a good base for families with young kids; the town has lots of motels with pools, as well as minitrain

Tips The Peripatetic Pet

In hot weather, *never* leave your pet inside a parked car with the windows rolled up. In fact, it's not a good idea to leave a pet inside a hot car with the windows rolled down, either.

Make sure your pet is wearing a name tag with the name and phone number of a contact person. "Smart" ID tags like Smart-i-Tag **(www.smartitag.com)** serve this function.

rides, streams suitable for splashing around, easy hikes, and the distraction known as Story Land.

TRAVELING WITH PETS

Some places allow pets, some don't. I've noted inns that allow pets, but even so I don't recommend showing up anywhere with a pet in tow unless you've cleared it over the phone with the innkeeper ahead of time. Note that many establishments have only one or two rooms (often a cottage or room with exterior entrance) set aside for guests traveling with pets, and they won't be quite so happy to see Fido if the "pet room" is already occupied. Also, it's common for a surcharge (usually $10–$20 per pet, per night) to be added to your bill to cover the extra cleaning effort needed by housekeeping staff.

Several websites dispense tips and list animal-friendly lodgings and campgrounds: **www.petswelcome.com**, **www.pettravel.com**, and **www.travelpets.com** together contain thousands of property and campground listings. Also note that all **Motel 6** hotel properties accept leashed, "well-behaved" pets, though this chain is pretty rare in northern New England.

Keep in mind that dogs are prohibited on most hiking trails and must be leashed at all times on federal lands administered by the National Park Service (which includes **Acadia National Park** in Maine). Pets are allowed to hike off-leash in the **White Mountain National Forest** in New Hampshire and the **Green Mountain National Forest** in Vermont, but you must control them by voice. No pets are allowed at any time (leashed or unleashed) at **Baxter State Park** in Maine. Some other Maine state parks do allow pets on a leash.

8 SUSTAINABLE TOURISM/ECOTOURISM

Every time you take a flight or drive a car, carbon dioxide is released into the atmosphere. Although one could argue that any vacation that includes an airplane flight or use of a car can't be truly called "green," you can still contribute positively to the environment while on vacation. Choose forward-looking companies that embrace responsible development practices and help preserve destinations for the future. An increasing number of sustainable tourism initiatives can help you plan a family trip and leave as small a "footprint" as possible.

Responsibletravel.com, run by a spokesperson for responsible tourism in the travel industry, contains a great source of sustainable travel ideas.

You can find eco-friendly travel tips, statistics, and touring companies and associations—listed by destination under "Travel Choice"—at the International Ecotoursm Society (TIES) website, **www.ecotourism.org**. Also check out **Conservation**

Tips It's Easy Being Green

We can all help conserve fuel and energy when we travel. Here are a few simple ways you can help preserve your favorite destinations:

- Whenever possible, choose nonstop flights; they generally require less fuel than those that must stop and take off again.
- If renting a car is necessary, ask the rental agent for the most fuel-efficient model available. Not only will you use less gas, but you'll also save money at the tank.
- At hotels, request that your sheets and towels not be changed daily. You'll save water and energy by not washing them as often, and you'll prolong the life of the towels, too. (Many hotels already have programs like this in place.)
- Turn off the lights and air-conditioner or heater when you exit your hotel room.

International (www.conservation.org) which, with *National Geographic Traveler,* annually presents **World Legacy Awards** to those travel tour operators, businesses, organizations, and places that have made a significant contribution to sustainable tourism.

Whale-watching is popular from some parts of the Maine coast. For information about the whales you'll be glimpsing (and how to respect them), visit the **Whale and Dolphin Conservation Society** (www.wdcs.org). For info on traveling lightly in general, see **Tread Lightly** (www.treadlightly.org).

9 SPECIAL INTEREST TRIPS & TOURS

OUTDOORS-ORIENTED TRIPS

One rewarding way to spend a vacation is to learn a new outdoor skill or add to your knowledge while on holiday. You can find plenty of options in northern New England, ranging from formal weeklong classes to 1-day workshops. Here are three of the best:

- **Learn to fly-fish on New England's fabled rivers.** Among the region's most respected schools are the two offered on-site by the region's outdoor equipment powerhouses: **Orvis** (✆ **888/235-9763** for retail, **866/531-6213** for fly-fishing classes) in Manchester, Vermont; and **L.L.Bean** (✆ **800/441-5713**) in Freeport, Maine. L.L.Bean also offers a number of workshops on many *other* outdoor skills through its outstanding **Outdoor Discovery Program;** call ✆ **888/552-3261** for information about the program.
- **Learn about birds and coastal ecosystems in Maine.** Budding and experienced naturalists can expand their understanding of marine wildlife while residing on 333-acre Hog Island in Maine's wild and scenic Muscongus Bay through the **Maine Audubon Society,** 20 Gilsland Farm Rd., Falmouth, ME 04105 (✆ **207/781-2330;** www.maineaudubon.org). Famed birder Roger Tory Peterson once taught birding classes here, and I can personally vouch

for Maine Audubon's educational programs. Call or visit their lovely headquarters, just north of Portland.

- **Sharpen your outdoor skills.** The **Appalachian Mountain Club,** 5 Joy St., Boston, MA 02108 (✆ **800/372-1758** or 617/523-0636; www.outdoors.org), offers a full roster of outdoor adventure classes, many taught at the club's Pinkham Notch Camp at the base of New Hampshire's Mount Washington. You could learn outdoor photography, wild mushroom identification, or backcountry orienteering. In winter, ice-climbing and telemark-skiing lessons are taught in the White Mountains. Course fees often include accommodations, and most are reasonably priced. Call or write for a catalog.

Northern New England also especially lends itself to outdoorsy adventures that combine fresh air and exercise with Mother Nature as your instructor in a vast, beautiful classroom. For special-interest trips of an even more active type, see "The Active Traveler," below.

HISTORIC TOURS

Historic New England is a nonprofit foundation that owns and operates 36 historical properties around New England, ranging from places built in the 17th century to the present, including a number of properties profiled in this book.

Members get access to all of the organization's properties for free and receive a number of other benefits, including a subscription to *Historic New England* magazine; a guide to the group's properties; and invitations to members-only events and other perks. Memberships cost $45 per year for individuals or $55 for an entire household.

For more information on Historic New England and its properties, visit the group's website at **www.historicnew england.org**, or call the organization's Boston headquarters at ✆ **617/227-3956.**

ESCORTED GENERAL INTEREST TOURS

Escorted tours are structured group tours with a group leader. The price usually includes everything from airfare to hotels, meals, tours, admission costs, and local transportation.

Despite the fact that these tours require big deposits and predetermine nearly all of your hotels, restaurants, and itineraries, many people crave the sort of structure they offer. And it's true—they do let you sit back and enjoy a trip without having to drive *or* worry about the little details. They take you to a maximum number of sights, in the minimum amount of time, usually with the least amount of hassle. They're particularly convenient for people with limited mobility, and they can be a great way to make new friends.

On the downside, though, you get little opportunity for interaction with locals. Escorted tours are generally jam-packed with activities, leaving little room for individual whims. And they often focus on only the most heavily touristed sites, so you might miss out on some off-the-beaten-track gems.

Still, if you're interested, dozens of companies operate bus and van tours of northern New England. **Tauck World Discovery** in Norwalk, Connecticut (✆ **800/788-7885;** www.tauck.com), is just one of the many outfits offering fall foliage tours of northern New England, for instance—they even have a resident "foliologist" (and no, that isn't really a word) on staff to monitor the peak leaf color in various spots. Tauck's "Grand Autumn in New England" tour covers all three of the states in this book and includes overnight stays in hotels and inns in the region for 6 of its 11 nights.

Consult your travel agent for additional options. And for even more information on escorted tours—including a list of useful questions to ask before booking your trip—see our own website at **www.frommers.com/planning**.

10 THE ACTIVE TRAVELER

Northern New England is an especially great destination for those who want to get as far away as possible from big buildings and noisy car horns. Hiking, canoeing, and skiing are among the most popular outdoor activities here, but you can also try rock climbing, sea kayaking, mountain and road biking, sailing, mountaineering, or snowmobiling. The farther north you go in the region, the more remote and wild the terrain becomes.

For some quick pointers on where to head, see the section "Enjoying the Great Outdoors" in the regional chapters of this book. (More detailed information on local services and outfitters is included in each section, when appropriate.)

GENERAL ADVICE

The best way to enjoy the outdoors here is to head for **public lands;** these are the places where the natural landscape has been best preserved. The wildest areas in northern New England include Vermont's **Green Mountain National Forest,** New Hampshire's **White Mountain National Forest,** and Maine's **Baxter State Park** and **Acadia National Park.** Use this book to help pick out the best area for what you want to experience. I have mentioned a few outfitters in this guide; you will often find lots more local adventure-travel outfitters and suppliers in the towns around the fringes of (and sometimes within the boundaries of) these parks.

Once you've zeroed in the area you want to visit, try to stay put. I've run across many gung-ho travelers who try to bite off too much—they want to go bicycling in Vermont, hiking in the White Mountains, and then maybe kayaking off the coast of Maine. All in one week. That's a good formula for a nervous breakdown (or at least a close relationship with your rental car).

So pick one area, settle in for a few days or a week, and spend the long summer days exploring locally by foot, canoe, and/or kayak. This will give you enough time to enjoy that odd extra hour lounging around a remote backcountry lake, or camping in the backcountry. You'll also learn a lot more about the area you're in. In my experience, few travelers regret planning to do too *little* on their vacations to northern New England, but plenty of visitors regret having tried to do too *much.*

HIRING A GUIDE

People used to hire guides just to ensure that they would later be able to find their way out of the woods. With development now encroaching on so many once-pristine areas of northern New England, it's now sometimes useful to have guides help you find your way into the woods and away from civilization's reach. Clear-cuts, second-home developments, and trails teeming with weekend hikers are obstacles to be avoided—and a good local guide is the best way I know to locate the most alluring (and least congested) spots.

Basically, you've got three options: Hire a guide, sign up for a guided trip, or dig up the essential information yourself. Guides of all kinds can be hired throughout the region, from grizzled fishing hands who know local rivers like their own living rooms to young canoe guides attracted to the jobs because of their enthusiasm for the environment.

Maine also has a centuries-old tradition of guides leading "sports" into the backwoods for hunting and fishing, although many now have branched out to include recreational canoeing and more specialized interests, such as bird-watching. Professional guides are certified by the state; you can learn more about hiring Maine guides by contacting the **Maine Professional Guides Association,** P.O. Box 336, Augusta, ME

04332. The association's website (www.maineguides.org) features links to many of its members.

In Vermont, contact the **Vermont Outdoor Guide Association,** P.O. Box 10, N. Ferrisburgh, VT 05473 (✆ **800/425-8747** or 802/425-6211; www.voga.org), whose members can help arrange adventure-travel tours, instruction, and lodging. The VOGA website is a good place to get ideas for an outdoor vacation, with links to outfitters and outdoor-oriented inns.

Elsewhere, contact chambers of commerce for suggestions about guides.

GUIDED TOURS

The phenomenon of guided tours in northern New England has exploded in the past decade, both in number and variety. These tours range from 2-night guided inn-to-inn hiking trips to weeklong canoe and kayak expeditions. The reputable outfitters working this territory include the following:

- **Allagash Canoe Trips,** P.O. Box 932, Greenville, ME 04441 (✆ **207/237-3077;** www.allagashcanoetrips.com), is a family operation that leads 7- to 9-day canoe trips down Maine's notably wild Allagash River, as well as other local lakes and rivers. You provide a sleeping bag and clothing; everything else is taken care of.
- **BattenKill Canoe Ltd.,** 6328 Historic Rte. 7A, Arlington, VT 05250 (✆ **800/421-5268** or 802/362-2800; www.battenkill.com), runs personalized, guided canoeing and walking excursions in Vermont as well as abroad; these trips have character. The nights are spent at quiet inns.
- **Country Walkers,** P.O. Box 180, Waterbury, VT 05676 (✆ **800/464-9255** or 802/244-1387; www.countrywalkers.com), has a glorious color catalog (more like a wish book) outlining supported walking trips around the world. Among the offerings: walking tours in coastal Maine and north-central Vermont. Trips generally run 4 to 5 nights and include all meals and lodging at appealing inns.
- **Maine Island Kayak Co.,** 70 Luther St., Peaks Island, ME 04108 (✆ **207/766-2373;** www.maineislandkayak.com), has a fleet of seaworthy kayaks for camping trips up and down the Maine coast, as well as to places like Canada and Belize. The firm has a number of 2- and 3-night expeditions every summer and has plenty of experience in training novices.
- **New England Hiking Holidays,** P.O. Box 1648, North Conway, NH 03860 (✆ **800/869-0949** or 603/356-9696; www.nehikingholidays.com), has an extensive inventory of trips, including weekend trips in the White Mountains, as well as more extended excursions to the Maine coast, Vermont, and even overseas. Trips typically involve moderate day hiking coupled with nights at comfortable lodges.
- **Vermont Bicycle Touring,** 614 Monkton Rd., Bristol, VT 05443 (✆ **800/245-3868;** www.vbt.com), is one of the more established and well-organized touring operations, with an extensive bike tour schedule in North America, Europe, and New Zealand. VBT offers several trips apiece in both Vermont and Maine, including a 6-day Acadia trip with some overnights at the Asticou and Bar Harbor inns.

FOR MORE INFORMATION

Guidebooks to the region's backcountry are plentiful and diverse. **L.L.Bean**'s headquarters in Freeport, Maine (plus a half-dozen outlet stores scattered in the three states), as well the **Green Mountain Club**'s head office in Waterbury, Vermont (see below), all stock excellent selections of local guidebooks, as do bookshops throughout the region—and even many gas stations. An exhaustive collection of New England outdoor guidebooks for sale may be found online at **www.mountain wanderer.com**, a company based right in the White Mountains of New Hampshire. The **Appalachian Mountain Club,** 5 Joy St., Boston, MA 02108 (✆ **800/372-1758** or 617/523-0636; www.outdoors.org), publishes a number of definitive guides to hiking and boating in the region.

Map Adventures, P.O. Box 15214, Portland, ME 04112 (✆ **207/879-4777**), is a small firm that publishes a growing line of good recreational maps covering popular northern New England areas, including the Stowe and Mad River Valley areas, the Camden Hills of Maine, Acadia National Park, and the White Mountains. See what they offer online at **www.map adventures.com**.

Local outing clubs are also a good source of information, and most offer trips to nonmembers. The largest of the bunch is the Appalachian Mountain Club, whose chapters run group trips almost every weekend throughout the region, with northern New Hampshire especially well represented. Another active group is the **Green Mountain Club,** 4711 Waterbury-Stowe Rd., Waterbury Center, VT 05677 (✆ **802/244-7037;** www.greenmountain club.org).

11 STAYING CONNECTED

TELEPHONES

Generally, hotel surcharges on long-distance and local calls are astronomical, so you're better off using your **cellphone** or a **public pay phone.** Most convenience stores in northern New England sell **prepaid calling cards** in denominations of up to $50; for international visitors these can be the least expensive way to call home. Many public pay phones at airports now accept American Express, MasterCard, and Visa credit cards directly. Local calls made from pay phones in most of northern New England cost from 25¢ to 50¢ each; pennies aren't accepted.

Most long-distance and international calls can be dialed directly from any phone. **For calls within the United States and to Canada,** dial 1 followed by the area code and the seven-digit number. **For other international calls,** dial 011 followed by the country code, city code, and the number you are calling.

Calls to area codes **800, 888, 877,** and **866** are toll-free.

For **collect** or person-to-person calls, dial the number 0, then the area code and number; an operator will come on the line, and you should specify whether you are calling collect, person-to-person, or both. If your operator-assisted call is international, ask for the overseas operator.

For **local directory assistance** ("information") in most towns in northern New England, dial ✆ **411;** for long-distance information, dial 1, plus the appropriate area code, plus ✆ **555-1212.**

CELLPHONES

Just because your cellphone works at home doesn't mean it'll work deep in the woods of northern Maine—or even at that rustic country B&B, thanks to our nation's (and the region's) fragmented and competing cellphone coverage systems. You may or may not be within your roaming area, even if you have a national calling plan. It's a good bet that your phone will work in the region's major cities, so look over your wireless company's coverage map on its website before heading out, to be sure; T-Mobile, Sprint, and Nextel are particularly weak at covering rural areas here.

If you're not from the U.S., you'll be appalled at the poor reach of the **GSM wireless network** (which is used by much of the rest of the world) here. Your phone will probably work in most cities and

Online Traveler's Toolbox

Savvy travelers know that it's a great idea to use online resources when planning a trip. Here are a few websites I bookmark:

- **Airplane food** (www.airlinemeals.net)
- **Airplane seating** (www.seatguru.com and www.airlinequality.com)
- **Maps** (http://maps.yahoo.com and http://maps.google.com)
- **MasterCard ATM locator** (www.mastercard.com)
- **Universal currency converter** (www.xe.com/ucc)
- **Visa ATM locator** (www.visa.com)
- **Weather** (www.intellicast.com and www.weather.com)

interstate corridors in northern New England, and along much of the southern Maine coast; but it definitely *won't* work in most of the rural areas, which means nearly all the rest of the region. You also may or may not be able to use SMS (in other words, send text messages home).

INTERNET & E-MAIL

Larger cities in northern New England, such as Portland and Burlington, always have a couple of **cybercafes;** in small towns, though, it's often hit-or-miss (usually miss).

Most **airports** in the region have either **Internet kiosks** that provide basic Web access for a per-minute charge, or **Wi-Fi access** free or for a charge. (In first-class lounges, it's almost always free.) **FedEx Office** branches (such as the one in the center of Portland, off Monument Square) offer computer stations with fully loaded software plus Wi-Fi access.

Starbucks coffee shops, which are spreading ever deeper into the region, have a partnership with AT&T allowing free Wi-Fi access if you create and then use a "Starbucks card" once per month.

Northern New England's **public libraries** are also surprisingly generous about offering Internet access, nearly always for free; you may need to submit a driver's license or library card or other piece of identification as a deposit. Avoid **hotel business centers,** though, which often charge exorbitant rates.

Business hotels and a surprising number of northern New England's inns, motels, and even campgrounds are also offering Wi-Fi hotspot access, often free (the more expensive the hotel, the more likely it is that there will be a charge).

12 TIPS ON ACCOMMODATIONS

"The more we travel," said an unhappy couple one morning at a New Hampshire inn, "the more we realize why we go back to our old favorites time and again." The reason for their grumpiness? They had been forced to switch rooms at 2 o'clock in the morning because rain began dripping onto them through the ceiling.

They're hardly the first victims. Northern New England is famous for its plethora of country inns and bed-and-breakfasts (B&Bs), which offer a wonderful alternative to the sort of cookie-cutter, chain-hotel rooms that line most U.S. highways from coast to coast. But (as this unhappy couple learned) there are *reasons* why some people prefer the cookie-cutter hotels. In a chain hotel, you can be reasonably sure that water won't drip through your ceiling in the middle of the night. At the inns, you sometimes get drips, creaks, and quirks with the territory. (Stick to two- and three-star recommendations in this book if you want to avoid such quirkiness.)

Still, every **inn** and **B&B** listed in this guide yields a decent—often a high-quality—experience. Just keep in mind that every place is different, and you need to match the personality of the place with your own. Some inns are more polished and fussier than others; this is a rural area, so some properties (even places calling themselves "resorts," which in some cases is just a bald-faced lie) lack the luxury-hotel amenities—such as in-room phones, air-conditioning, and Wi-Fi access—to which business travelers have grown accustomed to in chain hotels. If you need these things, call the hotel ahead and ask about them—and read my listings carefully (including the listings details at the end of each write-up).

SAVING ON LODGINGS

As I mention above (in "Money & Costs"), inns and hotels in northern New England are surprisingly expensive during peak season. So you'll need some strategies to save a buck without compromising your experience. Here are a few of my favorites:

- **Ask about special rates or other discounts.** You might qualify for AAA, corporate, student, military, senior, frequent flier, trade union, teacher, or another discount.
- **Dial directly.** When booking a room in a chain hotel, you'll often get a better rate by calling the individual hotel's front desk rather than the chain's main number.
- **Book online.** Many hotels offer Internet-only discounts or last-minute specials. Others supply rooms to online brokers like Priceline, Hotwire, Expedia, and Hotels.com at rates much lower than any you can get by booking through the hotel itself. Snoop around online and check.
- **Remember the law of supply and demand.** Resort hotels are most crowded (and therefore most expensive) on weekends. But that means discounts are usually available for midweek stays. Business hotels in downtown locations are busiest during the *week,* so you can expect discounts over the weekend—even on holiday weekends, if the city isn't a major destination *during* that holiday weekend. Conversely, don't expect any discounts on Memorial Day, July 4th, or Columbus Day weekends—prices shoot through the roof as a crush of tourist traffic heads north to New England on these dates.
- **Look into group or long-stay discounts.** If you come as part of a large group, you should be able to negotiate a bargain rate. Likewise, if you're planning a long stay, you might qualify for 1 free night per 7-night stay.
- **Sidestep excess charges and other hidden costs.** Many hotels have the unpleasant practice of nickel-and-diming guests with opaque surcharges. When you book a room, ask what's included in the room rate, and what costs extra. Avoid dialing direct from hotel phones, which can be exorbitant. Don't dip into the minibar unless you're truly desperate: Five bucks for a cola or a can of nuts isn't helping your budget. Finally, ask about local taxes and service charges, which can increase the cost of a room substantially, by 15% or more. Some hotels also tack on involuntary "service charge" of 10% to 15%. (The rates listed in this guidebook don't include service charges or sales taxes.) Other charges could include a pet fee ($10 or more per day per pet), a foliage-season surcharge ($10–$50 per room),

Fun Facts Inn vs. B&B: Everybody Wins

The difference between an inn and a B&B may be confusing for some travelers. A couple of decades ago, inns were full-service affairs, whereas B&Bs consisted of private homes with an extra bedroom or two and a homeowner looking for a little extra income. Bathrooms (or even just *a* bathroom) were shared communally. Plenty of these old-style B&Bs still operate throughout northern New England, of course; I've occupied quite a few evenings sitting in well-used living room with a kindly owner, watching TV as if visiting with a forgotten aunt and chatting about the news, weather, and Red Sox. Other B&B owners barely gave me the time of day, just took my money (cash only) and plunked down a heavy room key, then vamoosed.

But B&Bs are, more and more these days, professionally run affairs where guests have private bathrooms, duck in and out of a separate common area with some wine or chocolates to dip into, and get the benefit of quite professional service. The owners live in apartments tucked away in the back (or off-property), prepare sumptuous breakfasts in the morning (some B&Bs even offer "candlelight breakfasts"), and offer a high level of service. Most of the B&Bs in this guide are of the more professionally run variety (though several still have shared bathrooms).

The main difference between inns and B&Bs—at least in this book—is that inns usually serve dinner (and sometimes lunch). B&Bs, as a rule, cook breakfast only. Readers shouldn't infer that B&Bs are more informal or in any way inferior to full-service inns. With a little luck, you'll stumble onto an example of Ralph Waldo Emerson's stated ideal of simple contentment: "Hospitality consists in a little fire, a little food, and an immense quiet." Amen to that, Mr. Emerson.

and a "resort fee" (15%–20% tax at certain resorts). Some hotels even tack on a $1 per day fee for the in-room safe, whether you use it or not.

- There are a handful of **all-inclusive resorts** in northern New England; these are pricey, but you also get more, so they could work out as a bargain. Here, "all-inclusive" usually means that you get two to three meals daily, plus use of the resort's sports equipment (such as canoes and kayaks) for your rate. Golf will probably cost extra, though.
- Carefully consider your hotel's meal plan. If you enjoy eating out and sampling local cuisine, choose a Continental plan (B&B) or a **European plan** (no meals). You're occasionally forced to choose a **Modified American plan (MAP),** which includes breakfast and dinner (but no lunch), or an American plan, which includes all three meals. If you must choose a MAP and you really want to dine out at night, see if you can get a free packed picnic lunch at the hotel instead of dinner.
- **Book an efficiency unit.** A room with a kitchenette lets you shop for groceries and cook your own meals. This is a big money saver, especially for families—and you get to sample the local produce and seafood, too. Many budget-priced motels in this region include efficiency units.
- **Consider enrolling in "frequent-stay" programs.** Frequent guests can accumulate points or credits to earn free

Tips Nail Down That Cancellation Policy!

When making reservations, it's essential that you get down (in writing, via printed-out website confirmation, or by e-mail) some confirmation of your hotel's or inn's exact **cancellation policy.** Since they're going to take your credit card as a deposit in almost every case, you'll need this information in case your trip is waylaid for any reason at all—or in case the front desk loses the booking. (It happens. *A lot.*)

There's quite a variety of policies on cancellation out there. Some places give you all your money back if you cancel early enough; a cutoff of **24 hours before arrival is standard** as a deadline, but some lodging establishments require *1 week's advance notice* for a cancellation to get a full refund, and some will let you cancel at 4pm or even 6pm on the day of arrival. Most properties will **charge you 1 night's stay** as a penalty if you miss the cancellation cutoff. And a few give you nothing back, no matter what.

hotel nights, airline miles, tickets, and other goodies. Perks are awarded by not only chain hotels and motels (Hilton HHonors, Marriott Rewards, and Wyndham ByRequest, to name a few), but some individual inns and B&Bs, too.

- **Check to see if the hotel charges extra for additional guests.** All room rates published in this guide are for two people sharing one room. Most places charge $20 or more per extra adult guest sharing your room. Don't assume that children traveling with you will stay for free—usually they can, but at some expensive resorts, they can't—and don't assume that every room with two beds can hold four adults. Many can't.
- **Ask about minimum-stay requirements and multiday discounts.** Many inns now require guests to book a minimum of 2 nights or more during the busiest times (holiday weekends, peak ski season, and peak fall-foliage season). These policies are mentioned in the accommodations listings where known, but check anyway—or just walk in and ask. Innkeepers sometimes develop sudden amnesia when faced with a chance to sell that last empty room on a summer Saturday night, even though the hotel has a policy against booking 1-night weekend stays in summertime.

LANDING THE BEST ROOM

There are tricks to getting a better room. Start by joining a hotel's **frequent-stayer program,** which might make you eligible for upgrades. And always ask for a corner room—they're often larger and quieter, with more windows and light.

Also, ask questions like these when you book your room:

- What's the view? Some travelers will pay less for a room facing a parking lot. But you came here to see New England's wonderful leaves, beaches, and hillsides, and you might be willing to pay extra for that knockout view. Or they might *give* it to you for free, just because you asked nicely.
- Does the room have air-conditioning, a heater with a thermostat, and ceiling fans? Do the windows open?
- How far is the hotel (and room) from the beach, ski resort, apple orchard, or whatever it is you came to see?

If you're not happy with the room you get assigned, *ask for another one.* Most lodgings will accommodate you. If they won't? Take your business elsewhere.

4

Suggested Northern New England Itineraries

I strongly emphasize that you should not overreach when planning your trip. Many distant travelers view this trip as their only chance to see northern New England, and then drive madly across the region in a valiant effort to see the Green Mountains, the White Mountains, the Maine coast, and certainly a moose up in those Maine woods—all in a week or so.

This is a formula for disappointment, since you'll end up seeing little except the inside of your car. New England has few attractions that lend themselves to pit-stop tourism—you pay an entry fee, look around for a few minutes, take some photos, grab a snack, and get back on the road to the next "attraction." New England is best seen by moving rather slowly, by foot or canoe or bike. The happiest visitors to the region are those who stay awhile in one spot, getting to know it more intimately through well-crafted day trips.

With that in mind, here are some suggested itineraries that can even be combined, depending on your schedule.

1 THE BEST OF VERMONT IN 1 WEEK

You can get a good taste of Vermont in less than a week. This trip involves about 2 or 3 hours of driving daily, if you don't linger (though I wholeheartedly recommend doing so). You can also scout out places to which you'd like to return and explore in depth.

Days 1 & 2: Burlington ★★

Burlington is Vermont's biggest, most diverse, most cultured city. It's certainly worth spending a couple of days here. After checking into your room, head out to explore. Depending on the weather, rent bikes or in-line skates—or strap on a pair of walking shoes—and spend some hours cruising the city's excellent **Burlington Bike Pathway** (p. 184).

Make sure to budget plenty of time for exploring the pedestrian-only **Church Street Marketplace** (p. 190; keep an eye out for the popcorn guy hawking sugared kettle corn in summer), as well as the University of Vermont campus just up the hill.

Each night, have dinner at one of Burlington's many excellent midpriced restaurants. Don't forget to catch a **minor-league ballgame** at the city's ballpark. The local team has a name that reflects the mythical sea monster plying the waters of Lake Champlain.

Day 3: Shelburne ★★ & Middlebury ★

Depart southward in the morning to **Shelburne** and spend most of the day exploring the remarkable **Shelburne Museum**

(p. 183). If you are so inclined, go see the splendid horses at the **Morgan Horse Farm** (p. 152), operated by the University of Vermont.

Afterward, drive south to the classic town of **Middlebury** and spend the night at a country inn. The town **waterfall,** visible from the bridge right on Main Street, makes a great photo spot. If you're an art lover, explore the campus and art museum of little **Middlebury College** (p. 151), walking distance from downtown.

Day 4: In & Around Dorset ★★ & Manchester ★★

From Middlebury, drive south on Route 7, detouring over to Proctor (just north of Rutland) to visit the **Vermont Marble Museum** (p. 147). You'll be amazed at the famous sculptures and edifices that are carved, built, enhanced, or faced with the local stone.

Later, continue east on Route 4 almost to the New York border, then go south on Hwy. 30 through **Dorset** and **Manchester,** both classic Vermont small towns with scenic vistas. If you're a history fan, you'll love **Hildene** (p. 93), the former estate of Robert Todd Lincoln, son of the assassinated president.

Spend the night in Manchester, Dorset, or Arlington—being sure to leave time late in the day for **outlet shopping** (p. 102) in Manchester and a stop at the flagship **Orvis** outdoors shop.

Day 5: Grafton ★★★ & Woodstock ★★★

Today, head east on Hwy. 30 into the Green Mountains, then follow Hwy. 35 north to the village of **Grafton.** Wander around this lovingly preserved town, and buy some cheese at the local cheese factory before heading northward toward the town of **Woodstock.** (Break out those maps if you crave the back roads.)

Be sure to sit a spell on Woodstock's lovely town green, taking some photographs of the covered bridge beside it. You can walk from the center of town to the underrated **Billings Farm and Museum** (p. 126). Drop in to a local pub or coffee shop for a pint or a cup, and try to stay overnight here or nearby.

Day 6: The Mad River Valley

After exploring Woodstock in the morning, head west on Route 4 with a detour to **Plymouth** ★★ to visit the **President Calvin Coolidge State Historic Site** (p. 140), which is also the site of yet another **cheese factory.** Hey, you can't get enough Vermont cheddar, right?

Continue through **Killington** and up scenic Route 100 to the Mad River Valley. If it's winter and you're a skier, you may be in heaven, as the ski hill here is Vermont's most laid-back.

Overnight in **Warren** ★★ or **Waitsfield** ★★—dropping in the cute **Warren General Store** (p. 158) for souvenirs—and, if time permits, rent a bike or take a tour on **Icelandic ponies** (p. 158).

Day 7: Back to Burlington

Spend your final day of this tour working your way back to Burlington.

On the way, spend an hour or two in the lovely little capital city of **Montpelier** ★★—grab a coffee, browse the used books, and glimpse the handsome capitol dome. If you're interested, check out the immense working quarries in **Barre.**

You may be pressed for time, but your kids won't let you miss the **Ben & Jerry's factory tour** (p. 163) in **Waterbury** ★★. There's plenty of shopping around here, too, so give in.

End your trip with dinner in **Burlington** ★★ at one of the restaurants you missed on your first visit—even if it's just **Al's** (p. 188) in South Burlington.

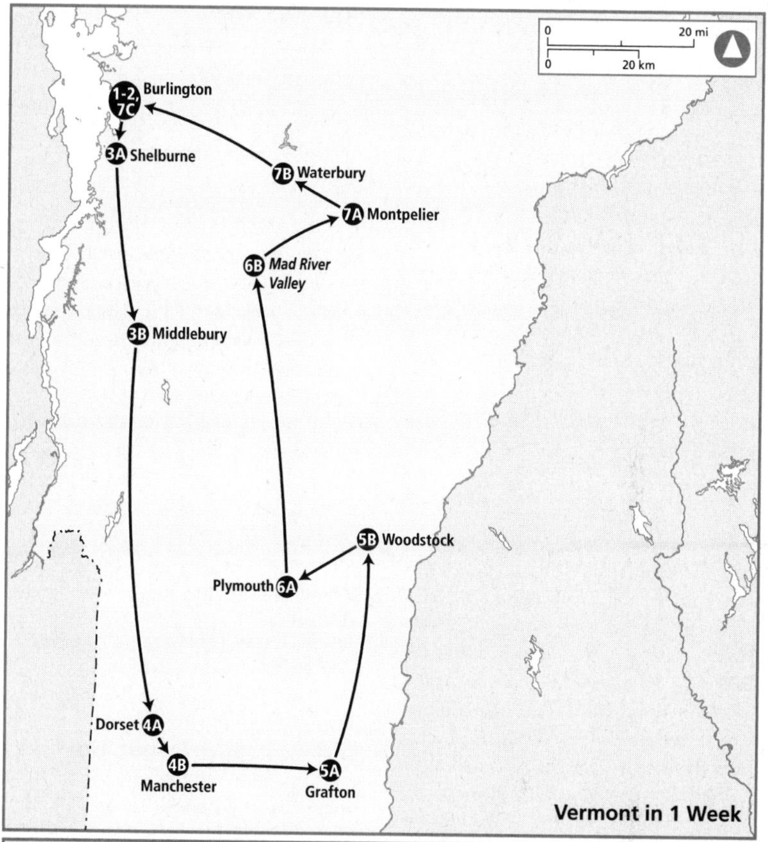
0
20 mi
0
20 km
1-2, 7C Burlington
3A Shelburne
7B Waterbury
7A Montpelier
6B Mad River Valley
3B Middlebury
5B Woodstock
Plymouth 6A
Dorset 4A
4B Manchester
5A Grafton
Vermont in 1 Week

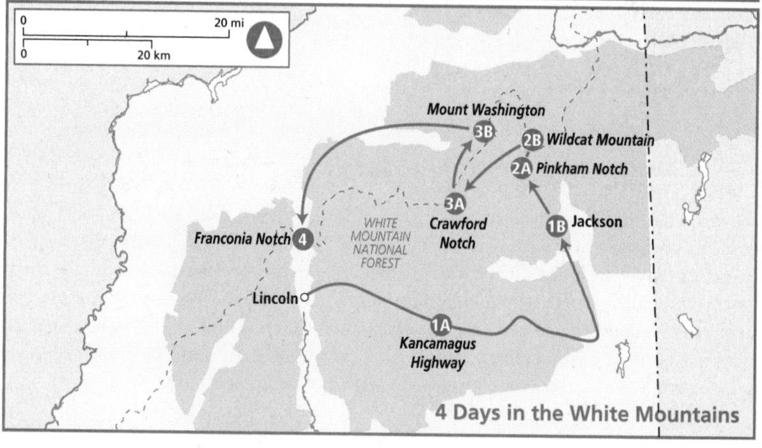
0
20 mi
0
20 km
Mount Washington
3B
2B Wildcat Mountain
2A Pinkham Notch
3A Crawford Notch
1B Jackson
Franconia Notch 4
WHITE MOUNTAIN NATIONAL FOREST
Lincoln
1A Kancamagus Highway
4 Days in the White Mountains

2 FOUR DAYS AFOOT IN THE WHITE MOUNTAINS

New Hampshire's White Mountains reveal extraordinary natural grandeur from the roadside, and provide the opportunity to explore mountain crags and crystalline streams.

Day 1: Doing the "Kanc"

Start at the town of Lincoln, at exit 32 of I-93, and drive to North Conway via the scenic **Kancamagus Highway** ★★★ (p. 266), stopping for some short hikes or a picnic. Indulge in a few shopping forays in town, and savor the views of the Mount Washington Valley. Head to the village of **Jackson** to check in for the night.

Relax before dinner at **Jackson Falls** ★ (p. 257), or take a bike ride up Carter Notch Road or other back roads in the hills above the village.

Day 2: Pinkham Notch

Stay another night in Jackson, and spend the day exploring by foot around **Pinkham Notch** ★★ (p. 255). Stop at **Glen Ellis Falls** (p. 255) en route to the base of Mount Washington. Park at Pinkham Notch, and then hike to dramatic **Tuckerman Ravine** (p. 255) for a picnic lunch.

Return to your car and continue north to the **Wildcat** ★ (p. 256) ski area. Take the chairlift to the summit for spectacular views of Mount Washington, the Presidential Range, and the Carter Range. Return to Jackson for the night.

Day 3: Mount Washington

Retrace your path down Route 16 and back to Route 302, turn right, and drive through **Crawford Notch** ★★ (p. 259). If weather and time allow, hike to one of the scenic waterfalls.

Go to the **Mount Washington Cog Railway** (p. 262) on the far side of the Notch. Take the train ride to the summit of **Mount Washington** ★★★ (dress warmly).

On your return, stop by the grand **Mount Washington Resort** for a celebratory snack.

Day 4: Franconia Notch

Continue west on Route 302 to Route 3. Turn left (south) onto I-93, then drive through scenic **Franconia Notch** ★★ (p. 269). Visit some of the scenic attractions (such as **Flume Gorge,** p. 269, or the **tram ride to Cannon Mountain**, p. 270) as time permits.

3 THE BEST OF THE MAINE COAST IN 2 WEEKS

Maine's coastline does not cater to hurry-up tourism. It has too many dead-end peninsulas to backtrack along and too many inlets that cleave the coast far inland, forcing visitors to drive great distances from one rocky, wave-beaten point to the next.

If you establish a couple of good home bases, it can work wonders, since you can then explore farther afield. Most of this trip heads north along U.S. Route 1, which has slow-moving traffic in high summer season. However, take heart: You'll have more time to soak up the views, which are pretty good, particularly north of Bath.

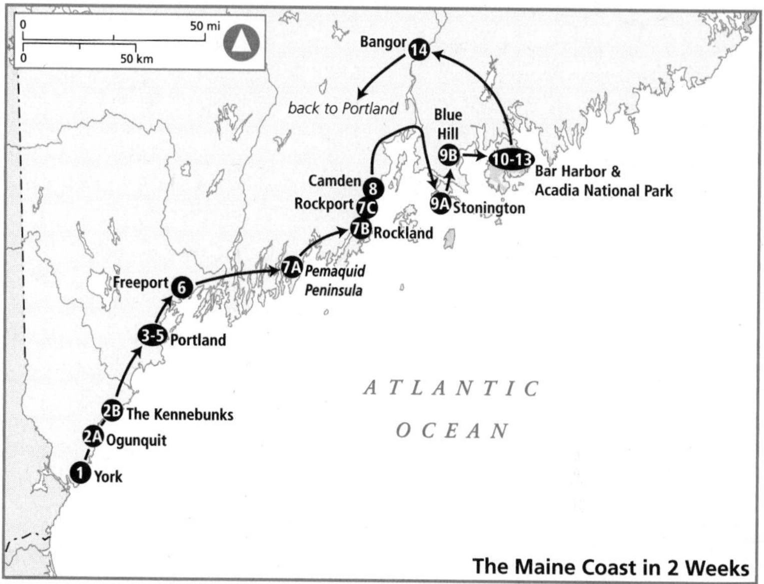

The Maine Coast in 2 Weeks

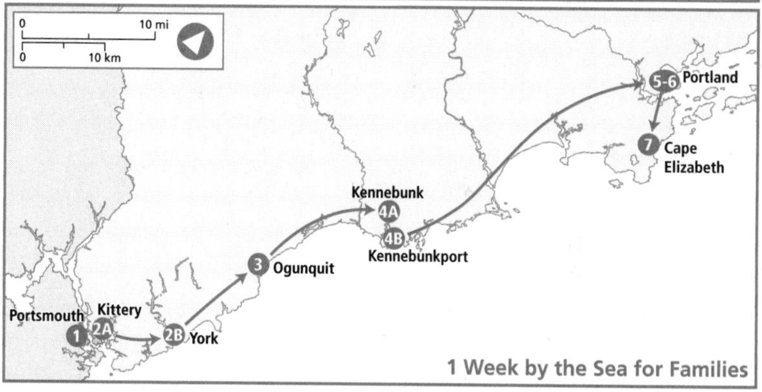

1 Week by the Sea for Families

Day 1: York ★★

Drive into Maine from the south on I-95, and head immediately for **York Village** (the first exit). Spend some time snooping around the historic homes of the **Old York Historical Society** (p. 283), and stretch your legs on a walk through town or the woods.

Drive northward through **York Beach** (stocking up on saltwater taffy at the **Goldenrod,** p. 286), and spend the night near the beach.

Day 2: The Kennebunks ★★

On your way north to the Kennebunks, take a quick detour and visit the excellent **Ogunquit Museum of American Art**

(p. 288). The Kennebunks are certainly worth a day if you enjoy old New England and luxury accommodations. There are some particularly fine inns and bed-and-breakfast establishments here.

Kennebunk, the lesser-known of the twin towns (they're separated by a tidal river), is quite the mixed bag. It's notable for the so-called Wedding Cake House, a fine public beach, a monastery (yes, really), and an outlet store selling Tom's of Maine natural personal-care products, among other attractions.

Across the river in **Kennebunkport,** you can stroll the leafy town, gawk at the Bush (as in former president) family compound from a distance—those Secret Service guys mean business—and have a relaxed dinner at one of the fine local restaurants. There's also a small shopping district, and plenty of pleasure boats and yachts moored in the harbor.

Days ❸, ❹ & ❺: Heading North to Portland

With the right route, getting to Portland can be as fun as being there. You can hit the antiques shops lined up along parts of Route 1 as you drive northward. If you're in a hurry or traveling in summer, avoid the crowds on Route 1 by taking I-95.

In **Portland** ★★★ by afternoon, you should collect tourism information and devise a schedule. Plan to stay in the city or on a nearby beach for up to 3 days, shopping for jewelry, souvenirs, or even kites; taste-testing chowder recipes and microbrewed beers; and just soaking up the salty air and atmosphere. Don't forget to take a walk along the **Eastern Promenade** (p. 304) or a day cruise to **Peaks Island** (p. 278) on a local ferry.

Day ❻: Freeport ★★★

Head north early to beat the shopping crowds at the outlet haven of Freeport. (You can't leave too early for **L.L.Bean**—p. 316—it never closes!). Spend your day trolling the flagship Bean store, the Bean offshoots (L.L.Kids, and the like) nearby, and the dozens of outlet shops that have sprung up in Bean's wake. For lunch or dinner, get in the car and explore the local side roads, being sure to grab a bite at one of the atmospheric local lobster shacks, such as **Harraseeket Lunch and Lobster** (p. 319).

Stay at a local inn or B&B, or backtrack to Portland for the night if you must; it's about a half-hour by car.

Days ❼ & ❽: Camden ★★ & Penobscot Bay

Heading north from the Freeport-Bath-Brunswick area, detour down to **Pemaquid Point** (p. 321) for a late picnic and to watch the surf roll in. Then head back to Route 1 and set your sights on Camden, Rockport, and Rockland, small and charming seaside towns at the heart of Penobscot Bay.

Rockland ★, which you'll reach first, is the workaday half of the equation. The best places here are the arty cafes and the excellent museum and restaurants. Nearby, **Rockport** ★★ is a tiny harbor town with excellent views and a small main street.

Finally, head a few miles north to wander around downtown **Camden** ★★, poking into shops and galleries. Hike up one of the impressive hills at **Camden Hills State Park** (p. 328), hop a **ferry** to an island (North Haven and Isleboro are both great for biking), sign up for a daylong sail on a **windjammer,** or just spend a long afternoon unwinding at one of the local pubs, chowder houses, or with an ice cream and a hot dog down at the harbor.

Then turn in. This town goes to bed early anyway.

Day ❾: Blue Hill ★★ & Deer Isle

From Camden, drive up and around the head of Penobscot Bay and then down the bay's eastern shore. The roads here are great for aimless drives, but aim for **Stonington** ★★, far down at the end of the peninsula. If distant **Isle au Haut,** visible from town docks, makes you pine for an offshore adventure, plan on a boat trip out early the next morning, secure lodging for the night, and adjust your schedule accordingly.

Next, head to scenic **Blue Hill** ★★ for dinner and lodging. I love the views from here, and the combination of a Maine fishing town and new-blood bookshops and restaurants is quite appealing. Also, take a spin around the peninsula to smaller towns such as **Blue Hill Falls** and **Brooklin,** where you'll see boatyards, old-fashioned general stores (post offices included), and Maine ingenuity holding it all together. *This* is the real Maine.

Days ⑩, ⑪, ⑫ & ⑬: Bar Harbor ★★ & Acadia National Park ★★★

Bar Harbor is a great base for exploring **Mount Desert Island,** which is well worth 4 days on a Maine itinerary. You may want to stay at least 2 nights in Bar Harbor, especially if you have children along. It provides access to comforts and services such as a movie theater, souvenir shops, bike and kayak rentals, free shuttle buses all over the island, and numerous restaurants. Yes, it's a lot more developed (perhaps too much so) than the rest of the island, but think of it as a supply depot.

Hike, bike, boat, or do whatever you must to explore the island and **Acadia National Park** (p. 340)—in my humble opinion, one of America's finest. Though it lacks in size, it makes up for it through intimate contact with nature. Explore the island at your own pace, via a beginner's **kayak trip** down the eastern shore, a **hike** out to **Bar Island,** or a **mountain bike trip** along one of the many **carriage roads** built by the Rockefeller family. Only bicycles and horses are allowed on these roads, making them a tranquil respite from the island's highways, which—almost unbelievably—do get crowded in summer.

The scenic **Park Loop Road** is a great introduction to what's in store for you later (crashing waves, big mountains, drop-dead-gorgeous views). Make sure to get your park pass—one that lasts more than a day.

While exploring the rest of the island, be sure to hit some of the towns without parks, too. **Northeast Harbor** ★★ and **Southwest Harbor** ★★ are two fishing towns that have been partly transformed by tourism into tiny centers of art, music, and shopping. However, they still have tiny stores where fishermen shop for slickers and Wonder Bread.

What about those things you wanted to do, but didn't have time for? Do them on your last day in Acadia. Cap off your visit with a cold-water dip at **Sand Beach** (p. 345) and tea and popovers at **Jordan Pond House** (p. 348). Watch a sunrise from the top of **Cadillac Mountain** (p. 346). Take a quick last hike up the **Bubbles** (p. 348). Paddle a canoe on **Long Pond.** Or just enjoy one last lobster atop a wooden pier.

Day ⑭: Back to Portland

On your last day, you may want to stop in **Bangor,** home to horror author Stephen King. Bangor is really the only cultural center in the vastly empty spaces of inland northern Maine, so stock up (and fuel up) here while you've got the chance. Heading home, you don't need to drive south on Route 1. In fact, it's far quicker to bypass the coast and use I-95—part of which takes in the Maine Turnpike, a toll road, that zips you south and out of Vacationland. Until next time.

4 A WEEK BY THE SEA FOR FAMILIES

A family can easily spend a pleasant week or so exploring the beaches, boats, cobblestones, shops, museums, and attractions of coastal New Hampshire and Maine.

Day ❶: Portsmouth ★★

Portsmouth is a great place to begin a tour of the coast and a good base for exploring local parks and beaches. Be sure to visit New Castle Island for its historic streets; the outstanding collection of oceanside state parks lining Route 1A in Rye; the gardens of pretty **Prescott Park** (p. 208); and the **Strawbery Banke** (p. 209) by the waterfront with its many historic buildings, museums, and restorations—and an ice-cream stand. In town there are plenty of shops and restaurants.

Day ❷: York ★★★ and Kittery ★

Only a 10-minute drive north, these twin towns offer a lot for families. **York** has a dynamite lighthouse (with homemade ice cream nearby), an amusement arcade, several excellent beaches, and a candy store where kids can watch taffy being pulled. You can buy boxes, of course, to take home; half the fun is deciding which candies to buy. **Kittery** is more for adults, but its extensive set of outlet stores also appeals to teen shopaholics.

Days ❸ & ❹: Ogunquit ★★ & the Kennebunks ★★

A 15-minute drive north leads you to **Ogunquit,** which has enough distractions for a few days with the family. In addition to a main street full of shops, restaurants, and cafes, it has a main beach that's a vast stretch of powdery sand at low tide and has some of Maine's warmest ocean water (which isn't saying much!). **Perkins Cove** (p. 288) has sea views, ice-cream and candy shops, an excellent small bookstore, and lots of souvenirs for sale.

A bit farther north, the **Kennebunks,** which consist of the twin towns of **Kennebunk** and **Kennebunkport** (summer home to the Bush family), are a great base for your next day. Here you'll find plentiful shopping, white clapboard homes, and more lobster and seafood restaurants than you can shake a fork at. If you've got time, drive out to the point of land where Secret Service guys guard the famous Bush compound.

Days ❺ & ❻: Portland ★★★

A 25-minute car ride will take you to **Portland,** which is a joy for families to explore. The **Children's Museum of Maine** (p. 304) is almost exactly in the center of Portland proper, making it a good jumping-off point for a tour of the city. The excellent **Portland Museum of Art** (p. 305) is right next door, providing teens and college-age family members with something different to do.

In the historic **Old Port** (p. 302), Exchange Street is the key shopping address, though the side streets have much to offer. The city's tourist office—stocked with free info—is at the end of Commercial Street, in the new Ocean Gateway (past the ferry docks). Kids will enjoy the ice-cream shops, boats, and quirky gift stores in this neighborhood.

The **Maine Narrow Gauge Railroad Co. & Museum** (p. 304) combines a leisurely, short train ride to the foot of the cliffs framing Portland's east end with an educational museum.

Another great experience is a cruise around Casco Bay on the **Casco Bay Ferry** (p. 306) lines that depart from a terminal at the foot of Franklin Arterial (across from the Hilton Garden Inn). You can take anything from a 20-minute run to a half-day mail-boat cruise. Two good destinations are **Peaks Island**—a favorite among mothers pushing baby strollers, with easy-to-cruise streets and Portland views—and **Long Island,** with an excellent beach.

If your kids are crazy about baseball, an outing at Hadlock Field watching the **Portland Sea Dogs** (p. 306) can't be beat; it's one of my favorite minor-league parks.

Finally, young and old alike enjoy the sunrises, sunsets, picnics, sailboat views, swing sets, and ball fields of the park along the **Eastern Promenade** (p. 304). It's one of Portland's true gems, and the perfect place to cap off a visit.

Day 7: Cape Elizabeth ★★

While staying in Portland, plan to spend at least one afternoon hitting the string of beaches and lighthouses off Route 77 in the quiet suburb of **Cape Elizabeth** and surroundings, just 15 minutes from the city.

Kids will especially enjoy the **Two Lights** and **Portland Head Light** lighthouses; the eats at **Two Lights Lobster Shack;** and romping around in the sand and surf on **Crescent, Scarborough,** and **Willard beaches.**

5

Southern & Central Vermont

Vermont's rolling, cow-spotted hills, shaggy peaks, sugar maples, and quaint towns clustered along river valleys give it a distinct sense of place. Still mostly rural (even if a few slices are gradually becoming more suburban), this state is filled with the dairy farms, dirt roads, and small-scale enterprises that bring joy to the hearts of back-road travelers. And the towns are home to an intriguing mix of old-time Vermonters; back-to-the-landers who showed up in VW buses in the 1960s and never left—many got involved with municipal affairs or put down business roots (think Ben & Jerry); and newer, moneyed arrivals from New York or Boston who came to ski or stay at B&Bs and ended up buying second homes. Some of those second homes ended up becoming first homes.

This place captures a sense of America as it once was—because here, it still *is.* Vermonters share a sense of community, and they still respect the ideals of thrift and parsimony above those of commercialism. (It took years of haggling for Wal-Mart to get approval to build its first big-box store in Vermont.) Locals prize their villages, and they understand what makes them special. A Vermont governor once said that one of his state's strengths was knowing "where our towns begin and end," and even if that seems overly simplistic, it also speaks volumes, because so many East Coast small towns have been swallowed up by a creeping megalopolis and an erosion of local identity.

For travelers, Vermont remains a superb destination of country drives, mountain rambles, and overnights at country inns. A good map opens the door to back-road adventures, and it's not hard to get a taste of Vermont's way of life. The numbers tell the story: Burlington, Vermont's largest city, counts just 39,000 year-round residents; Montpelier, the state capital, about 8,000; Brattleboro and Bennington, perhaps 12,000 and 16,000, respectively; and Woodstock, just 3,000. The state's total population is just a shade over 600,000, making it one of only a handful of states with more senators (2) than representatives (1) in Congress.

Of course, numbers don't tell the entire story. You have to let the people do that. Former Governor Howard Dean made a national splash in 2004 as a presidential candidate speaking (and screeching) with unusual candor. That was more or less in tune with the state's hard-won identity as a place of its own separate peace. For 14 long years during the late 1700s, in fact, Vermont *did* function as an independent republic, a historical moment that many Vermonters still savor with surprising pride—and that many wish to repeat.

More than 70 years ago, Nobel prize–winning author Sinclair Lewis wrote: "I like Vermont because it is quiet, because you have a population that is solid and not driven mad by the American mania—that mania which considers a town of 4,000 twice as good as a town of 2,000. Following that reasoning, one would get the charming paradox that Chicago would be 10 times better than the entire state of Vermont, but I have been in Chicago and not found it so."

So what's it like up there? Southern and central Vermont are defined by rolling hills, shady valleys, and historic villages. Throughout you'll find antiques shops and handsome inns, fast-flowing streams, and inviting restaurants. The southern edge is anchored at each corner by the towns of Bennington and Brattleboro, like pushpins; between them, running northward, is the impressively obdurate spine of the Green Mountains, much of which is part of the Green Mountain National Forest and all of which rewards explorers who consider dirt roads and quiet hiking tracks to be irresistibly tempting.

Here and there you'll find remnants of former industries—marble quarrying around Rutland, converging train tracks at White River Junction—but mostly it's still rural living here: cow pastures high on the hills, clapboard farmhouses under spreading trees, maple-sugaring operations in spring, and the distant sound of timber being felled from a woodlot on the far side of a high ridge. These steep hills are also the site of many of the state's most popular ski resorts, including Okemo, Killington, Sugarbush, and Mount Snow.

Though it is the closest part of northern New England to New York City, southern Vermont has somehow mostly resisted the encroachment of city-dwellers, except within ski resorts during a busy winter weekend and on any road leading to a bright maple leaf in October.

But even in these hectic moments—which are really not all *that* hectic—southern and central Vermont remain wonderful introductions to a place that is both rugged and lovely.

1 ENJOYING THE GREAT OUTDOORS

Arizona has the Grand Canyon, Florida has the Everglades, California has Hwy. 101, New York has the canyons of Manhattan. Vermont? Vermont has the Green Mountains. But you know what? I'll take *it* over all the others.

The Green Mountains aren't so much a destination as they are part and parcel of Vermont itself. These rolling old hills, crumpled up like the first pages of a novel, form a north-south spine from Massachusetts all the way to the Canadian border. These mountains not only define Vermont's look, feel, and character, but also offer wonderful recreational opportunities for visitors, especially those attracted to hiking, snowshoeing, cross-country skiing, and the like. These hills are nearly a perfect medium: less dramatic and more forgiving than the harsh White Mountains of New Hampshire, friendlier and more accessible than the big spruce-fir forests of Maine, cooler and less humid than the hazy Blue Ridge Mountains. You just feel at home here. And in a great (or even just a good) foliage year, I'd argue they're as beautifully colored as any range of mountains in the world.

About half a million acres make up the Green Mountain National Forest, and within its bounds you'll find some of the best hiking and mountain biking in the entire Northeast. Outdoorsy travelers don't need to restrict themselves to the national forest lands, though. Vermont's state forests and parks also possess exceptional hiking trails and lakes perfect for swimming and boating, and many privately owned lands are also open to low-impact recreation. Good campgrounds abound, too.

This mixture of wilderness and civilization gives Vermont much of its character. One of the great pleasures of exploring the state, whether by foot, bike, or canoe, is cresting a hill or rounding a bend and suddenly spying a graceful white steeple or a sturdy red wooden silo in the distance. These human markings are as integral to Vermont's landscape as its cows, maple trees, and rolling ridges, and just as pleasing.

BACKPACKING The **Long Trail** runs some 270 miles from Massachusetts to the Canadian border. The nation's first long-distance hiking path, this high-elevation trail remains one of its best today, following gusty ridges, dipping into shady cols, and crossing federal, state, and private lands on its nearly due-north run. Open-sided shelters along the trail are spaced about a day's hike apart; still, to hike the entire length requires stamina and experience.

The best source of information about backcountry opportunities is the **Green Mountain Club,** 4711 Waterbury-Stowe Rd., Waterbury Center, VT 05677 (✆ **802/244-7037;** www.greenmountainclub.org), which publishes the *Long Trail Guide* ($18.95, or $17 for club members). The club's headquarters and visitor center are on Route 100 between Waterbury and Stowe, about 4 miles north of the Stowe interstate exit. (It's just north of Cold Hollow Cider Mill.) The information center/bookstore is open daily in summer, usually 9am to 5pm, with slightly shorter hours (and closed Sun) the rest of the year. Annual membership dues, which get you a newsletter and discounts on guides, are $40 for an individual or $50 for a family.

BIKING Vermont's back roads offer some of the most attractive biking in the Northeast. Even Route 100—the main north-south thoroughfare burrowing up the middle of the state like a drunken zipper—is inviting for stretches, particularly between the Killington and Sugarbush ski resorts. While the steep hills on some back roads can be excruciating for those who've spent too much time behind a desk, scrutiny of a map should reveal other routes that follow rivers, valleys, or lake shores and offer less grueling pedaling. As a bonus, Vermont's local bike clubs are excellent, offering many free or inexpensive guides that lead you past covered bridges, farmlands, and views you surely never would have found yourself.

Vermont also lends itself to superb **mountain biking.** Abandoned county and town roads allow for superior backcountry cruising; most of the Green Mountain National Forest's trails are also open to mountain bikers. (The Appalachian and Long trails, however, are *not* open to bikes.) Mountain bikes are prohibited on state-park and state-forest hiking trails, but they are allowed on gravel roads—and this is a state with a *lot* of gravel roads. The Mount Snow and Jay Peak ski areas, among others, allow you to bring your bike up to blustery ridges via lifts or gondolas, from where you can use gravity as your best friend (or a potential enemy, if your brakes are balky) all the way down. The **Craftsbury Outdoor Center** (p. 196) is your best bet if you're looking for back-road cruising through farmland rather than forest.

Organized inn-to-inn bike tours are a great way to see the countryside by day while relaxing in relative luxury at night. These tours are typically self-guided, with luggage transferred for you each day by vehicle—a big help. Try **Vermont Bicycle Touring** (✆ **800/245-3868;** www.vbt.com), based in Bristol, or **Bike Vermont** (✆ **800/257-2226** or 802/457-3553; www.bikevt.com), based in Woodstock.

CANOEING Good stretches of river for padding include the Battenkill in southwest Vermont, the Lamoille near Jeffersonville, the Winooski near Waterbury, and the Missisquoi from Highgate Center to Swanton Dam. The whole of the historic Connecticut River, while frequently interrupted by dams, allows for uncommonly scenic paddling through rural farmlands. Especially beautiful is a 7-mile stretch between Moore and Comerford dams near Waterford. Rentals are easy to come by near Vermont's major waterways; just check the local Yellow Pages.

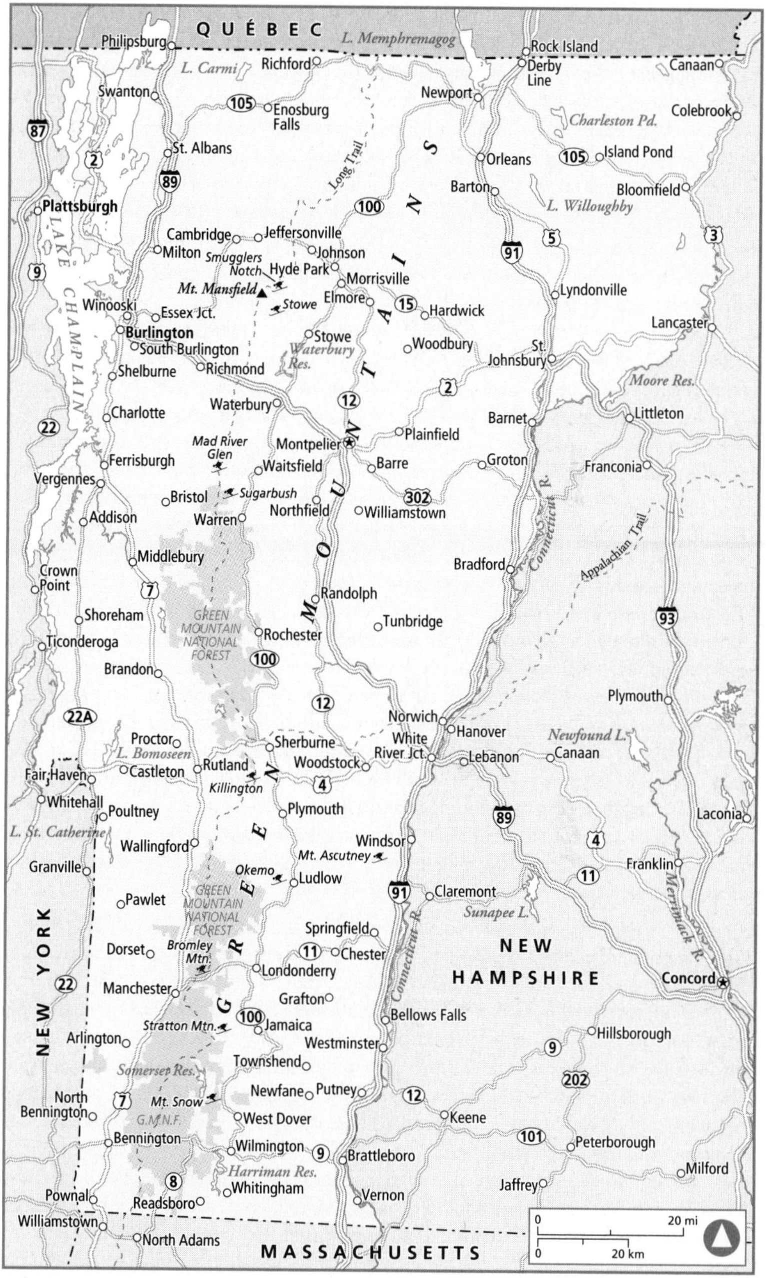
QUÉBEC
L. Memphremagog
Philipsburg
Richford
L. Carmi
Rock Island
Derby Line
Canaan
Swanton
Newport
Enosburg Falls
Colebrook
Charleston Pd.
St. Albans
Long Trail
Orleans
Island Pond
Barton
Bloomfield
L. Willoughby
Plattsburgh
LAKE CHAMPLAIN
Cambridge
Jeffersonville
Johnson
Milton
Smugglers Notch
Hyde Park
Morrisville
Mt. Mansfield
Stowe
Elmore
Hardwick
Lyndonville
Winooski
Essex Jct.
Burlington
South Burlington
Stowe
Waterbury Res.
Woodbury
Lancaster
St. Johnsbury
Shelburne
Richmond
Moore Res.
Charlotte
Waterbury
Barnet
Littleton
Mad River Glen
Montpelier
Plainfield
Ferrisburgh
Waitsfield
Barre
Groton
Franconia
Vergennes
Sugarbush
Bristol
Northfield
Williamstown
Addison
Warren
Connecticut R.
Appalachian Trail
Middlebury
Bradford
Crown Point
Randolph
Shoreham
GREEN MOUNTAIN NATIONAL FOREST
Tunbridge
Ticonderoga
Rochester
Brandon
Plymouth
Norwich
Hanover
Proctor
L. Bomoseen
Sherburne
White River Jct.
Newfound L.
Canaan
Lebanon
Fair Haven
Castleton
Rutland
Woodstock
Killington
Whitehall
Poultney
Plymouth
Laconia
L. St. Catherine
Wallingford
Windsor
Mt. Ascutney
Franklin
Granville
Okemo
Ludlow
Claremont
Pawlet
Sunapee L.
Springfield
Merrimack R.
Dorset
Bromley Mtn.
Chester
NEW HAMPSHIRE
NEW YORK
Manchester
Londonderry
Connecticut R.
Concord
Grafton
Stratton Mtn.
Jamaica
Bellows Falls
Hillsborough
Arlington
Westminster
Townshend
Somerset Res.
North Bennington
Mt. Snow
Newfane
Putney
Keene
G.M.N.F.
West Dover
Bennington
Wilmington
Brattleboro
Peterborough
Harriman Res.
Milford
Pownal
Readsboro
Whitingham
Vernon
Jaffrey
Williamstown
North Adams
MASSACHUSETTS
GREEN MOUNTAINS
0 20 mi
0 20 km
87
2
89
105
100
9
15
2
12
22
302
7
100
12
22A
4
89
4
11
91
11
22
100
9
202
7
12
101
9
8
5
3
91
93
105

For inn-to-inn canoe-touring packages (usually 4 to 5 days in length), contact **BattenKill Canoe Ltd.,** 6328 Rte. 7A, Arlington, VT 05250 (✆ **800/421-5268** or 802/362-2800; www.battenkill.com), based halfway between Arlington and Manchester Center.

The **Upper Valley Land Trust,** 19 Buck Rd., Hanover, NH 03755 (✆ **603/643-6626;** www.uvlt.org), oversees a network of primitive campsites along the Connecticut River. Canoeists can paddle and portage its length and camp along the riverbanks. Two of the campsites are accessible by car. Call for a brochure or visit the group's website.

A good general guide to the territory is Roioli Schweiker's *Canoe Camping Vermont & New Hampshire Rivers* ($16.95), published by the Countryman Press.

FISHING Both lake and river fishing can be excellent here, if you know what you're doing: Little Vermont contains nearly 300 lakes of 20 acres or more, plus hundreds of smaller bodies of water and countless miles of rivers and streams.

Novice fly-fishermen would do well to stop by the famed **Orvis Company Store** (✆ **802/362-3750**), on Route 7A in Manchester, for some friendly advice, then try out some tackle on the store's small ponds. If time permits, sign up for an Orvis fly-fishing class and have an expert critique your technique and offer some pointers, too.

Vermont's rivers and lakes are home to more than a dozen major species of sport fish, including landlocked salmon, four varieties of trout (rainbow, brown, brook, and lake), and largemouth and smallmouth bass. The 100-mile-long Lake Champlain attracts its share of enthusiasts angling for bass, landlocked salmon, and lake trout. To the south, the Battenkill is perhaps the most famous trout river in the eastern U.S. (thanks in part to its close proximity to Orvis), though some veteran anglers say it has lost its luster. The Walloomsac and West rivers also contain decent-size trout. And don't overlook the Connecticut River, which the Fish and Wildlife Department used to call "the best-kept fishing secret in the Northeast." Oops.

Fishing licenses are required and are available by mail from the state or in person at many sporting-goods and general stores. License requirements and fees change from time to time, so write or call for a complete list: **Vermont Fish & Wildlife Dept.,** 103 S. Main St., #10 South, Waterbury, VT 05671 (✆ **802/241-3700**). For more information, check the department's website at **www.vtfishandwildlife.com**. You can also now **buy your fishing license online,** at the website **www.vtfwdsales.com**. For nonresidents of Vermont, it costs $41 for a calendar-year license. Youths receive discounts, and state residents enjoy *big* discounts.

HIKING Vermont hosts a spectacular mix of hiking trails, from woodland strolls to rugged mountain treks. The two premier long-distance pathways in Vermont are the Appalachian and Long trails (see "Backpacking," above); day hikes are easily carved out of these longer trails. The **Green Mountain National Forest** (www.fs.fed.us/r9/gmfl) has something like 500 miles of hiking trails, for starters. Any of the four Green Mountain offices are good stops for picking up maps and requesting hiking advice from rangers. The **main office** is on Main Street in Rutland (✆ **802/747-6700**). District **ranger offices** are in Middlebury (✆ **802/388-4362**), Rochester (✆ **802/767-4261**), and Manchester (✆ **802/362-2307**).

In addition to this vast national forest, the state of Vermont also owns and maintains about 80 state forests and parks. Guides to hiking trails are essential to getting the most out of a hiking vacation. Recommended guides include the Green Mountain Club's *Day Hiker's Guide to Vermont* and *50 Hikes in Vermont* (published by the Green Mountain Club), both widely available in bookstores throughout the state.

Picking the Perfect Slope: A Field Guide

Choosing a ski resort in Vermont can be tough—there are so many options! So I've done the legwork for you. Here's a quick primer on who should look where:

- **Expert skiers** and **snowboarders** who crave **big mountains,** steep faces, and a lively **après-ski scene:** Killington, Sugarbush, Stratton, Mount Snow, and Stowe.
- **Families** and **intermediate-level skiers:** Okemo, Bolton Valley, and Smuggler's Notch.
- Skiers craving New England rustic **charm:** Ascutney, Burke, and Jay Peak.
- **Hippie** and **gonzo** skiers: Mad River Glen.
- **Budget-conscious** skiers and those who prefer **smaller mountains:** Middlebury Snow Bowl, Bromley, Maple Valley, and Suicide Six.
- The **shortest drive** from New York: Mount Snow.

For more information on ski conditions online, check the website **www.skivermont.com**.

SKIING Vermont has been eclipsed by upscale western and Canadian ski resorts during the past several decades, but to many, it's still *the* capital of **downhill skiing** in the United States. The nation's first ski lift, in fact—a rope tow—was rigged up to a Buick engine in 1934 on a hill near Woodstock, and the first lodge built specifically to accommodate skiers in the U.S. was at Sherburne Pass (now known as Killington).

Today the Green Mountains are dotted with ski resorts of every shape, size, feel, and price level—so many that it can be daunting for the first-time visitor to pick one. For a sense about which of the many ski resorts here are best for which skiers, see "Picking the Perfect Slope: A Field Guide," above.

Vermont is also blessed with 50 or so **cross-country ski** facilities, from modest mom-and-pop operations all the way up to elaborate destination resorts that make their own snow (though it's hard to believe that's ever necessary in Vermont). Some of these tracks are stitched together by the 200-mile Catamount Trail, which runs the length of the state parallel to, but at lower elevations than, the Long Trail. For more information, contact the **Catamount Trail Association,** 1 Mill St., Ste. 350, Burlington, VT 05401 (✆ **802/864-5794;** www.catamounttrail.org). For a free brochure listing all cross-country skiing facilities, contact the **Vermont Department of Tourism and Marketing** (✆ **800/VERMONT** [837-6668] or 802/828-3237).

The best general advice I can give cross-country skiers is to head north and to higher elevations, where you can usually find the most *and* fluffiest snow. Among the snowiest, best-managed destinations: the **Trapp Family Lodge** (p. 172) in Stowe and the **Craftsbury Nordic Center** (p. 196) in the Northeast Kingdom and the **Mountain Top Inn's** ridge-top property near Killington (p. 139).

Inn-to-inn ski touring is growing in popularity. **Country Inns Along the Trail** (✆ **800/838-3301** or 802/247-3300; www.inntoinn.com), based in Forest Dale between Rutland and Middlebury, offers self-guided, 4-night trips along the Catamount

Trail connecting inns in central Vermont for $625 to $699 per person (double occupancy), including all lodging and meals. Customized trips can also be arranged from this outfitter.

SNOWMOBILING Vermont has a surprisingly well-developed network of snowmobile trails throughout the state, plus a central clearinghouse organization that grooms and maintains trails: **VAST,** the Vermont Association of Snow Travelers (✆ **802/229-0005;** www.vtvast.org), in Barre. VAST produces a helpful newsletter that can help point you and your machine in the right direction; the group also sells an all-inclusive annual pass ($65–$90 for state residents, $95–$130 for nonresidents), allowing you access to all of the trails maintained, signed, and groomed by its 140 or so local clubs around the state. Without the pass, you can't use VAST trails. The pass is not mandatory, but it is certainly helpful if you want to expand your options.

If you don't have your own "sled," snowmobile rentals are somewhat difficult to come by in Vermont (contact VAST for information on rentals), but guided tours are fairly easy to arrange. In southern Vermont, **High Country Tours,** based about 8½ miles west of Wilmington (✆ **800/627-7533** or 802/464-2108; www.high-country-tours.com), is one experienced outfit offering tours in the national forest lasting between 1 hour ($75 for one rider, extra for a second) and a full day ($285 for one rider, $385 for two riding together).

2 BENNINGTON, MANCHESTER & ENVIRONS

Bennington: 143 miles NW of Boston; 126 miles S of Burlington. Manchester: 24 miles N of Bennington

Southwestern Vermont is the turf of Ethan Allen, Robert Frost, Grandma Moses, and Norman Rockwell—some pretty heavy hitters, arts-wise. The place might thus seem familiar even if you've never been here until now. Over the decades, this region has subtly managed to work itself deep into America's cultural consciousness, identity, and sense of wistful nostalgia about its past.

The region is sandwiched between the Green Mountains to the east and the rolling hills along the Vermont–New York border to the west. If you're coming from Albany or the southwest, the first town you're likely to hit is **Bennington,** a commercial center that offers up low-key diversions for residents and tourists alike. Northward toward **Rutland,** the terrain is more intimate than intimidating, with towns clustered in broad and gentle valleys along rivers and streams. Former 19th-century summer colonies and erstwhile lumber and marble towns exist side by side, offering pleasant accommodations, good food, and—in the case of **Manchester Center,** at least—pretty good big-brand-name outlet shopping. There are also an unusual number of lovely **covered bridges** and iconic **country stores** in this part of the state.

Interestingly, southern Vermont's icons of sophisticated culture—from outlet shops and ski resorts to fly-fishing stores and fancy inns—are all within easy striking distance of the Green Mountains, enabling you to both enjoy the outdoors by day *and* pull goose-down duvets over yourself at night. As a bonus, **shuttle buses** now cruise the southern mountain towns, most touching base in Manchester during their perambulations; you don't even need a car, though one is certainly very useful here for back-roading.

This region attracts its share of weekend celebrities, shoppers, gourmands, and those simply looking for a brief and relaxing detour to the elegant inns and B&Bs for which the region is so widely known.

ATTRACTIONS ●
Bennington Battle
 Monument **3**
Bennington College **1**
The Bennington Museum **5**
Hemmings Sunoco **7**

ACCOMMODATIONS ■
The Four Chimneys Inn **4**
Paradise Motor Inn **6**
South Shire Inn **8**

DINING ◆
Alldays & Onions **10**
Blue Benn Diner **8**
Pangaea **2**

SOUTHERN & CENTRAL VERMONT

5

BENNINGTON, MANCHESTER & ENVIRONS

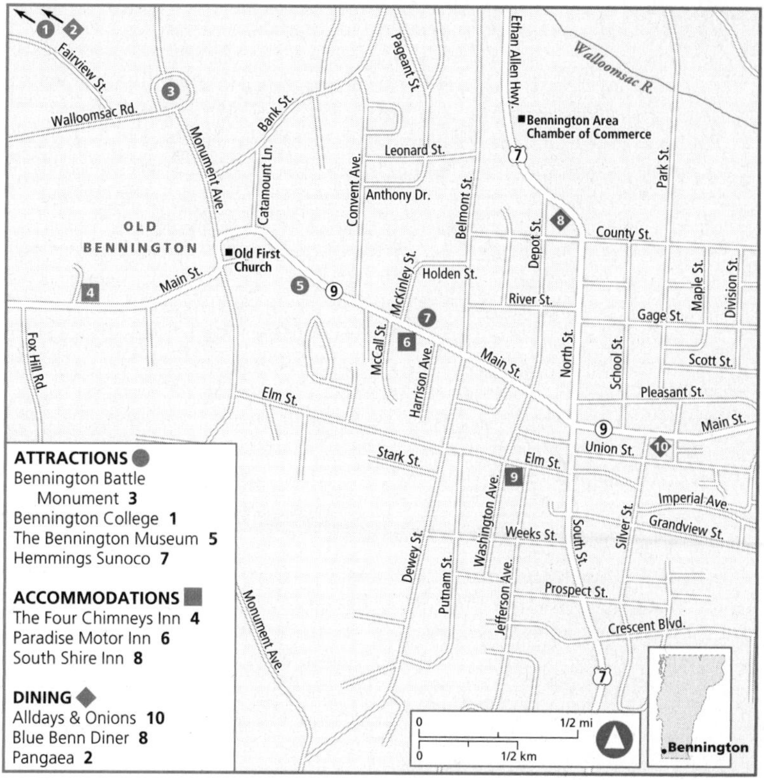

BENNINGTON ★

Bennington (motto: "Where Vermont Begins") is somehow Vermont's third-largest city, even though it feels a lot more like a one-stoplight town. The place owes its fame (such as it is) to a handful of eponymous moments, places, and things. There's the Battle of Bennington, fought in 1777 during the American War of Independence (which was actually fought in New York State); Bennington College, a small, prestigious liberal-arts school just outside town; and Bennington pottery, which traces its ancestry back to the original factory in 1793 and is still prized by collectors for its superb quality.

Today visitors will find a Bennington of two faces. Historic Bennington (more commonly known as **Old Bennington ★★**), with its white clapboard homes, sits atop a hill west of town off Route 9; look for the mini–Washington Monument obelisk and you're there. It's a gem of a neighborhood, especially if you fancy old homes and additional cows. Views materialize as you continue uphill and west from here on Route 7. The surrounding countryside, though defined by rolling hills, has fewer abrupt inclines and slopes than many other parts of Vermont, so go back-roading around here for a bit if you can.

Tips 7 Up: Choosing the Best Route

When driving through southern Vermont, note that there are *two* Route 7s. Running high along the foothills is the newer **Route 7,** a sort of parkway with limited access and (in places) double lanes, enabling a speedy and scenic trip up the valley toward Manchester and Rutland or back down to Bennington. It passes through a range of absolutely empty foothills (I challenge you to spot a person or even a cow from your car), offering some of the best foliage views you'll find on a U.S. highway; there are pull-off areas to take the photos I know you'll want to take. Drawback? There are only a few exits onto and off this highway; you might miss something in between, and if your kids suddenly need a break, it's 10 miles to the next exit. But if you're in a hurry—or want to snap great, expansive views of foliage without any buildings in the background—take this route.

Meandering along the valley floor, on the other hand, is **Route 7A** (in slightly pretentious fashion, it's usually called "Historic Rte. 7A"). This road is a much more leisurely ride—you'll encounter lots of locals, and some stopping-and-waiting in the village centers you'll pass through—with plenty of diversions along the way, including antiques shops, outlet stores, farm stands, historic buildings and inns, and a covered bridge. Both routes are nice. Choose according to your mood and needs.

Downtown Bennington, on the other hand, is a pleasant but no-frills commercial center stocked with real estate offices, plumbers, diners, coffee and sub shops, and stores that still sell things people actually need—not so much a tourist destination as a supply depot. The downtown is compact, low, and handsome, boasting a fair number of architecturally striking buildings. In particular, don't miss the stern marble Federal building (formerly the post office) with six fluted columns, at 118 South St.

Essentials

GETTING THERE Bennington is at the intersection of Vermont state routes 9 and 7. If you're coming from the south, the nearest interstate access is via the New York State Thruway at Albany, about 35 miles away. (But you have to drive through the city of Troy first, which takes time; figure 45 min. or more from the Thruway to downtown Bennington.) From the east, I-91 is about 40 miles away at Brattleboro.

VISITOR INFORMATION The **Bennington Area Chamber of Commerce,** 100 Veterans Memorial Dr. (✆ **800/229-0252** or 802/447-3311; www.bennington.com), maintains a **visitor center** on Route 7 about 1 mile north of downtown, near the veterans' complex and a small park. This office is open weekdays 9am to 5pm year-round, and also on weekends from mid-May until around mid-October. There's also a **downtown welcome center** (✆ **802/442-5758**) in a former blacksmith shop at South and Elm streets; look for the big blue flag. Operated by the *other* BBC—the Better Bennington Corporation, of course—it's open Monday through Friday year-round, and has a big map of the area to orient you.

Exploring the Town

Bennington's main claim to fame is the Battle of Bennington, which took place just outside town (across the New York state line, actually) on August 16, 1777. A relatively minor skirmish, it nevertheless had pretty major implications for the eventual outcome of the American Revolution.

It happened this way: The British devised a strategy to defeat the colonists and were putting it into play. Divide the colonies from the Hudson River up through Lake Champlain, they figured, and then concentrate their forces to defeat first one half of the Americans and then the other half. As part of this strategy, the British General John Burgoyne was ordered to attack Bennington and capture supplies that had been squirreled away by Continental militias. He came upon Colonial forces led by General John Stark, a veteran of Bunker Hill; after a few days playing cat-and-mouse, Stark ordered an attack on the afternoon of August 16, proclaiming, "There are the redcoats, and they are ours, or this night Molly Stark sleeps a widow!" (Or so the story goes.)

In less than 2 hours it was all over, and a rout for the underdogs—the British and their Hessian mercenaries were defeated, with more than 200 casualties, while the victorious Colonials lost only 30 men. The British would soon suffer another embarrassing setback at the Battle of Saratoga not far away, and these two losses effectively ended the idea of dividing and conquering; the British never recovered, and eventually lost the war.

This battle is commemorated by northern New England's most imposing monument. You can't miss the **Bennington Battle Monument** ★★ (✆ **802/447-0550**) if you're passing through the area—turn off the main road (Rte. 9) in Old Bennington's little traffic circle to visit it. This 306-foot obelisk of blue limestone atop a low rise was dedicated in 1891. It resembles a shorter, paunchier Washington Monument. (This is *not* the battle site; that's about 6 miles northwest of here. This monument marks the spot where American munitions were stored.) The monument's viewing platform, which is reached by elevator, is open daily from 9am to 5pm from mid-April through October. A small fee ($2 adults, $1 children ages 6–14) is charged. On holidays and during the last 2 weeks of every year, the monument is lit up.

Near the monument, you'll find distinguished old homes lushly overarched with ancient trees. Be sure to spend a minute exploring the **old burying ground** ★, where

The Bridges of Bennington County

There are five (count 'em, five) covered bridges within a short drive of downtown Bennington, all of them red and all of them photogenic. Get in your car and snap photos of a few of 'em. Three of the bridges are very near Bennington College, on or just off **Route 67A,** which is a sort-of continuation of Route 7A northwest of town. The **Silk Road Bridge** and **Paper Mill Village** bridges are right on 67A; just off that route, a turnoff (Murphy Rd.) leads to the **Henry Bridge** (which was restored in the 1990s).

There are two more bridges in **Arlington.** Right in the village center, turn east off Route 7A onto East Arlington Road and follow it a few miles south to find the high **Chiselville Bridge.**

The most famous of the five bridges, however, is probably the **West Arlington Bridge** ★, reached by following Route 313 (Batten Kill Rd.), a clearly marked turnoff from Arlington's village center, 4 or 5 miles west. This bridge not only sits right beside a lovely little country church, but also straddles the famous Battenkill River and stands within a stone's throw of Norman Rockwell's former home (see "Arlington, Manchester & Dorset," later in this chapter).

Moments "I Had a Lover's Quarrel with the World."

That's the epitaph on the tombstone of Robert Frost, who is buried in the cemetery behind the 1806 First Congregational Church where Route 9 makes two quick bends west of downtown and down the hill from the Bennington Monument. Signs point the way to the Frost family grave. Travelers often stop here to pay their respects to the man many still consider to be *the* true voice of New England. (Frost was born in California, but was raised in Massachusetts from the age of 11 and lived mostly in New Hampshire and Vermont the rest of his life.) Closer to the church, look for the old tombstones—some decorated with urns and skulls—of other Vermonters who lived much less famous lives.

the great poet Robert Frost and several Vermont governors are buried; see "I Had a Lover's Quarrel with the World," below. The chamber of commerce also provides a walking-tour brochure that helps you make sense of this neighborhood's formerly vibrant past.

Bennington College ★, just northwest of downtown Bennington, was founded in the 1930s as an experimental women's college. It later went co-ed and garnered a national reputation as a leading liberal-arts school with a special reputation for teaching writing: The Pulitzer Prize–winning poet W. H. Auden, novelist Bernard Malamud *(The Natural),* and novelist John Gardner all taught here. In the 1980s, Bennington produced a fresh wave of prominent young authors, including Donna Tartt, Bret Easton Ellis, and Jill Eisenstadt. The pleasant campus north of town is worth wandering; to get there, take the North Bennington Road (Rte. 67A) turnoff north of downtown (near the Bennington Square Shopping Center) and follow it about 2 miles north. There are also three attractive **covered bridges** near the college. (See "The Bridges of Bennington County," above.)

A fun local find is **Hemmings Sunoco** (✆ **802/447-9652**), a gas station at 216 W. Main St. (just west of downtown on Rte. 9, across from the Paradise Motor Inn). This isn't just *any* gas station, though—it's also headquarters for the *Hemmings Motor News,* a monthly publication considered essential reading for vintage-car collectors. You can tank up here. (It's full-service!) year-round; from May through October, ask to take a free escorted peek at the **car museum** ★★ in the storage area. You can also buy auto-related souvenirs, such as old Route 66 signs and model cars, inside.

The Bennington Museum ★★ Finds This eclectic and intriguing collection is one of the best small museums in northern New England. The museum traces its roots back to the 1850s, although it has occupied its current stone-and-column home overlooking the valley since "only" 1928. The expansive galleries here feature a range of exhibits on local arts and industry, including early Vermont furniture, glass, paintings, and Bennington pottery. Of special interest are the many colorful primitive landscapes by Grandma Moses (1860–1961), who lived much of her life nearby. (This museum has the largest collection of Moses paintings in the world.) There's also lots of American glass; a globe by James Wilson, the nation's first globe maker; a Windsor chair once owned by Ira Allen, who wrote the state's constitution; and a 1925 Martin Wasp luxury car (only 16 were ever made, hand-crafted in Bennington by Karl Martin btw. 1920 and 1925). Rotating special exhibits bring in serious art that's sometimes unrelated to local history, such as a show of rarely shown works by Renoir, Monet, and Degas or a show of Haitian quilts. This is a great find.

75 W. Main St. (Rte. 9 btw. Old Bennington and the town center). ✆ **802/447-1571.** www.benningtonmuseum.org. Admission $9 adults, $8 seniors and students, free for children 17 and under, $19 family. Nov–Aug Tues–Mon 10am–5pm; Sept–Oct daily 10am–5pm.

Where to Stay

The Four Chimneys Inn ★★ This 1912 Colonial Revival catches your eye as you roll into Bennington from the west; it's right at the edge of Old Bennington, and the towering Bennington Monument looms just over its shoulder. Set back from Route 7 on a big, nicely landscaped lot, the three-story mansion features—no surprise—four prominent chimneys. Guest rooms are divided among the main inn, an ice house, and a carriage house; they're spare, whitewashed, and flower-printed rather than luxe, with rather simple furniture and dated carpeting. Still, some units sport real fireplaces burning real wood, and many have nice Jacuzzis, four-poster beds, and/or mountain views from patios. I like room no. 11 because it has its own private porch and more windows than most of the other units; the brick carriage house (room no. 9) has a cathedral-type ceiling. Upper-floor and ice-house units, on the other hand, feel a bit cramped because of the odd-angled ceilings. This place had been fading in recent years, but is improving once again under its pleasant new owners, Pete and Lynn Green (who also married at the inn).

21 West Rd. (Rte. 9, just west of downtown), Bennington, VT 05201. ✆ **802/447-3500.** Fax 802/447-3692. www.fourchimneys.com. 11 units. $125–$295 double. Rates include full breakfast. 2-night minimum stay foliage and holiday weekends. AE, DISC, MC, V. Children 12 and over accepted. **Amenities:** Dining room. *In room:* A/C, TV, hair dryer.

Paradise Inn ★ Kids Paradise by the dashboard light? Maybe. This is perhaps Bennington's best motel, even if prices have shot up in recent years. It's clean and well managed, sits across from the Hemmings gas station (see above), and is walking distance to town. The tidy, generously sized accommodations are further bolstered by such surprising amenities as full kitchens in some of the suites, tennis courts, a heated pool, and a decent coffee shop. The very central location and neighborhood views aren't bad, either. Try to reserve a spot in the North Building, in spite of its dated 1980s styling—each unit has an outdoor terrace or balcony. The more up-to-date Office Building is done in Colonial Revival style. Furniture and carpeting are of the same quality/blandness as any mid-level chain business hotel.

141 W. Main St., Bennington, VT 05201. ✆ **800/575-5784** or 802/442-8351. Fax 802/447-3889. www.theparadisemotorinn.com. 77 units. $70–$145 double; $110–$220 suite. AE, DISC, MC, V. **Amenities:** Restaurant; exercise room; heated outdoor pool; 2 tennis courts; Wi-Fi (free, in lobby). *In room:* A/C, TV, kitchen (some units), Wi-Fi (free, some units).

South Shire Inn A locally prominent banking family hired architect William Bull in 1880 to design and build this Victorian home, with leaded glass on its bookshelves and intricate plasterwork in the main dining room. Five guest rooms in the main inn building are furnished with handsomely carved canopy or poster beds and working fireplaces (burning Duraflame logs, not wood); the two best rooms here are probably the former master bedrooms (Otto and Gold), with their king beds and tile-hearth fireplaces. Four newer, more modern guest rooms—with names like "Jim Dandy"—are located in an adjacent carriage house. They each sport extra amenities and lovely exposed pine flooring (rooms in the main inn have all been carpeted). All four of these rooms have televisions with DVD players, ceiling fans, and Jacuzzis.

124 Elm St., Bennington, VT 05201. ✆ **888/201-2250** or 802/447-3839. Fax 802/442-3547. www.southshire.com. 9 units. $125–$185 double; foliage season $155–$265 double. Rates include breakfast. 2-night minimum stay during foliage season. MC, V. Not appropriate for children. *In room:* A/C, TV/DVD (some units), fridge (1 unit), hair dryer.

Where to Dine

Alldays & Onions ★ AMERICAN This casual downtown eatery is named for a real company, an obscure early-20th-century British car manufacturer (proprietors: William Alldays and John Onions). Why? I'm not sure. But I do know locals flock here to eat tasty sandwiches, salads, and soups; it's one of the town's go-to family restaurants. Expect anything from pot roast and turkey with the fixin's, to seafood pasta, grilled steaks, burgers, and tortellini. More ambitious items might include a Southwestern-spiced steak or stir-fried soba noodles, but stick with traditional favorites. Breakfast, served on Saturday and Sunday only, is also good.

519 Main St. ✆ **802/447-0043.** www.alldaysandonions.com. Breakfast items $2–$8, sandwiches $3–$7, main courses $15–$19 at dinner. AE, DISC, MC, V. Mon–Wed 11am–3pm; Thurs–Fri 11am–3pm and 5–9pm; Sat 7:30am–3pm and 5–9pm; Sun 9am–1pm.

Blue Benn Diner Value DINER Diner fans make long pilgrimages to Vermont to eat at this 1945 Silk City classic—so classic it still has jukeboxes, and I remember the daily specials being magic-markered onto paper plates and hung up helter-skelter by the counter for years. (They finally got a printer to at least *print* them before hanging.) Those specials still often include vegetables, rice, soup or salad, rolls, and rice pudding with your entree. Fancy and vegetarian fare is sometimes available—think grilled portobello mushrooms on sourdough. But order any of the New England diner staples such as turkey with gravy, fried fish, yummy slabs of cornbread French toast, big delicious omelets, fruity pancakes, homemade doughnuts, or the signature dessert: butterscotch Indian pudding, served warm with a scoop of vanilla ice cream.

314 North St. (Rte. 7). ✆ **802/442-5140.** Breakfast $2–$6, sandwiches and entrees $2–$6, dinner specials $8–$10. No credit cards. Mon–Tues 6am–5pm; Wed–Fri 6am–8pm; Sat 6am–4pm; Sun 7am–4pm.

Pangaea ★★ INTERNATIONAL This upscale little culinary campus is a bit hard to find (tucked away in workaday North Bennington), but it's worth trying to locate. Chef/owner Bill Scully delivers good meals (using local and organic ingredients whenever possible) in five distinct dining spaces, including a tavern, a deli (across the street), and a fine-dining room. Start with something intriguing, such as Vermont boar-and-brie Wellington, spring rolls, or some fried oysters. Entrees could include a pan-roasted breast of Long Island duck, maple-glazed pork loin, steak frites, or seared diver scallops on a potato croquette; sauces are accented with hints of Asia and France. There's a cozy lounge next door, serving a lighter menu of burgers, pasta, cassoulet, salads, stir-fries, and beers that wouldn't be out of place in a Manhattan bar. The small card of desserts is notable, especially for the chocolate cake.

1–3 Prospect St., North Bennington. ✆ **802/442-7171.** Lounge items $10–$21, main courses $19–$24. V, MC. Tues–Sun 5–9pm. From Bennington, go west on Rte. 9 a half-mile, turn right onto Rte. 67A near Hemmings, and continue 4½ miles to North Bennington. Restaurant is in center of village.

ARLINGTON, MANCHESTER & DORSET ★★★

The rolling Green Mountains are rarely out of view when you're traveling through this part of the state. In midsummer the lush green landscape gives Ireland a run for its money—various hues of emerald can be seen in the forests blanketing the mountains, the

Tips Sticker-Shock Alert!

With its proximity to the New York State Thruway (which is about 40 miles west, at Albany), the Manchester area attracts a disproportionate number of affluent weekenders from the Big Apple and its metro areas. Some innkeepers here estimate that half of *all* their annual business originates from the City That Bloomberg Built. As a result, the price of inns and restaurants here tend to be higher than in the rest of the state. So don't consider Manchester to be representative (price-wise) of the rest of Vermont. Because it just isn't.

meadows in the valley, and even the moss growing along the many tumbling streams. It soon becomes obvious how these mountains earned their name.

And this string of closely spaced villages is Vermont at its most Vermonty, making them an ideal destination for a romantic getaway, antiquing trip, or even a serious outlet shopping trip. All three towns are worth visiting, and each has its own unique charm and vibe; you can even visit all three in a single day, if you sleep locally and get up early.

Arlington ★★ has a town center that borders on the microscopic. With its auto-body shop, hub-of-town gas station/convenience store, ice-cream shop, and redemption center (all remnants of a time when the main highway passed right through town), this is a real, functioning Vermont village. It also has a great riverside campground, an unusual number of good farmhouses-converted-into-inns on the surrounding roads, and Norman Rockwell. So there. It's about 8 miles south of the Manchesters, on Route 7A.

Manchester ★★★ (also sometimes called Manchester Village) and **Manchester Center** share a blurred town line and proximity, but maintain very different characters. The more southerly Manchester has an old-world, old-moneyed elegance and a prim, campuslike main street centered on the resplendently columned Equinox Resort. There's also a neat row of shops, a wonderful golf course, a town library, a former Lincoln home, and a fly-fishing museum. Just a mile and a half north along Main Street, Manchester Center is the major mercantile center for these parts; it almost feels like a small city, with its dozens of outlet stores (offering discounts on big-name clothing, accessories, and housewares), doughnut shop, big-box grocery store, golden-arched fast food, and surprising traffic jams at the main intersection.

Dorset ★★, an exquisitely preserved little village of white clapboard architecture and marble sidewalks, is one last worthy visit when in the area. It's a bit farther north; to get there, follow Route 30 north out of Manchester Center for about 7 miles. You'll roll right into the center of town.

Essentials

GETTING THERE Arlington, Manchester, and Manchester Center all lie north of Bennington on Historic Route 7A, which runs parallel to and west of Route 7; you can take either route. Dorset is north of Manchester Center on Route 30, which diverges from Route 7A in Manchester Center.

VISITOR INFORMATION The **Manchester and the Mountains Regional Chamber of Commerce** (✆ **800/362-4144** or 802/362-2100; www.manchestervermont.net) maintains a year-round information center at 5046 Main St. (Rte. 7A N.) beside the small village green in **Manchester Center.** It's open Monday through Saturday from

10am to 5pm; from Memorial Day weekend through October, it's also open on Sundays from noon to 5pm and until 7pm on Friday and Saturday nights. If you're staying in **Arlington,** that hamlet maintains its own small self-serve visitor information center at the Stewart's gas station on Route 7A. Just take what you need.

For information on outdoor recreation, the **Green Mountain National Forest** maintains a district ranger office (✆ **802/362-2307**) in Manchester on Route 11/30, east of Route 7. It's open Monday through Friday from 8am to 4:30pm.

Exploring the Area

Arlington has long been associated with the painter and illustrator Norman Rockwell, who lived here from 1939 until 1953. Arlington residents were regularly featured in Rockwell's covers for the *Saturday Evening Post.* "Moving to Arlington had given my work a terrific boost. I'd met one or two hundred people I wanted to paint . . . the sincere, honest, homespun types that I love to paint," Rockwell later wrote of his experiences here.

Visitors can catch a glimpse of this long relationship at the small, 19th-century Carpenter Gothic–style church in the middle of town (beside the gas station) housing the **Norman Rockwell Exhibition** ★ (✆ **802/375-6423**). This small museum features many of the painter's famous magazine covers, along with photographs of the original models (and the obligatory gift shop selling Rockwell prints); you might even find one of the former models working here as a volunteer or attending a reunion. From May through October, it's open daily from 9am to 5pm; the rest of the year, from 10am to 4pm. Admission is $4 for adults; children enter for free. (This is *not* to be confused with the more "seriously" operated Norman Rockwell Museum in Stockbridge, MA.)

North of Arlington, **Manchester** has long been one of Vermont's most moneyed resorts, attracting prominent summer residents such as Mary Todd Lincoln and Julia Boggs Dent (wife of Gen. Ulysses S. Grant) back in the day. The town is still well worth visiting just to wander its quiet streets, which are bordered by distinguished homes dating from the early Federal period; huge, lovely sugar maples line the streets and go bright orange in October. Even the sidewalks are made of irregular marble slabs. (The village is said to possess 17 miles of such sidewalks, castoffs from some of the state's marble quarries.) When you tire of exploring, simply stroll into the Equinox Resort on Main Street for a drink or a bite (or, best of all, an overnight sleep).

On Route 30, 7 miles north of the bustle in Manchester Center, is the village of **Dorset.** Fans of American architecture owe it to themselves to visit. While not as grand as Manchester Center, this town of white clapboard and black-and-green shutters has a quiet, appealing grace. The elliptical green is fronted by early homes that are subtly elegant; in the right light, the village feels more like a Norman Rockwell painting than many Norman Rockwell paintings.

Museums & Historic Homes

American Museum of Fly Fishing ★★ **Finds** If you loved *A River Runs Through It,* you're probably crazy about fly-fishing, and you'll probably go crazy for this museum: It's home to the world's largest collection of angling art and items under one roof. The complex, which includes a gallery space, library, reading room, store, and historical resources, was specially built for the purpose. You can browse through an impressive collection of antique rods (including some owned by Daniel Webster, Ernest Hemingway, and Winslow Homer), reels, and 200-year-old flies, plus photos, instructional videos, sketchbooks, and historical items. (A Greek historian wrote of a fly-fishing-like practice in A.D. 200; who knew?) This is a surprisingly fun place to while away an hour; about

Vermont's Honest Abe Connection

Robert Todd Lincoln was the only son of assassinated U.S. President Abraham Lincoln and his wife, Mary Todd Lincoln, to survive to maturity; the other three boys in his family all died before the age of 18.

Robert earned big bucks working as a corporate attorney and later served as Secretary of War and an ambassador to Britain. He also stepped in as president of the Pullman Company—makers of those deluxe train cars—from 1897 until 1911 following the death of founder George Pullman. Though he was sleeping at the White House when his father was shot and killed, Lincoln was coincidentally present at two other presidential assassinations (James Garfield's and William McKinley's). And he infamously committed his own mother to an insane asylum after his father's assassination. Quite a life. He died right here at Hildene on July 26, 1926, a week shy of his 83rd birthday.

the only thing missing is, well, fish. The museum is neatly positioned right between the Equinox and the Orvis fly-fishing store.

4104 Main St. (Rte. 7A), Manchester. ✆ **802/362-3300.** www.amff.com. Admission $5 adults, $3 children 5–14. Tues–Sun 10am–4pm. Closed major holidays.

Hildene ★★ As you first drive up the pretty gravel road to this estate, you might not realize that you're face to face with U.S. history *and* natural history. Robert Todd Lincoln, son of the former U.S. president (see "Vermont's Honest Abe Connection," below), summered in this stately 24-room Georgian Revival mansion between 1905 and 1926 and enjoyed showing off its remarkable features—including a sweeping staircase and a 1908 Aeolian organ with a thousand pipes (you can hear it played during the house tour). This place was built with an eye toward quality, rather than showiness or stuffiness. Lincoln also had formal gardens (designed after the patterns in a stained-glass window) planted on a gentle hill outside, with outstanding views of the flanking mountains—one of southern Vermont's most popular wedding spots every summer and fall. The home and lovely, expansive grounds can be viewed only on group tours that start at an informative visitor center; budget 2 to 3 hours for the tour plus extra time exploring the pretty grounds and diversions. (In summer there are fun wagon rides to the Hildene farm for $1, and cross-country skiing and snowshoeing are allowed with admission to the grounds in winter.)

Historic Rte. 7A (just south of Equinox Resort), Manchester. ✆ **802/362-1788.** www.hildene.org. Admission to grounds only $5 adults, $3 children 6–14; house tours $13 adults, $5 children, free for children 5 and under. Daily 9:30am–4:30pm.

Southern Vermont Art Center ★★ This fine-art center is well worth the short detour from town to find it. Located in a striking Georgian Revival home surrounded by more than 400 hillside acres overlooking land that once belonged to fly-fishing magnate Charles Orvis, the center consists of a series of galleries displaying works from its well-regarded collection, as well as frequently changing exhibits of contemporary Vermont artists. An inventive and appealing modern building across the driveway displays even more of the permanent collection. Check the center's schedule before you arrive; you may be able to sign up for an art class or workshop while you're in town. Also, leave time to enjoy a light lunch at the **Garden Cafe** and wander the lovely grounds, exploring both the sculpture garden and the woods beyond.

West Rd., Manchester. ✆ **802/362-1405.** www.svac.org. Admission $8 adults, $3 students, free for children 12 and under. Tues–Sat 10am–5pm; Sun noon–5pm. From Equinox Resort, bear left onto West Rd. at Reluctant Panther inn and continue approx. 1 mile.

Area Skiing

Bromley Mountain Ski Resort ★ (Kids) Bromley is a great place to learn to ski if you don't already know how. Gentle and forgiving, the mountain features long, looping, intermediate runs that are tremendously popular with families and beginners; *SKI* magazine once named it the second-best ski destination in the entire country for families. The slopes are mostly south-facing, which means they receive the warmth of the sun and protection from the harshest winter winds. There's one ski school here for kids ("Mighty Moose"), another for adults; the base-lodge scene here is mellower than at many other resorts; and the experience is nearly guaranteed to be relaxing. Even snowboarders and telemark skiers are made to feel very welcome. This is *not* a fancy-pants resort, however, and there are no quintuple-diamond, by-the-seat-of-your-pants runs here; if you crave that, bypass Bromley.

3984 Rte. 11, Peru (P.O. Box 1130, Manchester Center, VT 05255). ✆ **866/856-2201** or 802/824-5522. www.bromley.com. Adult lift tickets $39–$68 day, $55–$58 half-day; discounts for youths and seniors.

Stratton Mountain Ski Resort ★★ Founded in the 1960s, Stratton labored in its early days under the belief that Vermont ski areas needed to be Tyrolean to be successful—hence the Swiss-chalet feel of the architecture. For awhile this mountain felt like Vail's poor country cousin. In recent years, though, Stratton has worked to shed its image as a haven of alpine quaintness. In a bid to attract a younger, edgier set, new owners spent more than $25 million in improvements, mostly in snowmaking. Now this mountain is consistently ranked among the nation's best-groomed by skiers, and also picks up big kudos for its lifts, dining choices, and customer service. The slopes here are especially popular with snowboarders; expert skiers should check out Upper Middlebrook, a twisting run off the summit.

5 Village Lodge Rd., Stratton Mountain, VT 05155. ✆ **800/787-2886** or 802/297-4000. www.stratton.com. Adult lift tickets $72–$84, $59–$71 half-day; discounts for seniors, children, and any lift tickets bought online.

Other Outdoor Activities

HIKING & BIKING Scenic hiking trails ranging in difficulty from "very challenging" to "easy-as-an-after-dinner-stroll" can be found in the hills a short drive from town. At the Green Mountain District Ranger Station in Manchester (see "Visitor Information," above), ask for the free brochure listing hiking trails easily reached from the town.

A scenic drive 30 to 40 minutes northwest of Manchester Center takes you to the **Delaware and Hudson Rail-Trail,** approximately 20 miles of which have been built in two sections in Vermont. The southern section of the trail runs about 10 miles from **West Pawlet** to the state line at **West Rupert,** over trestles and past vestiges of former industry, such as the old Vermont Milk and Cream Co. Like most rail-trails, this one is perfect for exploring by mountain bike. You'll bike sometimes on the original ballast, other times through grassy growth. To reach the trail head, drive north on Route 30 from Manchester Center to Route 315, then continue north on Route 153. In **West Pawlet,** park across from the old-timey general store (a good place to pick up refreshments), then set off on the trail southward from the old D&H freight depot across the street. The trail also passes through **Lake St. Catherine State Park** in **Poultney.**

The hills around Manchester are full of other great touring rides, too; your headquarters should be **Battenkill Sports Bicycle Shop** (✆ **800/340-2734** or 802/362-2734), at 1240 Depot St. in downtown Manchester Center. It's a wonderful little place, with free local bike maps, great bikes for sale, and a range of rentals from hybrids to touring cycles to mountain bikes ($30 per day; locks and helmets are included).

CANOEING For a duck's-eye view of the rolling hills, stop by **BattenKill Canoe Ltd.** (✆ **800/421-5268** or 802/362-2800; www.battenkill.com) at 6328 Rte. 7A (about halfway btw. Arlington and the Equinox Resort). This friendly outfit offers daily canoe rentals for exploring the Battenkill River and surrounding areas. Trips range from 2 hours to all day, and the firm specializes in multiple-night, inn-to-inn canoe packages. The shop is open daily in season (which runs from about May–Oct) from 9am to 5:30pm, and Wednesday through Friday only during the rest of the year—but check ahead if you're coming during those months.

FLY-FISHING Why not learn from the best? Aspiring anglers can sign up for fly-fishing classes taught by skilled instructors affiliated with **Orvis** (✆ **800/235-9763**), the famous fly-fishing supplier and manufacturer based in Manchester. The shop's 1- and 2-day classes ($235 per person per day, with occasional 2-for-1 deals) include instruction in knot-tying and casting, plus some catch-and-release fishing on a company pond and the Battenkill River. Classes are held from late April until mid-October. Room rate discounts are sometimes available at the Equinox Resort (see "Where to Stay," below) for visiting Orvis students.

Where to Stay

The choices below mostly fall into the "luxury country inn" category, but there are plenty of other options in this valley, too.

For **B&Bs,** beyond the inns I have listed below, think **Arlington.** The small, 3-room **Whitney House Inn** (✆ **802/375-9701;** www.whitneyhouseinn.com) in the village center and the big, rustic **Hill Farm Inn** (✆ **800/882-2545;** www.hillfarminn.com) on a sprawling working farm 3 or 4 miles north, at 458 Hill Farm Rd. (turn off Rte. 7A at BattenKill Canoe), are each very well liked by my readers. Both include a full, tasty breakfast with your rate ($130–$150 per night at Whitney House, $110–$250 per night at Hill Farm), and both are exceptionally friendly.

For those who want to save money, drive south from Manchester **along Route 7A** (toward Arlington). As you leave town and roll through the flat farmlands, you'll come upon a number of budget choices, including the barn-red **North Shire Lodge** (✆ **888/339-2336** or 802/362-2336; www.northshirelodge.com), which seems to keep guests happy. You'll also pass by several 1950s-era, family-owned **motor-court-style motels and cottages** scattered along the highway. I can't vouch for all these places, but they are probably acceptable—so long as you're not expecting luxury, perfection, or valet parking. Think of it as car-camping with a roof over your head, and you'll be all right.

Note that local traffic whizzes pretty fast along Route 7A; don't let your young kids wander outside at these properties, or across the road, unsupervised.

Barnstead Inn ★ Value If you're feeling shell-shocked by local room rates, consider this place within walking distance of Manchester's commercial center. Most of the guest rooms are housed in an 1830s hay barn; many are decorated in a rustic country style, some exposing the barn's burnished old beams. Expect vinyl bathroom floors, industrial carpeting (but at least it's *nice* carpeting), and a mix of motel-modern and antique furnishings in most rooms. The most interesting units include the two above the office (with two double beds, and showing off those beams) and any of the pricier suites—including the renovated Green River Suite, with a lovely fireplace of big, hand-laid stones, Persian-style rugs, a kitchenette, and a two-person Jacuzzi. A few rooms here are even priced at less than $100, which is remarkable. (On the other hand, a few of those suites nearly touch $300.) All in all, a good value and one of the closest lodgings to the outlet mall.

349 Bonnet St. (P.O. Box 988), Manchester Center, VT 05255. ✆ **800/331-1619** or 802/362-1619. www.barnsteadinn.com. 15 units. $89–$165 double, $110–$299 suite; foliage-season rates higher. MC, V. Children 13 and over welcome. **Amenities:** Outdoor pool. *In room:* A/C, TV, hair dryer, Wi-Fi (free).

Barrows House ★ Within easy strolling distance of Dorset is this compound of eight Early American buildings, set on 12 landscaped acres studded with birches, firs, and maples. Built in 1784, the main house has been an inn since 1900, and its white exterior is most beautiful when the lawn is also blanketed with white snow. The inn's primary distinctions are its historical lineage and convenience to the village; the rooms are more comfortable than elegant, with sturdy dressers, bedside tables, and the like. (Some readers have mentioned that certain buildings are not aging well.) Some units have gas or wood fireplaces, while several cottages (one of which doubles as the pool house) offer additional space and privacy for families. This place will definitely please history and Rockwell buffs; those looking for luxury amenities, though, might prefer a place in Manchester Village. The inn's superb **restaurant** (p. 99) serves a clubby menu of upscale continental cuisine—roast duck, salmon, seared tuna, grilled steaks, lobster rolls—in a nicely glassed-in dining room.

Rte. 30, Dorset, VT 05251. ✆ **800/639-1620** or 802/867-4455. Fax 802/867-0132. www.barrowshouse.com. 28 units. $125–$195 double; $150–$255 suite and cottage. Rates include breakfast. MAP plans also available. 2-night minimum stay Sat–Sun and some holidays. AE, DISC, MC, V. Pets allowed in 2 cottages. **Amenities:** Restaurant/bar; bikes; heated outdoor pool; sauna; 2 tennis courts. *In room:* A/C, TV (some units), fridge (2 units), no phone (1 unit).

Dorset Inn ★★ Set in the center of genteel Dorset, this three-story former stagecoach stop was built in 1796 and claims to be the oldest continuously operating inn in Vermont. With more than two dozen rooms, it's large as Vermont inns go, yet very professionally run by its newest owners, the Bryants—who also own the **Mountain Top Inn & Resort** in Mendon (p. 143). Prices are surprisingly reasonable given the competition in Manchester, and the Bryants have upgraded everything from room decor to the restaurant. Guest rooms, some located in a well-crafted addition next door that dates from the 1940s, are named for famous local people and places (Frost, Saddleback, Marsh, Owls Head). They're furnished in upscale country style, in a mix of reproductions and antiques, including some canopy and sleigh beds. All units are air-conditioned, though a few still lack televisions and most don't have telephones; about one-quarter have Jacuzzi tubs, sitting rooms, and fireplaces. The excellent **restaurant** and **tavern** (see "Where to Dine," below) feature chef Thom Simonetti's use of local and regional ingredients. A small, newish day spa provides treatments and pampering.

8 Church St. (at Rte. 30), Dorset, VT 05251. ✆ **877/367-7389** or 802/867-5500. Fax 802/867-5542. www.dorsetinn.com. 25 units. $185–$425 double. Rates include full breakfast. MAP plans available. Packages available. AE, MC, V. Pets allowed by prior permission. Children 6 and over welcome. **Amenities:** Restaurant; bar; spa. *In room:* A/C, TV (most units), no phone (most units), Wi-Fi (in all but 2 units; free).

Finds Handling Birds of a Feather

The Equinox Resort offers a variety of activities, ranging from archery to off-road driving, but one of the most interesting experiences you can have here is handling and flying a bird of prey at the **British School of Falconry.** Trained falconers give participants an up-close-and-personal look at these beautiful raptors, mostly Harris hawks, with programs ranging from an introductory lesson ($110 for 45 min.) to a 2½-hour lesson incorporating hawk handling and archery training ($345; 1 free guest allowed). Participants must be at least 12 years old. (✆ **802/362-4780;** www.equinoxresort.com/thingstodo/falconry/)

The Equinox Resort & Spa ★★★ Now owned by the HEI hotel group, the venerable Equinox is changing with the times, yet it remains a longtime New England favorite. Its white clapboard and stately columns define Manchester and southern Vermont. The place's roots date to 1769, but don't be misled: This is a modern resort complete with a full-service spa, lovely indoor pool, scenic golf course, free business center, and extensive sports facilities. Rooms are moderately sized, but have just been retouched by a multimillion-dollar renovation project; think earth tones, new linens, and custom-made beds. The resort also owns and has upgraded the nearby **1811 House** (which had been one of the best B&Bs in the state)—a place of cozy rooms, authentically uneven pine floors, and antique furniture—as well as the adjacent **Charles Orvis Inn.** Suites in the Orvis Inn are big and modern, and use of a private billiards room is included. The resort offers plenty of activities on its 1,300-plus acres of grounds, including skeet shooting, falconry (see "Handling Birds of a Feather," above), and guided hikes up beautiful (but steep) Mount Equinox. Of the resort's three restaurants, the **Chop House** (see "Where to Dine," below) is best, but only operates half of each week. The **Marsh Tavern** is nearly as good and opens daily, serving both pubby and formal lunches and dinners, while the **Falcon Bar** is not to be missed—an outdoor brazier has recently been added, making it a convivial place to sip drinks beneath the stars.

3567 Rte. 7A (P.O. Box 46), Manchester Village, VT 05254. ✆ **800/362-4747** or 802/362-4700. Fax 802/362-4861. www.equinoxresort.com. 183 units. Main inn peak season $299–$449 double, $449–$849 suite; off season $169–$399 double, $399–$649 suite; Charles Orvis Inn $499–$899 suite. AE, DISC, MC, V. **Amenities:** 3 restaurants; bar; babysitting; bikes; concierge; golf course; exercise room; indoor and outdoor pools; room service; sauna; spa; 3 tennis courts. *In room:* A/C, TV, hair dryer, Wi-Fi (free).

The Inn at Manchester ★★ Finds It looks like just another Vermont residence outside, but this is a special B&B. Built in the late 19th century, the structure was converted to an inn in 1978. It's just a half-mile from the budget shopping that draws so many to Manchester, yet also nearly within sight of the village, resort, and golf course. I've yet to ever meet anyone with a bad word to say about this place, from the location to the rooms to the amazing hospitality. Rooms are in the main inn and an adjacent carriage house dating from the mid-1800s, both decorated with art and sculpture from around the world. The public spaces are whitewashed and lovely, with fireplaces, staircases, and wingback chairs tucked throughout its various corners and angles. Most of the 18 rooms and suites have televisions (no phones, though), and some also have poster beds and/or good direct views of Mount Equinox. All units feel clean and fresh, with distinctive looks—the Sage Suite is popular for its walk-out deck, sitting room, whirlpool tub, and that Equinox view. Owners Frank and Julie Hanes are as helpful as can be; their dog, Chai, is described as a "furball of joy." Four acres of gardens and grounds, a brook, and a lazy front porch complete the peaceful experience.

3967 Main St. (Rte. 7A), Manchester Village, VT 05254. ✆ **800/273-1793** or 802/362-1793. Fax 802/362-3218. www.innatmanchester.com. 18 units. $155–$235 double; $205–$295 suite. Rates include full breakfast. AE, DISC, MC, V. **Amenities:** Outdoor pool. *In room:* A/C, TV (most units), hair dryer, no phone, Wi-Fi (free).

Palmer House Resort Motel ★ What is a "resort motel"? Well, it's *not* a resort. But it *is* several notches above the run-of-the-mill motels that dot southern Vermont, and this place has long been surprisingly popular given the fancier and cheaper options in the valley. Owned and operated by the same family for about a half-century, its rooms are furnished with antiques and other unexpected niceties; ask for one of the somewhat larger rooms in the newer rear building if you value space. In 2000, 10 spacious suites were added, each with a king bed, sitting room, gas fireplace, two-person Jacuzzi, and private deck overlooking a trout-stocked pond and the mountains beyond—these are much more expensive than regular rooms, and somewhat bland, but they will do as a romantic retreat when the luxury inns in town are booked solid. The buildings are set on 22 nicely tended acres, and the motel even has its own small par-3 golf course. (There's no charge—just walk into the office and get some clubs.)

5383 Main St. (Rte. 7A), Manchester Center, VT 05255. ✆ **800/917-6245.** ✆/fax 802/362-3600. www.palmerhouse.com. 50 units. $95–$185 double; $190–$300 suite. 2-night minimum stay some weekends. AE, DISC, MC, V. Children 12 and older welcome. **Amenities:** 9-hole par-3 golf course; exercise room; Jacuzzi; 2 pools (1 outdoor, 1 heated indoor lap); sauna; 2 tennis courts. *In room:* A/C, TV, fridge, hair dryer, Wi-Fi (free).

The Reluctant Panther ★★★ New owners took over this luxury inn, a quick walk from the Equinox, in the fall of 2005—and a month later, the historic main house burned to the ground. Unbelievably, it reopened within a year and is now a true luxury inn, where once had stood a quirky B&B with a '70s vibe. Gone is the all-purple paint job; all rooms now sport a fireplace (or two), whirlpool tub, thick duvets, fluffy robes, and flatscreen TVs. In the main house, the woodsy Akwanok room is furnished with Orvis nightstand lamps and a birch headboard handcrafted in the Adirondacks, while Lady Slipper sports a claw-foot Jacuzzi and king poster bed. Other rooms are decorated according to themes, too: horses in the John Morgan Suite; flowery murals in the Florist Suite; green hues in the Fallen Spruce Suite. In the outbuildings, I like the Garden Suite's living room and see-through fireplace, as well as the expansive Panther Suite's four-poster bed, grandiose bathroom, and regal, columned Jacuzzi. The Pond View Suite, in the carriage house, is bigger than many Vermont cottages. The **dining room** (see "Where to Dine," below) is outstanding; a pub menu is also served on a patio (weather permitting) and in the Panther Pub.

17–39 West Rd., Manchester Village, VT 05254. ✆ **800/822-2331** or 802/362-2568. Fax 802/362-2586. www.reluctantpanther.com. 20 units. $179–$759 suite. Rates include full breakfast. AE, DC, DISC, MC, V. Pets allowed on limited basis ($50 per night). **Amenities:** Restaurant; pub; exercise room. *In room:* A/C, TV/DVD, CD player, hair dryer, Wi-Fi (free).

West Mountain Inn ★★ Sitting atop a grassy bluff at the end of a dirt road a half-mile from Arlington center, this rambling, white-clapboard building with the stone walkway is extremely appealing when you approach it. The farmhouse dates back a century and a half, and it's a perfect spot for travelers looking to find that "real" Vermont inn. Guest rooms, named for famous Vermonters, are nicely furnished in country antiques and Victorian reproductions; they vary widely in size and shape, but even the smallest has lots of charm and character. The expansive Rockwell Kent Suite offers a four-poster canopy bed in a very wood-paneled bedroom, plus a wood-burning fireplace in a sitting room with French-style couches. A delightful little wood cottage in back has been divided up into three units (the living room is shared among guests), and three town houses have also been carved out of a former millhouse (wow, this *is* Vermont) on the grounds. These feature TVs, river views and, in one case, a kitchen. There's a hundred-year-old post-and-beam barn on the grounds, often rented for weddings and reunions, and the 150 acres of meadows are good for exploring. In addition to the included breakfast (optionally, you can skip it for a discount in the town houses), the dining room also serves hearty regional dinners nightly in a wood-paneled dining room. Nice place.

River Rd. (at Rte. 313), Arlington, VT 05250. ✆ **802/375-6516.** Fax 802/375-6553. www.westmountaininn.com. 20 units. $175–$310 double; town houses $185–$299. Rates include full breakfast except for town houses. MAP plans available. 2-night minimum stay Sat–Sun. AE, DISC, MC, V. **Amenities:** Restaurant. *In room:* A/C, TV (some units), kitchenette (some units), no phone, Wi-Fi (in inn units; free).

Where to Dine

In addition to the selections below, most of the **inns** listed above offer good to excellent dinners on-site in their dining rooms, often in romantic settings. But there's also a cluster of quite good cafes, bistros, and restaurants on the **hill leading up out of Manchester Center** (Rte. 11/30) into the heart of the Green Mountains.

The best of these eateries might be the continental **Bistro Henry** ★★ (✆ **802/362-4982;** www.bistrohenry.com), run by a husband and wife who left Manhattan's kitchens 20 years to live and cook here. The Bronsons' food is expensive (for Vermont, not Manhattan) yet up to snuff: seared scallops with lemon-ginger risotto, steaks, chops, beef tournedos, and a daily fish dish, all with Provencal and Italian accents. Desserts come from the attached bakery, run by Dina Bronson.

For cheap grub, locals usually head for **downtown Manchester Center** and its agglomeration of Chinese food, gas-station fare, pizza, golden arches, and family restaurants serving heavy fare.

For a beer, I prefer either the Equinox's bar in Manchester Village (see "Where to Stay," above) or **Mulligan's** (✆ **802/362-3663**), a locals' sort of place kitty-corner across Route 7A from the Equinox resort and the town library. The food is nothing special, but the atmosphere is *Cheers*-like. It's open daily from around noon to 10pm.

And I *always* pick up a half-dozen (or more) sinkers for the trip home at **Mrs. Murphy's Donuts** (✆ **802/362-1874**), a locals-only spot right beside the outlet strip in Manchester Center. You won't find cake-style doughnuts this good anywhere else in New England; anything maple, apple, or filled with cream or custard is good, too.

Barrows House Restaurant ★★ CONTINENTAL Chef Lauren Wilcox delivers inn cuisine that's better than it has to be at this Dorset compound's house eatery (see "Where to Stay," above), infusing everything with Continental sensibilities. Example: You can begin with Maine crab cakes or a creamy seafood chowder full of New England veggies—but you can also start with a sweet-pea vichyssoise, Kahlúa-crusted brie, or an unusual leek crème brûlée. Daring indeed. The menu includes both small plates and entrees. The small plates (which are rather pricey) range from mini racks of lamb with a Vermont goat cheese-pistachio crust to half-servings of beef tenderloin, veal piccata, shellfish strudel, and the like. Entrees run to roasted duck, full racks of lamb, prime rib, and salmon. And watch for great rotating seasonal specials like mushroom-cheese bisque, fruit gazpacho, diver scallops, summer lobster rolls, coconut-curried shrimp, seared tuna, salmon *en croute,* or a grilled rib-eye with a brandy and peppercorn demi-glace and buttermilk-battered onion rings.

Rte. 30, Dorset (in Barrows House). ✆ **800/639-1620** or 802/867-4455. www.barrowshouse.com. Small plates $14–$20, main courses $22–$35. AE, MC, V. Daily 8–9:30am (to 10am Sun) and 5:30–9pm.

Chantecleer ★★★ CONTINENTAL If you enjoy top-rate Continental fare, but are put off by the stuffiness of Euro-wannabe restaurants, this is the place for you. Rustic elegance is the best description for Chantecleer, which cooks some of the best food in southern Vermont—inside a century-old dairy barn! Just outside Dorset, the restaurant's tidy exterior doesn't hint at how pleasantly romantic the interior is, even if it feels almost Pennsylvania Dutch. (Ignore the mounted cow's head above the bar; Baumann bought it at a local antiques shop.) The owner, Swiss chef Michel Baumann, changes his menu frequently. Appetizers lean toward seafood, especially shellfish (mussels, oysters, escargot). For the main course, he might feature a pistachio-encrusted rack of Colorado lamb one night, roasted duckling with a berry sauce or medallions of duck and venison another; especially good is the Dover sole, served with a compound butter. Whatever you eat, you must finish with Baumann's delicious "Matterhorn" sundae—Vermont ice cream shingled with toasted hazelnut nougatine and topped with Swiss and French hot fudges.

Rte. 7A (3½ miles north of Manchester Center), East Dorset. ✆ **802/362-1616.** www.chantecleerrestaurant.com. Reservations recommended. Main courses $28–$45. AE, MC, V. Wed–Sun 6–9pm. Closed 1st 3 weeks of Nov and Apr to mid-May.

The Chop House ★★★ STEAK Truly great steakhouses are thin on the ground in Vermont (family-style restaurants, on the other hand, are everywhere). Therefore, foodies noted with interest the 2008 opening of this mostly steak restaurant in the Equinox Resort (see "Where to Stay," above) in Manchester Village, a resort that strangely had lacked a fine dining option until now. Top chef Jeffrey Russell broils the expected porterhouses, rib-eyes, and filet mignons—get the excellent house sauce on the side—bakes potatoes, creams spinach. All good. And, smartly, he draws from the deep well of excellent cheeses and meats available from Vermont's own artisanal producers. But Russell also sets up strong appetizers that would be right at home on a Manhattan menu: chilled lobster cocktails, iceberg wedge/blue cheese salads, bisque, and one of the best mozza-tomato salads anywhere outside of Italy or New Yawk.

3567 Rte. 7A, Manchester Village (in the Equinox Resort). ✆ **800/362-4747** or 802/362-4700. Reservations recommended. www.equinoxresort.com. Main courses $18–$65. AE, MC, V. Thurs–Sun 5–10pm.

Dorset Inn Restaurant ★★ NEW AMERICAN The Dorset Inn's (see "Where to Stay," above) restaurant and tavern are newly conceived, with a new chef and a "slow food"-themed kitchen that plays the Vermont down-home card wisely and well. This is New England home cooking, trumped up and heavily incorporating the great seasonal foods available within the state's borders. Start with smoked local pheasant with apple pâté, PEI mussels, Maine crab cakes, or a plate of locally crafted cheese. Or go off the map by ordering fries with bourbon ketchup. Entrees are solidly New England: roasted turkey croquettes with peas, mashed potatoes, gravy, and cranberry sauce; burgers of local beef; a three-meat meat loaf; slow-cooked lamb stew; chicken pappardelle; and a roasted-corn polenta with local ricotta, veggies, and red-pepper pesto. Desserts are also stellar and (mostly) regional, from maple-pumpkin cheesecake with candied walnuts to apple crumble, crème brûlée, and New England bread pudding with maple. You can even order a bowl of Ben & Jerry's. Brunch, unusually, is served from Friday through Sunday and with a Cajun accent.

8 Church St. (Rte. 30), Dorset (in the Dorset Inn). ✆ **877/367-7389** or 802/867-5500. www.dorsetinn.com. Reservations recommended. Brunch items $12–$16, main courses $14–$28. AE, MC, V. Mon–Thurs 8–9:30am and 5–9pm; Fri–Sun 8am–2pm and 5–9pm.

Little Rooster Cafe ★ **Value** DINER You've got to love a place where the seats are painted like birds' nests. They really take the farm motif to the extreme at this spot near the outlets and the traffic circle, but they add gourmet twists as well. Breakfast choices might include Cajun omelets, corned-beef hash (with béchamel sauce!), or flapjacks with Vermont maple syrup (natch). Lunchtime features creative sandwiches—a good roast beef sandwich with sauerkraut and a horseradish dill sauce, for instance. This is the best non-inn spot in town for eggs, pancakes, or a filling lunch, and quite affordable.

Rte. 7A S., Manchester Center. ✆ **802/362-3496.** Breakfast and lunch items $4.50–$8.50. No credit cards. Daily 7am–2:30pm. Closed Wed in off season.

Mistral's at Toll Gate ★★ FRENCH This place is a little hard to find, a left turn off Route 11/30 as you ascend east into the mountains above Manchester Center. But it's worth it. The best tables are along the windows, which overlook a lovely creek spotlighted at night. Inside the tollhouse of a long-since-bypassed byway, the restaurant is a romantic mix of modern and old. The French menu changes seasonally, with dishes that might range from fish to cannelloni stuffed with lobster to a grilled piece of filet mignon served with a Roquefort-stuffed ravioli. This kitchen is run with skill by the chef and his wife, who have been doing an admirable job since before foodies discovered Vermont; plenty of *Wine Spectator* awards testify to that.

Toll Gate Rd. (east of Manchester off Rte. 11/30), Manchester Center. ✆ **802/362-1779.** Reservations recommended. Main courses $22–$32. AE, MC, V. July–Oct Thurs–Tues 6–9pm; Nov–June Thurs–Mon 6–9pm.

The Reluctant Panther ★★★ NEW AMERICAN This award-winning dining room—part of the renovation of the inn by the same name (see "Where to Stay," above)—has become one of the best fine-dining options in Manchester. The handsome dining space looks out onto Mount Equinox and a small pond; waitstaff are professional; and the cuisine never disappoints. The kitchen reaches for and attains a high level with

Finds Sweet-Toothing It in Manchester

When you're in the mood for sweets (or if you've gotten on someone's bad side and want to make up quick), head for **Mother Myrick's Confectionery** (✆ **888/669-7425;** www.mothermyricks.com). This former ice-cream parlor is a bit hard to find, tucked into a minimall on Route 7A (roughly across from the Orvis shop). Once there you can indulge in such treats as dipped chocolates, caramels, Key-lime pies, birthday cakes, luscious butter-crunch candies (made from toffee and Cabot Creamery butter, then rolled in ground almonds and cashews), and the signature "Lemon Lulu" pound cake. They'll even box up and freeze a cake for traveling if you let them know a little in advance.

cuisine that's both New American and Continental, with flair (and plenty of wine sauces). Starters could include such things as tuna tartare with an avocado cream, hearty soups, a risotto of truffles and green peas, or a blue-cheese tart. For the main course, you might choose from a mint- and vanilla-rubbed loin of lamb, pan-seared pheasant, butter-poached Maine lobster over freshly made fettuccine, braised pork cheeks, or a sea of pan-seared diver scallops swimming around an island of cauliflower "cloud" topped with seared spinach and a truffle. Desserts are stunning and beautifully presented; the wine list is long and well chosen, though predominantly of California vintages.

17–39 West Rd., Manchester Village. ✆ **800/822-2331** or 802/362-2568. www.reluctantpanther.com. Reservations required. Main courses $22–$32. AE, DC, DISC, MC, V. Tues–Sat 5:30–9:30pm.

Shopping

Manchester Center has one of the best concentrations of outlet shops in New England, both in terms of the number of shops in a compact area (it's very walkable and parkable, so you won't get tired) and the quality of the merchandise.

Among the designers and retailers with outlet shops here are: Brooks Brothers, Coach, Betsey Johnson, Cashmere Mill Shop, BCBG Max Azria, Giorgio Armani, Kate Spade, Polo Ralph Lauren, and Theory; good stuff, with something for shoppers young and old. Most of the shops are in minimall clusters in and around the busy little intersection at the heart of town. They're generally open daily from 10am until 6pm, except on Sunday, when they close an hour earlier; and during holiday seasons, when these hours are sometimes extended. Hungry from shopping and window-shopping? In season there's an outdoor stand scooping **Ben & Jerry's** ice cream, and a brand new cafe serves good sandwiches, lunches, and coffee to the shopped-out masses.

If your interests include fishing or rustic, outdoorsy fashion, though, head instead for **Orvis,** the Manchester-based local company that has crafted a worldwide reputation for manufacturing top-flight fly-fishing equipment and the associated gear. The massive, wood-framed **Orvis Company Store** ★★★ (✆ **802/362-3750**) in between Manchester and Manchester Center sells housewares, men's and women's clothing—both for daily wear and sturdy outdoor use—plus, of course, more fly-fishing equipment than you'll ever need. Two small ponds just outside the shop allow prospective customers to try the gear before buying. A sale room, with even more deeply discounted items, is directly behind the main store. It's open daily 9am to 6pm, except Sundays, when it opens from 10am to 5pm.

Remember *books?* Near the middle of Manchester Center, at the intersection of Route 7A and Route 30, there's a good place to get 'em: the **Northshire Bookstore** (✆ **800/437-3700** or 802/362-2200; www.northshire.com), open daily. It's not as big as a chain store, but so what? The shop stocks an excellent hand-picked choice of titles, plus there's a cafe and frequent author readings—check the store's website for the current schedule.

3 THE SOUTHERN GREEN MOUNTAINS

Brattleboro: 105 miles NW of Boston; 148 miles SE of Burlington

The southern Green Mountains *are* Vermont. If you've developed a notion of what New England looks like but haven't actually been there yet, this is the sort of place you're thinking of—small villages in valleys flanked by steep and leafy hillsides, cows on those

ATTRACTIONS ●
Brattleboro Museum &
 Art Center **8**
Latchis Theatre **6**
Vermont Jazz Center **9**

ACCOMMODATIONS ■
The Artist's Loft **3**
Latchis Hotel **5**

DINING ◆
Brattleboro Food Co-op **7**
Mocha Joe's **4**
Peter Havens Restaurant **2**
T.J. Buckley's **1**

SOUTHERN & CENTRAL VERMONT

THE SOUTHERN GREEN MOUNTAINS

5

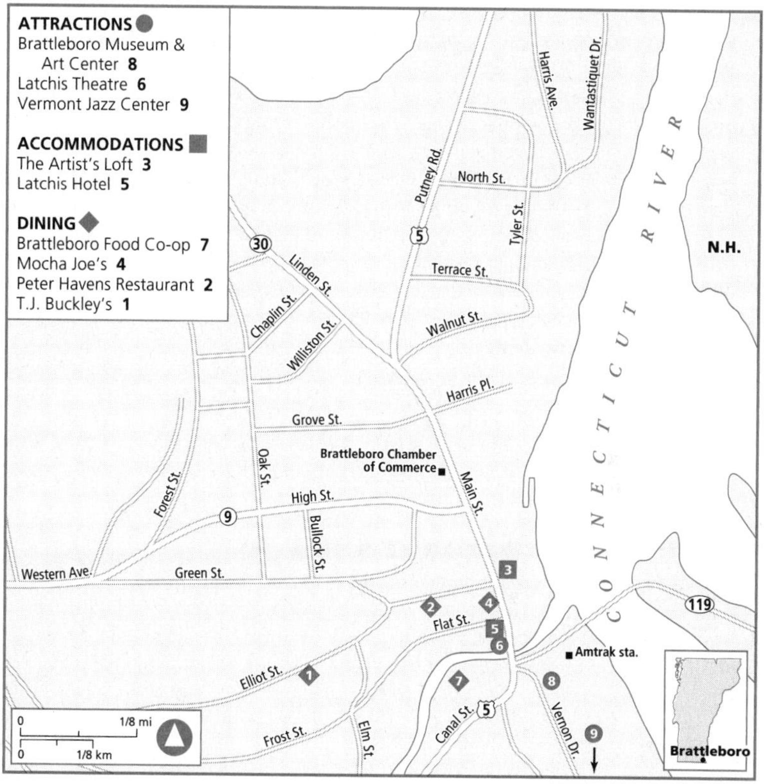

hillsides, white clapboard inns, wood smoke wafting upward at night, and diners where the men wear Red Sox caps pulled low.

The hills and valleys around the bustling town of **Brattleboro,** in Vermont's southeast corner, have some of the state's best-hidden treasures. Driving along the main valley floors—on roads along the West or Connecticut rivers, or on Route 100—is only moderately interesting. So to really soak up the region's flavor, turn off the main roads and wander up and over rolling ridges into the narrow folds of mountains hiding peaceful villages. If it looks as though the landscape hasn't changed all that much in the past 2 centuries, well, that's because it hasn't.

This region is well known for pristine and historic villages like **Wilmington** and **Marlboro, Putney** and **Jamaica, Newfane** and **West Dover, Townshend** and **Grafton.** Not to mention **Chester.** The list goes on, almost without end. You can't help stumbling across these places as you explore, and no matter how many other people have found them before you, you'll often feel like they're your own personal discoveries.

One good strategy is to stop awhile in Brattleboro, stock up on supplies or sample some local food or music, and then set off into the heart of the mountains, settle into a

Tips Information Building on the Superhighway

The best source of information for this region is the big, state-operated **Guilford Welcome Center** (✆ **802/254-4593**) on I-91 just south of Brattleboro (and just north of the Massachusetts border). Open 24 hours a day year-round, this attractive, cathedral-ceilinged building was inspired by Vermont's barns—it even has a weather vane on top! It's practically a tourist command post, filled with maps, brochures, and videos on activities in the region. Helpful staffers are on hand to dole out up-to-the-minute information, make reservations in a pinch, and otherwise guide you through the wonders of southern Vermont, but they're never pushy about it. The vending machines and spotless bathrooms within are an oasis for weary travelers with kids or infants; outside, there are often bake sales in good weather. One complaint: You can reach here only from the interstate, and only coming from the south.

remote inn, and continue exploring on foot or by bike. (In winter you can even tour the snowy hills on cross-country skis or snowshoes.) But even a tour by car, with camera poised at ready, can't go wrong.

WILMINGTON ★ & MOUNT SNOW ★

High in the hills on a winding mountain road partway between Bennington and Brattleboro, **Wilmington** retains its charm as an attractive village in spite of its location at the crossroads of two busy highways. Definitely a tourist town—for a light bulb, haircut, or quart of milk, head for Bennington or Brattleboro instead—Wilmington has a selection of antiques shops, boutiques, and pizza joints. Except on busy holiday weekends, when it's inundated by visitors driving SUVs, it still feels mostly like a gracious, untroubled mountain village.

From Wilmington, the ski resort of **Mount Snow** is easily accessible to the north via Route 100, a road that is brisk, busy, and close to impassable on sunny weekends in early October as the foliage reddens. Heading north, you'll first pass through **West Dover,** a classically attractive New England town with a prominent steeple and acres of white clapboard.

Between West Dover and the ski resort, it quickly becomes evident how developers and entrepreneurs discovered the area in the years following the founding of Mount Snow in the 1950s. Some regard this stretch of highway as a monument to lack of planning. While development certainly isn't dense (this is *not* **North Conway**), the buildings represent an unsavory mélange of architectural styles, the most prominent of which might be called Tyrolean Chicken Coop. (Many of these buildings began life as ski lodges, but have since morphed into boutiques, inns, and restaurants.)

The silver lining to all that? The unruly development here prompted Vermont to pass a progressive and restrictive environmental law known as Act 250, which has preserved many *other* parts of the state from the same fate.

When you're driving in the Mount Snow area, remember that you're not restricted to Route 100, either. The area is jam-packed with smaller roads—of pavement, gravel, and dirt—that make for excellent exploring (if your shock absorbers can take it; don't stray too far off the main roads in a sports or rental car). Be sure to get a good map or buy a

DeLorme atlas of Vermont before plunging in, and make sure you've got snow tires on if it's winter. You'll need them. They don't call it Mount Snow for nothing.

Essentials

GETTING THERE Wilmington is at the junction of routes 9 and 100. Route 9 offers the most direct access. The Mount Snow area is north of Wilmington on Route 100.

VISITOR INFORMATION The **Mount Snow Valley Chamber of Commerce** (✆ **877/887-6884;** www.visitvermont.com) maintains a visitor center on West Main Street. Open daily year-round from 10am to 5pm, the chamber offers a room-booking service, which is helpful for booking smaller inns and B&Bs; they also put together a comprehensive guide to the region. (To investigative or book on-the-mountain accommodations, however, it's best to check with **Mount Snow**'s lodging bureau at ✆ **800/451-4211** or 800/245-7669 directly.)

The Marlboro Music Festival

The renowned **Marlboro Music Festival** ★★★ is a series of summertime classical concerts, performed by accomplished masters as well as by highly talented younger musicians, on weekends from mid-July through mid-August in the agreeable village of **Marlboro,** east of Wilmington on Route 9. The musical retreat was founded in 1951 and has hosted countless noted musicians (including Pablo Casals, who participated btw. 1960 and 1973). Concerts take place in the 700-seat auditorium at Marlboro College, and advance ticket purchases are strongly recommended; call or write for a schedule and a ticket order form. Ticket prices usually range from about $15 to $35 per concert. Between late August and mid-June, contact the festival's winter office at 1616 Walnut St., Ste. 1600, Philadelphia, PA 19103 (✆ **215/569-4690**); in summer, write Marlboro Music at Box K, Marlboro, VT 05344, or call the box office at ✆ **802/254-2394.** The website is **www.marlboromusic.org**.

Outdoor Pursuits

Mountain Biking

Mount Snow was among the very first ski resorts to foresee the widespread appeal of mountain biking, and this region remains one of the leading destinations for those whose vehicle of choice has knobby tires. The first mountain-bike school in the country was established here in 1988 and still offers a roster of classes that are especially helpful to novices. Clinics and guided tours are also available.

Mount Snow Sports (✆ **802/464-4040**), inside the Grand Summit Hotel, offers bike rentals, maps, and advice from late May to mid-October. The resort has some 45 miles of trails; bikers can explore an additional 140 miles of trails and abandoned roads that lace the region. For a trail fee, you can take your bike to the mountaintop by gondola, then coast your way down along marked trails.

Downhill Skiing

Mount Snow ★ Mount Snow is noted for its widely cut runs on the front face of the mountain (disparaged by some skiers as "vertical golf courses"), yet it still remains an excellent destination for intermediates and advanced intermediates. More advanced skiers migrate to the North Face, another world of bumps and open glades. This is also a great spot for snowboarding. Because it's the closest Vermont ski area to Boston and New York (about a 4-hr. drive from Manhattan), the mountain can get more crowded than other Vermont hills on weekends—maybe that's why the resort's lift-ticket prices have surged in recent years? But Mount Snow's village is attractively arrayed along the base of the mountain; the most imposing structure is a balconied hotel overlooking a small pond, but the overall character here is still shaped mostly by unobtrusive smaller lodges and homes. Once famed for a groovy singles scene, the hill's post-skiing activities have mellowed somewhat and embraced the baby-boomer and family markets, though 20-somethings can still find a good selection of après-ski activities.

39 Mount Snow Rd., West Dover, VT 05356. ✆ **800/245-7669** or 802/464-3333. www.mountsnow.com. Adults $69–$75 day lift tickets, $54–$60 half-day; discounts for youths and seniors.

Cross-Country Skiing

The Mount Snow area offers excellent cross-country ski centers. The 9 miles of groomed trails at **Timber Creek Cross-Country Touring Center** (✆ **802/464-0999**), on Route 100 in West Dover near the Mount Snow access road, are popular with beginners, and they hold snow nicely, thanks to the high elevation. Day passes are $18 for adults, $12 for kids 12 and under; equipment rentals are available on-site.

Where to Stay

The Mount Snow area has a surfeit of lodging options, ranging from basic motels to luxury inns and slope-side condos; rates in most of them drop quite a bit in summer, when the region slips into a pleasant lethargy. In winter, though, the high prices reflect the relatively easy drive from New York and Boston.

The best phone call to make first is to **Mount Snow's lodging line** (✆ **800/451-4211** or 800/245-7669) to ask about vacation packages and condo accommodations.

Deerhill Inn ★★ The Deerhill Inn, on a hillside above Route 100 in West Dover with views of the rolling mountains, was built as a ski lodge in 1954, but subsequent innkeepers have given it more of a country gloss. Though the building is aging and isn't *quite* a "luxury inn," it's trying hard and it's more than acceptable as a rustic overnight in these parts. In summer the property features attractive gardens and a nice stonework pool; in winter the ski slopes are just a short drive away. Guest rooms vary from the small and cozy to the spacious, some with Jacuzzis and/or flatscreen TVs; several more are located in a motel-like annex (these rooms all have balconies). The Tamarack Room features a king bed, double Jacuzzi, and attractive stone fireplace; Dahlia has a Jacuzzi, small fireplace, and walk-out private deck. The "garden" rooms are cheaper and less luxe, but maybe more Cape Cod–charming. Dining room fare, available only to inn guests, is a highlight (the wine cellar is impressive), and all guests can use the two upstairs sitting rooms stocked with books.

14 Valley View Rd. (P.O. Box 136), West Dover, VT 05356. ✆ **800/993-3379** or 802/464-3100. Fax 802/464-5474. www.deerhill.com. 14 units. $145–$295 double; $240–$345 suite. Rates include breakfast. 2-night minimum stay Sat–Sun. AE, MC, V. Children 8 and over welcome. **Amenities:** Dining room; bikes; outdoor pool. *In room:* TV/DVD, CD player, no phone, Wi-Fi (free).

The Inn at Sawmill Farm ★★★ Finds The Inn at Sawmill Farm is spread over 28 acres on a former dairy farm, and it was one of the very first inns in New England to cater to affluent travelers. The very impressive wine cellar is a tip-off to what's to come at the inn, which has been in the same family ever since opening 40 years ago. Buildings and guest rooms on this property, some of which date back as far as 1797, are distinctive and cohesive, yet all were updated in contemporary country styling and Colonial reproduction furniture even as the room count was gradually doubled. There are now 10 rooms in the main house, 4 in an adjacent farmhouse, and 3 in former sheep's quarters, plus an entire carriage house and two cottages you can rent entirely. Many now have flatscreen TVs and/or whirlpool tubs. Among the most interesting units are the Victorian, flowery Cider House No. 2, with its rustic beams, marble double Jacuzzi, and oversized canopy bed, and the Woodshed, a quiet wooden cottage with cathedral ceiling, whirlpool tub, small loft, plenty of windows overlooking the woods and pond, and private deck for breakfasting. The Carriage House, the most expensive unit, is a small, pond-side home with a brick wood-burning fireplace, huge sleigh bed, and a wraparound deck. Standard rooms here, though, are similar to upscale inn rooms elsewhere in Vermont: king beds and tons of flowery wallpaper and well-worn Vermont charm, without the jetted tubs or modern amenities. All rates include breakfast, afternoon tea, and outstanding **five-course dinners** (see "Where to Dine," below). This place is not to be missed if you can pay the freight.

7 Crosstown Rd. (P.O. Box 367), West Dover, VT 05356. ✆ **800/493-1133** or 802/464-8131. Fax 802/464-1130. www.theinnatsawmillfarm.com. 20 units. Midweek $325–$425 double, $475–$625 suite; weekend $390–$525 double, $575–$750 suite plus 15% service charge. Rates include breakfast, afternoon tea service, and dinner. AE, DC, MC, V. Closed Apr–May. **Amenities:** Restaurant; exercise room; outdoor pool; tennis court. *In room:* A/C, TV (most units), hair dryer, Wi-Fi (most units; free).

Vintage Motel ★ **Value** This motel gives you a taste of the "real" Vermont: the thrifty one. A budget choice for travelers planning to spend little time in their rooms, the Vintage features basic units that are actually quite nice looking with industrial carpeting, TVs, phones, and durable furniture. There's a common room with a microwave and VCR, and this is one of the few motels I've seen with a driving range right on-site. In winter the place fills up with skiers and with local and visiting snowmobilers: A major trail passes through the motel's backyard.

195 Rte. 9 (P.O. Box 222), Wilmington, VT 05363. ✆ **800/899-9660** or 802/464-8824. www.vintagemotel.net. 17 units. $45–$85 double; $100–$200 suite. Rates include continental breakfast on weekends and holidays only. MC, V. 2-night minimum stay on weekends; 3 nights some holidays. Pets allowed in 3 units ($15 per pet). **Amenities:** Driving range; outdoor pool. *In room:* TV, fridge (some units), Wi-Fi (free).

Windham Hill Inn ★★★ Now a member of the exclusive Relais & Chateaux network, this inn is about as good as it gets if you're in search of a romantic Vermont getaway. Situated on 160 acres at the end of a dirt road in a high upland valley in West Townshend (about 20 miles/30 min. from Mount Snow), the inn was built in 1823 as a farmhouse and remained in the same family until the 1950s, when it was converted into an inn. Guest rooms are wonderfully appointed in elegant country style and floral prints, many with Jacuzzis or soaking tubs; balconies or decks; and gas fireplaces—and *all* of the rooms have good views. There isn't a bad room on the property, but especially nice are the Jesse Lawrence Room on the third floor, with its lovely modern soaking tub, plush chairs, cherry pencil-poster king bed, and gas stove; and Forget-Me-Not, on the second floor, which has a similar setup plus a window nook. An annex (the White Barn) contains eight units, the choicest of which is the great top-floor Meadowlook with lots of windows, fieldstone fireplace, soaking tub beneath a skylight, double shower—oh, and a big, open private deck. The inn's superb **dining room** ★ features creative Continental and New American cooking; outside, the pastoral acreage includes 6 miles of groomed cross-country ski trails.

311 Lawrence Dr., West Townshend, VT 05359. ✆ **800/944-4080** or 802/874-4080. Fax 802/874-4702. www.windhamhill.com. 21 units. $215–$295 double; $365–$465 suite. Rates include full breakfast. 2- to 3-night minimum stay Sat–Sun and some holidays. AE, DISC, MC, V. Turn uphill at West Townshend country store and continue uphill 1¼ miles to dirt road (Lawrence Dr.); turn right and continue to end. Children 12 and over welcome. **Amenities:** Restaurant; Internet (in lobby; free); outdoor heated pool; tennis court. *In room:* A/C, hair dryer.

There are only two really good choices in town at the moment, and they occupy diametrically opposite ends of the culinary spectrum: a local diner that has been here for years and is as unpretentious as humanly possible, and a luxe country inn offering upscale French cooking.

In between those extremes? There's a pub, a few sandwich shops, some upward-striving bistros, but I can't say I enjoyed and/or remember any of them well enough to recommend them other than **Anchor Seafood,** 8 S. Main St. (✆ 802/464-2112; www.anchorseafood.com). It's a basic fish house of the sort you usually find in Maine rather than Vermont, serving adequately prepared lobsters, fish platters, chowders, and steaks.

As usual in this area, you can also head for the slopes when hungry. Mount Snow's dining choices include a pubby, seasonal restaurant called **Harriman's** (✆ **902/464-1100,** ext. 6032; no lunch) inside the Grand Summit Hotel and a deli/coffee shop/country store serving hot breakfasts year-round.

Dot's ★ Value DINER Wilmington is proud of Dot's, a Main Street (literally) institution that has stubbornly remained loyal to its longtime clientele by continuing to serve good, inexpensive food in the face of the bistro-ization of the rest of the village. This is your classic Vermont diner, from the cool neon sign right down to the pine paneling, swivel stools at the counter, and checkerboard-patterned linoleum tiles. It's regionally famous for its chili (kicked up with jalapeño peppers), but other good choices include great pancakes, French toast, shakes, daily chicken specials, hot open-faced sandwiches, and the Cajun skillet: a medley of sausage, peppers, onions, and fries sautéed and served with eggs and melted Jack cheese. There's now a second, newer Dot's—known as "Dot's of Dover"—in **Dover** (✆ **802/464-6476**), 7 miles north on Route 100.

3 E. Main St., Wilmington. ✆ **802/464-7284.** Breakfast items $3–$7, lunch and dinner items $3–$13. DISC, MC, V. Daily 5:30am–8pm (to 9pm Fri–Sat).

The Inn at Sawmill Farm ★★ CONTINENTAL More than 20,000 bottles of wine fill the wine cellar of this top-rated inn (see "Where to Stay," above), which has earned a coveted "Grand Award" from *Wine Spectator* magazine and stocks a big selection of oh-so-fine Latours, Margaux, and various Burgundies. The wine is one of the reasons the house restaurant consistently attracts well-heeled diners. Chef/proprietor Brill Williams often incorporates game (rabbit, pheasant, venison) into the menu, in true French tradition; also look for choices like roasted poussin stuffed with shallots, a salmon filet with a sorrel cream sauce, or potato-encrusted sea bass with mushrooms—even something off-the-wall like the long-popular Indonesian curried chicken breast. The signature dessert is a sundae of dark chocolate, butter, and nut sauce. This isn't the best inn dining in the state, but it's good, and the barn/farmhouse atmosphere is romantic. Bring your wallet, though—you'll spend a lot here. (Nonguests should ask for a menu version with prices listed.)

7 Crosstown Rd., West Dover. ✆ **800/493-1133** or 802/464-8131. www.theinnatsawmillfarm.com. Reservations recommended. Main courses $28–$39. AE, DC, MC, V. Daily 6–9:30pm. Closed Apr–May.

BRATTLEBORO ★

Set in a scenic river valley, the commercial town of **Brattleboro** is more than just a wide place in the road to fill the gas tank and stock up on provisions (though some parts of town do lend themselves best to that). In fact, this compact, hilly former mill town has a funky, slightly dated charm; its rough brick textures have aged well, although you will note a suspiciously high concentration of ex-flower children who moved here, grew up, cut their hair, and settled in to operate many local enterprises and institutions—some with a New Agey tinge.

Brattleboro was actually Vermont's first permanent settlement. (The first *attempt* at settlement was at Isle La Motte on Lake Champlain in 1666, but that didn't take.) Soldiers protecting the Massachusetts town of Northfield built an outpost in 1724 at Fort Dummer, about 1½ miles south of Brattleboro's present downtown—the site is now a small **state park** with a campground—and this city eventually became the local center for trade and manufacturing. The busy manufacturers here included the Estey Organ Co., which supplied countless home organs carved in ornate Victorian style to families across the nation.

Today Brattleboro is *still* the commercial hub of southeastern Vermont, positioned right at the strategic junction of I-89, routes 5 and 9, and the Connecticut River. It's the most convenient jumping-off point for anyone arriving from the south via the interstate. If you're looking for supplies, you'll find a strip-mall area of big grocery stores, gas stations, and chain restaurants located just north of the city center on Route 5 (the main street), near the traffic circle connecting with Route 9. For more interesting shopping, take the time to comb through downtown's nooks and crannies.

Brattleboro has long seemed immune to the stresses of modern life, but one modern inconvenience has made a belated appearance: traffic. Lower Main Street, near one of the bridges to New Hampshire, can back up in the direction of town, even leading to a bit of un-Vermontlike horn-honking. Other than that, though, life here is mostly tranquil and neighborly.

Essentials

GETTING THERE There's no airport nearby, but Brattleboro is easily accessible by car via exits 1 and 2 on **I-91.** From the east or west, Brattleboro is best reached via **Route 9,** which comes in from Albany and Bennington to the west and Keene, New Hampshire, to the east. From New York City via Hartford, it's about 3 hours without traffic, up to 4 hours with traffic.

Brattleboro is a stop on **Amtrak**'s (✆ **800/872-7245;** www.amtrak.com) once-daily *Vermonter* service from Washington, D.C., and New York to northern Vermont. From New York's Penn Station, the ride takes about 5½ hours and costs $48 one-way; from Washington's Union Station, it's about 9 hours and $103 per person. Brattleboro's own Union Station sits by the river in a stone building at 10 Vernon Ave. (Rte. 142), just downhill from Main Street's concentration of shops.

Greyhound (✆ **800/231-2222;** www.greyhound.com) also stops in Brattleboro, running two buses daily from New York's Port Authority bus terminal. The ride takes 5½ hours and costs $60 one-way, but as little as $44 if nonrefundable and booked online. The bus station is tucked away behind a Citgo gas station in the Route 5/9 traffic circle on the north side of town (about 2½ miles from the train station).

A handy, free black-and-white shuttle bus known as **the MOOver** (✆ **802/464-8487;** www.moover.com)—it's spotted to look remarkably like a cow (don't you love Vermont?)—connects the two stations two or three times a day. I repeat: This combination of dairy goodness and liberal social programming could *only happen in Vermont.* Use it.

VISITOR INFORMATION The **Brattleboro Chamber of Commerce** office at 180 Main St. (✆ **877/254-4565** or 802/254-4565; www.brattleborochamber.org) dispenses tourist information when it's open for business (Mon–Fri 8:30am–5pm; closed holidays).

Exploring the Town

Here's a useful two-phase strategy for exploring Brattleboro: Park. Walk. The commercially vibrant downtown is blessedly compact, and strolling it is the best way to appreciate its human scale and handsome commercial architecture. A town of cafes, bookstores, antiques stores, and outdoor recreation shops, it invites casual browsing without an itinerary.

One shop of quirky note, though, is **SAM'S Outdoor Outfitters** (✆ **802/254-2933;** www.samsoutdooroutfitters.com) at 74 Main St.; you can't miss the long red sign sloping down Main Street. This place is filled to the eaves with every sort of hiking, camping, and fishing gear; it's open daily. (This is the original, but there are now 2 branches nearby in Bellows Falls and Keene, New Hampshire, as well.)

A good stop for kids and curious adults is the **Brattleboro Museum & Art Center** ★ (✆ **802/257-0124;** www.brattleboromuseum.org), housed inside the city's 1916 train station at 10 Vernon St. (Rte. 142), near the bridge to New Hampshire. Wonderful exhibits here highlight the history of the city and the Connecticut River Valley, and there's also plenty of both classic and contemporary sculpture and art from local and regional artists. The museum is open Thursday through Monday, 11am to 5pm (closed in Mar). Admission costs $6 for adults, $4 for seniors, $3 for students, and free for children 5 and under.

Nightlife in this town? Beyond the pub and brewery scene? Why, yes. There's classical music in summer from nearby music schools in **Marlboro** (p. 105) and **Guilford.**

And there's music right here in town, thanks to the under-the-radar **Vermont Jazz Center** ★ (✆ **802/254-9088;** www.vtjazz.org) at 72 Cotton Mill Hill, a side street off South Main Street close to the Amtrak station, south of the core downtown area. The center is located in suite no. 222 of the factory complex; talented performers, mostly from the New York scene, work tasty riffs and improvisations here year-round. Tickets cost $20 per person. Check the website for the latest schedule.

Don't miss the Art Deco **Latchis Theatre** ★★ (✆ **802/246-1500;** www.latchis.com) at 50 Main St., either. Normally, you don't go on vacation to go to the movies, but this theater screens everything from Michael Moore documentaries to art films, Japanese animated films, and interesting mass releases on three screens. Tickets cost $7.50 per adult, and $5.50 for children, seniors, and matinee shows. The theater hosts musical performances like local benefits, small orchestral concerts, and gospel shows, too. It shares the same building as the Latchis Hotel (see "Where to Stay," below).

About 1½ miles outside town on Route 30 is **Tom and Sally's Handmade Chocolates,** 485 West River Rd. (✆ **800/827-0800** or 802/254-4200; www.tomandsallys.com), a sort-of boutique chocolate shop purveying handmade confections and seconds from the factory on-site. (The chocolate body-paint kit comes complete with two brushes; that's all I'm going to say about it. You take it from there.) Tours are also given of the factory, Monday through Saturday between 10am and 2pm—though they're pricey at a cost of $7 per adult and $2.50 per child. (Samples are included, but I'm pretty sure it's *not* an all-you-can-eat deal.)

Outdoor Pursuits

A soaring aerial view of Brattleboro can be found atop **Wantastiquet Mountain** ★, just across the Connecticut River in Chesterfield, New Hampshire. (Figure on a round-trip of 3 hr. to drive over, hike up, hike down, and drive back.) To reach the base of the "mountain" (which is really more of a hill), cross the river on the two green steel bridges, then turn left on the first dirt road; go just ⅕ mile and park in a parking area on the right.

The trail begins here, via a carriage road (stick to the main trail and avoid side trails) that winds about 2 steep miles up through a forest and past open ledges to a summit marked by a monument dating from 1908. You gain about a thousand feet in elevation during the walk. From the top, you'll be rewarded with sweeping views of the river, town, and landscapes beyond.

The **Vermont Canoe Touring Center** (✆ **802/257-5008**), open seasonally, is at the intersection of Route 5 and the West River north of town. This is a great spot to rent a canoe or kayak to poke around for a couple of hours, half a day, or a full day. Explore locally, or arrange for a shuttle upriver or down. The owners are helpful about providing information and maps to keep you on track. Among the best spots, especially for birders, are the marshy areas along the lower West River and a detour off the Connecticut River, known locally as "the Everglades" (insert tongue-in-cheek *here*). Get a gourmet sandwich to go at the Brattleboro Food Co-op (see "Where to Dine," below) and make a day of it.

Bike rentals and advice on day-trip destinations are available at the **Brattleboro Bicycle Shop,** 165 Main St. (✆ **800/272-8245** or 802/254-8644; www.bratbike.com). Hybrid bikes, ideal for exploring area back roads, can be rented by the day or week. It's open daily from spring through summer, closed Sundays in fall, and closed Sundays and Mondays until March.

Where to Stay

Budget-priced chain motels flank Route 5 north of Brattleboro, especially around the Route 5/9 traffic circle leading to Keene, New Hampshire. Most of these are quite impressive, more on the order of truck stops; the best choice here is probably the **Hampton Inn Brattleboro,** 1378 Putney Rd. (✆ **800/426-7866** or 802/254-5700; www.hamptoninn.com). But it isn't as cheap as most of the other motel options, and it's hardly an "inn." Double-room rates generally fall into the $140 to $160 per night range (substantially cheaper when booked ahead online, higher in fall and on holidays). Some suites have small refrigerators, microwave ovens, kitchenettes, and/or Jacuzzi tubs, making those rooms a good choice for traveling families.

Fortunately, **inns** abound in this part of Vermont, and some are priced quite affordably.

Chesterfield Inn ★★ About a 10-minute drive east of Brattleboro in New Hampshire, this attractive inn sits in a field just off the busy state highway; but inside, it's quieter and more refined than you would expect. The original farmhouse dates back to the 1780s but has been expanded and modernized. Nine guest rooms are located in the main inn, plus six more in cottages nearby; all are spacious and comfortably appointed in a mix of modern and antique furniture, plus a fridge, CD player, television, and phone. The two priciest units have fireplaces, double Jacuzzis, and private decks with mountain and meadow views, but more than half of the other rooms *also* have fireplaces burning either wood or gas. The inn's chef also serves dinner six nights a week to guests and nonguests alike; see "Where to Dine," below, for details.

20 Cross Rd. (Rte. 9), W. Chesterfield, NH 03466. ✆ **800/365-5515** or 603/256-3211. Fax 603/256-6131. www.chesterfieldinn.com. 15 units. $175–$345 double. Rates include breakfast. 2-night minimum stay foliage season and holidays. AE, DC, DISC, MC, V. Pets welcome in 6 back units. **Amenities:** Restaurant; babysitting. *In room:* A/C, TV, CD player, fridge, hair dryer, minibar, Wi-Fi (free).

Colonial Motel & Spa (Value) Operated by the same family for 3 decades, this sprawling compound set back from Route 5 is well maintained and offers the best value in town; choose it over the chain motels back in town. Opt for the back building's larger, quieter rooms, furnished with armchairs and sofas. Free local calls are included with your

Finds Loft in Space

The Artist's Loft B&B, 103 Main St. (✆ **802/257-5181;** www.theartistsloft.com), features one—count it—one guest suite, but if it's available, it makes a good, funky base in this town between mid-September and mid-May. A spacious, bright third-floor suite with a living room in a historic building right in the middle of town, the suite faces away from traffic and toward the river. It's run by Patricia Long and William Hays, who also operate an art gallery. (Some of Hays' paintings adorn the unit.) The place is air-conditioned and includes a phone, private bathroom, satellite television, and Wi-Fi access. Rates are $138 to $178 per night, depending on the season and whether you want an optional breakfast for two.

room, and there's a cozy lounge and basic restaurant on-site. But this motel's best feature is its 75-foot indoor lap pool in the spa building, where there's also a sauna and a simple fitness center. A second pool is maintained outdoors for those hot summer afternoons.

Putney Rd., Brattleboro, VT 05301. ✆ **800/239-0032** or 802/257-7733. www.colonialmotelspa.com. 68 units. $60–$85 double; $85–$140 suite. Rates include continental breakfast (Mon–Fri only). AE, DISC, MC, V. Take exit 3 off I-91; turn right and continue a half-mile. **Amenities:** Restaurant; bar; exercise room; Jacuzzi; 2 pools (1 indoor lap, 1 outdoor); sauna. *In room:* A/C, TV, Wi-Fi (free).

Latchis Hotel This downtown hotel fairly leaps out in Victorian-brick Brattleboro. Built in 1938 in understated Art Deco style at one of the city's busiest intersections (right at the foot of the commercial district), the Latchis was once the cornerstone for a small chain of hotels and theaters. It no longer has its own orchestra or commanding dining room, but the movie theater (showing great films) remains, and the place still has an authentic—if at times outdated-feeling—flair. Some units have been upgraded over the past few years, with newer furnishings and sunny art prints on the walls; other rooms and hallways, however, are badly showing their age. About two-thirds of the rooms have limited views of the river, though those views include the sounds of cars crawling down Main Street early every morning. If you need quiet, sacrifice the views and ask for a room in back. You can walk to the museum, food co-op, or shops of Main Street from here without breaking a sweat.

50 Main St., Brattleboro, VT 05301. ✆ **800/798-6301** or 802/254-6300. www.latchis.com. 30 units. $80–$170 double; $145–$200 suite. Rates include continental breakfast. AE, MC, V. **Amenities:** Restaurant. *In room:* A/C, TV, fridge, hair dryer, Wi-Fi (free).

Where to Dine

Brattleboro is surprisingly thin on good dining options, considering the fresh-foods movement that has hit Vermont full force. This is still a mill town at heart, and the dining choices reflect it: Even sophisticated locals often go for pizza, takeout, or pub grub.

In addition to the choices listed below, the subterranean coffee shop **Mocha Joe's** ★ (✆ **802/257-7794;** www.mochajoes.com), at 82 Main St., is a collection point for locals. It sports a friendly, laid-back vibe, brews a good cup of joe or espresso, and pours fresh-squeezed "-ades" in the summer. Expect a few dudes with weird beards, a few workmen, a few geeks, and some local purveyor of quartz crystals or art. Try the maple latte if you're craving something different.

Brattleboro Food Co-op ★ Finds DELI Selling wholesome foods since 1975, this huge store also has a deli counter great for takeout meals. Grab a quick and filling lunch that won't *necessarily* be tofu and sprouts—you can also get a smoked turkey and Swiss cheese sandwich or a crispy salad. Check out the eclectic selection of wines and cheeses as well as the natural bath products (some locally made) and the hand-cut steaks in the butcher section. Sausages are made and stuffed on premises, too, and the place is renowned for "case lot specials:" deep discounts on oversized quantities of health food. (Stash a case of organic cheese puffs in the trunk for the road.) The store section stays open until 9pm every night, a boon in early-closing Vermont. The co-op, located in a small strip mall downtown near the New Hampshire bridge, has lots of parking—though the minimall plaza is hard to notice as you whiz downhill and around the town's main bend.

2 Main St. (in Brookside Plaza, on right at bottom of Main St. hill). ✆ **802/257-0236.** www.brattleborofoodcoop.com. Sandwiches $3.50–$6, prepared foods usually around $4–$5 per lb. MC, V. Mon–Sat 8am–9pm; Sun 9am–9pm.

Chesterfield Inn ★★ CONTINENTAL Chesterfield Inn chef Robert Nabstedt buys fish from the Boston market, adds local vegetables and game, and serves up dining room fare that's better than it has to be. This doesn't feel like New Hampshire at all (except for the emphasis on game, maybe). Feast on items like tea-smoked duck breast served over sesame and peanut-flavored soba noodles; grilled swordfish with a wasabi-Key lime vinaigrette; maple- and bourbon-basted barbecued shrimp over an autumn risotto; seared scallops over pappardelle; an elk *osso bucco* with ragout; herb-encrusted racks of lamb; or even a vegetarian Thanksgiving meal of baked, maple-glazed acorn squash stuffed with a cranberry-pumpkin seed stuffing. Finish with cinnamon-espresso crème brûlée, apple-berry crisp, chocolate cake, or a piece of Kentucky Derby pie.

20 Cross Rd. (Rte. 9), West Chesterfield, NH. ✆ **800/365-5515** or 603/256-3211. www.chesterfieldinn.com. Reservations recommended. Main courses $19–$29. MC, V. Mon–Sat 5:30–9pm.

Peter Havens Restaurant ★ AMERICAN/SEAFOOD You're likely to feel at home right away in this locally popular dining spot, which has just 10 tables. Housed in a pleasantly contemporary building, the kitchen might or might not bowl you over (quality seems uneven at times, entree to entree), but you'll be impressed by the menu of choices at least. The kitchen has perhaps moved even more in the direction of seafood than it had leaned before (though that has always been a specialty of the place) with a change in ownership; scallops, oysters, mussels, and seared tuna are now just as likely—no, more so—to be the night's star as duck or steak. The bar is convivial and popular, but make a reservation if you're visiting on a weekend: The place gets packed with a mix of locals and tourists.

32 Elliot St. ✆ **802/257-3333.** www.peterhavens.com. Reservations strongly recommended. Main courses $19–$24. MC, V. Tues–Sat 6–9pm.

T. J. Buckley's ★★ NEW AMERICAN Brattleboro's best restaurant, little T. J. Buckley's, is housed in a classic old diner on a dim side street—but this is *far* from diner food. Instead, it's kitchen theater. Renovations such as slate floors and golden lighting have created an intimate space that seats fewer than 20 when full; no secrets exist among the chef, sous-chefs, and server, all of whom remain within a couple dozen feet of each other and you throughout the meal as they cook and serve it and you gape in awe. (The whole place—kitchen plus seating—is smaller than the kitchens of most other restaurants.)

Fun Facts Yes, Syrup: Maple's Journey from Tree to Table

Maple syrup is at once simple and extravagant. Simple, because it's made from the purest ingredients available (light, water, weather); extravagant, because it's an expensive luxury that takes a lot of human labor and wood-fueled heating to get right.

Two elemental ingredients combine to create maple syrup: sugar-maple sap and fire. Sugaring season slips in between northern New England's painfully long winter and its frustratingly short spring, usually lasting 4 or 5 weeks, typically beginning in early or mid-March. As warmer, sunny days begin to alternate with freezing nights, the sap in maple trees begins to run from deep in its roots up toward the branches overhead, heading for the new shoots that will become buds and leaves. Sugarers drill shallow holes into the trees and insert small taps to short-circuit this process, and buckets (or, increasingly, lengths of synthetic plastic tubing) are hung from the taps to collect the sap bit by bit as it drips out the holes.

The collected sap is then boiled down ("boiled off" is the proper New England term). The equipment for this ranges from simple backyard fire pits, cobbled together from concrete blocks, to elaborate commercial-capacity sugarhouses using oil or propane burners. It requires between 32 and 40 *gallons* of sap just to make *one* gallon of supermarket syrup, so a lot of boiling has to happen to get from here to there. (The real cost of syrup isn't the sap or labor; it's all the fuel and time required to boil it down to the finished product.)

Vermont is the nation's unchallenged capital of maple syrup production, cranking out nearly *1 million* gallons a year, an industry whose full economic value statewide may be in the several tens of millions of dollars. The fancier inns and restaurants in the state serve local maple syrup with breakfast; local diners, though, sometimes charge a $1 supplement for the real stuff, or else you get that awful flavored corn syrup prevalent in most of the rest of the nation. (If you get the fake stuff, always ask a waitress if the real stuff is available.)

You can also pick up the real thing in practically every grocery store in the state, but I'm convinced it tastes better if you buy it straight from the farm. Look for handmade signs or maple-leaf icons touting syrup for sale posted at the ends of driveways around the region *throughout* the year. Drive on up, knock on the door, and get out your cash—no, people in houses don't take credit cards. Usually.

A number of Vermont's sugarers invite visitors to inspect the process and sample some of the fresh syrup (sometimes over snow) in the early spring. A list of sugarhouses that open to the public year-round is posted online at **www.vermontmaple.org/open-year-round.php** by the **Vermont Maple Sugar Makers' Association** (✆ **802/763-7435**). There's also a mass open-house event in late March known as Vermont Maple Open House Weekend; go if you can.

Iconoclastic chef/owner Michael Fuller's menu is always limited, with just a few entree choices each night, but the food nearly always dazzles in its execution. Expect the usual New American appetizers and entrees: beet carpaccios, wondrous pâtés, crab, seared scallops, steak, duck, fish dishes of the day. All beautifully prepared and presented, sometimes more adventurously than you might expect. (Whatever Fuller feels like making, he makes—*his* way.) ***Note:*** The tab for a dinner party of three or more *will* run into the hundreds, so hit a bank first (well, not in the John Dillinger sense) and bring a wad of big bills.

132 Elliot St. ✆ **802/257-4922.** Reservations strongly recommended. Main courses $27–$35. No credit cards. Winter Thurs–Sun 6–9pm; rest of year Wed–Sun 6–9pm.

PUTNEY ★★

The sleepy village of **Putney** (pop. 2,600 and holding) is something like Brattleboro, but *more* so: Once a farming town, it's now a mixture of New England and New Age. (Much of this is thanks to the Putney School, a somewhat alternative boarding school founded in 1935 whose well-bred students tend a real farm when they're not attending college-prep classes.) This village is now home to an uncommonly high number of physical therapists, writing counselors, life coaches, freelance social workers, and their ilk.

Yet there's little tension between old and new here; instead, it's infused with a sort of pleasant ennui, and while you're likely to see more dreadlocks here than in any other New England village of the same size, there are also still plenty of dairy farms, furniture makers, auto-body shops, bed-and-breakfast inns, and even—improbably—a great joint to get barbecue ribs. This is still New England, not Sedona.

Putney's free-spirited character has a history. In the early 19th century, a cousin of President Rutherford B. Hayes named John Humphrey Noyes settled here with a band of followers known as Perfectionists. For a few years, they quietly formed a commune on some land and practiced a sort of way-before-the-'70s free love (except Noyes called it "complex marriage"). "In a holy community there is no more reason why sexual intercourse should be restrained by the law than why eating and drinking should be," Noyes wrote.

Needless to say, when word of such practices leaked out, the prim Vermonters in town were less than pleased. Noyes was arrested in 1847. The 1960s and 1970s brought another wave of free thinking through town, but today the area is once again mostly known for good local cheese products, the farm school, and one of New England's best little natural-foods stores. Lacking only a big mountain, this is a fine place to get off the highway and explore small-town Vermont for a day or two.

Essentials

GETTING THERE Putney is approximately 12 miles north of Brattleboro on Route 5. Take exit 4 off I-91, then turn right. You'll be in town in a minute or two.

VISITOR INFORMATION There's no formal information center in Putney (it's too small), but a pretty good unofficial town website can be found online at **www.putney.net**. The town's official website, also good, is at **www.putneyvt.org**.

Finally, the town's natural-foods store (see "Where to Dine," below) maintains a very active **bulletin board** with free papers, tacked-up notices, and plenty of chitchat about local art shows, music performances, and other cultural events.

Exploring the Town

Putney is an arts and crafts destination, with at least a dozen artisans living and working in or very near the village. The 3-day **Putney Craft Tour** (www.putneycrafts.com) in late November showcases much of their work by opening up these artists' studios to the public. The compact village center also features several intriguing restaurants and shops with global imports, antiques, and used books.

About 7 miles north of town on Westminster West Road (which splits off from the main street in the center of town), **John Ewald and Peggy O'Toole** ★ (✆ **802/387-6661**) produce outstanding sculptured and painted ceramic tiles with an emphasis on naturalistic themes (check out the amazingly lifelike trout and flowers) in their studios. It's definitely worth a drive if you enjoy ceramics; you've probably not seen ceramics like these elsewhere.

Basketville, 2 Bellows Falls Rd. (✆ **800/258-4553** or 802/387-5509; www.basketville.com), dates to 1842, owned and operated by Vermonters ever since (though the company's website explains that the baskets are actually made in China). As you can probably guess from the name, its primary trade is in baskets—in far more styles than you thought possible. A sprawling store stocking Shaker-style baskets, Native American–style ash baskets, pine buckets, and plenty more Americana (wicker and rattan furniture, silk flowers, and so forth), it's just north of the village center on Route 5.

Savory, award-winning cheese (the *New York Times* has raved about it) is made in Putney at **Vermont Shepherd Cheese,** 281 Patch Farm Rd. (✆ **802/387-4473;** www.vermontshepherd.com). The creamy and rich cheeses have a brown rind and are aged in a cave on the property; you'll find it at fine restaurants and in better food shops along the eastern seaboard. (But check Vermont natural-foods co-ops for it as you ramble through the state.) Though the factory tours have been discontinued, there's a farm stand on-site where you can buy the cheese. It's a little tricky to find, though; from the center of Putney, turn north onto Westminster Road at the burned shell of the former general store, then continue 6 or 7 miles north. Bear right onto Patch Road; the right turn to the farm and cheese stand is about a half-mile farther along.

Where to Dine

There's a decent New England–style diner, called (of course) the **Putney Diner** (✆ **802/387-5433**), at 82 Main St. in the middle of town, open daily 6am until 8pm. Just across the road at 133 Main St., the **Front Porch Cafe** (✆ **802/387-2200**), inside the Putney Tavern, serves good light lunches—think comfort food but with upscale twists—and coffee and pastries daily except Mondays. It's open from 7am to 4pm.

Finally, for something healthier, head south on Main Street toward the interstate on-ramps. Right across from Curtis' barbecue pits is the **Putney Food Co-op** ★★ (✆ **802/387-5866;** www.putneycoop.com), a superlative place to stock up on organic local milk, goat cheese, maple syrup, produce, and other products for the drive home. It's one of my favorite natural foods stores on the East Coast. The coffee bar/deli has baked goods, coffee, and healthier-than-thou soups, sandwiches, and salads, too. It's open daily until 8pm.

Curtis' BBQ ★ BARBECUE Just uphill from exit 4 off I-91, you can smell the aroma of Southern-style barbecue sizzling over flaming pits before you see it. This classic roadside joint, situated on a more or less empty lot next to a gas station, has a heap of charm despite itself. The self-serve restaurant consists of two blue school buses—yes, you read that right, blue school buses—plus a newer, open-sided shed for dining. Guests take their plunder to picnic tables scattered about the lot. Place your order, grab a seat, dig in, and enjoy. In addition to the ribs, the barbecued chicken is surprisingly good, and so are the few side dishes available. Note that Curtis closes down and wisely packs up his grilling tools after foliage season and heads south, only to return faithfully like the geese each spring. But also note that his family has recently opened a second location in the village of Chester, about 30 miles north (p. 119).

Rte. 5, Putney. ✆ **802/387-5474.** www.curtisbbqvt.com. Ribs $7–$26, other items $3–$11. No credit cards. Thurs–Sun 10am–sunset. Usually closed Nov–Mar.

GRAFTON ★★★ & CHESTER ★

One of Vermont's most scenic and well-preserved villages, **Grafton** was founded in 1763 and soon grew into a thriving settlement. By 1850 the town was home to a population of 10,000 . . . sheep. It also boasted a hotel that provided shelter for guests on the stagecoach road between Boston and Montreal. A cheese cooperative was organized in 1890, and a soapstone industry flourished here for a time. But as the agriculture and commerce shifted west and to bigger cities, Grafton became a shadow of a town—by the Depression, many of the buildings here were derelict.

Then something remarkable happened. In 1963 Hall and Dean Mathey of New Jersey created the Windham Foundation. A wealthy relative who had recently died entrusted the two brothers to come up with a worthy cause for her fortune; it took a few years, but they eventually hit on Grafton, where their family had summered. The Matheys began purchasing and restoring the dilapidated center of town, including the old hotel. This foundation eventually came to own some 55 buildings and 2,000 acres around town—even the cheese cooperative was revived. The village sprung back to life, and it's now teeming with history buffs, antiques hounds, and tourists (instead of farmers and merchants). The Windham Foundation has taken great care in preserving this gem of a village, even to the point of burying utility lines so as not to mar the village's landscape with wires.

To the north, **Chester** is less pristine and more lived-in: There are actual grocers, diners, and gas stations here. Yet the downtown area has a pleasant, neighborly feel and attractive old architecture; you can also find a handful of boutiques and shops along the main road. Chester is a great stop for antiquing, too, with several good dealers in the area. If you're heading north of town along Route 103, be sure to go slowly through the Stone Village, a neighborhood of well-spaced, austere stone homes lining the roadway. Some are rumored to have been safe havens on the famous Underground Railroad once upon a time.

Essentials

GETTING THERE Take I-91 to Bellows Falls (exit 5 or 6), and follow signs to town via Route 5. From here, take Route 121 west for 12 miles to Grafton. Or for a more scenic route, follow Route 35 north from Townshend for about 3 miles, take the left fork, and continue 7 more miles into Grafton.

VISITOR INFORMATION Grafton's informal **information center** is located in a gift shop inside the Grafton Inn's Daniels House, adjacent to the Daniels House Cafe (it's right behind the Old Tavern). The town also maintains a somewhat basic website at **www.graftonvermont.org**. For information about Chester, contact the **Okemo Valley Chamber of Commerce** (✆ **802/228-5830;** www.okemovalleyvt.org) in Ludlow. There's also seasonal information on Chester's village green.

Exploring the Town

Grafton is best seen at a slow pace, on foot, when the weather is welcoming. A picnic is a good idea, especially if it involves a chunk of the excellent local cheddar. Unfortunately, none of the grand (and privately owned) historic homes you see in the village are open for tours; it's a village to be enjoyed with aimless walks outdoors. Don't expect to be overwhelmed by grandeur, but keep a keen eye out for telling historical details.

Start at the **Grafton Village Cheese Co.** ★ (✆ **800/472-3866;** www.graftonvillagecheese.com), a small, modern building where you can buy a snack of the great, award-winning cheese and peer through plate-glass windows to observe the cheese-making process. (No tours are allowed for sanitary reasons.) It's open daily, 10am to 5pm. Sometimes they sell big wheels of the cheese at deep discounts, too.

From the cheese shop, follow the trail over a nearby covered bridge, then bear right on the footpath along a cow pasture to the cute **Kidder Covered Bridge.** Head into town via Water Street, and then turn onto Main Street. In the village center, white clapboard homes and shade trees abound, about as New England as it gets.

On Main Street, stop by the **Grafton Historical Society Museum** ★ (✆ **802/843-1010;** www.graftonhistory.org)—open Friday to Monday from Memorial Day through Columbus Day (and daily during foliage season)—to peruse photographs, artifacts, and memorabilia of Grafton. The suggested donation is $3 per adult. Afterward, have a look at **The Old Tavern at Grafton** ★★, the impressive building that anchors the town and has served as a social center since 1801. Partake of a beverage at the rustic Phelps Barn Lounge or a meal in one of the dining rooms. (There's also an inn here; see "Where to Stay," below.) From here, make your way back to the cheese factory by wandering along pleasant side streets. Or if you'd like to see Grafton from a different perspective, inquire at the inn about a horse-and-buggy ride.

More active travelers, whether visiting in winter or summer, should head for the **Grafton Ponds Recreation Center** (✆ **802/843-2400**), just south of the cheese factory on Route 35. Managed by the Old Tavern, Grafton Ponds offers mountain-bike rentals and access to a hillside trails system in summer and fall (with a new mountain-bike park incorporating plenty of BMX tricks, like switchbacks and teeter-totters). In winter the Center grooms almost 20 miles of trails and maintains a warming hut. The 1-mile Big Bear loop, running high up the flanks of a hill, is especially appealing; travel counterclockwise so you can walk up the steep hill and enjoy the descent. Ski and snowshoe rentals are available; a day trail pass costs about $16 for adults, $14 for seniors and students, and $10 for children ages 6 to 12 (free for ages 5 and under).

Where to Stay

If you're seeking a more luxurious experience than the two inns I've listed below, the wonderful **Windham Hill Inn** (p. 107) is only about 15 miles away in **West Townshend.** From Grafton, take either Route 35 S. or Route 121 E.; the inn is just off Windham Hill Road.

Hugging Bear Bed & Breakfast Kids Young kids might like this place for its single-minded devotion to a particular toy. A turreted, Queen Anne–style home right on Chester's Main Street, it's filled to the brim with teddy bears, including a 5-foot teddy in the living room and some 250 or more scattered about the house. (In an attached barn, another 10,000 are for sale at the Hugging Bear Shoppe, which attracts serious collectors from around the world.) The rooms themselves? They're country-simple, themed around—you guessed it—the bears. Expect bear sheets, bear wallpaper, bear light-switch plates, bear shower curtains, and the like. Nothing fancy here, but (true bear connoisseurs take note) "Panda-monium" has a panda theme, while "Pooh and Piglet's Hideaway" is all Pooh, all the time. The included country breakfast is big, and five of the six units are air-conditioned.

244 Main St., Chester, VT 05143. ✆ **800/325-0519** or 802/875-2412. www.huggingbear.com. 6 units. $125–$150 double. Rates include full breakfast. 2-night minimum stay Sat–Sun and holidays. AE, DISC, MC, V. *In room:* A/C (5 units), no phone.

The Old Tavern at Grafton ★★ This beautiful, well-managed historic "inn" is actually a series of rooms spread throughout the village. Only about a dozen rooms are in the handsome, colonnaded main building, which dates from 1801 (and has slightly sloping corridors as a result), while the remainder are in the nearby Homestead and Windham properties across the road. All are decorated in antiques, Americana themes, and some upscale design touches (mostly; all rooms have phones, but none have televisions). These rooms are far from basic B&B digs. Room nos. 6 and 8 feature lovely, bridal-looking white canopies over the beds. Units in Windham "Cottage" are similar to those in the main building; again you find a number of snow-white canopy beds. Units in the Homestead "Cottage" (which isn't a cottage at all, but rather two historic homes joined together), on the other hand, have more of a modern, hotel-like character. Ask the hotel staff about the clock at the entrance. Finally, the Cricketers Suite is in yet another building, and has a small refrigerator, coffeemaker, and whirlpool tub where toddlers are welcome. In all, six units have suitelike layouts.

Rtes. 35 and 121 (P.O. Box 9), Grafton, VT 05146. ✆ **800/843-1801** or 802/843-2231. Fax 802/843-2245. www.old-tavern.com. 30 units. $150–$245 double; $195–$400 suite. Rates include breakfast. MAP plan rates available. 2- to 3-night minimum stay on winter weekends, holidays, and in foliage season. AE, MC, V. Closed Mar to mid-Apr. Children 4 and under welcome in Homestead Cottage and Cricketers Suite. **Amenities:** Restaurant; pub; bikes; Jacuzzi; swimming pond; tennis court. *In room:* Fridge (1 unit), Wi-Fi (most units; free).

Where to Dine

Curtis' All American Restaurant ★ Finds AMERICAN How great is this? Curtis Tuff, proprietor of the legendary (but seasonal) Curtis' in Putney (p. 116) has a daughter named Sarah. (Actually, he has 7 children, but that's not the point.) This youngest daughter knows how to do 'cue. *And* she decided to open this branch in Chester and keep it open year-round. True, the place has all the atmosphere of a break room at an auto shop, but the great ones always do. Sarah and her partner grill the same great ribs and chicken that the master does (he didn't pass on the magic sauce recipe, however), even when it's *snowing,* and they also do some things Curtis doesn't: chopped pork and chicken; smoked brisket (Fri nights only); beers and wines from a bar; side dishes like loaded-up potato skins; an actual roof between you and the elements; and a weekend buffet that's all-you-can-eat. Feels like I've gone to heaven, or at least back to north Georgia. "Southern" doesn't get any better than this in the North, folks; do not miss this place if you're passing through. They even have a kids' menu.

908 Rte. 103 S., Chester. ✆ **802/875-6999.** Main courses $4–$14. MC, V. Wed–Thurs and Sun 11am–8pm; Fri–Sat 11am–9pm.

LUDLOW & OKEMO

Centered on a former mill that once produced fabrics and then, later, aircraft parts, **Ludlow** has an unpretentious made-in-Vermont character that seems miles from the prim grace of white clapboard Grafton. There are plenty of basic services here. Things feel a bit strung out and centerless, though, because there's really only one street (the highway, headed elsewhere); you can't really walk around enjoyably from place to place. Low-key and unassuming, Ludlow has transformed into a somewhat hip destination thanks to the skiers who arrive by the busload to ski **Okemo Mountain,** a once-sleepy resort that has come back to life in recent years and is a pretty good family or beginning-skier destination.

Ludlow is notable for being one of the few ski towns in New England that didn't go all Tyrolean and over-the-top with ski huts, chalets, outlets, and/or boutique shops after the arrival of the skiing masses. This place *still* lacks pizzazz, splashy nightlife, or fancy restaurants today. Some longtime visitors like it just fine that way. Others, though, may find the place boring. That's when it's time to hit the slopes.

Essentials

GETTING THERE Ludlow is situated at the intersection of routes 193 and 100. The most direct route from an interstate is to take exit 6 off I-91, then follow Route 103 west to Ludlow; it should take 30 to 40 minutes to get there.

VISITOR INFORMATION The **Okemo Valley Regional Chamber of Commerce** (✆ **802/228-5830;** www.okemovalleyvt.org) staffs a helpful information booth at the Okemo Marketplace, on Mountain Road, year-round.

Exploring the Area

The history of Ludlow and its surrounding region is the subject of the **Black River Academy Museum** ★ (✆ **802/228-5050**), on High Street near the village green. Open from spring through early fall, the museum includes an exhibit on President Calvin Coolidge, who graduated from the academy (that is, prep school) in 1892. Other exhibits explore the role of industry and farming in the Black River Valley, and provide a look at life in a Finnish community. Roughly from Memorial Day through Labor Day it's open Tuesday through Saturday, noon to 4pm; admission is free.

Skiing

Okemo ★★ (Kids) Okemo fans like to point out a couple of things. First, this is one of the few family-owned ski resorts left in New England: It has been owned by Tim and Diane Mueller since 1982 (who now also own Mount Sunapee in New Hampshire; p. 235). It offers more varied and challenging terrain than ever. It doesn't attract as many ski yahoos as a place like Killington; this is first and foremost a mountain for families who enjoy the slopes and a friendly base area that isn't too intimidating to kids—there's even day care. The well-maintained half-pipes (with music) are popular with snowboarders, and there's excellent cross-country skiing, too. In recent years, Okemo has expanded to take in the slopes of adjacent Jackson Gore Peak, another family-friendly move that included construction of a new inn, fitness center, and two golf courses. Parents should note that the resort offers discounts for young adults (ages 13–18) and seniors (ages 65–69), and deeper discounts for juniors (ages 7–12) and "super seniors" (70 and over).

Ludlow, VT 05149. ✆ **802/228-4041** or 800/786-5366 for lodging. www.okemo.com. Adults $72–$79 day lift tickets, $54–$59 half-day; discounts for seniors and youths.

Where to Stay

Lodging choices in this area are a bit limited, but what there is, is excellent. See below for my two recommended choices. During ski season, you can also contact the **Okemo Mountain Lodging Service** (✆ **800/786-5366;** www.okemo.com) for information about availability and making reservations in slopeside condominiums with kitchens.

A Road Trip to Bellows Falls

A trip southeast through the ravine of Proctorsville Gulf to the riverside village of **Bellows Falls** is an option when you have an unscheduled day (or bad weather strikes) while you're in Ludlow. The town has a rough-edged industrial charm, rather than picture-postcard beauty.

Set in a deep valley at the edge of the Connecticut River, Bellows Falls went through several booms, each time riding a wave of technology. America's first canal was constructed here in 1802, offering a way for boats carrying freight to bypass the tumultuous town falls (which are still dramatic—in spring). After trains eclipsed the canal, this became a junction of railroad lines, providing a fresh infusion of cash. Advances in paper, farm machinery manufacturing, and hydroelectric power also lifted the town's economic fortunes—a wave that crested and broke, leaving the mills (and locals) high and dry once again.

Get a glimpse of earlier times via the town's varied architecture. The compact downtown is mostly of Victorian brick, watched over by the town hall's crenellated **clock tower**—it looks a little like it could be perched above a square in Venice. This handsome commercial architecture attests to the town's former affluence (check out the Romanesque post office near the former canal site). A well-written brochure guides visitors on a walking tour of Bellows Falls, offering a quick tour of the centuries, from the remains of the early canal to examples of Craftsman-style homes dating from the 1920s. The brochure is available at the **Great Falls Regional Chamber of Commerce,** 17 Depot St., Bellows Falls, VT 05101 (✆ **802/463-4280;** www.gfrcc.org).

What else can you do here? Investigate the roster of local artists who are beginning to move into town. Or stop by the visitor center at the **hydroelectric dam** in town for a tour of the clever fish ladder with its canal-like locks; when it opened in 1982, this device enabled the reintroduction of salmon to the upper Connecticut River.

The Governor's Inn ★★ (Finds) This regal village home, built in 1890 by eventual Vermont Governor William W. Stickney (thus the name), is the picture of Victorian elegance and B&B perfection. The lobby and common room, both with gas fireplaces, are richly hued with time-worn hardwoods. Guest rooms vary in size; some are smallish, but all are comfortably appointed with antiques. A few have gas fireplaces or stoves and some have two-person Jacuzzis. The plush top-floor suite comes with a whirlpool tub, skylight, and quirky top-floor angling; Jessica's Room features a little telescope for stargazing (or skier-watching); and most of the other rooms are decorated in lacy, flowery linens, wallpapers, and prints. There's a public computer for checking e-mail, a bar, and a front porch for rocking and reading on. In addition to cooking big, delicious breakfasts, co-owner Cathy Kubec (a trained chef) teaches cooking seminars here. Her husband, Jim, helps keep things running, and both appear to enjoy it immensely. Don't miss afternoon teas, featuring Cathy's baked goods.

86 Main St., Ludlow, VT 05149. ✆ **800/468-3766** or 802/228-8830. www.thegovernorsinn.com. 9 units. $149–$269 double; $199–$299 suite. Rates include full breakfast and afternoon tea. AE, DISC, MC, V. Children 12 and over welcome. **Amenities:** Dining room; bar. *In room:* A/C, TV/DVD (most units), hair dryer, no phone, Wi-Fi (free).

The Inn at Water's Edge ★ Just a short drive north of Okemo Mountain, this 150-year-old house sits on the banks of the Black River, off Route 100. It has been renovated and updated in a florid Victorian style. The attached barn has a lounge good for relaxing, with an oak pool table, chess set, leather couches, and a mahogany bar that was actually imported from England. Guest rooms in the barn over the pub are smallish and darker than those in the main building. Room no. 11, upstairs in the main house, is a good choice—it's bright and appealingly furnished, with corner windows and wood floors. Nearly all rooms have richly carved headboards, fireplaces, and Jacuzzi tubs; otherwise, they're kept New England–spare. The dining room serves four course meals nightly (which are excellent; $25 extra per person), and there's an outdoor patio with lake views in good weather. This inn also goes out of its way to encourage outdoor exercise with free bikes, canoes, a swimming beach, and snowshoeing and cross-country ski trails, as well as packages that save you a bundle by including the price of lift tickets. If you can handle a few odd rules, you might really like it.

45 Kingdom Rd., Ludlow, VT 05149. ✆ **888/706-9736** or 802/228-8143. Fax 802/228-8443. www.innatwatersedge.com. 11 units. $125–$250 double plus 15% service charge. Rates include full breakfast. MAP rates $50 higher. AE, MC, V. Children 12 and over welcome. **Amenities:** Dining room; bar; bikes; Jacuzzi. *In room:* A/C, no phone, Wi-Fi (some units; free).

Where to Dine

Most inns in the Ludlow area, including those listed above, also serve good dinners to the paying public. The **Okemo** ski resort also maintains a flight of restaurants serving Italian food, pizzas, fancy New American–style sandwiches, and more.

For a lower-brow night out with the kids, think about **Wicked Good Pizza** (✆ **802/228-4131;** www.wickedgoodpizza.com), at 117 Main St. (Rte. 103), at the eastern edge of town. It's the local option for pizzas, calzones, and subs, and they'll even sell you a slice (there are rotating daily specials). However, they don't take plastic.

Harry's Café ★★ **Finds** INTERNATIONAL Along a dark stretch of highway north of Ludlow, you'll pass this brightly lit cafe with a red neon sign indicating HARRY'S over the door. At 50 miles an hour, it looks like either a hamburger joint or a biker roadhouse, but it's not. Instead, this is an appealing family restaurant with a menu spanning the globe; owner Trip Pearce, a former lobster fisherman and seafood chef, named the place for his dad. He cooks anything from New York sirloin steaks and jerked scallops to curries, seafood medallions, grilled breast of duck, charred chicken with peanut sauce, pork chops, or ravioli. There's also a kids' menu. Thai fare is a house specialty on Thursdays, which feature Thai prix fixe meals (in the middle of Vermont). Dessert should be mousse or an ice-cream sundae with the house hot fudge. Pearce sells his sauces to take home, too.

Rte. 103 (5 miles north of Ludlow), Mount Holly. ✆ **802/259-2996.** www.harryscafe.com. Reservations recommended in winter. Main courses $13–$21. AE, MC, V. Wed–Sun 5–10pm.

4 WOODSTOCK & ENVIRONS ★★

Woodstock: 16 miles W of White River Junction; 140 miles NW of Boston; 98 miles SE of Burlington

For more than a century, the resort community of **Woodstock** has been considered one of New England's most exquisite villages, and its attractiveness has benefited from the largesse of some of the country's most affluent citizens. Even the surrounding countryside is mostly unsullied—it's pretty difficult to drive here via any route that *isn't* pastoral and

ATTRACTIONS ●
Billings Farm & Museum **5**
Marsh-Billings-Rockefeller
 National Historic Park **4**
Woodstock Green **3**
Woodstock Historical Society **7**

ACCOMMODATIONS ■
Shire Riverview Motel **12**
Woodstock Inn & Resort **2**
The Woodstocker Inn B&B **1**

DINING ◆
Bentley's **9**
Osteria Pane e Salute **11**
The Prince & the Pauper **6**
Village Butcher Shop **8**
Woodstock Coffee & Tea **10**

SOUTHERN & CENTRAL VERMONT

5

WOODSTOCK & ENVIRONS

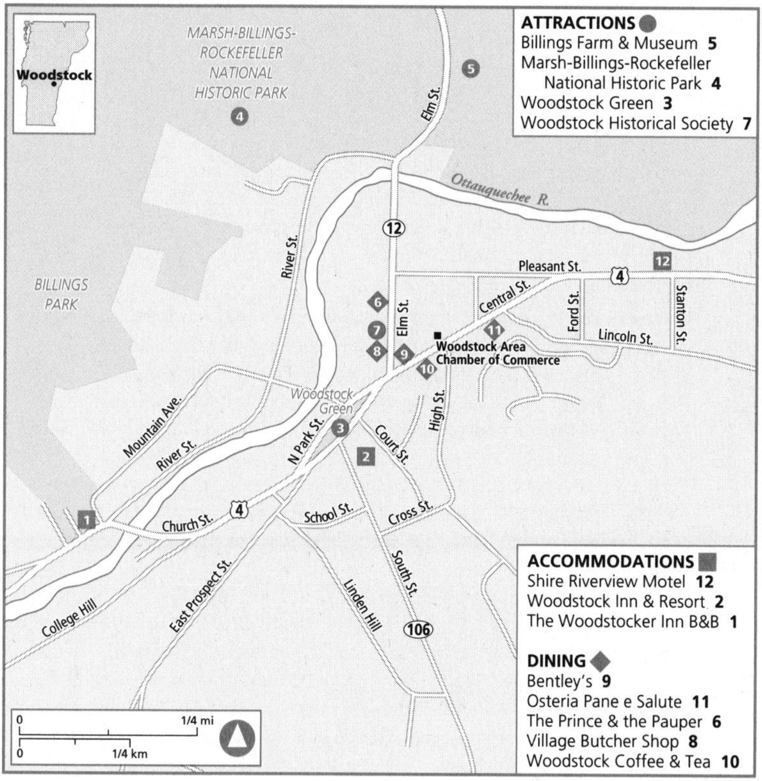

scenic, and by the time you're here you're already feeling as if you're in another era. Few New England villages can top Woodstock for grace and elegance; the tidy downtown is compact and neat, populated by a handful of shops, galleries, and boutiques. The lovely village green is surrounded by handsome homes, creating what amounts to a comprehensive review of architectural styles of the 19th and early 20th centuries. You could literally throw a stone (but don't) from the town center and hit a very attractive covered bridge.

In addition to Woodstock, this region also takes in nearby **White River Junction, Quechee,** and **Norwich,** three towns of distinctly different lineages along the Connecticut River on the New Hampshire border. In fact, while here you'll also want to cross that river over to **Hanover, New Hampshire** (p. 229), a lovely town that's also home to brainy, beery Dartmouth College.

WOODSTOCK ★★

Much of Woodstock is on the National Register of Historic Places already, and—as if that weren't enough—the Rockefeller family deeded 500 acres surrounding **Mount Tom** (see "Hiking," below) to the National Park Service just to protect even *more* of it from developers. Downtown Woodstock could probably be renamed "Rockefeller National

Leaf-Peeping Etiquette: A Viewer's Primer

Every October, tens of thousands of tourists (and more than a few locals) descend upon the best stretches of road in Vermont, New Hampshire, and—to a lesser extent—Maine to get a free look at the amazing natural spectacle of maple, oak, birch, and beech leaves turning fiery reds, oranges, and yellows. If the weather has been just right—clear, ice-cold nights after gradually cooler days are best; a warm or rainy September can kill the whole deal—it's as breathtaking as a van Gogh painting. To fully appreciate the spectacle, here's my eight-step insider program. Follow these simple rules, and you'll enjoy this year's foliage season more than ever:

1. **Plan ahead.** Leaf-peeping means big bucks to regional tourism, so each state now has set up a website and/or **toll-free hotline** giving daily updates on the areas and times of peak foliage (see section 1, "When to Go," in chapter 3). Use them; Mother Nature is notoriously crafty about the timing, intensity, and location of the best leaves year-to-year. Get a map and a good highlighter; mark it up, and give it to your co-pilot.
2. **Find a secret spot.** Check local magazines such as *Yankee, Vermont Life,* and *Down East;* check the travel section in big regional newspapers such as the *Boston Globe* or the *Rutland Herald.* Ask a local at the diner over doughnuts. Whatever it takes.
3. **See the leaves at a less-trafficked time,** if at all possible. First and foremost, **come midweek** if you can; traffic is considerably worse on Saturday and Sunday. Otherwise, try to see the foliage very late in the afternoon or early in the morning. (The light of early morning and near-sunset is great for showing the lovely colors of the leaves.) Early Sunday mornings are the lowest-traffic times in New England—folks are at church, you see—so that's an option. But setting

Park," for all the attention and cash that family has lavished on it. (Yes, Rockefeller money also built the faux-historic Woodstock Inn and paid to bury unsightly utility lines around town to preserve its character.)

The village, on the banks of the gently flowing Ottaquechee River, was first settled in 1765 and rose to prominence as a publishing center at one time: No fewer than *five* newspapers were being published in this tiny town in 1830. It soon began to attract wealthy families seeking cool solace from the big city summers. To this day, Woodstock feels as though it should have a prestigious prep school right off the green, and it comes as a real surprise that it doesn't. A Vermont senator, in the late 19th century, said "the good people of Woodstock have less incentive than others to yearn for heaven," and that still (partly) applies today.

The town is also a center for winter outdoor recreation. In fact, the very first ski tow (a rope tow powered by, yes, an old Buick motor) in the U.S. was built in 1933 at the Woodstock Ski Hill near the present-day Suicide Six ski area. There are no huge mountains hereabouts, and maybe that's why this is no longer the center of Vermont's skiing universe (I guess Stowe is)—but that's actually a good thing. Low-key Woodstock is getting more upscale, no doubt about it, but it remains one of my 10 favorite small towns out on a Saturday or, especially, Sunday afternoon in peak season is asking for a trip on Highway Pokealong. Try to avoid it.

4. Once you've selected your route and travel dates, **do not creep** along the road 20 miles below the prevailing speed limit so that you can get the best digital camera shots without stopping. There *will* be people behind you. A lot of people. Find a turnout, viewpoint, or parking lot off the road. This is particularly important for those driving an RV.
5. **Do not inch over** to the side of the road into the guard rails in an area where there's no pullout, necessitating a squeeze-by of two lanes of traffic. Find a real pullout. State officials helpfully provide these for you (sometimes); at other times, wait until you find a spot where the breakdown lane is actually the width of your car, and hit the hazards.
6. My super-secret tip for avoiding traffic jams? **Rent a bike** or strap on hiking shoes. If you're physically able, you've suddenly got access to tons of scenic back roads and mountain paths, as well as leaf-route handbooks written by the diehards who make up local bike and hiking clubs. And you won't find much, or any, auto traffic on these routes. To start, contact the local hiking club (the Appalachian Mountain Club and Long Trail are two; see section 9, "Special Interest Trips & Tours," in chapter 3) or the local bike shop.
7. ***Do not* say** "We're leaf-peepers!!" when questioned about your reasons for visiting. Is any explanation necessary here?
8. ***Do* eat local pie.** Again, no explanation is necessary. New England villages and diners are famous for their pies, and pie (preferably apple, but blueberry and pumpkin will do) just tastes better in front of great foliage. A scoop of vanilla or maple ice cream won't hurt, either.

in New England: a great place in summer, winter, or fall to hike, bike, skate, cross-country ski, snowshoe, or simply window-shop or leaf-peep.

Speaking of leaves, Woodstock's excellent state of preservation and outstanding local foliage haven't gone unnoticed. The secret is out, and this place draws hordes of travelers during peak foliage season (usually early to mid-Oct). During that time, the town green is practically obscured by the tour buses continually circling it and parking illegally around it. Ideally, that's when you will want to come; just don't expect quiet and peaceful streets when you get here.

Essentials

GETTING THERE Woodstock is located 13 miles west of White River Junction on Route 4 (take exit 1 off I-89). It's about 20 miles due east of Killington and Rutland, also via Route 4.

VISITOR INFORMATION The **Woodstock Area Chamber of Commerce,** 18 Central St. (© **888/496-6378** or 802/457-3555; www.woodstockvt.com), staffs a helpful information booth on the green, open daily from June through October. If you can't make it there (but you can, really), the chamber's website is a great quick reference to all the key local sights, eats, and inns—with hyperlinks. (If you don't know what a hyperlink is, go to the green.)

Exploring the Town

The heart of the town is the shady, elliptical **Woodstock Green.** The famous Admiral George Dewey spent his later years in Woodstock, and some local wags might try to convince you that the green was laid out in the shape of Dewey's flagship. This seems like a plausible explanation for the cigar-shaped green—but it's false. The green was already here—and shaped that way—in 1830, 7 years before Dewey was born. Oh well. Maybe it clinched his decision to move here.

Anyway, you can learn much more about local history by wandering into the **Woodstock Historical Society** ★ (✆ **802/457-1822;** www.woodstockhistorical.com) at 26 Elm St. Housed in the 1807 **Charles Dana House,** this beautiful home has rooms furnished in Federal, Empire, and Victorian styles, and has displays of dolls, costumes, and early silver and glass. The Dana House museum and adjoining buildings with more exhibits are open to the public, but only from late June through the end of October and only Friday to Sunday, noon to 4pm. Admission is $5 to the Dana House (which includes tours on the hour), or $3 to view only the gallery and barns sections, which are open the same dates but only until 3pm.

Billings Farm and Museum ★★★ Kids This remarkable working farm offers a striking glimpse into a grander era when Vermont was still Rockwellian—as well as an introduction to the oddly interesting history of scientific farming. This farm museum was the creation of Frederick Billings, a native Vermonter who was credited with completing the Northern Pacific Railroad. (Billings, Montana, is named after him.) Billings returned home to create a managed forest along the principles of the pioneering ecologist George Perkins Marsh, who was born right here in Woodstock and once lived on this estate. As a 19th-century dairy farm, it was renowned for its scientific breeding of Jersey cows (and also its fine architecture, particularly its gabled 1890 Victorian farmhouse). A tour includes hands-on demonstrations of farm activities, exhibits of farm life, a look at an heirloom kitchen garden, and a visit to active milking barns. Programs for kids include wagon rides, preschool activities, and sleigh rides; there are also many holiday events. Since they're so close to each other, adults would do well to buy the 2-day combination ticket granting admission to the farm and the national historic park (see below).

River Rd. (approx. a half-mile north of town on Rte. 12; P.O. Box 489), Woodstock. ✆ **802/457-2355.** www.billingsfarm.org. Admission $12 adults, $11 seniors, $6 children 5–15, $3 children 3–4, free for children 2 and under; combination ticket with national historic park $17 adults, $13 seniors. May–Oct, Sat–Sun of Thanksgiving weekend, and Christmas week daily 10am–5pm; rest of year Sat–Sun 10am–5pm.

Marsh-Billings-Rockefeller National Historic Park ★★★ Billings Farm and the National Park Service have teamed up to manage this newer park, the first and only national park focused on the history of conservation. It's more or less right across the street from the Billings Farm (see above), and is closely related. Here you'll learn more about the life of George Perkins Marsh, the author of *Man and Nature* (1864), one of the first and most influential books in the history of the environmental movement. You'll also learn more about how Woodstock native/rail tycoon Frederick Billings, who read *Man and Nature,* eventually returned and purchased Marsh's boyhood farm, putting into practice many of the principles of stewardship Marsh espoused. The property was later purchased by Mary and Laurance Rockefeller, who in 1982 established the nonprofit farm; a decade later, they donated more than 500 acres of forest land and their elaborate

Fun Facts Glory Road

When visiting Woodstock, history buffs might also want to take a walk across the river to the historic **River Street Cemetery.** The gravestones here include the final resting places of 11 African-American veterans of the 54th Massachusetts Volunteer Infantry—the first known African-American fighting unit in American history, and the Civil War regiment immortalized in the 1989 Hollywood film *Glory* (for which actor Denzel Washington won an Academy Award). You reach this little burial ground by strolling down River Street (cross the covered bridge and turn right) 1 block to the cemetery on the left.

Victorian mansion, filled with exceptional 19th-century landscape art, to the Park Service. Visitors can tour the mansion, walk the graceful carriage roads surrounding Mount Tom, and view one of the oldest professionally managed woodlands in the nation. Mansion tours accommodate only 12 people at a time, so advance reservations are highly recommended; check in at the visitor center, located inside a carriage barn, to reserve one (or call ahead).

54 Elm St. (P.O. Box 178), Woodstock. ✆ **802/457-3368.** www.nps.gov/mabi. Free admission to grounds; mansion tour $8 adults, $4 seniors, free for children 15 and under; combination ticket with Billings Farm $16 adults, $12 seniors, $15 children 16–17. Late May–Oct daily 10am–5pm.

A Side Trip to Quechee

About 5 miles east of Woodstock is the riverside village of **Quechee** ★ (*kwee*-chee). The town once revolved spiritually and economically around the mills on the local waterfalls; today, the mill building is home to **Simon Pearce Glass** ★★ (✆ **800/774-5277** or 802/295-2711), at 1760 Main St. Inside the former Downer's Mill, Pearce makes and sells fine glassware and pottery—the complex houses his glassmaking operation, retail store, and well-regarded restaurant (see "Where to Dine," below). Visitors can watch glassblowing here daily from a downstairs viewing gallery, and potting on the weekends. The store is open daily until 9pm.

Birders and other wildlife aficionados will enjoy a trip to the **Vermont Nature Center** ★ (✆ **802/359-5000**), at 6565 Woodstock Rd. (which is Rte. 4). The center began life as a rescue center for two dozen species of birds of prey that had been injured and could no longer survive in the wild: bald eagles, great horned owls, peregrine falcons, saw-whet owls, and an array of hawks. But the center has now expanded to an all-purpose nature center, with programs on animal behavior and natural phenomena throughout the year. From May through October, it's open daily from 10am to 5pm; the rest of the year, it's open shorter hours (generally Wed–Sun 10am–4pm, but check ahead). Admission is $10 for adults, $9 for seniors, and $8 for children ages 3 to 18.

There's also a kitschy, touristy attraction just outside the village on Route 4, **Quechee Gorge;** for more on that, see "Hole-y Cow! A Visit to Quechee Gorge" on p. 128.

Outdoor Pursuits

BIKING The rolling, hilly terrain around Woodstock is ideal for exploring by road bike for those in reasonably good shape. Most roads lead to great bike rides; just grab a good map and go. Need a rental? Some inns rent bikes, but anyone can stroll into **Start House Ski & Bike** (✆ **802/457-3377;** www.thestarthouseskiandbike.com), at 28 Central St.,

Tips Hole-y Cow! A Visit to Quechee Gorge

Five miles east of town, Route 4 crosses **Quechee Gorge,** which has reliably sucked in bus- and carloads of tourists for decades. (Yes, me too; I remember going there as a child.) The sheer power of the glacial runoff that carved the 165-foot-deep gorge perhaps 13,000 years ago must have been awesome. Equally impressive, though, is the engineering that took place over the chasm afterward. The gorge was first spanned in 1875 by a wooden rail trestle; the current steel bridge was constructed in 1911, also for the railroad; and then the tracks were torn up in 1933 and replaced by Route 4.

The best view is from the bottom of the gorge, accessible via a well-graded gravel path that descends south from the parking area on the gorge's eastern rim. A round-trip walk on this path should take no more than 45 minutes. If you're just planning to snap some quick pics from up top and move along, resist the macho temptation to climb over the protective fencing separating you from the edge. (Trust me, people do.) It's there for a reason.

which stocks a wide range of rides for hire and will also advise you on lovely local trips, such as one along pretty River Road.

HIKING **Mount Tom** ★★ is the prominent hill overlooking Woodstock, and its low summit has great views over the village and to the Green Mountains. It's part of the Marsh-Billings-Rockefeller National Historic Park, but you can ascend the mountain right from the village: Start at **Faulkner Park** ★★, a town-owned park named after Mrs. Edward Faulkner, who had the oddly zigzagging trail up the mountain built to encourage locals to exercise. To reach the trail head from the green, cross the Middle Covered Bridge (visible from the green) and continue straight ahead on Mountain Avenue. The road bends left and soon arrives at the grassy park; from here, it's less than an hour to the summit.

The trail winds uphill gradually, employing one of the most slowly climbing sets of switchbacks you'll ever see. Designed after once-popular "cardiac walks" in Europe, this trail makes hikers feel as if they are walking miles, only to gain a few feet in elevation. But at least you'll keep your heart rate down. The gentle trail eventually arrives at a clearing overlooking town, good for a rest and some photos. From here, a steeper, rockier, more demanding trail continues about 300 more feet up to the summit. From the top, you can follow a carriage path down to Billings Farm or retrace your steps back to the park and village.

HORSEBACK RIDING Experienced and aspiring equestrians head to the **Kedron Valley Stables** ★ (© **800/225-6301** or 802/457-1480; www.kedron.com), about 4½ miles south of Woodstock on Route 106. A full menu of riding options is available, from 1-hour beginners' lessons (about $50) to a 5-night inn-to-inn excursion (in the past, about $1,600 per person, including all meals and lodging; call for current pricing). The stables also rent out horses to experienced riders for local trail rides; offer seasonal **sleigh and carriage rides** ★; and maintain an indoor riding ring for inclement weather. In spring there's a maple syrup operation here as well. Kedron Valley is open daily except on Thanksgiving and Christmas—but credit cards aren't accepted.

SKIING The area's best cross-country skiing is at the Woodstock Inn & Resort's **Nordic Center** ★★ (✆ **802/457-6674;** www.woodstockinn.com), at the Woodstock Country Club, just south of the village center on Route 106. The center maintains about 38 miles of trails in two trail networks. It's not all flat, either; the high and low points along the trail system vary by some 750 feet in elevation. The ski center has a lounge and restaurant, as well as a large health and fitness center accessible via the ski trail. Lessons and tours are available. Skiing here is free if you're a Woodstock Inn guest; it costs $16 per day for nonguests (discounts for youths and half-day tickets). Skis and snowshoes can be rented on site, and there's a small discount for inn guests on the rental fees.

The ski hill **Suicide Six** ★ (✆ **802/457-6661;** http://suicide6.com) has an intimidating name, but at just 650 vertical feet, it doesn't pose much of a threat to either life or limb. Owned and operated by the Woodstock Inn (just like the Nordic Center), this family-oriented ski resort (which opened in 1934 using a gas-powered rope tow) has a couple of double chairs, a J-bar for beginners, two dozen lifts, and a modern base lodge. Beginners, intermediates, and families with young children alike will be content here; expert skiers won't. Again, inn guests always ski free—a big boon if you're staying there. For all others, lift tickets cost $38 to $57 for adults, with discounts for seniors and youths. It's located about 2 miles north of the village, on Pomfret Road (take Rte. 12 north past the Billings Farm and Museum, and bear right).

If you need a rental and won't be staying at the inn, or just want to shop around competitively for prices, also check out **Start House Ski & Bike** (✆ **802/457-3377**). It's right in the heart of the downtown at 28 Central St.

Where to Stay

Kedron Valley Inn ★★ (Kids) You might recognize this inn, one of Vermont's oldest, even if you've never been here: For years, it was featured in the background of Budweiser's Christmas TV commercials (the ones with Clydesdales stomping bravely through the snow). In a complex of Greek Revival buildings at a tiny crossroads 5 miles south of Woodstock, guests rooms are beautifully furnished in antiques, reproductions, poster beds, and heirloom quilts; about three-quarters have wood-burning fireplaces, and a few even have Jacuzzis. Rooms in the newer, motel-like log building by the river are less expensive, with canopied beds, custom oak woodwork, and solid fireplaces; one (a simple

> **Tips** **Beer Here Now!**
>
> In Bridgewater Corners, a little crossroads a few miles west of Woodstock on Route 4—near the junction of Route 4 with Route 100A—sits the brewery that is headquarters to the **Long Trail Brewing Co.** (✆ **802/672-5011;** www.longtrail.com). The company's easy-to-drink ales are renowned throughout the region, and if you visit you'll learn why.
>
> Self-guided tours of the brewery are offered daily, but even if you don't have time for that, drop by anyway for free samples of the current seasonal brews (ask the bartender to set you up); nosh on a basket of free popcorn; buy a six-pack or T-shirt at the small gift shop; or hunker down for some burgers and beer on the patio, with its woodsy views. The surrounding hillsides are beautiful in autumn and winter.

two-level suite) even has a private streamside terrace and kitchenette. Unit nos. 12 and 17 in the main house, both suites reached via stairs, are among the most popular, as both have lovely period fireplaces and double Jacuzzis. There are two dining spaces, a formal dining room and a tavern, and the inn's own spring-fed pond features a sandy beach, toys for kids, and a lifeguard.

10671 South Rd. (Rte. 106), South Woodstock, VT 05071. ✆ **800/836-1193** or 802/457-1473. Fax 802/457-4469. www.kedronvalleyinn.com. 26 units. $155–$195 double, $195–$245 suite; foliage season and Christmas week $195–$315 double, $370 suite. Rates include breakfast. AE, MC, V. Closed Apr and briefly prior to Thanksgiving. Pets $15 per night. **Amenities:** Restaurant; pub; swimming pond; Wi-Fi (in public rooms; free). *In room:* A/C, TV, fridge (some units), kitchenette (1 unit), no phone.

The Shire Riverview Motel ★ **Value** The convenient Shire Motel is within walking distance of the green and the rest of the village, and with its attractive Colonial decor, it's *far* better appointed than your average motel; this is no Motel 6. Rooms are bright and have more windows than you might expect, most facing the river that runs behind and far below the property. At the end of the second-floor porch there's a veranda where you can sit on rockers overlooking the amazing view and enjoy a cup of coffee. You pay more for rooms with a similar river view; luxury-level rooms add amenities like porches, Jacuzzis, or more antique furniture. No, it's not a luxury inn—walls, plumbing, and linens won't be brand new or top-quality. But for a motel, this place offers incredible views and is both friendly and decently priced.

46 Pleasant St., Woodstock, VT 05091. ✆ **802/457-2211.** www.shiremotel.com. 42 units. $88–$228 double; foliage season rates higher. AE, MC, V. *In room:* A/C, TV, fridge, Wi-Fi (free).

Woodstock Inn & Resort ★★★ This is possibly central Vermont's best full-scale resort. In a rambling brick building right beside the town green, this inn appears to be a venerable and long-established institution with its valet parking and apparently antique look. But it's not: It opened in 1969 (backed by Rockefeller money), though it looks centuries older and fits Woodstock like a glove. Inside, guests are greeted by a broad stone fireplace, the appealing smell of wood smoke, plenty of exposed woods, and sitting areas tucked throughout the giant open lobby. Guest rooms are tastefully decorated in country pine or a Shaker-inspired style—the best units, in the newer wing (built in 1991), have plush carpeting, refrigerators, and fireplaces. In recent years the inn has angled for a more contemporary look and younger clientele; most units have recently been refitted with new king size bedding and added amenities like high-speed Internet in all rooms. One huge bonus here is that all guests get *free* use of the inn's downhill and **cross-country ski facilities,** all nearby (free shuttle), with discounts for golf at the golf course. The fitness center has squash courts, racquetball, and steam room, though I've found the inn's dining experiences middling. That's okay; you'll love it here anyway.

14 The Green, Woodstock, VT 05091. ✆ **800/448-7900** or 802/457-1100. Fax 802/457-6699. www.woodstockinn.com. 141 units. $149–$434 double; $360–$664 suite. 2-night minimum stay Sat–Sun. AE, MC, V. **Amenities:** 2 restaurants; bar; babysitting; bikes; concierge; golf course; putting green; health club; indoor and outdoor pools; room service; 12 tennis courts. *In room:* A/C, TV, fridge (some units), hair dryer, Wi-Fi (free).

The Woodstocker Inn B&B ★★ **Finds** At the foot of Mount Tom, this 1830-built inn—so yellow it's impossible to miss—is owned by two Brits who display mighty fine hospitality and win awards for it. They also continue to do amazing renovations, including some of the best bathroom fixtures I've ever seen in a B&B. (Half the fun is figuring out how to work the various taps and contraptions.) Throughout, the lovely original pine floors are exposed, and everything is spotless. The romantic bathroom in the Westminster unit features cast-iron claw-foot tubs, side by side beneath a skylight; while the Richmond suite's big recliners face a Bose home-theater system, and its bathroom sports a jetted tub and double-nozzled shower. A library, a back garden, and baskets of complimentary chocolate bars add to the comfort level, while breakfasts are a high point: Expect homemade or locally sourced yogurt, muesli, compote, sausage, bacon, and tomatoes, served in a breakfast room sporting a new woodstove and doors opening onto a patio. The inn is powered by "green" fuel and fitted in organic duvets, recycled-paper tissues, energy-efficient lighting and appliances, and natural bath products. One of my favorites.

61 River St., Woodstock, VT 05091. ✆ **802/457-3896.** Fax 802/457-3897. www.woodstockervt.com. 9 units. $130–$395 double. Rates include full breakfast. MC, V. Children not allowed. *In room:* A/C, TV, hair dryer, no phone, Wi-Fi (free).

Where to Dine

In addition to the choices listed below, you can pick up provisions downtown at the **Village Butcher Shop** (✆ **802/457-2756**), at 18 Elm St. (right beside the Gillingham & Sons general store). Staff here make up big picnic sandwiches and good homemade desserts, and they're open from 7am 'til 6pm daily. **Woodstock Coffee & Tea** ★ (✆ **802/457-9268;** www.woodstockcoffeeandtea.com), nearby at 43 Central St., is a friendly, laid-back coffeehouse right beside the rushing river with coffee, chai, teas, hot cider, and inventive coffee drinks. (Try a Café Hawaiian if you like coconut milk.)

An even better, if pricier, place to grab food on the go is at the **Woodstock Farmers' Market** ★ (✆ **802/457-3658;** www.woodstockfarmersmarket.com), a mile west of the Woodstocker B&B on Route 4. It's not a roving outdoor market, as you might think, but rather a full-blown gourmet emporium under a roof with outstanding selections of artisanal cheese, ice creams, chocolate, wines, and the like. There's also a deli and plenty of local and organic produce. The market is open daily except Monday, but closes by 7pm (6pm on Sun).

You can grab a quick bite of a different sort right beside Queechee Gorge (see "Hole-y Cow! A Visit to Quechee Gorge," above) in Queechee at the **Farmers Diner,** 5573 Woodstock Rd. (✆ **802/295-4600;** www.farmersdiner.com). The diner serves blue-plate specials, using ingredients mostly from local Vermont farmers.

For upscale fare, in addition to the choices listed below, **Osteria Pane e Salute** (✆ **802/457-4882;** www.osteriapaneesalute.com), upstairs at 61 Central St., has won awards but cut back on its hours—such is life in rural Vermont. From Thursday through Sunday night, though, it serves glasses of wine and the best Italian food in these parts; try to book ahead if you can, either in the wine bar or the dining room.

Bentley's AMERICAN Bentley's is literally and spiritually at the center of town, and it sometimes feels like the *only* dining choice in town at midday or after 9 o'clock at night. The dining room, on two levels and beyond an England-feeling bar (except for the Red Sox on the tube), affects a Victorian elegance. The kitchen here never dazzles you, though. Expect burgers and big sandwiches for lunch, while the dinner menu is more refined, leaning toward chicken, shrimp, steaks, and the like. The monster-size chicken quesadillas are decent (if you skip the guacamole); the Caesar salads, not so much. Steak or salad are probably safe picks. It's often very crowded here at night both at the bar and in the dining room, when it becomes the closest thing Woodstock has to a "scene." Try to reserve a table if you'll be coming on a weekend night.

3 Elm St. ✆ **877/457-3232** or 802/457-3232. www.bentleysrestaurant.com. Reservations recommended for parties of 4 or more. Main courses $10–$15 at lunch, $8–$26 at dinner. AE, DC, DISC, MC, V. Mon–Thurs 11:30am–9:30pm; Fri–Sat 11am–10pm; Sun 11am–9pm. Later for cocktails and dancing on weekends.

The Prince and the Pauper ★★ NEW AMERICAN It takes a bit of sleuthing to find this spot, down Dana Alley (next to the Woodstock Historical Society's Dana House), but it's worth the effort. This is one of Woodstock's best meals, in an intimate but surprisingly informal setting. Start with a drink in the taproom, then move over to the rustic but elegant little dining room. The a la carte menu features grilled sirloin with garlic-herb butter and fries, sesame-crusted seared salmon with a Thai ginger sauce, roasted chicken with shiitake-Madeira wine sauce, panko-coated Jonah crab cakes, and smoked baby back ribs with coleslaw. But the prix-fixe menu, available daily except Saturdays and holidays, is even better. You might begin with Maine smoked salmon on toast, lobster ravioli, goat cheese soufflé, or French onion soup spiked with Vermont apple cider, then move on to five-spiced duck, boneless rack of lamb baked in puff pastry, grilled ahi tuna, or a piece of potato-encrusted Arctic char. There's also an inexpensive choice of gourmet hearth-baked pizzas, as well. Everything's good here, and it's a fairly unique venue: unfancy, yet fancy-feeling.

24 Elm St. ✆ **802/457-1818.** www.princeandpauper.com. Reservations recommended. Bistro main courses $18–$23, prix-fixe dinners $48. AE, DISC, MC, V. Sun–Thurs 6–9pm; Fri–Sat 6–9:30pm. Lounge opens at 5pm.

Simon Pearce Restaurant ★★ NEW AMERICAN The setting here can't be beat. Housed in a restored 19th-century woolen mill with wonderful views of a waterfall, Simon Pearce is a collage of exposed brick, pine floorboards, and handsome wooden tables and chairs. Meals are served on Simon Pearce pottery and glassware—if you like your place setting, you can buy it afterward at the sprawling retail shop in the mill. The atmosphere is a good mix of formal and informal. Chef Josh Duda's lunch menus include curried chicken salads, beef and Guinness stew, lamb burgers, shepherd's pie, a Maine lobster club sandwich, and crispy calamari with field greens. At dinner look for entrees like horseradish-crusted blue cod with crisped leeks, pan-seared salmon with Japanese vegetables and citrus-miso sauce, grilled top sirloin with Yukon gold potatoes, or roasted chicken with ancho chilies. For dessert? I've seen bittersweet chocolate pudding cake with a cappuccino semifreddo, roasted-apple tarts, blackberry cobbler, and a walnut meringue on the menu—with Vermont organic ice cream and Quechee-made sorbet for backup.

1760 Main St. (inside the Mill), Quechee. ✆ **802/295-1470.** www.simonpearce.com. Reservations recommended for dinner (not accepted for lunch). Main courses $13–$17 at lunch, $22–$30 at dinner. AE, DC, DISC, MC, V. Daily 11:30am–9pm.

WHITE RIVER JUNCTION, WINDSOR & NORWICH

White River Junction is a Vermont rarity: an industrial-era town that was built on the fruits of industry, not on farmlands, dairy fields, or stone quarries. Industry, in this case, was a railroad. How dramatically did the iron horse change things? Well, in 1847 the place consisted of just a single farmhouse; by 1862, however, five different rail lines had built terminals here and the town was bustling, noisy, and full of grit and commerce. Trains have suffered a well-documented decline since that golden era, and White River slipped from prominence right along with them; when the mighty steam trains and the lonesome whistle shut down, so did this town. Ever since, it has struggled to get back to its feet.

A half-hour or so south of White River down I-91, **Windsor** is rightfully considered the birthplace of Vermont. It was here that the treaty separating the state from Massachusetts was drafted and signed, and the town today celebrates both its industrial heritage (which was considerable, at one time) and a new wave of fresh artistic blood.

Just to the north of White River, **Norwich** is a peaceful New England farm town slightly off the beaten track—a farm town in transition. The town has a fine selection of wood-frame and brick homes, and boasts a superb restaurant and a science museum for kids. First settled in 1761, Norwich has long-established ties with **Hanover, New Hampshire,** across the river. Many Dartmouth College faculty and staff still commute to work from Norwich, and the two towns even share a school district.

Essentials

GETTING THERE White River Junction is easily reached via either I-89 or I-91, which converge just south of town. Norwich can be reached from exit 13 on I-91, or by driving north from White River Junction on Route 5.

White River is served by one daily **Amtrak** (✆ **800/872-7245;** www.amtrak.com) train from New York City, an inexpensive trip of just $48 one-way—though it takes 7 hours to make the trip. The bus ride on **Greyhound** (✆ **800/231-2222;** www.greyhound.com) from New York costs about $10 more than the train, and takes up to 90 minutes longer.

VISITOR INFORMATION The **Upper Valley Regional Chamber of Commerce** (✆ **802/295-6200;** www.uppervalleychamber.com) staffs an information center near the railroad station in downtown White River Junction. It's open daily during summer and foliage season (but only until 4:30pm), and shorter hours (or closed) during the off season. Call the chamber for more information if you expect to be heading here.

Exploring the Region

White River Junction's compact downtown is clustered near the river and a confusion of old train tracks. It's easy to get a glimpse of the town's history with a brief excursion on foot or by car. This downtown was never particularly cheerful or quaint—the bustle of rail yards has always overpowered it—but it manages to retain a rugged charm in the face of strip-mall sprawl that keeps expanding along the ridge above town. With an exception or two, though, downtown rolls up its sidewalk at dusk. There's no museum, but a monument of sorts to White River's rail heritage can be found near the Amtrak station (built in 1911), where an 1892 Boston & Maine locomotive, along with a caboose, are on display.

A few miles south of White River Junction is the historic town of **Windsor** ★. Asahel Hubbard put Windsor on the map in the early 19th century when he moved here from Connecticut and invented the hydraulic pump. Other ingenious inventions followed, not only from Hubbard but also from his relatives and inspired Windsor residents: the coffee percolator, the underhammer rifle, the lubricating bullet, and an early variant of the sewing machine, among others.

Learn about this fascinating period in American history at the **American Precision Museum** ★, 196 Main St. (✆ **802/674-5781;** www.americanprecision.org). Its collections commemorate Windsor's role as birthplace of the state's machine-tool industry, and home to countless inventors and inventions. The museum has large, dark, and heavy machinery, and looks closely at the technology behind the Industrial Revolution. It's located in the 1846 Robbins and Lawrence Armory (itself a historic site), and opens from

Memorial Day through the end of October, daily 10am to 5pm. Admission is $6 for adults, $4 for students, and free for children 5 and under. Entire families can enter for $18.

On Route 5 a few miles north of Windsor sits the **Windsor Industrial Park,** which is more interesting than it sounds. The focus here is on local crafts, and it's the home of some of **Simon Pearce's** manufacturing (of pottery and glass) operations.

There's crafting of another kind going on, as well, at the brewery owned by Boston-based **Harpoon Brewery** ★ (✆ **888/HARPOON** [427-7666] or 802/674-5491; www.harpoonbrewery.com). The brewery was originally built by Catamount Brewing, one of the first of the Vermont microbreweries, and Harpoon bought it in 2000; both Harpoon and Catamount beers are now produced here. The **free brewery tour,** Fridays and Saturdays only at 3pm (tour limited to first 30 people who show up), provides a quick education in the making of a fine beer plus samples of beers with names like UFO Hefeweizen. There's also a beer garden where you can eat sandwiches and bratwurst and sample more beers (though not for free). The store and beer garden close Mondays from November through April; the tours run year-round, through rain or sleet or snow or hail—just not on national holidays or during the brewery's 2-day Oktoberfest.

Also in Windsor is the new **Cornish Colony Museum** ★ (✆ **802/674-6008;** www.cornishcolonymuseum.org), commemorating the artists' colony that once thrived a short hop across the Connecticut River. (Cornish is home to the lovely **Saint-Gaudens National Historic Site;** p. 233). This museum focuses not only on the work of Augustus Saint-Gaudens, but also on the paintings of Maxfield and Stephen Parrish, among other artists affiliated with the colony. It's located inside the old firehouse at 147 Main St. in Windsor, and opens Tuesday to Saturday from 10am to 5pm and Sunday from noon until 5pm. In winter the museum opens from 10am to 4pm, Thursday through Sunday.

Finally, just outside Norwich—on the east side of Route 5 S.—are the interesting headquarters, bakery, and baking school run by the esteemed **King Arthur Flour** company, which makes some of the best baking flours in America. **The Baker's Store** ★ (✆ **802/649-3361** or 800/827-6836) is open Monday through Saturday until 6pm and Sunday until 4pm. In addition to its all-natural breads and a useful ongoing program of baking demonstrations and classes here, there's also a good supply of high-quality cookware for sale.

Fun for Kids

Montshire Museum of Science ★★ Kids The Montshire is a modern, attractive, hands-on place that draws kids (and parents) back for repeat visits. The museum is situated on a beautiful hundred-acre property sandwiched between the interstate and the Connecticut River (yet it's within walking distance of downtown Hanover). Exhibits are housed in an open, soaring structure inspired by local barns; there are both live animals and interactive exhibits that teach math and science on the sly while answering children's questions. Ever wonder how the air moves, makes sand dunes, and keeps planes in the sky? You'll find out. There's a special play area for the very young, with aquariums and bubble-making exhibits; outside, a science park masquerades as a playground, and nature trails wend through a riverside property of tall trees and chirpy birds. Special exhibits have included a series of shows entitled "Dinosaur Days"—featuring you-know-who.

1 Montshire Rd., Norwich. ✆ **802/649-2200.** www.montshire.org. $12 adults, $10 children 2–17, free for children 1 and under; special exhibits $2 additional. MC, V. Daily 10am–5pm. Take exit 13 off I-91 and head east; look for museum signs almost immediately.

Where to Stay

Thanks to its location at the crossroads of two interstates, White River Junction is home to several chain hotels near the highways. Your best bet is to cruise along Route 5, reached by exit 11 off I-91, and comparison-shop.

If you're craving a fine inn or bed-and-breakfast, you could also try Hanover, New Hampshire (p. 234), 2 minutes across the Connecticut River bridge from Norwich. On the other end of the spectrum, a small clutch of affordable motels clusters around the little airport and strip malls in West Lebanon, New Hampshire; see chapter 7 for details.

Juniper Hill Inn ★★ About 12 miles south of White River Junction in Windsor is this inviting retreat, set high atop a hill overlooking the Connecticut River Valley. The 1902 Colonial Revival manor home is a true period piece, more mannered and elegant than many similarly priced inns. Palladian windows, a slate roof, and six chimneys grace the exterior; the richly appointed great hall features coffered paneling. Common rooms are spacious and lovely—especially the library with its leather wingback chairs—and are reason enough to stay. Each of the 16 guest rooms is unique, but all feature thoughtful amenities. (Most have either wood-burning or propane fireplaces.) The lovely dining room is quietly romantic, with classical styling; dinner is served by reservation, with a day's advance notice requested, and guests rave about the straightforward offerings of steaks, lobster, lamb, and fish.

153 Pembroke Rd., Windsor, VT 05089. ✆ **800/359-2541** or 802/674-5273. Fax 802/674-2041. www.juniperhillinn.com. 16 units. $115–$285 double. Rates include full breakfast. 2-night minimum stay during foliage season, holiday weekends, and for fireplace rooms Sat–Sun. DISC, MC, V. Closed Apr and 2 weeks in early Nov. Dogs accepted in 3 units. Children 12 and over welcome. **Amenities:** Restaurant; outdoor pool. *In room:* A/C, CD player, hair dryer, no phone, Wi-Fi (some units; free).

Norwich Inn ★ Many of the rooms in this historic inn—parts of which date way back to 1797—are furnished with brass and canopy beds. History buffs should opt for one of the 16 comfortable rooms in the main inn, rather than those in the motel-style annex out back where rooms are less expensive. The main building is also allegedly host to one uninvited guest: the ghost of Mary Walker, who (according to local lore) must atone for her sin of selling bootleg liquor at the inn during Prohibition. Perhaps in her memory, the inn operates **Jasper Murdock's Alehouse,** probably one of America's tiniest breweries, which also serves some mighty good burgers. There's a dining room as well, where President James Monroe, while passing through on horseback, dined in 1817.

325 Main St. (P.O. Box 908), Norwich, VT 05055. ✆ **802/649-1143.** www.norwichinn.com. 27 units. $99–$239 double. Rates include continental breakfast. AE, DC, DISC, MC, V. Dogs allowed in motel section only. **Amenities:** Dining room; pub. *In room:* A/C, TV, hair dryer, Wi-Fi (free).

Where to Dine

The choices below are a good sampling of the wide spectrum of New England dining: from diner to fancy food.

However, there's much better hunting/grazing across the bridge in **Hanover, New Hampshire** (p. 238). There you'll find one of New England's best natural-foods stores (with plenty of picnic takeout meals); loads of coffee shops and pizza and ethnic restaurants catering to the local college students; and pubs, breweries, and fancy restaurants catering to those students' parents and professors.

Carpenter & Main ★★ FRENCH/FUSION It replaced another popular French restaurant in the same space, but Carpenter & Main hasn't settled for second-best; if anything, it upped the ante in the Upper Valley. The space here is divided into a tavern bistro section and then two more formal dining rooms. Main courses run to things like a steamed Maine lobster tail paired with one that's been deep-fried in bread crumbs (the whole mess served with Asian stir-fried veggies and plum sauce); three treatments of rabbit (braised, pan-seared, and cured as a pancetta); steaks of local Vermont-bred beef; or striped bass served with clams and vegetables. Veggie items like artichoke gnocchi and fettuccine with asparagus are also on the menu. Finish with a cheese plate, chocolate-caramel tart, ice-cream sundae, or panna cotta. The bistro menu is lighter and more Franco, with items such as pâté, escargots, frites, crisped duck confit, wine-steamed mussels, and changing daily specials. Of course there's a wine list here, and it's thankfully heavy (for once) on wines that are actually from France.

326 Main St., Norwich. ✆ **802/649-2922.** www.carpenterandmain.com. Reservations recommended for main dining room (not accepted for bistro). Main courses $18–$26. MC, V. Wed–Sun 5:30–10pm. Main dining room Wed–Sun 6–9pm.

Polka Dot Restaurant *Finds* DINER Places like this are disappearing fast. Classic diner fare is served up daily at this downtown White River diner, a relic of the day when railroad crews working the freight and passenger lines swarmed in for lunch. (Amtrak still makes a daily stop across the street.) The diner's interior is painted robin's-egg blue, the walls are hung with railroad photos and train models, and the locals on stools still talk Red Sox, even in winter. Get eggs and coffee at the counter, or relax in a booth and order old New England diner standards like liver and onions, burgers, fried fish platters, home fries, and tripe (yes, tripe). At breakfast, try the homemade doughnuts if they have some. This isn't your classic brushed-steel-diner-car, but the Dot has the food and atmosphere of one anyway.

N. Main St. (at Joe Reed Dr.), White River Junction. ✆ **802/295-9722.** Breakfast and lunch items $2–$5, dinner items $5–$8. No credit cards. Tues–Sun 5am–2:30pm.

5 KILLINGTON & RUTLAND

Killington: 12 miles E of Rutland; 160 miles NW of Boston; 93 miles SE of Burlington

In 1937 a travel writer described the village near Killington Peak as "a church and a few undistinguished houses." The rugged, remote area was isolated from Rutland by imposing mountains, and accessible only through the daunting Sherburne Pass.

But that was before Vermont's second-highest mountain was developed into the Northeast's largest ski area, and before a wide, 5-mile-long access road was slashed through the forest right up to the mountain's base. (It was also before Rte. 4 was widened and upgraded, improving access to Rutland considerably.) Today Route 4 is one of the most heavily traveled routes through the Green Mountains, and that writer would be hard-pressed to recognize this area today; a sea of condos, restaurants, and other tourist-related entities has moved in and taken possession of the pass.

So know this: **Killington** is plainly *not* the Vermont pictured on calendars and postcards. The region around the mountain boasts Vermont's most active winter scene, with loads of distractions both on and off the mountain. The area has a frenetic, where-it's-happening feel in winter. (That's *not* the case in summer, when the vast, empty parking lots trigger a mild, where-did-everybody-go panic, tempered by relief at the sinking prices of lodging.) The people happiest here are (a) skiers who like their skiing BIG; (b)

Tips **Commuting to Classic New England**

If you're in search of a classic New England experience while skiing Killington at the same time, consider staying in or around quaint **Woodstock** (p. 129) and commuting the 20 miles to and from the slopes. It's not a quick ride, but it's **scenic.** Or you can stay at one of the resorts tucked into the folds of other nearby mountains, such as the Mountain Top Inn in **Mendon** (p. 143).

singles in search of aggressive mingling on the mountain; and (c) travelers who want a wide choice of lodgings, eats, and fun stuff to do—and are willing to sacrifice a good portion of Vermont's usual charm in exchange for that.

About a dozen miles to the west, the city of **Rutland** lacks immediate charm, too. It's a working-class city with compact downtown, a rich history, and a wide array of convenient services for travelers—most of them arrayed along two cluttered edge-city strips that inch uncomfortably close to the city center, which is too bad. But the city is also home to a huge annual state fair each fall. If you like the action of Killington but not the prices, sleeping down here in the valley in Rutland and then driving 25 or 30 minutes up to the ski area in the morning—or taking the local shuttle bus there—will work just fine. If you don't mind waking up to zero scenery, that is.

KILLINGTON

Killington lacks a town center, a single place that makes you feel you've arrived, and perhaps it lacks a soul as well; Killington is, basically, "wherever you parked." This town is so tied to the ski hill that it actually renamed itself after the mountain and resort in 1999; before that, it had been called Sherburne.

Since the mountain was first developed for skiing in 1958, dozens of restaurants, hotels, and stores have sprouted up along **Killington Road** (which shoots off Rte. 4 at a sudden angle) to accommodate the legions of skiers who descend upon the area during the ski season, which typically runs from October well into May, and sometimes even into June. I'll be honest: I sort of detest Killington Road. I hate the way it looks physically—strung out, clear cut, unattractively landscaped—and the culinary offerings along its sides are very average at best. But this is the only access road in; it's a fact of life if you're skiing here. Learn to find the few diamonds in the rough.

The **ski area** itself is massive, stretching to encompass *seven* mountainsides, including Pico Peak. It's considered the biggest resort in the northeastern U.S., with plenty of everything—glade skiing, terrain parks, snowboarding pipes, gondola lifts, the longest mogul trail east of the Mississippi, and so on and so forth. The resort also maintains five **lodges** ★ (see "Lodging No Complaints: A Field Guide to Killington," below), which are the center of the action on-slope—these are actually much more fun than almost anything and everything on the access road, but you've obviously got to have a lift ticket to partake.

Until a proposed "village" concept comes more fully to life, Killington *is* its access road. Brightly lit and highly developed, there's nothing on it of the real Vermont. Suburban-style theme restaurants dot the road, plus dozens of hotels and condos ranging from fancy to not. Breeze through, picking your spots.

GETTING THERE **Killington Road,** the main access road to the mountain, extends southward off routes 4 and 100. (The point is still marked on some older road maps as "Sherburne.") This turnoff is about 10 or 12 miles (25 min.) east of Rutland, on your right. Coming from Woodstock to the east, on the other hand, the turnoff is about 20 miles west (40 min. driving time) via the same highway—but turn left.

Amtrak (✆ **800/872-7245;** www.amtrak.com) offers a daily service from New York City to Rutland (the **Ethan Allen**). The ride takes a shade under 6 hours and costs $65 one-way. From Rutland there are connecting shuttles to the mountain and various resorts—or you can call a taxi.

If you're staying in Rutland, the Marble Valley Regional Transit District (✆ **802/773-3244;** www.thebus.com) operates the **"Ski Bus"**—a very handy daily shuttle service between Rutland and Killington. The ride costs just $2 per person, one-way—and it's *free* for points along East Mountain Road, the other major road traversing some sections of the resort.

Some local hotels and inns also offer shuttles from tiny **Rutland airport,** from which **Cape Air (800/352-0714;** www.capeair.com) operates several daily flights to and from Boston's Logan International Airport.

VISITOR INFORMATION The **Killington Chamber of Commerce** (✆ **800/337-1928** or 802/773-4181; www.killingtonchamber.com) has information on lodging and travel packages, and staffs an information booth on Route 4 at the base of the access road; it's open weekdays from 9am to 5pm, shorter hours on weekends.

For information on accommodations in the area and travel to Killington, contact the resort's **lodging service** (✆ **800/621-6867**) directly.

Downhill Skiing

Killington ★★ A love-it or hate-it kind of place, New England's largest and most bustling ski area offers more vertical drop—and variety of experiences—than any other New England resort. It's certainly exciting here; you've got to give it that. You'll find a huge choice of slope types across the seven peaks here, from long, narrow, old-fashioned runs to killer moguls high on the mountains' flanks or tree-glade skiing. This is *the* Vermont choice of serious skiers. (That said, it's also the skiing equivalent of the Mall of America: a huge operation, run with efficiency and not much personality, where tickets and passes are referred to as "products.") It's easy for kids to get separated from friends and family, and the resort seems to attract boisterous packs of young adults, so families should stick to Ramshed (the family area) or head to another resort such as **Sugarbush** (p. 159), **Stowe** (p. 170), or **Suicide Six** (p. 129). But for a big-mountain experience, with lots of evening activities and plenty of challenging terrain, this is still a great choice—maybe Vermont's best. For more detail on the various ski lodges at Killington and which one is best for you, see "Lodging No Complaints: A Field Guide to Killington," below.

4763 Killington Rd., Killington, VT 05751. ✆ **800/621-6867** or 802/422-6200. www.killington.com. Adults $77–$82 day lift tickets; discounts for children and seniors.

Cross-Country Skiing

Nearest to the ski resort (just east of Killington Rd. on Rte. 100/4) is **Mountain Meadows Cross Country & Snow Shoe Area** ★ (✆ **802/775-7077** or 802/775-0166; www.xcskiing.net), with more than 35 miles of trails groomed for both skating and classic skiing. The trails are largely divided into three sections, with beginner trails closest to the

Lodging No Complaints: A Field Guide to Killington

The key to Killington is knowing its various personalities. The five lodges here each dispense slightly different food, fun, skis, and general atmosphere.

The **K-1 Lodge** ★★ is the most fun place for miles around, by far. It's the place to meet a partner, go on a ski date, and see the best views. Not only do you get up here (at 2,500 ft. of elev., not bad) via a zippy express gondola, but there also are plenty of skiing trail choices from here. Even better, food-wise, you can find anything from pizza to sushi to chicken wraps to trailside waffles. Or just grab an espresso on the go. Literally.

Snowshed Lodge is ground zero for adult skiing and snowboarding instruction. This is also where you rent equipment, or get it fixed if it breaks. Translation? You'll probably end up here at some point. There's an unimpressive food court, but also a pub with cold beers on draft.

Ramshead Lodge is the HQ of the kids' skiing and snowboarding schools, and it's also where you find the day care center. Dining options are kid-friendly, of course. This is the resort's most family-friendly section.

Bear Mountain is where extreme-skiing nuts come. There are terrain parks, a snowboarding Superpipe, and the Outerlimits—the longest (and steepest dropping) mogul trail in the East. If you're thinking about training for the Olympics, this is a good place to find out if you've got the right stuff. The deli has a deck overlooking some of the most rad sections.

Finally, the **Skyeship Lodge** has another fast gondola—this one in two stages—which goes up to Skye Peak. There is a true bar here, way up on the mountain, selling hot spiked drinks; no kidding. Otherwise the food options are somewhat limp.

lodge, an intermediate area a bit farther along, and an advanced 6-mile loop farthest away. Rentals and lessons are available at the lodge. For adults, a 1-day pass is $19, and a half-day (after 1pm) pass is $16. Kids ages 6 to 12 pay $8 per day, $6 per half-day.

The intricate network of trails at the **Mountain Top Nordic Ski & Snowshoe Center** ★★ (**© 802/483-6089;** www.mountaintopinn.com), part of the Mountain Top Inn (p. 143), has long had a loyal local following. (It was one of the first commercial cross-country ski facilities in the East.) The 35-mile trail network offers pastoral views through mixed terrain, most of it groomed for classic and skate skiing. Trails here are often deep with snow, owing to the inn's ridge-top position high in the hills. Adults pay $20 for 1-day trail passes, $16 for half-day passes (after noon). This is challenging and picturesque terrain.

Other Outdoor Pursuits

MOUNTAIN BIKING Mountain biking comes in two forms at Killington: barreling down the mountain, or exploring back roads on your own. Something like 45 miles of trails at the ski resort are opened to mountain biking, and one of the gondola lines (the K-1) is equipped to haul bikes and riders to the summit. After enjoying the great views, riders then give their forearms—rather than their thighs—a workout applying the brakes as they bump some 1,700 vertical feet back down the slopes. A trail pass is $14 for adults;

a trail pass plus two gondola rides up the mountain is $22; a trail pass plus *unlimited* gondola rides is $35 per day (go for that one). All these rates are heavily discounted for bikers age 12 and under.

Killington's **Mountain Bike Shop** (✆ **802/422-6232**) is located in the Base Lodge and is open from late June through mid-October. They do repairs, sell sports drinks, and rent bikes; adult rates start at $35 for 2 hours and run up to $49 for a full day, again discounted for junior riders. Helmets are required (small additional charge).

Bikes are also available for rent—along with sound advice on local trails—from **True Wheels Bike Shop** (✆ **877/487-9972** or 802/422-3234; www.truewheels.com), in the Basin Ski Shop near the top of Killington Road. Rentals range from around $45 a day for a low-end bike to around $65 for a bike with rock shocks and disc brakes (half-day rates also available; helmets are included). Reservations are helpful during holidays and busy times.

GOLF Vermont is loaded with fine golf courses, public and private, lovely in summer and outstandingly scenic in fall. The acknowledged top course is **Green Mountain National Golf Course** ★★★ (✆ **888/483-4653** or 802/422-4653; www.gmngc.com) on Route 100, about 3 miles north of the Route 100/Route 4 junction. Greens fees run from $59 to $69 per adult, not including the cost of a motorized cart (mandatory Fri–Sun and holidays). Discounts are available if you begin after 3pm. Rentals, instruction, and a driving range are also available.

HIKING Area hikers often set their sights on **Deer Leap Mountain** ★★ and its popular 3-hour loop to the summit and back. The trail begins at the Inn at Long Trail (see "Where to Stay," below), off Route 4 at Sherburne Pass. Park your car across from the inn, then head north through the inn's parking lot onto the Long Trail/Appalachian Trail and into the forest. Follow the white blazes (you'll return on the blue-blazed trail you see entering on the left). In about .5-mile, you arrive at a crossroads. Here the **Appalachian Trail** veers right and heads for New Hampshire's White Mountains and Mount Katahdin in Maine, while Vermont's **Long Trail** runs along the left fork.

Take the Long Trail. After some hiking through forest and rock slab for .5-mile or so, turn left at the signs for Deer Leap Height. Great views of Pico and the Killington area await you in less than another .5-mile. After a snack break, continue down the steep, blue-blazed descent back to Route 4 and your car. The entire round-trip is about 2.5 miles.

A Historic Site

President Calvin Coolidge State Historic Site ★★ Kids Even in death, the nation's most taciturn president didn't get much respect. But a trip to this historic site should restore Silent Cal's reputation once and for all among visitors, who'll get a strong sense of the man reared in this mountain village. The only president born on Independence Day, Coolidge was shaped by the strong sense of community and the harsh weather and isolation of his high upland valley. He's still a hero to Vermonters. The historic district consists of a group of about a dozen unspoiled buildings open to the public, plus a number of other private residences that can be observed from the outside only. Coolidge grew up here, and in August 1923 in his boyhood home—the Coolidge Homestead, open for tours—Vice President Coolidge was awakened and informed that President Warren Harding had died. His own father, a notary public, administered the presidential oath of office. Coolidge is buried in the cemetery across the road, where every July 4th a wreath is laid at his simple grave in a quiet ceremony. The bright foliage in the surrounding hills is another reason to visit here.

Moments **When Less Is More**

I've heard a story about former President Calvin Coolidge worth repeating; whether it's true or not, I just can't say. It goes like this: A young lady once walked up to the great man and told Silent Cal she had just bet her gal-pals that she could get the famously reticent Coolidge to say three words or more.

Coolidge: "You lose."

Now that's a Vermonter for you.

Also be sure to stop in at **Plymouth Artisan Cheese** (✆ **802/672-3650;** www.plymouthartisancheese.com), just uphill from the Coolidge Homestead. Founded in the late 1800s as a farmer's cooperative by Coolidge's father, this business was owned by the president's son until the late 1990s. The factory is open daily, on the same seasonal schedule as the historic site. It's free to tour.

3780 Rte. 100A, Plymouth. ✆ **802/672-3773.** Admission $7.50 adults, $2 children 6–14, $20 family. Late May to mid-Oct daily 9:30am–5pm.

Where to Stay

Skiers, especially families, headed to Killington for a week or so of skiing should consider the **condominium** option. A number of condo developments spill down the hillside and along the low ridges flanking the access road, varying in elegance, convenience, and size.

Among the complexes the resort owns and/or manages, **Highridge** features units with saunas, fireplaces, and two-person Jacuzzis, along with access to a compact health club; **Sunrise Village** is more remote, with a health club and easy access to the Bear Mountain lifts; **Fall Line** ★ is the luxury digs, with a private sports center (hot tub, indoor pool, exercise room), free Wi-Fi, washers/dryers, Jacuzzis, and killer views. Killington also manages condos at **Trail Creek, Pico Mountain,** and **Pinnacle.** Rates in these condos fluctuate widely, depending on luxury level, time of year, number of bedrooms, and number of days you plan to stay; obviously winter is the most expensive time, with foliage season right up there with it. You can score excellent deals in summer. Figure on winter prices starting around $120 per double unit (for a midweek, 5-day package, no lift ticket included) but quickly zooming upward from there for weekends, skiing, or extra-nice rooms. The condos can get expensive, but remember—in winter, some condo **rates include lift tickets.**

Talk to a representative at the **Killington Lodging Bureau** (✆ **800/621-6867;** www.killington.com), and check online for special deals. (Killington will also help you book a stay at area inns and motels that it does *not* own.)

There are also some moderate- and budget-priced motels and hotels as you ascend the mountain on **Route 4** from Rutland to Killington, some chain properties and some privately owned; these vary in quality, price, and experience, but are almost all uniformly bland.

Blueberry Hill Inn ★★ The simple, homey Blueberry Hill Inn, dating from 1813, lies in the heart of the Moosalamoo recreation area amid 180 acres of property, about 45 minutes northwest of Killington Resort—it's halfway to Middlebury. With superb hiking, biking, canoeing, swimming, and cross-country skiing all around, it's a good stop for those who enjoy the outdoors. An inn brochure put it like this: "We offer you no radios, no televisions, no bedside phones to disturb your vacation." There are also no Jacuzzis or fancy fireplaces (and quite a few double and twin beds), surprising given the (seasonally) high room rates. Instead, you get a clean room, solid construction, plenty of wood, and lots of Americana-themed quilts. The original inn building houses four units; an attached conservatory contains three loft-style rooms, all reached via stairs, and there are four more in a pondside 1987 addition plus one small, woody cottage. Family-style meals are served in a rustic dining room with a great stone fireplace and original wooden beams. The menu is Continental, with fusion touches—things like snapper cakes with guacamole and roasted free-range chicken. There's also a cross-country ski center on the property; a day pass is about $20.

1307 Goshen-Ripton Rd., Goshen, VT 05733. ✆ **800/448-0707** or 802/247-6735. Fax 802/247-3983. www.blueberryhillinn.com. 12 units. $129–$189 double; foliage and holiday season $322–$414 double. Rates include breakfast. MAP rates $100 additional. MC, V. **Amenities:** Babysitting; bikes; sauna; Wi-Fi (in public areas; free). *In room:* No phone.

Inn at Long Trail ★ Kids The Inn at Long Trail is situated in an architecturally undistinguished building (3 stories of beige), poised at an ecologically important crossroads: the intersection of the highway (Rte. 4) and the Long and Appalachian trails at the Sherburne Pass. It's also only a 10-minute drive from Killington's ski slopes. More importantly, the innkeepers get high marks for sustaining a rustic experience with real hospitality; young hikers and families seem to enjoy the place. This just feels like Vermont. The interior here is far more charming than the exterior: Tree trunks support beams in the lobby, which also sports log furniture and banisters carved from birch. The oldest rooms in the inn (built in 1938 as an annex to a long-gone lodge) are furnished simply, in ski-lodge style—but more modern suites with fireplaces, telephones, TVs, and (sometimes) Jacuzzis and fireplaces are housed in a motel-like annex. Go for those. The dining room is fun, with a stone ledge that pokes right through the wall from the mountain behind the inn; it serves straight-ahead family fare plus a kids' menu. There's also a pub.

709 Rte. 4, Killington, VT 05751. ✆ **800/325-2540** or 802/775-7181. Fax 802/747-7034. www.innatlongtrail.com. 19 units. Summer and fall $79–$110 double; foliage season and holiday weekends $195–$225. All rates include breakfast; foliage and holiday rates also include dinner. 2-night minimum stay weekends and during foliage season. AE, MC, V. Closed late Apr to late June. Pets allowed with prior permission. **Amenities:** Dining room; pub; Wi-Fi (in public areas; free). *In room:* TV (some units), no phone (some units).

Killington Grand Resort Hotel ★★ Kids This is a good (though pricey) choice for travelers seeking contemporary accommodations right on the mountain. More than half of the units have kitchen facilities, and most are quite spacious, though decorated in a generic country-condo style. There's a choice of standard queen-bedded rooms; studios; suites with sitting rooms; and 2-bedroom, 2-bathroom penthouses with full kitchens and gas fireplaces. Some of the units here can sleep up to eight people—this resort has really placed an emphasis on catering to families. You pay a premium for this convenience, but that convenience is hard to top during ski season. Staff here are more helpful than those at your typical big ski resort, and you can literally ski right onto the mountain from your room (or walk to the resort's golf course) via a special bridge. A shuttle runs you to Killington Road if you must sample the nightlife. There's a great health club here (two Jacuzzis with views, a big heated pool), plus a newer addition—the **Killington Grand Spa,** offering Swedish massage, Vichy showers, stone massages, nail care, and more.

228 E. Mountain Rd. (near Snowshed base), Killington, VT 05751. ✆ **877/4-KTIMES** (458-4637). Fax 802/422-6881. www.killington.com. 200 units. Fall and winter $336–$395 double, suites from $508; off-peak $129–$310 double, suites from $175. 5-night minimum stay during Christmas and school holidays;

2-night minimum stay Sat–Sun. AE, DISC, MC, V. **Amenities:** 2 restaurants; 2 bars; children's programs; concierge; health club and spa; Jacuzzi; outdoor pool; room service; sauna; spa; 2 tennis courts. *In room:* A/C, TV/DVD, fridge (some units), hair dryer, kitchenette (some units), Wi-Fi (free).

The Mountain Top Inn & Resort ★★ It really *is* on top of a mountain. Situated on 1,300 ridge-top acres, this pond-side property about 25 minutes from Killington sports one of Vermont's best inn views and a relaxing, summery feel, from the expansive front porch of Adirondack chairs to croquet games and equestrian programs. Carved out of a former turnip farm, the inn has left its heritage far behind: Even the lowest-priced rooms have been updated in woods, leathers, and tartan. Luxury rooms and suites come wonderfully outfitted with such modern amenities as flatscreen TVs, sofas, double-sided fireplaces, jetted tubs, and kitchenettes. The standard rooms are smaller and simpler but still come with fresh paint, rocking chairs, and views. Activities abound here: horse riding, clay-bird shooting, fly-fishing lessons, free canoeing and kayaking on the pond, dog-sledding (yes, really), and performances of jazz and orchestral music. The inn also rents five cabins on the grounds described as rustic (but they're quite nice, with TVs and big fireplaces), and can also arrange a stay in local ski chalets. The hospitality level here is very high, even if some staff are on the inexperienced side. This is among southern Vermont's most relaxing resorts. The dining room and tavern (see "Where to Dine," below) are pretty good, too.

195 Mountain Top Rd., Chittenden, VT 05737. ✆ **800/445-2100** or 802/483-2311. Fax 802/483-6373. www.mountaintopinn.com. 55 units. $160–$445 double; $315–$545 suite; $205–$575 cabin. Resort fee of 15% additional. 2-night minimum stay weekends; 3-night minimum stay some holidays. Pets welcome in cabins only ($25 fee). AE, MC, V. **Amenities:** 2 restaurants; bar; outdoor pool. *In room:* A/C, TV, fridge (some units), kitchenette (some units).

Where to Dine

If you like wings, especially *free* wings, you'll be in heaven on Killington Road. But if you're looking for something adventurous or delicious, you'll find instead an astonishing level of culinary mediocrity—bland pasta, tired pizza, and soggy nachos served by harried staff, for the most part. These restaurants are spots to carbo-load a tired family after a long day on the slopes, nothing more; if you're with a group, you might not mind sacrificing quality for convenience and some booze. Just don't expect a foodie adventure.

Fortunately, there are a few escape hatches. Hemingway's (see below), a short drive away, is one of Vermont's best fine-dining restaurants. And on the same flat, busy stretch of Route 4 as Hemingway's is **The Pasta Pot** (✆ **802/422-3004**), a locals' sort of place that's good for families or when you're in a pinch late at night. Here you'll find some of the best garlic bread in Vermont, plus good dressings on the salads. The main meals are pizza, Italian seafood dishes, and standard pasta-and-red-sauce fare—good enough, and full of local color. (A dog, or relatives of the owners, might show up at closing time.) Because there's a small attached bar, this place stays open later than many other restaurants in the area. It's closed Monday through Wednesday, however.

There's also **Peppino's** ★ (✆ **802/422-3293;** www.peppinoskillington.com), which is an exception: a decent restaurant on the access road. This place serves home-cooked Italian meals, too, but also well-chosen glasses of wine and mixed drinks—it's a cut above the place described above, with prices to match. The interior, however, is oddly unbefitting of a fine-dining experience.

Charity's 1887 Saloon & Restaurant PUB FARE Come here to drink; food is an afterthought. Bustling and laid-back, it's a place where the grub is big and simple (wings, cheddar burgers, shrimp; rinse, repeat) and the crowd young. The barnlike interior is adorned with stained-glass lamps, spittoons, and Victorian prints, but centered around a handsome old bar that was crafted in Italy. The menu has expanded a bit over the years to take in pastas (including a Cajun version), stuffed mushroom caps, healthier sandwiches, turkey burgers, and the like; give 'em credit for that. Who was Charity? She worked an old profession in the bartop's original American home. Ask a staffer if you want to know more.

Killington Rd. ✆ **802/422-3800.** www.charitysrestaurant.com. Reservations not accepted. Main courses $7–$25 at lunch, $10–$25 at dinner. AE, MC, V. Daily 11:30am–10pm.

Choices Restaurant and Rotisserie ★ *Finds* CONTINENTAL Locals like this unpretentious place on the access road, and indeed it's one of the best on the mountain (not saying much, but still). Full dinners come with salad or soup and bread, and they restore calories lost out on the slopes or the trail. Seafood and fresh pastas are a specialty (try the various permutations of fettuccine, most of them quite tasty), plus meats from a roaring front-and-center rotisserie. There's no theme, really, other than a Continental touch; you might just as well find curry, snails, or lamb chops on the menu as a smoked-salmon potato pancake, fish salad, nachos, or a cut of filet mignon dolled up with blue cheese. The atmosphere is nothing to write home about, and prices are higher than at the burger joints nearby, but the quality of the food and care taken in preparation are mostly ace.

Killington Rd. (at Glazebrook Center). ✆ **802/422-4030.** Main courses $10–$28. AE, MC, V. Wed–Thurs and Sun 5–10pm; Fri–Sat 5–11pm.

Hemingway's ★★★ CONTINENAL Killington seems an unlikely place for a culinary adventure, yet award-winning Hemingway's provides one. Set back from an arrow-flat stretch of highway (look sharp for it), Hemingway's is an elegant spot—one of the best restaurants in northern New England ever since it opened in 1982. Located in the 1860 Asa Briggs House (a former stagecoach stop), the restaurant seats guests in one of three formal areas; the two upstairs rooms are especially well appointed in linens, crystal goblets, and fresh flowers. Ted Fondulas' food draws heavily on Vermont game and produce, with lots of French and rural Italian accents. You might begin with Maine scallops, cooked three ways; a "fallen" goat cheese soufflé with honey; good cream of garlic soup; or rabbit potpie. The splendid main courses, which change seasonally, could take in cod and Maine lobster, cooked with sweet corn, vanilla, and chives; a cut of roasted King salmon served with white beans and truffles; herbed poussin with truffled potatoes; seared breast of duck, served with pears and a duck strudel; or fennel-encrusted veal and a cheddary corn cake. Finish with a Vermont cheese plate or desserts such as apple cider "soup" with cranberry sorbet, or a peppery Florentine wafer with dark chocolate mousse and cassis berries. Dress neatly—shorts or T-shirts are out of place here.

4988 Rte. 4 (btw. Rte. 100 N. and Rte. 100 S.). ✆ **802/422-3886.** www.hemingwaysrestaurant.com. Reservations highly recommended. Main courses $28–$34, prix-fixe and tasting menus $35–$75 per person. AE, MC, V. Wed–Sun 6–9pm; also select Mon–Tues during ski and foliage seasons (call ahead). Closed mid-Apr to mid-May and early Nov.

Highlands Dining Room ★★ NEW AMERICAN The Mountain Top Inn & Resort's dining room delivers surprisingly sophisticated cuisine from a woodsy, folksy perch—a place where jackets are requested of gentlemen, but there are also racks of moose antlers for lighting and accouterment. Chef Shawn Casey combines influences: Meals could begin with an appetizer of tuna tartare with spicy couscous and yogurt; a Vermont cheese-and-sausage board; corn-fried calamari with fried basil and a chipotle aioli; or healthy salads of fresh produce, truffles, mozzarella, and the like. Move on to filet mignon with potato cakes, a rack of veal, pan-seared ahi tuna served over jasmine rice, or fresh ravioli stuffed with foraged wild mushrooms and Asiago cheese. The attached **Highlands Tavern** serves a simpler and lower-priced (but equally fine) menu of wings, sandwiches, burgers, chili, and (after 5pm) tasty bistro meals like chicken potpie, fish and chips, or T-bone steaks—with the big added bonus of outdoor terrace seating in front of the resort's signature pond and view. A great spot.

195 Mountain Top Rd., Chittenden, VT 05737. ✆ **800/445-2100** or 802/483-2311. Reservations recommended. Appetizers $10–$14, main courses $24–$35. AE, DC, MC, V. Main dining room daily 6–9pm. Tavern daily noon–2pm and 5:30–9:30pm.

Wally's American Grill AMERICAN This 1950s-retro restaurant is a festive, upbeat place—often crowded with visitors and locals who've just come off a long day on the slopes. In a strip-mallish complex near the top of Killington Road, the place's interior sets a good mood. The menu here is just diner fare, expanded for a slightly sophisticated clientele; expect omelets, malted waffles, eggs, hot cakes, and combo specials at breakfast, and check out the active orange juice. Lunch brings salads and sandwiches with Quebec-style *poutine* (fries with gravy) on the side; dinner, the usual American entrees of shrimp, pasta, lobster ravioli, salmon, and steaks. There are plenty of beers on tap here, plus cocktails and mixed drinks. Wally's is probably best as a fill-'er-up breakfast spot, not a dinner engagement.

Killington Rd. ✆ **802/422-3177.** Breakfast items $4–$7, lunch and dinner main courses $8–$17. AE, DC, MC, V. Sun–Thurs 7am–9pm; Fri–Sat 7am–midnight.

Nightlife

Most of the nightlife options here involve guys still wearing their baseball caps indoors, bobbing up and down to rock, pop, country, or faux-electronica. Yikes. There are few fine arts to speak of, save the **Vermont Symphony Orchestra**'s (✆ **800/876-9293** or 802/864-5741; www.vso.org) annual tour, which touches down at the Mountain Top Inn & Resort (see "Where to Stay," above) in summer and in downtown Rutland during winter.

Outback Pizza ★ The music tends to be mellower here than at other spots along the Killington Road, with acoustic dudes playing live on weekends. It's nothing special, rather a place to go if you want to chill with pals to six-strings, some cold ones, and some wood-fired pizza. After hours, Outback morphs into a (not-so-taboo) nightclub called **Tabu.** Note the resourceful beer-mug cooling system. 2841 Killington Rd. ✆ **802/422-9885.** Cover varies.

Pickle Barrel Killington's largest, loudest nightclub, the Barrel occasionally ropes in B-list national acts (Eddie Money, Little Feat), but usually it's more obscure, youngish alterna-pop. There are four bars on three levels; the menu has Long Trail ales and chicken sandwiches. 1741 Killington Rd. ✆ **802/422-3035.** www.picklebarrelnightclub.com. Cover free to $20.

Wobbly Barn The Wobbly—a steakhouse as well as a live venue—has been a staple at Killington since 1963; it's the mountain's de facto nightlife capital, and home to the resort's annual winter kickoff bash. Well known for its happy hour, the Barn packs in weekend crowds dancing and mingling late to tunes from live bands you've surely never heard of before (Split Roast Muppet? The Bus Drivers?). The steak-and-rib house is attached. 2229 Killington Rd. ✆ **802/422-6171.** www.wobblybarn.com. Cover charge weekends (discounted if you dine first).

RUTLAND

Rutland is a no-nonsense, blue-collar city that never had a reputation for charm or grace. Today it's undergoing a slight renaissance thanks to new residents who enjoy the small-city atmosphere, free summer outdoor concerts, cheap real estate, and quick access to the mountains—Killington is just minutes away. But this place remains working-class at heart, and it probably always will. It's somehow the *second-largest city* in Vermont, which seems unbelievable once you've been here, but it's true. (Bennington is a close third.)

Set in the wide valley flanking Otter Creek, Rutland was built on Vermont's once-proud local marble trade, which operated out of bustling quarries in nearby Proctor and West Rutland. By 1880 this city boasted more residents than Burlington and had acquired the distinguished appellation of "Marble City." Many fine homes from that era line downtown's streets, and the intricate commercial architecture—which also incorporates a fair amount of marble—hints at Rutland's former prosperity.

Rutland is the regional hub for central Vermont, with a daily newspaper and a long line of big box stores, fast-food chain restaurants, and businesses stretched out along crowded Route 7 both north and south of the downtown center. (The local airport is nearby, too.) At times, this downtown comes perilously close to looking like one big, outdated strip mall; the concept of zoning got here too late, if it ever got here at all. Still, Rutland has the feel of a real place full of real people eating normal food—a good antidote when you've spent a little too much time in cuckoo-clock shops or the lift lines.

Essentials

GETTING THERE It's easy to get to Rutland. From New York City, it's about a 4½-hour drive via the New York State Thruway; from Boston it's closer, about 3 hours via I-89.

The city sits right at the intersection of two old U.S. highways, Route 7 and Route 4. Burlington is 65 miles north and Bennington is 55 miles south, both via Route 7 and both about a 90 minutes' drive away. Woodstock is 25 miles (45 min.) east on Route 4, through the mountains.

Amtrak (✆ **800/USA-RAIL** [872-7245]; www.amtrak.com) runs one daily train to and from New York up the Hudson River Valley; the ride to Rutland takes a little less than 6 hours (arriving after dark) and costs $65 to $70 one-way.

Surprisingly, Rutland is also served by several daily direct flights from Boston on **Cape Air** (✆ **800/352-0714;** www.capeair.com); the flight takes about an hour.

VISITOR INFORMATION The **Rutland Region Chamber of Commerce,** 256 N. Main St., Rutland, VT 05701 (✆ **800/756-8880** or 802/773-2747; www.rutlandvermont.com), staffs an information booth at the corner of Route 7 and Route 4 W. from Memorial Day until Columbus Day. The chamber's main office is open year-round, weekdays from 8am to 5pm.

FESTIVALS The **Vermont State Fair** ★ (✆ **802/775-5200;** www.vermontstatefair.net) has attracted fairgoers for more than a century and a half—since 1846 to be precise. Expect a conjunction of clowns, carnival rides, snacks, and live music from big-time country music acts with "The" in their names (The Gatlin Brothers, The Oakridge Boys), not to mention Bingo, cows, a demolition derby, and plenty more (but what more could you want?). Admission is $1 to $10 per adult, depending on the date, with big discounts for kids. There's also a small charge for parking (free to $3 per day). The fair is held for 10 days beginning in early September, just after Labor Day. Look for the expansive fairgrounds on Route 7, just south of the city center on the right-hand side as you leave town. Gates open at 8am daily.

Exploring the Town

A stroll through Rutland's historic downtown might delight architecture buffs. Look for the detailed marblework on many of the buildings, such as the Opera House, the Gryphan's Building, and along Merchants Row. Note especially the fine marble exterior of the Chittenden Savings Bank at the corner of Merchants Row and Center Street. Nearby South Main Street (Rte. 7) also has a good selection of handsome homes built in elaborate Queen Anne style.

Shoppers can look for small finds at a variety of unique downtown shops tucked under awnings here and there. Among those worth seeking out is **Michael's Toys ★**, 64 Merchants Row (✆ **802/773-3765;** www.michaelstoys.com), which will leave young kids wide-eyed. It's located at the head of a creaky Dashiell Hammett–esque stairway in a second-floor workshop filled with rocking cows, wooden trucks, and hand-carved wooden signs. (All it lacks are elves.) The shop is generally open Monday through Saturday.

Another stop worth making, especially as a rainy-day diversion, is the **Chaffee Art Center ★**, at 16 S. Main St. (✆ **802/775-0356;** www.chaffeeartcenter.org). Housed in a fairy-tale-like 1896 building with a prominent turret and mosaic floors in its archway vestibule—it's on the National Register of Historic Places, the glorious parquet floors now restored to their original luster—the arts center showcases the local talent from Rutland and the hills beyond. While it owns no permanent collections, the center does feature changing exhibits of local work, much of it for sale. It's open daily Wednesday to Saturday from 10am to 5pm, and Sunday from noon to 4pm; admission is by donation.

Outside of Town

When in Rutland, one good detour to make is to the town of **Proctor,** about 6 miles northwest of the city center. (Take Rte. 4 W., then turn onto and follow Rte. 3 N.) This quiet town is nestled in the folds of low hills; some of its homes and bridges are made of the local **marble,** a tipoff that this was once a huge center of commerce for quarrying, cutting, and shipping out the fine-grained local marble—which was used in the U.S. Supreme Court and Lincoln Memorial, among other important structures.

In the early 1990s, the quarries and factory closed down, but the heritage lives on at the expansive, popular **Vermont Marble Museum ★** (✆ **800/427-1396** or 802/459-2300; www.vermont-marble.com), which touts itself as the world's largest marble exhibit. View an 11-minute video about marble, walk through "Earth Alive" displays about local geology, see a sculptor working in marble, and explore the Hall of Presidents, with life-size bas-relief sculptures of all the past presidents. The sheer size of this former factory is impressive. The gift shop has a great selection of reasonably priced marble products.

The museum is open daily from mid-May through October, 9am to 5:30pm, and closed the rest of the year. Admission is $7 for adults, $5 for seniors, $4 for students 13 to 18, and free for children 12 and under. (Prices are $1 cheaper if you book them in advance.) Look for signs to the exhibit from Route 3 in Proctor.

Where to Stay & Dine

As lodging goes, Rutland is both rich and impoverished. The city's one true inn recently closed down, and B&Bs are not to be found. On the other hand, the city has an unusually wide selection of roadside **motels and chain hotels,** mostly clustered on or along **Route 7** either right downtown or just south of town, in the lower-to-middle price range for the most part. None of these is much better or different from any of the others. Check with the chamber of commerce (see "Visitor Information," above) if you need help weeding through and booking one of these, though most can easily be booked online from the comfort of your own home.

The dining scene is little better, though I fully expect culinary talents to discover this fact and move in soon; the chef at **Table 24** (see below) has already done so. If you're hankering eggs or hotcakes in the morning, though, **Clem' & Co.** (✆ **802/747-3340**) at 3 Center St.—known around town simply as "Clem's"—is a locally popular breakfast spot.

Little Harry's ★ INTERNATIONAL Little Harry's is an offshoot of the wonderful Harry's Café outside Ludlow (p. 122). This one is located in downtown Rutland, on the first floor and in the basement of a strikingly unattractive building; yet the place itself has a wonderfully eclectic menu, just like its papa. Main courses could range from grilled steak sandwiches to jerked chicken, cioppino to duck in a hot, hot red Thai curry (there's *always* something Thai on the menu here). Appetizers are equally eclectic: Marinated olives, gazpacho, pad Thai, and hummus might make appearances. The food here spans the globe, so it's likely anyone can find something he or she likes—so long as you don't mind venturing outside America with your palate.

121 West St. (at Merchants Row). ✆ **802/747-4848.** Reservations recommended. Main courses $11–$17. AE, MC, V. Daily 5–10pm.

Table 24 ★★ AMERICAN A welcome addition to the once-moribund Rutland dining scene, Table 24 serves up hearty lunches of soup, salad, meatloaf, chicken potpie, chicken with mashed potatoes, and burgers—you get the idea. These are cooked with a little more flair and care than your mom-and-pop diner would, though, and the restaurant uses Vermont-sourced ingredients wherever possible. Dinner is the real star—diner staples, but also things like baby back ribs, maple-glazed tenderloin, tamari-flavored trout, grilled steaks with compound butter, pan-roasted salmon, *carne asada* salads, and wild mushroom raviolis. Again, it's diner and bistro fare, but trumped up and better. Desserts choices include chocolate cake, ice-cream sundaes, bread pudding, and your classic banana cream pie. The high ceiling, exposed rafters, and a long, copper-top bar add to the restaurant's convivial feeling.

24 Wales St. (just off Rte. 4). ✆ **802/775-2424.** www.table24.net. Reservations recommended. Lunch items $5–$11, dinner main courses $13–$25. AE, MC, V. Mon–Sat 11:30am–9pm.

6 Northern Vermont

The top of Vermont gives you a good slice of both ends of the state's spectrum. It's here where you're most likely to see a dairy farmer driving a snowplow at 5 in the morning (his winter job), then stroll down the street to the town coffeehouse and stand in line behind a "local" who recently moved here from New York, ordering his daily organic, free-trade cup of joe.

At the western edge of the state, along the shores of huge Lake Champlain, is **Burlington:** the state's biggest and most lively city, ringed by fast-growing suburban communities and chock-full of microbrews, the arts, and recent blow-ins. But drive an hour east and you're deep in the heart of the **Northeast Kingdom,** the state's least developed and most remote region, which is only now slowly being discovered as a place for second homes. Dairy cows and tractor parts still largely rule the roost here.

Travelers can find a great variety of activities within and between these two extremes: exploring a few of Lake Champlain's many rural islands, dining in Burlington's amazingly creative restaurants, hiking the Long Trail across the state's most imposing peaks, mountain biking abandoned lanes past covered bridges and flame-colored maple trees, and poking through quirky museums. In winter, excellent resort-style skiing can be found at Stowe and Jay Peak, among other mountains, and there's also plenty of snowshoeing, ice fishing, town-common ice rink hockey and figure skating, and cross-country skiing for little to no cost.

You can also photograph outstanding foliage and buy apples, milk, cheddar cheese, and maple sugar right from their sources—plus Ben & Jerry's ice cream and a bevy of local gourmet foods.

These northern reaches of the state are far enough from the Boston–New York megalopolis that weekend crowds tend to be lighter than in the southern half, and the sense of space here is more expansive thanks to that big lake and those big mountain peaks.

Above all, savor the improbable existence of this region, which remains more steadfastly "old New England" than any other part of the five-state region in an age of Wi-Fi, PDAs, second homes, fast cars, and discount airlines. Here you're still more than likely to share the highway with a 20-year-old pickup or even a draft horse, and the local country store is probably still stocked with feed and nails rather than stuffed teddy bears or tiny tins of city-priced maple syrup. It might not stay this way forever, though. See it now, before it's too late.

1 MIDDLEBURY ★★

Middlebury: 35 miles S of Burlington; 85 miles N of Bennington; 65 miles NW of White River Junction

Middlebury is a gracious college town set among rolling hills and empty, pastoral countryside (dotted with barns and cows, it has to be added). The town center is idyllic in a New-England-as-envisioned-by-Hollywood way, and for many travelers it's *the* perfect combination of small-town charm, close access to the outdoors (the Adirondacks and Green Mountains are both pretty close at hand), and a dash of sophistication. (Foodies, rejoice.)

The worldly influence of a college (and its international student body), relocated artisans, and assorted other out-of-staters who've blown in here has led to the establishment of a natural foods store, ethnic restaurants, a microbrewery, and more arts, crafts, and books than you'd expect to find in a place several times its size—especially in Vermont.

The town centers around an irregular, sloping green topped by the commanding Middlebury Inn and surrounded by quaint shops. The whole tableau is then lorded over by the fine, white-steepled Congregational Church, built around 1806. Otter Creek tumbles dramatically through the middle of town as a steep, almost gorge-like waterfall, and the downtown area is flanked by a historic district with vestiges of former industry (including a former marble works). Middlebury has some 300 structures listed on the National Register of Historic Places, and about the only disruption to this perfect little scene is the sound of farm and delivery trucks downshifting as they drive the main routes through and around town, headed somewhere else.

Middlebury College, within walking distance of downtown's southern edge, doesn't dominate the village, and in fact you can spend an entire visit here without even noticing it. The students are quiet and mostly stay on campus, and the place coexists nicely with the town. (One possible reason: The college has a solid reputation for its liberal-arts program. All those students are busy studying.) Middlebury College is also well known for its intensive summer language programs—students commit to total immersion, taking a pledge not to use English while they're enrolled in it—so don't be surprised if you hear folks gabbing in exotic tongues as you walk through the town in summer.

Middlebury is also home to several good inns. Just keep both eyes on the road when driving around: There are lots of pedestrians here, and some rather strange traffic patterns encircling the green. Do all your sightseeing *outside* the car, and be on your toes behind the wheel.

ESSENTIALS

GETTING THERE Middlebury is on Route 7, almost exactly midway between **Rutland** and **Burlington,** about 30 miles (45 min.) from both of Vermont's largest cities. From New York City, it takes 5 or more hours to get here by car.

One popular route is to drive to the village of Fort Ticonderoga, then take a **cable ferry** (✆ **802/897-7999**) across Lake Champlain. Some form of ferry boat has crossed the lake here since way back in 1759; this one operates from May through October, about three times per hour from 8am until 6pm; the cost for autos is a steep $8 one-way, $14 round-trip, but it takes just 7 minutes. In very severe weather, the ferry doesn't run, but this is Vermont: It almost always does run.

VISITOR INFORMATION The **Addison County Chamber of Commerce,** 2 Court St. (✆ **802/388-7951;** www.addisoncounty.com), is in a handsome, historic white building just off the green, facing the Middlebury Inn. Brochures and assistance are available Monday through Friday during business hours (9am–5pm), and sometimes on Saturday and Sunday as well (from early June through mid-Oct). Ask for a map and guide to downtown Middlebury, which lists local shops and restaurants and is published by the Downtown Middlebury Business Bureau.

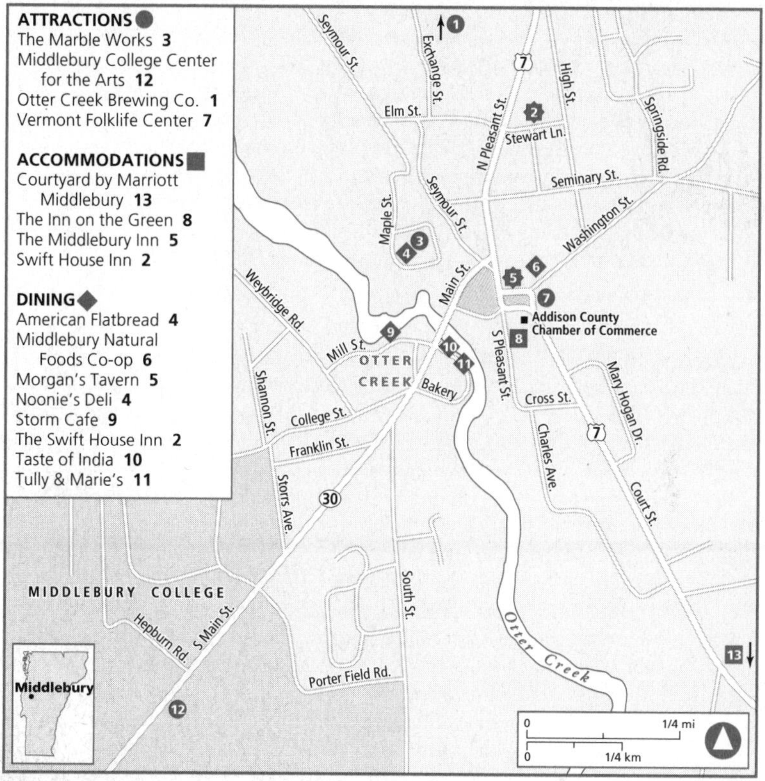

EXPLORING THE TOWN

The best place to begin a tour of Middlebury is at the Addison County Chamber of Commerce's information center (see above); be sure to request the chamber's self-guided **walking-tour** brochure.

The tiny main street has plenty of things to see—used-book shops, cafes, souvenir and stationery shops, and the like. It's a bit cutesy, but you'll find enough shopping interest to occupy an hour or two. The **Vermont Folklife Center** ★ (✆ **802/388-4964;** www.vermontfolklifecenter.org), at 88 Main St., is a gallery of changing displays of local art from Vermont and beyond—visual art, but also music. The gift shop sells heritage books, foods, baskets, and other traditional crafts. The center is open Monday through Saturday from 10am to 5pm, Sunday 11am to 4pm; admission is by donation.

Take the footbridge over the river and find your way to **The Marble Works,** an assortment of wood and rough-marble industrial buildings on the far bank, converted to a handful of interesting shops and restaurants (p. 155).

Atop a low ridge with beautiful views of the Green Mountains to the east and farmlands rolling toward Lake Champlain in the west, prestigious **Middlebury College** ★

Finds Fit to Be Tied

Any aficionado of bow ties will enjoy dropping by **Beau Ties Ltd.** (**✆ 800/488-8437;** www.beautiesltd.com) at 69 Industrial Ave. This cottage industry actually began as a retirement project. Now the firm designs, manufactures, and sells a distinctive line of old-fashioned bow ties—including some rather festive holiday-themed ties—from a utilitarian building here in Middlebury. (Past customers have included such bow-tied luminaries as popcorn magnate Orville Redenbacher and TV celebrity Charles Osgood). You're welcome to come see the tie-makers at work during weekday business hours; a mile north of downtown, turn west off Route 7 onto Exchange Street, then turn right a half-mile later onto Industrial Avenue.

(founded in 1800) has a handsome, well-spaced campus of gray limestone and white marble buildings best explored on foot. The architecture of the college is primarily Colonial Revival, giving it a rather stern Calvinist feel. The view from the marble **Mead Memorial Chapel** ★, built in 1917 and overlooking the campus green, is especially nice.

At the edge of campus is the **Middlebury College Center for the Arts,** which opened in 1992. This architecturally engaging center houses the good little **Middlebury College Museum of Art** ★★ (**✆ 802/443-5007;** http://museum.middlebury.edu), with a sampling of European and American art both old and new. Classicists will enjoy the displays of Greek painted urns, vases, and bits of stone frieze, as well as Florentine panels, a Rembrandt etching, and other Renaissance and Baroque artworks. Modern-art aficionados can check out the permanent and changing exhibits.

The museum is located on Route 30 (S. Main St.), and opens Tuesday through Friday from 10am to 5pm, Saturday and Sunday noon to 5pm. (It's closed during the second half of Dec and early Jan, when college is out of session.) Admission and parking are free.

Just 2 miles outside Middlebury is the famous **Morgan Horse Farm** ★★ (**✆ 802/388-2011**), dating to the late 1800s and now owned and operated by the University of Vermont. Col. Joseph Battell, who owned the farm from the 1870s to 1906, is credited with preserving the Morgan breed, a horse of beauty and stamina. With guided tours from May through October daily from 9am to 4pm, the farm also has a picnic area and gift shop. Admission is $5 for adults, $4 for teens, $2 for children ages 5 to 12, and free for kids 4 and under. To reach the farm, take Route 125 to Weybridge Street (which is also Rte. 23), head north for ¾ mile, turn right at the sign for the farm, and continue about 2 more miles. (As a bonus, the fall foliage around here can be stunning.)

Brewhounds should schedule a stop at the **Otter Creek Brewing Co.** ★, 793 Exchange St. (**✆ 800/473-0727;** www.ottercreekbrewing.com), for a quick tour and samples of the well-regarded beers, including the flagship Copper Ale, a robust Stovepipe Porter, and the organic Wolaver's line. The visitor center and gift shop are open daily; the free tours are given three times per afternoon (except Sun). Late September brings a 3-day Oktoberfest event to the brewery.

OUTDOOR PURSUITS

BICYLING The many two-lane paved, gravel, and dirt roads in these parts—many passing through Rockwell-esque landscapes of cows, barns, hay, covered bridges, and more cows—means there's abundantly good cycling in central Vermont. The **Central**

Vermont Chamber of Commerce (✆ **802/229-4619;** www.central-vt.com) in Barre publishes a good free handbook for some scenic bike rides in the region. Pick it up at a state tourist info kiosk or locally. It's also published online at the chamber's website, **www.central-vt.com/visit/biketour.**

HIKING The Green Mountains roll right down nearly to Middlebury's eastern doorstep, making for easy access to the mountains. Stop by the Green Mountain National Forest's **Middlebury Ranger District office,** south of town on Route 7 (✆ **802/388-4362**), for guidance and information on area trails and destinations. Ask for the brochure listing day hikes in the region.

One recommended walk for people of all abilities—and especially those of literary sensibilities—is the **Robert Frost Memorial Trail ★**, dedicated to the memory of New England's poet laureate. Frost lived in a cabin on a farm across the road for 23 summers. (The cabin is now a National Historic Landmark.) It's on Route 125, about 6 miles east of Middlebury's village center. The trail itself is a relaxing, easy mile-long loop with excerpts of Frost's poems posted on signs all along the way—a wonderful idea. There's also information about the natural history of the trail area. This is a nice taste of the local mountains, with a pleasant poetic tint thrown in. If you have questions about the trail, call the ranger office (see above), which administrates it.

SKIING Downhill skiers looking for a low-key, low-pressure mountain invariably head to **Middlebury College Snow Bowl** (✆ **802/388-4356**), near Middlebury Gap on Route 125 east of town. Founded in 1939, this ski area has a vertical drop of just over 1,000 feet served by a few chairlifts. The college ski team uses the area for practice, but it's also open to the public for about half what you'd pay at Killington. Adult day lift tickets are $30 weekdays, $34 on weekends and holidays, with discounts for youths, students, and senior citizens—and if you're over 70, it's free! You can also buy a half-day ticket. The chairlift opens at 9am daily but shuts down by 4pm due to the early darkness of a New England winter.

Cross-country skiing is also enjoyed nearby at the **Rikert Ski Touring Center ★** (✆ **802/443-2744**), also owned and run by Middlebury College. It's at the college's **Bread Loaf Campus,** 12 miles away (and up in the mountains) via Route 125. The center maintains about 25 miles of machine-groomed trails through a lovely winter landscape. Adult day passes are $15; rentals and half-day passes ($10) are also available.

WHERE TO STAY

There's a trio of significant **inns** in town, and all three of them are outstanding—you simply can't go wrong with any of them, though you'll pay for the privilege. Of these three, the Middlebury Inn is fanciest and most professional, but the Swift House Inn has arguably better food and hospitality, while the Inn on the Green probably feels most like your kindly New England aunt's place. Take your pick; they're all wonderful in their own way.

If you're looking to save a few dollars, the outskirts of Middlebury, especially Route 7 south of the village green, are home to a clutch of budget motels and inns, some locally owned and some chain-run. These are frankly mostly aging and wearing out their welcomes, but they're uniformly cheap—$100 a night or less, in most cases. But buyer beware.

By far the best choice in these parts, especially for families, is the 89-room **Courtyard by Marriott Middlebury** (✆ **800/388-7775** or 802/388-7600) on Route 7 a half-mile south of the village green. Yes, it's a chain and nothing special, but it supplies the basics plus an indoor pool. Some big spa suites have gas log fireplaces, Jacuzzi tubs, and fuller amenities, but all rooms come with hair dryers, coffeemakers, and free high-speed Internet access. There's also a coin-op laundry on the hotel premises.

The Inn on the Green ★★ This handsome, robin's-egg-blue village inn occupies a house that dates from 1803 (it was Victorianized with its mansard tower later in the 19th century). It's both historic and comfortable, one of three excellent lodging experiences within shouting distance of the town green. Rooms here are furnished in a mix of solid antiques and reproductions (pencil-poster beds, sleigh daybeds, and the like). Exposed wooden floors and boldly colored walls of harvest yellow, peach, and burgundy help lighten the architectural mood of the house, and everything was freshened and renovated in the mid-1990s to upgrade with the times. The suites are most spacious, but every unit offers enough elbow room; those in the front of the house are wonderfully flooded with afternoon light. A continental breakfast (delivered to your room) is always included, though there are no Jacuzzis or fireplaces; this is not a luxury property, but rather a cozy Vermont experience.

71 S. Pleasant St., Middlebury, VT 05753. ✆ **888/244-7512** or 802/388-7512. www.innonthegreen.com. 11 units. $119–$199 double; $199–$329 suite. Rates include continental breakfast. 2-night minimum stay Sat–Sun. AE, DC, DISC, MC, V. *In room:* A/C, TV, hair dryer, Wi-Fi (free).

The Middlebury Inn ★★ The most upscale experience in the village, the Middlebury Inn rambles along the main village square. Its impressive brick facade with a long, colonnaded front porch is as much a landmark as anything in town. The inn traces its roots to 1827, when Nathan Wood built the Vermont Hotel; the property now consists of three buildings housing 70 modern rooms. Units here are mostly on the big side, outfitted with either a sofa or upholstered chairs; Colonial-reproduction furniture; and vintage bathroom fixtures. Room nos. 116 and 246 are spacious corner units entered via foyers; no. 129, though smaller, has a four-poster bed, view of the green, and Jacuzzi. Rooms in the Porter Mansion next door also have a pleasantly historic feel, but the adjacent Courtyard annex is a standard-issue motel with double- and twin-bedded units beneath its cutesy veneer. Stick with the main inn or the mansion. An upscale **dining room/tavern** (see "Where to Dine," below) and a newish day spa ratchet up the luxury level even further, and all of the inn's guests receive complimentary passes to the nearby Vermont Sun fitness center—the best such facility in central Vermont, with an Olympic-sized pool and loads of workout equipment.

14 Court Sq., Middlebury, VT 05753. ✆ **800/842-4666** or 802/388-4961. Fax 802/388-4563. www.middleburyinn.com. 70 units. Mon–Fri $88–$245 double, $240 suite; Sat–Sun $98–$270 double, $270–$375 suite. Rates include continental breakfast. AE, DC, MC, V. Pets allowed in some rooms. **Amenities:** Restaurant; tavern; spa. *In room:* A/C, TV, hair dryer, Wi-Fi (in main inn; free).

Swift House Inn ★★ This historic complex of three whitewashed houses sits on a hillside 2 blocks from downtown Middlebury, and it was always a favorite of ours. But several waves of recent ownership have improved it with such touches as a friendly wine bar, improved pricing of the excellent **house restaurant ★★** (see "Where to Dine," below), and a "green" designation from the state of Vermont for environmentally sound practices. The five rooms in the roadside Gate House are lowest-priced and have a B&B feel, and have also been updated with newer, more upscale carpets, gorgeous wooden floors, and bathrooms. Nine units in the main Federal-style inn, built in 1814, are thoroughly imbued with the history of the place (a Vermont governor lived here at one time); inside, it's decorated in antiques and reproduction furnishings. And the carriage house's six suites are ideal for honeymooners and business travelers. They're the biggest and most luxurious, almost all of them furnished with Jacuzzis and fireplaces.

25 Stewart Lane, Middlebury, VT 05753. ✆ **866/388-9925** or 802/388-9925. Fax 802/388-9927. www.swifthouseinn.com. 20 units. Main inn $130–$200 double; gate house $110–$150 double; carriage house $235–$270 suite. Rates include full breakfast. Packages available. 2-night minimum stay some weekends. AE, MC, V. **Amenities:** Restaurant; room service (breakfast only). *In room:* A/C, TV, hair dryer, Wi-Fi (in main inn; free).

Waybury Inn ★ Photos of Bob Newhart and "Larry, his brother Darryl, and his other brother Darryl" grace the wall behind the desk at this 1810 inn. That's because the inn was featured in the classic TV show *Newhart*—the exterior, anyway, which was painted white for television. (The interior was created on a Hollywood sound stage.) The architecturally handsome Waybury is now green on the outside, but it has loads of integrity within in a simple, farmhouse sort of way. (Poet Robert Frost was a frequent guest back in the day.) The rooms here vary in size and price, as they do in most old inns; the more you pay, the more space you get. Two of the rooms are suites, with sitting rooms, four-poster king beds, Jacuzzis, and claw-foot tubs. Romantic types will love the fact that room no. 9, the Robert Frost Suite, has a secret stash of previous guests' notes, while the New England Room features the work of local artist Warren Kimbell. Two dining spaces and a tavern serve good food, especially the **Pine Room ★** with its inventive Continental menu. Front-facing rooms feel a bit noisy when nighttime highway traffic zooms by. This is about 5 miles southeast of Middlebury proper.

457 E. Main St. (Rte. 125, approx. 1½ miles past Rte. 7 S. turnoff), East Middlebury, VT 05740. ✆ **800/348-1810** or 802/388-4015. Fax 802/382-8926. www.wayburyinn.com. 13 units, 1 with detached private bathroom in the hall. $105–$190 double; $185–$285 suite. Rates include breakfast. AE, DISC, MC, V. Pets allowed with restrictions (call first). **Amenities:** Restaurant. *In room:* A/C, no phone, Wi-Fi (free).

WHERE TO DINE

In addition to the eateries listed below, Middlebury possesses an abundance of delis, sandwich shops, and the like—perfect for a quick lunch or a picnic. Among the best are **Noonie's Deli** (✆ **802/388-0014;** www.nooniesdeli.com), at 137 Maple St. in the Marble Works complex, which is locals' top choice for thick sandwiches on fresh breads; and **Taste of India** (✆ **802/388-4856**), hidden away down 1 Bakery Lane (downhill off Main St.), with inexpensive lunch specials.

But my favorite casual bite in town, by far, remains the local branch of **American Flatbread ★★** (✆ **802/388-3300;** www.americanflatbread.com), also in the Marble Works, open Tuesday through Saturday evenings from 5 to 9pm. They bake up some of the best pizzas I've ever tasted, before a roaring fire in a wonderfully homey atmosphere. Look for the chef's daily special pizzas, salads, and even desserts. (Apple-cinnamon crepes with fresh cream? Count me in.) I adore this place, in case you couldn't already tell.

All three restaurants will do takeout for you. There's also a small, good natural-foods store, the **Middlebury Natural Foods Co-op** (✆ **802/388-7276**), at 1 Washington St., just uphill from the Middlebury Inn. It's open daily from early morning until 7pm.

Morgan's Tavern ★ AMERICAN The house restaurant of the venerable Middlebury Inn (see "Where to Stay," above) delivers the sort of resort fare that you'd expect in a place like this. This is straight-ahead American resort cooking, playing it safe in its approach but with a bit of a snooty French influence (which is a good thing). Expect lunches of Waldorf chicken and Caesar salads (with homemade dressings), clam chowder, crab cakes, sandwiches, and burgers—plus the occasional wild card like a blue cheese-leek tart or homemade pâté. Dinner is fancier: starters of escargot with garlic butter, or shrimp cocktail; entrees such as filet mignon with garlic mashed potatoes, grilled miso and mirin-flavored salmon, monkfish served with langoustines, broiled rib-eye steaks, roasted chicken with wild mushrooms . . . and an incongruous slab of meat loaf. The wild card at night? Maybe the grilled buffalo steak with burgundy sauce.

14 Court Sq., Middlebury, VT 05753. ✆ **800/842-4666** or 802/388-4961. www.middleburyinn.com. Reservations recommended. Lunch items $7–$10, dinner main courses $11–$25. MC, V. Breakfast daily 7–10am; lunch daily 11am–2pm; dinner Wed–Sun 5:30–8:30pm.

The Storm Cafe ★★ NEW AMERICAN This tiny, casual spot with great river views on the ground floor of a stone mill in Frog Hollow is a chef-owned restaurant popular with locals and travelers alike. The menu is simple, but great care is taken in the selection of ingredients and cooking. The salads are especially good. Interesting lunch selections include "The Berber" (pan-fried salmon in African spices on a baguette, with lemon aioli), a chicken cheesesteak with hot peppers and cheddar, and a spicy pile of Prince Edward Island mussels steamed in wine. Dinner brings appetizers and main courses of pan-seared diver scallops, duck confit sliders, beet carpaccio, grilled polenta cakes, pan-roasted chicken with liver crostini, grilled beef filets, several pasta dishes, and a daily seafood special. Desserts are killer, too—try *not* to order a Snickers blonde brownie sundae, chocolate decadence cake, banana cream pie, or crème brûlée, but I bet you'll cave in. There's a tiny wine list, too. Ultra-fancy this place is not, but locals enjoy it, and for very good reasons.

3 Mill St. ✆ **802/388-1063.** www.thestormcafe.com. Reservations recommended. Main courses $7–$9 lunch, $17–$24 dinner. MC, V. Mon 11:30am–2:30pm; Tues–Sat 11:30am–2:30pm and 5–9pm; Sun 5–9pm.

Swift House Inn ★★ CONTINENTAL This inn restaurant consists of two dining rooms on the ground floor of the main house. It's a wonderfully homey place to get a fancy meal right in town, in a lovely setting. Since chef Zach Corbin came on board, the menu has moved away from American cuisine toward French shores, yet it remains top-notch in execution. Begin with homemade duck sausage over cassoulet beans, a lovely smoked salmon "Napoleon" of potatoes, fish, capers, and crème fraîche; country pâté; or house salads. Main courses could run to Long Island breast of duck with caramelized apples, grilled entrecôte of beef with mashed potatoes, flounder almondine, or fresh agnolotti pasta stuffed with spinach and ricotta cheese then topped with Parmesan cream sauce. There's also a second, bistro-style menu here with slightly lighter entrees (and prices): Expect burgers and upscale-yet-healthy presentations of fish. Some tables in the dining room look out onto the inn's grounds—and, by default, sunset over the mountains to the west. Ask for one.

25 Stewart Lane. ✆ **802/388-9925.** www.swifthouseinn.com. Reservations recommended. Main courses $15–$21. AE, MC, V. Wed–Sun 5:30–9pm.

Tully and Marie's NEW AMERICAN/FUSION Tully and Marie's is an Art Deco–inspired restaurant overlooking Otter Creek, in an almost hidden location down a narrow alley. (Try for a table perched over the water.) The menu is New American cuisine, but with heavy influences from Asia and Mexico. At lunch, expect burgers, burritos, and an array of sandwiches and wraps filled with crab, salmon, brie, or meat and cheese. At dinner, you might find pad Thai, grilled sea scallops, house-smoked pork barbecue, fajitas, pan-blackened salmon, jerked chicken, steak, or curry. It's an adequate central bite.

7 Bakery Lane. ✆ **802/388-4182.** www.tullyandmaries.com. Reservations recommended weekends. Main courses $7–$8 at lunch, $10–$24 at dinner. AE, MC, V. Daily 11:30am–3pm and 5–9pm (to 10pm Fri–Sat). Closed Wed in winter.

2 MAD RIVER VALLEY ★★

Warren: 3 miles S of Waitsfield; 205 miles NW of Boston; 43 miles SE of Burlington

The long, narrow, outstandingly scenic Mad River Valley is one of Vermont's better-kept secrets, enfolding the cute villages of **Warren** and **Waitsfield** while remaining completely out of the view of hurrying interstate travelers. The valley has a bit of a Shangri-La quality to it; in places, little seems to have changed since it was settled in 1789 by a handful of Revolutionary War veterans.

Since 1948, ski-related development has competed with the dairy farms that had been the backbone of this region for centuries—but the newcomers haven't been too pushy or obnoxious, so far. Save a couple of telltale signs, you could drive Route 100 through **Warren** and **Waitsfield** and never realize you're just a couple miles downhill of some of the choicest skiing in the entire state. There's no rampant condo or strip-mall development here, and the valley seems to have learned from the sprawl that afflicts such resort areas as Mount Snow and Killington. (Even the Mad River Green, a tidy strip mall on Rte. 100 just north of Rte. 17, is disguised as an old barn; it's scarcely noticeable from the main road.) Some Vermont travelers say the valley still looks much like the Stowe of 30 years ago. That's a good thing.

The region's character becomes less pastoral along the access road to the **Sugarbush** ski resort, however; at least the best inns and restaurants tend to be tucked back into the forest or set along rushing streams. Make sure you get good directions before setting out in search of accommodations or food in this valley, and try not to do so at night unless absolutely necessary—hardly any of the roads in this part of Vermont are lit by streetlights. (That's why you're in Vermont, remember?)

Hidden up a winding valley road, **Mad River Glen,** the area's *older* ski area, has a pleasantly dated quality that pointedly sticks a thumb in the eye of rock-stardom (we're looking at you, Sugarbush and Killington). It has an almost crunchy granola sort of charm, cute and unprepossessing, and it's many Vermonters' favorite ski hill for that very reason.

ESSENTIALS

GETTING THERE **Warren** and **Waitsfield** are close to each other on Route 100, north of **Killington** and south of **Waterbury**—figure on almost an hour's drive from either Burlington or Killington. The quickest access from a major interstate is via exit 10 (Waterbury/Stowe) off I-89; then you drive about 20 miles south on Route 100 until you hit Waitsfield. Warren is 5 or 6 more miles down the same road.

VISITOR INFORMATION The **Mad River Valley Chamber of Commerce** (✆ **800/828-4748** or 802/469-3409; www.madrivervalley.com) is at 4601 Main St. (that's Rte. 100) in **Waitsfield,** inside the General Wait House, which is next to the elementary school. It's open daily during regular business hours in summer, foliage season, and ski season; during slower times of the year, it sometimes closes weekends, or closes earlier.

One unique way to explore this region is atop an Icelandic pony. The **Vermont Icelandic Horse Farm** ★ (✆ **802/496-7141;** www.icelandichorses.com), on North Fayston Road in Waitsfield (turn west off Rte. 100 near the airport), specializes in tours on these small, sturdy horses. Full- and half-day rides are available daily. Or to really get to know both the countryside and the horses, sign up for a multiday trek ranging from 1 to 5 nights and including lodging at area inns, meals, your horse, and a guide. (In winter, try **skijoring,** best described as "skiing behind a horse.") A 2-day, 2-night trip begins at $600 per person, but contact the farm for current pricing information or to make reservations.

BIKING A rewarding 14-mile **bike trip** ★★ along paved roads begins at the village of Waitsfield. Park near the covered bridge, then follow East Warren Road past the Inn at Round Barn Farm and up into hilly, farm-filled countryside. (Don't be discouraged by the long hill at the outset.) Near the village center of Warren, turn right at Brook Road to connect to Route 100. Return north on bustling but scenic Route 10 to Waitsfield, minding the traffic carefully.

Clearwater Sports, at 4147 Main St. (Rte. 100) in Waitsfield north of the covered bridge (✆ **802/496-2708;** www.clearwatersports.com), has rented mountain bikes, snowshoes, kayaks, and skis out of a blue-and-white Victorian-era house since 1975; these folks are well-liked locally. Staff members are helpful, offering suggestions for routes and tours. The shop is open daily, year-round.

HIKING Hikers in search of good exercise and a spectacular view should strike out for 4,000-foot (yes, 4,000) **Mount Abraham** ★★, west of Warren. Drive west up Lincoln Gap Road (it leaves Rte. 100 just south of Warren Village) and continue to the crest, where you cross the intersection with the Long Trail. Park here and hike north on the trail; after about 2 miles, you reach the Battell Shelter. Push on another .8 mile up a steep ascent to reach panoramic views atop the summit. Enjoy, and then retrace your steps. Allow 4 or 5 hours for this round-trip hike.

For a less demanding adventure that still yields great views, head *south* from Lincoln Gap Road on the Long Trail. In about .6 mile, look for a short spur trail to **Sunset Rock** ★, with sweeping westward vistas of the farms of the Champlain Valley, Lake Champlain, and the knobby Adirondacks beyond. A round-trip hike here takes a little more than an hour.

Finds Country Comfort: Warren's General Store

The attractive **Warren Store** (✆ **802/496-3864;** www.warrenstore.com) anchors the little village of **Warren,** once a timber-cutting town but now the de facto headquarters for legions of laid-back Mad River skiers and cyclists. Set along a stream, this store has uneven floorboards, a pot-bellied stove, and a good selection of sandwiches with cute names like the "Turkey Tumble" and the "Pesto-palooza." This being modern Vermont, the store also now stocks gourmet foods and a small selection of wines. It's a very popular spot for bicycle riders to assemble for a bite pre-, mid-, or post-ride. (Get coffee and a sandwich at the back deli counter, then enjoy it on the deck overlooking the river.) The store is in Warren Village, just off Route 100 south of the Sugarbush Access Road. It's usually open until 7pm (6pm on Sun).

WINTER SPORTS Downhill skiing opportunities are abundant in the valley (see "Skiing," below). But you can *also* cross-country ski and snowshoe. The outdoorsy folks at Clearwater Sports (see "Biking," above), on Main Street in Waitsfield, rent snowshoes and telemark skis—and also dispense advice—in winter. Mad River Glen (see "Skiing," below) maintains an outstanding **telemark skiing area,** served by chairlifts. Don't know how to do those turns? Enroll in one of the many private or group classes offered at Mad River. The standard 2-hour beginner course costs $80 and *includes a ticket* for the beginner's lift, while private instruction is $65 per hour.

SKIING

Mad River Glen ★★ Finds Mad River Glen is at once the radical dude and the Zen master of Vermont's skiing universe—a place whose motto is still "Ski it if you can!" High-speed detachable quad chairs? Forget it; up until 2007, the main lift here was a 1948 *single*-chairlift that slowly creaked its way a mile up to the summit. Snowmaking? Nope. This hill functions according to the whims of Mother Nature. Snowboarding? No, it's forbidden. Gourmet restaurants? A lodge? Toll-free number? Fancy website? No, no, no, and definitely not. Mad River long ago attained cult status among "soul skiers" (for lack of a better term), and its fans seem determined to keep it this way. Owned and operated by a cooperative since 1995, it claims to be the only cooperatively owned ski area in the country—you can even buy a small share of the resort yourself, and get discounts on tickets afterward. But don't mistake this gentler approach for easier skiing; the slopes here are twisting and narrow, hiding some of the steepest drops in New England. (Nearly half of Mad River's runs are classified as "expert.") A ski school, kids' program, and telemarking classes are all offered, and care is taken here to both preserve and explain the mountain's ecology. Tickets are pretty affordable, too, especially midweek. A renegade spirit perseveres here, even in the face of the sport's (and Vermont's) inexorable process of upscaling. If you're interested in a different skiing experience, or one that's more "ecotouristy," this is it.

P.O. Box 1089, Waitsfield, VT 05673. ✆ **802/496-3551.** www.madriverglen.com. Adults $39–$66 day lift tickets, $35–$51 half-day; discounts for youths and seniors.

Sugarbush ★★ Now more than a half-century old, Sugarbush is a fine intermediate-to-advanced ski resort comprising several mountains linked by a long, high-speed chairlift that crosses several ridges. (A shuttle bus offers a warmer way to traverse the hills, and the resort also recently acquired a "Snow Cat" transporter.) The number of high-speed lifts, plus the excellent snowmaking, makes this a desirable destination for serious skiers—and there have been serious improvements over the past decade. But this is not Killington. The "Bush" remains a pretty low-key area with great intermediate cruising runs on its north slopes and challenging, old-fashioned expert slopes on Castlerock Peak. Mount Ellen features a terrain pipe and half-pipe, and the resort has made "green" strides by fueling all its equipment and shuttle buses with biodiesel (vegetable oil and/or reused waste oil). This is a good choice if you seek great, exciting skiing but find Killington's sprawl a little overwhelming.

1840 Access Rd., Warren, VT 05674. ✆ **800/537-8427** or 802/583-6300. www.sugarbush.com. Adults $77–$82 day lift tickets, $62–$67 half-day; discounts for youths and seniors.

WHERE TO STAY

In addition to the places listed below, think about Sugarbush's **condos.** While that resort isn't completely overrun by condos, it manages several hundred condominiums near the mountain, with accommodations ranging from one to four bedrooms; guests have access to amenities including a health club and five pools. (An even newer, more luxurious complex of apartments called **Clay Brook** was completed in 2006. Check here first if you want fancy digs.) The resort manages the **Sugarbush Inn,** as well.

From these condos, biodiesel-powered shuttle buses zip guests to and from the slopes and other facilities at Sugarbush (but not at Mad River). Rates vary widely, and most rooms are sold as packages that include lift tickets in winter. To discuss or book any of these resort-owned options, call Sugarbush's main switchboard at © **800/537-8427** and ask for lodging services.

Inn at the Mad River Barn (Value) This classic 1960s-style ski lodge attracts a clientele that's nearly fanatical in its devotion to the place. One reason might be its charismatic (and opinionated) owner Betsy Pratt, who was co-owner of the Mad River Glen ski area before she created and sold it to the cooperative that runs the mountain now. Accommodations are in a two-story barn behind the white clapboard main house, and in an annex building (a bit fancier but with less character). *Don't* come expecting a fancy place—carpets and furniture tend toward the threadbare—but rather to relax in a ski-lodge/aunt's-home/youth-hostel-like atmosphere. It's all knotty pine and rustic Americana here; the spartan guest rooms and countrified common spaces (there's a mounted moose head by the stone fireplace, for instance) get visitors feeling at ease right away. Visitors can swim in the lovely pool a short distance away from the inn beside a grove of birches of maples.

2849 Mill Brook Rd. (Rte. 17), Waitsfield, VT 05673. © **800/631-0466** or 802/496-3310. Fax 802/496-6696. www.madriverbarn.com. 15 units. $75–$150 double; holiday and foliage-season rates higher. Rates include breakfast. 2-night minimum stay holidays and Sat–Sun in winter. AE, DISC, MC, V. **Amenities:** Exercise room; outdoor pool; sauna. *In room:* TV (most units), fridge (some units), no phone, Wi-Fi (most units; free).

Inn at the Round Barn Farm ★★ (Finds) You pass through a covered bridge just off Route 100 to arrive at one of the most romantic and distinctive-looking B&Bs in northern New England, a regal barn and farmhouse on 235 sloping acres with views of fields all around. The centerpiece of the inn is the Round Barn, a beautiful 1910 structure used for weddings, art shows, even Sunday church services. Guest rooms are furnished in an elegant, understated country style with wingback chairs, poster beds, love seats, marble gas fireplaces, and luxe trimmings. The less expensive units in the older section of the home are comfortable, if comparatively small; the larger luxury units sport soaring ceilings beneath old log beams, and include such extras as Jacuzzis and cable televisions. There's also one suite (the Abbott), with plenty of those original beams plus CD and DVD players, a steam shower, Jacuzzi, and pullout sofa bed. Surprisingly, no dinner is served here (there isn't even a bar); but you'll still love the place anyway.

1661 E. Warren Rd., Waitsfield, VT 05673. ©/fax **802/496-2276.** www.innattheroundbarn.com. 12 units. $165–$315 double; $285–$315 suite. Rates include breakfast. 3-night minimum stay during holidays and foliage season. AE, DISC, MC, V. Closed Apr 15–30. Children 15 and over welcome. **Amenities:** Indoor pool; cross-country ski center. *In room:* A/C, TV/DVD, hair dryer, no phone (some units), Wi-Fi (most units; free).

The Pitcher Inn ★★★ This inn is one of New England's most expensive, luxurious, refined—and most interesting. Set in the timeless village of Warren, the business *and* inn were rebuilt from the ground up in 1993 after a fire leveled the 19th-century home that had previously stood here; now only the barn is original. Yet architect David Sellers has created a space seamlessly blending modern convenience, whimsy, and classic New England decor while paying deep respect to the Old Vermont with "themed" rooms taking that concept to new heights. There isn't a bad room in the house; all 11 are designed with gracefulness and a sense of humor, and they've been compared to elegant puzzles—each is almost like a miniature modern art installation. The carved goose on the ceiling of the Mallard Room, for example, is attached to a weathervane on the roof; it rotates with the vane to indicate wind direction. The Trout Room feels like a riverside campground with its antique oars, a desk for fly-tying, a porch extending over a rushing steam, and a fireplace of river stones. The Mountain Room has antique snowshoes and a brick fireplace of Vermont stone. And so on. Most rooms have wood-burning or gas fireplaces, all have Jacuzzis, and most have steam showers; among the choices are a pair of 2-bedroom suites in the barn.

275 Main St. (P.O. Box 347), Warren, VT 05674. ✆ **802/496-6350.** Fax 802/496-6354. www.pitcherinn.com. 11 units. $425–$650 double; $800 suite. Rates include breakfast and afternoon tea. Packages available. 2-night minimum stay Sat–Sun; 3-night minimum on holiday weekends; 5-night minimum at Christmas. AE, MC, V. Children 15 and under accepted in suites only. **Amenities:** Restaurant; babysitting; Jacuzzi; room service; spa. *In room:* A/C, TV/VCR, CD player, hair dryer, Wi-Fi (free).

West Hill House ★★ (Finds) If you go strictly by guests' comments, this is the best B&B in the entire Western world. It might not be *that,* but it's excellent—I challenge you to find someone with one bad word to say about it. Under the watchful ownership of Peter and Susan MacLaren since 2006, this is among the more relaxed inns in the valley, in part because of its quiet hillside location, in part because of the easy camaraderie among guests and hosts. Set on a lightly traveled country road, the inn offers the quintessential New England experience just a few minutes from the slopes of Sugarbush. Built in the 1850s, the farmhouse boasts three common rooms, including a bright, modern addition with a handsome fireplace for warmth in winter, an outdoor patio for summer lounging, and a game room with a pool table. Guest rooms are decorated in an updated country style, and all of them now sport air-conditioning; memory-foam mattresses on the beds; gas fireplaces or woodstoves; and steam showers or Jacuzzis. The Paris Suite, inspired by the MacLarens' time living near Versailles, is perhaps most lovely. The owners are unfailingly kind, even supplying snowshoes in winter if you wish some, while in summer they maintain lovely perennial gardens and ponds. A lovely find.

1496 W. Hill Rd., Warren, VT 05674. ✆ **800/209-1049** or 802/496-7162. www.westhillbb.com. 8 units. $140–$200 double; $185–$250 suite. Rates include breakfast. 3-night minimum stay preferred for foliage and holiday weekends; 2-night minimum stay other weekends. AE, DISC MC, V. Children 12 and over welcome. **Amenities:** Honor-system bar. *In room:* A/C, TV/VCR, hair dryer.

WHERE TO DINE

Pizza and burgers are easy to find near Sugarbush, but if you want something more, there's a superlative pizza place here—worth visiting even if you're not a big pizza fan. On Friday and Saturday nights only, **American Flatbread ★★** (✆ **802/496-8856;** www.americanflatbread.com) on Route 100 in Waitsfield serves terrific-tasting, organic-flour pizzas to the public from 5:30 to 9pm. Founder George Schenk's delicious vision is pizza-as-whole food, and this was his original restaurant of what is now a small, thriving northern New England chain and frozen-pizza operation. Get there up to an hour early and put your name on the waiting list; no reservations are taken. The chef also creates inventive weekly salad and nonpizza entree specials.

You can pick up thick, inexpensive sandwiches on fresh bread at most any **country store** in the area, such as the **Warren Store** (✆ **802/496-3864;** www.warrenstore.com) on Main Street in Warren; they also serve breakfast and lunch daily. And **Ake's Den**

(✆ **802/496-9000**), at the junction of routes 100 and 17 in Waitsfield, is a long-popular hangout spot with sports on the TV and pubby food from the kitchen.

For a fancy meal, the **Pitcher Inn** ★★ (see "Where to Stay," above) is superlative, and many other area inns also open their kitchens to the public. **The Green Cup Café** (✆ **802/496-4963;** www.greencupvermont.com), at 40 Bridge St. in Waitsfield, overlooks a covered bridge; it's a good spot for a cup of coffee and a bite, or even a surprisingly fancy dinner that drew mention in the *New York Times.* It's closed Wednesday and Thursday.

The Common Man ★★ CONTINENTAL It sounds like a pub, but this Common Man is anything but. Housed in a century-old barn, the interior is soaring and dramatic. Chandeliers, floral carpeting on the walls (it works), and candles on the tables create a relaxed feel. You'll be halfway through your meal before you notice there are no windows. The menu is far more ambitious than skiers' grub. Start with a Cortland apple salad, beets with goat cheese fondant, PEI mussels with garlic and shallots, or peppery, thin-sliced seared beef. Main courses here are solidly Continental: things like lump crab cakes with shrimp mixed in, skilled-roasted chicken breast with Gruyère cheese, grilled pork tenderloin, breast of duck, steak with blue cheese sauce, a buttery lobster-scallop gnocchi, and a nightly fish special. You can also get plates of that great Vermont artisanal cheese. The good selection of beer and wines completes the package.

3209 German Flats Rd., Warren. ✆ **802/583-2800.** www.commonmanrestaurant.com. Reservations recommended in peak season. Main courses $13–$24. AE, DISC, MC, V. Daily 6–9pm in ski season; Tues–Sat 6–9pm rest of the year.

John Egan's Big World Pub & Grill ★ Kids PUB FARE/INTERNATIONAL Extreme skier John Egan starred in a bunch of Warren Miller skiing films and still teaches radical moves at Sugarbush, but he *really* took a risk when he opened this restaurant at the junction of routes 17 and 100 in Waitsfield. It has worked out well. In a 1970s-style motel dining room decorated with skiing memorabilia (including a bar made of ski sections signed by skiing luminaries), the restaurant features a wood-fired grill and serves an above-average pub menu with flair and worldliness. Sure, there are burgers and salads galore, but you can also order a rack of lamb cooked right on the wood fire; spicy Asian noodles; Thai shrimp; Hungarian goulash; boneless pork loin chops in a Dijon mustard sauce; rotisserie chicken; or a steak. (Lobsters and salmon sometimes make appearances, too.) There's a decent list of California wines and Vermont beers to wash it down with, plus a kids' menu.

Rte. 100 at Rte. 17, Waitsfield. ✆ **802/583-3033.** www.bigworldvermont.com. Main courses $10–$28. AE, MC, V. Daily 5–9:30pm; Sun also 10am–2pm.

3 MONTPELIER, BARRE & WATERBURY

Montpelier: 13 miles SE of Waterbury; 9 miles NW of Barre; 178 miles NW of Boston; and 39 miles SE of Burlington

Montpelier ★★ might be the most down-home, low-key state capital in the nation (and it's definitely the one with the smallest population). The glistening, iconic gold dome of Vermont's capitol building is practically the only showy or pretentious thing in the entire city; behind it, there's no cluster of mirror-sided skyscrapers, but rather a thickly forested hill. This town, it turns out, isn't a self-important center of politics, just a small town that happened to become the home of state government.

Fun Facts Taste of Success: The Story of Ben & Jerry

A clutch of doleful cows standing amid a bright green meadow on Ben & Jerry's ice-cream pints has almost become *the* symbol of Vermont, but Ben & Jerry's cows—actually, they're Vermont artist Woody Jackson's cows—also symbolize friendly capitalism (or "hippie capitalism," as some prefer).

The founding of this company is legend in small-business circles. Two friends from Long Island, Ben Cohen and Jerry Greenfield, started the company in Burlington in 1978 with $12,000 and a few mail-order lessons in ice-cream making. The pair experimented with flavor samples obtained free from salesmen, and sold their product out of an old downtown gas station. Embracing the outlook that work should be fun, they gave away free ice cream at community events, staged outdoor movies in summer, and plowed profits back into their local community. This free-spirited approach, plus the exceptional quality of the product—their machines stir out most of the air bubbles as the ice cream freezes, creating a denser ice cream that's more expensive to manufacture—built a hugely successful corporation.

Since then they've faced tough competition from a zillion other upstart gourmet ice-cream makers, plus a gradual national shift toward healthier diets. Yet Ben and Jerry are still at it. Though the friends sold their interest to the huge multinational food concern Unilever—a move that raised not a few eyebrows among its grass-roots investors—its heart and soul (and manufacturing operations) remain squarely in Vermont.

The **main factory** in Waterbury might be Vermont's most popular tourist attraction. The plant is located about a mile north of I-89 on Route 100, and the grounds have almost a Woodstockian feel to them. During summer, crowds arrive early, milling about and making new friends while waiting for the half-hour **factory tours** to begin. Tours are first come, first served, and run at least every 30 minutes from 9am to 9pm from July to mid-August (last tour departs at 8pm). Tour hours are shorter the rest of the year, but they're always running from at least 9am to 5pm. The afternoon tours fill up quickly, so get there early to avoid a long wait.

Once you've got your ticket, browse the small museum (learn the long, strange history of Cherry Garcia), buy a cone of your favorite flavor at the scoop shop, or lounge along a promenade scattered with Adirondack chairs and picnic tables. Tours cost $3 for adults, $2 for kids and seniors, and free for children 11 and under. There's also a package deal where you get a tour, a T-shirt, and a pint of the good stuff for $21—only worth it if you love the T-shirt.

Kids can enjoy the "Stairway to Heaven," which leads to a playground, and a "Cow-Viewing Area," which is self-explanatory. The tours are informative and fun, and conclude with a sample of the day's featured product. For more information, call ✆ **866/BJ-TOURS** (258-6877) or 802/882-1240.

Restaurants, coffee shops, and cultural offerings have flowed here as a result, and it's an agreeable place to pass an afternoon or stay the night if you want to know how small-town Vermont ticks. Yes, the capitol building is worth a quick visit, as is the local historical society; more than that, though, Montpelier is worth visiting simply to experience a small, clean New England town that's friendly, cultured, and easy to stroll around. It's also very close to the Green Mountains and key attractions like the Ben & Jerry's ice-cream factory.

The city is centered around two main boulevards: State Street, lined with handsome, government buildings; and Main Street, where many of the town's stores and restaurants are found. Everything's compact here. The downtown sports a pair of hardware stores, decent small-town shopping, and one of the best art movie houses in northern New England: the **Savoy Theater** (✆ **802/229-0509** or 802/229-0598; www.savoytheater.com), where concession prices are almost criminally low.

Nearby **Barre** (pronounced "Barry") is more commercial and less charming, with a blue-collar, red-state ethos. It was once the hub of Vermont's huge granite quarrying industry, and you can still see granite curbstones lining Barre's long Main Street, not to mention signs for many businesses carved from it. Barre attracted talented stone workers from Italy and Scotland (there's a statue of Robert Burns here), who helped give the turn-of-the-20th-century town a lively, cosmopolitan flavor.

About 10 miles west of Montpelier, **Waterbury** ★ is at the junction of Route 100 and I-89, making it a commercial center by default if not by design. Set along the Winooski River, it has sprawled along the valley more than other Vermont towns, possibly because the flood of 1927 nearly leveled the town—or else because the town has attracted an inexplicable number of food companies (Ben & Jerry's ice-cream empire, Green Mountain Coffee's growing java business, Cold Hollow Cider Mill's cider operations) that have built factories and outlets in what were once dairy pastures. With its position between Montpelier and **Burlington,** plus easy access to **Stowe** and Sugarbush, Waterbury has lately been attracting city dwellers from both within and outside of Vermont looking for a quieter lifestyle.

Waterbury's downtown, with its brick commercial architecture, sampling of handsome early homes, Amtrak station, and shops and restaurants, is worth a brief tour. But most travelers are either stopping to gas up or looking for "that ice-cream place." Despite its drive-through quality, Waterbury makes a decent overnight base for further explorations of the Green Mountains, Burlington (just 25 miles west), or nearby Montpelier.

ESSENTIALS

GETTING THERE Montpelier is accessible by car via exit 7 off I-89. For Barre, take exit 8; Waterbury is just south of exit 10 (the same exit as Stowe). Burlington's **airport** (code: BTV), with daily flights from New York, is about 45 miles away by car.

Amtrak (✆ **800/872-7245;** www.amtrak.com) runs one daily train (the *Vermonter*) from New York City to Montpelier. The trip takes a long 8½ hours, but costs only $56.

Greyhound (✆ **800/231-2222;** www.greyhound.com) runs buses to Montpelier, as well. From New York City, the ride takes 8 hours (change buses in White River Junction) and costs about $80 one-way; from Boston, it's a 4-hour ride costing about $55 each way.

VISITOR INFORMATION The **Central Vermont Chamber of Commerce** (✆ **802/229-4619;** www.central-vt.com) is on Stewart Road in Montpelier, just off exit 7 of I-89. Turn left at the first light; it's a half-mile farther on the left. The chamber is open weekdays from 9am to 5pm.

EXPLORING MONTPELIER & BARRE

Start your exploration of Montpelier with a visit to the gold-domed **State House** ★ at 115 State St. (✆ **802/828-2228**), guarded out front by a statue of Ethan Allen. Three capitol buildings have risen on this site since 1809; the present building retained the portico

Finds Written in Stone: A Trip to Hope Cemetery

For a poignant display of a nearly lost art, visit Barre's **Hope Cemetery,** on a hillside in a wooded valley north of Barre on Route 14. (From the middle of town, follow Maple Ave. north.) This cemetery, established in 1895, is filled with columns, urns, and human figures carved from the wonderfully fine-grained local granite. It's more than just a memorial park; it's a kind of outdoor museum celebrating the remarkable talent of local stonecutters, many of whom were immigrants.

designed during the height of Greek Revival style in 1836. Modeled after the temple of Theseus in Athens, it's made of Vermont granite (of course). You can take a self-guided tour anytime the capitol is open, any weekday (except holidays) from 8am to 4pm. Free *guided* tours are offered every half-hour between July and mid-October, Monday through Friday from 10am to 3:30pm and Saturday from 11am to 2:30pm. The informative and fun tour is worthwhile if you're in the area, but not worth a major detour.

Next door to the State House is the **Vermont Historical Society Museum** (✆ **802/828-2291;** www.vermonthistory.org) at 109 State St. The museum is housed in a brick replica of the elegant old Pavilion Building, a once-prominent Victorian hotel, and it contains a number of Vermont artifacts such as a gun once owned by Ethan Allen, Colonial powder horns, and wood carvings. It mostly deals in Colonial history, though—there's not much on recent decades. From May through mid-October, it's open Tuesday to Saturday from 10am to 4pm. Admission is $5 for adults, $3 for students or seniors, and $12 for families. There's also a gift shop on the premises.

Rock of Ages Quarry ★★ When in or around Barre, listen for the deep, throaty hum of industry. That's the Rock of Ages Quarry, still operating high on a hill above town in the aptly named hamlet of Graniteville. A visitor center presents informative exhibits, a video about quarrying, a glimpse of an old granite quarry (no longer active), and a selection of granite gifts. Self-guided tours of the old quarry are free. For a look at the active quarry (the world's largest), sign up for a guided half-hour tour on a shuttle; an old bus groans up to a viewer's platform high above the 500-foot, man-made canyon, where workers cleave huge slabs of fine-grained granite and hoist them out using 150-foot derricks anchored with miles (yes, miles) of spider-web-like steel cable. It's an operation to behold. There's also an exhibit that lets you try your hand at blasting and cutting stone by hand yourself, with the following instructions: "Grab the gun, squeeze the trigger, and feel the pulsating throb of up to 110 PSI of abrasive and air leap from the nozzle as you learn to cut in stone." And what red-blooded American male could resist an offer like that?

560 Graniteville Rd., Graniteville, VT 05654. ✆ **802/476-3119.** www.rockofages.com. Visitor center mid-May to Oct Mon–Sat 9am–5pm, also Sun 9am–5pm in foliage season only; quarry tours 9:15am–3:35pm whenever visitor center is open; self-guided tours possible Mon–Fri 8am–3:30pm (closed holidays). Self-guided tours free, small charge for narrated tours. From Barre, drive south on Rte. 14, turn left at lights by McDonald's; watch for signs to quarry.

HIKING CAMEL'S HUMP

A short drive from Waterbury is **Camel's Hump ★**, the state's fourth-highest peak at 4,083 feet (and *the* highest one without a ski area). Its distinctive profile is clearly visible from a number of points in central Vermont, including I-91. Once the site of a

Victorian-era summit resort, the mountain attracts hundreds of hikers annually, who ascend a demanding trail to the barren, windswept peak. This isn't a place to get away from crowds on sunny summer or fall foliage weekends, but if you're a serious hiker, it's well worth the effort for the spectacular views and the alpine terrain along the high ridge.

The mountain itself is part of a **state park,** which is free to enter, though the park has no true visitor center and can be difficult to locate. There are several parking areas inside the park, none of them anywhere close to the summit.

One popular round-trip loop-hike is about 7.5 miles (plan on 6 hr. or more of hiking time), departing from the Couching Lion Farm, 8 miles southwest of Waterbury on Camel's Hump Road (ask locally for exact directions). At the summit, seasonal rangers are on hand to answer questions and admonish hikers to stay on the rocks to avoid trampling the rare and delicate alpine grasses, which in Vermont are found only here and on Mount Mansfield.

WHERE TO STAY

Despite this being a state capital, there are not a lot of good lodging options in Montpelier. Consider staying at the condos in **Stowe** (p. 173), the inns in the **Mad River Valley** (p. 159), or any of the many lodgings in **Burlington** (p. 185) if you can't find a good bed in Montpelier. All these areas are within 45 minutes' drive of the city.

The **1850 River House** (✆ **800/208-4008;** www.1850riverhouse.com) is a simple, friendly B&B on Route 2 in the village of Middlesex (about 6 miles north from Montpelier). Room rates are very reasonable: $110–$125 per night for a double room, $175 per night for the suite. As a bonus, it's practically beside the Red Hen Baking Co. cafe and bakery (see "Where to Dine," below). They'll take your personal check, but *not* your credit card.

In Montpelier

Capitol Plaza Hotel ★ The favorite hotel of folks here to do business with the state government, this four-story brick hotel is centrally located (right across from the capitol) and thus makes a good base for visitors to town. The small lobby has a Colonial cast to it; guest rooms on the three upper floors adopt a light, faux-Colonial tone and have more amenities than you might expect. It has the feel of a place best suited for conventions—clean, comfortable, and convenient digs, nothing more. The more expensive rooms add wingback chairs, Ralph Lauren bedding, and high-speed Internet access, while three still-fancier suites add Jacuzzis, fridges, sofas, and bigger televisions.

100 State St., Montpelier, VT 05602. ✆ **800/274-5252** or 802/223-5252. Fax 802/229-5427. www.capitolplaza.com. 56 units. $116–$162 double and suite; foliage season higher. AE, DISC, MC, V. **Amenities:** Restaurant. *In room:* A/C, TV, fridge (in suites), hair dryer, Wi-Fi (free).

In Waterbury

The Old Stagecoach Inn (**Value**) This handsome columned and gabled home, within walking distance of Waterbury's little downtown, is full of interesting detailing: painted wood floors, two porches, an old library with a stamped tin ceiling, and a chessboard. Built in 1826, the house was gutted and revamped in 1890 in ostentatious period style by an Ohio millionaire. After years of disuse, it was converted to an inn in the late 1980s by owners who preserved the home's historical touches; there are still Oriental rugs, an organ, a tapestry, and a parrot. Eight guest rooms and three suites are furnished mostly in oak and pine furniture and antiques, but this building is aging and could perhaps use a touch-up; this isn't a polished, luxury-inn experience in any way. Still, the price is right if you're looking to save, and the breakfasts are good. Two third-floor rooms show off their original exposed beams and skylights, while three back rooms share one bathroom and feel a bit more like paying to stay in some family's farmhouse than an actual vacation.

18 N. Main St., Waterbury, VT 05676. ✆ **800/262-2206** or 802/244-5056. Fax 802/244-6956. www.oldstagecoach.com. 11 units, 3 with shared bathroom. $75–90 double with shared bathroom; $100–$130 double with private bathroom. Rates include breakfast. 2-night minimum stay during peak periods. AE, DISC, MC, V. **Amenities:** Restaurant. *In room:* TV (some units), Wi-Fi (free).

WHERE TO DINE

Unlike good beds, dining options in Montpelier are numerous. That's largely due to the influence of the wonderful **New England Culinary Institute (NECI)** campus on the edge of town. **La Brioche Bakery & Cafe** (✆ **802/229-0443**), which is essentially NECI's pastry laboratory, occupies a key corner at State and Main streets. A deli counter here offers baked goods such as croissants and baguettes. Get them to go, or settle into a table in the afternoon sun outdoors. It's open daily from as early as 6am, usually until 6pm (to 2pm Sun).

I've also spent many an afternoon inside the cleverly named **Capitol Grounds** ★, at 27 State St. (✆ **802/223-7800;** www.capitolgrounds.com), a stone's throw from the gold dome of the state capitol building. It's not affiliated with NECI, but it's one of my favorite coffeehouses in New England—a great, youthful spot to order an espresso, hot chocolate, tea, or bite to eat while you peer out at the goings-on of town, watch snow fall, or leaf through the newspaper. You'll find everyone from mothers and their kids to State House interns, bike messengers, and environmental activists hanging out here planning insurrections. Especially notable are the selection of house-blended chai teas (they're complex and peppery, rather than sweet and cloying) and good sandwiches to eat in or take out. Great restroom decor, too.

Montpelier has a very active **farmers market,** operating both indoors and outdoors, depending on the weather. Every Saturday morning from May through October, outdoor vendors array along State Street from 9am until about 1pm; the rest of the year, the market happens *twice* a week (first and third Sat of the month) at the Vermont College of Fine Arts' gymnasium on the corner of East State Street and College Street from 10am until 2pm.

Beer connoisseurs: Do *not* pass by the **Three Penny Taproom** ★ (✆ **802/223-8277;** www.threepennytaproom.com), at 108 Main St., without sampling a few beers and a plate or two of food. Right beside the NECI restaurants (see below), it looks like any other pub from the outside. It's not. The kitchen actually serves a raft of upscale snacks (pork belly, anyone?), tapas-style. Meanwhile, the bar features more than a dozen carefully selected microbrews on draft and dozens more in bottles, drawn chiefly from New England but also from the West Coast and—of course—Belgium. This is a place seriously committed to promoting both the art of craft brewing (in a state fast becoming king of the microbeer movement) and of cooking good food.

Very close to the 1850 River House (see "Where to Stay," above) a few miles northwest of town, the **Red Hen Baking Co.** ★ (✆ **802/223-5200;** www.redhenbaking.com) on Route 2 in Middlesex serves good sandwiches and soups daily from early morning through dinner time. It's just off exit 9 of the interstate.

Finally, don't overlook the **food vendors** camped right out in front of the State House during the lunch hour—last time I was in town, a Thai cook dispensed delicious pad Thai and other quick, hot lunches at a fraction of what you'd pay in a restaurant.

In Montpelier

Main Street Grill & Bar ★★ NEW AMERICAN This modern restaurant serves as classroom and ongoing exam for students of the New England Culinary Institute. It's not unusual to see knots of students, toques at a rakish angle, walking around. You can eat in the first-level dining room, watching street life through the broad windows, or hang out in the homey bar downstairs. The menu changes often, but keeps a "farm-to-table" thread going throughout the year. Lunch might be a poached pear and Stilton salad or a bowl of clam chowder to start, followed by a hangar steak salad, grilled salmon, fried calamari, crab cakes, pulled-pork tacos, fish and chips, or something similar. Dinner is heavier, of course, and could feature a grilled leg of lamb, pan-roasted chicken, steaks, grilled venison, pasta with mussels, or a butternut squash risotto (vegetarian dishes are always on the menu). There are beer specials during the weekdays, and a popular prix-fixe Sunday brunch emphasizes fresh omelets and a meat-carving station.

The downstairs **Chef's Table ★★** dining room is a more upscale experience but is sometimes rented out for private or corporate events; call about its current status and daily specials if you're interested in trying it.

118 Main St. ✆ **802/223-3188** (Grill & Bar) or 802/229-9202 (Chef's Table). www.necidining.com. Main courses $4–$12 lunch, $12–$19 dinner. AE, DISC, MC, V. Tues–Sat 11:30am–2pm and 5:30–9pm; Sun 10am–2pm and 5:30–9pm.

Restaurant Phoebe ★ CONTINENTAL It's simple yet fancy. Right on Montpelier's main restaurant row, Phoebe offers a combination of the familiar—pastas, local beef—and the unusual or upscale: entrees like quail, side dishes like fried artichokes. Lunch could be a burger, a piece of grilled salmon with peppers and a pesto cream sauce, or a grilled chicken panini. Dinners run to items like roasted pork loin, steaks, pan-roasted Coho salmon, and house-made fresh fettuccine, while the pastry chef is especially inventive: He turns out desserts like a flourless chocolate mascarpone torte, tequila-spiked agave cheesecake, and crème brûlée flavored with Meyer lemons and ginger.

52 State St. ✆ **802/262-3500.** www.restaurantphoebe.com. Main courses $7–$13 lunch, $12–$21 dinner. AE, MC, V. Mon 11:30am–2pm; Tues–Thurs 11:30am–2pm and 5:30–9pm; Fri–Sat 5:30–9pm.

In Waterbury

Hen of the Wood ★★ NEW AMERICAN Chef Eric Warnstedt, noted in *Food & Wine* as an up-and-coming chef to watch, has made this open-kitchen concept work since opening in 2005 in a space right in downtown Waterbury. He now has a devoted local following. The menu leans on ideas borrowed from France (duck breast, a wild mushroom tartine) and Italy (a sheep's milk gnocchi), but most of the preparations are solidly New American: steamed mussels; a board of local bread, cheese, and prosciutto; seared Maine sea scallops with an olive butter; grass-fed rib-eye steaks with a tarragon-inflected aioli; and short ribs braised in red wine. There are also plenty of artisanal cheeses to sample here—the place is practically a master class in the modern art of Vermont cheesemaking (try Twig Farm's "2-Milk Round")—plus a long wine list.

92 Stowe St. ✆ **802/244-7300.** www.henofthewood.com. Reservations recommended. Main courses $16–$28. MC, V. Tues–Sat 5–9pm.

Marsala Salsa ★ Value Kids CARIBBEAN/MEXICAN And now for something completely different. The owner of Marsala Salsa was born in the Caribbean, raised on the cuisine of India, and once worked at a Mexican restaurant. The result? A happy hybrid of international cuisines, served at very reasonable prices. The restaurant is inside a funky storefront in Waterbury's historic downtown, and has been decorated with a light touch. Mexican entrees might include carne asada, *bistec picado* (chopped, peppery steak), or fajitas of charbroiled chicken or sirloin with a tasty homemade avocado-lime butter. If you're more partial to Indian or Caribbean food, try the curries, vindaloo, tandoori chicken, or grilled shrimp with creamy jerk sauce. Kids get their own menu featuring a little taco pizza, mini-tortillas, and chicken fingers, while sweet dessert choices include deep-fried bananas, pumpkin flan, gelati, and a coconut cream caramel.

13–15 Stowe St. ✆ **802/244-1150.** Reservations recommended Sat–Sun. Main courses $10–$16. MC, V. Tues–Sat 5–9pm.

4 STOWE

Stowe: 10 miles N of Waterbury; 35 miles E of Burlington; 75 miles NE of White River Junction

There's no other place in Vermont quite like **Stowe.** A wonderful destination in summer, fall, or winter—and one of Vermont's original winter vacation resorts—it's set in beautiful hills beneath bigger mountains. Yet it's also struggling with growing pains, as condo developments and strip-mall-style restaurants have arrived en masse. The village's main street has mostly preserved its New England character and great views of the surrounding mountains and farmlands, but this is one of the few places in the state where you'll find yourself cursing out traffic as a 2-mile line snakes through the center of town on a weekend.

This area has always attracted a more affluent traveler than, say, Killington or Okemo. Perhaps that fact has helped downtown Stowe remain quaint, quiet, and compact; it's home to what may be Vermont's most graceful church spire (atop the Stowe Community Church). Because the ski hill is a few miles away from this main street, there's actual life here year-round: the town doesn't experience that awful emptiness many ski towns do in summer. You can explore it on foot or by bike thanks to sidewalks and a recreation path, which *isn't* the case at ski towns that have built huge parking lots and condo clusters everywhere.

Tucked into the roads leading to and from the mountain are an amazing array of lodging and restaurants. Most of them are strung out along **Mountain Road** (Rte. 108), which strikes off northwest from the village center all the way to the base of Mount Mansfield and the Stowe **ski resort.** Along this well-, well-traveled road you'll find an almost never-ending line of motels, inns, resorts, restaurants, pizza places, ski shops, bars, and even a three-screen cinema. Some of these businesses are tastefully tucked out of view of the main road, and some aren't; the chief complaint about the road, though, is traffic, which invariably backs up at day's end in winter and in foliage season, making a trip into the village an experiment in blood-pressure management. Fortunately, a **free trolley bus** connects the village with the mountain during ski season (mid-Dec to Mar); even if your car gets snowed in, you can still kick back and enjoy the weekend.

Not a skier? That's okay; you can still play. **Mount Mansfield** (Vermont's tallest) is a lovely driving or hiking trip, ablaze with foliage in fall to photograph and full of plenty of rewarding views in summer. **Smuggler's Notch** is one of New England's most fun passes to squeeze your car through. And the concentration of **resorts** here rivals anywhere else in New England. Period.

Tips The Vermont Ski Museum

As you schuss through little downtown Stowe, the **Vermont Ski Museum** (✆ **802/253-9911;** www.vermontskimuseum.org), at 1 S. Main St., makes a good quick stop for ski buffs. It's filled with memorabilia and exhibits on such topics as the history of ski lifts, and the interesting Vermont Ski Hall of Fame is on the mezzanine level. Inductees include Mead Lawrence (who won two medals in the 1950 Winter Olympics) and Billy Koch (a silver medalist in 1976), both of whom trained in Vermont. The museum is open most days of the year from noon to 5pm (but closed Nov and mid-Apr to May). Technically it's free to enter; the suggested donation is $3 per adult or $5 per family.

ESSENTIALS

GETTING THERE Stowe is on Route 100, about 10 miles north of Waterbury; simply take I-89 to exit 10 and head north, continuing past all the tourist stuff until you reach the village center. In summer Stowe can also be reached from **Burlington** or **Montpelier** (after some back-roading) via Smugglers' Notch on **Route 108.** This scenic pass, which squeezes narrowly between rocks, is *not* recommended for RVs or trailers, but it *is* one of the state's most scenic drives. The pass is closed in winter, and absolutely packed with parked cars on both shoulders (try squeezing past *that*) in October.

Stowe has no direct train or bus service, though **Amtrak**'s (✆ **800/872-7245;** www.amtrak.com) *Vermonter* service does make one daily run from New York City to Waterbury, 10 miles away. The ride takes nearly 9 hours and costs $56 one-way. Once there, though, you'll probably have to call a local taxi.

VISITOR INFORMATION The **Stowe Area Association** (✆ **877/467-8693** or 802/253-7321; www.gostowe.com) maintains a great, professional **tourist information office** right in the village center at 51 Main St. It's open 9am to 8pm weekdays, plus 10am to 5pm weekends during summer, fall-foliage season, and winter ski season (during other seasons, weekend hours are more limited). The staff here can help you book a room even on short notice, give you enough maps and brochures to keep you reading all week long, and point you to a good restaurant. They also maintain clean restrooms.

The **Green Mountain Club** (✆ **802/244-7037;** www.greenmountainclub.org), a statewide association devoted to building and maintaining walking trails in the mountains, has its headquarters and **visitor center** on Route 100 between Waterbury and Stowe.

SPECIAL EVENTS The weeklong **Stowe Winter Carnival** (✆ **802/253-7321;** www.stowewintercarnival.com) has been held annually in January since 1921. The fest features a number of wacky events involving skis, snowshoes, and skates, as well as nighttime entertainment. Don't miss the snow-sculpture contest or snow golf, played on a snow-covered course.

DOWNHILL SKIING

Stowe Mountain Resort ★★★ Stowe was one of the first, and one of the classiest, ski resorts in the world when it opened in the 1930s. Its regional dominance has eroded somewhat over the years since—Killington, Sunday River, and Sugarloaf, among other resorts, have snagged big shares of the New England ski market, and iconic hills like Mad

DINING ◆
Blue Moon Cafe **13**
Harvest Market **10**
Michael's on the Hill **16**
Mr. Pickwick's **12**
The Shed **8**

ATTRACTIONS ●
Smuggler's Notch **1**
Stowe Mountain
 Resort **2**
Vermont Ski Museum **15**

ACCOMMODATIONS ■
Golden Eagle Resort **11**
Green Mountain Inn **14**
Inn at the Mountain **3**
Stone Hill Inn **6**
Stoweflake **9**
Stowe Motel **7**
Topnotch **4**
Trapp Family Lodge **5**

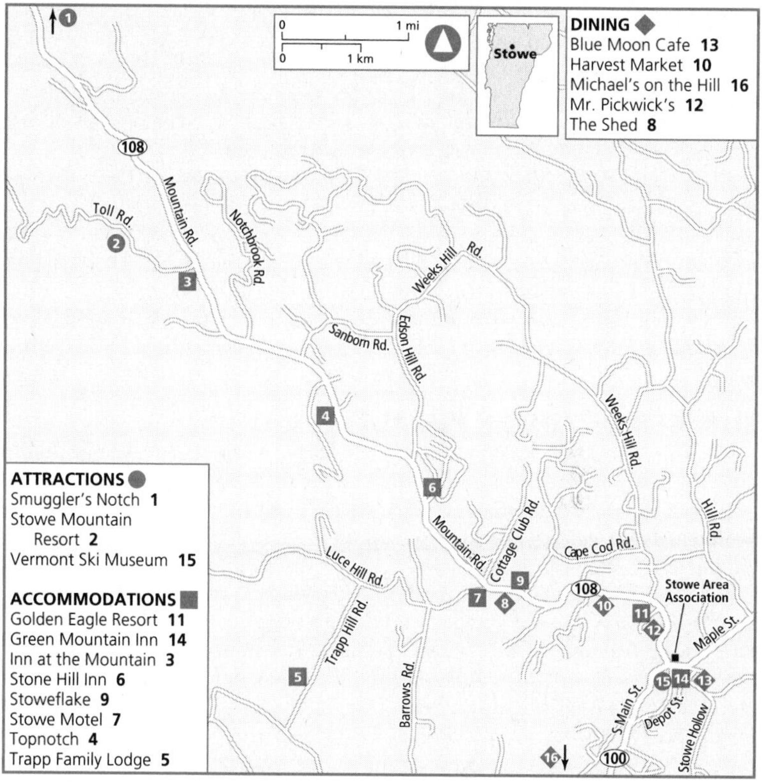

River and Jay Peak carved out niches, too. But this resort still has loads of charm and plenty of excellent runs, and it's still one of the best places to get that full New England ski experience: a combination of beautiful ski trails and pastoral Vermont views. This is a tremendous challenge for advanced skiers, with winding, old-style trails—especially notable are the legendary "Front Four" trails (National, Starr, Lift Line, and Goat), which have humbled more than a handful of folks. The mountain also has several good, long lifts that go all the way from bottom to top—not the usual patchwork of shorter lifts you find at many other ski areas. For après-ski, the resort operates the very tony **Stowe Mountain Lodge** (see "Where to Stay," below) and maintains a couple of upscale restaurants with bar areas—not to mention the obligatory spa.

5781 Mountain Rd., Stowe, VT 05672. ℂ **800/253-4754** or 802/253-3000. www.stowe.com. Adults $57–$89 day lift tickets, $68–$71 half-day; discounts for youths and seniors.

CROSS-COUNTRY SKIING

Stowe is an outstanding destination for cross-country skiers, offering several groomed ski areas with a combined total of more than 100 miles of trails traversing everything from gentle valley floors to challenging mountain peaks.

The **Trapp Family Lodge Nordic Ski Center** ★★ (✆ **800/826-7000** or 802/253-8511; www.trappfamily.com) on Luce Hill Road was the nation's first cross-country ski center. It remains one of the most gloriously situated in the Northeast, set atop a ridge with views across the broad valley and into the folds of mountains flanking Mount Mansfield. The center maintains some 30 miles of groomed trails (plus perhaps another 60 miles of ungroomed backcountry trails) on 2,700 acres of rolling forestland; basically, for the cross-country ski nut, this is sheer heaven. Rates are $22 per adult for a full-day trail pass (less for kids and half-days), and $25 per day to rent skis.

Good ski touring is also enjoyed at the **Stowe Mountain Resort Cross-Country Touring Center** (✆ **800/253-4754** or 802/253-3000), with about 20 miles of groomed trails and 25 miles of backcountry trails at the base of Mount Mansfield. Full-day passes cost $18 to $23 for adults, about half that much for children ages 6 to 12; private and group lessons are also available here.

The **Edson Hill Manor** (see "Where to Stay," below) maintains a **Ski Touring Center** (✆ **800/621-0284** or 802/253-7371) with 15 miles of wooded trails just off Mountain Road.

SUMMER OUTDOOR PURSUITS

Stowe's name is synonymous with winter recreation, but it's also a great summer destination. The area's lush, rolling hills are great for hiking and biking—and all of it's towered over by craggy **Mount Mansfield,** Vermont's highest peak.

You have several options for getting to the top of Mansfield. The **auto toll road** ★★ (✆ **802/253-3500**), part of the Stowe Mountain Resort, traces its lineage back to the 19th century, when it served horse-drawn vehicles bringing passengers to a former hotel near the mountain's crown. (That hotel was demolished in the 1960s.) Drivers now twist their way up the road and park in a lot, but there's still a ways to go to the summit. A **2-hour hike** along well-marked trails is required to get to the tippy-top, which offers unforgettable views of Lake Champlain and the Adirondacks. The toll road is open 9am to 4pm from mid-May until mid-October. The fare is a steep $24 per car, but that price covers up to six passengers (it's $6 per additional person if you have more than six—you don't, right?). Climbing the mountain on foot is free, but bicycles and motorcycles are prohibited.

Another option is the **Stowe gondola** ★ (✆ **802/253-3500**), which whisks visitors to the summit at the Cliff House Restaurant. Hikers can explore the rugged, open ridgeline, and then descend on the gondola before twilight. The gondola runs from mid-June to mid-October. The full round-trip costs $23 for adults, $19 for seniors, and $15 for children ages 6 to 12. There are family discounts, and you can also pay for a one-way ride. The lift is open 10am to 5pm daily in season.

The budget route up Mount Mansfield—the most rewarding, but of course the most physically demanding—is entirely **on foot** ★, with at least nine options for an ascent. This requires a good map. Ask for the *Visitor's Guide Hiking Map* at Stowe Mountain's guest services desk, the local tourism office, your inn, or the Green Mountain Club headquarters on Route 100 (about 4 miles south of Stowe's village center)—it's open weekdays, and the GMC can also offer you advice on other area trails.

Another local attraction is the **Stowe Recreation Path** ★★, winding for more than 5 miles from behind the Stowe Community Church and up the valley toward the big mountain, ending behind the Topnotch Tennis Center. This appealing pathway is heavily used by local walkers, hikers, and bikers in summer; in winter it becomes an equally

Tips: Squeezing Through Smugglers' Notch

Don't forget to drive through **Smugglers' Notch ★★**, Stowe's most scenic point accessible *without* skis. From the center of town, follow Route 108 west about 5 miles, past all the resorts, restaurants, and shops. The road, closed in winter, finally begins to hairpin and climb its way through the notch. You can park on the shoulder and hike the Long Trail or one of several others of varying degree of difficulty up **Mt. Mansfield.** A handy little information booth (looks a little like Camp Jellystone) right near the top of the pass is staffed from spring through summer by helpful young folks. Remember to sign in to the log book if you're doing a long hike—some of the trails are difficult, and weather can change up top in a hurry. In fall, the road here slows to a crawl as leaf-peepers ogle and snap pictures—an eye-popping but dreadfully slow ride. Come early morning if possible.

popular cross-country ski trail. Get onto the pathway at either end, or at points where it crosses side roads leading to Mountain Road. No motorized vehicles or skateboards are allowed.

According to the tourism office, some 300 bikes can be rented from shops near the Rec Path. Among those renting them is **AJ's Ski & Sports,** at 350 Mountain Rd. (✆ **800/226-6257;** www.ajssports.com), renting touring, mountain, hybrid, tandem, and even "baby jogger" bikes from its path-side location.

Fans of paddle sports (get it?) should seek out **Umiak Outdoor Outfitters ★**, at 849 S. Main St. in downtown Stowe (✆ **802/253-2317;** www.umiak.com). The folks here offer a slew of guided river trips (flat water or light rapids), with or without instruction. (My advice: Learn how to roll that kayak.) You can rent a canoe, kayak, or raft on your own. And the same outfit guides outstanding snowshoeing tours by moonlight in winter—some culminating in gourmet dinners. The outfitter is open daily 9am to 6pm.

Anglers should allow ample time to peruse **The Fly Rod Shop** (✆ **802/253-7346;** www.flyrodshop.com), located on Route 100 about 2 miles south of the village. This well-stocked shop sells fly and spin tackle and camping gear, and rents canoes and fishing videos.

WHERE TO STAY

Stowe is blessed with the highest concentration of **luxury resorts** in New England: there are *five* in this little village, plus several smaller inns that vault into the ultra-luxe category.

Of course, not everyone wants to travel high on the hog all the time. There are also plenty of basic **motels** along Mountain Road serving travelers who don't want or need to stay in the resorts, though I have found that they do vary widely in quality. One of the best value-priced options is the **Stowe Motel** (see below), which has wonderful outdoorsy amenities thrown in for free with your rate.

Or, for getting *really* close to nature, **Smugglers' Notch State Park** (✆ **802/253-4014** or 888/409-7579) maintains a 35-site campground from mid-May through late October. Its sites cost $16 to $27 per night. **Underhill State Park** ✆ **802/899-3022** or

888/409-7579), halfway up Mt. Mansfield, also offers campsites, reached via a steep gravel road. (You must walk in to your site carrying your tent a short distance from the parking area, and the access road is too steep for RVs.) Sites here cost $16 to $25 per night; the park is open from mid-May through mid-October.

Golden Eagle Resort ★ (Kids) Of the numerous lodgings lined up along Mountain Road, few are more family-friendly than this one. The Golden Eagle gets it right with a children's play area, three pools, two ponds for fishing, a regulation tennis court, 80 acres of private woods laced with hiking trails, and even a small spa offering kids' massages. Adults enjoy the place, too, particularly the romantic cottages and suites with fireplaces and whirlpools behind the main building. Standard units are more basic, but some do have sitting areas or porches. The small spa area includes a popular indoor Jacuzzi, and a cafe serves breakfasts of local eggs, dairy, and bacon. Don't come if you're expecting white-glove service, valet parking, or a fancy restaurant; but the Golden Eagle is perfect for casual families. The hotel also rents out several apartment units with full kitchens and kitchenettes.

511 Mountain Rd. (P.O. Box 1090), Stowe, VT 05672. ✆ 800/626-1010 or 802/253-4811. Fax 802/253-2561. www.goldeneagleresort.com. 94 units. $99–$199 double, $144–$299 suite; winter, holidays, and foliage season $149–$264 double, $199–$539 suite. AE, DISC, MC, V. **Amenities:** Cafe; 3 pools (2 outdoor, 1 indoor); spa; tennis court. *In room:* Fridge, Wi-Fi (some units; free).

Green Mountain Inn ★★★ (Finds) There are four true resorts on the road to Stowe Mountain, but this is the fifth—a totally different experience, because it's right in the village center. (Actually, it *is* the village center.) The handsome, historic inn is your best choice if you're seeking a New England history lesson along with your pampering. Guest rooms are spread out among several buildings old and new; rooms are tastefully decorated in an early-19th-century motif that befits the 1833 vintage of the main building. More than a dozen units have Jacuzzis and/or gas fireplaces, and the Mill House has rooms with CD players, sofas, and Jacuzzis that open into the bedrooms from behind folding wooden doors. The deluxe Mansfield House (which opened in 2000) adds double Jacuzzis, marble bathrooms, and 36-inch TVs with DVD players; all these expensive rooms are superb. Other rooms are smaller and simpler, but still offer a good taste of Vermont. The inn's restaurant, **The Whip** ★, is highly regarded by guests and locals for its Continental cooking.

18 Main St., Stowe, VT 05672. ✆ **800/253-7302** or 802/253-7301. Fax 802/253-5096. www.greenmountaininn.com. 100 units. $139–$319 double; $249–$769 suite. 2-night minimum stay summer and winter weekends and in foliage season. AE, DISC, MC, V. Pets allowed in some rooms (call ahead; $20 per night). **Amenities:** 2 restaurants; exercise room; Jacuzzi; heated outdoor pool (year-round); limited room service; sauna; steam room. *In room:* A/C, TV, hair dryer, Wi-Fi (free).

Inn at The Mountain ★ Owned and operated by Stowe Mountain Resort, this was for years the resort's "official" hotel near the base of the mountain—until the resort built the luxe Stowe Mountain Lodge, which now overshadows the Inn. Not a fancy place but rather a low-key spot, this is more like an upscale motel than an inn, though the clean, attractive rooms here are more spacious than your average motel rooms. Inside you'll find veneer furniture, small refrigerators, and tiny balconies facing the pool or the woods.

5781 Mountain Rd., Stowe, VT 05672. ✆ **800/253-4754** or 802/253-3000. www.stowe.com. 33 units. $119–$359 double, apts and town houses higher; holiday season rates higher. 5-night minimum stay Christmas week. AE, DC, DISC, MC, V. **Amenities:** Restaurant; exercise room; Jacuzzi; outdoor pool; limited room service; sauna; 9 tennis courts; Wi-Fi (in lobby; free). *In room:* A/C, TV, fridge.

Stone Hill Inn ★★ (Finds) With just nine rooms, the contemporary yet romantic Stone Hill Inn offers personal service and a handy location partway between Stowe village and the mountain. It's a very fancy place, with luxe amenities and furnishings in every room: four-poster king beds, Egyptian cotton towels, gas fireplaces that front double Jacuzzis in the oversized bathrooms, and flatscreen TVs with DVD players and VCRs. Suite layouts are all roughly similar, yet each room somehow has a distinct color scheme and feel; fabric and wall hues of gold, purple, bordeaux, and the like put one in mind of a French chateau. The high-ceilinged common rooms sport fireplaces and billiards tables, while a guest pantry offers complimentary beverages around the clock. Breakfast is served in a bright dining room, and snacks are set out each evening. An outdoor hot tub is good for a relaxing soak, and the inn has snowshoes and a toboggan for guests to use. Stone Hill may lack history, but that's all it lacks—this is a place of quiet, luxury, and romance.

89 Houston Farm Rd. (off Mountain Rd.), Stowe, VT 05672. ✆ **802/253-6282.** www.stonehillinn.com. 9 units. $330–$425 double. Rates include breakfast. 2-night minimum stay Sat–Sun and foliage season; 3-night minimum stay holiday weekends; 4-night minimum stay Christmas week. Closed Apr and Nov. AE, DC, DISC, MC, V. Not suitable for children. **Amenities:** Jacuzzi. *In room:* A/C, TV/DVD, hair dryer, no phone, Wi-Fi (free).

Stoweflake ★★ This resort with the cutesy name is on Mountain Road en route to the mountain, less than 2 miles from the village. It has gone on a sprucing-up program lately, adding better amenities to its most expensive rooms. As a result, the newest guest rooms are now as nice as those at Topnotch (see below)—they're regally decorated and have amenities such as two phones and wet bars. The resort has several categories of guest rooms in two wings; the "superior" rooms in the old wing are a bit cozy, okay for an overnight, but you're better off requesting "deluxe" level or better if you will be staying a few days. Many of these units have tubs with jets. The spa and fitness facilities are adequate, even if they lack the over-the-top elegance of Topnotch's (what, no waterfalls?). There's a decent-size fitness room with Cybex equipment, a squash/racquetball court, co-ed Jacuzzi, and a small indoor pool. Stoweflake also manages a small collection of fine town houses nearby. All rooms and town houses are wired for either high-speed Internet or Wi-Fi—free of charge.

1746 Mountain Rd. (P.O. Box 369), Stowe, VT 05672. ✆ **800/253-2232** or 802/253-7355. Fax 802/253-6858. www.stoweflake.com. 95 units. Peak winter season $170–$270 double, $390 suite; holiday season $180–$290 double, $340 suite; off season $150–$250 double, $360 suite. 2-night minimum stay on most weekends; 4-night minimum stay during holidays. AE, DC, DISC, MC, V. **Amenities:** 2 restaurants; babysitting; bikes; children's center; health club; indoor and outdoor pools; racquetball/squash court; limited room service; spa; 2 tennis courts. *In room:* A/C, TV, fridge (some units), hair dryer, either Wi-Fi or high-speed Internet (free).

Stowe Motel ★ (Value) This is one of the very best choices in Stowe if you're traveling on a budget. Units are spread out among three buildings; rooms are basic, but some have couches and coffee tables, and all have small fridges, air conditioners, televisions, and phones. The slightly more expensive efficiency units add two-burner stoves for in-room cooking. Surprisingly, you also get access to expansive grounds, tennis courts, a pool, hammocks, and an outdoor hot tub—a great setup for such a reasonably priced sleep. (You can often get a double room for around $100, a true steal in Stowe.) They will even rent or let you borrow snowshoes or mountain bikes. If you need more space, the motel rents out a few local houses and apartments nearby, some with hot tubs, washer/dryers, and the like. Again: a steal of a deal.

 2043 Mountain Rd., Stowe, VT 05672. ✆ **800/829-7629** or 802/253-7629. Fax 802/253-9971. www.stowemotel.com. 60 units. $75–$190 double. AE, DISC, MC, V. Pets allowed (1 per room, $10 per night). **Amenities:** Bikes; Jacuzzi; outdoor heated pool; tennis court. *In room:* A/C, TV, fridge, Wi-Fi (free).

Topnotch ★★★ The boxy, uninteresting exterior of Topnotch hides a surprisingly creative interior and upscale facility (voted one of the top resort spas in the U.S. by *Condé Nast Traveler* readers). The main lobby is in ski-lodge style, with lots of stone, wood, and a huge moose head on the wall; guest rooms are attractively appointed, mostly in country pine. Some units have wood-burning fireplaces, some have Jacuzzis, and third-floor rooms sport cathedral ceilings. The main attraction is the huge 35,000-square-foot **spa ★**, free for guests (nonguests pay a $50 fee). This spa has such nice touches as fireplaces in the locker rooms and a range of aerobics classes, weight training programs, and revitalizing treatments for face, skin, and body. Outdoors you can ramble on 120 acres of grounds, doing anything from horseback riding to cross-country skiing. There also is indoor tennis. Three pools (2 outdoor, 1 indoor) and a Jacuzzi help loosen after-ski muscles.

4000 Mountain Rd., Stowe, VT 05672. ✆ **800/451-8686** or 802/253-8585. Fax 802/253-9263. www.topnotchresort.com. 92 units. $180–$320 double, $315–$755 suite; holidays $380–$495 double, $500–$860 suite. 6-night minimum stay Christmas week. AE, DC, DISC, MC, V. Pets allowed. **Amenities:** 2 restaurants; concierge; exercise room; Jacuzzi; 3 pools (1 indoor, 2 outdoor); limited room service; sauna; spa; tennis courts (4 indoor, 10 outdoor). *In room:* A/C, TV, fridge, hair dryer, Wi-Fi (free).

Trapp Family Lodge ★★ Of Stowe's big four resorts, this one can claim the best views *and* the most history. It's a different experience from the other three, but for the outdoors enthusiast or *Sound of Music* fan, it can't be beat. You know the story: The Trapp family fled Nazi Austria under the cover of darkness and wound up on this lovely Vermont hillside, farming, singing, and eventually building a lodge. (The original burned in 1980; this is a copy.) Two of Maria's grandchildren now manage the resort and have gently tugged it into the 21st century: The newly added bakery, microbrewery, gorgeous fitness center with outdoor hot tub and indoor pool, and luxury wing testify to that. Even standard rooms are big, many with expansive balconies and views of the Green Mountains. (Ask about a corner unit.) Family suites like no. 421 are positively huge, while a half-dozen luxury suites in the newer Millennium Wing feature touches like wood-burning fireplaces, kitchenettes, wine glasses, or stylish European-style bathrooms with Jacuzzis and open showers. You can even sleep in Maria's own room, which sports a full brick fireplace, full kitchen, four-poster bed, and the best views in the house. (Her suite also overlooks the quiet family cemetery.) Hiking, biking, and skiing trails interlace 2,000-plus acres of grounds (see "Cross-Country Skiing," p. 171), and the lodge now rents mountain bikes. The restaurant still leans toward meaty Austrian fare, but even that's evolving with the arrival of a new chef.

700 Trapp Hill Rd. (P.O. Box 1428), Stowe, VT 05672. ✆ **800/826-7000** or 802/253-8511. Fax 802/253-5740. www.trappfamily.com. 120 units. $195–$585 double, $295–$880 suite. Rates include meals during holidays and foliage season. 3-night minimum stay Presidents' Day weekend and foliage season; 5-night minimum stay Christmas week. AE, DC, MC, V. Depart Stowe westward on Rte. 108; in 2 miles bear left at fork near white church; continue up hill, following signs for lodge. **Amenities:** 2 restaurants; babysitting; bikes; health club; Jacuzzi; 3 pools (1 heated indoor, 2 outdoor); limited room service; sauna; 4 tennis courts. *In room:* A/C, TV, fridge (some units), Wi-Fi (free).

WHERE TO DINE

Packing a picnic? The **Harvest Market ★**, at 1031 Mountain Rd. (✆ **802/253-3800;** www.harvestatstowe.com), is a great place for picking up takeout gourmet. You can browse Vermont products and imports, or snag fresh-baked goods to bring back to the ski lodge or take for a picnic on the bike path. It's open daily until 7pm.

Blue Moon Cafe ★★★ NEW AMERICAN Delectable crusty bread on the table, Frank Sinatra crooning in the background, and local art on the walls are clues that this isn't a typical ski-area restaurant in any way, shape, or form. Just a short stroll off Stowe's *real* main street, inside an older home with a contemporary interior, the Blue Moon offers what's probably the town's top fine dining—it's amazing that they're so low-key about it. The restaurant's wonderful menu changes pretty much every week, so half the fun of eating here is that you never know what's going to be on the menu until you open it. Start out with the appetizer of the moment, whether that happens to be a grilled sweet potato-and-orange salad with frisée and pecans, some lamb skewers, a piece of smoked trout, or a preparation of Maine crab cakes. Then move on to entrees such as filet of sole with lemon, capers, and roasted potatoes; mahi mahi with a mango salsa *and* a chipotle pineapple sauce; a grilled half chicken with chutney; a grilled lamb steak; or New York strip served with cognac cream and crispy fried onions. There are also a few changing small plates each week, which are even more inventive than the regular menu—rock shrimp risotto and venison burrito are two that have popped up on the menu, for instance. Finish with the popular Belgian chocolate pot, some homemade sorbet, or whichever mousse, tart, or cheese plate happens to be on the card.

35 School St. ✆ **802/253-7006.** www.bluemoonstowe.com. Reservations recommended. Small plates $13, main courses $18–$31. AE, DISC, MC, V. Sun–Thurs 6–9pm (Fri–Sat to 9:30pm).

Michael's on the Hill ★★★ NEW AMERICAN In a farmhouse on the hill and highway leading up to Stowe village, Michael's does New American like few others in the area. There are three dining spaces: a porch with plenty of windows looking out on the mountains; the elegantly arched Trout Room; and a woody-rustic, renovated barn. The menu is stunning in its new interpretations of classical Continental cuisine, Vermont-style. Appetizers might include a roasted corn soup with mint, a Maine crab cake with an asparagus tart, beer-steamed mussels, pumpkin soup with curry and local cheddar, a crab rissolé with lemon aioli, or Vermont quail. Entrees run to things like a Moroccan lamb loin chop with merguez sausage, roasted strip loin with truffled mashed potatoes and marrow, lobster ravioli, trout meunière, or riesling- and spice-braised rabbit served with polenta. This is truly an exciting place to dine. And if you're day-tripping in Waterbury village, don't miss the little cafe (✆ **802/882-2700**) at Waterbury's train station with gourmet products; it's run by the same owners.

4182 Waterbury-Stowe Rd. ✆ **802/244-7476.** www.michaelsonthehill.com. Reservations recommended. Main courses $25–$43. AE, MC, V. Wed–Mon 5–9:30pm.

Mr. Pickwick's ★★ **Finds** PUB FARE/CONTINENTAL Mr. Pickwick's is a pub and restaurant inside the Ye Old English Inne. Ignore the silly spelling and the over-the-top faux Englishness of the place, because this restaurant is actually very good. Run since 1983 with creative gusto by British expats, it's an enjoyable place to eat. Begin by admiring the decor while relaxing at handsome wood tables in the booths (dubbed *pews*). Sample from among some 150 beers or 21 casks (many of them British) before studying the much-changed lunch menu—they still do fish and chips and bangers and mash here, sure, but now the food is mostly things like Caesar salads, an inventive onion soup, mulligatawny, Kobe burgers, duck confit (!), and a rocket salad of pears in wine, Stilton cheese, and fresh herbs. Dinner has become something much more interesting and upscale than it used to be, too: grilled fish, Statler chicken, delicious pasta, various steaks, prosciutto-wrapped kangaroo (yes, really) served with a chocolate plum sauce, pan-seared elk medallions, game stew, or whatever else the owners feel like finding and cooking.

Tips Après-Ski Beer

It's pretty easy to find good beer in the Stowe area. About 10 miles north of Stowe, in the hamlet of **Morrisville,** you can visit the small **Rock Art Brewery** ★ (✆ **802/888-9400;** www.rockartbrewery.com) and buy beer or attend charity tastings. On busy Mountain Road in Stowe, **The Shed** (✆ **802/253-4364**) has expanded its brewing from simple ales to a wide range of microbrews for its happy, après-ski crowd.

You could also head 10 miles south to **Waterbury,** home to the newish **The Alchemist Pub and Brewery** (✆ **802/244-4120;** www.alchemistbeer.com), though the proprietor may be taking himself a little too seriously: He says he has "a hard enough time letting someone else *pour* my beer, let alone watch it walk out the door to an uncertain future." Hopefully he'll get over that.

Anglophiles, fear not: The beef Wellington and oyster-kidney pie are still safe and sound on the menu.

433 Mountain Rd. ✆ **802/253-7558.** www.mrpickwicks.com. Reservations accepted for parties of 6 or more. Main courses $10–$18 at lunch, $18–$36 at dinner. AE, DC, MC, V. Daily 11am–1am.

The Shed PUB FARE/BREWERY Stowe has plenty of options for pub fare, but the Shed takes the prize for longest-running. Since it opened more than 3 decades ago, this informal place has supplied local skiers and tourists with filling food and camaraderie (join the "Hall of Foam" by ordering a microbrew sampler). A few craft brews are made right on the premise, but there are plenty more choices as well. The taproom has a pubby feel; the bright solarium in the rear is a better spot to eat Sunday brunch. Meals are pub fare and nothing special: nachos, burgers, ribs, fish and chips, chicken, shepherd's pie, sandwiches. Look for prime rib specials on the weekends.

1859 Mountain Rd. ✆ **802/253-4364.** Reservations recommended weekends and holidays. Main courses $8–$11 at lunch, $8–$21 at dinner. AE, DC, DISC, MC, V. Sun–Thurs 11:30am–10pm; Fri–Sat 11:30am–11pm.

5 BURLINGTON

Burlington: 215 miles NW of Boston; 98 miles S of Montreal; 154 miles NE of Albany, NY

Right at the doorstep of Lake Champlain, **Burlington** is Vermont's biggest city (though it isn't all *that* big). It's a vibrant college town—home to the University of Vermont, known locally as UVM—with flavors of hippie, yuppie, and vintage Vermont mashed and mixed in like a scoop of Ben & Jerry's super fudge chunk. Speaking of Ben & Jerry, they completely epitomize this place: two city hippies-gone-big-time who found the city to be their ideal testing ground. Later, when the brand exploded, they resisted the temptation to move their factory elsewhere. (Look for the sidewalk plaque at the corner of St. Paul and College sts. commemorating their original ice-cream shop.)

This city is so independent-minded that it elected a socialist mayor in 1981, Bernie Sanders, who captured the local mood so well that he's now the independent (and only

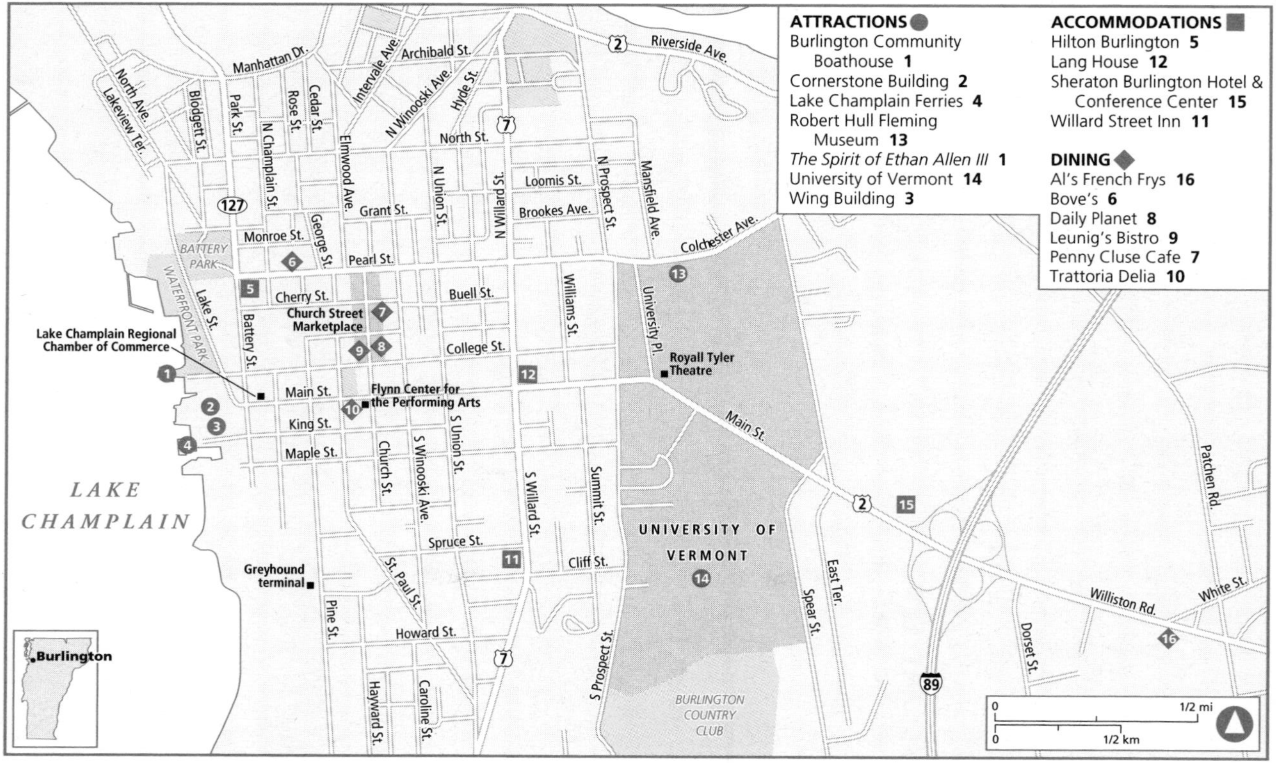
ATTRACTIONS
Burlington Community Boathouse 1
Cornerstone Building 2
Lake Champlain Ferries 4
Robert Hull Fleming Museum 13
The Spirit of Ethan Allen III 1
University of Vermont 14
Wing Building 3
ACCOMMODATIONS
Hilton Burlington 5
Lang House 12
Sheraton Burlington Hotel & Conference Center 15
Willard Street Inn 11
DINING
Al's French Frys 16
Bove's 6
Daily Planet 8
Leunig's Bistro 9
Penny Cluse Cafe 7
Trattoria Delia 10
LAKE CHAMPLAIN
Lake Champlain Regional Chamber of Commerce
Church Street Marketplace
Flynn Center for the Performing Arts
Royall Tyler Theatre
Greyhound terminal
UNIVERSITY OF VERMONT
BURLINGTON COUNTRY CLUB
BATTERY PARK
WATERFRONT PARK
Burlington
Riverside Ave.
Manhattan Dr.
Archibald St.
Intervale Ave.
N Winooski Ave.
Hyde St.
North Ave.
Lakeview Ter.
Blodgett St.
Park St.
Rose St.
Cedar St.
N Champlain St.
Elmwood Ave.
North St.
N Union St.
N Willard St.
Loomis St.
Brookes Ave.
N Prospect St.
Mansfield Ave.
Colchester Ave.
Grant St.
Monroe St.
George St.
Pearl St.
Cherry St.
Buell St.
Williams St.
University Pl.
Lake St.
Battery St.
College St.
Main St.
King St.
Maple St.
Church St.
S Winooski Ave.
S Union St.
S Willard St.
Summit St.
Spruce St.
Cliff St.
St. Paul St.
Pine St.
Howard St.
Hayward St.
Caroline St.
S Prospect St.
East Ter.
Spear St.
Dorset St.
Patchen Rd.
Williston Rd.
White St.
0 1/2 mi
0 1/2 km

socialist!) member of the U.S. Senate. Burlington was also the birthplace of the rock band Phish, legendary for their meandering jam sessions.

It's really no wonder that Burlington has become a magnet for those seeking an alternative to big-city life, though. The downtown occupies a superb position overlooking the lake and the Adirondack Mountains to the west. To the east, the Green Mountains rise dramatically, with two of their highest peaks (Mount Mansfield and Camel's Hump) stretching above an undulating ridge.

The downtown is thriving. The pedestrian mall (Church St.), a concept that has failed in so many other cities, *works* here: People stroll, eat, shop, and enjoy the relative lack of auto traffic. New construction has also brought chain and grocery stores downtown, reversing the flight to the suburbs and malls that has plagued most U.S. cities. How to enjoy this place? The city's scale is pleasantly skewed toward pedestrians, so walk everywhere whenever possible. Bad weather? Not to worry. The city's bus system is the most extensive in Vermont, and it's absurdly cheap: You can ride to the city airport for less than $2.

ESSENTIALS

GETTING THERE Burlington is at the junction of I-89, Route 7, and Route 2. From New York City, it's between a 5- and 6-hour drive via either I-91 and I-89 or the New York State Thruway; from Boston, figure on 3 to 3½ hours' driving via I-93 and then I-89.

Burlington International Airport (airport code: BTV), about 3 miles east of the city center, is served daily by nonstop flights on **Continental Express** (✆ 800/525-0280; www.continental.com) from Newark and Cleveland; **Delta Connection** (✆ 800/221-1212; www.delta.com) from Atlanta and New York's JFK; **JetBlue** (✆ 800/538-2583; www.jetblue.com) daily from New York City's JFK and Orlando; **United** (✆ 800/241-6522; www.united.com) from Chicago and Washington's Dulles airports; and **US Airways Express** (✆ 800/428-4322; www.usair.com) from New York City's LaGuardia, Philadelphia, and Washington's Reagan.

Auto rentals are available from a half-dozen national chains inside the terminal, or a bus ride into the city on a **CCTA bus** (bus no. 1; departs every 30 min., every hour on Sun) costs just $1.25.

Amtrak's (✆ **800/872-7245;** www.amtrak.com) *Vermonter* service offers one daily departure to **Essex Junction** (connected by bus to downtown Burlington) from New York, New Haven, Springfield, Massachusetts, and points beyond such as Baltimore and Washington, D.C. It's a cheap ride ($56 one-way) from New York—but it also takes more than 9 hours from New York.

Greyhound (✆ **800/231-2222;** www.greyhound.com) has a depot near the city center at 345 Pine St., with bus connections to Albany, Boston, Hartford, and New York. From New York, it's a long 10- to 14-hour slog (change in Boston), costing $68 one-way; but from Boston, it takes 4½ to 5 hours and costs $56 one-way.

VISITOR INFORMATION The **Lake Champlain Regional Chamber of Commerce,** 60 Main St. (✆ **877/686-5253** or 802/863-3489; www.vermont.org), maintains an information center in a brick building near the waterfront and a short walk from Church Street Marketplace. It's open weekdays only. (On weekends, helpful maps and brochures are left in the entryway for visitors.) In summer, an information kiosk is also staffed at the Church Street Marketplace, at the corner of Church and Bank streets.

The excellent free local weekly paper, *Seven Days* (www.7dvt.com), carries great local articles and dining reviews plus a very good listing of local events, exhibits, and happenings.

Moments **Initial Reservations**

The University of Vermont is always abbreviated—both officially and unofficially by alums and sports commentators—as UVM, never as UVT or UV. Ever wonder why? Well, there's actually a reason, and it has to do with the classics. The initials don't stand for University of Vermont, rather for *Universitas Virdis Montis* (in Latin: "University of the Green Mountains"). Now don't you wish you'd paid attention during Latin class?

SPECIAL EVENTS **First Night Burlington** (✆ **802/863-6005;** www.firstnightburlington.com) turns downtown into a stage on New Year's Eve. Hundreds of performers—from rockers to vaudevillians—play at nearly three dozen venues (mostly indoors) for about 10 hours beginning at 2pm. The evening finishes with a bang at the midnight fireworks. Admission is $15 for adults or $5 for children (a "family pack" reduces the cost for families) and covers most performances—some music performances require a small $2 to $3 supplement for admission.

The **Vermont Mozart Festival** (✆ **802/862-7352;** www.vtmozart.com) takes place in and around Burlington (and farther afield) for about 3 weeks from mid-July through early August. The festival also has a small winter series of Christmas and other performances (check the festival website for details). Ticket prices to individual concerts vary considerably; call or consult the online schedule.

ORIENTATION

Burlington basically comprises three distinct areas: the **UVM campus** on top of the hill, a **downtown** area centered around the active Church Street Marketplace, and a thin strip of **waterfront** running along Lake Champlain.

UNIVERSITY OF VERMONT Founded in 1791 (funded by a state donation of 29,000 acres of forest land), Vermont's public university has since grown to accommodate nearly 10,000 undergraduates, more than a thousand graduate students, and a few hundred medical students. The campus is set on 400 acres atop a small hill overlooking downtown Burlington and Lake Champlain to the west; it also has a pretty good view of the Green Mountains to the east. The campus is large, with more than 400 buildings, many of which were designed by noted architectural firms such as H. H. Richardson and McKim, Mead, and White. A controversial new student center opened in 2007, dwarfing surrounding buildings with both its size and its boxy design, but it's here to stay. What UVM *doesn't* have is the usual college strip of beery bars, bagel shops, and bookstores adjacent to campus. Downtown serves that function, 5 blocks away; College Street connects the two, as does the free **College Street Shuttle** (it looks like an old-fashioned trolley). The shuttle runs between Burlington's waterfront boathouse and the UVM campus year-round, every 15 to 30 minutes from 11am until 9pm. Use it.

CHURCH STREET Downtown centers around the largely traffic-free Church Street Marketplace, a pedestrian corridor that jumps with activity most of the year (see "Shopping," p. 190)—it's most fun in summer, obviously. This is the place to wander without purpose, people-watching and snacking. While the shopping and grazing are excellent here, don't overlook the superb historic commercial architecture that graces much of the area. A number of side streets radiate out from Church Street, too, with a mix of restaurants, shops, and offices.

THE WATERFRONT The waterfront has benefited from a multimillion-dollar renovation, which included new construction of buildings like the **Wing Building** (a quirky structure of brushed steel and other nontraditional materials). Next door is the **Cornerstone Building,** with a restaurant and offices (and better views of the lake due to its higher vantage point). Nearby the city's **Community Boathouse** is a good destination on a hot summer day (see "Outdoor Pursuits," below). Bear in mind that Burlingtonians accept a fairly liberal definition of the adjective "lakeside," though; in some cases, it can mean a shop or restaurant that's actually 300 feet away and with no sight of water.

EXPLORING BURLINGTON

Frankly speaking, there are not a ton of attractions in Burlington; instead the chief attractions are the lovely natural setting, the lakefront (which is mostly hidden from view), and the city's vibrant culture and counterculture. So if it's attractions you want, think about striking out into the countryside to nearby country towns like **Charlotte, Shelburne, Colchester, Underhill,** and **Jericho,** which hold some of the best sights.

Ethan Allen Homestead Museum A quiet retreat on one of the most idyllic, least-developed stretches of the Winooski River, this museum just north of the city center is a shrine to Vermont's favorite son; even today, centuries later, he and his Green Mountain Boys remain larger-than-life figures in this state. Though Allen wasn't actually born in Burlington, he settled here later in life on property confiscated from a British sympathizer during the Revolution. Inside this red reconstruction of a farmhouse, an orientation center gives an intriguing multimedia account of Allen's life, plus info about regional history. The admissions fees have recently been jacked up quite a bit (more than double, in some cases), for some reason.

Rte. 127, Colchester. ✆ **802/865-4556.** www.ethanallenhomestead.org. Admission $7 adults, $3 children 3–6, seniors $5, $25 per family. Mid-May to mid-Oct Thurs–Sat 10am–4pm; Sun 1–4pm. From city center, follow Pearl St. (at the northern end of Church St. Marketplace) to Rte. 127, then continue about 2 miles north. From I-89, take exit 17 to North Ave. or exit 15 to Rte. 15.

Lake Champlain Ferries ★★ Car ferries chug across the often placid, sometimes turbulent waters of Lake Champlain from Burlington to Port Kent, New York, between late May and early October, and it's a good way to cut out miles of driving if you're heading west toward the Adirondacks. It's also a great way to see the lake, leaves, and mountains on a pleasant, inexpensive 1-hour cruise. Reservations are taken for the Burlington route only, which operates 10 to 20 times per day when it's running. Travelers are advised to make reservations at least a day in advance. Two other ferries also cross the lake—much more quickly, in just 12 to 20 minutes—linking Grande Isle, Vermont, with Plattsburgh, New York; and Charlotte, Vermont, with Essex, New York. (***Note:*** Credit cards are not accepted for fares on these two shorter rides.) Between June and mid-October, narrated, musically accompanied, or dinner-inclusive lake cruises are also offered by the ferry company; call ✆ **802/864-9669** for details. Note that these three ferries are unaffiliated with the "cable ferry" at Ticonderoga, New York (p. 150), a fourth Champlain crossing.

King St. Dock. ✆ **802/864-9804.** www.ferries.com. Burlington–Port Kent $18 one-way car and driver, $4.95 additional adults, $2.20 children 6–12; Charlotte–Essex and Grande Isle–Cumberland Head $9.50 one-way for car and driver, $3.75 additional adults, $1.50 children 6–12; all round-trip fares slightly discounted. No credit cards for Charlotte and Grande Isle ferries.

Ethan Allen, Patriot & Libertine

In 1749 the governor of New Hampshire began giving away land to any settler willing to brave the wilderness that is Vermont (a territory whose ownership was still nebulous at that time). But two decades later, New York State's court *cancelled* those grants, opening the door for New York speculators to flood the region and push the original settlers out of the valleys—up into the less hospitable Green Mountains.

Unsurprisingly, that decision didn't sit well with those who had already settled. So they formed a network of military units—the Green Mountain Boys—to drive out the New Yorkers. A fellow named Ethan Allen headed up this new militia, launching a series of harrying raids against the impudent Gothamites. His Boys destroyed homes, drove off livestock, and chased those Big Apple sheriffs back across the border from whence they had come.

The American Revolution soon intervened. Allen and his Green Mountain Boys took up the revolutionary cause with equal vigor, helping to sack Fort Ticonderoga in 1775, rallying to the cause at the famed Battle of Bennington, and generally confounding the British for the remainder of the war. Allen's legend grew to ridiculous proportions during the war: He could supposedly bite the head off a nail (yeah, right), and was so tough (it was said in those days) that a rattlesnake once bit him—and promptly died.

While Allen's supposed exploits endured long after his death in 1789, he also left a more significant legacy: The fact of Vermont's statehood in 1791 (instead of being annexed by its bracketing states) was due largely to the independence and patriotism the place developed under Allen's leadership. And today you can't drive far in Vermont without seeing reminders of the patriot—parks and highways are named for him, inns boast he once slept in them, and you'll still hear an occasional tale about Allen's patriotic (or even his bawdy) exploits.

Robert Hull Fleming Museum ★ This University of Vermont facility houses a collection of art and anthropological displays, with permanent holdings of African, ancient Egyptian, Asian, and Middle Eastern art. A selection of paintings by 20th-century Vermont artists is also on permanent display, and changing exhibitions reflect various cultures around the globe. Call or check the museum website for the schedule of lectures and other special events, as well. (***Note:*** If you drive to the museum on weekdays, you must feed the museum's parking meters 75¢ per hour and also obtain a pass from the reception desk; on weekends, there's a free parking lot nearby.)

61 Colchester Ave. (UVM campus). ✆ **802/656-0750.** www.flemingmuseum.org. Admission $5 adults, $3 seniors and students, $10 family. Labor Day to Apr Tues–Fri 9am–4pm (Wed to 8pm), Sat–Sun 1–5pm; May to Labor Day Tues–Fri noon–4pm, Sat–Sun 1–5pm.

Shelburne Museum ★★★ Established in 1947 by one Electra Havenmeyer Webb, the Shelburne houses one of the nation's best collections of American folk and decorative art. The museum occupies three dozen buildings spread out across 45 rolling acres, about 7 miles south of Burlington, and no less than the *New York Times* has opined that "there is nothing like Shelburne in the museum universe." The holdings total some 150,000 items in all—the expected quilts, tools, duck decoys, and weather vanes, but also entire *buildings* gathered from around New England and New York, which are a highlight. The structures include an 1890 railroad station, an entire lighthouse, a stagecoach inn, an Adirondack lodge, and a Vermont round barn. Even a 220-foot steamship is eerily landlocked on the museum's grounds. More recent additions include a 1950s ranch house (furnished in '50s style) and the engaging Kalkin House, creatively constructed of prefab metal structures and other materials. Rotating special exhibits highlight specific aspects of Americana such as Shaker design, African-American quilt work, the art of John James Audubon, and similar topics. As if this weren't enough, there's an annual summer festival here highlighting Vermont cheeses, wines, and beers known as the Vermont Cheesemakers Festival.

Rte. 7 (P.O. Box 10), Shelburne. ✆ **802/985-3346.** www.shelburnemuseum.org. Summer admission $18 adults, $9 children 6–18; discounted rates after 3pm. Late May to mid-Oct daily 10am–5pm; selected buildings also Apr to late May and mid-Oct to Dec 31. (Call for information.)

The *Spirit of Ethan Allen* III ★ The vistas of Lake Champlain and the Adirondacks haven't changed much since Samuel de Champlain first explored the area in 1609—but travel sure has. This tour ship, holding 500 passengers on three decks (it's much larger than its predecessor), offers a more genteel touring alternative to taking a ferry ride. The enclosed decks are air-conditioned, and food and drink are served from a deli and cash bar. In addition to four-times-daily narrated tours (1½ hr.; sunset cruise more expensive than the others), there are many specialty trips involving lunch, brunch, dinner, music, or even a murder (dramatically, for mystery buffs; not a real one). Parking is available at an additional cost.

Burlington Boathouse. ✆ **802/862-8300.** www.soea.com. Narrated 90-min. tours $15–$20 adults, $6–$13 children 3–11; meal and specialty cruises $23–$48 adults, $12–$31 children 3–11. Narrated cruises daily mid-May to mid-Oct; specialty cruises mid-June to mid-Oct.

OUTDOOR PURSUITS

Burlington is blessed with numerous parks. Most popular is **Leddy Park ★★** on North Avenue, with a 1,800-foot beach, tennis courts, ball fields, walking trails, and a handsome indoor skating rink. **North Beach ★** (✆ **802/862-0942**), at 60 Institute Rd., also has a long sandy beach, plus a pricey campground with nearly 140 sites for those looking to pitch a tent or park an RV. The catch? Those sites cost $24 to $35 per night.

On the downtown waterfront, look for the city-owned **Community Boathouse ★** (✆ **802/865-3377**), a modern structure with a bit of Victorian flair. This place sees a lot of action during the short Vermont summer (as does the 900-ft. boardwalk adjacent to it). You can rent a sailboat or rowboat, sign up for kayak or sculling lessons, or just wander around and enjoy the sunset like the locals do.

Another of Burlington's hidden yet beguiling attractions is the **Burlington Bike Path ★★**, running 8 or 9 miles along an old rail bed fronting the shores of Lake Champlain. It's an easy, quiet trip through parks, past backyards, and along sandy beaches. You start near the boathouse and head north toward the Winooski River; it's definitely worth packing a lunch and exploring for a few hours on a sunny afternoon if you like bikes. From the north shore of the Winooski, pedal northward, picking up the Causeway Park trail, which lets you seemingly skim across the lake's surface by bike.

Moments **No Business Like Snow Business**

If you're a lover of science or nature, one of the more interesting day trips from Burlington is to the little hamlet of **Jericho,** about a 15- to 20-minute drive northeast on Route 15. Once there, find the **Old Red Mill Museum** ★ (✆ **802/899-3225;** www.snowflakebentley.com), maintained by the Jericho Historical Society.

This best part of the museum showcases America's finest repository of snowflake photographs, made by one Wilson Bentley—a local farmer and amateur naturalist who lived here from 1885 until 1931, devising the world's first camera designed to capture images of snowflakes. He photographed some 5,000 snowflakes in his lifetime, publishing articles in *National Geographic* and first advancing the idea that no two snowflakes are identical. The story of Bentley's determined pursuit of his studies is as entrancing as the photographs lining the walls, which reveal the amazing variety of crystalline structures created in snowstorms—many of them breathtakingly beautiful.

The museum is open daily from April through September, Wednesday through Sunday in winter. There's no admission charge.

WHERE TO STAY

Several excellent resort properties are located within a half-hour's drive of the city. If those are too rich for your blood, a number of chain motels cluster along Route 7 (Shelburne Rd.) in South Burlington, about a 5- to 10-minute drive from downtown. While they lack even a trace of New England charm, they're mostly clean, modern, and reliable.

Basin Harbor Club ★★ **Kids** This is one of Vermont's most peaceful resorts if your goal is to kick back and enjoy lake breezes and lovely scenery. The property is well integrated into its fine natural setting on the shores of Lake Champlain. Indeed, the best units aren't in the main inn but rather are the various cottages facing out onto the lake from their wooded, cliff-top perches; they feel wonderfully isolated, yet many sport fireplaces, comfy beds, work desks, sofas, and Jacuzzis. You won't find televisions here, so borrow or rent bikes, kayaks, canoes, or a speedboat; hit the little golf course; or grab a tennis racquet (lessons are available) and head to the clay courts. A good program of events and activities, including art classes and lectures, supplements your own walks in the nice gardens and lounging in the bright, Adirondack chairs on the lawn. Dining is at three good restaurants of various types—you choose from among B&B, MAP, or full dining plans in spring and fall, while all meals are included in summer rates—and the excellent kids' program completes the sense of having stepped into an upscale summer camp from another century. Summertime bonus: Thursday nights bring lobster dinners and live jazz to the beach.

4800 Basin Harbor Rd., Vergennes, VT 05491. ✆ **800/622-4000** or 802/475-2311. Fax 802/475-6545. www.basinharbor.com. 123 units. $147–$521 double; $262–$780 cottage. Rates include breakfast, lunch, and dinner mid-June to early Sept only. Rates do not include 18% service fee. B&B and MAP plans and rates also available. 2-night minimum stay some weekends. MC, V. Closed mid-Oct to mid-May. From

Burlington, follow Rte. 7 south about 20 miles, turn right onto Rte. 27A and follow into Vergennes; just after bridge, turn right onto Panton Rd. (watch for Basin Harbor signs), then bear right after 1½ miles onto Basin Harbor Rd.; continue about 5 more miles to resort. "Well-behaved" pets allowed in cottages ($10 per pet per night). **Amenities:** 3 restaurants; babysitting; bikes; children's programs; concierge; golf course; exercise room; outdoor pool; 5 tennis courts; watersports equipment/rentals. *In room:* A/C, fridge (some units), hair dryer, Wi-Fi (free; extra charge for larger bandwidth).

The Essex ★ This inn, just outside the fringe of Burlington's exurban sprawl, bills itself as "Vermont's Culinary Resort"—a big claim, given that there are so many great eats and wonderful inns in the state. It isn't quite up to the luxury level of the top-rank Vermont inns yet. True, the setting (20 acres of hillside) is majestic, the fitness center and rock-climbing course are great, and the cooking classes are a fun option. And some rooms—particularly the expensive suites outfitted for longer stays, built with full kitchens (including Hearthstone gas stoves)—are nice, gussied up with fireplaces, CD players, Jacuzzis, four-poster beds, and the like. Other units, though, are fairly ordinary for the high prices you pay. A spa was added in 2009, there's an airport shuttle and kids' play area, and the property offers several dining options. (See "Where to Dine," below.) This is a work in progress.

70 Essex Way, Essex, VT 05452. ✆ **800/727-4295** or 802/878-1100. Fax 802/878-0063. www.vtculinaryresort.com. 120 units. May–Oct $219–$349 double, $249–$579 suite; Nov–Apr $189–$289 double, $219–$489 suite. AE, DC, MC, V. **Amenities:** 2 restaurants; bikes; exercise room; golf course; heated outdoor pool; room service; spa. *In room:* A/C, TV, fridge (some units), Wi-Fi (free).

Hilton Burlington ★ This nine-story Hilton hotel—formerly a Radisson and then a Wyndham—has great views if you spend extra for a lakeside room. It's a sleek glass box built in 1976; renovations have kept the aging process mostly at bay. It's the most centrally located of any hotel in the city, tucked right between the waterfront and Church Street Marketplace, but otherwise nothing special. Rooms are standard chain-hotel fare. A few "cabana" units by the pool area are convenient for families, while executive-floor rooms add duvets and more amenities. The airport shuttle is a plus, and the staff is friendly and competent. I'd eat elsewhere, though—the breakfast and dining are middling at best.

60 Battery St., Burlington, VT 05401. ✆ **800/445-8667** or 802/658-6500. Fax 802/658-4659. www.hilton.com. 257 units. Summer $159–$269 double; winter $139–$179 double. AE, DISC, MC, V. Self-parking in garage $5.50 per day. **Amenities:** Restaurant; babysitting; concierge; exercise room; Jacuzzi; indoor pool; room service. *In room:* A/C, TV, hair dryer, Wi-Fi ($9.95 per day).

The Inn at Shelburne Farms ★★ The numbers behind this elaborate mansion on the shore of Lake Champlain tell the story: 60 rooms, 10 chimneys, 1,400 acres. It's a whimsical house, a tourist attraction in and of itself (in fact, there's an admission charge to the extensive farms on the property; see "Exploring Burlington," above). Yet from May through October, you can sleep here and pretend it's all yours. Built in 1899, the sprawling Edwardian "farmhouse" is a place to fantasize about the lifestyles of the rich and famous. Famous architect Frederick Law Olmsted helped design the grounds—the concept was an "agricultural estate" complete with grazing cows on the lawns and a sustainable dairy operation, but also super-plush (for the time) bedrooms and fittings. Today the property is aging, but looks fairly luxurious if a bit dated; expect French design touches, floral wallpapers, and a spare, whitewashed elegance to the rooms. Units here vary considerably in decor and amenities: About a quarter of the rooms share hallway bathrooms with other rooms, for example (the Oak Room is probably best of these)—but you can also rent luxurious digs like Overlook, the original master bedroom of owner Lila Webb, with its frilly draperies, big king bed, and great views of the lake, meadows, and grounds. The Louis XVI room was furnished with whitewashed furniture when the home was built in 1899, and that furniture is still here, complemented by a design scheme that was popular at that time.

1611 Harbor Rd., Shelburne, VT 05482. ✆ **802/985-8498.** www.shelburnefarms.org. 26 units, 7 with shared bathrooms. $155–$220 double with shared bathroom; $260–$465 double with private bathroom; $260–$380 cottage. 2-night minimum stay Sat–Sun. AE, DC, DISC, MC, V. Closed mid-Oct to early May. **Amenities:** Restaurant; babysitting; tennis court. *In room:* Kitchenette (2 units), Wi-Fi (in some main floor rooms; free).

Lang House ★ This stately, walk-up Queen Anne mansion (1881) sits on the hillside between downtown and the University of Vermont. It's appointed with rich cherry and maple woodwork. Rooms vary in size, though most have smallish bathrooms and quite small TVs, and are perhaps a bit on the pricey side for what you get. Two of the best rooms are corner units: no. 101 on the first floor, and no. 202 on the second floor, with a sitting area tucked into the turret. Breakfast is good, and the owners have a liquor license, so they can sell you a bottle of wine or beer. All in all, a good experience. Only cautions? There's no elevator, and you're sleeping practically right on a big university campus with a national reputation for its parties. So you might *hear* some of that partying late at night.

360 Main St., Burlington, VT 05401. ✆ **877/919-9799** or 802/652-2500. Fax 802/651-8717. www.langhouse.com. 11 units. $165–$245 double. Rates include breakfast. AE, DISC, MC, V. *In room:* A/C, TV, Wi-Fi (free).

Sheraton Burlington Hotel & Conference Center ★ Perhaps the largest conference facility in Vermont, the Sheraton also does a decent job catering to travelers and their families. A sprawling and modern complex, it's just off the interstate a few minutes' drive east of downtown, on the strip leading to Burlington's airport (handy if you're flying in or out). Some units are more traditional-looking (furnished in wrought-iron beds or hardwood furniture), while others are more modern (flatscreen TVs in the club rooms, for instance), but all are more than adequate. There are plenty of business-hotel amenities here, too, like a nice indoor pool, a free fitness center, a business center, and a free airport shuttle center—families take note. Ask for a room facing east if you want views of Mount Mansfield and the Green Mountains.

870 Williston Rd., Burlington, VT 05403. ✆ **800/866-6117** or 802/865-6600. Fax 802/865-6670. www.starwoodhotels.com/sheraton. 309 units. $89–$229 double. AE, DC, DISC, MC, V. **Amenities:** Restaurant; lounge; exercise room; 2 Jacuzzis; indoor pool. *In room:* A/C, TV, hair dryer, Wi-Fi ($11 per day in guest rooms, free in public areas).

Willard Street Inn ★★ Finds This impressive and historic inn is housed in a splendid 1881 Queen Anne–style brick mansion a few minutes' walk from the university campus, and surely belongs in some sort of glossy "beautiful homes" magazine. All rooms are exceptionally well decorated in genuine and reproduction antiques. Some have down comforters and fireplaces, and many have interesting slopes, angles, and eaves; four-poster beds and handsome, not-too-frilly decor are the norm here. Among the best units are the third-floor Tower Room (in the turret), which boasts a small sitting area (with wicker furniture!) and the best views of the lake; and Champlain Lookout, on the second floor, with its spacious bedroom and bathroom and more great lake views. I like the antique tub in the Nantucket Room, too. Walk down the marble staircase and check out the marble-floored solarium, green lawns, and English gardens. This inn's owners really go the extra mile to ensure guests' satisfaction—breakfasts are universally raved about.

349 S. Willard St. (2 blocks south of Main St.), Burlington, VT 05401. ✆ **800/577-8712** or 802/651-8710. Fax 802/651-8714. www.willardstreetinn.com. 14 units, 1 with private bathroom across hall. $140–$250 double. Rates include full breakfast. 2-night minimum stay Sat–Sun. AE, DISC, MC, V. Children 12 and over welcome. *In room:* A/C, TV, Wi-Fi (free).

WHERE TO DINE

In addition to the choices listed below, another good upscale pick in the Burlington area is the **Starry Night Café** ★★ (✆ **802/877-6316;** www.starrynightcafe.com) on Route 7 in Ferrisburg, about 15 miles south of the city—past Charlotte and before Vergennes. Native Vermonter David Hugo serves eclectic Continental meals of duck, salmon, grilled chicken, steak, and the like Wednesday through Sunday nights.

And if you're casting about for picnic packings, Burlington has an uncommonly good natural-foods store (no shock there) with a cafe, the **City Market** (✆ **802/861-9700;** www.citymarket.coop) at 82 South Winooski Ave. It's open daily from 7am until 11pm.

Al's French Frys ★ (Finds) FAST FOOD Ignore the technically incorrect spelling. Al's is where *the* Ben and Jerry go to satisfy their french-fry cravings, so why shouldn't you? It's a must-hit roadside joint when you're in the neighborhood of the Burlington airport or driving through on the interstate. Al's is both fun and efficient, and the fries here (which you can order by the cup, pint, or even quart) draw locals back time and again. Other offerings—hamburgers, dogs, wraps, chicken strips, and grilled cheese sandwiches (for less than a buck)—are okay, nothing special. But you're here for the fries—add a side order of cheese or chili sauce if you want to get experimental with them. There's no beer here, but you can order cola, shakes (in five flavors), or—this being Vermont—a cup of plain or chocolate milk.

1251 Williston Rd. (Rte. 2, just east of I-89), South Burlington. ✆ **802/862-9203.** www.alsfrenchfrys.com. Fries $1–$4, sandwiches and burgers $2–$5. No credit cards. Mon–Thurs 10:30am–11pm; Fri–Sat 10:30am–midnight; Sun 11am–11pm.

Bove's ★ (Value) ITALIAN A Burlington landmark since 1941, Bove's is a classic red-sauce-on-spaghetti joint a couple blocks from the Church Street Marketplace. It's got real character, and only one or two items on the entire menu here cost more than 10 bucks—amazing. Grab a seat at a vinyl-upholstered booth, and sit down to a plate of spaghetti with butter sauce, meat sauce, sausage, meatballs, or a few other things. Choose any sauce and you can't go wrong: The red sauce is tangy, the vodka-cream sauce rich, the garlic sauce super-garlicky. These sauces are also now a thriving side operation, in case you want to take a jar home. Not hungry for pasta? Bove's also offers grinders (that's New Hampshire/Vermont lingo for a sub sandwich), veal cutlets, and fried clams, plus simple, sweet-ish desserts and daily specials like manicotti, stuffed peppers, lasagna, and chicken cacciatore. Takeout is no problem—they specialize in it.

68 Pearl St. ✆ **802/864-6651.** www.boves.com. Sandwiches $2–$6, dinner items $7–$10. No credit cards. Tues–Thurs 2–8:45pm; Fri–Sat 11am–8:45pm.

Butler's Restaurant and Tavern ★ REGIONAL/CONTINENTAL The house restaurant at the Essex (see "Where to Stay," above), Butler's is also a sort of auxiliary campus of the Montpelier-based New England Culinary Institute. On the tavern menu, expect slightly fancy takes on nachos, burgers, fish and chips, sandwiches, and chili—the BLT, to take just one example, is made of maple-glazed bacon and put together with truffled mayonnaise. The restaurant offers a more intimate experience and more ambitious fare: Entrees might run to homemade gnocchi, pan-seared diver scallops, porcini-dusted beef tenderloin with cheddar-flavored mashed potatoes, or a grilled top sirloin steak.

70 Essex Way, Essex Junction. ✆ **802/764-1413.** www.vtculinaryresort.com. Reservations recommended at Butler's (not necessary in tavern). Tavern menu $6–$15; restaurant menu $14–$23. AE, DC, DISC, MC, V. Restaurant daily 11:30am–10pm. Tavern daily 2–11pm.

The Daily Planet ★ **Finds** INTERNATIONAL Named for the newspaper where Superman's alter-ego Clark Kent works, (I think), this popular spot often fills with college students and/or downtown folks getting out of work. It's central (on Central St.) and feels cutting-edge, even though it's been here more than 20 years. The mild chaos in the dining room only adds to the experience, which begins with a fun, eclectic menu—better than you might expect given the pubby look to the place and its largely college-age clientele. Look for smoked salmon tostadas, green chili polenta with chèvre, pork carnitas, or Vietnamese beef sandwiches on the bar menu; lemon-poached tuna, cider-brined pork chops, rack of lamb with chimichurri sauce, and shrimp in yellow curry on the more substantial dinner menu. The vegetarian entrees here are among the very best in town. Desserts are creative and tempting, too—choices might include a lavender crème brûlée, a praline sundae, or a hazelnut-topped cheesecake. Don't forget to check the specialty martini menu (which includes a kicky chocolate mole version employing chipotle-flavored tequila) and the rotating art exhibitions.

15 Center St. ✆ **802/862-9647.** www.dailyplanet15.com. Reservations recommended for parties of 5 or more. Bar menu items $3–$13 at lunch, $9–$19 at dinner. AE, DISC, MC, V. Daily 5–11pm (until midnight Fri–Sat).

Leunig's Bistro ★ CONTINENTAL What an intriguing place for a meal Leunig's is. Named for an Australian cartoonist, this fun spot right on the Church Street mall (in a former A&W root beer shop) has a retro feel with its washed walls, marble bar, crystal chandeliers, and oversized posters. The inventive menu uses regional ingredients, prepared with a Continental (usually a French) hand. An upscale brunch is served Saturday and Sunday, with seasonally changing items such as gravlax crepes, eggs Benedict, and the like; weekday lunches run to good, upscale bistro-style sandwiches and soups (you can add truffled fries or foie gras to any lunch, if that gives you a sense of it). But dinner is where things *really* get cranked up and daring: On the nightly menu, you might find a grilled rack of lamb, a neat vegetable Napoleon, a filet mignon, a piece of pear-and-cardamom stuffed pork, a rack of wild boar, lamb shanks, or skate wings cooked in parchment paper. The side dishes, salads, and cheese plates here are also outstanding. (Truly adventurous foodies might want to try the $100 tasting menu for two: a little bit of everything.) Leunig's claims to offer "the panache of Paris, and the value of Vermont," and they just might be right about that.

115 Church St. ✆ **802/863-3759.** www.leunigsbistro.com. Reservations recommended. Main courses $6–$15 at lunch, $18–$26 at dinner. AE, DISC, MC, V. Mon–Thurs 11am–10pm; Fri 11am–11pm; Sat 9am–11pm; Sun 9am–10pm.

Penny Cluse Cafe ★ CAFE The Penny Cluse gets most local foodies' votes for "best breakfast" in the city, and they do indeed serve a mostly breakfast-centric menu. Just a block off the Church Street Marketplace, it's a casual, bright spot decorated in a vaguely Southwestern motif. Among the many excellent breakfast items here: pancakes made from buttermilk or gingerbread; banana bread with maple cream cheese; breakfast sandwiches; a "tofu scram;" and the Zydeco breakfast of eggs, black beans, andouille sausage, and corn muffins. Lunch plates range to chorizo tacos, chicken and biscuits, a smoked salmon plate, and good sandwiches—including some terrific veggie options. The breakfast prices are at the high end of the usual Vermont price scale for that meal, but they leave you satisfied, so you might not mind. Good coffees and teas abound, too.

169 Cherry St. ✆ **802/651-8834.** www.pennycluse.com. Breakfast and lunch items $5–$10. MC, V. Mon–Fri 6:45am–3pm; Sat–Sun 8am–3pm.

Trattoria Delia ★★ **Finds** ITALIAN Serving the best Italian food in Burlington, Lori and Tom Delia's eatery is in a low-traffic location, almost hidden through a speakeasy-like door beneath a large building. But Burlingtonites (Burlingtonians?) know exactly where it is—be sure to reserve ahead if you're coming on a summer weekend. Inside the place is culinary magic; genuinely Italian entrees like veal shanks, red-wine-braised wild boar, filet mignon in white-truffle butter, sirloin sautéed in chianti, seafood stew, and pasta dishes predominate. Go for bruschetta, tagliatelle alla Bolognese, spaghetti and Gulf shrimp baked in a parchment paper, or rigatoni baked in a clay pot with basil–tomato sauce and meat, then choose from the selection of dessert wines and desserts such as gelati, torte, tiramisu, and panna cotta. The wine list is good, as evidenced by a raft of *Wine Spectator* awards. This is real Italian food, upscale and delicious.

152 Saint Paul St. ✆ **802/864-5253.** www.trattoriadelia.com. Reservations recommended. Main courses $15–$28. DC, MC, V. Daily 5–10pm.

SHOPPING

The **Church Street Marketplace** is the focus of downtown Burlington. Running along 4 blocks that extend south from the elegant 1816 Congregational Church, this marketplace buzzes with a sort of European-central-square energy. While the marketplace has been discovered by a few national chain stores, it still includes lots of homegrown local shops, too. In summer take time to listen to the drummers, pan-flutists, and buskers and sample foods sold such as great kettle corn. Most of the shops listed below are either in the marketplace or within walking distance.

Bennington Potters North You can find a good selection of creative and elegant stuff (made in, yes, Bennington) for your dining-room table and kitchen in this handsome, century-old building just off Church Street. 127 College St. ✆ **802/863-2221.** www.benningtonpotters.com.

Frog Hollow Gallery ★ The Vermont State Craft Center's gallery, Frog Hollow has a broad selection of items from some of the best craftspeople in the state. You can pick up anything from pottery to woodwork to glassware in this place, which is located in a storefront in the Church Street Marketplace. 85 Church St., Burlington. ✆ **802/863-6458.** www.froghollow.org.

Kiss the Cook Located in the best stretch of the Church Street mall, this is a good spot to stock up on Vermont gourmet products. They also stock tons of cookware—Calphalon pans and Oxo gadgets, sure, but also a few handy New England gadgets like bean pots and apple peelers. 72 Church St. ✆ **888/658-5477** or 802/863-4226. www.kissthecook.net.

Pompanoosuc Mills ★ This upscale New England furniture chain, based near Norwich (p. 132), specializes in austerely simple hardwood furniture in cherry, birch, maple, and oak. Their Burlington showroom—once again, right on the pedestrian mall—also carries carpets, lamps, frames, and a selection of other decorative arts. 50 Church St. ✆ **800/718-8601** or 802/862-8208. www.pompy.com.

BURLINGTON AFTER DARK

Performing Arts

Flynn Center for the Performing Arts The Flynn Center is the anchor of Burlington's fine-arts scene. Run as a nonprofit and housed in a wonderful Art Deco theater dating from 1930, the organization puts on events ranging from touring Broadway productions to classical, rock, folk, and world-music concerts; dance performances; and even author readings. Call or visit the Flynn website for a schedule. 153 Main St. ✆ **802/863-5966.** www.flynncenter.org.

Royall Tyler Theatre Dramatic works performed by University of Vermont theater department students and faculty, as well as local theater groups, are staged in this handsomely designed performance hall. Shows range from Shakespeare to student-directed one-act plays, and the performance schedule continues throughout the year. University of Vermont campus. ✆ **802/656-2094.** www.uvmtheatre.org.

UVM Lane Series This university-run series brings renowned performers from around the country and the globe to Burlington for performances in local theaters, chapels, and the acoustically superb UVM Recital Hall. The series runs September through April. Performers have included folk and world-music stars, though the series is mostly classical of late. Various venues. ✆ **802/656-4455.** www.uvm.edu/laneseries.

Vermont Symphony Orchestra ★ In summer outdoor pops performances punctuated by fireworks take place at various locations around Vermont; in winter the classical series moves indoors, with regular performances at the Flynn Theatre. 2 Church St., Ste. 3B. ✆ **800/876-9293** or 802/864-5741. www.vso.org.

Nightclubs

Burlington sustains a thriving local music scene, though it's sometimes a bit hard to determine exactly *where* the best gigs are being played. Check the excellent local weekly paper *Seven Days* (free in boxes around town, and online at **www.7dvt.com**) as well as bulletin-board postings and local radio for information on festivals, concerts, and club shows.

Nectar's, at 188 Main St. (✆ **802/658-4771;** www.liveatnectars.com), is an odd amalgam—part funky-cafeteria-style restaurant, part lounge. Unsurprisingly, this is the place Phish got its start. Live blues, rock, folk, and jam bands play nightly, and there's no cover. On weekends it's packed with UVM students (and abuzz with elevated levels of hormonal energy, as a result); try midweek if you can. Look for the club's distinctive revolving neon sign, said to be the last of its kind in Vermont.

Right upstairs from Nectar's is **Club Metronome** (✆ **802/865-4563;** www.clubmetronome.com), a loud and loose nightspot offering a wide array of acts, including DJs, reggae artists, and singer-songwriters. You can dance or shoot a game of pool (or do both at once, as seems popular). This is a good place to sample the local talent, which is pretty impressive—bands like the Black Crowes (not from Burlington, but counterculture as all heck) got a toehold here before breaking out nationally. The cover charge can range from around $3 to $15.

6 THE NORTHEAST KINGDOM

St. Johnsbury: 60 miles N of White River Junction; 75 miles E of Burlington; 125 miles N of Brattleboro

Vermont's Northeast Kingdom has a wilder, more remote character than the rest of the state. Consisting of Orleans, Essex, and Caledonia counties, the region was given its memorable nickname in 1949 by Vermont Sen. George Aiken. What gives this region its character is its stubborn, old-fashioned insularity. It looks and feels *much* more like hard-scrabble parts of neighboring New Hampshire (which it faces across the Connecticut River) than the farmhouses and malls of Manchester, country stores of the Mad River Valley, or ski hills of Stowe. You won't find any designer fly-fishing shops in *these* parts.

The landscape here is open and spacious, its dairy pastures ending abruptly at the hard edge of dense boreal forests. The leafy woodlands of the south quickly give way to spiky woods of spruce and fir. Accommodations and services for visitors aren't plentiful or easy to find here, but a growing number of inns are sprouting up in these hills.

Because the sights and points of interest are somewhat sparse here, I have constructed a loose driving tour of the region—plus some suggestions for outdoor recreation, which is a good way to increase your enjoyment here. If your time is limited, though, at a minimum stop in **St. Johnsbury** (which holds two excellent attractions, the Fairbanks Museum and St. Johnsbury Athenaeum, and is right off the interstate highway). Also try to cruise through at least a couple of small towns here—**Craftsbury Common** is nice—before heading elsewhere. The fall foliage can be brilliant, too, although it arrives a bit earlier here (from late Sept to very early Oct, usually) than anywhere else in New England.

The entire tour described below, from Hardwick to St. Johnsbury by way of Newport, Derby Line, and Lake Willoughby, is about 90 miles by car. Allow at least a full day for it, though, if you plan to hike and/or bike in the region.

Visitor information for the region is available from the **Northeast Kingdom Chamber of Commerce** (✆ **800/639-6379** or 802/748-3678; www.nekchamber.com) at 51 Depot Sq. in downtown St. Johnsbury.

DRIVING TOUR THE NORTHEAST KINGDOM

START: **Hardwick**
FINISH: **St. Johnsbury**
TIME: **One full day**

Start your tour at Hardwick, which is at the intersection of routes 14 and 15, about 40 minutes' drive from both Stowe and Montpelier.

1 Hardwick

A small town with rough edges set on the Lamoille River, Hardwick has a single main street with some intriguing shops, a couple of casual, family-style restaurants, and one of Vermont's best natural foods stores (the Buffalo Mountain Food Co-op). A 2005 fire claimed part of this downtown block, but it has since been rebuilt.

From Hardwick, head north 7 miles on Route 14 to the turnoff to Craftsbury and:

2 Craftsbury Common ★★

An uncommonly graceful village, Craftsbury Common is home to a small academy and a large number of historic homes and buildings spread along a central green and the village's main street. The town occupies a wide upland ridge and offers sweeping views to the east and west; be sure to stop by the old cemetery on the

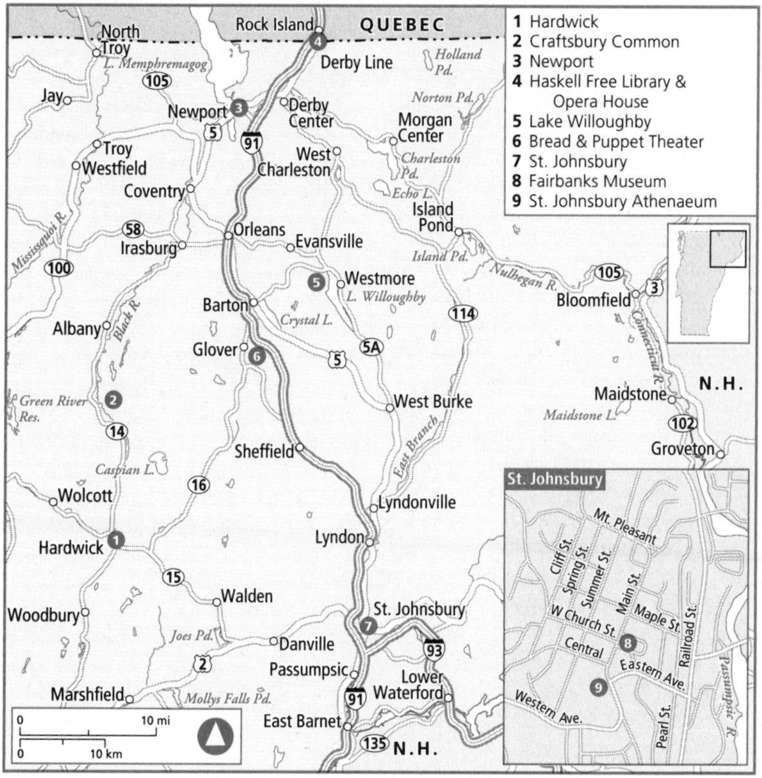

south side of town, too, where you can wander among historic tombstones of pioneers—they date back to the 1700s. Craftsbury is an excellent destination for mountain biking and cross-country skiing.

From Craftsbury, continue north to reconnect to Route 14. Pass through the towns of Albany and Irasburg as you head north. At the village of Coventry, veer north on Route 5 to the lakeside town of:

❸ Newport

This commercial (and commercial-looking) outpost is set on the southern shores of big Lake Memphremagog, a stunning 27-mile-long lake that's just 2 miles wide at its broadest point (the bulk of it actually lies across the border in Canada). From Newport, continue north on Route 5 (crossing under I-91) about 7 miles more to the border town of Derby Line. This outpost has a handful of restaurants and antiques shops; if you've got your passport, you can also park and walk across the bridge to poke around the Quebec town of Rock Island.

Back in Derby Line, look for the:

❹ Haskell Free Library & Opera House ★

At the corner of Caswell Avenue and Church Street, this handsome neoclassical building (✆ **802/873-3022;** www.haskellopera.org) contains a public library on the first floor and an elegant opera house on the second, which is modeled after the old Boston Opera House. The theater opened in 1904 with advertisements promoting a minstrel show featuring "new songs, new jokes, and beautiful electric effects." It's a beautiful theater, with a scene of Venice painted on the drop curtain and carved cherubim adorning the balcony.

What's coolest about this building, though, is that it lies half in Canada and half in the United States. (The Haskell family donated the building jointly to the towns of Derby Line and Rock Island.) A thick black line runs right beneath the seats of the opera house, marking the border between nations. Because the stage portion is set entirely in Canada, legends abound of frustrated U.S. marshals sitting in the audience watching fugitives perform on stage, free as birds. (Those stories are almost certainly false.) More recently, the theater has been used for an occasional extradition hearing. Performances still take place here. Tours are also available, from May through October, anytime during regular library hours; a $3 per person donation is suggested. (The library is open Tues–Sat.)

From Derby Line, retrace your path south on Route 5 to Derby Center and the junction of Route 5A. Continue south on Route 5A to the town of Westmore, on the shores of:

5 Lake Willoughby ★★

This underappreciated lake might be one of the most scenic in Vermont—it almost looks like something from Switzerland. Carved out by glaciers and set in an unpopulated area, the lake is best viewed from the north, where its shimmering sheet of water appears to be pinched between the base of two low mountains at its southern end. Route 5A as it runs along the lake's eastern shore is lightly traveled, thus good for biking or walking. For information about ascending the nearby mountains on foot, see "Outdoor Pursuits," below.

Head southwest on Route 16, which branches off Route 5A just north of the lake. Follow Route 16 through the peaceful villages of Barton and Glover. About 1 mile south of Glover, turn left on Route 122. On your left, look for the farmstead that serves as home to the:

6 Bread & Puppet Theater

For nearly 3 decades, Polish artist and performer Peter Schumann's Bread and Puppet Theater staged an elaborate annual summer pageant at this farm, attracting thousands of attendees who gaped at the theater's brightly painted puppets (crafted of fabric and papier-mâché, they could be an amalgam of Ralph Nader and Hieronymus Bosch). The huge puppets marched around the farm grounds, acting out dramas that typically featured rebellion against tyranny of one sort or another. It was like Woodstock, minus the music.

Alas, the event became too popular—and attracted drifters of questionable character. In 1998, a murder at an adjacent campground prodded Schumann to shut down the circus for a while. His troupe still designs and builds puppets here, however, and periodically takes its unique shows on the road—or offers live performances in Glover. (For the latest schedules, check the troupe's website, **www.breadandpuppet.org**.)

Between June and October, you can still visit the venerable, slightly tottering barn, home of the **Bread and Puppet Museum** ★ (✆ **802/525-3031** or 802-525-1271), which preserves many of the puppets from past events. This remarkable display shouldn't be missed if you're near the area. Downstairs, in former cow-milking stalls, smaller displays include mournful washerwomen doing laundry and King Lear addressing his daughters. Upstairs, the vast hayloft is filled with soaring, haunting puppets, some up to 20 feet tall. Admission is free, though donations are encouraged. It's open daily 10am to 6pm from spring through November.

From Glover, continue south through farmlands to Lyndonville, where you pick up Route 5 S. to:

7 St. Johnsbury

This is by far the largest community in the Kingdom, and its major center of commerce. First settled in 1786, the town enjoyed a buoyant prosperity in the 19th century, largely stemming from the success of platform scales (which were invented right here in 1830 by Thaddeus Fairbanks, and are still manufactured here). The place hasn't yet been overtaken by sprawl, outlet shops, boutiques, or brewpubs, and the downtown features an abundance of commercial architecture in two distinct neighborhoods connected by steep Eastern Avenue.

The commercial part of town lies along Railroad Street (Rte. 5) at the base of the hill, while the most visually pleasing section of town runs along Main Street at the top of the hill. There you'll find the local library (with its fine art museum), the St. Johnsbury Academy, and a second museum. This northern end of Main Street is also notable for its grand residential architecture.

In St. Johnsbury, at the corner of Main and Prospect streets, find the:

8 Fairbanks Museum ★★

This imposing Romanesque red-sandstone structure was constructed in 1889 to hold the accumulations of obsessive amateur collector Franklin Fairbanks, grandson of the inventor of the platform scale. Fairbanks was once described as "the kind of little boy who came home with his pockets full of worms." Some of his collections now displayed here include four stuffed bears, a huge moose with full antlers, art from Asia, and 4,500 stuffed native and exotic birds—just the tip of the iceberg. (In fact, it's sort of surprising there isn't an *actual* iceberg here as well.)

The soaring, barrel-vaulted main hall, which is reminiscent of an old-fashioned train station, embodies Victorian grandeur. Amid the assorted clutter, look for the, er, unique mosaics of John Hampson, who depicted famous moments in American history (Washington bidding his troops farewell and the like) entirely from mounted insects. In the Washington scene, iridescent green beetles form the epaulets, and the regal great coat was made using hundreds of purple moth wings. These works alone are worth the price of admission, and capture the peculiar oddity of the place.

The museum (✆ **802/748-2372;** www.fairbanksmuseum.org) is open Tuesday through Saturday from 9am to 5pm, and Sunday from 1 to 5pm; from April to October, it's also open Monday from 9am to 5pm. Admission is $6 for adults, $5 for seniors and children ages 5 to 17, and $18 per family (maximum of 2 adults). There's a planetarium ★ here as well—the only one in Vermont.

Also on Main Street, just south of the museum at 1171 Main St., find the:

9 St. Johnsbury Athenaeum ★★

Inside a brick building with a blunt mansard tower and prominent keystones over the windows, St. Johnsbury's public library houses an extraordinary little art gallery dating to 1873. It claims to be the oldest unadulterated art gallery in the nation.

Your first view of the gallery is spectacular. After winding through the cozy library and past a ticking regulator clock, you round a corner and find yourself gazing across Yosemite National Park—or, at least, a pretty good facsimile. The luminous 10×15-foot oil painting of the park here, ***The Domes of the Yosemite*** ★★★, was made by painter Albert Bierstadt in 1867, just 3 years after President Lincoln created the California park. Horace Fairbanks later bought it and built this gallery specifically for the painting. (Not everyone was happy about that. "Now *The Domes* is doomed to the seclusion of a Vermont town, where it will astonish the natives," groused the *Boston Globe*.) Natural light from a skylight only enhances the painting, and there's a viewing gallery at the opposite end of the hall.

That's not all there is here. Another 100 or so works fill the remaining walls of the museum. Most are copies, but there are a few originals from Hudson River School painters such as Asher B. Durand, Thomas Moran, and Jasper Cropsey.

The Athenaeum (✆ **802/748-8291;** www.stjathenaeum.org) is open weekdays from 10am to 5pm and Saturdays 9:30am to 4pm. Admission is free, but donations are encouraged.

DOWNHILL SKIING

Jay Peak ★★ Finds Just south of the Canada border, Jay Peak is a great choice for those who prefer to avoid the glitz and clutter of modern-looking ski resorts. Though some condo development has taken place at the base of this mountain, Jay still has the feel of a remote, isolated destination, accessible only via a winding road through thick woods—something you just can't find in the U.S. anymore. Thanks to its staggering snowfall (an average of about 30 ft. annually, more than anywhere else in New England), there's extensive glade skiing between the trees here, with views of nothing but trees and mountains. (They also make snow here if Mother Nature decides to take a break from it.) The resort's ski school specializes in training you to run the glades, so it's a good place for intermediate-to-advanced skiers to learn how to navigate the peak's exciting, challenging trails. In summer there's a golf course, aerial tram (similar to a gondola), and pool for families to enjoy. Be aware that lodging and dining are limited to what's on the mountain, and après-ski is nonexistent.

4850 Rte. 242, Jay, VT 05859. ✆ **800/451-4449** or 802/988-2611. www.jaypeakresort.com. Adults $67 day lift tickets, $49 half-day; discounts for youths, students, seniors, and VT residents.

OUTDOOR PURSUITS

HIKING At the southern tip of Lake Willoughby, two rounded peaks rise above the lake's waters. These are the biblically named Mount Hor and Mount Pisgah, both lying within the Willoughby State Forest. The summits are accessible via footpaths that are somewhat strenuous but offer excellent views.

To hike **Mount Pisgah** (elev. 2,751 ft.), look for parking on the west side of Route 5A, about 5¾ miles south of the junction with Route 16. The trail begins across the road and runs about 1.7 miles to the summit; it's a fairly difficult hike, steep in parts and potentially muddy, and the summit is all exposed ledges with no fences and a long drop down. Wear boots and be in good shape; allow at least 4 hours. To hike facing **Mount Hor** (elev. 2,648 ft.), drive 1½ miles down the gravel road on the right side of the parking lot, veering right at the fork. Park at the small parking lot, and continue on foot past the parking lot a short distance until you spot the start of the trail. Follow the trail signs to the summit, a round-trip of 3.5 to 4 miles. Views of the lake and surrounding countryside from both peaks are excellent.

CROSS-COUNTRY SKIING The **Craftsbury Outdoor Center** maintains more than 50 miles of cross-country trails through the gentle hills surrounding the village of Craftsbury. These forgiving, old-fashioned trails, maintained by the center's **Nordic Center ★★** division (✆ **802/586-7767;** www.craftsbury.com), emphasize landscape over speed. They even guarantee skiable snow from January until the second Sunday in March. A trail pass costs $10 per person per day, while a full setup of rental equipment costs just $15 per day more—an outstanding value, given the local scenery.

Another option is the **Highland Lodge Ski Touring Center** ★ (✆ **802/533-2647;** www.highlandlodge.com), on Caspian Lake in Greensboro, with more than 30 miles of roller-packed trails (some of which are further groomed) through rolling woodlands and fields. When you stay at the lodge (see "Where to Stay," below), you ski for free.

WHERE TO STAY

I won't lie to you: Lodging choices are thin on the ground up here in the Kingdom, and you'll possibly be forced to bunk down either in a chain motel or a less-than-luxe B&B carved out of someone's home (with the host family still living in it).

There are a couple of alternative options, though. When in Craftsbury Common, for instance, you can stay at the **Craftsbury Outdoor Center** (✆ **802/586-7767;** www.craftsbury.com) in an array of small, simple single and double rooms; nicer, bigger suite rooms; and full cabins with kitchens and living rooms. A night in a double room or cabin costs anywhere from $93 to $323 for two adults, plus an extra charge per child; rates are highest in winter and on weekends, but all rates include breakfast, lunch, and dinner.

Comfort Inn & Suites ★ This big chain hotel is about a mile south of St. Johnsbury's downtown district, up on a hill right where Route 5 crosses under the interstate. Built in 2000, it consists of more than 100 units and has a number of nice business-hotel touches, such as granite vanity counters, high-backed desk chairs, small fridges in every room, and a free continental breakfast. Rooms are pleasantly appointed, more like an inn than a motel chain, and the basement houses an appealing small pool, fitness center, and game room outfitted with air hockey and a billiards table. It's a good pick when you're tired of driving or with a family.

703 Rte. 5 S., St. Johnsbury, VT 05819. ✆ **866/464-2408** or 802/748-1500. Fax 802/748-1243. 107 units. $89–$149 double; $139–$399 suite. Rates include continental breakfast. AE, DISC, MC, V. From I-91, take exit 20. **Amenities:** Exercise room; indoor pool; sauna. *In room:* A/C, TV, fridge, hair dryer, Wi-Fi (free).

Highland Lodge ★ Built in the mid–19th century, this all-inclusive lodge has been accommodating guests since 1926. Just across the road from lovely Caspian Lake, it has 11 rooms furnished in a comfortable country style, plus 11 nearby cottages, most equipped with kitchenettes. A stay here is supremely relaxing: Summer activities include swimming, boating on the lake, cycling, and playing tennis on a clay court. In winter, the lodge maintains its own cross-country ski area (see "Outdoor Pursuits," above) with miles of packed and groomed trails. Behind the lodge is an attractive nature preserve for exploration. Rates here always include breakfast, dinner, and free use of the canoes, kayaks, and most of the other equipment scattered about the property (there's a charge for skis, snowshoes, mountain bikes, and sailboats). You can even get a single room here for a fair price—about 60% of the double-occupancy rates. But children and teens are charged an extra fee, depending on their age—from $105 for an 18-year-old to $45 for a 2-year-old. (Infants are not charged.)

1608 Craftsbury Rd., Greensboro, VT 05841. ✆ **802/533-2647.** Fax 802/533-7494. www.highlandlodge.com. 22 units. $237–$330 double. Rates include breakfast, dinner, and 15% service charge. Extra charge per child ages 2–20. DISC, MC, V. Closed mid-Mar to May and mid-Oct to Christmas. From Hardwick, take Rte. 15 east 2 miles to Rte. 16, then drive 2 miles north to East Hardwick. Follow signs 6 miles to inn. **Amenities:** Dining room; babysitting; bikes; children's program; tennis court; watersports equipment/rentals. *In room:* No phone, Wi-Fi (entire main inn and some cottages; free).

WilloughVale Inn ★★ An elegant inn on a low rise at the north end of Lake Willoughby, the WilloughVale offers stunning views across the water to the twin mountains bracketing the southern end of the lake. It's ideal for a quiet retreat with some books or a bicycle; Robert Frost stayed here in 1909 and even wrote a poem about it ("A Servant to Servants"). Rooms in the main lodge are tastefully appointed, much of their furniture crafted right here in Vermont. Some have private sections of porch and have been thoroughly updated with Jacuzzis, big-screen satellite televisions, gas fireplaces, and similar touches. The cottages—four right on the lake with kitchenettes (including the one Frost stayed in), plus three others nearby with lake views—give off a rustic, Adirondack-lodge feeling, albeit with modern comforts. All these cottages now have wall-unit air-conditioning and televisions, and some have fireplaces or Jacuzzis yet still feel rustic thanks to their exposed woodwork. Note that this inn's restaurant is seasonal, opening in spring and closing in fall; it serves good food with a superb view of the lake, but in winter you'll have to hunt for other options. (See "Where to Dine," below, for a few suggestions.)

793 Rte. 5A S., Westmore, VT 05860. ✆ **888/594-9102** or 802/525-4123. Fax 802/525-4514. www.willoughvale.com. 13 units. $115–$240 double; $180–$320 cottage. Weekly rates available (summer only). Rates include continental breakfast. 2-night minimum stay in cottages, and in lodge during July, Aug, and fall-foliage season. AE, MC, V. Closed Jan to mid-June. Small dogs sometimes accepted ($20 per night; call ahead). **Amenities:** Restaurant; tavern; bikes; watersports equipment/rentals. *In room:* A/C, TV/DVD, fridge (some units), Wi-Fi (free).

WHERE TO DINE

Dining options are similarly sparse here. Fortunately, a number of inns in this region include dinner service with their room rates. There are also local restaurants in most villages in the Kingdom, and gourmet food *is* finally slowly filtering in—try driving into **Lyndonville, Barton,** or **East Burke** and scanning the options.

Two of the best places I've found in the region are both in Lyndonville. **The Lyndon Freighthouse** ★★, at 1000 Broad St. (✆ **802/626-1400;** www.thelyndonfreighthouse.com), open daily 6:30am to 9pm, serves a hearty menu of nearly all-organic pastas, salads, omelets, burgers, and beers from early morning until relatively late at night. **Trout River Brewing** ★ (✆ **802/626-9396;** www.troutriverbrewing.com), whose motto is "Catch some Trout," is a small microbrewery on Route 5, serving very good pizza for dinner plus its own fresh-brewed beers. An instant fan of the beer? Buy a "growler" (glass jug), finish it, and refill it from the tap later on your trip at a discount.

On the other hand, if you enjoy "road food," one of my favorite truck stops on the east coast is the **P&H Truck Stop** ★ (✆ **802/429-2141**) in Wells River, right at exit 17 off I-91. The custardy, rich maple-sugar pie here (topped with a mound of meringue) is indescribably delicious—it reflects the influence of nearby Quebec—while blue-plate specials like turkey with gravy are also tasty and filling. The bread and doughnuts are homemade, naturally. It's a must-stop on the way to Jay Peak or St. Johnsbury, if only to check out the scene of Canadian truckers wolfing down the maple pie with big mugs of coffee. Fear not, though—plenty of local families eat out here, too.

Southern & Central New Hampshire

New Hampshire gets a pretty bad rap from the national press and late-night comedy. Some of it is deserved, but not all of it. No, it's not quite as postcard-worthy as Vermont, and no, it's nowhere near as lobster-obsessed as Maine. Yes, the state charges everyone, even residents, an annoying $2 to traverse a measly 15 miles of interstate highway. Beaches are practically nonexistent. The fields are too full of rocks, winter is much too long. That "Live Free or Die" license plate? It's for real: Granite Staters still mostly regard government as an annoyance, and zoning as a grand conspiracy to undermine their Constitutional property rights.

The last time I checked, the state still did not have any bottle-return laws, bills banning billboards, or legislation requiring motorcyclists to wear helmets, and no sales or income tax. Longtime New Hampshire resident Robert Frost once famously stated that "Good fences make good neighbors," and—even if things are changing with new arrivals from out of state—folks here still mostly agree with that proclamation.

Yet that's what makes this state so wonderful to visit: its authenticity. You'll hear *real* accents and see *real* ingenuity in action, not some fake Hollywood or historical-park version. (Remember, these are the same folks who took up arms against King George.)

The Granite State's rebellious attitude has had consequences, of course. Public services are partly funded by lottery sales and through a stiff "tourist tax" (9% on meals *and* hotels), or through high local property taxes that have hit residents hard. Legislators could create income and sales taxes—but they won't, not in this lifetime. That would be political suicide.

Get beyond New Hampshire's stubbornness, though, and it's a very good place to vacation—especially if you like incredible views, fall foliage drives, and maple syrup. Sure, you'll still find plenty of pickup trucks, pancake houses, hunting caps, and country-rock music here, but it's not *all* about flannel shirts and rifle racks anymore. Granite Staters do know how to have fun—the band Aerosmith formed in **New London,** and comedian Adam Sandler was born in **Manchester.** They've got Dartmouth College in the lovely small town of **Hanover,** too.

It's also a state blessed with the huge peaks of the **White Mountains** (see chapter 8), lovely lakes like **Lake Winnipesaukee,** outstanding foliage in the **Mount Monadnock** area, and increasingly good resorts and restaurants. You can toss a Frisbee on a beach; ride bikes along country lanes; or canoe or boat on a placid lake. Need a little city culture? **Portsmouth** is a great 1- or 2-day stop, a sort of miniature Boston with seafood, music, and history, while **Manchester** has a gritty Franco-industrial heritage.

The inns here are getting better, and local fare is always easy to find in diners and family restaurants. Most of all, you'll get a strong sense of the wily independence that has always defined New England.

1 ENJOYING THE GREAT OUTDOORS

You can find gentle outdoor recreation—lakes, hills, hikes—throughout much of central and southern New Hampshire, from canoeing on the meandering **Connecticut River** (which forms the border with Vermont) to sailing on vast **Lake Winnipesaukee.** (The White Mountains offer an entirely different set of options and challenges—big skiing, extreme hiking, and dizzying auto drives. See "Enjoying the Great Outdoors" in chapter 8 for the lowdown on outdoor pursuits in the White Mountains.)

CAMPING Nineteen of New Hampshire's state parks allow camping (one accepts only RVs, no tents). About half the parks are in or around the White Mountains. To make advance **reservations,** call New Hampshire's parks and recreation division (✆ **603/271-3628**); phone lines are open daily 9am to 4pm. Or call the campground directly, in season. Easier still, you can book a site online at the parks division's website, **www.nhparks.state.nh.us**. Remember that rates cover two adults and two children; more people, and you'll pay more. There's a 9% tax added to the posted rates.

New Hampshire also has more than 100 private campgrounds. The **New Hampshire Campground Owners Association** (✆ **800/822-6764** or 603/736-5540) publishes listings of its member campgrounds online at **www.ucampnh.com**.

CANOEING New Hampshire has plenty of quiet rivers and lakes good for paddling, and canoe rentals are widely available. In this southern portion of the state, good flat-water paddling can be found along both the **Merrimack** and **Connecticut** rivers. Virtually any lake or pond is also probably suitable for dabbling about with canoe and paddle, though you'll want to check locally before setting out. (And be aware of the stiff winds that can occur when crossing the biggest lakes, such as Winnipesaukee.)

CYCLING You can enjoy excellent cycling throughout the southern half of the state. Southwestern New Hampshire in the Mount Monadnock region is especially good for back-road cycling, especially around **Hancock** and **Greenfield**—the area fairly glows with foliage in October. Over on the east side of the state, a great way to take in sea breezes is to pedal along New Hampshire's diminutive coastline, following **Route 1A** ★★ from the beach town of **Hampton** up to the mini-metropolis of **Portsmouth**—passing through **Rye** and **Rye Beach** on the way, which are highlights. This coastal road can get a little crowded with RVs at times, but there's a path near the surf to make up for that annoyance.

The Granite State Wheelmen (www.granitestatewheelmen.org) is the state's recreational cycling club. It doesn't publish route maps, but the club does hold lots of weekly rides in pretty areas. You don't need to be a member to join these rides; check the group's website for a complete, updated listing of events.

Another useful resource is *Backroad Bicycling in New Hampshire* by Andi Marie Cantele (Countryman Press, 2004). So is *Bicycling Southern New Hampshire* by Linda Chestney (University Press of New England, 2000), though it's not easy to find a copy; check online.

FISHING A vigorous stocking program keeps New Hampshire's lakes and rivers full of fish. Brook trout (about half of all the trout stocked), lake trout, and rainbow trout are some of the species abundant in the state's waters. Other sport fish here include smallmouth and largemouth bass, landlocked salmon, and walleye.

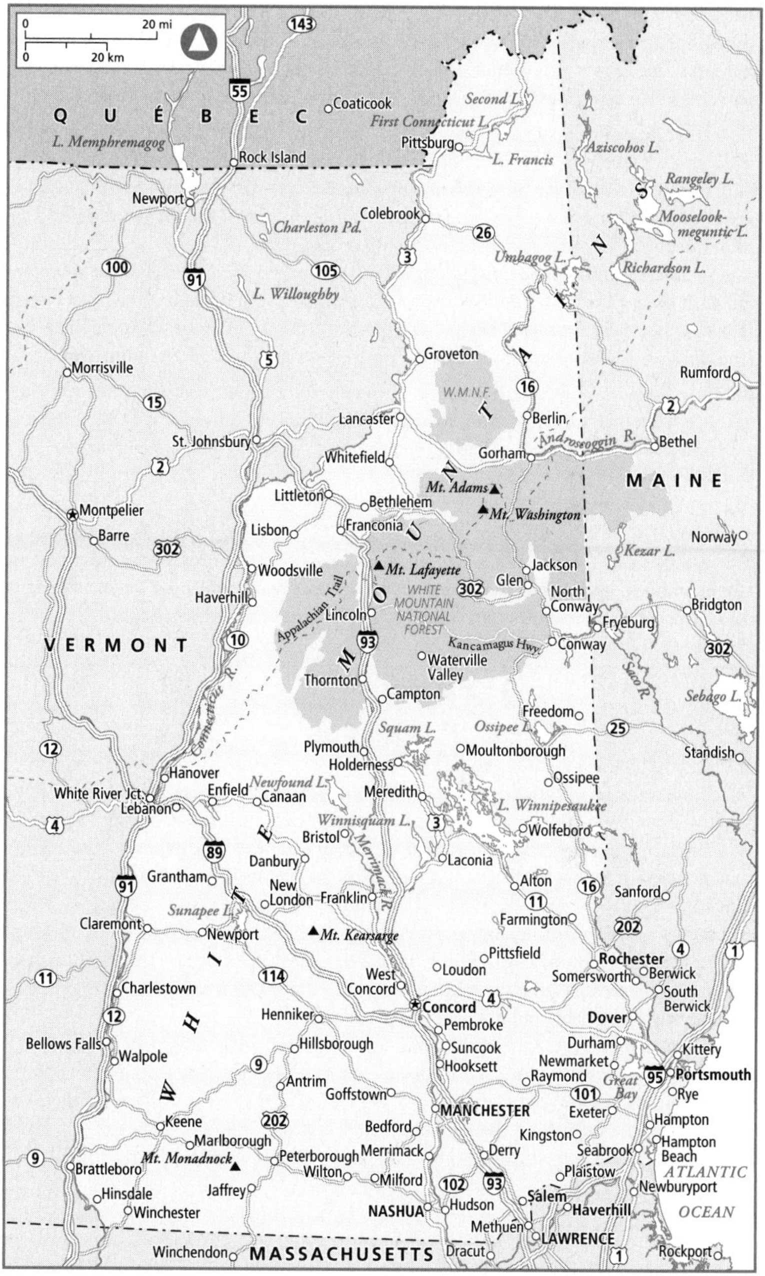
0
20 mi
0
20 km
QUÉBEC
L. Memphremagog
Coaticook
First Connecticut L.
Second L.
Pittsburg
L. Francis
Rock Island
Newport
Colebrook
Charleston Pd.
Aziscohos L.
Rangeley L.
Mooselookmeguntic L.
Umbagog L.
Richardson L.
L. Willoughby
Groveton
Morrisville
W.M.N.F.
Rumford
Lancaster
Berlin
St. Johnsbury
Androscoggin R.
Bethel
Whitefield
Gorham
MAINE
Littleton
Mt. Adams
Bethlehem
Mt. Washington
Montpelier
Barre
Lisbon
Franconia
Norway
Kezar L.
Woodsville
Mt. Lafayette
Jackson
Glen
Haverhill
WHITE MOUNTAIN NATIONAL FOREST
North Conway
Bridgton
Appalachian Trail
Lincoln
Fryeburg
VERMONT
Kancamagus Hwy.
Conway
Waterville Valley
Saco R.
Thornton
Campton
Sebago L.
Connecticut R.
Freedom
Squam L.
Ossipee L.
Plymouth
Moultonborough
Standish
Holderness
Hanover
Ossipee
White River Jct.
Enfield
Newfound L.
Canaan
Meredith
Lebanon
L. Winnipesaukee
Winnisquam L.
Bristol
Wolfeboro
Danbury
Laconia
Grantham
Merrimack R.
New London
Franklin
Alton
Sanford
Sunapee L.
Farmington
Claremont
Newport
Mt. Kearsarge
Pittsfield
Rochester
Loudon
Somersworth
Berwick
Charlestown
West Concord
South Berwick
Concord
Henniker
Dover
Pembroke
Bellows Falls
Hillsborough
Durham
Walpole
Suncook
Kittery
Hooksett
Newmarket
Portsmouth
Antrim
Raymond
Great Bay
Goffstown
Rye
Keene
MANCHESTER
Exeter
Bedford
Hampton
Marlborough
Kingston
Hampton Beach
Mt. Monadnock
Peterborough
Merrimack
Derry
Seabrook
Brattleboro
Wilton
Milford
Plaistow
ATLANTIC
Hinsdale
Jaffrey
Newburyport
Winchester
NASHUA
Hudson
Salem
Haverhill
OCEAN
Methuen
LAWRENCE
Winchendon
MASSACHUSETTS
Dracut
Rockport
WHITE MOUNTAINS
143
55
100
91
105
26
3
5
15
16
2
302
10
93
12
25
4
89
11
202
1
114
9
95
101
102

Fishing licenses are required for freshwater fishing, but not for saltwater fishing. For detailed information on the latest regulations, request material from the **New Hampshire Fish and Game Department** (✆ **603/271-3421**), or check the department website online at **www.wildlife.state.nh.us**. Fishing licenses for nonresidents range from $15 for 1 day to $35 for a week or $53 for the calendar year. (Salmon fishing requires a separate $11 permit.) It's easiest, by far, to buy these online in advance of your trip.

HIKING In southwest New Hampshire, the premier hike is **Mount Monadnock,** which local tourism folks claim to be one of the world's two most popular hikes—second only to Mount Fuji in Japan. That's a bit hard to believe, but on autumn weekends it *does* get mighty crowded here. The lone peak, rising regally above the surrounding hills, is a straightforward day hike accessible via any of several trails.

For other hiking opportunities, see *50 Hikes in the White Mountains* and *50 More Hikes in New Hampshire,* both written by Daniel Doan and Ruth Doan MacDougall (Backcountry Publications, 2004 and 2006). These can still be found at some New England libraries and bookstores, though it's simplest to buy through an online retailer.

SKIING New Hampshire has about 20 downhill ski areas, though none can really compare with the grand resorts of Stowe, Vermont (p. 170), or western Maine. However, this state's specialty is small skiing areas catering to families—places like Sunapee, Gunstock, Temple Mountain, King Pine, and Pats Peak, all with vertical drops of 1,500 feet or less and all with family-friendly amenities.

Ski NH (✆ **800/887-5464** or 603/745-9396), based in North Woodstock in the White Mountains, distributes a map of resorts and other information helpful when ski-trip planning. This organization also provides updated snow condition reports during the ski season; visit **www.skinh.com/Snow_Reports.cfm** for up-to-date reports.

2 THE SEACOAST

Portsmouth: 11 miles N of Hampton; 10 miles NE of Exeter; 55 miles N of Boston; 54 miles S of Portland

First-time travelers to New England are often surprised to learn that New Hampshire isn't landlocked—it actually has a coastline. Granted, it isn't much of one (just 18 miles), but this little strip manages to pack in a lot of variety (and real-estate value). The coastline has honky-tonk beach towns, eye-popping mansions in blue-blood villages, old forts, the odd fishing village, vest-pocket state parks with swaths of sand, and one historic seaport city with a vibrant maritime history and culture. Ecologically speaking, you can find sand dunes, hardwood forests, bird-friendly tidal inlets, and a complex system of salt marshes that has prevented development from overtaking the seacoast entirely by rendering the ground unstable for big buildings in those areas.

A short drive inland, Colonial-era historic towns and a slower way of life have so far resisted the inexorable creep of Boston's suburbs. Though strip malls are appearing throughout the region (especially along Rte. 1), most of the towns are holding their own, and several are establishing themselves as fertile breeding grounds for small-scale entrepreneurs who've shunned the fast life in bigger cities to the south.

EXETER ★

The southern New Hampshire town of **Exeter**—a bit inland, with no seacoast whatsoever—is classic, small-town New England. It has a small bandstand around which all the local traffic circles; some Revolutionary War history; a mixture of longtime locals and

recent blow-ins; some pretty big companies tucked among the trees; and varied commercial architecture in its compact but vibrant downtown. There's also wonderful residential architecture on the shady side streets—and the town produced novelist John Irving (a pen name; he was born John Blunt) of *The Hotel New Hampshire* and *The Cider House Rules* fame.

Bisected by the historic Squamscott River, which once provided power to mills, Exeter now boasts a fine, browsable selection of boutiques and shops, plus one of the nation's most famous prep schools (Phillips Exeter Academy), which is architecturally (if not yet totally culturally) integrated into the town and sports handsome buildings and green spaces. In short, Exeter is a good stop for a quick taste of old New England when you're dashing north for the coast.

Essentials

GETTING THERE Exeter is on Route 108. From Portsmouth or Boston, take exit 2 (Hampton) from I-95, but drive *west* (instead of east toward the Hampton beach) on the Route 101 parkway to Route 108. Exit again onto Route 108 (exit 11) and drive 2 miles south into town.

Moments Lincoln's Legacy—Sort Of

True history buffs walking around Exeter might want to stroll quickly past **11 Pleasant St.,** just across the High Street bridge, before they leave town. Claim to fame? Just this one: Abraham Lincoln's son Robert Todd—the only son of Abe's four who would live past his teenage years, and the man who would one day build the lovely Hildene estate (p. 93) in southern Vermont—lived here while attending Exeter Academy in the late 1850s. Hey, it's a tenuous connection to history, but when you can do anything in the steps of Honest Abe, why not?

VISITOR INFORMATION The **Exeter Chamber of Commerce,** 24 Front St., Ste. 101, Exeter, NH 03833 (✆ **603/772-2411;** www.exeterarea.org), distributes travel information from its offices Monday through Friday during business hours, roughly from 8:30am until 4:30pm.

Exploring the Town

Exeter is best viewed on foot. Downtown has an eclectic mix of architecture, from clapboarded Georgian homes to intricate brick Victorians. The center of downtown is marked by the **Swasey Pavilion,** a trim 1916 bandstand with an intricate floral mosaic on the ceiling. Brass-band concerts are still held here in the summer. Just up the hill is the imposing **Congregational Church,** built in 1798, with its handsome white spire. On Thursdays from mid-May through late October, a big **farmers' market** is held from 2:15 until 6pm along Swasey Parkway, along the river (off Water St.); local farms and live local folk music are featured.

The booklet *Walking Tour of Exeter,* published by the Exeter Historical Society during the 1990s, is available for a small fee at the American Independence Museum (see below), chamber of commerce (see above), and the local historical society (at 47 Front St.). If you're serious about getting to know the town for a few days, this guide and the map that comes with it offer a concise, well-written history of the town, plus interesting historical and architectural comments about notable buildings.

With or without the guide, the grounds of **Phillips Exeter Academy** ★, just southwest of the town center, are always worth a stroll. The predominant style is Georgian-inspired brick—it's hard to imagine misbehaving at a campus this stern, though that hasn't deterred generations of prep-school kids here. But look for anomalies, too, such as the 1971 prize-winning library designed by American architect Louis I. Kahn. It's on Front Street, near Abbot Place.

American Independence Museum ★ This small but good museum offers an insightful glimpse into Colonial life during hour-long tours of a colonial home from spring through fall. Displays inside the 1721 house include Revolutionary War and Colonial Revival artifacts and furniture, though you won't see the museum's most prized possession: 1 of just 25 original copies of the Declaration of Independence still known to exist. It turned up when someone got around to cleaning out the attic in the 1980s; owing to its great delicacy, the document is brought out only for special occasions, though copies are always on display. The homestead itself was built by John Taylor Gilman, an early governor of New Hampshire—among other functions, the house served as the state's treasury during the American Revolution. (Look for displays of early currency in the treasury room.) Descendants of Gilman occupied the home for decades; in 1902 it was acquired by the state's chapter of the Society of the Cincinnati, the oldest veterans group in the nation, and in 1991 the group finally opened the house to the public (society members still meet here twice a year). Every year on the third weekend in July, the museum hosts the free Revolutionary War Festival, attracting thousands of history buffs to the area; book your room well ahead if you come then.

1 Governor's Lane (1 block west of band shell, off Water St.). ✆ **603/772-2622.** www.independencemuseum.org. Admission $5 adults, $3 children 6–12, free for children 5 and under. Mid-May to early Nov Wed–Sat 10am–4pm (tours on the hour; last tour at 3pm); Nov to mid-May by appointment only.

Where to Stay

The Exeter Inn ★★ At the edge of the Exeter Academy campus and within easy walking distance of downtown, the big brick Exeter Inn is under new ownership. They're trying to put a new face on the place, and they've already succeeded to an extent. The inn—which mostly caters to parents and staff associated with Phillips Exeter—was built in 1932; with its prominent chimneys, it could easily pass for a campus building. Rooms are furnished in reproduction American antiques, including some canopy beds. There's a range of accommodations—a few king-size rooms and suites even have Jacuzzis, while others are standard or even a bit on the tiny side. Almost all are welcoming and homey, though—and the house restaurant **Epoch ★★** is *very* good, serving upscale meals sourced from local farms and fisheries such as tenderloin filets, baked cod, rack of lamb, poached salmon, roasted chicken, and steak. Things are looking up.

90 Front St., Exeter, NH 03833. ✆ **800/782-8444** or 603/772-5901. Fax 603/778-8757. www.theexeterinn.com. 46 units. $119–$259 double; $219–$349 suite. AE, DC, MC, V. **Amenities:** Restaurant. *In room:* A/C, TV, Wi-Fi (free).

The Inn by the Bandstand ★★ Finds Wandering through downtown Exeter, you almost can't help but notice this regal, yellow Federal-style home looming over the town's signature bandstand. An inn since 1992, the place is handsomely decorated in antiques and a few reproductions; some rooms have propane fireplaces, and some also sport Jacuzzis in the bathrooms. On the third floor are the two best rooms, beautiful Somerset Cottage and Lakeheath, each showing off the home's original, ruggedly hand-hewn oak beams (the home was built in 1809) plus touches like a wet bar, wrought-iron beds, a cozy brick fireplace (original to the home), handmade quilting, and the like. There's also complimentary port wine in each room, the innkeepers are friendly and helpful, and a full hot breakfast is included with your room. Conclusion? The history, detailing, and room size here make these rates a real bargain—this inn could surely charge more and get it. Tiny quibble: The central location is handy, but also a bit noisy when trucks downshift coming down the hill *next* to the bandstand. Otherwise, a wonderful inn.

6 Front St., Exeter, NH 03833. ✆ **877/239-3837** or 603/772-6352. www.innbythebandstand.com. 9 units. $139–$209 double; $179–$249 suite. Rates include full breakfast. 2-night minimum stay holidays and school-event weekends. AE, DISC, MC, V. *In room:* A/C, TV, CD player (some units), fridge (2 units), hair dryer, kitchenette (2 units), Wi-Fi (free).

Where to Dine

There aren't all that many restaurants in this town. In addition to the bakery listed below and the very good in-house gourmet restaurant **Epoch ★★** at the Exeter Inn (see "Where to Stay," above), there's also the **Tavern at River's Edge** (✆ **603/772-7393;** www.tavernatriversedge.com) at 163 Water St., a rather basic town gathering place serving pubby meals and beer (go for the beer; tolerate the food). And that's about it.

Loaf and Ladle ★ CAFE/BAKERY A handsome view of the river and colorful art are the only distractions from the baked goods and soups served up at this cafeteria-style eatery. It's sometimes hard to get a grasp of the menu, which is updated on chalkboards as the day progresses. (As one soup is drained by the diners, another follows on its heels.) Bowls come with hefty slabs of house-baked bread. Among the other baked goods, the cinnamon buns are especially good. Everything is made from scratch here, and vegetarian entrees are usually available. This place has been a local mainstay for years.

9 Water St. ✆ **603/778-8955.** www.theloafandladle.com. Main courses mostly $5–$8. AE, DISC, MC, V. Mon–Sat 8:30am–9pm; Sun 9am–9pm (closed 8pm Mon–Fri in winter).

PORTSMOUTH ★★

Portsmouth is a civilized little seaside city of bridges, brick, and seagulls, and is quite a gem. Filled with elegant architecture that's more intimate than intimidating, this bonsai-size city projects a strong, proud sense of its heritage without being overly precious. Part of the city's appeal is its variety: Upscale coffee shops and art galleries stand alongside old-fashioned barbershops and tattoo parlors. Despite a steady influx of money in recent years, the town still retains an earthiness that serves as a tangy vinegar for more saccharine coastal spots. Portsmouth's humble waterfront must actually be sought out; when found, it's rather understated.

This city's history runs deep, a fact that's evident on even a quick stroll through town. For 3 centuries, Portsmouth has been the hub of the coastal Maine/New Hampshire region's maritime trade. In the 1600s, Strawbery Banke (it wasn't called Portsmouth until 1653) was a major center for the export of wood and dried fish to Europe. Later it prospered as a regional center for trade. Just across the Piscataqua River in Maine (so important a connection that there are four bridges from Portsmouth to that state), the Portsmouth Naval Shipyard—founded back in 1800—evolved into a prominent base for the building, outfitting, and repairing of U.S. Navy submarines.

Today Portsmouth's maritime tradition continues with a lively trade in bulk goods; look for the scrap metal and minerals stockpiled along the shores of the river on Market Street. The city's de facto symbol is the tugboat, one or two of which are almost always tied up in or near the waterfront's picturesque "tugboat alley."

Visitors to Portsmouth will discover a surprising number of experiences in such a small space—good shopping in the boutiques that now occupy much of the historic downtown; good eating at many small restaurants and bakeries; great coffee; and plenty of history to explore in the form of historic homes, parks, gardens, and museums. As if that weren't enough, ocean beaches are just a couple minutes away.

Essentials

GETTING THERE Portsmouth is served by exits 3 through 7 on I-95. The most direct route to downtown is via Market Street (exit 7), the last New Hampshire exit just before the big bridge that crosses the river into Maine. Take that exit, then bear right (coming from the south) or left (from the north). You'll come straight into town. From Boston's Logan Airport, Portsmouth is about a 1-hour drive via I-95; from Portland Jetport or Manchester airport, the trip is an hour at most.

For once the bus is a viable option to Portsmouth, as well. **Greyhound** (✆ **800/231-2222;** www.greyhound.com) and **C&J** (✆ **800/258-7111** or 603/430-1100; www.ridecj.com) each run about five buses daily from Boston's South Station directly to Portsmouth (trip time: 1¼ hr.); C&J also runs trips from Boston's Logan Airport. Greyhound

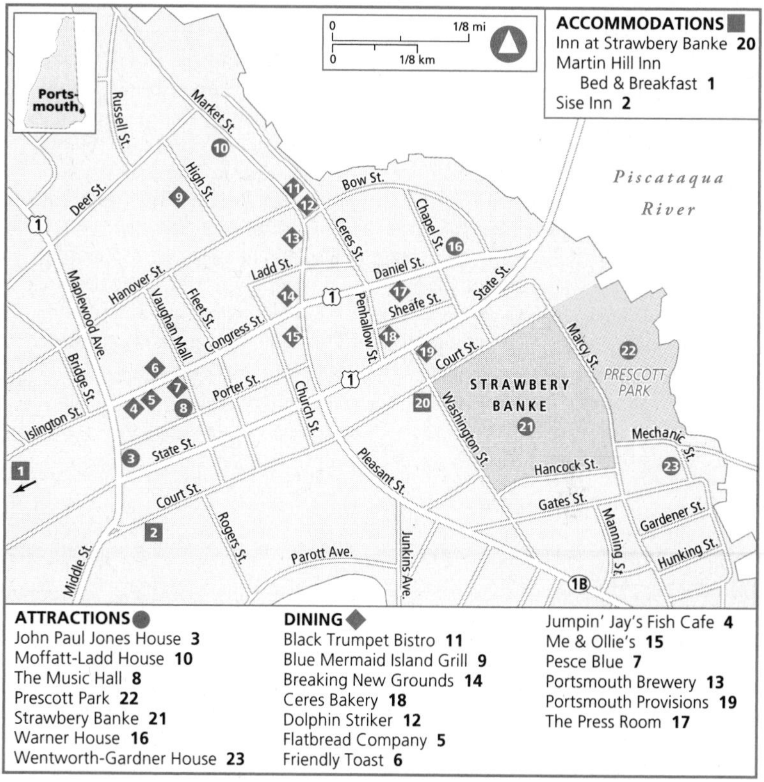

is probably the better choice, because it drops you off right in Market Square, while C&J calls at a modern but distant bus station about 5 miles south of the city. (There's a 50¢ "trolley" [bus] shuttle from the station into and back from the city about once an hour—though *no* shuttle runs on Sunday. Otherwise, you'll need to call a taxi or have a rental car outfit pick you up.)

A ticket from South Station costs $18 each way on either bus line; the trip from Logan Airport costs $24 one-way on C&J. From New York City, a one-way Greyhound ticket to Portsmouth costs about $48 and the ride takes about 6½ hours.

It's also possible to get here by train—sometimes. **Amtrak** (✆ **800/872-7245;** www.amtrak.com) runs five trains daily from Boston's North Station to downtown Dover, New Hampshire, about 12 miles from Portsmouth; a one-way ticket is $19 per person, and the trip takes about 90 minutes. So far, so good. You can then take a no. 2 **COAST bus** (✆ **603/743-5777;** www.coastbus.org) from Dover station to the center of downtown Portsmouth, a 45-minute trip that costs $1.50. However, this bus runs on a very limited schedule on Saturday, and not at *all* on Sunday, making this route impractical for weekend travel.

Tips Packing a Picnic

Portsmouth's **Prescott Park** is about as pretty a spot as you could ever find for an alfresco bite, with views of the harbor, a well-kept green, colorful flower gardens, summer music festivals, and vendors dispensing slushies and other fun treats in the summer. It's all free. There are a few benches, but tote a blanket just in case—the lawn makes a great spot for splaying out and catching some rays. Get provisions nearby at the aptly named **Portsmouth Provisions** (✆ **603/436-5104**), 2 blocks away at 148 State St. It's open daily from early in the morning until almost midnight. There's a good selection of beers; an attached sandwich counter, where a lot of locals eat lunch on the fly; and plenty of snacks and ice-cream products. Or just hit the vendors in the park for a hot dog, an ice cream, or a lemonade. In recent years, a summertime ice-cream shop has opened its doors across the street in Strawbery Banke, too.

VISITOR INFORMATION The **Greater Portsmouth Chamber of Commerce,** 500 Market St. (✆ **603/610-5510;** www.portsmouthchamber.org), has an information center on the road into town from exit 7—it's on the right, across from the piles of scrap metal. From Memorial Day to Columbus Day, it's open daily until at least 5pm every day (later Thurs–Fri). The rest of the year, the info center is open weekdays only. During summer, a staffed information hut opens in Market Square in front of the Breaking New Grounds coffee shop.

PARKING Most of Portsmouth can be easily explored on foot. Mind the rules and signs carefully when you park; parking can be tight in and around the historic district in summer, and officers will ticket. The city's municipal parking garage nearly always has space and costs 75¢ per hour; it's on Hanover Street, between Market and Fleet streets. The Strawbery Banke museum (see "A Magical History Tour," below) provides limited parking for visitors, as well.

A Magical History Tour

Portsmouth's 18th-century prosperity is evident in the Georgian-style homes and other mansions that dot the city. Strawbery Banke occupies the core of the historic area and is definitely worth a visit. If you don't have the budget, time, or inclination to spend half a day at Strawbery Banke, though, a local walking tour will take you past many other significant homes, some of which are maintained by various historical or colonial societies and are open to the public. A helpful map and brochure, *The Portsmouth Trail,* is available for free at the information centers and hut.

Tired from touring? Take a break at **Prescott Park** ★★, between Strawbery Banke and the water. (See "Packing a Picnic," above.) It's one of the best municipal parks in New England. The water views, lemonade vendors, benches, grass, lovely gardens, and full card of festivals make it worth a visit. There's a calendar of events at the park festival website, **www.prescottpark.org**.

John Paul Jones House ★ This yellow, handsome, three-story 1758 home is easy to miss, simply because it's parked right at one of Portsmouth's busiest traffic intersections a few blocks down State Street from the Market Square area. Yet it's worth finding—and near several excellent restaurants. Scottish Revolutionary War hero Jones ("I have not yet begun to fight") didn't build it; he's believed to have lived in it during the war while here to oversee construction of his sloop, the *Ranger* (probably the first ship ever to sail under the U.S. flag; a model is on display). The house is immaculately restored and maintained by the Portsmouth Historical Society, which formed in 1917 to protect it from the wrecking ball. Interestingly, Jones sailed out of Portsmouth the next year and never returned.

43 Middle St. (corner of State St.). ✆ **603/436-8420.** Admission $6 adults, free for children. Memorial Day to Oct daily 11am–5pm (last tour at 4:30pm). Closed Nov to mid-May.

Moffatt-Ladd House & Garden ★★ Built for a family of prosperous merchants and traders, this 1763 home is as notable for its elegant gardens as it is for the home's great hall and elaborate carvings. Now a National Historic Landmark, it belonged to a single family from 1763 until 1913, when it became a museum. As a result, many of the furnishings here have never left the premises; aficionados of Early American furniture and painting, take note.

154 Market St. ✆ **603/436-8221.** www.moffattladd.org. Admission to house and gardens $6 adults, $2.50 children 11 and under; gardens only $2 per person. Tours mid-June to mid-Oct Mon–Sat 11am–5pm; Sun 1–5pm (last tour at 4:30pm). Closed mid-Oct to mid-June.

Strawbery Banke ★★★ In 1958 the city of Portsmouth was finalizing plans to raze this neighborhood (which was settled in 1653!) to make way for "urban renewal." A group of local citizens resisted the move, and they prevailed, establishing an outdoor history museum that's become one of the largest and best in New England. Today the attraction consists of 10 prime downtown acres and more than 40 historic buildings, some restored with period furnishings, others featuring historic exhibits. (The remainder can be viewed only from the outside, but are mostly well restored.) The focus is on the buildings, architecture, and history rather than silly re-enactors in kingly costumes. The neighborhood surrounds an open lawn (formerly an inlet) and has a settled, picturesque quality; several working crafts shops demonstrate colonial skills and craftwork. The most intriguing home might be the Drisco House, half of which depicts life in the 1790s and half of which shows life in the 1950s—nicely demonstrating how houses grow and adapt to each era.

Visitor center at 14 Hancock St. (at Marcy St.) ✆ **603/433-1100.** www.strawberybanke.org. Summer admission $15 adults, $10 children 5–17, free for children 4 and under, $40 per family; winter rates discounted. May–Oct daily for self-guided tours 10am–5pm; Nov–Apr 90-min. guided tours on the hour Sat–Sun only 10am–2pm; extra tours in Dec. Look for directional signs posted around town.

Warner House ★ Finds This house, built in 1716 for a local merchant and ship owner, was later the New Hampshire governor's mansion for a time during the mid–18th century (when Portsmouth was the state capital). After a period as a private home, it was opened to the public in the 1930s. The stately brick structure with graceful Georgian architectural elements is a favorite of architectural historians for its wall murals (said to be the oldest such murals still in place in the U.S.), early wall marbleizing, and original white pine paneling. It, too, is a bit hard to find, although it's very close to Market Square—from the square, walk past the post office toward the steel Memorial Bridge; look to your left for a brick house with dormers and a white picket fence.

150 Daniel St. ✆ **603/436-5909.** www.warnerhouse.org. Admission $5 adults, $4 seniors, $2.50 children 7–12, free for children 6 and under. Mid-June to mid-Oct Tues and Thurs–Sat noon–4pm. Closed mid-Oct to mid-June.

Finds Snooping Around the South End

Most travelers to Portsmouth tend to hit Strawbery Banke, do a little shopping at the downtown shops, grab a bite or a cup coffee, then hustle onward to southern Maine's beaches. To get a fuller sense of Portsmouth, though, take the time to stroll a bit off the beaten track in some of its downtown neighborhoods. The area around the Wentworth-Gardner House (sometimes locally called "the South End") is one great place to snoop around—a mix of twisting roads, lanes too narrow for SUVs, fish restaurants, fishing boats, historic properties, and wooden houses in various condition. It's a taste of the real Portsmouth, both the 18th-century version and the current fishing-village version.

Wentworth-Gardner House ★★ Arguably one of the best-looking mansions in the Seacoast region, this is considered one of the nation's prime examples of Georgian architecture. The yellow 1760 home features many period elements, including pronounced *quoins* (blocks on the building's corners), pedimented window caps, plank sheathing (to make the home appear as if made of masonry), an elaborate doorway with Corinthian pilasters, a broken scroll, and a paneled door topped with a pineapple (even then, the symbol of hospitality). Perhaps most memorable is its scale—though a grand home of the Colonial era, it's fairly modest in size. Once again, you need to look carefully for this house; it's wedged between Prescott Park and Geno's Chowder Shop on Mechanic Street. Walk down the street that juts off from the base of the little bridge beside the park.

50 Mechanic St. (at Gardner St.). ✆ **603/436-4406.** www.wentworthgardnerandlear.org. Admission $5 adults, $2 children 6–14, free for children 5 and under. Mid-June to mid-Oct Thurs–Sun noon–4pm. Closed mid-Oct to mid-June. From the Prescott Park rose gardens (across from Strawbery Banke), walk 1 block and make a left toward the bridge. Take right onto Mechanic St. just before crossing the bridge; house is 2 blocks farther on right, at corner of Gardner St. and before Hunking St.

Where to Stay

In addition to the options listed below, also see the **Portsmouth Harbor Inn and Spa** in chapter 9; it's just across the river in Kittery, a quick walk from downtown.

Inn at Strawbery Banke ★ This little inn is tucked away in a simple but old (built in 1814) home on Court Street, a very central base for exploring Portsmouth: Strawbery Banke is just a block away, and Market Square is just 2 blocks away. The owner has done a nice job of taking an antique home and making it comfortable for modern guests. Though rooms are tiny and simply furnished, they're brightened by stenciling, pencil-poster beds, wooden shutters, and beautifully preserved pine floors (one has a private bathroom down the hall). Two sitting rooms are stocked with TVs, phones (there are none in the rooms), and plenty of books; breakfast is served in the dining room. Note that stairs to upper-floor rooms are a bit steep.

314 Court St., Portsmouth, NH 03801. ✆ **800/428-3933** or 603/436-7242. www.innatstrawberybanke.com. 7 units, 1 with detached bathroom. Mar–Oct $160–$170 double; Nov–Feb $100–$115 double. Rates include full breakfast. 2-night minimum stay Sat–Sun in Aug and Oct. AE, DISC, MC, V. Children 10 and over welcome. *In room:* A/C, no phone.

Martin Hill Inn Bed & Breakfast ★ This B&B is in a residential neighborhood a half-mile west of Market Square, and consists of two attractive buildings: a main house (built around 1815) plus a guesthouse built 35 years later. Rooms have queen-size beds, writing tables, and sofas or sitting areas, and are appointed in handsome wallpapers, antiques, and four-poster or brass beds; some even have private porches. There are no televisions in this inn's rooms, however. A stone pathway leads to a small water garden. The full breakfast here might consist of johnnycakes, "goldenrod" eggs, quiche, nutty waffles, or cooked fruit—a good start to the day. There are a number of rules at the inn, however (check-in is limited to 4–6pm; there's a mandatory $3 charge for housekeepers' tips on your first night; children 11 and under aren't accepted; and so forth), so just be aware of those before arriving.

404 Islington St., Portsmouth, NH 03801. ✆ **603/436-2287.** www.martinhillinn.com. 7 units. May–Nov $140–$210 double; rest of year $105–$160 double. 2-night minimum stay summer and holiday weekends. Rates include full breakfast. MC, V. Children 12 and over welcome. *In room:* A/C, Wi-Fi (free).

Sise Inn ★ This Queen Anne–style home in the downtown district was built for a prominent merchant in 1881; the hotel section was added a century later. The effect is mostly harmonious, though, as the antique stained glass and oak trim mesh with the contemporary design elements. Some rooms have antique armoires, updated Victorian styling, or whirlpool or soaking tubs. I like no. 302, a bi-level, two-bedroom suite with a claw-foot tub; no. 406, a suite with soaking tub and private sitting room; no. 120, with its private patio; and no. 216 (in the carriage house), with a working sauna, two-person whirlpool, and lovely natural light.

40 Court St. (at Middle St.), Portsmouth, NH 03801. ✆ **877/747-3466** or 603/433-1200. Fax 603/431-0200. www.siseinn.com. 34 units. $119–$199 double; $159–$279 suite. Rates include continental breakfast. AE, DISC, MC, V. *In room:* Wi-Fi (free).

Wentworth by the Sea ★★★ The reopening of this historic resort in 2003 was a major event. A photogenic grand hotel of white paint and red accents, it was built on a lovely spot on New Castle Island in 1874 but later shut down. Today it's operated jointly by a Maine firm and Marriott in professional, luxurious fashion. As befits an old hotel, rooms vary in size, but most are spacious with good views of ocean or harbor; especially interesting are the suites that occupy the three turrets. Some units have gas-powered fireplaces or private balconies in addition to the spruced-up bathroom fixtures, detailing, and furnishings. The luxury suites beside the water are truly outstanding: They have water views, modern kitchens, and marble bathrooms with Jacuzzis—plus access to a private dock-side pool. A full-service spa offers a range of treatments, and there's a handsome lounge area as well as an excellent **dining room ★** in the main building; in summer a seasonal deck grill opens adjacent to the Marina Suites. You can also golf at the lovely 18-hole Wentworth golf course (a 5-min. walk down the road), even though it's a private club and separately owned.

588 Wentworth Rd. (P.O. Box 860), New Castle NH 03854. ✆ **866/240-6313** or 603/422-7322. Fax 603/422-7329. www.wentworth.com. 161 units. Peak season $259–$459 double, $439–$559 suite, $599–$899 marina suite; off season $179–$229 double, $259–$329 suite, $359–$599 marina suite. AE, DISC, MC, V. From downtown, take Rte. 1A (Miller Ave.) 1 1/3 miles south; turn left onto Rte. 1B and continue 1 1/2 miles to hotel. **Amenities:** 2 restaurants; bar; 2 pools (1 indoor, 1 outdoor); spa. *In room:* A/C, TV, hair dryer, Internet (free), kitchenette (some units).

Where to Dine

Beyond the options listed below, you could visit the dining room or grill at the **Wentworth by the Sea** resort (see "Where to Stay," above), on Route 1B a few miles south of the city—chef Daniel Dumont's Continental fare is outstanding, served beneath a

Tips Portsmouth: Coffee Capital

Portsmouth has perhaps the best cafe scene in northern New England, nearly comparable to Cambridge's or Boston's and better than Portland's or Burlington's. There are numerous places in the compact downtown alone where you can get a decent-to-very-good cup of coffee and better-than-average baked goods; new coffeehouses open all the time. My favorite spots to quaff a coffee drink or pot of tea with a book include **Breaking New Grounds,** 14 Market Sq. (✆ **603/436-9555**), with outstanding espresso shakes, good tables out on the square, and late hours; the tie-dyed **Friendly Toast,** 113 Congress St. (✆ **603/430-2154;** www.thefriendlytoast.net), serving a fun variety of eggs and other breakfast dishes all day long; and **Me and Ollie's,** 10 Pleasant St. (✆ **603/436-7777;** www.meandollies.com), known locally for its good bread, sandwiches, and homemade granola. And there are several *more* bakeries and coffee shops within shouting distance of Market Square, plus a great cafe a couple miles up Route 1 in Kittery (p. 285).

If you want a bit more of a bite to go with your coffee, the funky **Ceres Bakery,** 51 Penhallow St. (✆ **603/436-6518;** www.ceresbakery.com), on a side street off the main square, has a handful of tiny interior tables; grab a sandwich, cookie, or slice of cake to go and walk to the waterfront rose gardens nearby.

remarkable (and original) frescoed dome. Entrees might include grilled swordfish, lobster with filet mignon, seared yellowfin tuna, a clambake, or a lobster pie. Men are asked to wear collared shirts. The resort's **Latitudes** grill has a simpler menu but offers something the main inn doesn't—an outdoor patio, softly lit at night, of tables with lovely views overlooking the water. The grill is open from late spring through the end of summer.

Downtown Portsmouth's casual dining scene got a shot in the arm with the opening of a branch of the terrific **Flatbread Company** (✆ **603/436-7888;** www.flatbreadcompany.com) pizzeria at 138 Congress St. It's *the* place to eat a terrific organic-wheat crust pizza.

Black Trumpet Bistro ★★ BISTRO Formerly known as Lindbergh's Crossing, this bistro changed ownership in 2007—to Lindbergh's chef, Evan Mallett, who has settled in nicely. He cooks exotically spiced comfort food in an intimate, two-story building within a former warehouse. The menu, composed of small plates, medium plates, and full entrees, is influenced by the south of France, Spain, Africa, and Latin America. You can partake of starters like saffron Provençal fish soup, octopus with chorizo, bacalao salad, mussels steamed in porter, or a Moroccan-spice beet soup. Among the entrees, try something like wild mushroom and ricotta crepes; bison short ribs; roasted chicken; or fish with a sauce, such as habanero-banana cream. The side dishes are uniformly inventive and healthy, wild-foraged mushrooms make frequent appearances, and the wine list is strong. If you don't have reservations and they're full, sit at the bar.

29 Ceres St. ✆ **603/431-0887.** www.blacktrumpetbistro.com. Reservations recommended. Small plates $6–$15, main courses $20–$27. AE, DC, MC, V. Sun–Thurs 5:30–9:30pm; Fri–Sat 5:30–10pm.

Blue Mermaid Island Grill ★★ Finds GLOBAL The Blue Mermaid is a Portsmouth favorite as much for its good food as for its refusal to take itself too seriously. A short stroll west of Market Square, in a historic area called the Hill, it's unpretentious—folk tunes play in the background, and service is casual yet professional. The menu is adventurous in a low-key, global way, leaning toward the Caribbean—but they really run the table. You might try a burrito, tortilla pizza, or sesame-crusted seared cod sandwich for lunch, or a dinner of braised beef short ribs in guava-soy sauce served with corn bread; Bimini-style grilled chicken with bananas and walnuts in a bourbon-coconut (!) sauce; paella; barbecued mahi mahi with mole sauce; or spicy "rasta pasta" (saw that one coming). Or, for fun, you can also make a dinner out of several of the funky small-plate offerings, like chicken-and-jack-cheese wontons, lobster quesadillas, Jamaican beef patties, and veggie spring rolls. They also cook steaks and seafood on a wood-fired grill, plus burgers, pasta, and pizzas. Libations include local draft brews, of course, but also a wine list and a menu of fruity tropical mixed drinks, fun margaritas, and martinis. A fascinating place—try it out.

409 The Hill (at Hanover and High sts., facing the municipal parking garage). ✆ **603/427-2583.** www.bluemermaid.com. Reservations recommended for parties of 6 or more. Main courses $6–$12 at lunch, $16–$24 at dinner. AE, DISC, MC, V. Mon–Fri 11:30am–9pm; Sat noon–10pm; Sun noon–9pm.

Dolphin Striker ★ SEAFOOD/AMERICAN In an old brick warehouse down on one of Portsmouth's most charming streets, the Dolphin serves traditional New England seafood dishes—some of them dressed up in new ways, such as a mushroom-crusted filet of cod or a piece of salmon "lacquered" in tomato-y balsamic vinaigrette and then grilled. But the Maine lobster potpie hasn't changed since, well, probably 1700, and you can also get pan-seared scallops, curried monkfish, bouillabaisse, and other fishy dishes. Seafood avoiders can find refuge in the beef Wellington, steak au poivre, chicken carbonara, or grilled pork chop. The main dining room here has a rustic, public-house atmosphere with wide pine-board floors and wooden furniture; downstairs is a comfortable pub known as the Spring Hill Tavern, with quite good acoustic acts. There's also a lighter, tavern-style menu of burgers, sandwiches, fish and chips, lobster rolls, and the like.

15 Bow St. ✆ **603/431-5222.** www.dolphinstriker.com. Reservations recommended. Main courses $18–$27. AE, DC, DISC, MC, V. Daily 5–11pm.

Jumpin' Jay's Fish Café ★★ Finds SEAFOOD One of Portsmouth's best-loved eateries, Jay McSharry's signature eatery is the place for anyone who wants to eat a fish cooked in something other than a deep-fryer. A sleek and spare dining room dotted with splashes of color and white Corian table tops, it features an open kitchen and a polished-steel bar. People seem to have fun eating here, one reason Jay's attracts a younger, more culinary-attuned clientele than most other spots in town. The fresh catch of the day is posted on the blackboards; you pick your fish and the way you want it cooked, then pair it with one of the sauces, such as an orange-sesame glaze, a lobster velouté, a citrusy mustard sauce, a butter sauce, or simply olive oil with herbs. (Up to a half-dozen fish make it onto the menu on a given night, depending on what's fresh.) Starters include escargots, fish stews, crab cakes, and fried oysters; a few pasta dishes are also available. The food here is great, and the attention to detail by the kitchen and waitstaff is admirable. This is one of Portsmouth's iconic spots, a place that wouldn't feel right anywhere else.

150 Congress St. ✆ **603/766-3474.** www.jumpinjays.com. Reservations recommended. Main courses $16–$21. AE, DISC, MC, V. Mon–Thurs 5:30–9pm (summer to 9:30pm), Fri–Sat 5–10pm; Sun 5–9pm.

Pesce Blue ★★ SEAFOOD/ITALIAN Another excellent seafood eatery in downtown Portsmouth? Indeed. Here James Walter serves with a strong Italian accent. Lunch might be a piece of grilled flatbread topped with smoked salmon; a "salad" of mussels,

Tips Seabrook Side Trip: Lobsters Galore!

If you're driving Route 1 or I-95 south of Portsmouth, heading to or from Massachusetts, make a detour along **Seabrook's** Route 286 for some of the best lobsters in New Hampshire—and the amazing spectacle of two (gently) competing shacks facing off right across the road from each other.

Brown's (✆ **603/474-3331;** www.brownslobster.com) got here first, and it's a bit more like the typically unadorned shack you'd find in, say, Downeast Maine: It's just a low shack over the water. Its patio also frames a view of Seabrook's infamous nuclear power plant—which, yes, is still actively splitting atoms. (If your lobster starts glowing, put it down. I'm kidding.) **Markey's** (✆ **603/474-2851**) opened later and more closely resembles a small-town diner. Cutthroat competition? Hardly: If one place runs out of something, the other will send someone across the street with extra supplies. To find the pounds from I-95, take exit 60, merge onto Route 286, and drive east a few miles until you cross a bridge; the pounds are on the other side of the water. From Hampton Beach, head south on coastal Route 1A a few miles and turn inland (west) on Route 286. The pounds are a few hundred yards ahead.

San Marzano tomatoes, marinated olives, and capers; or a cut of pan-roasted haddock with baccala-whipped potatoes and ramps. Plenty of antipasti are available as well. Dinners run to crisp pieces of sockeye salmon, lasagna made from the house lamb sausage, oil-poached halibut, mixed seafood grills, great small plates of things such as tuna tartare with pickled apples and capers, or an entire salt-baked branzino. Don't overlook the pastas, either—seasonal pumpkin gnocchi in a nutmeg cream sauce, orecchiette with Bolognese sauce, or spaghetti with clam sauce. Desserts have included mascarpone cheesecake, fennel panna cotta, molten chocolate cake, and olive oil-orange cake topped with vanilla cream. On Sunday, the kitchen serves an upscale brunch of truffled lobster frittatas, buttermilk pancakes, poached eggs, lobster rolls, niçoise salads, and the like.

103 Congress St. ✆ **603/430-7766.** www.pesceblue.com. Main courses $9–$21 at lunch, $14–$26 at dinner. AE, DISC, MC, V. Mon–Fri noon–2pm and 5:30–9pm; Sat 5:30–9:30pm; Sun 10am–2pm.

Portsmouth Brewery ★ PUB FARE In the heart of the historic district (look for the tipping tankard suspended over the sidewalk), New Hampshire's first brewpub opened here in 1991 and still draws a loyal clientele with its superb beers and fun atmosphere. The tin-ceiling, brick-wall dining room is open, airy, echoey, and redolent of hops. Brews are made in 200-gallon batches and include specialties such as Old Brown Dog ale and a delightfully creamy Black Cat Stout—plus some cool offbeat styles like cream ale, "California common," Flanders Red (a Dutch-style red ale), a "braggot" (a medieval style), and plenty more. The eclectic menu complements the beers and holds its own; it includes the expected pizzas, burgers, fish and chips, and sandwiches (including a "steak bomb"), of course, but also offers a changing selection of specials that trot the globe adventurously—things like Asian rice noodles in a coconut broth, oven-baked ziti, and a meatloaf spiked with chipotle peppers.

56 Market St. ✆ **603/431-1115.** www.portsmouthbrewery.com. Reservations accepted for parties of 10 or more. Main courses $9–$26. AE, DC, DISC, MC, V. Daily 11:30am–12:30am.

The Press Room AMERICAN Locals flock here for the good atmosphere, live music, and easy-on-the-budget prices rather than fancy cuisine. A downtown favorite since 1976, the restaurant boasts that it was first in the area to serve Guinness beer—and, indeed, the interior has a rustic, Gaelic sort of charm. On cold days, a fire burns in the woodstove while drinkers throw darts beneath heavy wooden beams. Choose from a menu of inexpensive selections such as quesadillas, nachos, salads, burgers, wraps, and stir-fries, or order a heavier (but still cheap) meal of blackened haddock, steak tips, or jambalaya. The live jazz here is justifiably popular (see "Portsmouth After Dark," below). 77 Daniel St. ✆ **603/431-5186.** www.pressroomnh.com. Reservations not accepted. Sandwiches $4–$7, main courses $7–$13. AE, DISC, MC, V. Sun–Thurs 5–11pm; Fri–Sat 11:30am–11pm.

Portsmouth After Dark

Performing Arts

The Music Hall ★★ This historic theater near Market Square dates to 1878 and was more recently restored to its former glory by a local arts group. A variety of shows are staged here, from lots of film to comedy revues, *The Nutracker,* and concerts by visiting pop artists like David Crosby, Graham Nash, and the great Lyle Lovett. Call or check the website for a current calendar. 28 Chestnut St. ✆ **603/436-2400.** www.themusichall.org.

The Press Room ★ A popular local pub and eatery (see "Where to Dine," above), the Press Room also offers casual entertainment almost every night, either upstairs or down. It's best known locally for copious amounts of live jazz; the club brings in quality performers from Boston and beyond. You might hear beat poetry or blues on occasion, too. 77 Daniel St. ✆ **603/431-5186.** www. pressroomnh.com. Cover varies.

Spring Hill Tavern Quality acoustic noodling, live jazz, classical guitar, and/or low-key rock are on top most nights of the week here in the pub located right downstairs from the popular Dolphin Striker seafood restaurant (see "Where to Dine," above). Expect anything from a seasoned New Orleans–style blues band to a local singer-songwriter's nascent efforts. There are also sometimes fun free-form jam sessions. 15 Bow St. ✆ **603/431-5222.** www.dolphinstriker.com. Cover varies.

3 MANCHESTER & CONCORD

Manchester: 51 miles W of Portsmouth; 53 miles NW of Boston; 19 miles S of Concord

Tourists tend to overlook the two Merrimack Valley cities of **Manchester** and **Concord,** making tracks instead for the big lakes and White Mountains to the north or the beaches and lobsters to the east. That isn't necessarily a mistake—frankly, neither city deserves billing as a top tourist destination. Still, both have made efforts to increase their touristic offerings in recent years, and both are highly representative of the *real* New Hampshire: the one that still remembers its industrial heritage and a time when big rivers powered huge, prosperous mills cranking out American goods for transport and export the world over.

The two cities are different from each other. Manchester is the biggest city in northern New England (pop. 110,000, about the size of Portland and South Portland, Maine, combined)—yet the downtown feels fairly compact. Its industry grew up entirely around the falls of the Merrimack River; today the city tries to make the most of its industrial heritage, and has converted and updated many of the grandly monolithic brick riverside mills into shops and condos. It's something of a surprise to find these brick mastodons still grazing at river's edge—inhabited not by millworkers but by swimming pools, print shops, and computer geeks.

Concord is slowly becoming a more arty enclave, and it's worth a stop for its modern, engaging history museum and wonderful planetarium, which commemorates local schoolteacher Christa McAuliffe—the teacher who perished in the space shuttle *Challenger* explosion in January 1986.

MANCHESTER

The history of Manchester is the history of its mills. Brick buildings still line both shores of the Merrimack River today. The industrial age has long since passed, but you'll still be impressed by the mills, now converted into restaurants, offices, university classrooms, and technology centers.

If you're interested, there are plenty of traces of Manchester's rough history as a mill town in the working-class bars and shotgun houses, too, and many tips of the hat to its deep Franco-American heritage. Thousands of French-Canadians (men and women, boys and girls) migrated south across the border to work in the local mills during the late 19th century, and their descendants still live, work, play, go to Mass, and eat *poutine* (fries served with curdled cheese and chicken gravy) here.

Manchester still has a grittier, more urban feel than anywhere else in the three states covered in this book. (Streetwise comic actor Adam Sandler grew up here.) As such, it's best used as a place for stocking supplies, visiting the fine-art museum, and getting a glimpse of the region's proud industrial heritage. Then: onward.

Essentials

GETTING THERE Manchester is accessible from both I-93 and I-293. By car, coming from the south, the easiest route downtown is by taking exit 2 off I-293 and then following Elm Street into town.

Manchester Regional Airport (airport code: MHT) is a growing regional air hub, and you can sometimes score amazingly cheap flights to this city if you check in advance or subscribe to airline fare-sale announcements. **Southwest Airlines** (✆ **800/435-9792;** www.southwest.com) was first to utilize the airport heavily, and it's still the lynchpin here, flying in from Florida, California, Baltimore, Chicago, and Philadelphia.

Other airlines now serve Manchester, too, including **Delta** and its subsidiary Delta Connection (✆ **800/221-1212;** www.delta.com), which flies in from Atlanta, Dallas, and New York's JFK; **Continental** (✆ **800/525-0280;** www.continental.com), from Newark and Cleveland; **United** and United Express (✆ **800/241-6522;** www.united.com), from Chicago and Washington, D.C.; and **US Airways Express** (✆ **800/428-4322;** www.usair.com), flying in from New York's LaGuardia, Charlotte, Atlanta, Philadelphia, and Nashville.

From the airport, get into the city by renting a car (plenty of options at the terminal), taking a private shuttle van, riding a Manchester Transit Authority bus (30 min., $1.50 one-way; service 5:45am–5:45pm on weekdays only), or taking a $15 cab ride. Reach the airport by phone at ✆ **603/624-6556,** or check its website at **www.flymanchester.com** for other questions.

Bus service to Manchester is provided by **Greyhound** (✆ **800/231-2222;** www.greyhound.com), but the bus only stops at the city's airport, *not* downtown. From Boston, the ride takes an hour and costs about $19 one-way; from New York City, it takes an inconvenient 6½ to 7 hours (must change in Boston) and costs about $70 each way.

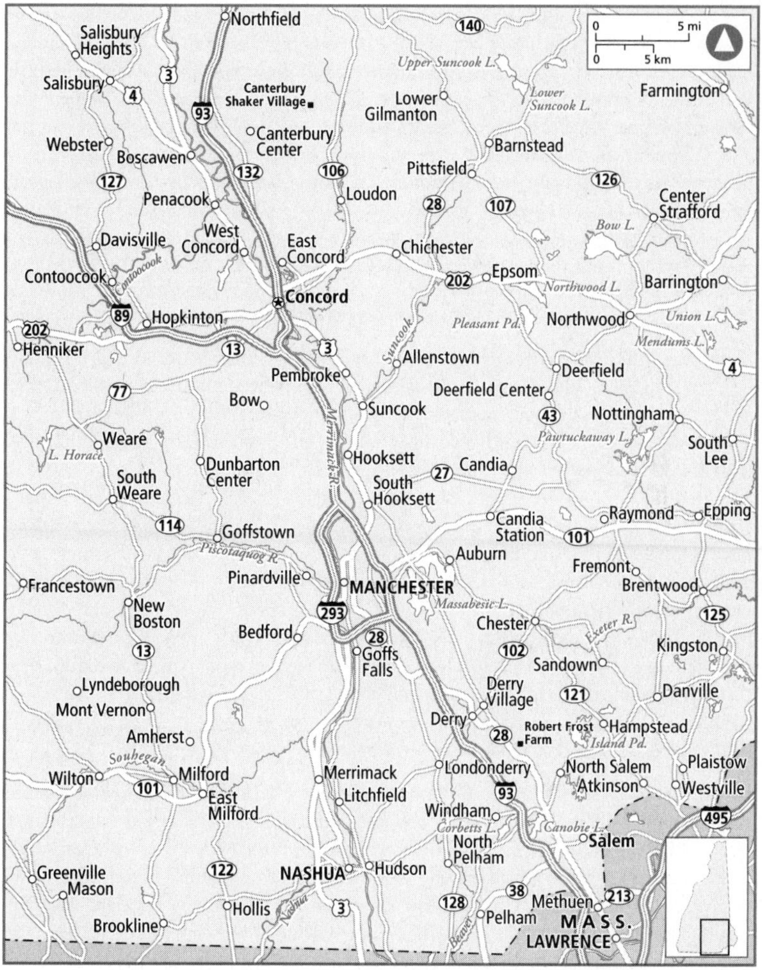

VISITOR INFORMATION The **Greater Manchester Chamber of Commerce** (✆ **603/666-6600;** www.manchester-chamber.org) dispenses brochures, maps, and a handy city guide from a facility at the corner of Elm and Merrimack streets. Its offices open daily from 8:30am to 5pm except Friday, when they close at 4pm.

Exploring Manchester

The two main thoroughfares traversing the mill district are **Commercial** and **Canal** streets, both of which parallel the Merrimack on its eastern bank right at the foot of the landmark green Notre Dame bridge. From here, on the hillside above the mill area, you can see a range of housing. Workers lived in the tenements, while their bosses occupied more stately homes higher up—all of them walking distance from the mills.

Currier Museum of Art ★★ (Finds) One of northern New England's premier art museums is a huge surprise in this industrial city. Housed in an elegant, classical 1932 Beaux Arts building a few blocks from Manchester's main drag, the Currier benefited from major renovations in the late 1990s and a second expansion in 2008. The permanent collections include some 12,000 works of European and American art, with fine pieces by Degas, Picasso, Monet, and John Singer Sargent. Look for the haunting Edward Hopper work *The Bootleggers.* In addition to its extensive holdings of paintings and sculpture, the museum also possesses fine exhibits of silver, glass, furniture, and pewter. An annex property, the **Zimmerman House** (see below), was designed by the famed architect Frank Lloyd Wright.

150 Ash St. ✆ **603/669-6144.** www.currier.org. Admission main museum only $10 adults, $9 seniors, $8 students, free for children 6 and under, free to everyone Sat 10am–noon. Sun–Mon and Wed–Fri 11am–5pm; Sat 10am–5pm. From I-93 take exit 8, bearing right onto Bridge St.; continue 1½ miles and turn right onto Ash St.; continue 2 blocks to museum. Free parking on Prospect St. (2 blocks beyond Ash St.).

Millyard Museum ★★ (Finds) Right inside one of Manchester's brick behemoths (known simply as "Mill no. 3") at the corner of Commercial and Pleasant streets, this is an intriguing local museum operated by the Manchester Historical Association. It's a good first stop when you've just blown into town and want to learn some local history with the kids. A permanent exhibit called "Woven in Time" traces the history of the Merrimack River and the region, from Native American times to its role as an economic powerhouse and a magnet for immigrants. This particular mill building, you'll learn, once belonged to the Amoskeag Manufacturing Co.—for a time, the *world's* single largest manufacturer of cotton textiles. You'll also learn a bit about other notable Manchester natives, from Revolutionary War hero Gen. John Stark to *Peyton Place* author Grace Metalious. Some of the items in the collection here are downright fun: a curly neon shoe-store sign, a fire department's hand-operated pumper tub, and some of the looms from the mill that spun so many thousands (millions?) of textiles. Well done.

200 Bedford St. ✆ **603/622-7531.** www.manchesterhistoric.org. $6 adults, $5 seniors and students, $2 children 6–18, free for children 5 and under, $18 family. Wed–Sat 10am–4pm.

Robert Frost Farm ★★★ One of several New England locations that lays a claim to the poet Robert Frost, this white-clapboard farmhouse in Derry (about 8 miles southeast of Manchester, on Rte. 28) is the most significant of them all. It was Frost's home from 1901 until 1909, where he first worked on a farm and first began learning and writing about his fellow Granite Staters, whose taciturn rhythms of speaking and living would soon pervade his best work. The home's original wallpaper patterns have been restored to look just as they did when Frost and his wife lived here (she gave birth to their three children in one of the rooms); it's almost as though they never left. Those nickmarks in the soapstone sink? Made by Frost while sharpening knives. You can also learn about the historical moment in which Frost lived, listen to occasional free readings of his poetry, and explore a network of trails through surrounding forests and fields that helped inspire the great poet. There aren't many places like this left in the world today—places where nature and art intersect, and have both been preserved purely for the appreciation of both, rather than to create tourist traffic. I highly recommend a visit.

122 Rockingham Rd. (Rte. 28), Derry. ✆ **603/432-3091.** www.robertfrostfarm.org. $7 adults, $3 children 6–17, free for children 5 and under, free for all NH residents. Grounds open year-round. Farmhouse and barn mid-June to Aug daily 10am–5pm; early May to mid-June and Sept to mid-Oct Wed–Sun 10am–5pm. Closed mid-Oct to early May.

SEE Science Center ★★ (Kids) Housed on the upper levels of the good Millyard Museum (see above), the SEE science museum focuses on hands-on, interactive science exhibits rather than Manchester's past. If you're visiting one sight, you might as well visit the other—though you'll pay a second fee for everyone, as there are no combo tickets available. Kids can try out a gyroscope, periscope, "whisper room," electricity machines, and a "moonwalk" exhibit, learning about gravity, light, sound, and other science concepts while having fun at the same time. But don't miss the best exhibit of all here, something much more low-tech than all that: the LEGO MillProject, a remarkable miniature-scale model of the downtown and mill yard as they might have looked in 1900. It's the world's largest permanent LEGO construction. (So many little plastic "bricks" were used to build it that they would stretch to Boston and back, lined up end-to-end!)

200 Bedford St. (upstairs inside the Millyard Museum). ✆ **603/669-0400.** www.see-sciencecenter.org. Admission $6, free for children 1 and under. Mon–Fri 10am–4pm; Sat–Sun 10am–5pm.

Zimmerman House ★★★ From the 1930s through the 1950s, architect Frank Lloyd Wright designed a number of so-called Usonian homes—designed to be compact, useful, elegant, and inexpensive to build. The low-slung Zimmerman House, built in a Manchester residential neighborhood in 1950, was one such home, though the owners didn't really cut corners. Wright designed the entire building, the furniture, the gardens—*everything,* right down to the hexagonal napkins in the dining room, the Japanese paper lamps, and the sleek, wooden Fallingwater-esque mailbox. Throughout, the home features luxe touches such as Georgia-cypress trim and red-glazed brick. Only five Wright homes were built in the entire Northeast, and this is the only one open to the public. It's not only a precious architectural gem, though; it also offers a rare window into 1950s and 1960s America. Visitors are shuttled to the house from the Currier Museum (see above) by van; the tours take 1½ to 2 hours, after which you're whisked back to the museum. Advance reservations are required, and make them *well* ahead if your heart is set on touring the house. If you can't get a spot and just want to sneak a peek, the home is located at 223 Heather St. (at Union St.); a few houses west on Heather is *another* Wright home that's privately owned, but can be viewed from the curb.

C/o Currier Museum of Art, 150 Ash St. ✆ **603/669-6144.** www.currier.org. Standard tours $18 adults, $17 seniors, $16 students, $8 children 7–17 (price includes admission to Currier Gallery). Tours Mon and Thurs–Fri 2pm; Sat 10:30am, 12:30, and 3pm; Sun 11:30am and 1:30pm. Reservations required. Children 5 and under not permitted. Tours depart from the Currier Gallery.

Where to Stay

Manchester offers very few interesting overnight options for travelers, though there are plenty of chain hotels clustered near the airport and even a few surprisingly close to downtown's best attractions.

Besides the small B&B listed below, the most centrally located downtown hotel is probably the boxy **Radisson Hotel Manchester** at 700 Elm St. (✆ **800/395-7046** or 603/625-1000; www.radisson.com), right across from green Veterans Memorial Park. This big, 250-room hotel runs a complimentary airport shuttle and maintains a small indoor pool, fitness center, and sauna. It's about a mile southwest of the Currier Museum—take Bridge Street to Elm.

Ash Street Inn ★ This 1885, three-floor Victorian home-converted-to-B&B has the requisite pointy tower, but it's more interesting to travelers for its very central position—just a block or so from the great Currier Museum of Art (see "Exploring Manchester," above). There's lots of lovely original stained glass work throughout this house, from the front door to the living room to the tower, and it's all unified by an intriguing "sunburst" theme. Surprisingly, all five rooms have phones with voicemail, televisions, free Wi-Fi, bathrobes, and Egyptian cotton sheeting; otherwise, they're decorated in a spare, woody, country-simple style with solid sleigh beds, writing desks, or other furniture pieces. As seems appropriate in a place like this, the innkeepers serve a full afternoon tea three times a week (extra charge); breakfast, though, is included in your rate and served either in a dining room or—weather permitting—on a sun porch. This inn offered a special package deal in 2009 including a room plus a tour of both the Zimmerman House and Currier Museum for one price.

118 Ash St., Manchester, NH 03104. ✆ **603/668-9908.** www.ashstreetinn.com. 5 units. $139–$259 double. Rates include full breakfast. AE, DISC, MC, V. Children 12 and over welcome. *In room:* A/C, TV, hair dryer, Wi-Fi (free).

Quality Inn Manchester Airport ★ A short drive from downtown Manchester in the bedroom community of Bedford (about 4 miles south of the Currier Museum and across the river), this is not just another chain hotel, despite the drab name. In fact, it's a sprawling, architecturally unique hotel right on the site of a once-historic grist mill—offbeat, to say the least. For years it was a favored haunt of reporters, politicians, and even presidential candidates, who liked to conduct interviews right in front of the miniature covered bridge. Rooms are simply furnished but comfortable. Pricier rooms have writing desks and small refrigerators; all rooms have free Wi-Fi access, ironing boards, and other business-hotel amenities. The property is very close to malls, movie theaters, interstate highways, and the city airport, which limits the charm somewhat but adds convenience to the process of getting into the city, stocking up, and getting out.

121 South River Rd., Bedford, NH 03110. ✆ **877/424-6423** or 603/622-3766. Fax 603/625-1126. www.qualityinn.com. 175 units. $105–$199 double. Rates include continental breakfast. AE, DC, DISC, MC, V. Pets allowed ($25 per pet). **Amenities:** Restaurant; lounge; exercise room; 2 pools (1 indoor, 1 outdoor); limited room service; sauna. *In room:* A/C, TV, fridge (some units), hair dryer, Wi-Fi (free).

Where to Dine

Chez Vachon ★ (Finds) DINER Manchester's French-Canadian heritage lives on at this popular diner, a short drive across the river from the central downtown area. A nondescript place with a Coca-Cola sign out front, it's in an area of triple-decker homes in the old Francophone part of town. And the menu, as you'd expect, is diner fare—but it's diner fare angled toward Franco favorites like *poutine,* crepes, bologna omelets, baked apples, pork pie, salmon pie, baked beans, and pressure-fried chicken. Even though it isn't exactly healthful, you simply can't find food like this anywhere else in the lower 48. This is a good spot for aficionados of road food and travelers on a budget; families with kids will note a kids' menu of pancakes—just as unhealthy, but in smaller portions.

136 Kelley St. ✆ **603/625-9660.** www.chezvachon.com. Main courses $2–$8. DISC, MC, V. Daily 6am–2pm. Cross river on Bridge St. (turns into Armory St.), turn right at 2nd light, and take left at top of hill onto Kelley St.

Lakorn Thai ★ THAI Over the past 15 years or so, Thai food has gone from being a real rarity to becoming fairly commonplace around in New England, even in small towns. Some of it is *very* commonplace (which is to say, pretty bad). But Lakorn Thai is one of the better Thai places in northern New England, hidden in a storefront in a strip mall on the west bank of the Merrimack en route to the malls and airport. The usual Thai dishes can be found here, but it's probably best to order pad Thai or the curries.

470 S. Main St. ✆ **603/626-4545.** Main courses $5–$8 at lunch, $9–$13 at dinner. AE, DISC, MC, V. Mon–Sat 11:30am–3pm and 5–9pm; Sun 4–8:30pm. From downtown, follow Maple St. or Elm St. to Lake St.; turn right (west), and cross the Granite St. bridge; turn left on S. Main St. and continue ½ mile to strip mall on left.

CONCORD ★

Concord, set on a narrower stretch of the Merrimack than Manchester is, is lorded over by the gold-leafed dome of New Hampshire's State House. This is one of America's smallest state capitals (pop.: 42,000), and it feels small. With all this government business going on, it also feels a bit more "proper" than surrounding towns—at least until you cross beneath interstate highway and reach the strip malls, which look like strip malls anywhere in America.

Still, the **downtown** is attractive. Within a few blocks of "the dome," you can pick out a wide range of architectural styles—commercial brick architecture with elaborate cornices, grand Richardsonian state office buildings, and buildings that draw heavily on classical tradition. All three northern New England state capitals do everything on a small scale, and small-town friendliness is the rule here, too. (Think Montpelier, minus the Birkenstocks and organic veggies.)

Though the **river** runs right through town, the city has curiously turned its back on it. Downtown is blocked off from the riverside by I-93, parking lots, and commercial plazas. You have to drive north or south, looking carefully and using maps, to even find the river's shores.

But, fortunately, there's one good spot for a stroll along its banks—the preserve and conservation center that also serves as headquarters of the **Society for the Protection of New Hampshire Forests** ★ (✆ **603/224-9945;** www.spnhf.org). It's located at 54 Portsmouth St. in East Concord, just across the river. From I-93, drive north past the city, take exit 16, and follow signs to the conservation center. (If you're coming from Maine or Portsmouth via Rte. 4, take exit 2 and follow Rte. 132 north.) Trails through the property, which total about 100 acres of grounds in all, are open to the public daily from dawn until dusk. The rustic, energy-efficient society **headquarters building** is also worth a quick look inside—it's open weekdays during business hours.

Essentials

GETTING THERE Concord is at the junction of I-93 and I-89, about 25 minutes' drive from Manchester Airport. From New York City, it's a 4- to 4½-hour drive; from Boston, it's a little more than an hour.

By bus, the city is served throughout the day by **Concord Coach** (✆ **800/639-3317;** www.concordcoachlines.com) buses to and from Boston's South Station and Logan Airport ($15 one-way, round-trips discounted); the trip takes 1 hour and 20 minutes, a bit longer from the airport. There's also one daily **Greyhound** (✆ **800/231-2222;** www.greyhound.com) bus on the same route (1¾ hr.; $17 one-way). From New York, a change at the bus station in Boston is required, and the total cost is about $70 each way; it takes 6½ hours or more for the trip.

VISITOR INFORMATION The **Greater Concord Chamber of Commerce** (✆ **603/224-2508;** www.concordnhchamber.com) is located inside the Grappone Conference Center at 40 Commercial St., about 3 minutes' drive from downtown. (From I-93, take exit 15W and follow the blue TOURIST INFO signs.) It's open year-round on weekdays (9am–5pm), and also on weekends during the summer and fall tourist seasons.

Exploring Concord

McAuliffe-Shepard Discovery Center ★★ Kids Beneath a glass pyramid on the city's technical-college institute, just north of the downtown area (you'll need a car to get there), the McAuliffe Planetarium is the state's wonderfully appropriate memorial to the Concord schoolteacher who died in the 1986 *Challenger* space-shuttle explosion. It also commemorates astronaut Alan B. Shepard, Jr., the Manchester native who—as every New Hampshire child knows—was the first American in space, for 16 minutes in 1961. (He later hit two golf shots on the moon.) A 92-seat theater presents several hour-long astronomy shows throughout the week, showcasing a high-tech computerized projection system. Shows are tailored to different interests and age levels; to avoid disappointment, be sure to ask about the intended age level of a particular show *before* buying your ticket. There's also an observatory with a telescope—look through that thing and you'll be amazed at the depth and detail in the night sky. There are some intriguing exhibits in the waiting area to look at before shows, and you can buy astronomy-related trinkets in a gift shop.

2 Institute Dr. (at New Hampshire Technical Institute). ✆ **603/271-7827.** www.starhop.com. Admission $9 adults, $8 seniors and students, $6 children 3–12. Daily 10am–5pm (to 9pm Fri). From downtown, take I-93 to exit 15E, then take exit 1 (Fort Eddy Rd.) and follow signs. From the east (Rte. 4), take exit 1 and follow signs.

Museum of New Hampshire History ★ The New Hampshire Historical Society's museum is in a sturdy, stone-faced warehouse that dates from 1870. Exhibits here focus on New Hampshire's 19th-century heritage and include several interactive displays. Permanent holdings, including a stagecoach, occupy the first floor; upstairs you'll find interesting exhibits that change throughout the year—one chronicled President Abraham Lincoln's 1860 anti-slavery speaking tour of this state, for example. A "fire tower" pokes through the roof and allows glimpses of the Merrimack River and the State House dome. Also don't miss the **historical society's headquarters and library ★★** nearby at 30 Park St., the museum's former home; the handful of paintings and furniture on display here are nice, as is the comprehensive library of historical materials. But most impressive is the massive, columned building itself, wrought from New Hampshire granite—it's like something from ancient Greece. The rotunda inside is also intriguing. The portal sculpture above the front door is by Daniel Chester French, the New Hampshire native who also sculpted Lincoln for the Lincoln Memorial in Washington, D.C. From the museum, circle around behind the State House dome to find the library.

6 Eagle Sq. (across from the State House, 1/2 block off Main St.). ✆ **603/228-6688.** www.nhhistory.org/museum.html. Admission $5.50 adults, $4.50 seniors, $3 children 6–18, free for children 5 and under, $17 family. Tues–Sat 9:30am–5pm; Sun noon–5pm (July to mid-Oct and Dec also Mon 9:30am–5pm). Free parking in museum lot off Storrs St.

State House ★★ You can't miss this gold-domed state capitol, which is big—and has to be. New Hampshire's state legislature consists of 412 members, making it the third-largest legislative body in the entire English-speaking world (only the U.S. Congress and the British Parliament are bigger.) That's odd, given Granite Staters' chronic mistrust of government—but it also means even the smallest town is well represented. The legislature still occupies its original chambers here, in an 1819 Greek Revival building that's the nation's oldest continuously used state capitol. Both chambers were restored in the mid-1970s, and visitors can catch a glimpse of its hallowed halls during a self-guided tour of the building. Stop by the visitor center in room 119 and pick up a map and brochure, then wander halls lined with portraits of dour legislators. Especially impressive are the portrait of Benning Wentworth (New Hampshire's first governor) and the statue of revered native son Daniel Webster, who stands guard on the lawn in front of the building.

107 N. Main St. (in State House Plaza). ✆ **603/271-2154.** Free admission. Self-guided tours Mon–Fri 8am–4:30pm; guided tours for groups of 10 or more only.

Where to Stay

In addition to the hotel listed below, Concord has a good supply of lower-priced hotels and motels catering primarily to business travelers. Check along **Hall Street,** which runs roughly parallel to (and sometimes right under) I-93 as it bisects the city—there are a number of chain properties along here.

The Centennial ★★ This 1892 brick mansion with twin turrets sits about a half-mile from downtown, and was always popular with business types. But a recent change in ownership and makeover have transformed it into a sleek, stylish boutique hotel (with rates to match) that reminds one more of New York than New Hampshire. The mansion has been thoroughly modernized within, and most guests now enter through glass doors facing the parking lot in back rather than through the pedimented main entrance. Room sizes and configurations vary greatly; some suites offer sitting areas or reading nooks in the mansion's turrets, and some open up to private decks. All units are done up with sleek cherry furniture, pillow-topped beds with fine linens, art prints, DVD players, flatscreen TVs, minibars, and terrycloth robes. The hotel's upscale New American restaurant, **Granite,** is one of the fanciest in Concord (see "Where to Dine," below).

96 Pleasant St., Concord, NH 03301. ✆ **800/360-4839** or 603/227-9000. Fax 603/225-5031. www.thecentennialinn.com. 32 units. $100–$200 double; $180–$270 suite. Rates include continental breakfast. 2-night minimum some weekends. AE, DC, DISC, MC, V. **Amenities:** Restaurant; bar; exercise room. *In room:* A/C, TV/DVD, hair dryer, minibar, Wi-Fi (free).

Where to Dine

Most of Concord's downtown restaurants serve the usual American fare, or derivatives thereof: Italian-American, Chinese-American, pub fare, and so forth.

For true fine dining, the best bite in town is the Centennial hotel's **Granite ★★** (✆ **800/360-4839** or 603/227-9000) restaurant at 96 Pleasant St., serving breakfast, lunch, and dinner (except no lunch Sat and a brunch service on Sun). Chef Matt Lee cooks dinners of pork tenderloin, potato-wrapped cod, grilled swordfish, and pan-roasted duck. Lunches run to curries, soups, sandwiches, and salads, plus a few dinner items in smaller portions.

Susty's ★ Value VEGETARIAN About 20 miles east of Concord on Route 4, Susty's serves some of the best vegetarian fare in all of northern New England. That's right: Absolutely no animals were harmed during the making of this restaurant. Yet the food—tofu pie, thick soup, and whatever else the kitchen cooks up—is surprisingly hearty and tasty. Staff and clientele lean toward the hippie-dippy/New Age-y, yes, but I've seen regular-looking folks eating here, too. The pastries and baked goods are very good.

159 1st New Hampshire Turnpike (Rte. 4 at junction of Rte. 202), Northwood. ✆ **603/942-5862.** Main courses $3–$7. No credit cards. Thurs 11am–8pm; Fri–Sat 11am–9pm; Sun 11am–8pm.

4 THE MONADNOCK REGION ★

Peterborough: 71 miles NW of Boston; 38 miles SW of Manchester, NH

New Hampshire's southwestern corner is a pretty region of rolling hills, small villages, rustic farms, winding back roads, and amazing fall foliage. What the area lacks in major attractions, it makes up for in peacefulness and bucolic charm—plus one good-sized mountain. The inns here tend to be more basic and less luxurious than those in southern Vermont, but their prices do appeal to budget travelers. This is also becoming a popular area for Bostonians seeking a respite from city life, and in fall thousands of them stream north to the region for the excellent leaf-peeping, which is by all account some of the best in New England.

There aren't many museums or fancy restaurants around here. The preferred activities are woodland strolls, back-road cycling trips, afternoons reading on the porch, and obscure country-store exploration.

PETERBOROUGH ★★

Peterborough, settled in 1749 in a river valley at the confluence of two rivers, has successfully pulled off the economic transition from the Colonial and industrial eras to the modern one without sacrificing its soul. That's a neat trick, one that much of small-town New England still hasn't quite figured out how to perform. The town and its neighbors have carved out a new identity for themselves as centers of publishing and light technology—the *Old Farmer's Almanac* and *Yankee Magazine* are both published in nearby Dublin, and the outdoor-gear manufacturer Eastern Mountain Sports is based here.

In the literary universe, Peterborough remains everlastingly famous for having inspired playwright Thornton Wilder to write *Our Town,* sometimes said to be the most frequently staged play in American history. It's also home to the **MacDowell Colony,** founded in 1907 to provide peaceful short-term retreats for artists, musicians, and writers to create without the distractions of cooking (or working).

Peterborough is well worth a look—its town hall (known here as the Town House) is one of the finest in the three northern England states—and so are many of the tiny villages scattered in the countryside around Mount Monadnock.

Essentials

GETTING THERE Peterborough is situated between **Keene** and **Nashua** on Route 101; reach it from Boston (about 90 min. away) via Route 3 or I-93 to Nashua. From New York and Hartford, take I-91 north to Brattleboro, Vermont; exit and cross the river on Route 9 to Keene; and continue east on Route 101 to Peterborough—it takes about 4 hours in all.

A decent map is *essential* for exploring the many fine little villages and towns nearby, as the winding state and county roads have no rhyme or reason to them.

VISITOR INFORMATION The **Greater Peterborough Chamber of Commerce** (✆ **603/924-7234;** www.greater-peterborough-chamber.com) provides advice either over the phone or at a year-round information center at 10 Wilton Rd. (just east of the intersection of rtes. 101 and 202). The center is always open weekdays during business hours, and it's also open on Saturday from 10am to 3pm during the peak tourist season, from mid-June through the end of October.

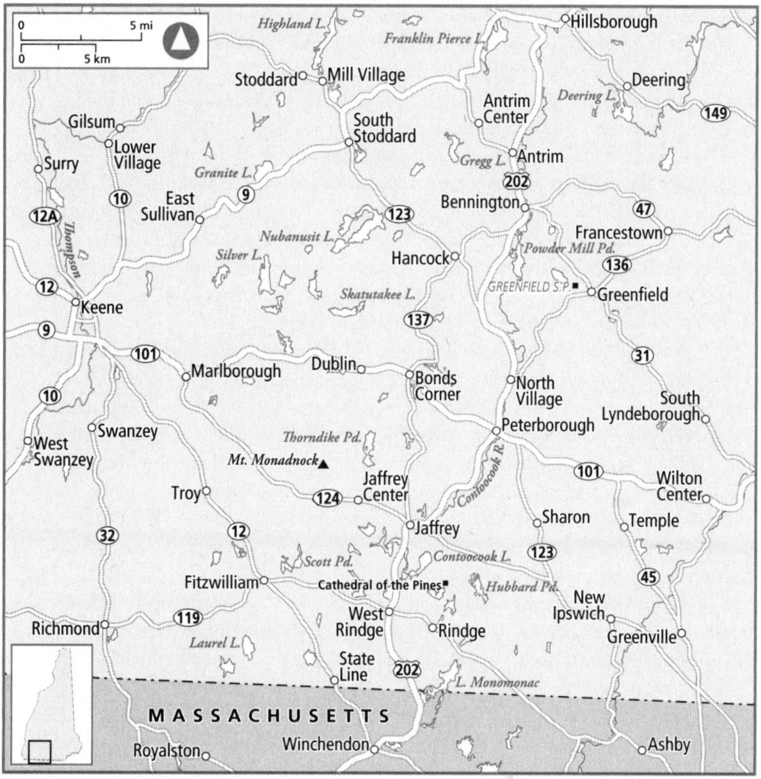

Exploring the Peterborough Area

Peterborough's downtown is a good place for walking around and browsing, with a compact clutch of decent art galleries, bookstores, antiques shops, and boutiques in the village center. Also worth visiting is the **Sharon Arts Center** (✆ **603/924-2787;** www.sharonarts.org), with a great selection of eclectic local crafts, including pottery, glasswork, paintings, and ironwork. There's a spacious, attractive gallery in Depot Square, and a satellite gallery just down the block at 30 Grove St.

The three dozen or so villages surrounding Peterborough and the city of **Keene** (20 miles west) have a strongly traditional New England demeanor; you half expect to hear town criers wandering through the squares, offering news. I've chosen five representative villages to tour. Begin in Peterborough and visit two towns north of Peterborough, or three towns south of it.

About 10 miles north of Peterborough on Route 123, **Hancock** ★ is a picture-postcard-perfect New England village with a quiet street of early homes. Settled in 1764, it was renamed in 1779 after the first signer of the Declaration of Independence. A former cotton-farming center (yes, really), the village is also home to an eponymous inn—one of the oldest in the region (see "Where to Stay," below). Even farther north along Route 123, **Marlow** ★ and **Stoddard** are also scenic villages good for snapping photos in.

About 10 miles east of Hancock via routes 202 and 47, **Francestown** ★ (incorporated in 1752) is rife with remarkable Federal homes, and it also has a general store, an inviting library, and an 1801 meetinghouse. Until 1891, when the local quarry closed, Francestown was famed for producing some of the finest soapstone in the world.

Three more interesting towns are clustered *south* of Peterborough, where the foliage is spectacular. **Fitzwilliam,** 16 miles southwest at the intersection of routes 12 and 119, is presided over by the columned Fitzwilliam Inn. The village features a triangular green with a Civil War obelisk (dedicated to "soldiers who died for their country in the rebellion of 1861"); a cast-iron Victorian fountain; some wonderful Greek Revival homes facing the green; and an impressively columned 1817 church that's been the town hall since 1858. You'll also find several good antiques shops here.

Just 8 miles east of Fitzwilliam on Route 119, **Rindge** was settled in 1736 and boasts a large meetinghouse (which is also a Congregational church). The town has a very small university, plus good views of Monadnock. Two miles north of the village center, just off Cathedral Road (look for signs), is Rindge's most famous site, the lovely **Cathedral of the Pines** ★★ (✆ **603/899-3300;** www.cathedralofthepines.org) on Hale Hill Road. This outdoor "cathedral" is set on an open knoll amid a stately grove of swaying pines, with views toward Mount Monadnock. It's a quietly spectacular spot, with wooden benches, fieldstone altars, and pulpits. (The cathedral was built by the parents of Lt. Sanderson Sloane, a bomber crewman who died in World War II.)

The grove was seriously damaged in a winter 2008 ice storm, but a reconstruction project is ongoing. The site is open daily from May through October 9am to 5pm for self-touring (guided tours are given only to groups); leave a donation if you visit. Pets and smoking are not allowed here.

Finally, 8 miles north of Rindge on Route 124 is one of the best-looking towns of them all: **Jaffrey Center** ★★, which is west of **Jaffrey** (a bigger, more commercial market town). Jaffrey Center is an aristocratic little roadside village all but hidden in the maples and filled with notable homes and small, tidy barns. If you're in a hurry and can't visit all the towns on this minitour, Jaffrey Center is only about 9 miles from downtown Peterborough—take Route 202 south to Jaffrey, turn right, and continue 2 miles to find it.

Outdoor Pursuits

Mount Monadnock ★★ rises impressively above the gentler hills of southern New Hampshire. Though only 3,165 feet high (about half the height of Mount Washington in northern New Hampshire), it has a solitary grandeur. Its knobby peak was scaled by such New England literary luminaries as Ralph Waldo Emerson and Henry David Thoreau back in the day, when ascents were still rare. Today, though, more than 100,000 hikers follow their lead and head for the summit each year. It's *not* a place for solitary walks. Some 40 miles of trails (30% of which can be cross-country skied) lace the patchwork of public and private lands on the various slopes of the mountain.

The most popular and best-marked trails leave from near the entrance to **Monadnock State Park** ★★ (✆ **603/532-8862**), about 4 miles northwest of Jaffrey Center off Route 124. (Head west on Rte. 124; after 2 miles, follow the park signs to the north.) A round-trip hike up and down the most direct, crowded routes (the **White Dot** and

> **Fun Facts What's a Monadnock, Anyway?**
>
> If you look up the world "monadnock" (say ma-NAD-uh-knock) in the dictionary today, it says the meaning is "mountain that sticks up above the surrounding flat countryside"—well, approximately. The mountain, which was named by local Native Americans, gave us the science word. Really.

White Cross trails, which begin at the end of a paved road) should take someone in decent shape 3 to 4 hours—keep your eyes on the trail and be careful, as some sections are steep and some sections involve broken-up rock or ledges.

The final ascent is pretty steep; if you're afraid of heights, stop at one of the overlooks on the way up and snap pictures. You can just see Boston and bits of all the New England states from the tippy-top if you know where to look. The state park is open year-round (a ranger is on duty in summer). Admission costs $4 for adults, $2 for children 12 and over. No pets are allowed in this park. There's also camping at about two dozen sites in a small camping area, some available by reservation only; the sites cost $25 per night, and there are no water or electrical hookups whatsoever.

About an 18-mile drive north of Monadnock, not far from Hancock and Peterborough, is a smaller park that's nevertheless a gem: **Greenfield State Park** ★ (✆ **603/547-3497**) on Route 136, open from late May through Labor Day (weekends only until late June). The 400-acre park is great for both car campers and geology buffs. It was profoundly shaped by glaciers during the last ice age, and eskers, bogs, kames, and other intriguing geological formations can easily be spotted (ask a ranger to point them out). The park also maintains a small beach on scenic **Otter Lake,** plus a separate 900-foot beach set aside just for campers—there are about 250 wooded, well-spaced campsites here costing $25 per night (no electrical hookups). On summer weekends, this campground bustles, but from Monday through Friday, it's usually a peaceable oasis.

The day-use fee for the park is $4 per adult and $2 per child ages 6 to 11.

Where to Stay

Benjamin Prescott Inn Col. Benjamin Prescott fought at the Battle of Bunker Hill before retiring to Jaffrey in 1775. This three-story farmhouse built by his sons dates from 1853, a handsome yellow Greek Revival building on an (often busy) road about 2 miles east of Jaffrey's town center. Throughout the inn, there's a strong sense of history and a connection to the past. All 10 rooms have ceiling fans and phone jacks (phones are provided on request), while the two suites are air-conditioned; otherwise, rooms are very simply furnished—cranberry-hued Col. Prescott's Room is furnished with two armchairs and a writing desk, Susannah's Suite has a narrow brass bed and a sitting room with a couch. Guests can wander the farmlands beyond the inn or hike Monadnock, just a short drive down the road.

433 Turnpike Rd. (Rte. 124), Jaffrey, NH 03452. ✆ **888/950-6637** or 603/532-6637. Fax 603/532-1142. www.benjaminprescottinn.com. 10 units. $95–$160 double; peak season $120–$195 double. Rates include full breakfast. 2-night minimum some holidays and peak-season weekends. AE, MC, V. Children 12 and over welcome. *In room:* A/C (2 units), no phone, Wi-Fi (free).

Birchwood Inn (Value) This quiet retreat offers rooms at affordable prices and a thoroughly British experience. Thoreau visited the inn during one of his many rambles through New England; neither the town nor the inn seems to have changed much since. A handsome, historic brick farmhouse with a white-clapboard ell, it's in the middle of the crossroads town of Temple near the town grange and a park with three war memorials. (It's also an easy stroll to a historic cemetery with headstones dating back to the 18th century.) The inn itself is decorated in an informal country style and operated by a pair of affable guys; all its rooms and suites are named for important cities in England, each with a different theme (musical instruments, train memorabilia, country-store) bordering on the kitschy. Rooms have small TVs with DVD players, there's Wi-Fi access throughout, and an on-site tavern opens 5 nights a week, serving actual English-style pub food and beer.

340 Rte. 45 (P.O. Box 23), Temple, NH 03084. ✆ **603/878-3285.** Fax: 603/878-2159. www.thebirchwoodinn.com. 5 units. $89–$139 double. Rates include full breakfast. 2-night minimum stay during foliage season. No credit cards. Drive 1½ miles south on Rte. 101. Children 11 and over welcome. **Amenities:** Restaurant; pub. *In room:* TV/DVD, no phone, Wi-Fi (free).

Hancock Inn ★★ The Hancock Inn, built in 1789, claims to be New Hampshire's oldest. You'll find classic Americana inside, from creaky floors and braided oval rugs to guest rooms appointed in understated Colonial decor. The Rufus Porter Room has an evocative full-length wall mural from the inn's early days, plus two fireplaces, while the Ballroom has a high, vaulted ceiling (it really used to be the ballroom) and Jacuzzi. The Bell Tower Room comes furnished with a cannonball king-size bed, gas fireplace, and Jacuzzi—it overlooks the garden. And the Moses Eaton Room features the designs of Eaton, a famed stencil artist who lived in this town for a time. This inn has the same historical charm as other historic inns in this area, but with more upscale rooms. The food is good, too.

33 Main St., Hancock, NH 03449. ✆ **800/525-1789** or 603/525-3318. www.hancockinn.com. 14 units. $150–$260 double; $260–$290 suite. Rates include breakfast. AE, DC, DISC, MC, V. Pets allowed in 1 unit. **Amenities:** Restaurant. *In room:* A/C, TV, hair dryer, Wi-Fi (most units; free).

Monadnock Inn In the middle of one of New Hampshire's most gracious villages, this lovely, architecturally eclectic inn (formerly called the Inn at Jaffrey Center) was built around 1830. After years of decline, it got a much-needed makeover in 2000, when all its rooms were updated in traditional New England style—some with four-poster or canopy beds. Units that formerly shared a bathroom all got their own bathrooms, and fixtures such as aging claw-foot tubs were refurbished. The building is definitely showing its age, but it's still a conveniently placed sleep in a pretty village. Some rooms have TVs; all have goose-down comforters. The lawns and porches are attractive, and the inn's friendly innkeepers serve better meals than you'd expect in the **restaurant** ★★ and pub. The village's churches and lanes are within walking distance.

379 Main St. (P.O. Box 484), Jaffrey Center, NH 03452. ✆ **877/510-7019** or 603/532-7800. Fax 603/532-7900. www.theinnatjaffreycenter.com. 11 units. $110–$160 double. Rates include continental breakfast. Minimum stays required during foliage and holiday weekends. MC, V. **Amenities:** Restaurant; pub. *In room:* No phone, Wi-Fi (most units; free).

Where to Dine

Three of the four inns listed above maintain restaurants serving dinner to both their own guests and the public, and they're actually quite good. Even if you're not staying at one of them, think about taking a drive to Hancock, Jaffrey Center, or Temple for dinner—just be sure you can find the way. There are few streetlights on these country roads. (A competent GPS system might do a world of good.)

At lunchtime, I recommend a stop at the sandwich bar-slash-coffee shop Twelve Pine in Peterborough (see below). Or drive west to the little college city of **Keene,** with a compact main street and a great shopping-mall-in-a-mill—there are numerous choices of ethnic food, pizzas, diner fare, and deli sandwiches; excellent coffee shops; and even a few fancy bites.

Acqua Bistro ★★★ BISTRO Acqua Bistro is the Monadnock region's best gourmet meal for miles, hands down. Hidden off Peterborough's main streets, near Twelve Pine and the Sharon Arts Center, it's in a modern, agreeable dining space overlooking a little stream. The kitchen offers fusion twists on Continental fare. Small plates and entrees could run to tea-smoked duck, ginger-crusted scallops, rib-eye steaks, salmon, seared tuna, grilled organic chicken breast, duck, or a gourmet burger. There's always something intriguing on the menu for vegetarians, as well as creative thin-crust pizzas with alternative toppings like chicken sausage, shrimp with wasabi cream, and chipotle barbecue baked in a stone oven. There's a good wine list, house cocktails, a full martini menu—you can order a cheese plate or other light meal from a special bar menu if you're not overly hungry. What more could you ask for? Oh, this: Sunday mornings feature a great, stylish brunch.

9 School St. (in Depot Sq.), Peterborough. ✆ **603/924-9905.** www.acquabistro.com. Reservations accepted for parties of 5 or more. Main courses $14–$25. MC, V. Tues–Sat 4–10pm; Sun 11am–10pm; off-season hours may be shorter.

Peterborough Diner (Kids) DINER This classic throwback to the 1940s is hidden on a side street, but it's worth finding. Behind the faded exterior is a cozy diner of wood, aluminum, tile, and ceiling fans, plus a jukebox. The meals are just as you'd expect: filling, cheap, basic. Look for hot-oven grinders sided with fries, plates of hot turkey with cranberry sauce, and veal parmigiana. A few fancier items like chicken cordon bleu are also on the menu, but you don't come for those—you come for milkshakes and banana splits. Or order a "belly buster," which is three of everything: eggs, slices of bacon, slices of toast, sausage patties, pancakes, and slices of French toast. Keep your doctor on speed-dial.

10 Depot St., Peterborough. ✆ **603/924-6710.** www.peterboroughdiner.com. Breakfast items $2–$6, lunch and dinner items $4–$8. AE, DISC, MC, V. Mon–Fri 6am–9pm (to 8pm in winter), Sat–Sun 7am–8pm.

Twelve Pine ★ (Finds) DELI This inviting deli and market, in an airy former railroad building behind Peterborough's main street, has been here since 1996. It's a great spot to nosh and linger; select a pre-made meal or sandwich from a deli counter, bring it to a table, eat, repeat. Sandwiches are made with homemade bread and heaping fillings; excellent cheeses are available by the pound, and fresh juices and good gourmet coffees round out the meal. On your way out, stock up on gourmet foods to go in the market and wine shop. In an age of megalithic whole-foods stores, it's refreshing to see a home-grown version still holding its own—and then some.

11 School St. (in Depot Sq.), Peterborough. ✆ **877/412-7463** or 603/924-6140. www.twelvepine.com. Sandwiches around $6, other items priced per pound. MC, V. Mon–Fri 8am–7pm; Sat 9am–5pm; Sun 9am–4pm.

HANOVER ★★

If your idea of a perfect New England experience involves a big green park surrounded by old brick buildings and smart people, visit **Hanover,** a university town in the Connecticut River Valley about a half-hour's drive north of **Cornish** and right across the river from **Norwich** (p. 132). Settled in 1765, the town was first home to early colonists who were granted a charter by King George III to establish a college here. That school was named for the second Earl of Dartmouth, its first trustee, and ever since has had a profound impact in shaping the town.

The handsome, oversized village green marks the border between college and town. In summer it's a great place for strolling or lounging. The best way to explore Hanover is on foot, anyway, so your first job is to park your car—which can be trying during peak seasons (fall, plus whenever school is in session or there's a football game). Try the municipal lots west of Main Street if you can't find a meter. The chief attraction is the pretty campus of **Dartmouth College** itself, but downtown also offers plenty of fine restaurants, galleries, bookstores, and pubs.

Just south of Hanover on Route 120 is the working-class town of **Lebanon,** a commercial center. (If you're looking for the *New York Times,* look in Hanover; if you need a wrench, head for Lebanon.) Lebanon has its own attractive village green, plus a handful of shops and appealing restaurants. Nearby there's a mall carved out of an old brick powerhouse in **West Lebanon,** where there's also a tiny regional airport and a gaggle of big-box stores, fast-food restaurants, and chain hotels lined up along Route 12A.

Essentials

GETTING THERE Hanover is a bit off the interstate. From Boston, Concord, or Manchester to the south, take I-93 to I-89 N. From Brattleboro or St. Johnsbury, Vermont, take I-91. From Montpelier or Burlington, Vermont, take I-89 S. to I-91 N. in White River Junction, head north a few miles, then exit for Norwich and cross the river.

Amazingly, there is daily direct bus service to Hanover from both Boston and New York. **Dartmouth Coach** (✆ **800/637-0123;** www.dartmouthcoach.com) travels to and from Boston at least a half-dozen times per day, an easy 2½ hour ride costing $50 round-trip. From New York City, there's one Dartmouth Coach trip daily ($149 round-trip, 5 hr.)—it departs from the Yale Club, on Vanderbilt Avenue beside Grand Central Terminal.

Amtrak (✆ **800/872-7245;** www.amtrak.com) also runs one train daily (7 hr.; $56 one-way) from New York City to **White River Junction,** Vermont (p. 132), about 4½

Fun Facts Green Power

At the heart of Hanover is **Dartmouth College,** which has exerted a constant influence over the town's economic fortunes, liquor sales, and residential real-estate values almost since the moment it opened in 1769. But it's a pretty fair institution of higher learning, too: The college has produced more than its share of celebrated alumni, hallowed Ivy Leaguers like **Robert Frost, Nelson Rockefeller,** ex-Surgeon General **C. Everett Koop,** actress **Meryl Streep** (okay, she was an exchange student), even wacky-kid's-book author **Dr. Seuss.**

Another son of Dartmouth was the 19th-century politician and orator **Daniel Webster,** who argued for the survival of the college in a landmark case before the U.S. Supreme Court in 1816. (Two factions were vying for control of the school.) Webster offered a famous closing line: "It *is* a small college, gentlemen, but there are those who love it." And that has served as a sort of informal motto for the college's alumni ever since.

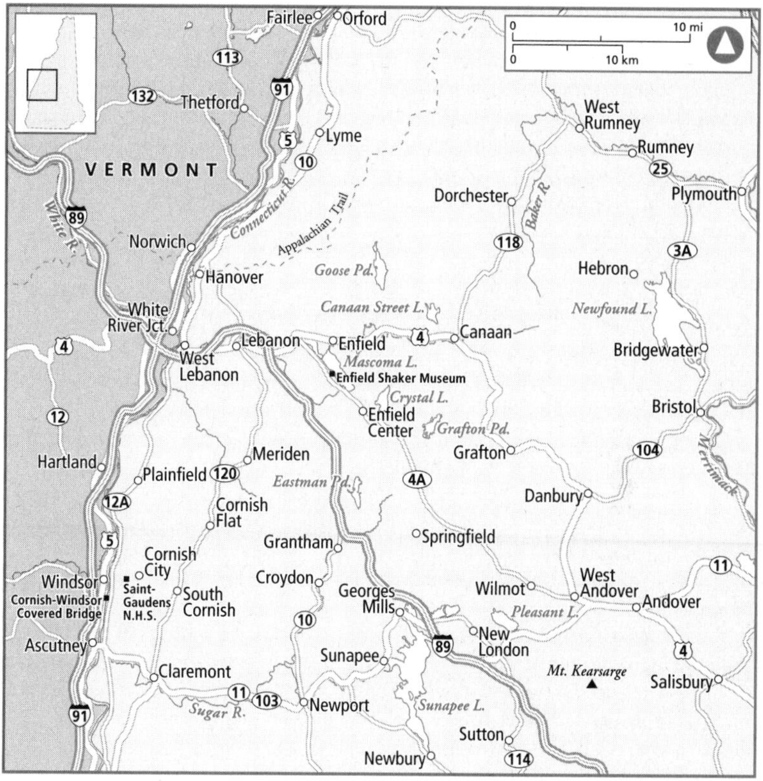

miles away. From there, you'll need to take a cab—or, I suppose, you could go on foot (a 90-min. to 2-hr. walk), but I would never recommend doing that after dark.

VISITOR INFORMATION Dartmouth College alumni and local chamber of commerce volunteers maintain an **information center** right on the town green daily from June through September. During the off season, head for the offices of the **Hanover Area Chamber of Commerce** (✆ **603/643-3115;** www.hanoverchamber.org) at 47 S. Main St., across from the town post office. It's open weekdays only, during normal business hours. Bonus: The chamber's members include businesses across the river in Norwich, Vermont (p. 132), too.

SPECIAL EVENTS In early to mid-February, look for the fantastic and intricate ice sculptures marking the return of the annual **Dartmouth Winter Carnival.** Call Dartmouth College's student affairs office at ✆ **603/646-3399** for more information on this traditionally beer-soaked event.

Exploring Hanover

Hanover is a great town to explore on foot, by bike, or even by *canoe.* Start by picking up a map of the **Dartmouth campus** at the college's information center on the green

Tips Orozco's Hidden Artwork at Dartmouth

Dartmouth's **Baker Memorial Library**—that tall, church-like building at the back of the green—houses a wonderful hidden treasure downstairs: a complete set of fresco murals by the Mexican painter José Clemente Orozco, who painted *The Epic of American Civilization* while teaching here from 1932 until 1934. The huge paintings, 24 panels covering 3,200 square feet, wrap around an entire study room—unnoticed by the chatting and snacking students. Ask for a fact sheet interpreting the colorful, metaphorical murals at the library's front desk.

(summer and fall only), or at The Hanover Inn (see "Where to Stay," below) across the street. Free guided tours of the campus are also offered during summer, and the expansive, leafy neighborhood is a delight to walk through—especially the fraternity district, believe it or not, which is full of grand old homes (the non-fraternities, I mean), ponds, and a golf course.

On the south side of the green, next door to The Hanover Inn, is the modern **Hopkins Center for the Arts** ★★ (✆ **603/646-2422**). Locally known as "The Hop," the center attracts national acts to its 900-seat concert hall and stages top-notch dance and theatrical performances in its Moore Theater. Wallace Harrison, the architect who later went on to fame for designing Lincoln Center in New York, designed this building. You can find a comprehensive schedule of upcoming events at the Hop at its website, **http://hop.dartmouth.edu**.

You can shop quite nicely in Hanover's little downtown. In addition to some fine gift and clothing shops, there are two outstanding bookstores standing nearly shoulder to shoulder. The huge **Dartmouth Bookstore** ★★, at 33 S. Main St. (✆ **603/643-3616**), was sold to Barnes & Noble's college bookstore division in 2005, but it remains mostly the same as it was before the changeover: a maze of good rooms of children's and travel books, calendars, music, textbooks, and a bargain section. The newspaper and magazine selection is exemplary, and the staff is unfailingly helpful—there's even an information desk for tracking down or ordering hard-to-find titles, staffed by actual adults. It's open daily, most days (except Sun) until at least 9pm.

The compact **Left Bank Books** (✆ **603/643-4479**) bookshop, a few doors down (and up the stairs) from the Dartmouth Bookstore at 9 S. Main St., is also good in its own way. Going upstairs, you wonder what you'll find; when you get there, the small space (with a good Hanover view) stocks a changing selection of mostly used poetry, fiction, philosophy, art books, cookbooks, and the like. The leftward tilt of the place is unmistakable, as is the owner's eye for a good read.

In addition to the attractions listed below, see p. 134 for more about the great, children-oriented **Montshire Museum of Science.** It's just a mile across the river in Norwich, Vermont.

Enfield Shaker Museum ★ A cluster of historic buildings on Lake Mascoma about a 20-minute drive southeast of Hanover, "The Chosen Vale" (as its first inhabitants called this valley) was founded in 1793. During the mid-1800s, this Shaker community counted 350 members and held 3,000 acres; today, however, the museum is state-owned. Dominating the village is the Great Stone Dwelling, an austere but gracious granite five-plus-story structure erected between 1837 and 1841. (At the time, it was the tallest building north of Boston.) A self-guided walking tour of the surrounding village—check out the Stone Mill Building, too—is free with admission.

447 Rte. 4A, Enfield. ✆ **603/632-4346.** www.shakermuseum.org. Admission $7.50 adults, $6.50 seniors, $5 college students, $3 children 10–17, free for children 9 and under. Mon–Sat 10am–5pm; Sun noon–5pm (last tour 4pm).

Hood Museum of Art ★★ Finds Often overlooked by visitors to Hanover (maybe because it's not even visible from the street, but rather set back behind other buildings), this modern, open structure beside the Hopkins Center houses one of the oldest college museums in the country. The permanent collection holds some 65,000 items, including a superb selection of 19th-century American landscapes; significant holdings of African, African-American, and Native American art and artifacts; and six stone reliefs dating from 900 B.C. Assyria. Special exhibits are frequent and high-quality—for one show, artist Fred Wilson arranged hidden and neglected items from the permanent collection in thought-provoking, sometimes disturbing ways. A 2009 exhibit highlighted the work of legendary mixed-media artist Robert Rauschenberg, who was an artist-in-residence at the college in 1963.

Wheelock St. ✆ **603/646-2808.** http://hoodmuseum.dartmouth.edu. Free admission. Tues–Sat 10am–5pm (Wed to 9pm); Sun noon–5pm. From the Hanover green, facing the Hopkins Center, cross Wheelock St. and take the footpath to the left of the Hopkins Center.

Moments Saint-Gaudens Gardens of Stone

There was a seriously thriving artists' colony in the little village of **Cornish,** about 20 miles south of Hanover, in the early 20th century; today the chief relic of those heady days is the **Saint-Gaudens National Historic Site ★★** (✆ **603/675-2175;** www.nps.gov/saga) off Route 12A, a remarkable little spot. The Irish-born sculptor Augustus Saint-Gaudens arrived here in 1885, having received an important commission to create a statue of Abraham Lincoln. His friend Charles Beaman, a Manhattan lawyer who owned several homes in the area, assured him he could find plenty of "Lincoln-shaped men" in the area. Saint-Gaudens came, found them, and stayed for the rest of his life, creating work that today fills American museums, cemeteries, and public parks. (He even designed a U.S. coin, the lovely "double eagle.")

Saint-Gaudens' hillside home and studio, Aspet—named for the village in Ireland where he was raised—are superb places to learn more about the artist. A brief tour of the house, kept mostly as it was when Saint-Gaudens lived here, provides an introduction to the man; you then tour outbuildings, where replicas of many of his most famous statues are on display. The 150-acre grounds are also laced by short nature trails where you can explore the hilly woodlands, passing streams and a millpond.

The historic site is a bit hard to find, located just off Route 12A (almost directly across the river from Windsor, Vermont). The grounds are open year-round, while the buildings are open to the public daily from late May through October, 9am to 4:30pm. Admission is $5 for adults, free for children 16 and under. (There's no charge to visit the grounds during the off season.)

Tips Side Trip: Newport, Sunapee & New London

While visiting the Hanover, Concord, or Cornish areas, don't forget to side-trip over to the Newport–Lake Sunapee region. The commercial center of the area is **Newport** ★★, a mill town with grit, character, and substantial history in a pretty valley setting. This town produced Sarah Josepha Hale, author of the children's poem "Mary Had a Little Lamb" and creator of the Thanksgiving holiday—President Lincoln was sufficiently impressed by her persistence to make it official. Hale was also among the first American women to serve as editor of a national publication *(Godey's Lady's Book).* Yet she's only one of the famous folks who grew up here.

The town's historical attractions include a quilt project documenting Newport's industrial past (including healthy numbers of Finn, Polish, Greek, and Italian immigrants); an antique 1815 Hunnemen "handtub," a wheeled apparatus built by an apprentice of Paul Revere and once used by firemen to pump water while fighting blazes (it's on display inside the Lake Sunapee Bank, at 9 Main St.); and a wooden **covered bridge** ★★, painstakingly built by a local craftsman to replicate the priceless original, which was sadly torched by an arsonist in 1993.

Drop by the town's **Richards Free Library** ★ (✆ **603/863-3430**), at 58 N. Main St., to get oriented; for my money, it's one of the best small-town libraries in New England. (Tantalizing historical tidbit: President Kennedy was supposed to accept a writing award at this library on the night of Nov 22, 1963. He politely declined, due to commitments in Dallas.) You'll find a few restaurants on Main Street as well. For more details, contact the helpful Newport Area Chamber of Commerce (✆ **603/863-1510**). A good, volunteer-run **info kiosk** is open on the town "common" (big green space) during the summer.

Ledyard Canoe Club ★ One idyllic way to spend a lazy afternoon in Hanover is by drifting along the Connecticut River in a canoe—assuming you know how to paddle one safely, that is. Dartmouth's historic boating club is just downhill from the campus at the river's bank. While much of the club's focus is on competitive racing, it's also a place where travelers can rent a boat for a few hours and explore the tree-lined river. (Instruction is also available.) Life jackets must be carried at all times, and worn by children and non-swimmers. The club is open daily from spring through mid-October.

Off W. Wheelock St. ✆ **603/643-6709.** www.dartmouth.edu/~lcc. Canoe and kayak rentals $10 per hour, $20 per day Mon–Fri, $30 per day Sat–Sun. Summer Mon–Fri 10am–8pm, Sat–Sun 9am–8pm; spring and fall Mon–Fri noon–6pm, Sat–Sun 10am–6pm. Open whenever river temperature is higher than 50°F (10°C), generally mid-May to mid-Oct. Turn upstream at the bottom of the hill west of the bridge; follow signs to the clubhouse.

Where to Stay

If you're not interested in staying in Hanover's signature (but pricey) inn, there are plenty of mid-priced chain hotel and motel properties clumped together along a strip just off the interstate in **West Lebanon,** 5 miles south of Hanover. Take exit 20 off I-89 to find them.

Six miles away, big **Lake Sunapee** ★★ is said to be one of the purest in the nation, and it's much deeper than it looks. Sunapee is a longtime favorite summer resort of Bostonians, and offers excellent swimming, boating, and fishing. The short, steep mountain across the way—which, together with the beach, forms **Mount Sunapee State Park** (✆ **603/763-5561**)—is a fine place to hike or catch a gondola ride for expansive foliage and lake views. There's a $4 charge ($2 for kids) to enter either the beach or mountain portions of the park; the ski hill itself is operated by the family-owned **Mount Sunapee Resort** (✆ **603/763-3500;** www.mountsunapee.com).

Early August brings one outstanding arts event to the park, the 9-day **Craftsman's Fair** ★ (✆ **603/224-3375;** www.nhcrafts.org). Expect high-quality handcrafted art pieces and great demonstrations and workshops (soap carving, pottery, and the like). Two-day admission tickets cost about $10 per adult, $8 per senior or student; children 11 and under are admitted for free.

The main harbor for the lake, **Sunapee Harbor,** is a few miles away at the junction of routes 103B and 11. This is the place to put in your boat, grab an ice-cream cone, or watch a sunset. You might see a famous face with your cone, too; members of the band Aerosmith own homes in the harbor area.

On the back side of the lake, pretty **New London** ★★ is an attractive college town with lots of fine homes and a few good restaurants. Without ever straying off Main Street, you can settle down for a full meal at the tony **Millstone** (✆ **603/526-4201;** www.millstonerestaurant.com); relax over coffee and sandwiches at **Ellie's Cafe** (✆ **603/526-2448;** http://elliescafeanddeli.com); or go British-pub-style with a shared "board" of bread, cheeses, sliced meats, and beer at **Peter Christian's Tavern** (✆ **603/526-4042;** www.peterchristianstavern.com).

There are also inns in **Norwich,** Vermont (a mile across the river from Hanover) and chain hotels in **White River Junction,** Vermont (a few miles downriver via I-91). See chapter 5 for details on lodgings in those towns.

The Hanover Inn ★★ The venerable white-and-brick Hanover Inn is one of the oldest lodgings in the region, yet it's also the Upper Valley's best-managed and most up-to-date luxury hotel—perfectly situated for exploring both the Dartmouth campus and the compact downtown. (The inn is located directly across Hanover's big central green from the college.) Built in 1780, most of the present-day five-story structure you see today was actually added in successive stages—in 1924, 1939, and, finally, 1968. This inn offers professional service, attractive rooms, fine dining, and subterranean walkways connecting you to the college's Hood Museum of Art and its Hopkins Center for the Arts. Rooms are trim and solid, as you'd expect; most have canopy or four-poster beds and down comforters, and some even overlook the pretty green. Going all out? The Baker Tower Suite features a wet bar, sitting space, and the best views. The inn's dining options include a fancy dining room (see "Where to Dine," below), a terrace of outdoor tables fronting the green, and a wine bistro (see below).

 Wheelock St. (P.O. Box 151), Hanover, NH 03755. ✆ **800/443-7024** or 603/643-4300. Fax 603/643-4433. www.hanoverinn.com. 92 units. From $259 double; from $309 suite. AE, DISC, MC, V. Valet parking $12 per day. Pets allowed ($15 per night). **Amenities:** 3 restaurants; 2 bars; babysitting; limited room service. *In room:* A/C, TV, hair dryer, Wi-Fi (free).

Where to Dine

Whether you're in a hurry or just need caffeinating, the **Dirt Cowboy Café** ★ (✆ **603/643-1323;** www.dirtcowboycafe.com), at 7 S. Main St., is my local spot for coffee and snacks. The beans are roasted right downstairs, then served upstairs in a number of inventive combinations (I like the *breve* shot best). They also mix smoothies and sell good baked items. Sit at a table, read a book, and just eavesdrop on professors and students discussing particle physics, the green revolution, or whatever else college kids talk about on their down time.

Another good spot for a quick bite or drink is **Zins winebistro** ★, an informal bistro serving about 35 wines by the glass (plus 25 beers) off the lobby of the regal Hanover Inn (see "Where to Stay," above) on Wheelock Street. It's open daily, serving light meals of sandwiches, salads, burgers, and grilled fish with the wine. Helpfully, they also offer a short menu of kids' meals.

Daniel Webster Room ★★ AMERICAN The main dining room in the Hanover Inn will appeal to anyone looking for fine dining in a formal New England atmosphere. The Colonial Revival–style room is reminiscent of a 19th-century resort hotel, with big fluted columns, floral carpeting, and regally upholstered chairs. Inn chef Jason Merrill has unveiled a new, much more contemporary New American/fusion-oriented menu in recent years: gingered tuna loin with wasabi rice cake and ponzu sauce, pappardelle with ragout made from local lamb, and a changing daily vegetable dish depending on what's being harvested is in—the heavy resort fare that used to fill the menu is mostly out. (They'll still grill you up a nice strip steak and side it with mashed potatoes, though, if you wish.) Tasty small-plate choices include items like shrimp-and-crab fritters, small grilled flatbread pizzas, crispy tofu with cashews, and pan-roasted day-boat scallops. At lunch, go low (chowder, a salad) or high (the lobster club); either way, it's excellent. Yes, the inn serves great breakfasts, too—New England classics (buttermilk pancakes with real maple syrup), but also bagels with lox, poached eggs, and a cinnamon brioche French toast.

Wheelock St. (in the Hanover Inn). ✆ **603/643-4300.** www.hanoverinn.com. Reservations recommended. Main courses $7–$21 at lunch, $12–$27 at dinner. AE, DISC, MC, V. Mon 7–10:30am and 11:30am–1:30pm; Tues–Fri 7–10:30am, 11:30am–1:30pm, and 6–9pm; Sat 7–10:30am and 6–9pm; Sun 11am–1:30pm.

Lou's **Value** BAKERY/DINER Lou's has been a Hanover institution since the 1940s, attracting hordes of students for breakfast on the weekends and a steady local clientele of working folk during the week. This is no-frills New Hampshire, just a black-and-white-checkerboard linoleum floor, maple-and-vinyl booths, and a harried yet efficient crew of waiters. Breakfast is served all day (real maple syrup on your pancakes costs extra, though), and the sandwiches, served on freshly baked bread, are huge. Locals know to pop in after the diner closes in the late afternoon; while the staff preps for the next morning's rush, you can buy the day's remaining baked goods (if any are left) until 5pm.

30 S. Main St. ✆ **603/643-3321.** http://lousrestaurant.net. Breakfast items $3–$7, lunch items $5–$8. AE, MC, V. Mon–Fri 6am–3pm; Sat–Sun 7am–3pm (opens 8am Sun in winter). Bakery daily to 5pm.

5 THE LAKE WINNIPESAUKEE REGION ★

Meredith: 40 miles N of Concord; 60 miles NW of Portsmouth; 110 miles N of Boston

Huge **Lake Winnipesaukee,** carved by glaciers from nearly the dead center of New Hampshire, is *easily* the state's biggest, with a 180-mile shoreline. Yet it's very irregularly shaped, edged with dozens of inlets, coves, and bays, and dotted by more than 250 islands. As a result, when you're actually out on the lake, it doesn't seem big at all. This lake gives the illusion of being a chain of smaller lakes and ponds, rather than one massive body of water.

If you're just wanting a quick, scenic cruise of the lake, the impressive **MS *Mount Washington*** ★★ (✆ **888/843-6686** or 630/366-5531; www.cruisenh.com) is the way to do it. This handsome, 230-foot-long vessel sails out of the honky-tonk port at **Weirs Beach** daily in summer at 10am and calls at **Wolfeboro** harbor (p. 239) before turning around (once a week, it turns around at **Alton Bay**). The boat holds more than 1,000 passengers and serves cocktails; day cruises (2½ hr. each) cost $25 to $40 for adults, less for children. Dinner cruises (with dancing!), foliage, and sunset cruises also frequently depart; check the boat's website for each season's schedule details.

Dozens of towns small and large ring the lake; of them, **Meredith** and **Wolfeboro** have the most services, plus pretty good views.

MEREDITH ★

The village of Meredith sits at the northwestern facet of diamond-shaped Winnipesaukee. There are good views across a nice bay from almost anyplace in town, but the place lacks quaintness—a very busy road cuts the little downtown off from the lake's shore, and strip malls have also intruded. Still, it's stocked with life's necessary services (restaurants, gas station, souvenir shops, pizza places, grocery stores), and the town is also home to several desirable inns and resorts.

Essentials

GETTING THERE Reach **Meredith** by taking I-93 to exit 23. Drive 9 miles east on Route 104 to Route 3, turn left, and continue downhill to the town and the lakefront.

Concord Coach (✆ **800/639-3317;** www.concordcoachlines.com) provides twice-daily bus service to Meredith from Concord, Manchester, and Boston's Logan Airport and South Station (the city bus terminal). The bus picks up and drops off in the parking lot on Route 3, beside the Aubuchon Hardware store (*not* in front of the store). The same bus also stops in the nearby villages of **West Ossipee, Moultonborough,** and **Center Harbor** at various car washes, general stores, gas stations, and laundromats (hey, this is

Fun Facts **What-the-Winnipesaukee?**

How do you say it? All together, now: Win-uh-pa-SOCK-ee. What does it mean? It's a little hazy. Either "Smile of the great spirit," in the tongue of local Abenaki peoples who were living here when colonists arrived, or possibly "Pretty lake in a high spot." (Pretty *big* lake would have been even better.) Both work for me.

 small-town New Hampshire, remember?). Consult the Concord Coach website for exact bus stop locations.

A ticket to any of these four towns from Boston costs $22 to $25 one-way, with a slight discount for round-trips.

VISITOR INFORMATION The **Meredith Area Chamber of Commerce** (✆ **877/279-6121** or 603/279-6121; www.meredithcc.org) maintains an office in the white house on Route 3 (on the left when driving down the hill from Rte. 104). It's open daily in summer, and open only weekdays in winter.

Exploring the Area

Meredith's Main Street ascends a hill from Route 3 at an elbow in the middle of town. A handful of shops, galleries, and boutiques offer low-key browsing. The creative re-adaptation of an early mill at the **Mill Falls Marketplace** has about 20 shops, including a well-stocked bookstore, pizzeria, ice-cream shop, and art gallery. It's connected to The Inns at Mill Falls (see "Where to Stay," below), at the intersection of routes 3 and 25.

One excellent fair-weather trip is an excursion out to 112-acre **Stonedam Island ★★**, one of the largest protected islands in the lake. You need a boat, canoe, or kayak to get there, obviously; check at the harbor about chartering a boat if need be. Owned by the Lakes Region Conservation Trust (✆ **603/253-3301;** www.lrct.org), the island has a self-guiding trail that winds through wetlands and forest; contact the trust for a map.

Where to Stay

The Inns at Mill Falls ★★★ This expanding complex is gradually dominating Meredith but has managed its growth pretty well so far. Accommodations are spread among four buildings, each subtly different, all well tended and comfortable. The main inn is in a former mill complex and has attractive, simple rooms. Units in the more upscale Chase House all have gas fireplaces; most also have balconies with rockers. The Inn at Bay Point is on 2,000 feet of lakefront, and most rooms have balconies with sensational views. In 2004 the inn unveiled Church Landing, a converted church right on the lakefront (it's connected to the other by a footpath). This annex offers rooms and suites with gas fireplaces, double Jacuzzis, and balconies. (Hallelujah!) A pool and health club were also added to this new section, as well as marina space and a restaurant—one of eight in the inns, ranging from sub sandwiches to sit-down finery.

312 Rte. 3, Meredith, NH 03253. ✆ **800/622-6455** or 603/279-7006. www.millfalls.com. 159 units. $109–$329 double; $159–$459 suite. Minimum stay some weekends. AE, DC, DISC, MC, V. **Amenities:** 8 restaurants; bar; babysitting; exercise room; Jacuzzi; indoor pool; limited room service; spa. *In room:* A/C, TV, hair dryer, Wi-Fi (free).

Where to Dine

There's not much gourmet fare around here at all. If you want to eat something fancy, dine in the dining rooms, taverns, and bistros of the Inns at Mill Falls (see "Where to Stay," above)—there are *eight* distinct dining spaces.

For lunch, there's always takeout on the town docks—ice cream, fried fish, nothing spectacular. Or, behind the resort on Main Street, **Abondante** (✆ **603/279-7177**) is a trattoria popular with locals. It has some atmosphere—maple floors, copper-topped tables, classical music—and serves sit-down meals along with fixing plenty of to-go orders. The menu is mostly pastas. They also sell breads, chocolates, and meat and cheese in a market and deli.

Moments Funspot: Video Geek Heaven

The lake town of **Laconia** should be avoided by travelers seeking "classic" New Hampshire—the town is better known for amusement parks than *On Golden Pond*–type vistas. Its **Weirs Beach** section is as ticky-tacky as New England gets.

But there's one roadside attraction here you absolutely shouldn't pass up if the words Atari, *Asteroids, Space Invaders,* or *Ms. Pac-Man* light your internal fires: **Funspot** (© **603/366-4377;** www.funspotnh.com). The lakeside amusement park bills itself as the world's biggest arcade, and the Guinness world-record folks agree. Whether that's true or not, though, this place has become the de facto East Coast capital of the video-gaming world. The first-ever perfect score in Donkey Kong, and a subsequent higher score, were achieved here; a documentary film, *The King of Kong,* was filmed here; and there's also an annual video game tournament. A little arcade museum on the third floor of the arcade archives classic gaming consoles that no longer see the inside of America's pizza parlors and mall arcades.

Not a video-game fan? The place also has a 20-lane candlepin bowling alley, indoor *and* outdoor miniature golf, and car shows. Seriously kitschy Americana here, folks.

Funspot is located on Route 3 in the center of Laconia, near the beach and **Interlaken Park.** It's open daily, year-round, until at least 10pm (later Fri–Sat nights)—though the park's outdoor portions close from Labor Day through Memorial Day.

Hart's Turkey Farm Restaurant Kids AMERICAN Hart's is bad news if you're a turkey. It's Thanksgiving every day of the year here; on a typical busy day, the place dishes up more than a *ton* of America's favorite bird to its loyal diners. Opened in 1954, it hasn't changed much since then. No gourmet cuisine here; this is a comfortable, New England–style family restaurant in a big, rambling space (biggest in the lakes region, say the proprietors). Service here is afflicted with the same rushed efficiency found in any place that sees lots of bus tours, but it's friendly enough. There's a gift shop where you can find even more turkeys—and they sell carryout fruit pies in the lobby. Strictly local color.

Junction of rtes. 3 and 104. © **603/279-6212.** www.hartsturkeyfarm.com. Main courses $10–$25, sandwiches less. AE, DISC, MC, V. Summer daily 11:15am–9pm; fall–spring daily 11:15am–8pm.

WOLFEBORO ★★

The handsome town of **Wolfeboro,** on Lake Winnipesaukee's eastern shore, claims to be the first-ever summer resort in the U.S. The available documentation makes a pretty good case for it, too: In 1763 John Wentworth, nephew of a former governor, was granted land for a summer estate on what's now called Lake Wentworth, a small lake connected to Winnipesaukee by a tiny river. Blue-blood types (and grand hotels) followed him to the area, and the village that prospered has been a great success both as a summer retreat and a year-round community.

In contrast to the low-brow tourist attractions of towns like **Weirs Beach,** this town has a more prim sensibility and takes its preservation very seriously. You'll find impeccably maintained 19th-century homes, attractive downtown shops, and a refined sense of place. (There's even a private boarding school.) You might even see a famous face at the hardware store or ice-cream shop—well-known celebrities and politicians sometimes vacation here, and some own summer homes in the area.

Essentials

GETTING THERE Lake Winnipesaukee's eastern shore is best explored using Route 28 (from Alton Bay to Wolfeboro) and Route 109 (from Wolfeboro to Moultonborough).

VISITOR INFORMATION The **Wolfeboro Area Chamber of Commerce** (✆ **800/516-5324** or 603/569-2200; www.wolfeborooonline.com/chamber) provides regional information and advice from its offices in a converted railroad station at 32 Central Ave., a block off Main Street. It's open daily in summer, weekdays only the rest of the year.

SPECIAL EVENTS The **Great Waters Music Festival** ★ (✆ **603/569-7710;** www.greatwaters.org) is an amazingly eclectic series held on the campus of Brewster Academy throughout summer. Performers really run the gamut, from swing (the Glenn Miller Orchestra) to jazz (Dianne Reeves, Wynton Marsalis) and even classical. But good old-fashioned folkies (Judy Collins, Arlo Guthrie, John Gorka) still seem to rule the roost.

Exploring Wolfeboro

Wolfeboro has a vibrant, compact downtown, easily explored on foot. Park near Depot Square and the Victorian-style train station, and stock up on brochures and maps at the chamber of commerce office. Behind the station, a trail runs along the old tracks past Back Bay to a set of small cascades.

Several **boat tours** of the lake depart from the docks just behind the shops on Main Street. One of the most fun is the wind-in-your-face, zippy half-hour tour aboard the ***Millie B.*** ★ (✆ **603/569-1080**), a 28-foot mahogany speedboat constructed by HackerCraft. (Ticket prices have zoomed in recent years, too: The ride costs $20 per adults, $10 for children ages 4–12.)

There's also quiet lake swimming at **Wentworth State Park** ★ (✆ **603/271-3556**), which has a nice beach and a shaded picnic area. The park is 5 miles east of Wolfeboro on Route 109. It's open daily mid-June to Labor Day. The entrance fee is $4 per adult, or $2 per child ages 6 to 11. No pets are allowed in the park.

Castle in the Clouds ★★ **Finds** About 15 miles north of Wolfeboro is this rather unusual, castle-like attraction. Boston shoemaker-turned-millionaire Thomas Gustave Plant built an eccentric stone edifice on top of a little mountain overlooking Winnipesaukee in 1913, at a cost of $7 million (in 1913 dollars!) as a retreat from his factory. Known as "Lucknow" at the time, the home is a sort of rustic, smaller San Simeon East, with cliff-hugging rooms, stained-glass windows, and unrivaled views of surrounding hills and lakes. Park at the carriage house; from there, you're led through the house by knowledgeable tour guides. Look for mannequin knights in suits of armor, old shotguns, exotic wood carvings, tusks—guy stuff, basically. Even if the castle isn't interesting to you, the 5,200-acre grounds and the views (which get even better in foliage season) are worth the price of admission alone. So is the access road, which is harrowingly narrow and twisty in spots but rewards the brave traveler with wonderful views and turnouts along the way. Bring. A. Camera. (A different road back downhill is uninteresting.) There's also a cafe at the top. This place is quirky and marvelous—but if it's rainy, skip it.

455 Rte. 171 (4 miles south of Rte. 25), Moultonborough. ✆ **603/476-5900.** www.castleintheclouds.org. Castle and grounds admission $12 adults, $9 seniors, $5 students 7–14, free for children 6 and under; grounds only $5 adults, free for children. Mid-May to late May Sat–Sun 10am–4:30pm; June to mid-Oct daily 10am–4:30pm. Closed mid-Oct to mid-May.

8

The White Mountains & Northern New Hampshire

In the same way that Vermont's Northeast Kingdom is quite different from its pastoral southern reaches, northern New Hampshire is very different from southern New Hampshire. The gentleman's farms, technology companies, summer homes, and sandy beaches disappear, replaced by iffy weather, tight budgets, Republicans, trucks, part-time jobs—and trees. No, not really—I'm oversimplifying. Sort of.

At the heart of this region are the tough White Mountains, northern New England's focal point for outdoor recreation. This high, windy range of peaks is a sprawling and rugged playground for hard-core kayakers, mountaineers, rock climbers, extreme skiers, mountain bikers, bird-watchers, and hikers. There's nothing "soft" about adventures here.

The **White Mountain National Forest** organizes and administrates most of this vast landscape, nearly 800,000 acres of rocky, forested terrain, more than 100 waterfalls, dozens of backcountry lakes, miles of clear brooks and cascading streams—you get the idea. An elaborate network of hiking trails (more than 1,000 miles' worth) dates back to the 19th century, when city folk took to these mountains to build character and experience nature first-hand. Pathways ranging from easy to vertical lace the forests, trade the rivers, and traverse knife-like ridgelines where the weather can change so quickly and dramatically it can do you in, if you're not ready for it.

The heart of the White Mountains is their highest point: 6,288-foot **Mount Washington,** an ominous, brooding peak that's often cloud-capped and mantled with snow both early and late in the season. It's so big, you can see it from Portland, Maine, 100 miles away. An often-blustery peak, it's accessible by cog railway, car, and foot, making it one of the more popular destinations in the region. You won't find untouched wilderness here, but you will find abundant natural drama.

Flanking Washington is the brawny **Presidential Range,** a series of similarly wind-blasted granite peaks which are similarly named for U.S. presidents and offer similarly eye-popping views. Beyond this range, plenty of lesser-known ridges also beckon hikers seeking an elemental test, too.

But even if your idea of fun *doesn't* involve steep, scary cliffs, near-vertical ski runs, and icy plunges into mountain streams, you can still enjoy the scenery around here via spectacular drives. The most scenic is the **Kancamagus Highway** between Conway and Lincoln, offering plenty of pullouts to picnic and snap great photos.

Towns are few and far between, but a handful are worth mentioning. **North Conway** is the lodging capital, with hundreds and hundreds of motel units and strip-mall and outlet shopping. **Loon Mountain** and **Waterville Valley** are condo villages attached to ski resorts. And **Bethlehem, Jackson,** and the **Franconia** and **Crawford notches** offer genteel main streets and old-style (or sometimes just old) hotels and inns.

1 ENJOYING THE GREAT OUTDOORS

BACKPACKING The White Mountains have some of the most challenging and scenic backpacking in the eastern U.S. The best trails are within the huge White Mountain National Forest, which encompasses several 5,000-plus-foot peaks and more than 100,000 acres of designated wilderness. The trails range from easy walks along bubbling streams to demanding ridgeline paths buffeted by fierce winds.

The **Appalachian Mountain Club** (© **603/466-2727;** www.amc-nh.org) is an excellent source of general information about the region's outdoors offerings. It's a major supplier of lodging, too. Eight sturdy **mountain huts** ★ (small cabins) offer bare-bones, bunkroom-style shelter and great campfire conviviality in dramatic settings; hearty breakfasts and dinners are included with your rates, which are about $90 per adult, less for kids. The AMC maintains a clutch of other cabins and lodges in the mountains, too, such as the 16-bed Shapleigh Bunkhouse in Crawford Notch (a bunk plus breakfast costs about $40 to $65 per non-AMC member) and the Joe Dodge Lodge in Pinkham Notch, which has some four-person family rooms.

The **Appalachian Trail** ★★★ passes through New Hampshire, entering the state at Hanover and running along the highest peaks of the White Mountains before exiting into Maine along the scenic, tough-to-climb **Mahoosuc Range** ★★ northeast of Gorham. The trail is well maintained in these stretches, though it tends to attract teeming crowds along the highest elevations in summer.

Everything you could possibly need for a day or overnight hike, including sleeping bags and pads, tents, and backpacks, is available at **Eastern Mountain Sports** (© **603/356-5433**), at a brand-spanking-new location taking a run at L.L.Bean-type greatness. It's located in the Settlers' Crossing mall (don't confuse it with Settlers' Green, a *different* mall) on Route 16/302 between Conway and North Conway (though closer to Conway). The store is open daily.

BIKING For some great routes and spots, consult *Backroad Bicycling in New Hampshire* (Countryman Press, 2004) by Andi Marie Cantel. The White Mountains have plenty of opportunities for mountain bikers, too; all trails are open to bikers unless noted otherwise. (Bikes are not allowed in the forest's "wilderness areas," however.) The upland roads outside Jackson allow for superb biking, for instance, as does the steep terrain around Franconia and Sugar Hill.

Bike rentals cost anywhere from $30 to $60 per day, depending on rental location and type of bike. **Great Glen Trails** (© **603/466-2333;** www.greatglentrails.com), near Mount Washington, and **Waterville Valley Base Camp** (© **800/468-2553;** www.waterville.com), at the southwest edge of the park, each provide bike rentals and maintain mountain bike trails. (Waterville Valley also has lift-serviced mountain biking down the ski hill.) At both facilities, the trail systems cost around $8 per person to use if you've brought your own bike. They're free to use if you get a rental.

CANOEING Canoeing is very big up here. In the corner of the state, 8,000-acre **Lake Umbagog** ★★ is home to bald eagles and loons, and is especially appealing to explore by canoe.

The **Androscoggin River** offers superb Class I to II white-water and swift flat-water canoeing upstream of **Berlin;** downriver from there, the river can get faintly noxious with mill effluent. Serious white water enthusiasts head for the upper reaches of the **Saco River** during spring runoff, when the Class III to IV rapids are intense, if relatively short-lived,

Moments Going Vertical at Tuckerman Ravine

The most impressive ski run in New Hampshire isn't served by any lift. **Tuckerman Ravine** (known locally as Tuck's) drops a scary, stomach-churning 3,400 feet from the shoulder of Mount Washington to the valley floor. It's a mecca for extreme skiers, who arrive from all over the country early every spring (the ridge is dangerously avalanche-prone during the height of winter), hike steeply up to the top from Pinkham Notch, then launch themselves almost vertically toward the bottom of a dramatic glacial cirque. The slope is sheer and unforgiving of any mistakes; ***only very advanced skiers*** should try. (Careless and overly cocky skiers are hauled out every year on stretchers, and sometimes people die.)

If you're in that upper-upper echelon in skill, the AMC's **Pinkham Notch Visitor Center** (✆ **603/466-2721**) can give you information about current conditions. There's also a volunteer-run website (www.tuckerman.org) with avalanche-warning updates. If you're *not* in that upper tier, lots of folks still hike up here just to sit on the rocks and watch—drinking beverages, tanning, tossing Frisbees, and oohing and ahhing at the thrills and spills.

along a 6½-mile stretch running parallel to Route 302. Inquire locally about outfitters and gear shops if you're staying near any of these areas.

HIKING The essential guide to hiking in this region is the Appalachian Mountain Club's *White Mountain Guide,* which contains up-to-date and detailed descriptions of every trail in the area. The guide is available at most bookstores and outdoor shops (even at some gas stations) in the region.

SKIING The best downhill ski areas in the White Mountains are Cannon Mountain, Loon Mountain, Waterville Valley, Wildcat, and Attitash Bear Peak, with vertical drops of 2,000 feet and all the services one would expect of a professional ski resort. See below in this chapter for details on these ski hills.

The state also boasts some two dozen cross-country ski centers. The state's premier cross-country destination is **Jackson** ★★ (✆ **800/927-6697** or 603/383-9355; www.jacksonxc.com), whose town cross-country association maintains more than 50 miles of lovely trails in and around the scenic village (near the base of Mount Washington). A trail pass at Jackson costs $19 per adult ($10 if you're only snowshoeing), $8 per child.

Two more good Nordic ski centers are located at **Bretton Woods Resort** (✆ **800/314-1752** or 603/278-3322; www.brettonwoods.com)—anchored by that huge, red-and-white hotel at the western entrance to Crawford Notch—and the spectacularly remote **Balsams/Wilderness** cross-country ski center (✆ **800/255-0600** or 603/255-3400; www.thebalsams.com), operated by the Balsams resort in the northerly reaches of the state. Adults will pay $15 to $17 per day to ski the trails at any of these facilities (with big discounts for kids and seniors), and any of them can rent you a set of good skis to get you on your way.

BACKCOUNTRY FEES

The White Mountain National Forest requires anyone using the backcountry—for hiking, mountain biking, picnicking, skiing, or any other activity—to pay a recreation fee. Anyone parking at a trail head must display a backcountry permit on the car dashboard;

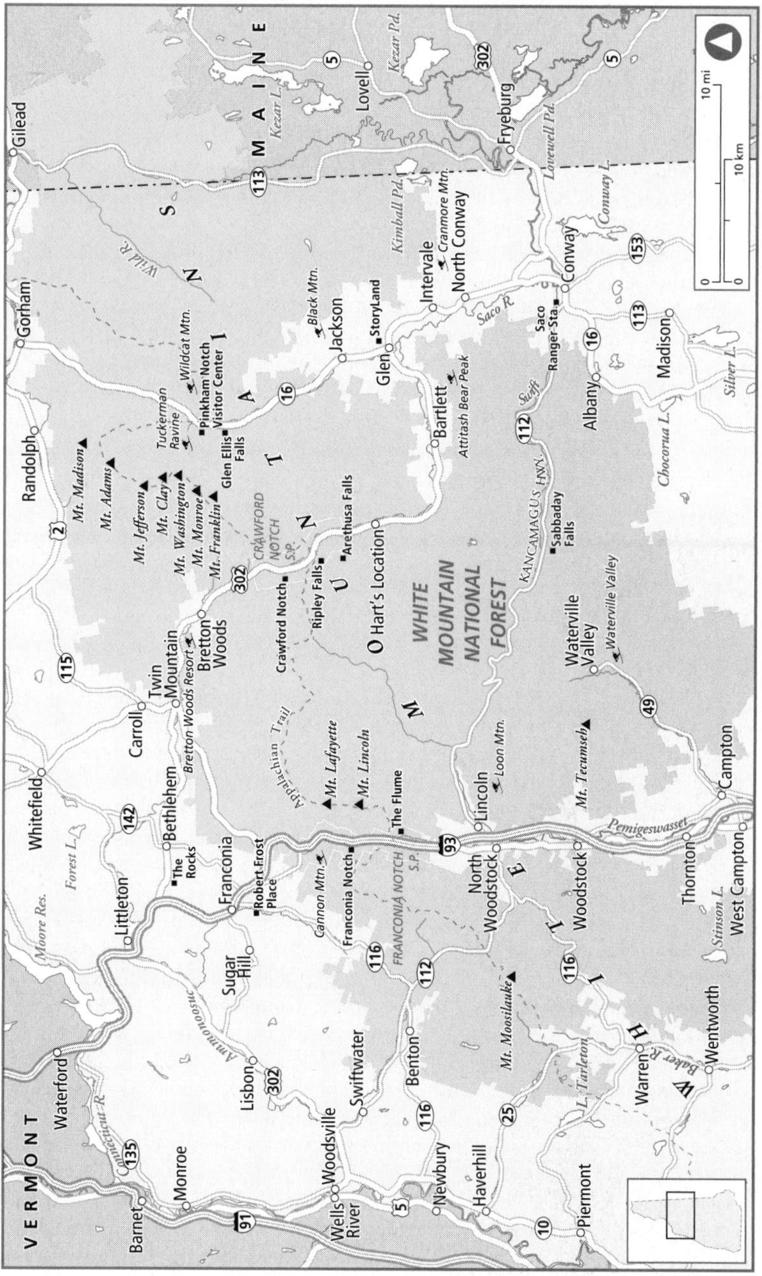

VERMONT
MAINE
WHITE MOUNTAINS
WHITE MOUNTAIN NATIONAL FOREST
CRAWFORD NOTCH S.P.
FRANCONIA NOTCH S.P.
Gilead
Gorham
Randolph
Whitefield
Carroll
Twin Mountain
Bretton Woods
Bretton Woods Resort
Bethlehem
The Rocks
Littleton
Franconia
Robert Frost Place
Sugar Hill
Lisbon
Waterford
Barnet
Monroe
Woodsville
Wells River
Swiftwater
Newbury
Haverhill
Benton
Piermont
Warren
Wentworth
West Campton
Thornton
Campton
Woodstock
North Woodstock
Lincoln
Loon Mtn.
The Flume
Franconia Notch
Cannon Mtn.
Mt. Lafayette
Mt. Lincoln
Appalachian Trail
Crawford Notch
Ripley Falls
Arethusa Falls
Hart's Location
Mt. Jefferson
Mt. Adams
Mt. Madison
Mt. Clay
Mt. Washington
Mt. Monroe
Mt. Franklin
Tuckerman Ravine
Pinkham Notch Visitor Center
Wildcat Mtn.
Glen Ellis Falls
Black Mtn.
Jackson
StoryLand
Glen
Bartlett
Attitash Bear Peak
Intervale
Cranmore Mtn.
North Conway
Conway
Saco Ranger Sta.
Saco R.
Albany
Madison
Silver L.
Chocorua L.
Conway L.
Kimball Pd.
Lovewell Pd.
Fryeburg
Lovell
Kezar L.
Kezar Pd.
Wild R.
Swift
KANCAMAGUS HWY.
Sabbaday Falls
Waterville Valley
Mt. Tecumseh
Mt. Moosilauke
Pemigewasset
Ammonoosuc
Connecticut R.
Moore Res.
Forest L.
L. Tarleton
Stinson L.
Baker R.
0 10 mi
0 10 km
2
5
10
16
25
91
93
112
113
115
116
135
142
153
302
49

those lacking a permit face a fine. Permits are available at ranger stations and many stores in the region. An annual permit costs $20, and a 7-day pass is $5. You can also buy a day pass for $3, but it covers only one site: the spot you bought it at. (If you drive anywhere else on the mountain later in the afternoon and park again, you'll have to pay the $3 all over again.) You're much better off with the 7-day or annual pass.

For more information, contact the **Forest Service's White Mountains office** (✆ **603/536-6100;** www.fs.fed.us/r9/white).

RANGER STATIONS & INFORMATION

The Forest Service's brand new **White Mountains National Forest headquarters** are located at 71 White Mountain Dr. in Campton (take exit 27 from I-93 and follow signs to reach it). The facility houses the Forest Supervisor's Office, Pemigewasset Ranger District staff, and a handy visitor center that's open daily, year-round, 8am to 4:30pm.

There are two more stations in the mountains: the **Saco Ranger Station,** at 33 Kancamagus Hwy., 300 feet west of Route 16 in Conway (✆ **603/447-5448**); and the **Androscoggin Ranger Station,** at 300 Glen Rd. in Gorham (✆ **603/466-2713**).

The National Parks Service also maintains two helpful year-round visitor centers. The **Gateway Visitor Center** ★ (✆ **603/745-3816**) is just off exit 32 of I-93, well stocked and in a good position en route to many attractions. It's open daily 8:30am to 4pm. Then there's the **Lincoln Woods Visitor Center** (✆ **603/630-5190**), about 5 miles east of Lincoln right on the Kancamagus Highway. There's a **suspension bridge** very near this visitor center, too, accessible via a footpath. It's open daily 8am to 5pm.

Finally, info and advice are also available at the **AMC's Pinkham Notch Visitor Center** (✆ **603/466-2721**), on Route 16 between Jackson and Gorham. The center is open daily, year-round, from 6am to 10pm. It has a cafe and a travel store, too.

CAMPING

The White Mountain National Forest maintains about two dozen drive-in campsites scattered throughout the region, from small to large. Campsites mostly cost in the $16 to $20 range per night. Online reservations are accepted at many of these campsites through the **National Recreation Reservation Service** (✆ **877/444-6777;** www.recreation.gov). Most of the mountains' campsites are rather basic—in fact, some have only pit toilets—but all of them are pretty well maintained. Remember that some sites require reservations at least a week in advance (in other words, no walk-ins), and 2- to 3-night minimum stays are enforced on certain Saturdays and Sundays during peak season.

Of all these **national forest campgrounds,** the biggest (and least personal) is **Dolly Copp Campground** (✆ **603/466-2713**), near the base of Mount Washington. Still, it has a superior location and great views from the open sites. Along the Kancamagus Highway, many travelers enjoy **Covered Bridge Campground** (✆ **603/447-2166**), about 6 miles west of Conway and adjacent to an 1858 covered bridge. (It's also a short drive to some delightful river swimming at the Rocky Gorge Scenic Area.) Both of these campgrounds are open only seasonally, from around mid-May until mid-October.

Backcountry tent camping is free throughout the White Mountains, and no permit is needed. (You *will* need to purchase a parking permit to leave your car at the trail head, however; see "Backcountry Fees," above.) Check with a ranger station and the forest service website about updated camping rules. Three-sided log lean-tos are also scattered throughout the backcountry, providing overnight shelter. Some of these are free; at others, a backcountry manager will collect a small fee from you. Again, contact any of the three ranger stations (see "Ranger Stations & Information," above) for details and locations of these campgrounds.

There are also 10 **state parks offering camping** in northern New Hampshire, including four in the White Mountains; most of them are pretty nice. Consult the state parks division's website (www.nhstateparks.org) or call them at ✆ **603/271-3628** for rates, reservations, and details. You can also now reserve these state campgrounds through the online system at **www.reserveamerica.com**.

2 NORTH CONWAY & ENVIRONS

North Conway: 150 miles N of Boston; 62 miles NW of Portland

For better or worse, **North Conway** is the commercial heart of the White Mountains. Outdoor purists abhor the place—except, maybe, when seeking a post-hike pizza and beer. Shoppers, on the other hand, are drawn magnetically to the outlets and other accoutrements of commerce perched along routes 302 and 16, the two highways that overlap in town. On rainy weekends and during foliage season, the road can resemble a linear parking lot. There's so much clutter here you often forget to look *up*—which is where the peaks of the Whites are standing quietly, behind a big grocery store.

Sprawl notwithstanding, North Conway is beautifully situated along the eastern edge of the broad and fertile Saco River valley (here usually called the Mount Washington Valley). Gentle, forest-covered mountains, some with sheer cliffs that could be distant cousins of those in Yosemite, border the bottomlands. Northward up the valley, hills rise in a triumphant crescendo to the blustery, tempestuous heights of Mount Washington.

But the central village is trim and attractive (if often congested), with an open green, some colorful shops, Victorian frontier-town commercial architecture, and a little train station. It's a good place to park, stretch your legs, and get a cup of coffee or a snack.

ESSENTIALS

GETTING THERE North Conway and the Mount Washington Valley sit on routes 16 and 302. Route 16 connects to the Spaulding Turnpike, then to I-95 to Boston and New York; Route 302 zigzags from Maine to Vermont. Traffic can be vexing in this valley on holiday weekends in summer, and it gets *really* bad on foliage weekends in fall, when backups several miles long are common. Try to plan around these busy times to preserve your sanity.

Concord Coach (✆ **800/639-3317;** www.concordcoachlines.com) runs two daily buses from Boston's South Station and Logan Airport, picking up and dropping off in **North Conway** at the Eastern Slope Inn (Rte. 16/302) and in **Conway** at the First Stop Market gas station on West Main Street (across from the high school). The cost is $30 one-way, $56 round-trip to South Station—a few dollars more each way for the airport—and takes about 4 hours.

VISITOR INFORMATION Contact the **Mount Washington Valley Chamber of Commerce** (✆ **877/948-6867;** www.mtwashingtonvalley.org), which operates year-round offices and a seasonal information booth, both opposite the village green. Staff can help arrange for local accommodations. The info booth is open daily in summer, weekends only in winter.

Cranmore Mountain Resort ★ Value Mount Cranmore claims to be the oldest operating ski area in New England, and ski pioneer Hannes Schneider did in fact practically single-handedly bring a new form of downhill skiing to America here beginning in 1939. (The resort was also famous, for half a century, for its tracked ski lift, known as the Skimobile—now sadly gone by the wayside.) Cranmore's slopes are unrepentantly old-fashioned, but the mountain has restyled itself as a snow-sports mecca—look for snow tubing, snow scooters, and ski bikes. These slopes aren't likely to challenge advanced skiers, but they delight many beginners and intermediates, as well as those who enjoy diversion with the ski toys. It's ideal for families, thanks to the relaxed attitude, range of activities, and not-outrageous ticket prices.

1 Skimobile Rd. (P.O. Box 1640), North Conway, NH 03850. ✆ **800/786-6754.** www.cranmore.com. Adults $55 day lift tickets; discounts for youths and seniors.

WHERE TO STAY

In addition the choices I've listed below, **Route 16** in North Conway is packed to the gills with basic motels (many family-run), which are affordably priced in the off season—you can sometimes find a room for as low as $50 per night in spring or late fall—but disappointingly expensive during peak travel times (summer, ski-season weekends, fall foliage season). They vary wildly in upkeep from place to place, though, and some are frankly just awful.

Luckily, a couple new B&B and inn properties are making waves in town. The **Red Elephant Inn Bed & Breakfast** ★ at 28 Locust Lane (✆ **800/642-0749** or 603/356-3548; www.redelephantinn.com) has super-friendly hosts and eight quirkily decorated theme rooms (from the Hippie Room and Domestic to Neiman Marcus) for $110 to $225 per night. The **Wyatt House Country Inn** ★ (✆ **800/527-7978** or 603/356-7977; www.wyatthouseinn.com), on Route 16 just north of the village, is a more traditional New Hampshire inn (whitewashed, weather vane, lawn) but has its own growing fan club, too—many rooms here have Jacuzzis. Rooms and suites cost $84 to $193 per night.

Briarcliff Motel Value Of North Conway's dozens of roadside motels, the Briarcliff is one of the best choices. Located about a half-mile south of the village center, this is your basic U-shaped motel with standard-size rooms, but all its units have been redecorated in rich colors, much like B&B rooms. You have to pay extra for a room with a "porch" and mountain view—and the porches are actually part of a long enclosed sitting area, each unit separated from its neighbor by cubicle-height partitions. So think twice about doing so. Need a soda, an iron, a microwave, a ski locker? Head for the common room; rooms don't have any of these things. But this is still a bargain, and well kept up.

Rte. 16 (P.O. Box 504), North Conway, NH 03860. ✆ **800/338-4291** or 603/356-5584. www.briarcliffmotel.com. 30 units. Summer and fall $99–$179 double; rest of year $69–$189 double. 2-night minimum stay holidays and foliage season. AE, DISC, MC, V. **Amenities:** Outdoor pool. *In room:* A/C, TV, fridge, Wi-Fi (free).

The Buttonwood Inn ★ Just a few minutes' drive from the outlets and restaurants, the Buttonwood has more of a classic country-inn feel than most other North Conway inns. It's set on 17 acres (with cross country ski trails) on the side of Mount Surprise in an 1820s-era home, with a tastefully appointed interior inspired by Shaker style. Most rooms are smallish and cozy, though two common rooms (one with a television, one with a fireplace) allow guests plenty of space to unwind. Two units have gas fireplaces, one has

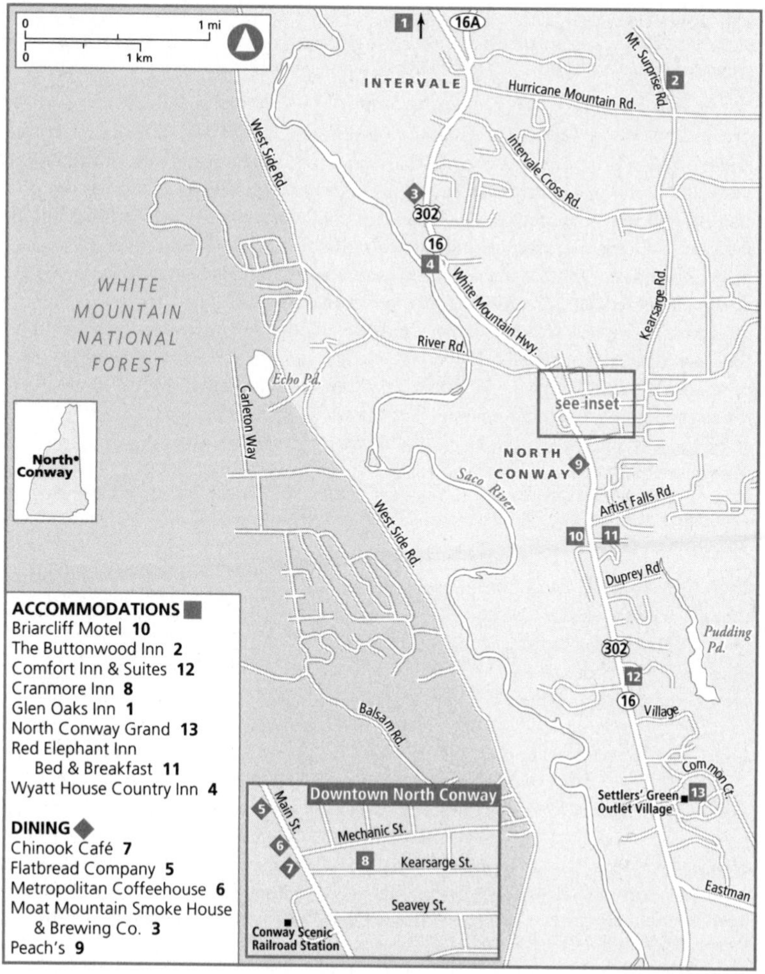

a Murphy bed, and one has a large Jacuzzi (it's also wheelchair accessible). The hosts are helpful with the planning of day trips, no matter your interests. Breakfasts are a hit.

64 Mt. Surprise Rd., North Conway, NH 03860. ✆ **800/258-2625** or 603/356-2625. Fax 603/356-3140. www.buttonwoodinn.com. 10 units, 2 with detached private bathroom. $99–$299 double. Rates include breakfast. 2- to 3-night minimum stay Sat–Sun and holidays. AE, DISC, MC, V. Closed Apr. "Well behaved" children 10 and over welcome. **Amenities:** Outdoor heated pool. *In room:* A/C, TV (some units), hair dryer, Wi-Fi (free).

Comfort Inn & Suites ★ (Kids) This tidy chain hotel consists entirely of "suites" (big rooms with low partitions; not separate rooms) spread out among three stories, giving travelers a bit more elbow room than the other motels in town. It's a good choice for families, because it's close to outlet shopping and near a pirate-themed miniature golf course. A few rooms have gas fireplaces. For a chain property, it's uncommonly well run.

2001 White Mountain Hwy. (Rte. 16), North Conway, NH 03860. ✆ **877/424-6423** or 603/356-8811. Fax 603/356-7770. www.comfortinn.com. 59 units. $99–$199 double; executive suites to $249. Rates include continental breakfast. AE, DISC, MC, V. **Amenities:** Exercise room; heated indoor pool. *In room:* A/C, TV, fridge, hair dryer, Wi-Fi (free).

Cranmore Inn ★ Kids The Cranmore Inn has the feel of a 19th-century boardinghouse—which is appropriate, because that's what it is. Open since 1863, this three-story Victorian home is a short walk from North Conway's village center. Its heritage—it claims to be the oldest continuously operating hotel in town—adds charm and quirkiness, but comes with occasional old-house drawbacks such as uneven water pressure and hallway bathrooms. Still, it offers good value thanks to its handy location, the hospitality of the innkeepers, and the nice rooms. Interestingly, some of the 16 units in the main inn consist of two bedrooms, connected in the middle by a private hallway bathroom; these are very family-friendly. Three big "kitchen units" are housed in an annex; these suites come with their own kitchens, gas woodstoves, separate dining rooms, living rooms, and even personal computers (but they don't include breakfast).

80 Kearsarge St. (P.O. Box 1349), North Conway, NH 03860. ✆ **800/526-5502** or 603/356-5502. www.cranmoreinn.com. 19 units, some with private bathroom across hall. June–Mar $89–$210 double; Apr–May $65–$155 double. Rates include full breakfast (except kitchenette units). 2-night minimum stay weekends, holidays, and in foliage season. DISC, MC, V. **Amenities:** Jacuzzi; outdoor pool. *In room:* TV (some units), kitchenette (some units).

Glen Oaks Inn ★ Just 10 minutes north of North Conway is a spur road that leads through the little village of Intervale, with several lodges and a feeling of being removed from the clutter of outlet shops. Glen Oaks was built here in 1850, and a mansard-roofed third floor was added when the home became an inn in 1890. Typical for the era, the rooms are small to medium-sized, and are decorated mostly with reproductions and some country Victorian antiques. Some rooms have private bathrooms across the hallways; some have fireplaces. The best units might be the two in nearby stone cottages—the Cottle Room has a wood-burning fireplace, wing chairs, and a small porch with Adirondack chairs, while the newer Forest Cottage has a two-person Jacuzzi and small refrigerator.

Rte. 16A (P.O. Box 37), Intervale, NH 03845. ✆ **877/854-6535** or 603/356-9772. Fax 603/356-5652. www.glenoaksinn.com. 11 units. $99–$219 double. Rates include full breakfast. 2-night minimum stay most weekends and holidays. AE, DISC, MC, V. Children 6 and over welcome. **Amenities:** Outdoor pool. *In room:* A/C, TV/VCR, fridge (some units), Wi-Fi (free).

North Conway Grand ★★ Kids If you're looking for convenience, amenities, and easy access to outlet shopping, this former Sheraton is a safe bet. Built on the site of North Conway's former airfield, it's a four-story, gabled hotel with a pond, adjacent (and architecturally similar) to Settlers' Green, one of the town's key shopping complexes. The hotel offers clean comfortable rooms with the usual chain-hotel furnishings. Recently, the hotel's amenities have been ramped up, including now-year-round access to the outdoor pool and Jacuzzi (the patio is heated); there's another brick-terraced pool inside with his-and-her saunas, plus a newly constructed outdoor kiddie pool and play area featuring spray jets and other fun features. Some suites have Jacuzzis, but even the simplest room type has a full flight of business-hotel amenities and a Nintendo video game setup for the kids.

Fun Facts **The Father of American Skiing (via Austria)**

Long before Arnold Schwarzenegger hit the golden shores of California, another Austrian was making waves—and creating sports history—here on the white-powder slopes of New Hampshire. Hannes (né Johannes) Schneider (1890–1955) was a cheesemaker-turned-famed ski instructor in the Austrian Alps who helped invent and refine some of the same basic stopping and turning maneuvers that all recreational downhill skiers use today. Two action films of Schneider schussing downhill were screened worldwide and helped jump-start downhill skiing as an activity on the continent.

When Adolf Hitler (another Austrian) assimilated his country into the German state in 1938, Schneider would not accept the Nazi decision, or its party line; as punishment, he was fired from his ski post and placed under house arrest. But Schneider escaped to the U.S. with his family and put down roots in North Conway, which offered similar mountain vistas—and the backing of a local businessman, a former student who was just then developing the new Mount Cranmore resort. Soon Schneider was a local wonderboy. He would later help train U.S. troops in mountain skiing techniques for World War II, and an annual ski race at Cranmore carries his name today.

Rte. 16 at Settler's Green (P.O. Box 3189), North Conway, NH 03860. ✆ **800/655-1452** or 603/356-9300. Fax 603/356-6028. www.northconwaygrand.com. 200 units. Summer $109–$219 double; off season $79–$149 double. AE, DC, DISC, MC, V. **Amenities:** Restaurant; children's programs; exercise room; Jacuzzi; 3 pools (1 indoor; 2 outdoor, 1 heated); sauna; 4 tennis courts. *In room:* A/C, TV/DVD, fridge, hair dryer, Wi-Fi (free).

WHERE TO DINE

North Conway is a hub of family-style restaurants, fast-food chains, and bars that happen to also serve food. If you want more refined dining, you're better off heading for the Inn at Thorn Hill in Jackson, about 10 minutes north (see "Mount Washington & Environs," below). Or check with your inn or hotel—it might serve decent resort fare (a smaller B&B won't offer dinner service, though).

For a good breakfast or lunch, look for the peach-colored house on Route 16 in North Conway—it's a wildly popular local breakfast and lunch spot called, naturally, **Peach's** ★ (✆ **603/356-5860;** www.peachesnorthconway.com). Expect eggs, Belgian waffles, sandwiches, and sweets. It's open daily from 7am until 2:30pm. The **Metropolitan Coffee House** (✆ **603/356-2332;** http://metcoffeehouse.com) is another good bet on Main Street. The free Wi-Fi, purple couches, and world music might keep you (or your teenager) there all day. It's open daily from 7am until 9pm.

There's also **Flatbread Company** (✆ **603/356-4470;** www.flatbreadcompany.com), an organic-pizza place inside the Eastern Slope Inn on Route 16, just north of the village center.

Chinook Café ★ CAFE/VEGETARIAN Located in Conway, a pretty village about a 10-minute drive south of North Conway, the Chinook Café serves healthy, vaguely gourmet fare for breakfast (polenta with goat cheese, oatmeal pancakes) and lunch (smoked salmon and white-bean-and-portobello sandwiches), with a good selection of vegetarian items, too. There are changing daily specials, and the homemade baked goods are a fitting conclusion to a hike.

80 Main St. (across from fire station), Conway. ✆ **603/447-6300.** Breakfast and lunch items $5–$7. MC, V. Daily 7:30am–3pm.

Moat Mountain Smokehouse and Brewing Co. ★ Finds BARBECUE/PUB FARE In a town starved for good eats, a lot of people end up here at Moat Mountain—the place in the valley for fresh, on-site brewed beer, smoked meats, and wood-fired pizza. It's casual and relaxed. Though this isn't nearly as good as barbecue cooked in the South (the real South, I mean, not southern New Hampshire), you can still choose from quite a selection of smoky barbecued items—brisket and ribs are especially popular. Other menu choices include burgers, sliders (miniburgers), quesadillas, and nachos—including a version with chicken and a mango-pineapple salsa. About a dozen beers are on tap most nights, many of them brewed in-house; these beers are the highlight of a trip here.

3378 White Mountain Hwy. (Rte. 16), North Conway (approx. 1 mile north of village). ✆ **603/356-6381.** www.moatmountain.com. Reservations not accepted. Main courses $7–$20. AE, MC, V. Daily 11:30am–9pm (until 10pm Fri–Sat).

SHOPPING

North Conway was one of northern New England's first major outlet centers. Now several hundred shops clump along the main drag, which extends some 3 miles northward from the junction of routes 302 and 16 in Conway into the village of North Conway itself.

Curiously, though, the outlet scene here has lagged here in recent years. But one outlet center has been a smashing success, expanding and absorbing much of the surrounding business into what is now a villagelike minimall. I'm talking about **Settlers' Green Outlet Village** (✆ **888/667-9636;** www.settlersgreen.com), and hard-core shoppers should make a beeline for it. The center has more than 60 shops, including heavy hitters like J. Crew, Coach, Brooks Brothers, Aeropostale, Harry & David, Nike, Under Armour, and Stonewall Kitchen.

Nearby is the popular **L.L.Bean** (✆ **603/356-2100**) factory outlet store, just north of Settlers' Green; it's just one of around a half-dozen outdoors-equipment manufacturers with retail stores or outlet stores in this town.

3 MOUNT WASHINGTON & ENVIRONS ★★★

Jackson: 8 miles N of North Conway

One of two gateway villages to **Mount Washington** ★★★ and its massive surrounding peaks, **Jackson** ★★ is a quiet place in a picturesque valley off Route 16. It's only about a 15 minutes' drive north of North Conway—yet this is a world apart. The compact village center, approached via a single-lane covered bridge, has retained its old-world elegance—reminders of a time when Jackson was the favored destination of the East Coast upper-middle-class types, who migrated in summer from East Coast cities to grand hotels and summer homes here.

After the Depression and the rise of the motel trade, though, Jackson and its old-fashionedness slipped into a protracted slumber—all the way until the roaring 1980s, when condo projects began sprouting in fields where cows had roamed, vacation homes began carpeting the hills, and the only two grand hotels that hadn't burned down or collapsed were spruced up.

Today, thanks to its revamped golf course and one of the most elaborate, well-maintained cross-country ski networks in the nation, Jackson has found renewed purpose as a resort in summer *and* winter. It's no longer undiscovered, but it does still feels a bit out of the mainstream, especially compared to the busy scene just to the south in the Conways.

ESSENTIALS

GETTING THERE Jackson is just off Route 16, about 11 miles north of North Conway. Heading north, look for the covered bridge on the right.

Surprisingly, **Concord Coach** (✆ **800/639-3317** or 603/228-3300; www.concordcoachlines.com) offers one daily bus to Jackson from Boston. Wait at the covered bridge and wave down the driver for the return trip. The trip takes 4 hours one-way and costs about $60 round-trip.

VISITOR INFORMATION The **Jackson Area Chamber of Commerce** (✆ **800/866-3334** or 603/383-9356; www.jacksonnh.com), based in offices at the Jackson Falls Marketplace on Route 16B, can answer questions about area attractions and make lodging reservations.

EXPLORING MOUNT WASHINGTON ★★★

Mount Washington, just north of Jackson in the heart of the White Mountain National Forest, is often described with impressive facts and figures that don't always succeed at evoking the windblown, hellishly scenic peak. But here are a few anyway.

At 6,288 feet, Washington is *the* highest mountain in the Northeast. It's also said to have some of the worst weather in the world, and it still holds the world's record for the highest surface wind speed ever recorded—231 mph in 1934, a record some Granite Staters take a perverse pride in. (There's a weatherman posted at the top of the mountain year-round, and there used to be a small TV crew here, too, documenting the craziness.) Winds topping 150 mph are routinely recorded here, a result of the mountain's position at the confluence of three major storm tracks.

Strangely, this is also the New England mountain with the most options for getting to its summit. Visitors can ascend via a special **cog railway** (see "Crawford Notch," later in this chapter); by car, along a snaky **toll road** to the summit; in an all-terrain vehicle (ATV), using the same road; in a guide-driven van; or **on foot.** You can even climb **by**

Tips You'll Never Walk Alone

Despite the raw power of its weather, Mount Washington's summit is *not* the place for those seeking true wilderness. The top is home to a train platform, a parking lot, a snack bar, a gift shop, a museum, and a handful of outbuildings housing a weather observatory. There are also plenty of crowds on clear days, all seeking that prized THIS CAR CLIMBED MT. WASHINGTON bumper sticker New England cars wear like badges of courage. Then again, the views here can't be beat, extending into four states and out to the ocean on a clear day. It's worth seeing, certainly. But keeping all those other folks out of the frame of your digital shots and camcorder footage? That's an extreme sport, too.

bike, though only twice a year—during two annual thigh-punishing races to the summit. The grade increases steeply to 22% near the top, where even pros have flipped over backwards trying to downshift in time.

The best place to learn about Mount Washington and its approaches is rustic **Pinkham Notch Visitor Center** (✆ **603/466-2721**), operated by the Appalachian Mountain Club. At the crest of Route 16 between Jackson and Gorham, the center offers overnight accommodations and meals at the adjacent Joe Dodge Lodge (see "Where to Stay," below), maps, a limited selection of outdoor supplies, and plenty of advice from its helpful staff. A number of hiking trails also depart from here, with several loops and side trips. It's open year-round.

About a dozen **trails** lead to the mountain's summit, ranging in length from about 4 to 15 miles. (Detailed information is available at the visitor center.) The most direct and dramatic way is via the **Tuckerman Ravine Trail** ★★★, which departs right from Pinkham Notch. It's a true full day's endeavor. Healthy hikers should allow 4 to 5 hours for the ascent, 2 to 4 hours for the return trip. Be sure to allow enough time to enjoy the dramatic glacial cirque of Tuckerman Ravine (see "Going Vertical," earlier in this chapter), which attracts extreme skiers to its sheer drops as late as June, and often holds patches of snow well into the summer.

The **Mount Washington Auto Road** ★★ (✆ **603/466-3988;** www.mountwashington autoroad.com) opened in 1861 as a carriage road and has since remained a wildly popular attraction. The steep, winding 8-mile road (with an *average* grade of 12%) is partly paved and incredibly dramatic; your breath will be taken away at one curve after another. The ascent will test your iron will; the descent will test your car's brakes. This trip is not worth doing, though, if the summit is in the clouds—wait for a **clear day.**

Located on Route 16 just north of Pinkham Notch, the road is open daily from early May until late October from 8am to 5pm (hours may be slightly different early or late in the season). The cost is $23 per vehicle and driver, plus $8 for each additional adult ($6 for extra children ages 5–12); it's $14 for a motorcycle and its operator. This price includes an audiocassette or CD narration pointing out sights along the way (available in English, French, or German) and the famous bumper sticker.

No trailers, RVs, or mopeds are allowed, which makes sense. But management has also imposed some other slightly curious vehicle restrictions to protect against breakdowns and logjams; for example, Acuras, Hondas, Saturns, Sterlings, and Jaguars with automatic transmissions must show a "1," "L," or "S" on the shifter to be allowed on the road; only H-3 version Hummers can ascend; and no Lincoln Continentals from 1969 or early are permitted. (Dang!) But most taxis and police cars are okay, so long as the first gear is operational.

If you'd prefer to leave the driving to someone else—or it's winter—**van tours** ascend throughout the day in safe weather, allowing you to relax, enjoy the views, and learn about the mountain from informed guides. The cost is $29 for adults, $25 for seniors, and $12 for children ages 5 to 12, and includes a short stay on the summit.

One additional note: The average temperature atop the mountain is 30°F (–1°C). (The record low was –43°F/–42°C, and the warmest temperature ever recorded atop the mountain, in August, was 72°F/22°C.) Even in August, bring backup just in case blustery, cold weather moves in suddenly. Wearing only shorts and a T-shirt, with nothing else as backup, is a bad idea.

Fun Facts **Mount Reagan, Maybe**

Move over, Henry Clay. The Presidential Range of New Hampshire's White Mountains will one day soon gain a Mount Reagan. Probably. What is now Mt. Clay—an impressive, 5,500-plus-foot peak running along the arm of rock between Washington and Jefferson, named for the Kentuckian who famously brokered the Missouri Compromise—was renamed by New Hampshire lawmakers in 2003. However, the state does not have final say in matters such as naming national forests. Final approval must be given by the U.S. Board of Geological Names, among other government pencil-pushers, and they haven't ruled on the matter yet.

EXPLORING PINKHAM NOTCH ★★★

The AMC's Pinkham Notch Visitor Center is at the height of land on Route 16. Just south of the center, look for signs to **Glen Ellis Falls** ★★, which is worth a quick stop because it's such an easy walk. From the parking area, you pass through a pedestrian tunnel and walk along the Glen Ellis River for less than 10 minutes until the path suddenly seems to drop off the face of the earth. The stream plummets 65 feet down a cliff here; observation platforms are situated at the top and near the bottom of the falls, some of this area's most impressive after a heavy rain. From the parking lot to the base of the falls is less than a half-mile walk.

From the same AMC visitor center, it's about 2.5 miles up to **Hermit Lake** and **Tuckerman Ravine** ★★★ via the Tuckerman Ravine Trail (see above). Even if you're not planning to continue on to the summit, the ravine—with its sheer sides and lacey cataracts—might be the most dramatic destination in the White Mountains. If you're in good shape, it's well worth the 2-hour hike in anything except miserable weather. The trail is wide and only moderately demanding. Bring a picnic and lunch on the massive boulders that litter the ravine's floor.

In summer an enclosed gondola known as the **Wildcat Express** ★ at the Wildcat Mountain ski area (see "Downhill Skiing," below) hauls passengers up the mountain for views of Tuckerman Ravine and Mount Washington's summit. The lift operates Saturday and Sunday from Memorial Day to mid-June, then daily through mid-October. The ski resort's base lodge is just north of Pinkham Notch on Route 16. It costs $15 per adult to ride the gondola, with discounts for seniors and kids, but it doesn't run in bad weather. There's now also a "ziprider," a zipline ride down a similar track—it costs $5 extra and you must be between 75 and 275 lbs. and between 4'4" and 6'8".

Too crazy for you? There's also **Frisbee golf** on the mountain ($10–$15 per person, depending on whether you brought your own disc or not).

CROSS-COUNTRY SKIING

Jackson regularly ranks among the top cross-country ski resorts in the nation. The reason is the nonprofit **Jackson Ski Touring Foundation** (✆ **800/927-6697** or 603/383-9355; www.jacksonxc.com), which created and maintains the extensive trail network. The terrain is wonderfully varied; many of the trails are rated "most difficult," which will keep advanced skiers from getting bored. But novice and intermediate skiers also have plenty of good options spread out along the valley floor.

Start at the base lodge, near the Wentworth Resort in the center of Jackson. There's parking here, and you can ski right through the village and into the hills. Gentle trails traverse the valley floor, with more advanced trails winding up the mountains. One-way ski trips with shuttles back to Jackson are available; ask if you're interested. Given how extensive and well maintained the trails are, passes are a good value at $19 for adults, $15 for seniors, and $8 for children ages 10 to 15. Rentals are available at the ski center (ticket/rental packages are available); snowshoes can be rented, too—there are specifically groomed trails for snowshoers.

DOWNHILL SKIING

Black Mountain ★★ Value Kids Dating back to the 1930s, Black Mountain was one of the White Mountains' pioneering ski areas. It hasn't gone all modern like many of New England's other ski hills; no, it remains a quintessential family mountain—modest in size, nonthreatening, ideal for beginners—though there's also glade skiing for more advanced skiers. A day here feels a bit like you've trespassed in some farmer's unused hayfield, which actually adds to the charm; this place isn't even on the radar of the Aspen set. The views of the Presidentials are very good, and a lift ticket is surprisingly inexpensive compared with the other resorts in the area—on a weekday, an adult can ski for less than $30, and that's just criminal. Bonus: Most of the 44 trails are pointed due south, so no frigid north winds blast your face. The resort also offers two compact terrain parks for snowboarders, as well as lessons, rentals, a day-care center for small kids, a ski school, and a base lodge with a cafeteria and pub. Nice place.

1 Black Mountain Rd. (P.O. Box B), Jackson, NH 03846. ✆ **800/475-4669** or 603/698-4490. www.blackmt.com. Adults $29–$39 day lift ticket, $26 half-day; discounts for seniors and youths.

Wildcat ★★ Set high in Pinkham Notch, Wildcat combines a rich heritage as a venerable ski resort with the best views of any ski area in the White Mountains. This mountain offers a bountiful supply of intermediate trails, as well as some challenging expert terrain. It's skiing the way it used to be—no base-area clutter, just a single lodge with an unpretentious cafeteria and a pub. That also means there are no on-slope hotels, condos, or other accommodations, but there are plenty of lodging options within an easy 15-minute drive of the mountain. Ask about ticket packages combining your lift ticket with downhill ski rentals and, if you need some, lessons.

Rte. 16, Pinkham Notch, NH 03846. ✆ **888/754-9453** or 603/466-3326. www.skiwildcat.com. Adults $65 day lift tickets, $45 half-day; discounts for seniors, teens, and children 6–12.

ESPECIALLY FOR KIDS

Parents with young children (age 10 and under) can buy peace of mind at **Story Land ★★**, at the northern junction of routes 16 and 302 (✆ **603/383-4186;** www.storylandnh.com). This old-fashioned (mid-1950s) fantasy village is filled with 30 acres of improbably leaning buildings, magical rides, cuckoo clocks, minitrains, fairy-tale creatures, a swan boat, and plenty of other enchanted beings. It's open weekends from 9am to 5pm from Memorial Day to mid-June; daily 9am to 6pm from mid-June to Labor Day; and again weekends only from 9am to 5pm through Columbus Day. Admission is about $25 per person for all visitors ages 4 and over; children 3 and under enter free.

WHERE TO STAY

Most inns in this area fall under the category of "classic New England inn," rather than "luxury country inn"—this is not Vermont. So long as you arrive *expecting* ceiling fans

Moments So Falls Jackson Falls

A warm weekday afternoon, an engrossing book, and **Jackson Falls** are a memorable combination. This wonderful cascade tumbles down out of Carter Notch (from the Jackson village, head up Carter Notch Rd. in front of the Wentworth Resort). Park along the notch road and find a sunny patch near the water, with views toward the valley. A few natural pools allow for great splashing around. Two caveats: It can get buggy early in the summer, and it gets crowded on Saturday and Sunday *all* summer.

instead of air-conditioning, creaky steam radiators, and similar quirks that come when 19th-century mansions haven't been thoroughly retrofitted for the 21st century, you won't be disappointed. And the setting *is* marvelous.

Eagle Mountain House ★ The white wooden Eagle Mountain House is a handsome relic that has happily survived the ravages of time, fire, and the fickle tastes of tourists. Built in 1916, the gleaming, classic, five-story hotel is set in an idyllic valley above Jackson. Guest rooms are furnished in a country-pine look with stenciled blanket chests, armoires, and feather comforters. You pay more for rooms with mountain views, though it's not really necessary to spend the extra cash—just plan to spend most of your free time lounging on the long, wide wraparound porch with views across the hotel's golf course and out to the mountains beyond.

179 Carter Notch Rd. (P.O. Box E), Jackson, NH 03846. ✆ **800/966-5779** or 603/383-9111. Fax 603/383-0854. www.eaglemt.com. 93 units. $69–$199 double; $129–$239 suite. 2-night minimum some weekends and peak periods. MAP plans available. AE, DISC, MC, V. "Limited" number of pets allowed with advance notice. **Amenities:** 2 restaurants; tavern; exercise room; Jacuzzi; outdoor pool; sauna; 2 tennis courts. *In room:* TV, fridge ($5 fee), Wi-Fi (some units; free).

The Inn at Thorn Hill ★ This elegant inn is a good choice for a romantic getaway. The classic shingle-style home (now swathed in light-yellow siding) was designed by famed architect Stanford White in 1895, just outside Jackson's village center and surrounded by wooded hills. Inside, the place has a comfortable Victorian feel. Rooms are luxuriously appointed—every room in the main house has a two-person Jacuzzi. There are also three cottages, done up in French country style, with air-conditioning and porches, and a half-dozen rooms in an adjacent carriage house. Some of the nicest units include the Katherine Suite, with a fireplace and two-person Jacuzzi, and the little yellow Notch View Cottage with its classic screened front porch and double Jacuzzi with a forest view. The hospitality here is excellent, and the **dining room's** ★★ three-course dinners (see "Where to Dine," below) are among the best in the valley. There's also quite a lovely spa area with a wooden sauna, whirlpool-like tubs, and a menu of services from hydrotherapy and facials to massages and yoga.

Thorn Hill Rd. (P.O. Box A), Jackson, NH 03846. ✆ **800/289-8990** or 603/383-4242. www.innatthornhill.com. 25 units. $169–$400 double; $309–$440 suite. Rates include full breakfast, afternoon tea, and dinner. 2- to 3-night minimum stay Sat–Sun and some holidays. AE, DISC, MC, V. Children 8 and over welcome. **Amenities:** 3 restaurants; bar; babysitting; Jacuzzi; limited room service; outdoor pool; spa. *In room:* A/C, TV/DVD, hair dryer, Wi-Fi ($6 per day).

Joe Dodge Lodge at Pinkham Notch ★ *Finds* Guests come to the Pinkham Notch Visitor Center more for the camaraderie than for the simplistic accommodations, yet they seem to always go away smiling; fresh air and good service will do that for you. Situated spectacularly at the base of Mount Washington, far from commercial clutter and with easy access to many hiking and skiing trails, the center is operated by the Appalachian Mountain Club somewhat like a tightly run youth hostel. Guests share bunkrooms, dormitory-style bathrooms, and optional meals at family-style tables in the main lodge. (A few private rooms provide double beds and family accommodations, with breakfast and dinner included in the prices, but you should try to book these ahead if possible.) The festive atmosphere is wonderful, as is the can't-be-beat location. You can also buy a trail lunch to-go in the cafeteria.

Rte. 16, Pinkham Notch, NH. (Mailing address: AMC, P.O. Box 298, Gorham, NH 03581.) ✆ **603/466-2721.** www.outdoors.org. 108 beds in bunkrooms of 2, 3, and 4 beds, all with shared bathroom. Private rooms $130–$150 double including breakfast and dinner. Bunkrooms peak season $51 per adult, $28 per child 15 and under (discount for AMC members); off season $43 per adult, $25 per child. MAP plans also available. Holiday rates higher. MC, V. Children 3 and over welcome. **Amenities:** Cafeteria. *In room:* No phone, Wi-Fi (free).

Wentworth Resort Hotel ★★ The venerable Wentworth sits in the middle of Jackson Village, all turrets, eaves, and awnings. Built in 1869, this Victorian shingled inn once consisted of a campuslike setting of 39 buildings (including a dairy and an electric plant), but it had edged to the brink of deterioration by the mid-1980s. Then the remaining buildings were refurbished, with a number of condominium clusters added around a refreshed golf course. Regular rooms are decorated with Victorian-inspired furnishings; suites (all with king-size beds) are stocked with such amenities as propane fireplaces, whirlpools, outdoor hot tubs, and claw-foot tubs. Visitors of stout constitution can stroll up the road and plunge into the icy waters of Jackson Falls; others can hang out in the hotel and eat in the very good **dining room** ★. Bear in mind that this building is aging, so some rooms have seen better days, but the 2009 addition of a luxury cottage ("Fairlawn") was a very positive sign: All eight expansive suites here have steam showers, either a whirlpool tub or an outdoor hot tub, multiple flatscreen TVs, a gas fireplace, and a sitting room.

1 Carter Notch Rd. (P.O. Box M), Jackson, NH 03846. ✆ **800/637-0013** or 603/383-9700. Fax 603/383-4265. www.thewentworth.com. 76 units. Peak season $214–$245 double, $314–$354 suite; off season $158–$168 double, $238–$278 suite. Rates include full breakfast and dinner. B&B and no-meals plans also available. AE, DC, DISC, MC, V. **Amenities:** Restaurant; golf course; outdoor pool; tennis court. *In room:* A/C, TV/DVD (some units), fridge (some units), Wi-Fi (free).

WHERE TO DINE

Most of the inns in town offer some form of dinner service and/or a pubby tavern right on their premises, though the quality level of food at these inns does vary. Check the write-ups above for more details.

In addition to the choices listed above and below, meals at the **Wildcat Inn & Tavern** (tel] **800/228-4245** or 603/383-4245) on Route 16A are decent. Main courses could include steaks, chops, rack of lamb, mushroom tarts, or lobster-flavored orzo. The tavern is a good place for a meal and a beer, with burgers and meatloaf in addition to entrees like barbecued pork sandwiches, salmon, and ribs.

The Inn at Thorn Hill ★★ NEW AMERICAN The romantic Inn at Thorn Hill is one of the best choices for a meal in the valley. The dining room faces the forested hill behind the inn. Start with a glass of wine from the wine list (the restaurant has won *Wine Spectator* awards of excellence), then browse the menu, which has leaned away from Asian accent to more solidly Continental and New American fare of late. A new chef, Peter Belmonte, joined the inn in 2009, so we'll see what direction he takes; so far, appetizers include things like saffrony mussel soup, chèvre tarts (yum), crab-and-melon salads with crème fraîche, and cucumber soup with toasted anise. Entrees could be a Maine lobster with a potato cake and fava beans; roasted chicken with a green pea risotto; steak frites with Bordelaise; or rack of lamb with a carrot puree. Desserts are great—in the past, they've included choices like a chèvre cheesecake, sour-cream panna cotta, and chocolate pavé. There's also a simpler "lounge menu" of burgers, fondue, salads, and the like. Wine-themed dinners are held throughout the year at the inn, and they're well worth attending.

Thorn Hill Rd., Jackson. ✆ **603/383-4242.** www.innatthornhill.com. Reservations recommended. Main courses $24–$36. AE, DISC, MC, V. Daily 6–9pm.

Thompson House Eatery ★ AMERICAN This friendly, old-fashioned spot in a 19th-century Cape-style "plank" farmhouse sits at the edge of Jackson's golf course. It attracts crowds for the fare, which is pricier than it used to be. You can dine both indoors and (in good weather) out. Elbow up at a communal table and meet fellow travelers while awaiting service and food; for lunch, expect a variety of fun deli-style sandwiches, plus turkey, meatloaf, BLTs, and a few salads. For dinner, prices spike upward and the fare becomes somewhat more refined—barbecue-spiced pork tenderloin, a seafood mélange cooked in sherry, lamb chops with mint jelly, bronzed duck breast, and even some vegetarian items like a Parmesan-crusted eggplant layered with smoked cheddar and portobello mushrooms. (You can also order lighter fare, like scallops or a mushroom dish called, I kid you not, "Fungus Among Us.") Desserts and martinis are excellent; there's also a bar with its own substantial menu.

193 Main St. (off Rte. 16A, near intersection with Rte. 16), Jackson. ✆ **603/383-9341.** www.thompsonhouseeatery.com. Reservations recommended for dinner. Main courses $8–$13 at lunch, $17–$31 at dinner. AE, DISC, MC, V. Thurs–Mon 11:30am–3pm and 5:30–9pm; Tues–Wed 5:30–9pm.

4 CRAWFORD NOTCH ★★

Crawford Notch is a wild, rugged mountain valley that angles right through the heart of the White Mountains. There's a surplus of history here. For years after its discovery by European settlers in 1771, this was an impenetrable wilderness—literally a barrier to commerce, because it blocked trade between the upper Connecticut River Valley and the busy harbors of Portland and Portsmouth. Eventually some plucky bunch got through the pass, and it finally developed into an important route.

Nathaniel Hawthorne immortalized the notch with a short story about a terrible real-life tragedy that struck here in August 1826. One dark and stormy night, the Willey family fled their home as a huge, rain-driven mudslide of boulders and trees roared down the mountain toward the valley floor. Wouldn't you know it, though? The river of destruction divided right above the house and spared the home entirely; all seven Willeys were killed because they *weren't* in the house. As I said, this story is real—and really sad. Though the house later burned, you can still visit the spot today—watch for signs to the WILLEY HOUSE HISTORICAL SITE when driving through the notch.

Route 302 plows through the notch, wide and speedy in its lower sections but then steeper and narrower as it approaches the defile of the notch itself. Modern engineering has taken most of the kinks out of the road, though, so you need to remind yourself to stop from time to time and enjoy the panoramas. The views *up* the cliffs from the road can be spectacular on a clear day.

By the way, don't get confused by directions and maps referring to the towns of **Twin Mountain** and **Bretton Woods.** Those two are the very *same* village; it simply has two different names.

ESSENTIALS

GETTING THERE Route 302 runs right through Crawford Notch for approximately 25 miles between the towns of **Bartlett** and **Twin Mountain.** From Portland, Maine, it's 2 hours or less of driving; from Boston, take Route 16 from Portsmouth (about 3 hrs.). Or from New York City, take I-91 to exit 17 (Wells River, Vermont) and crawl east along Route 302, a trip of about 6 hours one-way. Already in New Hampshire? From the central part of the state, take I-93 to exit 40 (Bethlehem) and head east.

VISITOR INFORMATION The **Twin Mountain–Bretton Woods Chamber of Commerce** (✆ **800/245-8946;** www.twinmountain.org) provides general information and lodging referrals from a booth near the intersection of Route 302 and Route 3. It's open from late May through mid-October.

HIKING

The Appalachian Mountain Club's **Highland Center at Crawford Notch** ★★ (✆ **603/278-4453**), on Route 302 in Bretton Woods, is a newish (2003) multipurpose facility on 26 acres of AMC-owned land. It's a great headquarters for hikes into the surrounding mountains. Under one roof, you can book a tour, hike the path that passes nearby (two AMC huts are each a short hike away), bunk down for the night in the Highland Lodge, eat communal dinners, and use L.L.Bean gear for free (yes, really). It's open year-round.

From late spring through fall, the center is also the hub for two AMC-operated **hiker shuttles** (✆ **603/466-2727**). These vans cruise the mountains daily from June through mid-September, and then on weekends through mid-October, depositing and picking up hikers; they're useful, though pricey—but if you haven't brought a car, this is really your only option. Rides cost $18 one-way, regardless of length; AMC members get a $2 discount.

SKIING

Attitash ★★ This is one of New England's most scenic ski areas, and Attitash is also a good mountain for families and skiers at the intermediate-to-advanced level. The resort consists of 70 or so trails across two peaks: 1,750-foot Attitash and adjacent Bear Peak. Dotted with rugged rock outcroppings and full of sweeping views of Mount Washington and the Presidential Range (there's also an observation tower on the main summit), this is an eye-popping place—with excellent skiing. Look for great cruising runs and a handful of challenging drops. Snowboarders can hone their skills at the terrain park. You can stay right on the mountain in the 143-unit summit hotel. As with many of these New Hampshire ski hills, though, the base area is sleepy at night; if you're looking for a beer or some live music, pile into the car and drive about 15 minutes to North Conway, where you'll find both of those things.

Rte. 302 (P.O. Box 308), Bartlett, NH 03812. ✆ **877/677-7669** or 603/374-2600. www.attitash.com. Adults $62–$69 day lift tickets, $48–$55 half-day; discounts for seniors, students, and children.

Bretton Woods (Mount Washington Resort) ★★ Kids In terms of sheer acreage, Bretton Woods/Mount Washington is New England's biggest ski resort; it's also possibly the most family-friendly. And it's at the foot of Mount Washington. What else could you ask for? The resort continues to do an award-winning job taking care of kids—there are tons of programs for the little ones here, and *SKI* magazine annually ranks it among the nation's best family ski areas. The low-key attitude is a big part of that. Accommodations are available both on the mountain and nearby, notably at the grand, red-roofed Mount Washington Resort (see "Where to Stay & Dine," below), though nightlife here mostly consists of a hot tub in your room or catching the late news on TV. Trails feature plenty of glades and wide cruising runs, perfect for beginners and families, as well as a few more challenging options for advanced skiers—they're not up to the most radical slopes in Vermont and Maine, though. There's also night skiing; four freestyle (snowboard) terrain parks; and—for those so inclined—an excellent cross-country ski center nearby. A great New Hampshire experience.

Rte. 302, Bretton Woods, NH 03575. ✆ **800/314-1752** or 603/278-1000. www.brettonwoods.com. Adults $66–$74 day lift tickets ($10 discount for Mt. Washington Resort guests); $50–$56 half-day; discounts for teens, young children, and seniors.

WATERFALLS & SWIMMING HOLES

Much of the mountainous land flanking Route 302 falls under the jurisdiction of 5,700-acre **Crawford Notch State Park** ★★ (✆ **603/374-2272**), established in 1911 to preserve lands that had largely been decimated by aggressive logging. The headwaters of the Saco River form in this notch, and what's generally regarded as the first permanent trail up Mount Washington departs from here. Several turnouts and trail heads invite a more leisurely exploration of the area as well. The trail network on both sides of Crawford Notch is extensive; consult the *AMC White Mountain Guide* or the *White Mountains Map Book* for more details.

Up the mountain slopes that form this valley, hikers can spot a number of lovely waterfalls, some more easily accessible than others. **Arethusa Falls** ★★ has the highest drop of any waterfall in the state, and the trail to the falls passes several attractive smaller cascades en route. It's especially beautiful in spring or after a heavy rain, when the falls are at their fullest. You can enjoy a 2.6-mile round-trip to the falls and back via either the **Arethusa Falls Trail,** or a 4.5-mile loop that takes in views from Frankenstein Cliffs (named for a landscape painter, not the monster-making doctor). If you're coming from the south, look for signs to the trail parking area just after passing the state park entrance sign. From the north, the trail head is a half-mile south of the Dry River Campground (see "Where to Stay & Dine," below). At the parking lot, use the sign and map to get your bearings, then cross the railroad tracks and start up the trail to the falls.

Tips Take a Dip in the Saco

During the dog days of summer, the bends and falls of the Saco River—which runs through this notch and valley—produce several good swimming holes just off the highway. They're unmarked and invisible from the road, but you can still find them. Here's how: Look for clumps of cars parked over on the shoulder of the road for no apparent reason. The trail you find there will either lead up a local mountain trail or, just as often, down to an oasis. You know what to do: Lather. Rinse. Repeat.

For another waterfall experience, continue north on Route 302 to the trail head for tumultuous **Ripley Falls** ★. This easy hike is a little more than a mile round-trip; look for the sign to the trail on the highway, just north of the trail head for **Webster Cliff Trail.** (If you pass the **Willey House** site, p. 259, you've gone too far.) Park at the site of the Willey Station and follow signs for the **Ripley Falls Trail,** allowing about a half-hour to reach the cascades. The best swimming holes are at the top of the falls.

A HISTORIC RAILWAY

Mount Washington Cog Railway ★★ Mount Washington's Cog Railway was a marvel of engineering when it opened in 1869, and it remains so today. Part moving museum, part slow-motion roller-coaster ride, the Cog Railway steams to the mountain's summit at a determined, "I think I can" pace of about 4 mph. But you'll still get some adrenaline thrills, especially when the train crosses Jacob's Ladder, a rickety-seeming trestle 25 feet high that angles upward at a grade of more than (!) 37%. Holy smokin' transmission, Batman. Passengers enjoy the expanding views on the 3-hour round-trip, which includes important stops to add water to the steam engine, check the track switches, and allow other trains to ascend or descend. A 20-minute stop at the summit gives you a little time to poke around. Caveats: This ride is noisy, breezy, sulfurous, and a little sooty; *don't* wear white. Dress warmly in a jacket and sweater that you don't mind getting a little dirty and you'll be okay. There's now also a shorter, 1-hour ride, operating twice daily all winter, through the lovely, snow-covered vistas.

Base Rd., Bretton Woods. ✆ **800/922-8825** or 603/278-5404. www.thecog.com. Fare $59 adults, $54 seniors, $39 children 4–12, free for children 3 and under; winter fares lower. MC, V. Memorial Day to late Oct daily (and Sat–Sun in May) usually on the hour 9am to 3 or 4pm. (Check website or call for schedule.) Reservations recommended. From Rte. 302, turn onto Base Rd. at Fabyan's Station Restaurant and continue 6 miles to railway base station.

WHERE TO STAY & DINE

If the Mount Washington Resort (see below) is full, there are two more adjacent properties owned by the same group offering affordable lodgings and comparable views: the **Bretton Arms Inn** (a simple, 34-room inn right next door to the big main hotel) and the more modern, almost motel-like **The Lodge** ★ (right across the highway). I prefer the Lodge, which has a nice rustic feel and balconies with better views. Call the resort's reservation line at ✆ **800/314-1752** or 603/278-1000 to book either property.

In addition to the choices below, the **Dry River Campground** (✆ **603/374-2272**) inside Crawford Notch State Park offers three dozen campsites in the notch for $18 to $25 per night.

Mount Washington Resort ★★ (Kids) At the foot of New Hampshire's highest peak, this five-story resort, with gleaming white clapboards and a cherry-red roof, almost looks like a Bavarian castle appearing out of the mist. Built in 1902, it once drew luminaries like Babe Ruth, Thomas Edison, and Woodrow Wilson. I love the 900-foot-long back porch, which looks directly up at the massive mountain and down onto the resort's golf course, pool, and tennis court. Guest rooms vary in size and decor, but many have grand views. Meals are taken in an impressive, lost-in-time octagonal dining room while an orchestra plays. There are lots of family and kids' programs and activities (such as fly-casting lessons), and new management (it's now owned by the Omni chain) is making overdue improvements. Though the hotel can still feel a bit unfinished at times, it remains a classic New England resort in an unbeatable setting—and service is improving with the management change.

Rte. 302, Bretton Woods, NH 03575. ✆ **800/314-1752** or 603/278-1000. www.mtwashington.com. 200 units. $145–$525 double; $910–$1,750 suite. Rates include breakfast and dinner. Minimum stay during holidays. AE, DISC, MC, V. **Amenities:** 2 restaurants; babysitting; bikes; children's programs (summer); concierge; 2 golf courses; Jacuzzi; 2 pools (1 indoor, 1 outdoor); room service; sauna. *In room:* TV, Wi-Fi (free).

Notchland Inn ★★ Off Route 302 on a wild section of Crawford Notch, this inn looks like a bit spooky at first glance, like that hotel in *The Shining.* Fear not; built of hand-cut granite in the mid-1800s, the Notchland is classy yet informal, perfectly situated for exploring the surrounding mountains. The front parlor was designed by Gustav Stickley, a founder of the Arts & Crafts movement, in a suitably wood-heavy style; check out the unique fireplace. Guest rooms are big and beautiful, outfitted with antiques, wood-burning fireplaces (all units), high ceilings, and thermostats. Most of the five suites have Jacuzzis and/or private decks; two are located in an adjacent former schoolhouse (the one upstairs has a wonderful soaking tub), and there are two newish cottages with modern touches like kitchens or wet bars. The optional five-course dinner is probably worth signing on for—any other food is a long, dark drive away. (Nonguests can dine here, as well.) And the foliage here is amazing in fall. But you'll pay for the location and experience: This is one of the pricier choices in the Whites. Note that the innkeepers own two dogs, who peaceably roam the property.

2 Morey Rd. (just off Rte. 302), Hart's Location, NH 03812. ✆ **800/866-6131** or 603/374-6131. www.notchland.com. 15 units. $195–$228 double; $280–$380 cottage and suite. Rates include full breakfast. 2- to 3-night minimum stay Sat–Sun, foliage season, and some holidays. AE, DISC, MC, V. Children 12 and over welcome. **Amenities:** Dining room; babysitting; Jacuzzi. *In room:* A/C (some units), CD, hair dryer, kitchenette (some units), no phone, Wi-Fi (free).

5 WATERVILLE VALLEY ★

Waterville Valley: 60 miles N of Concord; 95 miles NW of Portsmouth; 125 miles N of Boston

In the southwestern corner of the White Mountains is **Waterville Valley,** which occupies a lovely, remote valley at the head of a 12-mile dead-end road. Incorporated as a town in 1829, Waterville Valley became a popular destination for summer visitors during the spurt of mountain tourism that hit these mountains in the late 19th century. Skiers first started descending the slopes here in the 1930s when New Deal workers and local ski clubs carved a few trails out of the forest, but it wasn't until 1965—when a skier named Tom Corcoran bought up 425 acres in the valley—that Waterville Valley became a true "resort."

Few traces of the village's original history remain, and Waterville Valley today looks somewhat manufactured and out-of-place here in northern New England: a bit like what Disney might do, given a run at the Whites, perhaps. The "village" is reasonably compact, though you need to drive or take a shuttle to the ski slopes. Modern lodges, condos, and a handful of restaurants are all situated within a loop road. In the center is a "Town Square," a smallish mall-like complex with a restaurant and a few shops.

This is a reasonable choice for a luxurious, weeklong family vacation—the resort has plenty of planned activities for kids—but anyone in search of the "real" New England might want to skip this village in favor of the others described in this chapter.

ESSENTIALS

GETTING THERE Waterville Valley is located about 12 miles from I-93. Take exit 28 or exit 29 from the interstate, then follow Route 49 north and west to the resort.

VISITOR INFORMATION The **Waterville Valley Region Chamber of Commerce** (✆ **800/237-2307** or 603/726-3804; www.watervillevalleyregion.com) staffs an information booth on Route 49 in Campton, right off the exit ramp at exit 28 of I-93. Amazingly, it's open daily year-round, 9am to 5pm.

SKIING

Waterville Valley ★ Waterville Valley's local ski hill is your classic intermediate resort: The mountain's trails are kept uniformly wide and well groomed, and the whole place is compact enough that no one will get lost or confused and end up hurtling down a double-diamond trail by mistake. It's a good place to learn to ski or brush up on your skills, but the selection and steepness don't rival those of larger ski mountains to the north or in Vermont. A terrain park above the base lodge is popular with both advanced and beginning snowboarders, however.

1 Ski Area Rd. (P.O. Box 540), Waterville Valley, NH 03215. ✆ **800/468-2553** or 603/236-8311. www.waterville.com. Adults $67 day lift tickets, $57 half-day; discounts for 2nd day of skiing, students, children, and seniors.

WHERE TO STAY

The Waterville Valley resort maintains hundreds of condominium units in the valley—and these are actually your best choice when in the area, as the various inns and lodges are mostly aging.

The modern **Town Square Condominiums** ★★ (✆ **888/462-9887**) are an especially good choice: three-bedroom, two-bathroom units that sleep up to eight travelers each. Every unit is equipped with a full kitchen, several televisions, and a DVD player; some have Wi-Fi access, too (ask when booking). One-bedroom condos are harder to scare up but sometimes become available midweek. A rental here gives you access to a free shuttle bus, 1 hour daily of ice skating on the resort's indoor rink, a full card of recreation programs, and access to a health club.

Call the resort's dedicated lodging hotline at ✆ **800/468-2553** to get a fuller sense of the range of other condo choices and prices.

Golden Eagle Lodge ★ This dominating, contemporary-looking condominium project is centrally located in the village. From the outside, the shingle-and-stone edifice looks like one more of those grand mountain resorts from the 19th century. Inside, it's regal in a cartoon-Tudor kind of way: lots of stained wood, columns, and tall windows. Condo-like rooms accommodate two to six people in each of the one- or two-bedroom units, which have kitchens and basic cookware (handy, given the dearth of available eateries around here during crowded times). Despite the grandiose exterior, though, the furnishings and construction are rather basic and average, and are showing their age. Acceptable for families; romantic travelers might want to look elsewhere.

28 Packard's Rd., Waterville Valley, NH 03215. ✆ **888/703-2453.** Fax 603/236-4947. www.goldeneaglelodge.com. 118 units. Summer $103–$198 double; winter $103–$281 double; spring $88–$158 double; holiday rates higher. Minimum stay some holidays. AE, DC, DISC, MC, V. **Amenities:** Bikes; Jacuzzi; 2 pools (1 indoor, 1 outdoor). *In room:* TV, kitchenette, Wi-Fi ($9.95 per day).

WHERE TO DINE

The good news is that many of Waterville Valley's accommodations include kitchens, so you can prepare your own meals. The bad news? If you actually want to go out, the village offers a fairly limited choice of restaurants.

The White Mountain Athletic Club facility has its own restaurant, the **Wild Coyote Grill** ★ (✆ **603/236-4919;** www.wildcoyotegrill.com), located on the second floor, and it's actually one of the best places to sup in town. The kitchen serves a curious amalgam of hearty New England resort favorites (grilled venison, strip steaks, lobster, shrimp) and healthful fare: tofu-sweet potato ragout, curries, hibachi-cooked chicken, buffalo meatloaf, spring rolls, pear tarts, roasted-beet salads, and the like.

More basic pub fare can be enjoyed seasonally (as in, ski-seasonally) at the **Mad River Tavern** (✆ **603/726-4290;** www.madtav.com), just off exit 28 of I-93 in Campton. And high up on the summit, at altitude 4,000 feet, the resort runs a little mountain hut called **Schwendi Hutte,** serving beer and Swiss fondues (but also Starbucks coffee; sign o' the times).

A quick takeout Mexican joint, **The Flying Burrito Bros.** (✆ **603/236-8226;** apologies to Gram Parsons), is in the faux-old Olde Town Marketplace. However, it's open only on summer weekends.

6 LINCOLN, NORTH WOODSTOCK & LOON MOUNTAIN ★

Lincoln: 65 miles N of Concord; 100 miles NW of Portsmouth; 130 miles N of Boston

About 25 miles north of Waterville Valley are the twinned towns of **Lincoln** and **North Woodstock,** plus the nearby **Loon Mountain** ski resort (just east of Lincoln). These towns are all at the beginning (or end) of the **Kancamagus Highway,** a 35-mile highway from hell—er, make that one of the White Mountains' most scenic drives, except during peak fall foliage, when it becomes the former.

In Lincoln and North Woodstock, you'll find hardware shops, fast-food restaurants, and no-frills motels. Lincoln has embraced strip-mall development. North Woodstock has retained a bit of charm in its tiny village center. Neither will win awards for quaintness, though. Loon Mountain opened in 1966 and was criticized early on for its mediocre skiing, though some improvements since have brought the mountain a little more respect.

Clusters of condos blanket the lower hillsides of this narrow valley. Loon Mountain's base village is lively with skiers in winter, but in summer it has a ghost-town feel. There are a *few* charms here—local diners and cottages (slightly cheesy), attractions for kids, and that great highway drive. But, as is true of Waterville Valley, other towns in the White Mountains are more distinct and interesting than these three. If nothing in this section catches your eye, you're probably better off pressing onward to **Bretton Woods, Bethlehem,** "the Kanc" (see "The Kancamagus Highway," below), or even (gasp) the **Conways.**

ESSENTIALS

GETTING THERE By car, Lincoln is accessible from I-93 via exits 32 and 33. **Concord Coach** (✆ **800/639-3317** or 603/228-3300; www.concordcoachlines.com) also runs two daily buses from Boston's South Station and Logan Airport to **Lincoln** ($27–$32 one-way), about a 3-hour ride.

VISITOR INFORMATION The best, most comprehensive information source in the mountains is the **White Mountains Visitor Center** (✆ **800/346-3687** or 603/745-8720; www.visitwhitemountains.com) in North Woodstock, just east of I-93 at exit 32. It's stocked with tons of information and open year-round daily from 8:30am to 5pm, with later closing hours in summer. The **Lincoln-Woodstock Chamber of Commerce** (✆ **603/745-6621;** www.lincolnwoodstock.com) also has an information office in Depot Plaza on Route 112 in Lincoln, near the start of the Kancamagus Highway.

THE KANCAMAGUS HIGHWAY ★★★

The **Kancamagus Highway**—sometimes called "the Kanc" by locals—is among the White Mountains' most spectacular drives. Officially designated a National Scenic Byway by the U.S. Forest Service, this 35-mile roadway joins **Lincoln** and **Conway** through the 2,860-foot Kancamagus Pass. When this highway was built in the early 1960s, it opened up 100 square miles of wilderness, irking some wilderness advocates but quickly becoming popular among the majority of sightseers, who tour by car rather than shoe leather.

The two-lane route begins and ends along wide, tumbling rivers on fairly flat plateaus, but rises steadily to the pass; along the way, several rest areas allow visitors to pause and enjoy sweeping mountain views. This highway also makes a good destination for hikers, since a number of day and overnight trips can be launched right from the roadside. One simple, short hike along a gravel path (less than .3 mile each way) leads to **Sabbaday Falls** ★★, a cascade that's especially impressive after a downpour. A half-dozen national-forest campgrounds are also located along the highway.

To get the most out of the Kanc, take your time and make frequent stops. Think of it as a scavenger hunt—look for the covered bridge, cascades with good swimming holes, the historic home with the quirky story behind it, and spectacular mountain panoramas. All these things, and more, lie along the route.

HIKING

One level trail that's inviting for hikers of any level of fitness is the **Wilderness Trail,** along the East Branch of the Pemigewasset River. Head east on Route 112 (the Kancamagus Hwy.) from I-93 for 5 miles, then watch for the parking lot on the left just past the bridge. Both sides of the river are open to the public. The trail on the west side runs a little more than 3 miles to beautiful, remote Black Pond, while an abandoned railroad bed on the east side makes for smooth mountain biking.

Tips Kanc'ed-Out? More Driving Options

The *Kanc* is the most scenic drive in northern New Hampshire, but it's not the only one. In fact, other drives might suit you better if you're allergic to crowds. Try these options: **Route 302** through **Crawford Notch** and on to the little towns of **Bethlehem** and **Littleton; Route 16** north of **North Conway,** as it twists up through dramatic **Pinkham Notch** at the base of Mount Washington; fast **Route 2,** skirting the northern edge of these mountain ranges and offering wonderful views en route to the town of **Jefferson;** and **Route 25** through the mountains' southern foothills to Lake Winnipesaukee. Finally, **I-93** shoots right through the heart of spectacular **Franconia Notch** (p. 269), narrowing to just two lanes (one each way) out of deference to its vertical surroundings.

SKIING

Loon Mountain ★★ Situated on U.S. Forest Service land, Loon was long stymied in its expansion efforts by environmental concerns regarding land use and water withdrawals from the local river. The resort has been slowly reshaped over time, adding uphill capacity, glade skiing, improved snowmaking, and snowboarding areas. Its expansion has reduced some of the congestion of this popular area, but it's still somewhat crowded on busy winter weekends. Most of the trails cluster toward the bottom of the hill, and most are solid intermediate runs. Experts head for the north peak, with a challenging selection of advanced trails served by a triple chairlift; new in 2008 was the hill's first double-diamond run. The resort also added a snow-tubing park for kids (use the chairlift beside the Octagon Lodge), and the snow terrain parks for snowboarders include a few "secret" areas improvised by staff in random locations each winter—they must be happened upon to be enjoyed. Strides are being made here.

Rte. 112, Lincoln, NH 03251. ✆ **800/229-LOON** (5666) or 603/745-8111. www.loonmtn.com. Adults $73 day lift tickets, $63 half-day; discounts for 2nd day, seniors, and youths.

WHERE TO STAY

In addition to the choices listed below, the town of **Lincoln** offers a range of reasonably priced motels, cottages, and campgrounds that appeal to budget travelers.

Mountain Club on Loon ★ Right at the foot of Loon Mountain's slopes, the Mountain Club is a contemporary resort of prominent gables and glass, built during the real-estate boom of the 1980s. Managed for several years as a Marriott, the inoffensive decor reflects its chain-hotel heritage. Guest rooms are designed to be rented individually or as two-room suites; suites all have full kitchens, two bathrooms, king-size master bedrooms, and living and dining areas, some with almost cathedral-height ceilings. Those units are best, obviously, but also quite expensive. Other units are smaller. Guests receive membership in the Viaggio spa and health-club facilities, connected to the hotel via a covered walkway. The somewhat expensive rates here reflect the proximity to the slopes.

90 Loon Mountain Rd. (Rte. 112), Lincoln, NH 03251. ✆ **800/229-7829.** www.mtnclub.com. 351 units. $89–$264 double; $173–$309 suite. Resort fee of up to 25% not included in rates. AE, DISC, MC, V. **Amenities:** Restaurant; bar; concierge; health club; Jacuzzi; 2 pools (1 indoor, 1 outdoor); limited room service; sauna; spa; 2 tennis courts. *In room:* A/C, TV, kitchenette (some units), fridge (some units), hair dryer, Wi-Fi (free).

Wilderness Inn ★★ (Kids) The Wilderness Inn is at the southern edge of North Woodstock village—not quite the wilderness the name suggests. Still, it's a fun, friendly, handsome, bungalow-style home dating to 1912, and its interior sports heavy timbers in classic craftsman style, plus a spare mix of antiques and reproductions. In a common room, there are games to occupy your evening, and the front porch is also a fine place to hang out. As for the rooms, many are as country-simple and retro as your grandmother's spare bedroom, but some suites add poster beds, frilly linens, and, in some cases, a fireplace or Jacuzzi. The cottage outside the main inn is the best unit, with its sunnier decor, bright art, gas fireplace, and whirlpool tub. Breakfast is good, with kid-friendly pancakes plus crepes, eggs, French toast, and such. The innkeepers seem amicable and responsive. This is a good "sleeper" pick for families traveling through.

57 Rte. 3 (just south of Rte. 112), North Woodstock, NH 03262. ✆ **888/777-7813** or 603/745-3890. www.thewildernessinn.com. 8 units. $65–$165 double; $90–$175 suite and cottage. Rates include full breakfast. DISC, MC, V. *In room:* A/C, TV, no phone, Wi-Fi (free).

Woodstock Inn ★★ Finds The Woodstock Inn has a Jekyll-and-Hyde thing going on. In front it's a white Victorian on the main commercial strip—one of the few older inns in a forest of condos and modern resorts. Out back it sports a modern brewpub (in the former village train station) serving up hearty fare and ales to appreciative locals (see "Where to Dine," below). The guest rooms are spread out among the main inn and four other houses nearby; all units are individually decorated in a country Victorian style and furnished with both reproductions and antiques. Some rooms are pretty simple—two in the Deachman House even share a third-floor bathroom. But others, including all nine in the Cascade Lodge (where all the beds are constructed from knotty logs and tree trunks) and all three in the low-slung Sawyer House, have some form of a Jacuzzi. This property has expanded and upgraded in recent years, a welcome change in a town better known for its budget motels and snowmobile conventions than its luxury digs.

135 Main St. (Rte. 3), North Woodstock, NH 03262. ✆ **800/321-3985** or 603/745-3951. www.woodstockinnnh.com. 33 units, including 2 with shared bathroom and 2 with private hallway bathroom. $84–$224 double. Foliage-season rates higher. Rates include breakfast. AE, DISC, MC, V. **Amenities:** 2 restaurants; pub. *In room:* A/C, TV, fridge (some units), hair dryer, Wi-Fi (free).

WHERE TO DINE

Clement Room Grille/Woodstock Station ★ AMERICAN/PUB FARE At the Woodstock Inn, you can dine in the casually upscale Clement Room, on the inn's enclosed porch, or in the brewpub out back, housed in an old train station. The Clement Room has an open grill and fare that tries for originality—one house special combines double-layered steak filets with asparagus, crab meat, and hollandaise, for instance. (How many calories is *that?* Ah, never mind.) The pub has high ceilings and knotty pine, and

Finds All Aboard! For Dinner, That Is

Fancy dining is so scarce around here that the best meal isn't even served in a restaurant—it's on a train. The **Café Lafayette** ★★ (✆ **800/699-3501** or 603/745-3500; www.cafelafayette.com) operates within three restored Pullman rail cars that chug along a scenic tour through the western White Mountains while diners enjoy a multicourse meal served on white tablecloths. The evening ride lasts a little more than 2 hours, and includes homemade dinner rolls or potatoes, vegetables or salad, an entree, and dessert. (Wine and cocktails are available at an extra cost.) Meals are prepared on board, and the main courses run to solidly New American or Continental fare such as Chicken Cordon Bleu or pork tenderloin medallions in a pinot noir sauce.

The train runs 2 to 4 days per week from mid-May through the end of October. In summer boarding begins at 5:15pm on Tuesday, Thursday, and Saturday, and around 4:30pm on Sunday; check the train's website for spring and fall schedules and departure times. The station is located on Route 112 in **North Woodstock,** just on the west side of I-93 (take exit 32 coming from the north, exit 33 coming from the south; the depot is almost under the interstate). Reservations are recommended, though not essential. Tickets for the ride plus dinner cost from $73 to $83 per adult, and from $53 to $63 per child ages 6 to 11; the price depends on whether you want to dine in the Dome Car or on the regular level.

is decorated with vintage winter recreational gear—which I like. The menu takes in all the usual pub suspects: nachos, chicken wings, burgers, and pasta. Better than those are the house-brewed porters, stouts, and brown and red ales.

Main St. ✆ **603/745-3951.** Reservations recommended for Clement Room only. Main courses $9–$25. AE, DISC, MC, V. Clement Room Grille peak season daily 5:30–9:30pm. Woodstock Station peak season daily 11:30am–10pm; off season call ahead for hours at both restaurants.

7 FRANCONIA NOTCH ★★

Franconia: 80 miles N of Concord; 115 miles NW of Portsmouth; 145 miles N of Boston

Franconia Notch *is* New Hampshire. As travelers drive north on I-93, the Kinsman Range to the west and the Franconia Range to the east begin converging, and the two mountain ranges press inward on either side like a closing book, forming "the Notch." This narrow defile offers little in the way of civilization or services, but a whole lot of natural drama. Plan on a leisurely ride through the notch, allowing extra time to get out of your car and explore the local forests, peaks, and eateries. Too bad the Old Man of the Mountain isn't here anymore (see "The Old Man of the Mountain: Gone, but Not Forgotten," below)—then this drive would rank even higher on my must-do list of places in northern New England.

Interestingly, the area around the notch is just as developed for recreation—or more so—as equally rugged and much more famous Crawford Notch to the northeast (see section 4, earlier in this chapter). Outdoorsy types may enjoy it here more, as a result. Warning: You won't be alone. Day-trippers *have* discovered this place.

ESSENTIALS

GETTING THERE I-93 runs right through the Notch, narrowing from four lanes to two (and becoming the Franconia Notch Pkwy.) in its most scenic parts. Several scenic roadside pulloffs dot the route. The notch is about 2¼ hours by car from Boston via I-93, or about 5½ hours from New York City via I-84 and I-93.

Concord Coach (✆ **800/639-3317** or 603/228-3300; www.concordcoachlines.com) runs two daily buses from Boston, a 3½-hour trip that costs about $30 each way. There is no ticket office in Franconia; wait at Mac's Market, right off I-93 at exit 38.

VISITOR INFORMATION Information on the park and surrounding area is available at the **Flume Gorge & Gilman Visitor Center** (✆ **603/745-8391**), in the notch at exit 34A of I-93.

North of the notch, the **Franconia Notch Chamber of Commerce** (✆ **603/823-5661** in summer or 603/823-3450 in winter; www.franconianotch.org) maintains a helpful little hut of visitor information on Main Street next to the town hall, open spring through fall.

EXPLORING FRANCONIA NOTCH STATE PARK ★★

Franconia Notch State Park's (✆ **603/745-8391**) 8,000 acres, nestled within the much bigger White Mountain National Forest, host an array of scenic attractions easily accessible from I-93 and the Franconia Notch Parkway.

The Flume ★★ is a rugged 800-foot gorge through which the Flume Brook tumbles. A popular attraction as far back as the mid–19th century, it's 800 feet long, 90 feet deep, and as narrow as 20 feet at the bottom; visitors explore it by using a series of boardwalks and bridges on a 2-mile-long walk. If you're looking for an easy, quick hit of nature with the kids, this is worth the money. (But if you'll be in town for awhile, set off on one of the local hiking trails instead and seek your own sights without the crowds or cost.) The flume is open daily 9am to 5pm from early May through mid-October, weather permitting—it stays open a half-hour later in July and August. Admission costs $13 for adults, $9 for children ages 6 to 12, and is free for younger children. You can walk or snowshoe the grounds for free in the off season.

Echo Lake ★★ is a picturesquely situated recreation area with a 28-acre lake, handsome swimming beach (with lifeguards), and picnic tables scattered about—all within view of the peaks of Cannon Mountain and Mount Lafayette. It's a great place to bring the kids, even if no pets are allowed; and Lance Armstrong wannabes will appreciate the 8-mile bike path that runs alongside the lake and meanders up and down the notch. The beach is open daily from mid-June through early September 10:30am to 5:30pm—admission costs $4 per adult, $2 for children age 6 to 11, and is free for younger kids. Inexpensive canoe and kayak rentals are also available at the beach (last rental at 4:30pm); to find the lake, take exit 34C off I-93.

For a high-altitude view of the region, set off for the alpine ridges on the **Cannon Mountain Aerial Tramway** ★★ (✆ **603/823-8800**). This old-fashioned cable car serves the ski hill (see "Skiing," below) in winter; in summer it whisks up to 80 travelers at a time to the summit of the 4,180-foot mountain. Once up top, you can strike out on foot along the Rim Trail for superb views. Be prepared for cool, gusty winds, though. The tramway usually operates from mid-May through mid-October, and costs $13 round-trip for adults, $10 for children ages 6 to 12.

Fun Facts — The Old Man of the Mountain: Gone, but Not Forgotten

If you haven't been back to the Notch for a long while, you might notice something seriously different in the way it looks: The famous **Old Man of the Mountain** stone face, hanging high above Franconia Notch's **Profile Lake** and held there by chains, came suddenly crumbling apart in 2003 after a spring snowstorm and could not be restored. Local son Daniel Webster once famously wrote of the visage: "Men hang out their signs indicative of their respective trades; shoe makers hang out a gigantic shoe; jewelers a monster watch, and the dentist hangs out a gold tooth; but up in the Mountains of New Hampshire, God Almighty has hung out a sign to show that there He makes men."

Good stuff. This was almost certainly the state's most beloved natural attraction, and its collapse was a near-physically painful event for lots of Granite Staters. Don't expect to see the Old Man's vaguely Native American (or maybe vaguely Abe Lincoln-esque) face staring down the notch ever again, but he will live on in the official state emblem (seen on police cars, state offices, and highway route signs) as well as on postcards, calendars, and stamps. And of course, in the memories of longtime New Englanders.

HIKING

The Franconia Notch region is one of the most varied regions for White Mountain hikers to find a good track. It's easy to plan hikes ranging from gentle valley walks to arduous ascents of blustery granite peaks. Consult the *AMC White Mountain Guide* for a comprehensive directory of area hiking trails, or ask for suggestions at the information center.

Among my recommendations: A pleasant woodland detour of 2 hours or so can be found at the **Basin-Cascades Trail** ★★ (look for well-marked signs off I-93 about 1½ miles north of the Flume gorge). A popular roadside waterfall and natural pothole, the Basin attracts crowds who come to see pillows of granite scoured smooth by glaciers and water. But relatively few visitors continue to the series of cascades beyond. Look for signs to the trail, then head off into the woods. After about .5-mile of easy hiking, you'll reach **Kinsman Falls** ★★, a beautiful 20-foot cascade. Continue another .5-mile farther along to **Rocky Glen,** where the stream plummets through a craggy gorge.

For a more demanding hike, set off for **Mount Lafayette** ★, with its spectacular views of the western White Mountains. *Hikers should be experienced, well equipped, and in good condition* before attempting this route. Allow 6 to 7 hours to complete the tough hike. Another popular and fairly straightforward ascent begins up the **Old Bridle Trail,** which departs from the Lafayette Place's parking area off the parkway. The trail climbs steadily to the AMC's **Greenleaf Hut** (about 3 miles), with ever-expanding views along the way. From here, continue to the summit of Lafayette on the **Greenleaf Trail.** It's a little more than a mile to the top, but this stretch covers rocky terrain and can be quite difficult, especially if the weather turns on you.

When in doubt about conditions, ask other hikers or the AMC staff at **Greenleaf Hut;** there's no shame in turning back shy of the top.

SKIING

Cannon Mountain ★★ During downhill skiing's formative years, this state-run ski area was *the* place to ski in the East. One of New England's very first ski mountains, Cannon remains famed for its challenging runs and exposed faces, and the mountain still attracts skiers who are serious about getting down the hill in style. (The scenery is knockout-gorgeous, too—ranked second-best in the eastern U.S. by *SKI* magazine.) Many of the old-fashioned New England–style trails here are narrow and fun (but sometimes icy, because they're constantly scoured by the notch's winds), and the enclosed tramway is an elegant way to get to the summit. With no base-lodge scene to speak of, though, skiers must retire to inns in Franconia or Sugar Hill, or else retreat southward to the condo country that is Lincoln. Then there's this: Lift-ticket prices have shot up in the past 2 years, right in the middle of a global recession, to match those of other fancier resorts. (This had once been a great-value lift ticket.) What's that all about—state budget crisis, perhaps? Only time will tell.

Franconia Notch Pkwy., Franconia, NH 03580. ✆ **603/823-8800** or 603/823-7771. www.cannonmt.com. Adults $66 day lift tickets, $44 half-day; discounts for seniors, teens, and youths.

LITERARY HISTORY

The Frost Place ★★ Robert Frost lived in New Hampshire from the time he was 10 until he was 45. The Frost Place is a smallish, humble farmhouse where the poet once came with his family to escape the ravages of hay fever; it's one of several northern New England abodes he inhabited during his career. (Homes in Arlington, Vermont, and

Derry, New Hampshire, are also covered in this book, in chapters 5 and 7, respectively.) Today his former farmhouse is a quietly respectful tribute in the form of an arts center and gathering place for local writers. Walking the grounds, it's not hard to see how his granite-edged poetry evolved here at the fringes of the White Mountains. First editions of Frost's works are on display; a nature trail in the woods nearby is posted with excerpts from some of his poems. In early July every year, there's a **Frost Day** celebration with readings from resident poets and lectures. Pay the suggested donation; this is a special place.

Ridge Rd. (P.O. Box 74), Franconia. ✆ **603/823-5510.** www.frostplace.org. Admission free; suggested donation $5 adults, $4 seniors, $3 students 6–18. Late May to June Sat–Sun 1–5pm; July to early Oct Wed–Mon 1–5pm. Closed mid-Oct to mid-May. From Franconia, travel south 1 mile on Rte. 116 to Ridge Rd. (a gravel road); turn and follow signs a short way to the house, parking in lot below the house.

WHERE TO STAY

Franconia Inn ★ This inn is set on a quiet road in a bucolic valley about 2 miles from the village of Franconia. Built in 1934 after a fire destroyed the previous 1886 structure, the inn has an informal feel, with wingback chairs around a fireplace in one common room, and puzzles and books in a paneled library. Guest rooms are appointed in a relaxed country fashion; a few have gas fireplaces, a few have Jacuzzis. The inn is a haven for cross-country skiers—about 40 miles of groomed trails begin right outside the front door—and walkers will enjoy exploring the hundred-plus acres of grounds, as well. Other activities include horseback and glider rides, badminton, tennis, and croquet. **Breakfast ★★** is delicious, with plenty of gourmet choices available; it's served in a pretty, French-doored breakfast room.

1172 Easton Rd., Franconia, NH 03580. ✆ **800/473-5299** or 603/823-5542. www.franconiainn.com. 34 units. $115–$241 double and suite. Rates usually include breakfast. MAP rates also available. 3-night minimum stay on holiday weekends. AE, MC, V. Closed Apr to mid-May. **Amenities:** Restaurant; bar; bikes; Jacuzzi; heated outdoor pool; sauna; 4 clay tennis courts; Wi-Fi (in public areas; free). *In room:* No phone.

Sugar Hill Inn ★★★ This classic New England inn, with wraparound porch and sweeping mountain panoramas occupying 16 acres on lovely Sugar Hill, is as welcoming and comfortable a spot as you'll find in the Whites. A new owner purchased the inn in 2006, and so far he has improved the property substantially with central air-conditioning; an in-ground pool, the inn's first; a cottage; and a raft of new luxurious rooms. Rooms are graciously appointed in country style (poster beds, printed wallpapers, antique furniture); many also have gas Vermont Castings stoves for heat and atmosphere, and some of the suites and cottage units have double Jacuzzis. The **dining room ★★**, one of the area's best, serves upscale eclectic dinners in a cozy, fire-lit-tavern setting (see "Where to Dine," below). There's even a simple 9-hole golf course (unaffiliated with the inn) with a knockout view of the mountains literally right across the road. This was a good place before; now it's becoming a great one.

116 Rte. 117, Sugar Hill, NH 03586. ✆ **800/548-4748** or 603/823-5621. www.sugarhillinn.com. 12 units. $125–$265 double; $210–$410 suite and cottage. Rates include full breakfast. 2- to 3-night minimum stay in foliage season and holiday weekends. AE, MC, V. Closed Apr. Children 12 and over welcome. **Amenities:** Restaurant; outdoor pool; spa. *In room:* A/C (most units), hair dryer, no phone, Wi-Fi (in main inn; free).

WHERE TO DINE

In addition to the fun, cost-conscious eatery listed below, the two inns described above each serve gourmet dinners in dining rooms to their own guests and the general public. Both kitchens are very good to excellent.

The **Sugar Hill Inn's** dining room ★★ is a point of pride for the inn's latest owner, who himself received culinary training at the prestigious French Culinary Institute in New York (though he employs an executive chef). The four-course, prix-fixe (about $50 per person) dinners run to entrees such as maple-cured grilled pork, breast of duck, crispy sockeye salmon, and beef tenderloin. Salads and desserts are excellent as well.

The **Franconia Inn**'s candlelit dining room ★ serves classically resort-appropriate meals of crab, lamb, salmon, lobster bisque, and the like.

Polly's Pancake Parlor BREAKFAST/LIGHT FARE ★★ (Value) (Kids) This family-style eatery, in a shaggy wood-sided building dating from around 1830 a few miles uphill from the little village of Sugar Hill, is one of my favorite breakfast stops in New England (or anywhere). And the folks at the James Beard Foundation apparently agree: They awarded the pancake house a medal in 2006! Besides possessing possibly the best views of any pancake shop in the Western world, the restaurant serves a wonderful assortment of pancakes (order a combo of three; I like the chocolate chip and cornmeal versions). Of course, all are served with real New Hampshire maple syrup and maple sugar from the "sugar farm" on which Polly's sits. Kids love this place, and there's also a good gift shop for adults that doubles as a display for antique farm implements. They also serve sandwiches and salads (which is not why you're here), plus maple-inflected desserts (which *is*). Breakfast and American-road-food aficionados shouldn't miss it. It's open only from spring through foliage season, but you can mail-order the syrup by phone year-round.

672 Rte. 117, Sugar Hill, NH 03586. ✆ **800/432-8972** or 603/823-5575. www.pollyspancakeparlor.com. Most items $4–$10. May to late Oct Mon–Fri 7am–2pm; Sat–Sun 7am–3pm.

8 BETHLEHEM ★★

85 miles N of Concord; 115 miles NW of Portsmouth; 150 miles N of Boston

More than a century ago, **Bethlehem** was as populous as **North Conway** to the south, a place of numerous resort hotels, summer retreats, and even its own semi-professional baseball team. (I'm not kidding; Joseph Kennedy, patriarch of the Kennedy clan, once played for the team, you can look it up.) Bethlehem subsequently lost the race for the riches—or won, depending on your view of outlet shopping—and today it's once again just a sleepy town of lovely homes high on a hillside that's occasionally "discovered" by city folks passing through the area. It still feels refreshingly lost in time, and sometimes that's a good thing.

ESSENTIALS

GETTING THERE Bethlehem is about 3 miles east of **Littleton,** on Route 302. Get off I-93 at exit 40 and head east. Coming from the east, you also take Route 302—the town is about 15 miles past the resort at **Bretton Woods.**

VISITOR INFORMATION The **Bethlehem Chamber of Commerce** (✆ **888/845-1957;** www.bethlehemwhitemtns.com) has an information booth on Main Street across from town hall. It's open daily 10am to 4pm during the summer, weekends only during the rest of the year.

EXPLORING BETHLEHEM

Bethlehem consists of a Main Street, plus a small handful of side streets; it becomes more appealing as you get farther away from the I-93 end of town. Several antiques stores are clustered in what passes for a village center. For a better understanding of the town's history—which once was home to almost 40 resort hotels, though there's almost no evidence of them today—pick up a copy of *An Illustrated Tour of Bethlehem, Past and Present,* available at local shops. The informative guide brings to life many of the graceful old homes and buildings here, as well as some that *aren't* here anymore.

Harking back to its more genteel era, Bethlehem still has two well-maintained 18-hole golf courses amid beautiful North Country scenery, right on its main street; how many towns can you say *that* about? Both the municipal **Bethlehem Country Club** ★ (✆ **603/869-5745;** www.bethlehemccnhgolf.com), designed by famed course architect Donald Ross, and the private **Maplewood Country Club** ★★ (✆ **603/869-3335;** www.maplewoodgolfresort.com)—also designed by Ross, with a stone clubhouse—are on Route 302.

West of Bethlehem on Route 302 is a gem known as **The Rocks** ★★ (✆ **603/444-6228;** www.therocks.org), a classic Victorian gentleman's farm that today is a conservation center operated by the Society for the Protection of New Hampshire Forests—and a working Christmas tree farm, to boot. The original 1883 estate on 1,200 acres includes a well-preserved shingled house, handsome barn, and hiking trails that meander through the meadows and woodlands. It's a peaceful spot, perfect for a picnic, and there's a great history guide to accompany your walk (also available online). Best of all, admission is *free,* and the property is open daily from dawn to dusk.

WHERE TO STAY & DINE

Adair Country Inn ★★ Formerly a historic home, Adair opened as an inn in 1992, yet it remains one of the White Mountains' better-kept secrets. The peaceful Georgian Revival home dates from 1927, set on 200 acres very near what is now the interstate exit ramp. But don't worry about that; you won't see it or notice it. Guest rooms (most named for peaks in the Presidential Range) are impeccably furnished in a mix of antiques and reproductions; deluxe rooms have fireplaces. The best and most expensive unit is the Kinsman Suite, with a sleigh bed, Jacuzzi the size of a small swimming pool, library, gas stove, and little balcony looking out to the Dalton Range. The service is hospitable and top-rate. Nice place, and it's getting even better after a change in ownership.

80 Guider Lane (off exit 40 on I-93), Bethlehem, NH 03574. ✆ **888/444-2600** or 603/444-2600. Fax 603/444-4823. www.adairinn.com. 9 units. $195–$345 double; $325–$375 suite. Rates include full breakfast. 2-night minimum stay weekends and foliage season. AE, DISC, MC, V. Children 12 and over welcome. **Amenities:** Restaurant; tennis court. *In room:* A/C, hair dryer, no phone, Wi-Fi (free).

Coastal Maine

Humor columnist Dave Barry once suggested that Maine's state motto should be changed to "Cold, but damp."

That's cute, but it's also sort of true. Spring tends to last just a few blustery days. November features bitter winds alternating with gray sheets of rain. And the winter brings a mix of blizzards and ice storms—and it sometimes lasts 6 months.

But summer and fall are the big payoff for your year-long patience. You can drink in a huge dose of tranquillity during these seasons in Maine, and it's almost like medicine to city-jangled nerves.

Summer in Maine brings the smell of salt air; osprey diving for fish off wooded points; puffy cumulus clouds and fog banks building over the sea; and the haunting whoop of loons. It brings long, lazy days when the sun rises over the beaches and the Atlantic Ocean very early, well before travelers do—by 8 o'clock in the morning, it already feels like noon. It brings a special, haze-tinted coastal light that can't be described (but has been painted by some wonderful artists down through history). And summer brings lobsters!

Autumn is every bit as nice: brilliant foliage against rippling, blue bay waters; tart apples ripening in the orchards; the wonderful smell of wood smoke.

The trick is finding the *right* spot in which to enjoy the coast. The main road along Maine's coast, Route 1, is for long stretches an amalgam of convenience stores, fast-food restaurants, and shops selling slightly tacky souvenirs. And traffic isn't restricted to Route 1, either: Even the most beautiful places on this coast—the loop road, beaches, and most popular mountain peaks in Acadia National Park, for instance—can get pretty crowded in summer. Arriving without a room reservation in high season is just a bad idea.

On the other hand, Maine's remote position and size *can* work to your advantage sometimes. This state has an amazing 5,500 miles of coastline, plus 3,000 or so coastal islands. With a little homework, you can find that perfect little cove or island, book a room in advance, and enjoy coastal Maine's extremely lovely scenery without battling traffic jams, lines, or rising blood pressures.

Getting to know the locals here is fun, too. Their ancestors were mostly fishermen (as opposed to the farmers who colonized the rest of New England) and other seafaring folk, and today coastal Mainers—even transplanted ones—still exhibit a wry sense of humor and gregariousness. Need proof? There's a Bait's Motel—complete with worm-hanging-off-a-hook-shaped sign—in Searsport; a tiny street called Fitz Hugh Lane in Somesville; and an oil company called Midnight Oil in Newcastle. Take the time to get to know these local folks. You'll be glad you did.

For even more detailed coverage of this gorgeous coastline, pick up my other two books on the region, *Frommer's Maine Coast* and *Frommer's Maine Coast: Day by Day,* to supplement your travels. They're great resources for enjoying this region in even greater detail.

1 ENJOYING THE GREAT OUTDOORS

No New England state offers as much outdoor recreational diversity as Maine. Bring your mountain bike, hiking boots, sea kayak, canoe, fishing rod, and snowmobile—there'll be plenty for you to do here.

Even if your outdoor skills are rusty or nonexistent, you can brush up at **L.L.Bean Outdoor Discovery Schools** (✆ **888/552-3261;** www.llbean.com), which offers a comprehensive series of lectures and workshops that run anywhere from 2 hours to 3 days. Classes are held at various locations around the coast (and inland), covering a range of subjects from orienteering, fly-tying, cycle maintenance, and canoeing to kayaking and cross-country and telemark skiing. L.L.Bean also hosts popular canoeing, sea-kayaking, and cross-country-skiing festivals that bring together instructors, lecturers, and equipment vendors for 2 or 3 days of learning and outdoor diversion. Call for a brochure or check the website (**www.llbean.com/ods**) for a schedule.

See chapter 10, "Northern & Western Maine," for specific tips on enjoying the state's noncoastal lakes, mountains, and woods.

BEACHGOING Swimming at Maine's ocean beaches is for the hardy. The Gulf Stream, which prods plenty of warm water toward Cape Cod, cruelly veers east just short of Maine and leaves the state's 5,500-mile coastline washed by brisk Nova Scotia currents that originate in frigid Labrador. During summer, water temperatures along the southern Maine coast may top 60°F (16°C) during an especially warm spell where water is shallow, but it's usually colder than that; the average ocean temperature at Bar Harbor in summer is 54°F (12°C). Expect an electric-like shock of cold when you first touch bare feet to water.

Maine's beaches are mostly confined to the 60-mile southernmost stretch of coast between Portland and the New Hampshire border. Beyond Portland, a handful of fine sand beaches are worth visiting—including **Reid State Park** and **Popham Beach State Park**—but these are exceptions; rocky coastline defines almost all of the rest of Maine. These southern beaches are beautiful but popular. Summer homes occupy the low dunes in most areas, and mid-rise condos give **Old Orchard Beach** an unwelcome Florida-condo-country look.

Perhaps the best swimming beach is **Long Sands,** in York (in a part of town known as York Beach). The long, sandy strip is worth combing for miles—but check tide tables, as it mostly disappears at high tide. Another great beach is located in the resort town of **Ogunquit:** a 3-mile-long sandy strand with a somewhat remote character (except on hot summer weekends, when it's inundated).

Finally, there are a handful of scenic beaches just south of **Portland.** (See the "Portland" section, later in this chapter.)

BIKING **Mount Desert Island** and its **Acadia National Park** are the premier destinations on the Maine coast for cyclists, especially mountain bikers who prefer easy riding—the cycling here might be some of the most pleasant in America. About 60 miles of well-maintained carriage roads in the national park allow for superb cruising through thick forests and to rocky knolls with ocean views—and no cars are allowed on the grass or gravel lanes.

It's easy to rent mountain bikes in Bar Harbor (see section 7, "Mount Desert Island" later in this chapter, for details). The island's Park Loop Road, although often crowded with slow-moving cars, provides one of the most memorable road-biking experiences in Maine. The rest of the island is also good for highway biking, especially the quieter western half of the island, where traffic is much thinner.

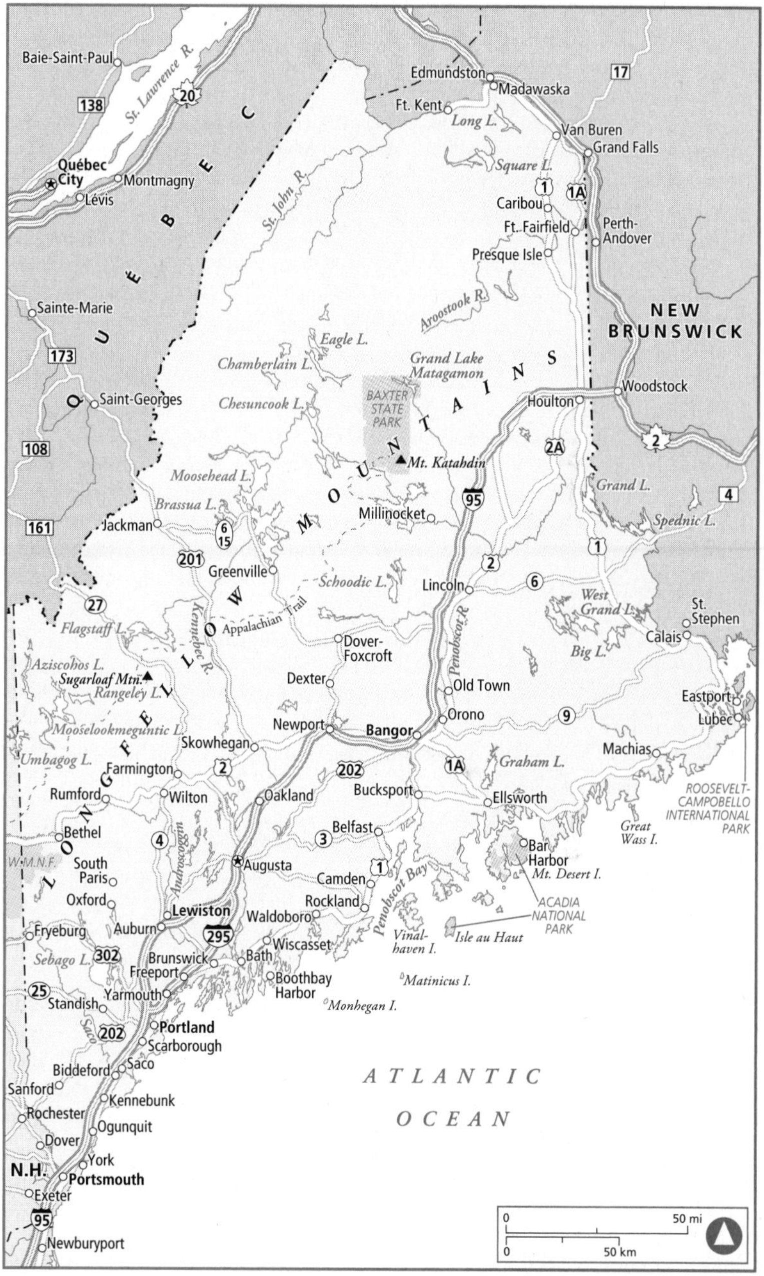
Baie-Saint-Paul
St. Lawrence R.
138
20
QUÉBEC
Québec City
Montmagny
Lévis
St. John R.
Sainte-Marie
173
Saint-Georges
108
161
Edmundston
Madawaska
17
Ft. Kent
Long L.
Van Buren
Grand Falls
Square L.
1
1A
Caribou
Ft. Fairfield
Perth-Andover
Presque Isle
Aroostook R.
NEW BRUNSWICK
Eagle L.
Chamberlain L.
Grand Lake Matagamon
BAXTER STATE PARK
Chesuncook L.
Woodstock
Houlton
2
2A
Mt. Katahdin
LONGFELLOW MOUNTAINS
Moosehead L.
Brassua L.
Jackman
6
15
95
Millinocket
Grand L.
4
Spednic L.
201
Greenville
Schoodic L.
Lincoln
6
West Grand L.
27
Flagstaff L.
Appalachian Trail
Kennebec R.
Penobscot R.
St. Stephen
Calais
Dover-Foxcroft
Big L.
Aziscohos L.
Sugarloaf Mtn.
Rangeley L.
Dexter
Old Town
Eastport
Mooselookmeguntic L.
Newport
Bangor
Orono
9
Lubec
Umbagog L.
Skowhegan
Machias
Farmington
2
202
1A
Graham L.
Rumford
Wilton
Oakland
Bucksport
Ellsworth
ROOSEVELT-CAMPOBELLO INTERNATIONAL PARK
Bethel
4
Androscoggin
Belfast
3
Great Wass I.
W.M.N.F.
South Paris
Augusta
1
Bar Harbor
Mt. Desert I.
Camden
Penobscot Bay
Oxford
Rockland
ACADIA NATIONAL PARK
Lewiston
Waldoboro
Fryeburg
Auburn
295
Isle au Haut
Vinalhaven I.
Wiscasset
Sebago L.
302
Brunswick
Bath
Freeport
Boothbay Harbor
Matinicus I.
25
Yarmouth
Standish
Monhegan I.
Saco
202
Portland
Scarborough
Biddeford
Saco
ATLANTIC OCEAN
Sanford
Kennebunk
Rochester
Ogunquit
Dover
York
N.H.
Portsmouth
Exeter
95
Newburyport
0
50 mi
0
50 km

And don't overlook the islands as destinations for relaxed biking. In Casco Bay, **Chebeague Island** offers a pleasant wooded excursion; **Peaks Island** is circled by a single paved road, with good views on the island's back side; and **Vinalhaven** and **North Haven** in Penobscot Bay and **Swan's Island** in Blue Hill Bay are also popular and scenic.

The Maine Department of Transportation publishes a booklet, *Explore Maine by Bike,* describing 25 popular bike trips around the state; log onto **www.exploremaine.org/bike** to get it (or to read it online). Maine DOT also publishes a map marked up with state biking information, including traffic volumes and road shoulder conditions along popular routes. You can order it by e-mailing the DOT, or call them at ✆ **207/624-3250.**

BIRDING Birders from southern and inland states enjoy expanding their life lists on trips to the Maine coast, because this region attracts migrating birds cruising the Atlantic flyway—and supports healthy populations of native shorebirds such as plovers (including the threatened piping plover), terns, whimbrels, sandpipers, and dunlins. Without any great effort, you'll see or hear herring, great black-backed gulls, common terns, common eiders, and loons. Get lucky and you might also spy Bonaparte's gull, laughing gulls, jaegers, and the Arctic tern. Downeast, near Lubec, look for members of the Alcidae family, such as razorbills and guillemot. Puffins nest on several offshore islands; tour boats to view puffins depart from Boothbay Harbor, Bar Harbor, and Jonesport.

For recent sightings of rare birds on the coast, check the **Maine Audubon Society's** constantly updated Web page: **www.maineaudubon.org/nature/birdalert.shtml**. (Sample weekly entry: TOP BIRDS THIS WEEK ARE: PINK-FOOTED GOOSE, CACKLING GOOSE, TUFTED DUCK, AMERICAN WHITE PELICAN, AND YELLOW-THROATED WARBLER.) Maine Audubon (✆ **207/781-2330**) is also the state's best source for bird news, bird trips, and education about birds in the state.

HIKING Acadia National Park has wonderful day hiking, though its trails can get a bit crowded during the peak summer season. ***50 Hikes in Southern and Coastal Maine,*** by John Gibson (Backcountry Publications), is a reliable directory to trails in Acadia and the Camden Hills area, as well as elsewhere. It's available at local bookstores or online. Also see "Getting Outside," in section 7, later in this chapter, for more details on hiking in the park.

SEA KAYAKING Paddlers come to the Maine coast from across the continent for the world-class sea kayaking found here. Thousands of miles of deeply indented coastline and thousands of offshore islands have created a sort of kayaker's playground. This sport can be extremely dangerous (when weather shifts, the seas can turn on you in a matter of minutes), but it can be very rewarding if you have the proper equipment and training.

The nation's first long-distance water trail, the **Maine Island Trail,** was created here in 1987. This 350-mile waterway winds along the coast from Portland to Machias, incorporating more than 150 state-owned and privately owned islands on its route. The **Maine Island Trail Association,** 58 Fore St., Ste. #30–3, Portland, ME 04101 (✆ **207/761-8225;** www.mita.org), helps maintain and monitor the islands, and its members are granted permission to visit and camp on them for free so long as they follow the restrictions (no visiting certain islands during seabird nesting season, for example). Contact the association about becoming a member; it's not expensive.

For novices, a number of kayak outfitters take guided excursions ranging from an afternoon to a week. The top outfitters include **Maine Island Kayak Co.** (✆ **207/766-2373;** www.maineislandkayak.com), on Peaks Island in the **Portland** area; and **Maine Sport Outfitters** (✆ **800/722-0826** or 207/236-8797; www.mainesport.com), on Route 1 in **Rockport** in the Midcoast region.

2 THE SOUTHERN MAINE COAST ★★

York: 45 miles SW of Portland; 10 miles NE of Portsmouth; 65 miles NE of Boston

Maine's southern coast runs roughly from the state line at Kittery to Portland, and this stretch is the primary destination of most travelers to the state. While it takes some work to find privacy or remoteness here, there are at least two excellent reasons to come: long, sandy beaches and a sense of history in the coastal villages (some of them, anyway).

Nearly all of Maine's best sand beaches lie along this stretch of coastline. Whether you prefer dunes, the lulling sound of breaking waves, or a carnival-like atmosphere in a beach town, you can find what you need here. The weather is highly variable, though: During a good Northeast blow (say, a 3-day winter storm), waves pound the shores, rise above the roads, and threaten beach houses built decades ago. But during balmy midsummer days, the sea can be as gentle as a pond, waves lapping timidly at the shore as the tide creeps in, inch by inch, covering tidal pools full of crabs, snails, and starfish.

Fun Facts Maine, Secret Getaway? Hardly.

Think of Maine as your own private getaway? Well, it can feel that way if you plan carefully, but you're hardly the first to get here. In fact, this coast has seen wave after successive wave of visitation, beginning at least 3 centuries ago when European newcomers tried to settle it, only to be driven off by Native Americans. (It's also locally believed that Vikings may have touristed—er, pillaged?—the region even longer before that.)

By the early 19th century, the coast had become settled, and it blossomed into one of the most prosperous places in all the U.S. Shipbuilders constructed brigantines and sloops, using stout pines and other trees floated downriver from Maine's North Woods; ship captains built huge, handsome homes in towns such as Searsport, Kittery, Bath, and Belfast; and merchants and traders built not only vast warehouses to store the booty from their excursions, but also their own grandiose homes.

Then things quieted down for a while, until landscape artists "rediscovered" Maine, bringing a fresh influx of city dwellers in their wake in the mid-to-late 19th century from Boston, New York, and Philadelphia, seeking relief from the heat and congestion of the city. They built huge, shingled estates facing the sea in places such as Bar Harbor and Camden. Then, at the beginning of the 20th century, a newly moneyed emerging middle class (a third wave?) showed up to discover Maine yet again, building smaller, less expensive bungalows by the shore in places such as York Beach, Kennebunk Beach, and Old Orchard Beach.

The 1980s brought a fresh wave of vacation-home building, but the past decade has *really* seen leaps and bounds in development of the tourist industry here as resorts become more luxurious and technology allows broader marketing than ever before. So it might feel like *yours*. Just remember: It's a lot of people's *ours*, too—and, actually, I'm okay with that.

One thing all the beaches here share in common is that they're all washed by the chilly Gulf of Maine, which makes for invigorating swimming—but I never fail to get in the water at least once, no matter how cold. (The salty water feels almost like a spa treatment.) Though the beach season here is brief and intense, running only from around July 4th until Labor Day (the first week of Sept), some towns are making an effort to stretch their tourist seasons into fall. However, this idea hasn't fully taken hold yet—the frigid waters might have something to do with that—and once Labor Day weekend is finished, these oceanside communities mostly slow down to a crawl.

KITTERY ★ & THE YORKS ★★

For travelers driving into Maine from the south, **Kittery** is the first town to appear after crossing the big bridge spanning the Piscataqua River from New Hampshire. Once famous for its (still operating) naval yard, Kittery is now better known for its dozens of factory outlets.

"The Yorks," just to the north, are three towns that share a name, but little else. In fact, it's rare to find three such well-defined and diverse New England archetypes within such a compact area. **York Village** ★ is full of 17th-century American history and architecture in a compact area and has a good library. **York Harbor** ★★ reached its zenith during America's late Victorian era, when wealthy urbanites constructed cottages at the ocean's edge; it's the most relaxing and scenic of the three. Finally, **York Beach** ★★ is a fun beach town with amusements, taffy shops, a small zoo, gabled summer homes set in crowded enclaves, a great lighthouse, and two excellent beaches with sun, sand, rocks, surf, surfers, and fried-fish stands.

Essentials

GETTING THERE Kittery is accessible from either **I-95** or **Route 1,** with well-marked exits. Coming from the south, the Yorks are reached most easily by taking I-95 N. toward (but not onto) the Maine Turnpike; exit just south of the turnpike entrance, and turn right. Coming from the north, pay your toll exiting the turnpike and then take the first exit, an immediate right. Go around the hairpin turn and you'll be pointing right into town.

Amtrak (✆ **800/872-7245;** www.amtrak.com) operates five trains daily from Boston's North Station (which does *not* connect directly to Amtrak's national rail network; you must take a subway or taxi from Boston's South Station first) into southern Maine. The station is outside Wells, about 10 miles away from the Yorks, and inland—not on the beach. A one-way ticket from Boston costs $19; the trip takes 1¾ hours. From Wells, you'll then need to call a local taxi or arrange for a pickup to get to your final destination on the beach.

No bus lines serve the stretch of southern Maine coastline between Kittery and Portland. However, two bus lines run regular buses daily from Boston's South Station to downtown **Portsmouth,** New Hampshire (see section 2 in chapter 7), which is so close to Kittery that you can actually walk over a bridge into Maine from Portsmouth. The lines are **Greyhound** (✆ **800/231-2222;** www.greyhound.com) and **C&J** (✆ **800/258-7111** or 603/430-1100; www.ridecj.com). A bus from New York City's Port Authority to Portsmouth costs about $48 one-way and takes about 6½ hours; from Boston, figure a fare of $18 to $24 one-way and a bit more than a 1-hour ride.

From late June through the end of August, daily except Saturday, a trackless "trolley"—a bus gussied up to *look* like an old-fashioned trolley, basically—links the two beaches (**Short Sands** and **Long Sands**) in York. The ride costs $2.50 each way. Hop on at any of the well-marked stops. There's also now a shuttle out to **Nubble Light,** a scenic

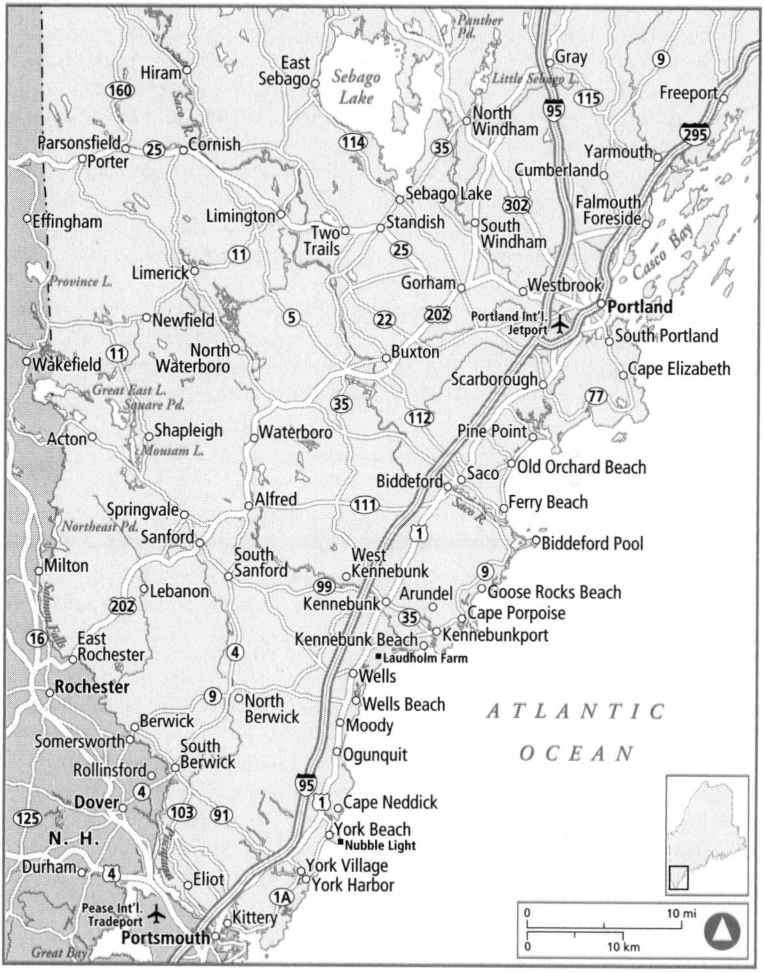

point too far for most folks to walk to (or take good pictures of) from the beaches; that ride costs $1 each way.

VISITOR INFORMATION The **Maine State Visitor Information Center** (✆ **207/439-1319**) is at a well-marked rest area on I-95. It's full of info and helpful staff; it has a pet exercise area and copious vending machines; and it's open daily from 8am to 6pm in summer, from 9am to 5:30pm the rest of the year. (The vending machines and restrooms are open 24 hr.)

The **Greater York Region Chamber of Commerce** (✆ **207/363-4422;** www.gatewaytomaine.org) also operates another helpful **visitor center,** one that mirrors the

Fun Facts Founding Father . . . Flop As a Wharf Owner

John Hancock is justly famous for his oversized signature on the Declaration of Independence, his tenure as governor of Massachusetts, and the insurance company and tall Boston building that were named for him. What's not so well known is his involvement as a proprietor of **Hancock Wharf,** a failed wharf-and-warehouse enterprise that went bust. Hancock never actually set foot on the wharf, but locals believed for years that he used it to stash arms, contraband, and/or goods he didn't want taxed by those tax-happy British. It now appears that wasn't the case, but it still makes for one of the many intriguing sites and stories in the **York Village** section of downtown York. (See "Exploring York," below, for more details on this neighborhood.)

Surprisingly, the wharf has a happy ending: It's more famous today than it was then, the only 18th-century warehouse still standing on the York River. It has been designated a National Historic Site, and the York Historical Society sometimes uses it to launch or receive the occasional historic boat passing through town.

shape of a stone cottage. It's across Route 1 from the Maine Turnpike access road (right beside the Stonewall Kitchen headquarters and cafe) on Stonewall Lane. In peak season, it's open Monday to Saturday from 9am to 5pm and Sunday from 10am to 4pm; from Labor Day through June, it's open Monday to Friday 9am to 4pm and Saturday from 10am to 2pm.

Exploring Kittery

Kittery has no true town center, but is instead made of several disconnected villages (all of them quite old) and a long, skinny shopping strip.

On the waterfront, such as it is, the historic **Portsmouth Naval Shipyard** faces Portsmouth, New Hampshire. This shipyard isn't open to the public for security reasons (they fix nuclear submarines here; cut 'em some slack), but you can visit the engaging displays at the **Kittery Historical & Naval Museum** (✆ **207/439-3080;** www.kitterymuseum.com) nearby to learn a bit about the history of subs, the shipyard's specialty. It's open daily from June through October 10am to 4pm and charges a small admission fee. Find it by taking Route 1 to the Kittery traffic circle, then exiting for Route 236 S. (Rogers Rd.) and continuing onto Rogers Road Extension.

From Kittery, it's easy to take Route 1 north to York. But it's much prettier to follow winding **Route 103** ★. This quiet road passes through the historic, lost-in-time village of **Kittery Point,** where homes seem to be just inches from the roadway and there are not one but *two* historic forts; both are parks open to the public.

Exploring York

York is split into several village centers, described above; the best for walking around in is **York Village** ★★, a fine destination for those curious about early American history. First settled in 1624, the village opens several homes to the public.

For a duck's-eye view of the local terrain, visit **Excursions Coastal Maine Outfitting Co.,** at 1740 Rte. 1 in **Cape Neddick** (✆ **207/363-0181;** www.excursionsinmaine.com). This outfitter offers sea-kayak rentals and tours ($60 per adult for a guided half-day excursion) along the local coastline. For more dramatic paddling, ask about sunrise, sunset, full-moon, and overnight kayaking trips. The shop is located on Route 1, between Ogunquit and York, 5 or 6 miles north of York's information center.

Old York Historical Society ★★★ York's local historical society oversees the bulk of the town's collection of historic buildings, some of which date to the early 18th century, and most of which are astonishingly well preserved or restored. Tickets are available to eight Old York–operated properties in all; one good place to start is at the barn-red **Old Gaol ★★**, which still has its (now-musty) dungeons and was built in 1719 as a jail to hold criminals, debtors, and other miscreants. It's the oldest surviving public building in the United States. Next, cross the street to the yellow **Jefferds Tavern ★**, near the **old burying ground ★**. Inside, changing exhibits document various facets of early life. A 10-minute walk along Lindsay Road brings you to **Hancock Wharf,** next door to the **George Marshall Store.** (Also nearby is the **Elizabeth Perkins House,** with its well-preserved Colonial Revival interiors.) Finally, just down the hill from the jail is the **Emerson-Wilcox House ★**, built in the mid-1700s and periodically added onto through the years; it's a virtual catalog of architectural styles and early decorative arts.

207 York St., York. ✆ **207/363-4974.** www.oldyork.org. Admission per building $5 adults, $4 seniors, $3 children 3–15; pass to all buildings $10 adults, $9 seniors, $5 children 4–15, $20 families. Museum and Old Gaol June to mid-Oct Mon–Sat 10am–5pm; some properties shorter hours.

Beaches

York Beach actually consists of *two* beaches, **Long Sands Beach ★★** and **Short Sands Beach ★**, separated by a rocky headland. Both have plenty of room for sunning and Frisbees when the tide is out. (When the tide is in, though, both become narrow and cramped.)

Short Sands fronts the honky-tonk town of **York Beach,** and it offers candlepin bowling, taffy-pulling machines, and video arcades. It's a better pick for families traveling with kids who have short attention spans. Long Sands runs along Route 1A, directly across from a line of motels, summer homes, and convenience stores. Parking at *both* beaches is metered from mid-May through mid-October; pay heed, as enforcement is strict and you must pay from 8am until 10pm, 7 days a week. (In the off season, they decapitate the meters—literally—and parking is then free and plentiful until spring.)

Where to Stay

Besides the properties listed below, York Beach is also stocked with plenty of condo and house rentals and motel rooms right on Long Sands Beach, plus a bunch more on Short Sands. The quality of these places is highly variable, though, since all the properties are individually owned. (At least all of them can truthfully boast that you can literally walk across the street to the beach.)

No matter where you stay, try to book ahead during high season. Failing that, turn up at the York visitor center (see "Visitor Information," above) to find vacancies if you have arrived without a room—which, in summer, is usually a bad idea.

Dockside Guest Quarters ★ David and Harriette Lusty established this quiet retreat in 1954, but more recent additions and new management (son David and his wife) haven't changed the friendly, maritime flavor of the place. Situated on an island connected to the mainland by a small bridge, the inn occupies nicely landscaped grounds shaded with maples and white pines. A few of the rooms are in the cozy main house, built in 1885, but the bulk of the accommodations are in small, shared, town-house-style cottages down by the water added between 1968 and 1998. These are simply furnished, but

Finds York Harbor's Sayward-Wheeler House

For those who'd like a taste of local history but lack the stamina for the full-court Old York visit, stop by the **Sayward-Wheeler House** ★ at 9 Barrell Lane Extension (behind the post office) in **York Harbor,** run by the group **Historic New England.** In this well-preserved merchant's home dating back to 1760, you'll see china captured during the 1745 Siege of Louisbourg, which routed the French out of Nova Scotia. It's open only two Saturdays per month, and only from June through mid-October. Tours are given hourly from 11am to 4pm. Admission is $5. For information, call the house (✆ **207/384-2454**) or the organization's office in Boston (✆ **617/227-3956;** www.historicnewengland.org).

bright and airy; most have private decks overlooking the entrance to York Harbor. Several also have woodstoves, fireplaces, and/or kitchenettes (though you do pay quite a bit extra for the kitchenette units and suites). The inn also maintains a simple restaurant (run by yet another son), and offers personalized boat tours of the harbor from its own private dock in addition to rowboats for guest use.

22 Harris Island Rd., York, ME 03909. ✆ **888/860-7428** or 207/363-2868. www.docksidegq.com. 25 units. $117–$265 double; $236–$312 suite. Rates include breakfast. 2-night minimum stay in summer. DISC, MC, V. Closed Jan–Apr and Mon–Fri in May, Nov, and Dec. From Rte. 1A in York Harbor, turn onto Rte. 103 and cross bridge over York River; make an immediate left and follow signs to end of road. **Amenities:** Restaurant; bikes. *In room:* A/C, TV, kitchenette (some units), Wi-Fi (in main house; free).

Portsmouth Harbor Inn and Spa ★★ This handsome 1899 home is just across the river from downtown Portsmouth, New Hampshire (p. 206), a pleasant, half-mile walk across a drawbridge. Rooms are tastefully restored and furnished in eclectic antiques, and though some are on the small side, all are boldly furnished and fun. Valora has ruby-red walls, harbor views, attractive antiques, and an above-average-size bathroom with historic accents. King George comes with a king-size bed (of course) and kingly skyline and bridge views. Dido's two single beds, meanwhile, can be adapted into an extra-long king. The whimsically decorated sitting room has two couches on which you can sprawl and browse through intriguing books. Spa services in an annex building are quite popular with guests.

6 Water St., Kittery, ME 03904. ✆ **207/439-4040.** Fax 207/438-9286. www.innatportsmouth.com. 5 units. Mon–Fri $120–$190 double; Sat–Sun $120–$200 double. Rates include full breakfast. 2-night minimum sometimes required. MC, V. Not recommended for children 11 and under. **Amenities:** Jacuzzi; spa. *In room:* A/C, TV/DVD, hair dryer, Wi-Fi (free).

Union Bluff Hotel ★★ With its turrets, dormers, and porches, the Union Bluff looks like a 19th-century beach hotel—except it was actually built in 1989, replacing the previous version (ca. 1870) of the hotel, which had burned in a fire. Inside, the hotel is modern if bland; but rooms have oak furniture, wall-to-wall carpeting, and small refrigerators, and the place seems to be getting better over time, not deteriorating like most beachside hotels do. There are about 20 rooms in an annex next door, but the main inn's rooms and views are better—the best units are the suites on the top floor and have beach vistas (and some have Jacuzzis, fireplaces, and decks overlooking the sea). It's amazing how low rates plummet here midweek and off season, when the hotel becomes among the most inexpensive places to stay in all of southern Maine; but weekends, even before and after summer, are quite expensive. Step outside and you're a half-block from Short Sands Beach, downtown T-shirt and shell shops, and the bowling alley and arcade. The hotel assigns one parking spot for each room, a boon because parking is very tight in Short Sands. But if you've brought an RV or a second car, you'll need to use the big parking lot adjacent to the hotel—bring lots of quarters.

8 Beach St. (P.O. Box 1860), York Beach, ME 03910. ✆ **800/833-0721** or 207/363-1333. www.unionbluff.com. 61 units. Mid-June to Aug $179–$279 double, $229–$379 suite; rest of year $59–$169 double, $89–$289 suite. AE, DISC, MC, V. **Amenities:** Restaurant; pub. *In room:* A/C, fridge (some units), Wi-Fi (free).

Where to Dine

In addition to the choices below, there are plenty of seafood and fried-fish joints in the area, plus a few options that go beyond the usual takeout fare. On Route 1 in Kittery, not far north of the island bridge to Portsmouth, the **Beach Pea Baking Co.** ★ (✆ **207/439-3555**) turns out outstanding sandwiches, breads, and pastries. Eat at one of the tables outside or on the front porch. It's open until 6pm (closed Sun).

York Village harbors a good little Italian family restaurant with atmosphere, **Fazio's** (✆ **207/363-7019**), at 38 Woodbridge Rd. (a side road near the town library). Directly on Long Sands in York Beach, **Sun & Surf** (✆ **207/363-2961**) has a takeout window serving fried seafood and ice cream, plus a dining room with standout ocean views and the usual family-restaurant fare: steaks, salads, fish, and pastas.

Finally, an impressive number of new restaurants have opened along the 8-mile stretch of **Route 1** ★ between York's information center and the next town, **Ogunquit,** over the past several years. You'll find everything here, from lobsters to burgers to high gourmet fare.

Bob's Clam Hut ★ *Finds* SEAFOOD Operating since 1956, Bob's manages to retain its old-fashioned feel—despite being surrounded on all sides by outlet malls, and with prices that have escalated way out of the "budget eats" category. The cooks still fry up heaps of clams and other seafood, toss them with fries and coleslaw into baskets, and send them out with tremendous efficiency. Order at the window, get a soda from the machine, and stake out a table inside or a picnic table out on the deck (with its lovely/unlovely view of marshes and busy Rte. 1) while waiting for your number to be called. The food is surprisingly light, cooked in cholesterol-free vegetable oil; the onion rings are pretty

Moments Shopping & Jam Sessions in York

Need a souvenir, but too weak with hunger to shop another minute? I've got you covered. At **Stonewall Kitchen**'s flagship store (✆ **207/351-2712**) on Stonewall Lane—that's just behind the huge tourist information complex at the corner of Route 1 and the access road leading to and from I-95 and the Maine Turnpike—you can sample the company's delicious jams before tucking into soups, salads, and sandwiches from the on-site deli (see "Where to Dine," below). Then, hunger and birthday lists both satisfied in one fell swoop, keep browsing through a good selection of handy kitchen accessories: knives, lobster bibs, graters, and the like. The staff is friendly and helpful. It's open daily; the shop closes at 8pm, while the cafe closes at 3pm.

good, but it's the plump clams that have inspired generations of fans to make return visits every summer. You can also get fish and chips quite cheaply if you're not a fan of big, pricey fried-shellfish baskets. Continuing with the unhealthy-yet-so-tasty theme, Bob's scoops up New Hampshire–made Annabelle's ice cream from an adjacent window—now that's overkill.

315 Rte. 1 (west side of Rte. 1, just south of outlets), Kittery. ✆ **207/439-4233.** www.bobsclamhut.com. Sandwiches $4–$13, dinner items $8–$29. AE, MC, V. Mon–Thurs 11am–7pm; Fri–Sat 11am–8pm; Sun 11am–7pm.

Goldenrod Restaurant Kids DINER Follow the neon to this seasonal beach-town classic, which is *the* place in York Beach for local color—it has been a summer institution here since 1896. Visitors and their kids love gawking through the plate-glass windows at ancient taffy machines hypnotically churning out taffy in volume (millions of candies a year). The restaurant, right behind the candy-making operation, is low on frills—it feels like long-gone New England, even if the food isn't all that impressive. Diners sit on stout oak furniture around a stone fireplace or elbow-to-elbow at an antique soda fountain; breakfasts are your basic New England diner standards, while for lunch and dinner you eat soups, burgers, and too-pricey sandwiches. But what saves the place is the **candy counter** ★, where you can line up to buy boxes of wax-wrapped taffy "kisses" (check the striping or coloring on the candy to know its flavor; I like the molasses and peppermint ones), almond-pocked birch bark, and other penny-candy treats. The shakes, malts, and sundaes are on the sweet side, but not bad.

2 Railroad Ave. (at Ocean Ave.), York Beach. ✆ **207/363-2621.** www.thegoldenrod.com. Breakfast items $2–$6, most lunch and dinner items $5–$8. MC, V. Memorial Day to Labor Day daily 8am–10pm (until 9pm in June); Labor Day to Columbus Day Wed–Sun 8am–3pm. Closed Columbus Day to Memorial Day.

Lobster Cove ★ Kids SEAFOOD Right across the street from the pounding surf of Long Sands Beach, dependable Lobster Cove is a good choice when the family is too tired to cook or drive off the beach. A "feed" is what you'll get here: Breakfast consists of standard diner choices like omelets, pancakes, and eggs Benedict, while lunch runs to burgers and sandwiches. But dinner is prime time, when cars with out-of-state plates pack into the little dirt lot and the shore dinner of lobster, corn on the cob, clam chowder, and steamed clams is hefty, popular, and good. Lobster pie is another old-fashioned New England favorite on the menu, and they also do lobster rolls, clam rolls, steaks, steamed clams with butter, and broiled seafood, too. Old-timey Maine dessert choices include a wild blueberry pie (a must-order, in season) or warmed bread pudding with whiskey sauce. They've got a liquor license and a long cocktail menu, as well. Inoffensive and unfancy it may be, but it fits the bill in certain situations.

756 York St. (south end of Long Sands Beach), York Harbor. ✆ **207/351-1100.** www.lobstercoverestaurant.com. Main courses $7–$21. AE, MC, V. Daily 8am–9pm.

Stonewall Kitchen Café ★★ CAFE Stonewall Kitchen's York-based gourmet foods operation took a step forward when it opened this quality, inexpensive cafe, smartly located right at its York headquarters next to the local tourist information office. The cafe serves simple, hearty items such as fish chowder, soups, lobster rolls, lobster BLTs, muffulettas (a New Orleans–style olive-salami sandwich), turkey wraps with cranberry spread, and many more; check the board to find out what's being served that day. Finish with a dessert such as lemon squares, brownies, or fresh-baked cookies. The cafe kitchen also prepares gourmet meals to go, and will do so up to an hour after the table service concludes. There's an espresso machine here, too.

2 Stonewall Lane (set back from Rte. 1), York. ✆ **207/351-2719.** www.stonewallkitchen.com. Sandwiches and salads $7–$11. AE, DC, DISC, MC, V. Mon–Sat 8am–3pm, Sun 9am–3pm; takeout available until 4pm.

Union Grill ★ AMERICAN/SEAFOOD Surprisingly, there aren't many upscale dining choices in the Yorks, so the Union Hotel's stab at "fancy" is a welcome development. Seafood predominates, though the menu wanders around. Start with a lobster corn dog, duck wings, calamari, or oysters on the half shell; then move on to a gourmet flatbread pizza (topped with Kobe short ribs, for instance) or entrees like a crusted lobster "mignon," seared scallops with dumplings, line-caught cod, or organic salmon. Landlubbers can go for a wild boar chop with béarnaise, crispy chicken with sweet potatoes, or a venison burger. Desserts are sweetish: a molten lava cake, a huge cookie, warmed bread pudding, or an oversized banana split with three gelati. It will be very interesting to see whether this place's lofty aspirations and high price point can make it in Short Sands—a place still so lowbrow, there's a gypsy palm reader on the main street.

8 Beach St. (in the Union Bluff Hotel), York Beach. ✆ **800/833-0721** or 207/363-1333. www.unionbluff.com. Main courses $11–$30. MC, V. Reservations recommended. Mid-May to mid-Oct daily 7–11am and 5–9:30pm; off season Thurs–Sun only. Pub daily 11:30am–10pm year-round.

Shopping

Kittery has become a shopping mecca ever since the arrival of little clusters of factory outlet shopping malls along both sides of Route 1. The lineup begins about 4 miles south of York. More than 100 of these outlets now flank the highway, in more than a dozen strip malls—not the prettiest sight in Maine, but if you're looking to score a deal, you just might find it beautiful.

Name-brand retailers with factory shops here purveying cut-rate designer stuff include Coach, Orvis, Samsonite, Gap, Adidas, Eddie Bauer, Banana Republic, Calvin Klein, Brookstone, and Polo Ralph Lauren, among many others. On rainy summer days, hordes of disappointed beachgoers head here and swarm the aisles; at those times, parking is especially tight.

Information on current outlets is available from the **Kittery Outlet Association.** Call ✆ **888/548-8379** or visit the website at www.thekitteryoutlets.com.

OGUNQUIT ★★

Ogunquit (oh-GUN-quit) is a bustling little beachside town that has attracted vacationers and artists for more than a century. Though certainly notable for its abundant and elegant summer-resort architecture and nightlife, Ogunquit is *most* famous for its 3½-mile white-sand beach, backed by grassy dunes and serviced by a beautiful seaside walking path, one of Maine's best. This beach is the town's front porch, and almost everyone ends up here at least once a day if the sun is shining.

Ogunquit's fame as an art colony dates to the 1890s, when Charles H. Woodbury arrived and declared the place an "artist's paradise." He was followed by artists like Walt Kuhn, Elihu Vedder, Yasuo Kuniyoshi, and Rudolph Dirks. During this same period, the town found another sort of fame, as well: as a quiet destination for gay travelers, and that following has continued to this day.

Despite its architectural gentility and overall civility, the town can become overrun with tourists and cars during summer weekends. If you despise crowds and the processes of jockeying for parking spots and beach space, visit during the off season or during summer weekdays instead.

Essentials

GETTING THERE Ogunquit is on Route 1, about halfway between York and Wells. It's accessible from both exit 7 (the Yorks) and exit 19 (Wells) of the Maine Turnpike, though you'll have to drive awhile from either exit.

Turn seaward at the confusing intersection at the center of town and follow Shore Road—the southernmost of the two spurs—to reach Perkins Cove and the best shops, accommodations, and restaurants. (For the best beach access, take the *other* prong of the intersection to Beach St.) Expect traffic to creep along Route 1 during summer weekends.

VISITOR INFORMATION The **Ogunquit Welcome Center** (✆ **207/646-2939;** www.ogunquit.org) is easy to miss: It's on the east side of Route 1, just south of the main intersection. The center is open daily from Memorial Day through Columbus Day (until 8pm during summer weekends), and daily except Sunday during the off season. Yes, it has restrooms.

GETTING AROUND Ogunquit's entrance is a horrid three-way intersection that seems intentionally designed to cause massive traffic tie-ups. Parking in and around the village is tight and relatively expensive for small-town Maine ($6–$15 per day in various lots). My advice? The town is best navigated on foot, by bike, or by using the local shuttle bus (see "Trolley Ho!," below).

Exploring Ogunquit

The village center is good for an hour or two of browsing among the boutiques, or sipping a cappuccino at one of the several coffee emporia.

From the village, you can walk to scenic Perkins Cove along **Marginal Way** ★★, a mile-long oceanside pathway that departs across from the Seacastles Resort on Shore Road. It passes tide pools, pocket beaches, and rocky, fissured bluffs, all worth exploring. The seascape can be spectacular, even if Marginal Way can get quite crowded with walkers during fair-weather weekends. Do like the regulars and locals do: Head out in the early morning for your walk.

Perkins Cove ★, accessible either from Marginal Way or by driving south along Shore Road and then veering left at the Y intersection, is a small, well-protected harbor that attracts lots of visitors (sometimes too many). A handful of galleries, restaurants, and T-shirt shops cater to tourists here. Also at the cove, an intriguing pedestrian drawbridge is operated by whomever happens to be handy.

Not far from the cove is the **Ogunquit Museum of American Art** ★★★, 543 Shore Rd. (✆ **207/646-4909;** www.ogunquitmuseum.org), one of the best small art museums in the nation (that's not just me talking; the director of New York's Metropolitan

Tips — Trolley Ho!

A number of trackless "trolleys" (✆ **207/646-1411;** www.ogunquittrolley.com)—actually buses—with names like *Dolly* and *Ollie* (you get the idea) run all day from mid-May to Columbus Day between Perkins Cove and the Wells town line to the north, with detours to the sea down Beach and Ocean streets. These trolleys are very handy, and they stop everywhere. (There's a map of stops posted online at **www.ogunquit.com/trolley.cfm**.) Rides cost $1.50 one-way (free for children); it's worth the expense to avoid driving and parking hassles and limits.

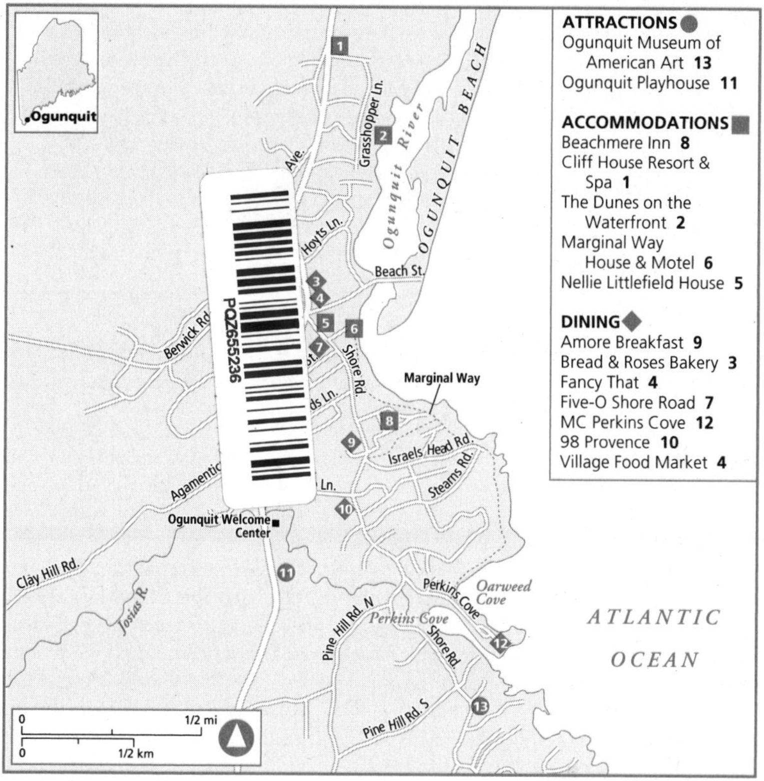

Museum of Art said so, too). It's open only in summer and early fall, however. Set back from the road in a grassy glen overlooking the rocky shore, the museum has a spectacular view that initially overwhelms the artwork as visitors walk through the door. But stick around for a few minutes—the changing exhibits in this architecturally engaging modern building of cement block, slate, and glass will get your attention soon enough; its curators have a track record of staging superb shows and attracting national attention, and the permanent collection holds work by seascape master Marsden Hartley and many members of the Ogunquit Colony, including Charles H. Woodbury, Hamilton Easter Field, and Robert Laurent.

The museum is open from July to October, Monday to Saturday from 10:30am to 5pm and Sunday from 1 to 5pm. Admission costs $7 for adults, $5 for seniors, and $4 for students; it's free for children 11 and under.

For evening entertainment, head for the **Ogunquit Playhouse** ★★ (✆ **207/646-2402;** www.ogunquitplayhouse.org), a 750-seat summer stock theater right on Route 1 (just south of the main intersection) with an old-style look that has garnered a solid reputation for its careful, serious attention to stagecraft. The theater has entertained Ogunquit since 1933, attracting noted actors such as Bette Davis, Tallulah Bankhead,

Tips Paying the Parking Piper

Ogunquit's beachside parking fees are the most exorbitant in Maine, hands down. (On the planet? Possibly.) The cost of leaving your car in the village varies quite a bit, depending on where you want to do so. It costs $15 to $20 per day at North and Footbridge beaches and two other satellite lots, while you pay by the hour (up to $4 per hour!) on Main Beach, Perkins Cove, and Cottage Street. My advice: Most hotels in town offer free parking for guests, so use them; the beach shuttle is cheaper than parking fees or a parking ticket. Also, there are private lots a few blocks from Perkins Cove that have charged a flat $7–$10 per day in previous summers (though that could be on the rise.)

Sally Struthers . . . er, and Lorenzo Lamas. Performances run from mid-May through mid-October, and tickets generally cost in the range of $30 to $45 per person.

Beaches

Ogunquit's **main beach** ★★ is more than 3 miles long when all of the pieces are considered together, though its width varies with the tides. This beach is livelier at its south end, near the town itself; it's more remote and unpopulated heading north, where there are dunes and, beyond them, clusters of summer homes.

The most popular access point is the foot of Beach Street, which runs into Ogunquit Village. This beach ends at a sandy spit, where the Ogunquit River flows into the sea; here you'll find a handful of informal restaurants. It's also the most crowded part of the beach. Less congested options here include **Footbridge Beach** (from Rte. 1, north of the village center, turn off onto Ocean Ave.) and—a few more miles north along Route 1—**Moody Beach** (turn onto Eldridge Ave. in **Wells**). Restrooms and changing rooms are maintained at all three beaches.

Where to Stay

In addition to the selections below, there are loads of family-owned budget- to moderately priced motel operations around town. Simply cruising Route 1 can yield dividends. (Don't forget your AAA card if you're a member.)

Beachmere Inn ★★ Kids In a town of motels, simple B&Bs, and condos, the Beachmere excels. Operated by the same family since 1937, this quiet, well-run cliff-top inn sprawls across a scenic lawn where repeat visitors have reclined for decades. Nearly every unit gives you an amazing look up or down the beach, and all have kitchenettes. The original Victorian section dates from the 1890s and is the most fun; it's all turrets, big porches, angles, and bright, beachy interiors. Next door is the modern Beachmere South, with spacious rooms and plenty of private balconies or patios—those on the end have absolutely knockout views. A new wing (Beachmere West) was added in 2008, with a small but nice little hot tub, exercise room, and children's play area; units in this wing have sitting rooms and bigger bathrooms. The adjacent Marginal Way footpath (see "Exploring Ogunquit," above) is terrific for walks and beach access, and groups can inquire about several off-property cottages a short walk away. The inn is now open year-round: You can rent snowshoes in winter to (carefully) stroll the path.

62 Beachmere Place, Ogunquit, ME 03907. ✆ **800/336-3983** or 207/646-2021. Fax 207/646-2231. www.beachmereinn.com. 53 units. June–Aug $175–$250 double, $275–$380 suite, $460 cottage; May and

Sept to mid-Oct $105–$220 double, $195–$265 suite, $270–$305 cottage; Apr and mid-Oct to early May $95–$160 double, $155–$195 suite, $235 cottage. Rates include continental breakfast. 3-night minimum stay in summer. AE, DC, DISC, MC, V. **Amenities:** Lounge; children's play room; Jacuzzi. *In room:* A/C, TV/DVD, kitchenettes (some units), Wi-Fi (in main inn; free).

Cliff House Resort and Spa ★★ This complex of modern buildings replaced a former grand hotel and now offers some of the best hotel-room ocean views in Maine—nearly a 360-degree panorama, in some cases. The rooms come in a number of different styles, most with comforts such as digital televisions and recliners; other updates include new beds and furniture in the Cliffscape wing and a covered corridor linking all terraces and guest rooms with the dining areas. A vanishing-edge pool fronting the sea does indeed seem to disappear into the blue yonder, and there's an upscale restaurant with knockout vistas. The state-of-the-art spa and fitness facility dispenses a wide range of soothing treatments and exercise programs.

Shore Rd. (P.O. Box 2274), Ogunquit, ME 03907. ✆ **207/361-1000.** Fax 207/361-2122. www.cliffhousemaine.com. 200 units. July–Aug $265–$310 double, $335–$360 spa room and suite; mid-Apr to June and Sept–Nov $175–$255 double, $225–$310 and suite. Meal plans available. 3-night minimum stay July–Aug and holiday weekends; 2-night minimum other weekends. AE, DISC, MC, V. Closed Dec to mid-Apr. No children in spa room units. **Amenities:** Restaurant; bar; health club; Jacuzzi; 3 pools (1 indoor, 2 outdoor); room service. *In room:* A/C, TV, hair dryer, Wi-Fi ($9.95 per day).

The Dunes on the Waterfront ★★ This classic motor court (built around 1936) somehow manages to be rustic yet elegant. It has made the transition into the modern luxury age more gracefully than just about any other vintage motel I've ever seen. The complex consists of a motel-like main building, but most guests come to stay in one of the 19 gabled cottages (painted white and trimmed in green shutters) scattered about the 12-acre grounds. Plenty of old-fashioned charm remains in here, as they've been decked out in vintage maple furnishings, oval braided rugs, maple floors, knotty pine paneling, and louvered doors. These cottages all have full kitchens, and many have wood-burning fireplaces as well. The complex is wedged between busy Route 1 and the ocean, but it

Moments **Doing Doughnuts in Wells**

Cruising the Wells-Ogunquit corridor of Route 1, foodies will want to check out venerable **Congdon's Doughnuts Family Restaurant & Bakery ★★** at 1090 Post Rd., which is just Rte. 1 (✆ **207/646-4219;** http://congdons.com). Clint and Dot "Nana" Congdon moved to Maine and opened a family-style restaurant in 1945; Nana's sinkers proved so popular that she relocated the whole operation to Wells 10 years later and went into the doughnut business full time. Chocolate-chocolate is ever-popular, but you can't go wrong with almost anything else among the dozens of choices—pillowy raised doughnuts; filled blueberry doughnuts; butter crunch, honey-dipped, sugar twist, and chocolate honey doughnuts . . . or one of the seasonal specials such as maple, apple, or pumpkin doughnuts. You can also eat diner meals here, most of which involve fried food and/or breakfast fare. Despite a newish drive-through window, this place retains its original character (and that includes the local characters dining inside). The secret? They use lard. Congdon's is open daily, except Wednesday, year-round from 6am to 2pm.

somehow stays quiet and peaceful; Adirondack chairs overlook a lagoon, and guests can borrow a rowboat to get across to the sandy beach without having to pay for parking.

518 Rte. 1 (P.O. Box 917), Ogunquit, ME 03907. ✆ **888/295-3863.** www.dunesonthewaterfront.com. 36 units. Summer $140–$345 double, $235–$435 cottage; spring and fall $95–$225 double, $160–$335 cottage. July–Aug 1-week minimum stay in cottages, 3-night minimum stay in motel. MC, V. Closed Nov to late Apr. **Amenities:** Outdoor pool; watersports equipment/rentals. *In room:* A/C, TV, fridge.

Marginal Way House and Motel ★ This simple, old-fashioned compound centers on a four-story, mid-19th-century guesthouse with summery, basic rooms and white-painted furniture. The whole complex is plunked down on a large, grassy lot on a quiet cul-de-sac, and it's hard to believe you're smack in the middle of busy Ogunquit. But you are: The beach and village are each just a few minutes' walk away. Room no. 7, despite its skinny twin beds, has a private porch and canopy and ocean views. The main building is surrounded by four more contemporary buildings that lack charm, but rooms here are mostly comfortable and bright. The "motel" building has only rooms with double beds, but the Wharf House has a cool quietude about it, enhanced by white linens and shady trees. Some units have little decks with views; all rooms have refrigerators and televisions, but none have phones. The property also maintains some one- and two-bedroom efficiency apartments (some have minimum stays); inquire when booking.

22–24 Wharf Lane (P.O. Box 697), Ogunquit, ME 03907. ✆ **207/646-8801.** www.marginalwayhouse.com. 30 units, 1 with private bathroom down hall. Early June to Labor Day $86–$208 double; mid-Apr to early June and early Sept to Oct $49–$146 double. $15 extra charge for more than 2 people (except kids age 2 and under). Minimum-stay requirements some weekends. MC, V. Closed Nov to mid-Apr. Pets allowed in off season only; advance notice required. *In room:* A/C (most units), TV, fridge, no phone, Wi-Fi (in most; free).

Nellie Littlefield House ★★ Finds Of the many B&Bs and boardinghouses filling downtown Ogunquit, this might be the friendliest. The handsome 1889 home stands at the edge of the town's compact commercial district and features elegant Queen Anne–style detailing. All rooms are carpeted and feature a mix of modern and antique reproduction furnishings; several have refrigerators. Rooms to the rear have private decks, although views are limited—mostly looking out on a motel next door. The most spacious room is the third-floor J. H. Littlefield suite, with two televisions and a Jacuzzi, and the most unique unit is probably the circular Grace Littlefield room in the upper turret, overlooking the street. The basement features a compact fitness room. Hospitality remains a strong selling point here.

27 Shore Rd. (P.O. Box 1341), Ogunquit, ME 03907. ✆ **207/646-1692.** www.nellielittlefieldhouse.com. 8 units. June–Sept $108–$230 double; Mar–May and Oct–Dec $85–$170 double; holiday rates higher. Rates include full breakfast. 3-night minimum stay on high-season weekends and holidays. DISC, MC, V. Closed Jan–Feb. Children 13 and over welcome. **Amenities:** Small exercise room. *In room:* A/C, TV, fridge (some units).

Where to Dine

The main strip, where Route 1 converges with Perkins Cove Road, is packed with bakeries, coffee shops, markets, and restaurants, and this has got to be the latest-open-hours town in Maine. Amazingly, many restaurants stay open until 10 or 11pm in summer. The seating area by Route 1 shared by several of these places is the town's prime people-watching spot.

Eateries here include the **Bread & Roses Bakery** (✆ **207/646-4227;** www.breadandrosesbakery.com), 246 Main St., which skillfully turns out cakes, cupcakes, mousses, and other sweets year-round. **Fancy That** (✆ **207/646-4118**) is a seasonal cafe nearby with sandwiches, hot panini, slices of Boston cream and other pies, and a Wi-Fi–equipped patio, great for people-watching. And the **Village Food Market** (✆ **207/646-2122** or 877/646-2122; www.villagefoodmarket.com), at 230 Main St., stocks good wines, ready-to-go meals, and staples, and it also has a small deli. Try the house red-eye coffee.

Amore Breakfast ★★ (Value) BREAKFAST Newly relocated down the village's main street in the Perkins Cove district, Amore is a breakfast-only place—but what a breakfast it is. (This is *not* a place for weight-watchers. But you're on vacation, right?) Look for numerous variations on the eggs Benedict theme (including a popular one with a big hunk of lobster on top), plus good Belgian waffles, a calorific bananas-Foster–style French toast with pecans outside and cream cheese inside, French toast topped with blueberries, and more than a dozen tasty variations on an omelet. Coffee is from a small-batch San Diego coffee roaster. And they've got heart, too: Annual benefit meals are held, with the proceeds going to care packages for a Dominican orphanage. Italian owner Leanne Cusimano deserves (and gets local) kudos.

309 Shore Rd. ✆ **866/641-6661** or 207/646-6661. www.amorebreakfast.com. Breakfast items $5–$14. MC, V. Summer daily 7am–1pm; off season closed Wed–Thurs. Also closed mid-Dec to Apr.

Arrows ★★★ NEW AMERICAN When owners Mark Gaier and Clark Frasier opened Arrows in a gray farmhouse outside town in 1988, they quickly put Ogunquit on the national culinary map. They've done so not only by creating an elegant and intimate atmosphere, but also by serving up some of the freshest, most innovative cooking in New England. The emphasis is on local products—often very local. The salad greens are grown in gardens on the grounds, and much of the rest is produced or raised locally. The food transcends traditional New England fare and is deftly prepared with exotic twists and turns. The menu changes nightly, but among the more popular recurring appetizers is a house-cured prosciutto—hams are hung in the restaurant to cure in the off season. Entrees might include roasted chicken stuffed with a sourdough-and-foie-gras stuffing; roasted halibut; tenderloin of pork with yam puree and pork dumplings; Maine-caught sole with a champagne glaze; or surf and turf (roasted rib-eye au poivre plus a chilled lobster cocktail). The wine list is top-rate. Note that there is a moderate dress code: Jackets are preferred for men, and shorts aren't allowed.

41 Berwick Rd. ✆ **207/361-1100.** www.arrowsrestaurant.com. Reservations strongly recommended. Main courses $41–$43, tasting menus $95–$135. MC, V. June to Columbus Day Wed–Sun 6–9pm; late Oct to Dec and mid-Apr to May Thurs–Sun 6–9pm. Closed Jan–mid Apr. Turn onto Berwick Rd. at Key Bank in the village center; restaurant is 2 miles along road, on right.

Five-O Shore Road ★★ SEAFOOD/FUSION A fine choice if you're looking for a more casual alternative to the more formal restaurants listed, Five-O is one of those spots where just reading the menu is a decent evening's entertainment. The formerly Caribbean-inspired menu has been transformed into one that veers all over the map. And the fun thing about eating here is that you can mix-and-match small plates, tapas-style, if nightly main courses like baby back ribs, rack of lamb, Delmonico steaks, quail, or fish don't grab you. Instead, you could eat some rope-grown Maine mussels, almond-crusted fried duck tenders, escargot with shallots, wild salmon poached in lobster-saffron bullion, molé-spiced pork, pâté, a cheese plate, or some hand-made onion rings with barbecue sauce. (Or just order a fresh Maine lobster in season, perhaps served over a bed of mussels steamed with blue cheese, sweet cream, and cracked pepper.) Five-O also has a cool cocktail lounge and club, and a strong wine list. Is this Maine or Manhattan? Either way, it's still a winner.

50 Shore Rd. ✆ **207/646-5001.** www.five-oshoreroad.com. Reservations strongly recommended in summer. Small plates $8–$13, main courses $14–$32. AE, DISC, MC, V. Valet parking. Memorial Day to Labor Day Mon–Fri 5–9pm, Sat–Sun 11am–2pm and 5–9pm; call for hours outside peak season.

MC Perkins Cove ★★★ SEAFOOD/NEW AMERICAN Chef-partners Mark Gaier and Clark Frasier (the M and C in MC) of Arrows (see above) have opened this bistro, which manages to be fun rather than stuffy. (Well, no bathing suits are allowed in the dining room, but still.) Expect big food, even on the "small" plates: Chopped salads, fried calamari, and oysters on half shells give way to more sophisticated starters like mussels steamed in a red curry sauce, rustic pizzas of ham and apple, or house-cured smoked salmon with dill. For your entree, choose a main dish such as a steamed lobster; a piece of sesame-encrusted, deep-fried trout; a Kobe burger; some grilled tuna; a hanger steak; or a piece of plank-roasted fish—then add aioli or another sauce and one of the so-called "evil carbos" (french fries, onion rings, and so on). Desserts might be best of all: Finish with a brown-butter brownie with vanilla ice cream, burnt orange caramel, and candied orange peel; mini whoopee pies; apple-blueberry turnovers with a mulled cider reduction; a bittersweet chocolate cake with chocolate sauce and pistachio crème anglaise; or peppermint-stick ice cream with cookies.

111 Perkins Cove Rd. ✆ **207/646-6263.** www.mcperkinscove.com. Reservations recommended. Main courses $8–$19 at lunch, $19–$31 at dinner. DC, DISC, MC, V. Late May to mid-Oct daily 11:30am–2pm and 5:30–11pm; rest of year closed Tues. Also closed Jan.

98 Provence ★★★ FRENCH How many good meals can you eat in one town? Find out. At this bistro, chef Pierre Gignac incorporates fresh, local ingredients (such as lobster) in a menu that changes thrice yearly to reflect the seasons but never gets too fusion-minded; instead, it's solidly French throughout. Start with lobster cooked in puff pastry with a sherried honey-ginger cream; Provençal fish stew; escargots with a Parmesan crisp and black trumpet mushrooms; rabbit fricassee; or the daily soup or mussel dish. (Yes, they have a daily, changing mussel dish.) Then move on to veal with wild mushrooms; a grilled boar chop with a chestnut croquette and pomegranate sauce; braised beef short ribs; a cassoulet of duck confit, lamb shoulder, and pork sausage; rack of lamb roasted with cumin and garlic; or the catch of the day. There's also now a daily bistro prix-fixe menu with lighter items (and prices)—the trio might be vichyssoise, stewed chicken, and lemon tart, for instance, or soft-shell crab with halibut confit and Provence-style nougat, served frozen. The summery, classy interior decor is about as close as you'll get in New England to a Provençal feel. Outstanding place.

262 Shore Rd. ✆ **207/646-9898.** www.98provence.com. Reservations recommended. Main courses $23–$28, prix-fixe menus $29–$39. AE, MC, V. Summer Wed–Mon 5:30–9:30pm; off season Thurs–Mon 5:30–9pm.

THE KENNEBUNKS ★★

"The Kennebunks" consist of the side-by-side villages of **Kennebunk** and **Kennebunkport,** both situated along the shores of small rivers and both claiming a very scenic section of the rocky coast.

The region was first colonized in the mid-1600s, and it flourished after the American Revolution when ship captains, boat builders, and prosperous merchants constructed imposing, solid homes in both towns. The Kennebunks are each famed for their striking historical architecture, shopping, dining, fine inns and hotels, ocean views (the Bush family owns a summer home here), and long, sandy beaches. Be sure to take time to explore both towns.

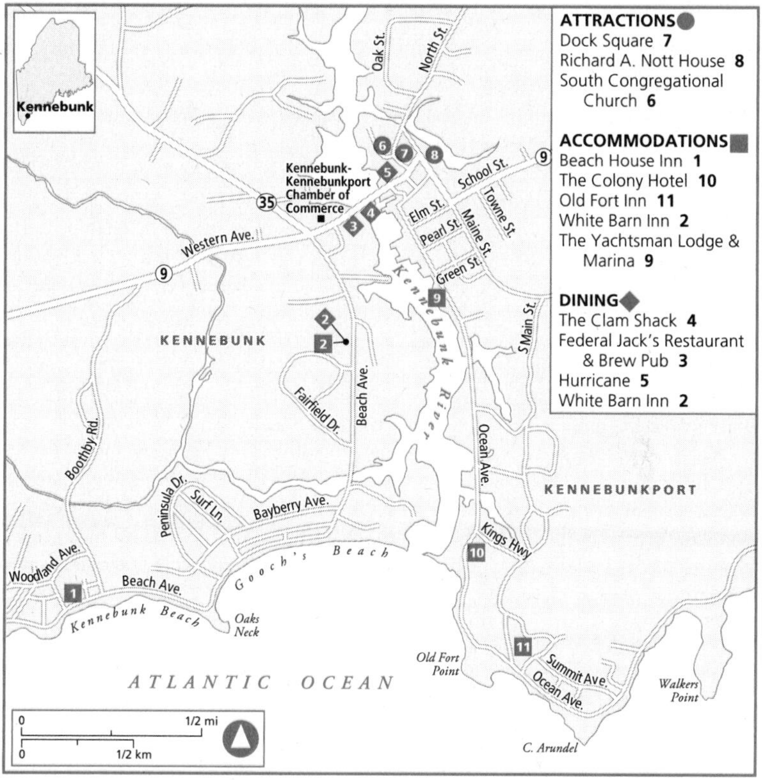

Essentials

GETTING THERE Kennebunk is just off exit 25 of the Maine Turnpike; turn left after the ramp, and follow signs east into town. You can also get here by taking Route 1 north from York and Ogunquit.

To reach Kennebunkport, take the exit for Kennebunk and continue through town on Port Road (Rte. 35) for about 3½ miles. At the traffic light, turn left and cross the small bridge.

VISITOR INFORMATION The helpful **Kennebunk-Kennebunkport Chamber of Commerce** (✆ **800/982-4421** or 207/967-0857; www.visitthekennebunks.com) can answer questions year-round by phone or in person at its offices at 17 Western Ave. (Rte. 9), beside the H.B. Provisions general store.

GETTING AROUND Several higher-end inns in these two towns offer shuttle services to the downtown areas. Otherwise, a local **trolley** (actually a bus that looks like a trolley) makes several convenient stops in and around the Kennebunks, and also serves the best local beaches; it picks up about once per hour from 10am until 4pm (3pm in spring and fall). But it's *expensive:* Your fare comes in the form of a day pass, and that costs $15 per adult or $5 per child ages 3 to 17. The upside? One ticket allows you unlimited jumping on and off all day long.

Call ✆ **207/967-3686** for details, or check the trolley's schedule online at **www.intowntrolley.com**.

Exploring Kennebunk

Kennebunk's downtown is inland, just off the turnpike, and is a dignified, compact commercial center of clapboard and brick.

If you're a history buff, the **Brick Store Museum** ★, 117 Main St. (✆ **207/985-4802;** www.brickstoremuseum.org), should be your very first stop in town. The museum hosts showings of historical art and artifacts throughout summer, switching to contemporary art exhibits in the off season. And they've got extensive local historic archives, too. The museum is housed in a former brick store plus three adjacent buildings renovated to a polish. Admission is free (though a $5 per person donation is suggested), and tours cost $5 per person. The museum opens Tuesday to Friday from 10am to 4:30pm, and Saturday from just 10am until 1pm.

The $5, 1½-hour **walking tours** ★ of Kennebunk's historic district (Maine's first) that set out from the museum are a must-do if you love history.

When en route to or from the coast, be sure to note the extraordinary homes that line Port Road (Rte. 35). This includes the famously elaborate **Wedding Cake House** ★, which you should be able to identify all on your own: It's a yellow-and-white stunner. Local lore claims the house was built by a guilt-ridden ship captain who left for sea before he and his bride could enjoy a proper wedding cake. Try to pull over to the shoulder and take a quick gawk.

Exploring Kennebunkport

Kennebunkport is the summer home of President George H.W. Bush, whose family has summered on an estate here for decades, and it has the tweedy, upper-crust feel that one might expect of the place. (Kennebunk, by contrast, feels more like a place where real people pump gas, portage kayaks, wait in line for license plates, and steer pickup trucks around town doing odd construction and painting jobs.)

Kennebunkport's historic village center features narrow streets that were laid out during the days when travel by boat and horse were still the ways people went; as such, it tends to create some traffic jams.

Dock Square has a bustling feel to it, with low buildings of mixed vintages and styles. The boutiques in the area are attractive, and many feature creative artworks and crafts, but sometimes they're a bit crowded. Kennebunkport's real attraction is found in the surrounding blocks, though, where side streets are lined with one of the nation's richest collections of Early American homes. Many of the beautiful Federal-style houses here have been converted to B&Bs (see "Where to Stay," below). And the amazing meetinghouse-style **South Congregational Church** ★★, the one with the big clock faces just off Dock Square at North and Temple streets, is well worth the short detour.

Also try to stop by the **Richard A. Nott House** ★★ (✆ **207/967-2751**), at 8 Maine St. (corner of Spring St.). This imposing Greek Revival house was built in 1853 and is a Victorian-era aficionado's dream. It remained untouched by the Nott family through the years and was donated to the local historical society with the stipulation that it remain forever unchanged. Tours run about 40 minutes; it's open from mid-June to mid-October, Tuesday to Friday from 1 to 4pm and Saturday from 10am to 1pm. (In summer it reopens for 2 hr. every night, 7–9pm.) Admission is $7 for adults, free for children.

Historic **walking tours** ★ of Kennebunkport also depart from here, and again they're well worth the time—you won't believe how many 19th-century homes are within spitting distance.

Finally, head out toward the ocean. **Ocean Drive** (marked by a post in Dock Sq.) runs out to and beyond the Bush compound at **Walkers Point** ★, and the route is lined with opulent summer homes. Take a quick look at the presidential palace, snap a pic, and move on—there's plenty more to see out here, including outstanding ocean and shore views.

Beaches

The coastal area around Kennebunkport is home to several of the state's best beaches. Southward across the river (technically, this is Kennebunk, though it's much closer to Kennebunkport) are **Gooch's Beach** ★★ and **Kennebunk Beach** ★★. Head eastward from the intersection of routes 9 and 35 along—yes—Beach Street past the White Barn Inn (see "Where to Stay," below), and in a few minutes you'll arrive at the ocean and a handsome row of eclectic, shingled summer homes.

The narrow road continues to twist past sandy strands and rocky headlands for a few miles, and this portion is well worth exploring, too. It can get congested in summer, though; avoid gridlock by parking and wandering on foot or by bike. (Also take note of local parking regulations: Only local residents are permitted to park along some stretches of these beaches. Check with your hotel reception desk if you're in doubt.)

Where to Stay

There's a serious shortage of budget digs in the Kennebunks. There *are* a few motels in Kennebunk proper, though none will knock your socks off—the **Turnpike Motel,** 77 Old Alewive Rd. (✆ **207/985-4404;** www.turnpikemotel.com), literally attached to the northbound turnpike exit; the **Econo Lodge** (✆ **207/985-6100;** www.econolodge.com), on Route 1 just south of downtown; and the **Gallery Motel and Cottages** (✆ **207/985-4543;** www.kennebunkcottages.com), near the Econo Lodge.

Beach House Inn ★★ This is a good choice if you'd like to be close to the people-watching, dog-walking action on and above Kennebunk Beach. The inn was built in 1891 but has been extensively modernized and expanded. The rooms here aren't necessarily historic, but most have Victorian furnishings and accents, plus nice framed photographs of beach landscapes. Suites have lovely panoramic views of the ocean across the road. But the main draw here is the lovely front porch, where you can stare out at the water and watch passing walkers and cyclists. The inn has bikes and canoes for guests to use, and provides beach chairs and towels, too.

211 Beach Ave., Kennebunk, ME 04043. ✆ **207/967-3850.** Fax 207/967-4719. www.beachhseinn.com. 35 units. Late June to mid-Sept $255–$390 double; early June to late June and mid-Sept to Oct $185–$399 double; Nov–Dec $155–$300 double. Rates include continental breakfast and afternoon tea. 2-night minimum Sat–Sun. AE, MC, V. Closed Jan–May. **Amenities:** Babysitting; bikes; canoes. *In room:* A/C, TV/VCR, CD player, hair dryer, Wi-Fi (free).

The Colony Hotel ★★ One of a handful of oceanside resorts that has actually preserved the classic New England vacation experience without fading into oblivion, this mammoth white Georgian Revival inn (ca. 1914) lords over the ocean at the mouth of the river on the Kennebunkport side. All rooms in the three-story main inn have been renovated; they're bright and cheery, simply furnished in summer-cottage antiques. Rooms in two of the three outbuildings carry over the feeling of the main hotel; the exception is the East House, a 1950s-era motel at the back edge of the property with uninteresting rooms. Staff encourages guests to socialize in the lobby, on the porch, on the putting green, even at a shuffleboard court that's lighted for nighttime play. Yes, the building is aging, and no—most rooms still don't have televisions. But if you're coming for proximity to the ocean, quiet, and casual elegance, you can find them here.

140 Ocean Ave. (P.O. Box 511), Kennebunkport, ME 04046. ✆ **800/552-2363** or 207/967-3331. Fax 207/967-8738. www.thecolonyhotel.com/maine. 123 units. Summer $149–$549 double; spring and fall $99–$399 double. Rates include breakfast. 3-night minimum stay summer weekends and holidays. AE, MC, V. Closed Nov to mid-May. Pets allowed ($30 per pet per night). **Amenities:** Restaurant; lounge; bikes; heated saltwater pool; room service. *In room:* A/C (some units), TV (some units), Wi-Fi (free).

Old Fort Inn ★★ The Old Fort tops some of the much better-known B&Bs in town. A sophisticated little inn, it sits on 15 acres in a quiet, picturesque neighborhood of late-19th-century summer homes 2 blocks from the ocean. Guests check in at a tidy antiques shop and park around back at the large carriage house, an interesting amalgam of stone, brick, shingle, and stucco. Rooms and suites here all have creature comforts yet retain the charm of yesteryear: They are solidly wrought and delightfully decorated with antiques and reproductions. About half the rooms have in-floor heated tiles in the bathrooms; all have such welcome amenities as plush robes, refrigerators, Aveda bath products, discreet self-serve snack bars, microwaves, and sinks. There are two large suites in the main house—light-filled no. 216 faces east, overlooking the attractive pool, for instance. A good, very full buffet breakfast is served in the main building daily; a free hour of tennis on a carefully kept court is included with your rate; and the inn now also offers massage and other spa services.

Old Fort Rd. (P.O. Box M), Kennebunkport, ME 04046. ✆ **800/828-3678** or 207/967-5353. Fax 207/967-4547. www.oldfortinn.com. 16 units. $125–$245 double; $295–$390 suite. Rates include full breakfast and 1 hr. free tennis. 2-night minimum stay weekends; 3-night minimum holiday weekends. AE, DC, DISC, MC, V. **Amenities:** Heated outdoor pool; tennis court. *In room:* A/C, TV, fridge, hair dryer, microwave, minibar, Wi-Fi (free).

White Barn Inn ★★★ As it has long done, the exclusive White Barn goes the extra mile to pamper its guests to no end, and it remains the state's best inn (with arguably its best dining room; see "Where to Dine," below). Upon checking in, guests are shown to a parlor and served a drink while valets gather luggage and park cars. The atmosphere here is distinctly European, with an emphasis on service and a polished international staff. Rooms are individually decorated in an upscale country style recently recast to emphasize simple, sea-inspired pastel colors. The biggest main-house unit, no. 8, feels most New England-y with its mix of the modern (double Jacuzzi, thick robes) and the classic: a two-sided fireplace, folding screens in the enormous bathroom, prints on the walls. Suites in the adjacent May's Cottage outbuilding are spectacular—each has a unique color theme, most have flatscreen TVs and/or whirlpools, and a few have great front porches. Across the road, several cottages on the Kennebunk River at a private marina offer cozy escapes, yet they're equipped with modern kitchens and bathrooms to go with their full river and harbor views. There are plenty of extra touches here, from fresh flowers to daily tea and scones, a new spa, a secluded outdoor pool behind a gate, and a pedicab whisking guests into the nearby town. And chef Jonathan Cartwright's resort cuisine? Sublime.

37 Beach Ave. (1/4 mile east of junction of rtes. 9 and 35; P.O. Box 560-C), Kennebunk Beach, ME 04043. ✆ **207/967-2321.** Fax 207/967-1100. www.whitebarninn.com. 25 units, 4 cottages. $310–$620 double; $540–$925 cottage and suite. Rates include continental breakfast and afternoon tea. 2-night minimum

Moments **Packing a Picnic on Cape Porpoise**

Cape Porpoise ★★ is a lovely little village, nearly forgotten by time, between Kennebunk and **Biddeford** that makes for a superb day trip or bike ride—and you've got to love the name, too. Find it by traveling about 2½ miles east of Kennebunkport along Route 9 (from Dock Sq., go out Spring St. and turn right at Maine St.). While in the village, think about packing a picnic and taking it to the rocks where the lobster boats are tied up—you can watch fishing boats coming and going, or train your binoculars on Goat Island and its lighthouse. What to eat? In the village center, drop by **Bradbury Brothers Market** (✆ **207/967-3939;** www.bradburybros.com) for staples, or the seasonal **Cape Porpoise Kitchen** (✆ **800/488-1150** or 207/967-1150; www.capeporpoisekitchen.com) for prepared gourmet meals, cheeses, and baked goods. The town also has two good **lobster shacks** ★, a handful of shops, and a postage-stamp-size library.

Sat–Sun; 3-night minimum holiday weekends. AE, MC, V. Free valet parking. **Amenities:** Bikes; concierge; outdoor heated pool; limited room service. *In room:* A/C, TV, Wi-Fi (free).

The Yachtsman Lodge & Marina ★★ The White Barn Inn took over this riverfront motel in 1997 and made it over into a much more appealing base for exploring the Kennebunkport side of the river. Within walking distance of Dock Square, its nice touches abound: down comforters, granite-topped vanities, high ceilings, CD players, and French doors that open onto patios just above the river. While the rooms here are all motel-size and all on one level, their simple, classical styling and fine amenities are far superior to anything you'd ever find at a roadside or even chain motel. (Room rates here are higher than you might expect, as a consequence of that.)

Ocean Ave. (P.O. Box 2609), Kennebunkport, ME 04046. ✆ **207/967-2511.** Fax 207/967-5056. www.yachtsmanlodge.com. 30 units. $189–$369 double. Rates include continental breakfast. AE, MC, V. 2-night minimum stay Sat–Sun and holidays. **Amenities:** Bikes; canoes. *In room:* A/C, TV/VCR, CD player, fridge, hair dryer, Wi-Fi (free).

Where to Dine

Also don't miss the **Clam Shack** (✆ **207/967-3321;** www.theclamshack.net), tucked up against the bridge linking the two Kennebunks (it's on the south/Kennebunk side). The owner opens this dumpling-plain shack every spring, and some surprisingly well-heeled folks roll up to the window to order fried clams, steamed lobsters, chowder, or the awesome lobster rolls on round French bread with butter and mayo.

Federal Jack's Restaurant and Brew Pub ★ AMERICAN This light, airy, and modern restaurant, named after a schooner built at Cape Porpoise a century ago, is tucked back from the bridge in a retail complex sitting oddly amid boatyards lining the south bank of the Kennebunk River. From the second-floor perch (look for a seat on the spacious three-season deck in warmer weather), you can gaze across the river toward the shops of Dock Square. The restaurant is best known for its Kennebunkport Brewing Co. ales, lagers, and porters, which they've been brewing here beneath the pub since 1992. An upscale menu to accompany your beer features the expected hamburgers, seafood, wings, calamari, and pizza, plus some nods to and twists on regional fare—glazed salmon, a lobster feed. Keep an eye on the menu, which might include something as upscale as a grilled-crab-and-havarti sandwich, lamb burger, or plate of tuna sashimi, or as downscale as a bowl of Texas chili and a simple hummus wrap. Yes, they have a kids' menu, and Sunday brunch is served from 11:30am to 2pm.

8 Western Ave., Lower Village (south bank of Kennebunk River), Kennebunk. ✆ **207/967-4322.** www.federaljacks.com. Main courses $2.95–$16, lobster dinners priced to market. AE, DISC, MC, V. Daily 11:30am–1am (late-night menu only after 9pm Sun–Thurs and after 10pm Fri–Sat).

Hurricane ★★ AMERICAN Brooks and Luanne MacDonald's Hurricane remains the best place in downtown Kennebunkport for a gourmet lunch or dinner. Its windows on the river and casual, maritime decor are perfect for a sea town where millionaires wander around in jeans and boat shoes. Lunch might start with a cup of lobster chowder, the "Ice Cube" (a block of iceberg lettuce with blue-cheese dressing, toasted pecans, roasted pears, and croutons), a lobster Cobb salad, a bento box of Maine seafood, or a salad; the main course could be a Cubano sandwich, a grilled tuna burger, or a three-cheese tortellini. Dinner entrees run to such items as a Mediterranean stew of Maine lobster and other local seafood; pan-roasted chicken with a pecorino macaroni-and-cheese; grilled beef tenderloin; brined pork chop with honeyed sweet potatoes; baked lobster stuffed with scallops, crab, and shrimp; or a slowly cooked rack of lamb. Finish with a dessert like vanilla bean crème brûlée, Key lime tart with coconut rum sauce, panna cotta, toffee-flavored bread pudding, or a course of cheeses—or, if it's around Christmas, ask if the egg nog cheesecake is on the menu.

29 Dock Sq., Kennebunkport. ✆ **207/967-9111.** www.hurricanerestaurant.com. Reservations recommended. Small plates $8–$25, main courses $19–$45. AE, DC, DISC, MC, V. Daily 11:30am–10:30pm (winter to 9:30pm).

Pier 77 Restaurant ★ REGIONAL Long a tony restaurant with a wonderful ocean view, Pier 77 was recently renovated and renamed by husband-and-wife team Peter and Kate Morency. The food, drawing on Peter's training at the Culinary Institute of America and 20 years in top kitchens in Boston and San Francisco, is more contemporary and skillful than almost anything else in Maine. Lunches run to comfort food: barbecued pork, spaghetti and meatballs, cheddar burgers, fried clams. The dinner menu leans toward traditional American favorites (pastas, steaks, lobster) as well, but there are also some slightly more adventurous dishes: A trio of duck courses and a tomato-y seafood stew have landed on the menu, for instance. The restaurant has earned *Wine Spectator*'s awards of excellence since 1993. A more casual section known as the Ramp Bar & Grill stays open all day, even between the lunch and dinner services.

77 Pier Rd., Cape Porpoise (Kennebunkport). ✆ **207/967-8500.** www.pier77restaurant.com. Reservations recommended. Main courses $9–$18 at lunch, $18–$30 at dinner. AE, MC, V. Restaurant daily 11:30am–2:30pm and 5–9pm. Ramp Bar & Grill 11:30am–9pm. Closed Tues Oct–Dec.

White Barn Inn ★★★ REGIONAL/NEW AMERICAN The White Barn Inn's (see "Where to Stay," above) classy dining room—carved out of a former barn, naturally, attached to the inn—attracts gourmands from across the nation. The barn itself is half the fun, with its cathedral-like space and an eclectic collection of country antiques displayed in the old hayloft; window displays are changed with the seasons. Chef Jonathan Cartwright's menu also changes frequently, nearly always incorporating local ingredients. You might start with his signature lobster spring roll (daikon radish, carrots, snow peas, and Thai sauce accent the lobster meat), or locally caught pan-seared diver scallops; glide through an *intermezzo* course of fruit soup or sorbet; then graduate to a pan-seared filet of salmon, a grilled chicken breast over creamed spinach, or a simply steamed lobster over fettuccine with cognac coral-butter sauce. Cartwright's special tasting menus run to seasonal items such as variations of oyster, sautéed smoked haddock rarebit, Québec foie gras roulade, or peekytoe crab with a roast pineapple salad. And the table service is astonishingly attentive and knowledgeable, capping the experience. It's no surprise at all to learn this is often selected one of America's top inn restaurants by readers of top travel magazines; it's simply Maine's best.

37 Beach Ave., Kennebunkport. ✆ **207/967-2321.** www.whitebarninn.com. Reservations recommended. Fixed-price dinner $91, tasting menu $125 per person. AE, MC, V. Mon–Thurs 6:30–9:30pm; Fri 5:30–9:30pm. Closed 2 weeks in Jan.

3 PORTLAND ★★

Portland: 106 miles N of Boston

Maine's largest city, salty **Portland** sits on a hammerhead-shaped peninsula extending into scenic Casco Bay. It's easy to drive right past the place on I-295, admiring the skyline at 60 mph, on your way to the villages, islands, and rocky points farther up the coast. People don't usually think about an urban experience while packing for a vacation in Maine.

But I can speak from direct experience: Portland is *well* worth an afternoon's detour, or even a whole weekend. This historic city has plenty of charm—not only in its renovated, touristy Old Port (a place of brick sidewalks, cobblestone streets, and fish)—but also throughout its lovely residential neighborhoods, some of which look out onto Casco Bay.

And it's a great base, too. From here, you can catch a 20-minute ferry to quiet offshore islands; drive 20 minutes to terrific lighthouses and beaches; browse through good antiques and boutique shops; drink excellent coffee and eat top-flight baked goods; photograph an amazing variety of historic mansions, churches, and other architectural treasures; and dine better than you can anywhere else in northern New England. (In this city, the Food Network is almost required viewing.) Blessed with an uncommon number of excellent restaurants and brewpubs for a city this size—the population totals just 100,000, and that's including all the suburbs—Portland eats and drinks *well.* So can you.

ESSENTIALS

GETTING THERE Coming from the south by car, downtown Portland is most easily reached by taking exit 44 off the Maine Turnpike (I-95), then following I-295 (which is free) into the city. Exit onto Franklin Arterial (exit 7), and continue straight downhill to the city's ferry terminal. Turn right onto Commercial Street, and continue a few blocks to parking meters and the visitor center on the right (see below). Get oriented there.

Amtrak (✆ **800/872-7245;** www.amtrak.com) runs a daily *Downeaster* service from Boston's North Station to Portland (passengers from other cities must change stations from South Station to North Station in Boston by taxi or subway). The train makes five round-trips daily (2½ hr. one-way), and a ticket costs $24 each way. From the station, downtown is a short city bus ride, or a drab 30- to 45-minute walk, away.

The regional line **Concord Coach** (✆ **800/639-3317** or 207/228-3300; www.concordcoachlines.com) connects Portland to Boston, with more than a dozen buses daily from Boston's bus station and Logan Airport. The trip takes about 2 hours and costs $21 to $26 one-way, $35 to $44 round-trip. Its bus terminal is set on Thompson Point Road (a 30- to 45-min. walk from downtown) next to the Amtrak station; from there, you can walk, but it's difficult. City buses and taxis also serve the terminal.

Greyhound (✆ **800/231-2222;** www.greyhound.com) provides bus service into Portland from both Boston and New York City. Several buses daily make the trip from Boston, which takes about 2 hours and costs $21 each way; from New York, there's only one bus per day (7 hr.), costing $47 each way. Greyhound's bus terminal is at 950 Congress St., about a mile downhill from, and south of, the downtown core—walking distance, though a long way.

Portland International Jetport (✆ **207/874-8877;** www.portlandjetport.org), airport code PWM, is the largest airport in Maine. It's served by flights from **AirTran** (✆ 800/247-8726; www.airtran.com), **Continental** (✆ 800/523-3273; www.continental.com), **Delta/Northwest** (✆ 800/221-1212; www.delta.com), **JetBlue** (✆ 800/538-2583; www.jetblue.com), **United Express** (✆ 800/864-8331; www.ual.com), and **US Airways** (✆ 800/428-4322; www.usair.com). The airport has grown by fits and starts in recent years but is still easily navigated. Many hotels in the city offer free shuttles to and from the airport; inquire when booking your hotel.

Car rentals are available from a half-dozen chain outfits at the terminal. Also, the no. 5 **Metro city bus** ($1.25) passes nearby about twice per hour (but once per hour, for shorter hours, on Sun); limos and vans can be called to pick you up; and a taxi into the city center costs about $20, tip included.

VISITOR INFORMATION The **Convention and Visitors Bureau of Greater Portland** (www.visitportland.com) maintains *four* information centers in and around the city. The **main info center** (✆ **207/772-5800**) is located on the new Ocean Gateway Pier, at the far-northern end of Commercial Street past the Casco Bay Ferry docks. Most of the time, it's open Monday to Saturday; in July and August, it also opens on Sunday, and it's closed the last two weeks of February.

You'll also find tourist information kiosks at the **Portland International Jetport** (✆ **207/775-5809**), near the baggage claim, open daily year-round; in **Deering Oaks Park** at the Forest Avenue exit of I-295, open at least six days a week year-round (closed Sun in Sept and June); and one ad hoc kiosk that opens up outside the **cruise ship terminal** on Commercial Street for 4 hours after any cruise ship arrives.

Portland also has a free weekly newspaper, the *Portland Phoenix* (**www.thephoenix.com/portland**), offering good listings of local events, films, nightclub performances, and the like. Copies are widely available at restaurants, bars, convenience stores, and in newspaper boxes on the curb.

EXPLORING THE CITY

Visitors to Portland usually begin with a quick stroll around the historic **Old Port** ★. Bounded by Commercial, Congress, Union, and Pearl streets, this area near the waterfront has some of the city's best commercial architecture, a clutch of boutiques, some of the state's best restaurants (seafood is a special strength here), and one of the densest concentrations of bars on the eastern seaboard. (Late on a weekend night, the young packs of drinkers here can get rowdy.)

Where to begin? Either at the foot of the port, along Commercial Street, or walking up or downhill along **Exchange Street**—the spiritual heart of the Old Port, with the most boutiques, eateries, and coffee shops. Narrow, attractive streets run off and around Exchange, as well. These alleys and intricate brick facades in the port area reflect the mid-Victorian era; most of this area was rebuilt following a devastating fire in 1866 that leveled the entire waterfront.

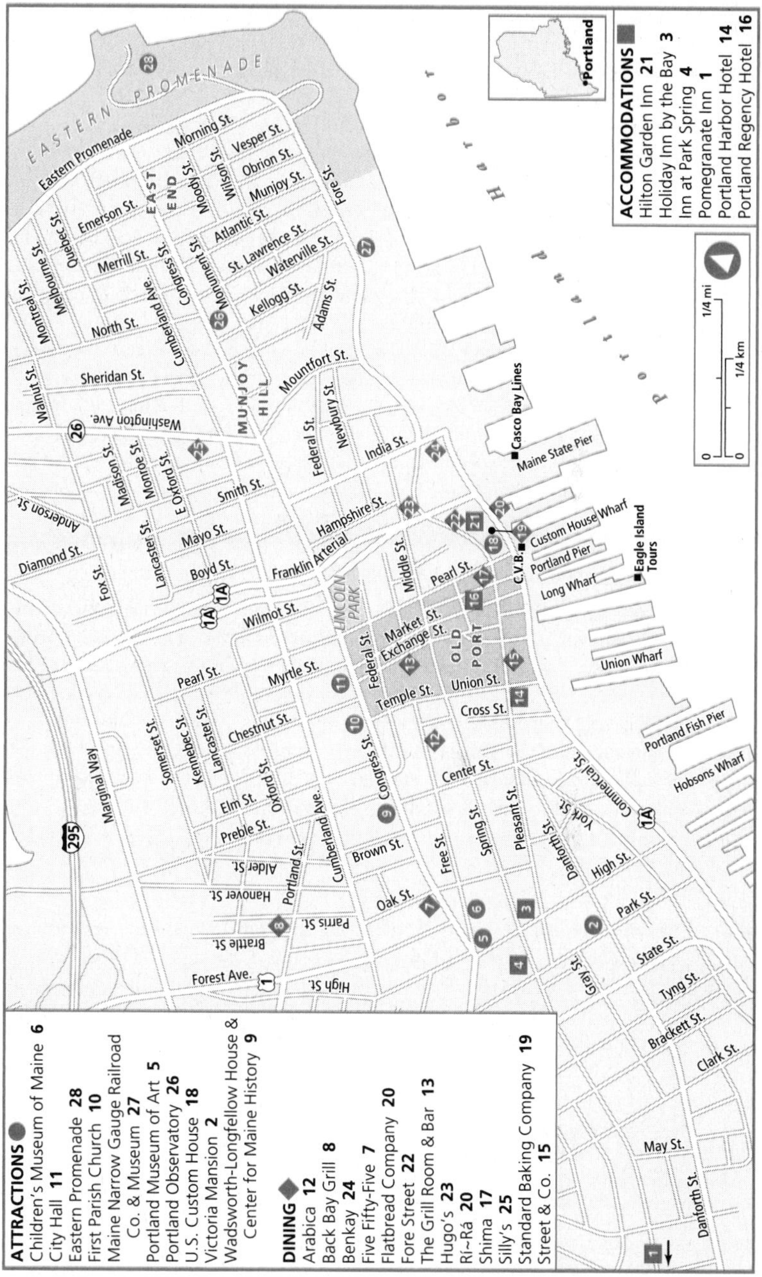

COASTAL MAINE 9 PORTLAND

Just outside the Old Port, don't miss the **First Parish Church** at 425 Congress St., a granite meetinghouse with an impressively austere interior that has changed little since 1826. A few doors down the block, Portland's **City Hall** is at the head of Exchange Street. Modeled after New York City's city hall, it was built from granite in 1909. In a similarly regal vein is the **U.S. Custom House,** at 312 Fore St. near the Old Port. The fine woodwork and marble floors here date to 1868.

The city's finest harborside stroll is along the **Eastern Prom Pathway** ★★, which wraps for about a mile along the waterfront beginning at the Casco Bay Lines ferry terminal at the corner of Commercial and Franklin streets. This paved pathway is suitable for walking or biking, and offers expansive views of the islands and sailboats in the harbor. The pathway skirts the lower edge of the **Eastern Promenade** ★★, a 68-acre hillside park with broad, grassy slopes extending down to the water. There's also a tiny beach here, though it's often off-limits for swimming. The pathway continues on to Back Cove Pathway, a 3.5-mile loop around tidal Back Cove.

Atop **Munjoy Hill,** above the Eastern Promenade, you'll find a cluster of good restaurants, grocers, and a coffee shop, not to mention the distinctive **Portland Observatory** (✆ **207/774-5561**) at 138 Congress St.: a quirky, shingled tower built in 1807 to signal the arrival of ships into port. Exhibits inside the tower provide a quick glimpse of Portland's past, but the real reason people come is for the great views from the top. It's open daily (when flags are flying from the cupola) from Memorial Day through Columbus Day, with guided tours from 10am until 5pm; the last tour leaves at 4:30pm. (In the middle of summer, the observatory stays open until 8pm for sunset viewing from on high.) Admission to the tower is $7 for adults, $4 for children ages 6 to 16.

Children's Museum of Maine ★ Kids The centerpiece exhibit in Portland's kids' museum—a stout, columned downtown building next to the art museum—is its *camera obscura,* a room-size "camera" on the top floor. Children gather around a white table in a dark room, where they see magically projected images that include cars driving by on streets, boats plying the harbor, and seagulls flapping by. This never fails to enthrall, providing a memorable lesson in the workings of lenses. That's just one attraction; there are plenty more, from a simulated supermarket checkout counter to a firehouse pole to a mock space shuttle that kids pilot from a high cockpit.

142 Free St. (next to the Portland Museum of Art). ✆ **207/828-1234.** www.childrensmuseumofme.org. Admission $6; free 5–8pm 1st Fri of the month. AE, MC, V. Mon–Sat 10am–5pm; Sun noon–5pm. Closed Mon Nov–Apr.

Maine Narrow Gauge Railroad Co. & Museum Kids During the late 19th century, Maine was home to several narrow-gauge railways, operating on rails that were just 2 feet apart. Most of these trains have disappeared, but this nonprofit organization is dedicated to preserving some of the few examples that remain. The small admission fee to the museum is waived if you purchase a more expensive ticket for the short ride on a little train that putters along Casco Bay at the foot of the Eastern Promenade. Views of the islands are great; the ride is slow and yawn-inducing, but young kids enjoy it.

58 Fore St. ✆ **207/828-0814.** www.mngrr.org. Museum admission $2 adults, $1 seniors and children 3–12; train fare (includes museum admission) $10 adults, $9 seniors, $6 children 3–12, free for children 2 and under. Memorial Day to Columbus Day daily 10am–4pm (trains run on the hour); rest of year Mon–Fri 10am–4pm. From I-295, take Franklin Arterial exit to Fore St.; turn left and continue to museum on right.

Portland Head Light & Museum ★★★ A short drive from downtown Portland, this 1794 lighthouse has been called one of the most picturesque in the nation. It's certainly one of the most-photographed; you'll possibly recognize it from advertisements, calendars, postcards, or posters. It was the first constructed in the new United States, commissioned by President George Washington; it began warning ships in 1791 and was manned by a keeper until 1989, when it was automated and the graceful keeper's house converted into a small museum focusing on the history of navigation. The lighthouse itself is still active, thus it's closed to the public. But you can stop by the museum, browse for lighthouse-themed gifts in a gift shop, and wander the lawns, cliffs, and other grounds of adjacent **Fort Williams Park,** which is a great place for a picnic, tossing around a Frisbee, strumming a guitar, or peering out to sea through the looking-glasses on the cliff top.

1000 Shore Rd. (in Fort Williams Park), Cape Elizabeth. ✆ **207/799-2661.** www.portlandheadlight.com. Free admission for grounds; museum $2 adults, $1 children 6–18. Park grounds daily year-round sunrise–sunset (until 8:30pm in summer); museum daily Memorial Day to Columbus Day 10am–4pm, Sat–Sun only mid-Apr to mid-May and mid-Oct to late Dec. From Portland, follow State St. across bridge to South Portland; bear left on Broadway. At 3rd light, turn right on Cottage Rd. (Rte. 77), which becomes Shore Rd.; follow several more miles to park on left.

Portland Museum of Art ★★★ Portland's top-rate art museum announces itself boldly with a high, thin, brick front wall, and indeed it was designed by the famous firm of I.M. Pei & Partners in 1983. Its holdings are superb, with art drawn from its own fine collections plus a parade of touring exhibits. (Summer exhibits are usually targeted at a broader audience and include the work of internationally famous painters.) The holdings are particularly strong in terms of American artists with Maine connections, such as Winslow Homer, Andrew Wyeth, and Edward Hopper; it also hosts fine displays of Early American furniture and crafts. The museum also shares the Joan Whitney Payson Collection with Colby College (the college borrows it for one semester every 2 years), which includes wonderful work by Renoir, Degas, and Picasso, among other titans. Special exhibitions have brought in the landscape paintings of Frederic Church, art by Native American high-school students from northern Maine, and a mysterious *Mona Lisa* that may have been a preparatory study for the famous work; who knows? Guided tours are given once daily at 2pm.

7 Congress Sq. (corner of Congress and High sts.). ✆ **207/775-6148.** www.portlandmuseum.org. Admission $10 adults, $8 seniors, $4 students 6–17; free admission Fri 5–9pm. Tues–Sun 10am–5pm (Fri to 9pm); Memorial Day to mid-Oct also Mon 10am–5pm.

Victoria Mansion ★★★ Finds Widely regarded as one of the most elaborate Victorian brownstone homes ever built in the U.S., this mansion (also known as the Morse-Libby House, but rarely called that) is oft-mentioned in books on American architecture. It's a remarkable piece of high Victoriana. Built between 1858 and 1863 for a Maine businessman who had made his fortune in New Orleans, the towering, slightly foreboding home is a prime example of Italianate style. Inside, craftsmen and artisans went to town with murals and other details; the decor is somber, yet the home offers an engaging look into a bygone era. It's a must for architecture buffs—or just snap a photo of the exterior from the sidewalk if you're pressed for time or don't want to buy the pricey admission ticket. The weeks leading up to Christmas bring special events and extra tours.

109 Danforth St. ✆ **207/772-4841.** www.victoriamansion.org. Admission $15 adults, $14 seniors, $5 children 6–17, $35 family, free for children 5 and under. May–Oct Mon–Sat 10am–4pm, Sun 1–5pm; late Nov to Dec daily 11am–5pm. Tours (45 min.) twice per hour. Closed Jan–Apr and Nov until day after Thanksgiving. From the Old Port, head west on Fore St., and veer right on Danforth St. at light (beside Yosaku sushi restaurant); proceed 3 blocks to the mansion on right, at corner of Park St.

Wadsworth-Longfellow House & Center for Maine History ★★ The Maine Historical Society's self-described "history campus" includes three buildings lined up along busy Congress Street in downtown Portland. Most local residents never give these buildings a second thought, but they're important. The austere brick Wadsworth-Longfellow House dates from 1785 and was built by Gen. Peleg Wadsworth, father of the noted poet Henry Wadsworth. It's furnished in an early-19th-century style, with many samples of Longfellow family furniture on display. Adjacent to the home is the Maine History Gallery, in a garish postmodern building (formerly a bank). Changing exhibits here explore the rich texture of Maine history. And just behind the Longfellow house is the library of the Maine Historical Society, a popular destination for amateur genealogists and Portland buffs. You have to be a history nerd to appreciate this place, but it's gold if you are.

489 Congress St. ✆ **207/774-1822.** www.mainehistory.org. Admission $8 adults, $7 seniors and students, $3 children 5–17. Wadsworth-Longfellow House May–Oct and Dec Mon–Sat 10:30am–4pm and Sun noon–4pm; tours on the hour. Closed Jan–Apr and Nov. History museum Mon–Sat 10am–5pm; Sun noon–5pm. Research library normally Tues–Sat 10am–4pm but hours vary.

ON THE WATER

Casco Bay Lines Seven of Casco Bay's islands have year-round populations and are served by scheduled ferries from downtown Portland. These ferries, which depart from a plain terminal at the north end of Commercial Street (across from the Hilton), provide an inexpensive way to view both the bustling harbor and these islands. Trips range from a 20-minute ride to Peaks Island (the most populous) to longer "mail boat" circuits taking in several quieter islands in one run. All these islands are well suited for walking or cycling; Peaks Island has a rocky back shore accessible by the island's paved perimeter road (bring a picnic lunch and a bike), while Long Island has a nice hidden beach. Cliff Island is the most remote of the six-pack, with a sedate turn-of-the-20th-century character. Fares are discounted by about half outside of peak season.

Commercial and Franklin sts. ✆ **207/774-7871.** www.cascobaylines.com. Summer $7.70–$12 round-trip; off season $4.10–$7.45 round-trip. Frequent departures daily 6am–10pm.

Eagle Island Tours ★ Eagle Island was the summer home of famed Arctic explorer and Portland native Robert E. Peary, who claimed in 1909 to be the first person to reach the North Pole. In 1904 Peary built a simple home on a remote, 17-acre island at the edge of Casco Bay—perhaps he wanted to preserve that polar feel of having no neighbors? Later he added flourishes in the form of two low stone towers. After Peary's death in 1920, his family kept up the home and later donated it to the state of Maine, which now manages it as a state park. The home is open to the public, maintained much as it was when Peary lived here, but you can get here only by taking your own boat or a charter boat. **Portland Discovery,** a local outfit offering various tours of Portland and the vicinity, sends a boat out from Portland's Long Wharf (the one with the boat-shaped restaurant) five times per week in summer; the 4-hour excursion includes a 1½-hour stopover on the island, which is lovely in and of itself. Bring a picnic.

Long Wharf (Commercial St.) ✆ **207/774-0808.** www.eagleislandtours.com. Admission $33 adults, $20 children 3–12 (fare includes state-park fee). July to Labor Day tour departs 10am Tues and Thurs–Sun.

MINOR LEAGUE BASEBALL

Portland Sea Dogs ★★ Value Kids This Double-A baseball team affiliated with the Boston Red Sox (a perfect marriage in baseball-crazy northern New England) plays its games at Hadlock Field, a small, attractive stadium a few miles from downtown (but close to the interstate highway) that retains an old-timey feel. It's a great place to catch a contest, especially on a summer night when the lights are on and ticket prices are a *steal.* (Get it?) Activities are geared toward families, with lots of entertainment between innings and food that's a couple notches above just hot dogs and peanuts. (Try the french fries, grilled sausages, and local brews like Shipyard, Sebago, and Geary's, available from the microbrew pavilion.) You'll almost certainly catch future pro stars in action, too—current Sox like Josh Beckett, Kevin Youkilis, Jacoby Ellsbury, and Jonathan Papelbon all did time here.

Hadlock Field, 271 Park Ave. ✆ **800/936-3647** or 207/879-9500 (ticket office). www.seadogs.com. Adults $7–$9, children 16 and under $4–$8. Season runs Apr to Labor Day.

WHERE TO STAY

If you're looking for something central, the **Hilton Garden Inn** at 65 Commercial St. (✆ **207/780-0780;** www.hiltongardeninn.hilton.com) is right across from the city's ferry dock. It's convenient to all the Old Port's restaurants, bakeries, and pubs—not to mention the islands of Casco Bay. You'll pay for the privilege of being in the heart of the waterfront, though: Double rooms mostly run from about $189 up to $369 per night.

The **Holiday Inn by the Bay,** 88 Spring St. (✆ **800/345-5050** or 207/775-2311; www.innbythebay.com), offers great views of the harbor from about half the rooms, along with the usual chain-hotel creature comforts. Peak-season rates are approximately $180 for a double. Budget travelers seeking chain hotels typically head toward the area around the Maine Mall in South Portland, about 8 miles south of the attractions of downtown.

Black Point Inn ★★ The Black Point Inn is a Maine classic. Built as a summer resort in 1873 on the same rocky point (Prouts Neck) memorialized by landscape painter Winslow Homer, it remains a great luxury choice—even if it is a lot smaller than it used to be. The property changed hands in 2007 and then emerged under new ownership; having sold off outlying cottages, they thereby slashed the inn's room count by approximately two-thirds. But the rooms that do remain, in the main inn, have been given a much-needed makeover. The interior of the inn is as elegant as ever, and views from the expansive porch (with its constant sea breezes) are as breathtaking as ever. If rates seem hefty, that's because they include breakfast, dinner, and views stretching both north and south along the coast. Homer's former painting studio is a short half-mile walk around the point. It takes about 20 minutes to drive to this inn from downtown Portland.

510 Black Point Rd., Scarborough, ME 04074. ✆ **207/883-2500.** Fax 207/883-9976. www.blackpointinn.com. 25 units. $420–$560 double; $540–$620 suite. Rates include full breakfast and dinner. AE, DC, DISC, MC, V. Free valet parking. Closed Nov–Apr. From Portland, drive south on I-295, getting off at Rte. 1 S. (exit 4); continue south 4½ miles to Rte. 207 intersection, turn left, and continue 5 miles south along Black Point Rd. to inn (on left). **Amenities:** Restaurant; babysitting; children's programs (summer only); exercise room; Jacuzzi; heated outdoor pool; limited room service; sauna. *In room:* A/C, TV/DVD, hair dryer, Wi-Fi (free).

Inn at Park Spring ★ This small, tasteful B&B is located on a busy downtown street in a historic brick home that dates back to 1835. It's well located for exploring the city on foot, and well kept by friendly owners John and Nancy Gonsalves. Guests can linger or watch TV in the front parlor, or chat at the dining table in the adjacent room (communal breakfasts here are a highlight—unless you're shy). The accommodations are all corner rooms, and most are bright and sunny. Especially nice is the Spring Room, with its queen sleigh bed, hardwood flooring, and wonderful views of the historic row houses along Park Street; and crimson-hued Gables, on the third (top) floor, which gets plenty of afternoon light and is furnished with a king bed, big sitting room, and nice bathroom. The Portland Museum of Art is only 2 blocks away, the Old Port about 10 minutes away, and great restaurants are within an easy walk.

135 Spring St., Portland, ME 04101. ✆ **800/437-8511** or 207/774-1059. www.innatparkspring.com. 6 units. Mid-Apr to Oct and holidays $129–$205 double; Nov to mid-Apr $99–$165 double. 2-night minimum stay Sat–Sun. Rates include full breakfast. AE, MC, V. No children 9 and under. *In room:* A/C, hair dryer, Wi-Fi (free).

Inn by the Sea ★★★ Not so much an inn as a luxury retreat, Cape Elizabeth's grand hotel has made the successful transition from relaxed seaside getaway to destination resort. Yet they've done it while retaining a wonderful sense of place: Suites and dining areas emphasize Maine-themed art and foods, while summery gardens and ocean views tantalize through the windows. An expansive **spa** was added in 2008, as were fireplace rooms and bi-level spa suites with double Jacuzzis. A further set of cottages (town-house-like suites) in an outbuilding add full kitchens and extra bedroom or bathroom space. Especially welcome is this inn's move toward green practices: It was the first hotel in Maine to burn biofuels, operate carbon neutrally, and employ printed-paper key cards. (Recycled materials and low-flow toiletry also predominate.) The house restaurant, **Sea Glass ★★**, is excellent, and the boardwalk path at the foot of the property leads down to one of southern Maine's best beaches—no admission ticket required. Kids' programs include walks and nighttime marshmallow roasts.

40 Bowery Beach Rd., Cape Elizabeth, ME 04107. ✆ **800/888-4287** (outside ME) or 207/799-3134. Fax 207/799-4779. www.innbythesea.com. 57 units. July–Aug $350–$419 double, $399–$789 suite; May–June and Sept–Oct $199–$209 double, $299–$509 suite; Nov–Apr $199–$209 double, $189–$369 suite. AE, DC, DISC, MC, V. Pets welcome in some units. **Amenities:** Restaurant; lounge; exercise room; Jacuzzi; heated outdoor pool; room service; sauna; spa. *In room:* A/C, TV/DVD, fridge (some units), hair dryer, kitchenette (some units), Wi-Fi (free).

Pomegranate Inn ★★ Housed in a dove-gray, 1884 Italianate home in Portland's lovely West End, this winning B&B is decorated with whimsy and elegance. Look for bold wall paintings by a local artist and eclectic antique furniture collected and tastefully arranged throughout. Each of the eight rooms is distinct, with painted floors and faux-marble woodwork. Most have gas fireplaces; the best room might be the one in the carriage house, which comes with its own private terrace (sliding doors lead out to a little garden) and a fireplace. Sit-down breakfasts are served in a cheery dining room.

49 Neal St., Portland, ME 04102. ✆ **800/356-0408** or 207/772-1006. Fax 207/773-4426. www.pomegranateinn.com. 8 units. Memorial Day to Oct $185–$295 double; rest of year $140–$225 double. Rates include full breakfast. 2-night minimum stay summer weekends and holidays. AE, DISC, MC, V. On-street parking. Take Spring St. to Neal St. and turn right. Children 16 and over welcome. *In room:* A/C, TV, Wi-Fi (free).

Portland Harbor Hotel ★★ Adjacent to Portland's bar scene on the corner of Fore and Union streets, this semicircular, town-house-like structure was designed to fit in with the much older brick facades that prevail in the surrounding Old Port. Yet it's quite modern inside, with many amenities and a boutique feel. An interior courtyard throws off European ambience; big, exquisite rooms are furnished with comfy queen- and king-size beds and spacious work desks. Even standard rooms are outfitted with armoires, duvets, two-line phones, large televisions, and deep bathtubs in granite-faced bathrooms, while deluxe rooms and suites add Jacuzzis and sitting areas. The house restaurant, **Eve's**

at the Garden, serves gourmet meals, and the front desk rents bicycles and helmets to aid your sightseeing.

468 Fore St., Portland, ME 04101. ✆ **888/798-9090** or 207/775-9090. Fax 207/775-9990. www.portlandharborhotel.com. 100 units. Mid-May to mid-Oct $229–$249 double, $329 suite; off season $159–$179 double, $259 suite. AE, DC, DISC, MC, V. Valet parking in garage $16 per day. **Amenities:** Dining room; bar; babysitting; bikes; concierge; exercise room; room service. *In room:* A/C, TV, hair dryer, Wi-Fi (free).

Portland Regency Hotel ★★ Centrally located on a cobblestone courtyard right in the middle of the Old Port, the Regency boasts one of the city's premier hotel locations. And it's got more than location—this is also one of the most architecturally striking luxury hotels in southern Maine. Housed in an 1895 brick armory, the hotel is thoroughly modern and offers attractive rooms, appointed and furnished with all the expected amenities. You can choose from several types of rooms and suites, each fitted to the place's unique architecture; for a splurge, ask about a luxurious corner room with a handsome (nonworking) fireplace, sitting area, city views out the big windows, and a Jacuzzi. The small health club is among the best in town (it includes a sauna and hot tub), and the basement level conceals both a restaurant **(Twenty Milk Street)** and the small **Armory Lounge** ★, a great, quiet place to sip a drink.

20 Milk St., Portland, ME 04101. ✆ **800/727-3436** or 207/774-4200. Fax 207/775-2150. www.theregency.com. 95 units. Early July to late Oct $249–$269 double, $289–$389 suite; off season $159–$219 double, $209–$329 suite. AE, DISC, MC, V. Valet parking $12 per day. **Amenities:** Restaurant; bar; babysitting; health club; Jacuzzi; limited room service; sauna; spa. *In room:* A/C, TV, minibar, Wi-Fi (free).

WHERE TO DINE

In addition to its raft of top-flight gourmet restaurants (the listings below are just a sampling; there are many more good-to-great places), Portland is also a city of creative cheap eats. Don't neglect local bakeries, coffee shops, and markets when you're trolling for a quick or takeout meal.

Standard Baking Company ★★ (✆ **207/773-2112**) at 75 Commercial St., for instance, is one of my favorite bakeries in all New England. Allison Bray and Matt James bake up great sticky buns (with or without nuts) and focaccia, plus top-rate breads, brioche, and cookies, in an aromatic space right beneath the Fore Street restaurant (see below). They brew good coffee here, too, and they're open daily.

Of the many coffee shops around the city, I most often end up at **Arabica** ★ (✆ **207/879-0792**), at 2 Free St., a locally owned business featuring house-roasted beans, a great choice of coffee drinks and teas, and pie, bagels, scones—even toast with peanut butter.

Expensive

Back Bay Grill ★★ NEW AMERICAN Back Bay Grill has long been one of Portland's best restaurants, with an upscale, contemporary ambience; the only trouble is finding it (it's near the city's main post office, far from most other sights). The menu, revamped seasonally, emphasizes local produce and meats as much as possible. Diners might start with some kicky Maine crab cakes, a saffrony mussel chowder, beef tartare with truffle flavors, foie gras served with crispy polenta, house-cured gravlax salmon, or local mussels steamed in white wine. Among the main courses, look for such dishes as filet mignon with gnocchi, breast of duck, salmon with couscous, Casco Bay cod in a tomato–lemon grass broth, two versions of lamb, or agnolotti stuffed with goat's-milk ricotta and spinach. Finish with crème brûlée, caramel ice cream with bourbon sauce, vanilla panna cotta, or a walnut and lemon crepe with mead-and-caramel sauce.

65 Portland St. ✆ **207/772-8833.** www.backbaygrill.com. Reservations recommended. Main courses $18–$35. AE, DC, DISC, MC, V. Mon–Thurs 5:30–9:30pm; Fri–Sat 5:30–10pm. From Congress St., take High St. downhill to Park Ave. and turn right (becomes Portland St.); continue 4 blocks to Parris St.

Five Fifty-Five ★★ NEW AMERICAN Has it already been 7 years? Steve and Michelle Corry opened this eatery on a somewhat moribund stretch of Congress Street, just when Portland's main drag was in need of a shot in the arm. It's been a marvelous hit. Sommelier Michelle, formerly of the White Barn Inn, oversees a cellar that reportedly brags of more than a thousand bottles of wine. Steve is a former brewer and NECI graduate named one of *Food & Wine*'s chefs to watch in 2007. His cuisine features small plates grouped into categories (green, savory, and so forth) that might include anything from soups, beet salads, and cheese plates to foie gras or full, meal-size plates like "the sticky pig" (a grilled pork chop with a honey glaze and apple butter), grilled veal, or truffled, lobster-flavored mac-and-cheese. Tasting menus bring in additional courses like crispy codfish, lobster, hanger steak with caramelized shallots, steak carpaccio, and hand-rolled pasta, while dessert options might include a chocolate-hazelnut upside-down cake with coffee and cardamom ice cream; old fashioned apple crisp with oats, Calvados, and crème anglaise; a sweet potato Napoleon with maple syrup; homemade ice cream; or warm cranberry-and-cream cheese tarts. The wine list, of course, is huge yet well selected.

555 Congress St. ✆ **207/761-0555.** www.fivefifty-five.com. Reservations recommended. Small plates $6–$15, main courses $31–$35, tasting menus around $60. AE, MC, V. Sun 9:30am–2pm and 5–9:30pm; Mon–Thurs 5–9:30pm; Fri–Sat 5–10:30pm.

Fore Street ★★ CONTEMPORARY GRILL Fore Street has emerged as one of northern New England's most celebrated restaurants. Chef Sam Hayward gets profiled in magazines like *Saveur* and *House Beautiful,* his restaurant was often in *Gourmet*'s 100 Best, and so forth. Hayward's secret is simplicity: Local and organic ingredients are used where possible, and the kitchen avoids fussy presentations. The dining space centers around a busy open kitchen where a team of chefs constantly stoke the wood-fired brick oven and grill, which feature prominently in the culinary philosophy here. The menu changes nightly, but entrees might run to spit-roasted pork loin, grilled duckling, grilled marinated hanger steak, or a piece of pan-seared bluefish; the wood-roasted mussels are also a big hit. Finish with a dessert such as chocolate soufflé, hand-dipped chocolates, or gelati—these are often accented in summer by seasonal Maine berries or fruits. Though it can be difficult to snag a reservation here on summer weekends, management always sets aside a few tables every night for walk-ins. Get there early and grab one.

288 Fore St. ✆ **207/775-2717.** www.forestreet.biz. Reservations recommended. Main courses $13–$29. AE, MC, V. Sun–Thurs 5:30–10pm (May–Oct Sun to 9:30pm); Fri–Sat 5:30–10:30pm.

Hugo's ★★★ NEW AMERICAN A decade ago this place was fading fast, but chef Rob Evans and partner Nancy Pugh bought the place and changed all that. Now it's arguably the most exciting place to eat in northern New England. Trained in star kitchens (French Laundry, the Inn at Little Washington), Evans brought a philosophy of using local ingredients and crafting unusual, exciting menus. (He was named "best chef in the Northeast" by the James Beard Foundation in 2009.) Evans offers a small-plate style of service of mid-sized, constantly changing portions of everything from sweetbreads with peanut and cilantro flavors to goat-cheese ravioli with molé sauce; raw Maine sea urchin over sticky rice; pan-fried Arctic Char; local cod baked in parchment paper; a combo plate of rib-eye, short ribs, potato puree, and onions; or crisped pork belly with fried pig's tail and a jalapeño marmalade. A nightly "blind" tasting menu (you don't find out what you ate until the end) expands the journey to six courses, and chef's menus (by advance reservation only) run to even more flights. Dessert could be a very upscale take on peanut butter cups, ice-cream floats, or an apple turnover jacked up with dates, bacon, pralines, and homemade butter ice cream. A good tapas menu (charcuterie, cheese plates) is served at the bar, and the same partners also run a Belgian fries-and-shakes shop, Duckfat, down the block.

88 Middle St. ✆ **207/774-8538.** www.hugos.net. Reservations strongly recommended. Plates $10–$25, tasting menus $75 and up. AE, MC, V. Tues–Thurs 5:30–9pm; Fri–Sat 5:30–9:30pm.

Street & Co. ★★ SEAFOOD Dana Street's intimate brick-walled bistro specializes in seafood, and it's possibly the city's best place to eat fish. You pass the open kitchen as you're seated in one of the two halves of a quirky dining room, then watch the talented chefs perform their magic in the tiny space. The fish is as fresh as can be (the docks are a block away), and they do lobster in interesting configurations (such as grilled and served over linguine in a buttery garlic sauce). Other fine choices include tuna, mussels, or the grilled catch of the day. Reservations are definitely recommended, although some tables are set aside for walk-ins; it can't hurt to check if you're strolling down Wharf Street and get hungry (try toward opening, rather than toward the middle of the service). During summer, outdoor seating is available at a few choice alfresco tables on a cobblestone alley: plain but atmospheric.

33 Wharf St. ✆ **207/775-0887.** www.streetandcompany.net. Reservations recommended. Main courses $14–$24. AE, MC, V. Mon–Thurs 5:30–9:30pm; Fri–Sat 5:30–10pm. Lounge opens 30 min. earlier.

Moderate

Beale Street BBQ ★★ Finds BARBECUE Beale Street BBQ owner Mark Quigg once operated a takeout grill on Route 1 near Freeport, but author Stephen King got wind of his cooking; soon he was catering movie shoots and opening a restaurant. Of all the barbecue joints in Maine, this is probably my favorite. It's got an appealing roadhouse atmosphere, friendly staff, and great smoked meats. Check the board for daily specials, which usually include a fish entree as well as Creole and Cajun offerings. But I nearly always stick to the barbecue sampler (from the menu: "AKA All You Really Need to Know About BBQ"): You get your choice of pulled pork, chicken, or beef brisket; sweet, crunchy corn bread; a half slab of ribs; a quarter chicken; delicious spicy smoked links; and a mound of barbecued beans and coleslaw. Two people can comfortably split it, and it's just $24.

725 Broadway, South Portland. ✆ **207/767-0130.** www.mainebbq.com. Reservations not accepted. Main courses $9–$18. MC, V. Daily 11:30am–10pm. From Portland waterfront, cross Casco Bay Bridge (Rte. 77) and turn right onto Broadway; continue about 1/3 mile to restaurant.

Benkay ★ Value SUSHI Among Portland's sushi restaurants, Benkay is hippest, usually teeming with a lively local crowd lured by the affordable menus. Chef Seiji Ando trained in Osaka and Kyoto; his sushi, sashimi, and maki rolls deliver a lot for the price, and there's a wide range of choices and combinations. Standard Japanese bar-food items such as tempura (deep-fried vegetables), *gyoza* (dumplings), teriyaki, *katsu* (fried chicken or pork cutlets), and udon (thick noodles) are also served. It stays open pretty late, too—until midnight on Friday and Saturday, which is handy in early-closing Portland. For dessert, consider the green tea ice cream: deliciously bitter . . . and good for you. Sort of.

2 India St. (at Commercial St.). ✆ **207/773-5555.** www.sushiman.com. Reservations not accepted. Main courses $7.95–$17. AE, MC, V. Mon–Thurs 11:30am–2pm and 5–9:30pm; Fri 11:30am–2pm and 5pm–midnight; Sat 5pm–midnight; Sun 5–9pm.

Flatbread Company ★★ (Kids) PIZZA This upscale pizzeria—an offshoot of the original Flatbread Company in Vermont, with a serious hippie tinge—might have the best waterfront location in town. It sits on a slip overlooking the Casco Bay Lines terminal, so you can watch fishermen and ferries while you eat. The inside brings to mind a Phish concert, with quirky decor and bearded staffers stoking wood-fired ovens, slicing nitrate-free pepperoni and organic vegetables, and the like. The laid-back, wood-smoky, family-fun atmosphere makes the place fun to enter; but the pizza is excellent and will keep you coming back. Organic salads are also available.

72 Commercial St. ✆ **207/772-8777.** www.flatbreadcompany.com. Reservations accepted for large parties only. Most pizzas $12–$15. AE, MC, V. Daily 11:30am–10pm.

The Grill Room & Bar ★★ AMERICAN It replaced the popular Natasha's in this same space, but the Grill Room—the place with the bull for a sign—didn't miss a stride: good food, served unpretentiously. Chef Harding Lee Smith, a Portland native, left Back Bay Grill to open this mecca to meat. Most items are cooked out on the open kitchen's wood-fired grills, but there's more than just cow here: yummy seared-tuna sandwiches on ciabatta and thin-crust pizzas, for example. Of course, you can always get a slab of steak (porterhouse, rib-eye, sirloin; the works) or a piece of grilled fish or chicken, and you're encouraged to do so. Choose from a card of tasty sauces ranging in description from "zippy" to "brandy cream," and you're good to go. The outdoor tables in Tommy's Park are ideal in summer, but my favorite feature of this place is its bar area with personable barkeeps, good beers on tap, and Red Sox on the tube. This is fast becoming a favorite local bite.

84 Exchange St. ✆ **207/774-2333.** www.thefrontroomrestaurant.com. Appetizers and pizzas $7–$12, main courses $13–$27. AE, DISC, MC, V. Daily 11am–2:30pm and 5–10pm (Sun to 9pm).

Rí Rá ★ PUB FARE This Old Port eatery is styled after an Irish pub, though it's somewhat fancier than *real* Irish pubs. (Patriots and Red Sox are on the TV instead of soccer—sorry, "footie.") They've got the decor right, at least: The doors were imported from a pub in Kilkenny, and the back bar and counter are from other public drinking houses in County Louth. Upstairs beyond the pub is a dining room with a view of the docks; look for smoked turkey wraps, fish and chips, meatloaf, shepherd's pie, and Guinness bread pudding, plus a few more upscale dishes such as crab-filled salmon, Derrybeg pork (which is glazed with apricot, mustard, and cider), and *boxty,* a scallion-potato pancake topped with parsley sauce and meat.

72 Commercial St. ✆ **207/761-4446.** www.rira.com. Main courses $9–$20. AE, MC, V. Mon–Sat 11:30am–10pm; Sun 11am–10pm.

Inexpensive

Shima ★ (Value) FRENCH/JAPANESE/SUSHI Just around the corner from the Regency hotel, Shima (Japanese for "island," and also the chef's last name) opened in the fall of 2009 and is run by a Japanese-Hawaiian sushi chef who also trained in France. You can tell this guy comes from these diverse backgrounds: The huge, creative menu features the expected sushi rolls, pork belly, and *omakase* (chef's choice) service that any self-respecting sushi joint or *izakaya* (bar) in Tokyo would. But it also veers off on interesting Hawaiian tangents (pineapples, bigeye), and employs creamy French sauces in more than a few spots. (Don't be surprised if a duck entree pops up, either.) The biggest surprise here is the price point: Nothing's outright expensive, and many items feel like a steal. Yet the quality is very good for a just-opened place. Hip music plays in the background, and service is on two levels—upstairs is my preference, though it's sometimes harder to snag a table there than on street level. Good debut.

339 Fore St. ✆ **207/773-8389.** Main courses $8–$20. DISC, MC, V. Mon–Fri 11:30am–3pm and 5:30–10pm, Sat noon–11pm.

Silly's ★ Finds Kids INTERNATIONAL Silly's has long been the favored cheap-eats joint of hip Portlanders. Situated on a busy commercial street near the Eastern Promenade, the interior is informal, bright, and funky, with mismatched 1950s dinettes and a hodgepodge back patio beneath trees. There's also a weird fascination with Einstein here, and like Einstein, the menu is creative. The place is noted for its roll-ups ("Abdullahs"), a series of tasty fillings piled into soft tortillas; try one with shish kabob and feta, or a "Diesel," made with pulled pork and coleslaw. Newer menu additions include a slop "bucket," which has a messy, layered-burrito feel. The fries are hand-cut, the burgers big and juicy, and there's beer on tap. Don't overlook the dessert menu of cookies, pies, ice creams, cakes, and big milkshakes—Silly's whips its shakes up with peanut butter, tahini, bananas, malt, or almost anything else you could imagine, plus a few things (cranberry sauce? marshmallow crispies? check) you couldn't have.

40 Washington Ave. ✆ **207/772-0360.** www.sillys.com. Most items $5–$13, pizzas to $18. MC, V. Tues–Sun 11am–9pm.

4 FREEPORT TO MIDCOAST MAINE

Bath: 33 miles NE of Portland. Boothbay Harbor: 23 miles E of Bath; 41 miles SW of Rockland

Veteran Maine travelers contend that the rocky, central stretch of the coast, long known as the "Midcoast," is both its most lovely *and* the part that's fastest losing its native charm—it's becoming too commercial, they say, too developed, too tacky, too fancy. These grousers have a point, especially along Route 1.

But get off the main roads and you'll swiftly find another Maine, full with some of the most pastoral, picturesque meadows, mountains, peninsulas, and harbors in the entire state.

The coast is best reached via Route 1, which you catch in **Brunswick** by taking exit 28 off I-295. Traveling north, highlights of this coastal route include the shipbuilding town of **Bath,** pretty little **Wiscasset,** and the Boothbay region on the southern end of the Midcoast; the lovely Pemaquid peninsula; lost-in-time **Monhegan Island;** and finally, the power trio of **Camden, Rockland,** and **Rockport** at the northern end of the Midcoast (which are covered in the next section, "Penobscot Bay").

Beyond local tourist huts and chambers of commerce, the best source of information for the Midcoast region in general is found at the **Maine State Information Center** (✆ **207/846-0833**), just off exit 17 of I-295 in Yarmouth, which isn't yet in the Midcoast—but you'll almost certainly pass through here to get there, so stock up. This state-run center is crammed with glossy brochures, and it's staffed with a helpful crew who can provide information about the entire state but is particularly well informed about the middle reaches of coast. It's open daily, year-round, and even when it's closed, the attached restroom facilities are open.

FREEPORT ★

If **Freeport** were a mall, L.L.Bean would be the anchor store. It's the business that launched this town to prominence, elevating its status from just another Maine fishing village near the interstate to one of the state's major tourist draws for the outlet centers that sprang up here in Bean's wake.

Freeport still has the look of a classic Maine village today, but it's a village that's been largely taken over by those outlet shops; most of the old historic homes and stores here have been converted into upscale stores purveying name-brand clothing and housewares at cut-rate prices. Banana Republic occupies an exceedingly handsome brick Federal-style home; a Carnegie library became an Abercrombie & Fitch, pumping club music (oh, the inhumanity); and even the McDonald's is housed in a tasteful, understated Victorian farmhouse, for crying out loud—you really have to look to find the arches.

Still, strict planning guidelines have managed to preserve most of the town's local charm, at least in the downtown section. (Huge parking lots are hidden from view off the main drag.) As a result, Freeport is one of the more aesthetically pleasing places to shop in New England—though even with these large lots, parking can be scarce during the peak season.

Expect crowds. Seeking out the real Maine? Ask directions off the main road to **South Freeport,** which consists of a boat dock, a general store, and a good lobster shack (see "Where to Dine," p. 319) on a point of land.

Seeking out a bargain? You've come to the right place.

Essentials

GETTING THERE Freeport is on Route 1, about 16 miles north of Portland. The downtown is reached by taking I-295 north to either exit 20 or 22, then following signs.

VISITOR INFORMATION The **Freeport Merchants Association** (✆ **207/865-1212** or 800/865-1994 [automated]; www.freeportusa.com), at 23 Depot St., is the closest thing to a local tourist office here. The association publishes a map and directory of businesses, restaurants, and overnight accommodations that's widely available around town.

Shopping

Freeport crams more than 140 retail shops between exit 20 of I-295 (at the far lower end of Main St.) and Mallet Road, the access road to exit 22 at the northern end of the main street. The bulk of these are "factory" or "outlet" stores, offering cut-rate prices on samples, seconds, and styles that never quite caught on. If you don't want to miss a single shop, get off at exit 17 and drive north on Route 1.

The bargains can vary from extraordinary to "huh?" Plan on wearing out some shoe leather and taking at least a half-day if you're really intent on finding the best deals. The

Finds Mapping Your Next Stop

Right across the road from the Maine State Information Center in Yarmouth (see above) is the **DeLorme Map Store** (✆ **800/642-0970;** www.delorme.com), open daily from 9am to 6pm (Sun to 5pm). You'll find a wide selection of maps here, including the firm's trademark state atlases and a line of CD-ROM map products. The store is fun to browse even if you're not a map buff, but what makes the place really worth a detour off the interstate is Eartha, "the world's largest rotating and revolving globe." The 42-foot-diameter globe occupies the entire atrium lobby and is constructed on a scale of 1:1,000,000. It's said to be the biggest satellite image of the Earth ever produced. Far out.

rotation of national chains here currently includes Abercrombie & Fitch, Banana Republic, Gap, Calvin Klein, Patagonia, North Face, Nike, Chaudier, Mikasa, Nine West, Timberland, and Maidenform, among many others.

Stores in Freeport are typically open daily 9am to 9pm during the busy summer and close much earlier (5 or 6pm) in other seasons; between Thanksgiving and Christmas, they remain open late once more.

In summer be sure to consult the schedule of **free music performances** on a big new tent-shaped stage behind L.L.Bean, sponsored by the retailer as the **L.L.Bean Summer Concert Series** ★, from mid-June through Labor Day. Some pretty important national folk and country acts (Kathy Mattea, Lonestar, Dar Williams) perform each summer. Did I mention that it's all *free?*

Cuddledown Cuddledown started producing down comforters in 1973 and now makes a whole line of products much appreciated in northern climes and beyond. Some of the down pillows are made right in the outlet shop, which also carries a variety of European goose-down comforters in all sizes and weights. Look for linens, blankets, moccasins, and home furnishings, too. 475 Rte. 1 (btw. exits 17 and 20). ✆ **888/235-3696.** www.cuddledown.com.

Tale of the Tags: Freeport vs. Kittery

When visiting the Maine coast, many travelers only find time to shop once. Trouble is, there are *two* significant outlet centers on the southern coast. How to choose? Here's my quick take:

In **Kittery,** located at the southern edge of Maine (see section 2, "The Southern Maine Coast," earlier in this chapter), the malls are clumped along Route 1 just a couple of miles north of the New Hampshire border. Though the area appears at first glance to be a conglomerated, single huge mall, in fact there are five or six distinct areas with separate entrances. Choose carefully before you make your turn!

Generally speaking, Kittery is better for the name-brand shopper who wants to hit a large volume of places in a short time. It's easier to do Kittery quickly than Freeport, because of the side-by-side arrangement of the various stores and the malls. The trade-off is the blandness of the experience: Each of these side malls offers vast parking lots and boring architecture, and you can't always safely walk from one mall to another—you need wheels.

Among Kittery's best places are a **Gap** outlet, a small but elegant **Coach** store, **Reebok, Stride-Rite, Seiko,** an **Orvis** sporting-goods outlet, and a useful **Crate & Barrel** store. The Indian-themed **Kittery Trading Post** is not all it's hyped up to be, but at least prices are low.

Additionally, there are a couple of good places here for a snack or meal, but nothing fancy; **Bob's Clam Hut** (p. 285) sells fried clams. For a sit-down meal, I like **The Weathervane,** a small New England fish-house chain that delivers value at moderate prices for families, but people usually order broiled or fried fish; again, nothing fancy.

Freeport is different. The outlets here are interspersed throughout Freeport's Main Street. That makes driving around town a headache, as pedestrians and cars bring things to a constant halt. My advice? Put on your walking shoes, park anywhere you can find a spot—even in a distant satellite lot—and hoof it.

Freeport Knife Co. ★ This store sports a wide selection of knives for kitchen and camp alike, including blades from Germany, Switzerland, and Japan. Look for their custom line, or just bring in your dull blade for a sharpening. They also sell replacement parts and do repairs on all brands of knives. 181 Lower Main St. ✆ **207/865-0779.** www.freeportknife.com.

L.L.Bean ★★★ Kids Monster outdoor retailer L.L.Bean traces its roots from the day Leon Leonwood Bean decided that what the world really needed was a good weatherproof hunting shoe. He joined a watertight gum shoe to a laced leather upper; hunters liked it; the store grew; an empire was born. Today L.L.Bean sells millions of dollars' worth of clothing and outdoor goods nationwide through its well-respected catalogs, and it continues to draw hundreds of thousands of customers through its doors to a headquarters building and several offshoots around town. The modern, multilevel main store is about the size of a regional mall, but it's very tastefully done with its own indoor trout pond and lots of natural wood. Selections include Bean's own trademark clothing, along

Bring a portable dolly or luggage rack to carry packages if you're expecting to make a lot of purchases.

Freeport's outlets generally offer a higher grade of product than Kittery's, and the stores have a great deal more architectural (and corporate) personality, too. You will actually find local, small manufacturers here, not just the big guys, and inventive big brands that go beyond the usual.

You can troll **L.L.Bean**'s factory stores (now tucked down below Main St. in a new complex) for top-grade outdoors equipment and clothing, but even just sticking to Main Street you'll come across plenty of finds.

If you love shopping and you seek quality, it's a genuinely enjoyable experience to stroll around for a day, taking a snack of chowder or lobster (see "Where to Dine," below); pausing to assess your finds; grabbing a soda, grilled hot dog, or ice cream from a vendor; then planning dinner somewhere. Parking and traffic are negatives to consider—you might cruise around a half-hour before finding a choice open spot. You'll also probably spend more in Freeport than in Kittery, as price tags are generally a little higher. (That's a purely subjective observation; I could be wrong.)

The winner? It's close, but I'll take Freeport only because it's walkable.

A third option to consider is the big **Maine Mall,** on a huge chunk of parking lot near the Portland Jetport in South Portland (easily reached off the Maine Turnpike via its own special exit). The options here are uniformly bland—this could be Anywheresville, America—and there are no outlet or factory stores. Still, there's something vaguely reassuring about being able to bop among **Macy's, Bath & Body Works, Victoria's Secret, Pottery Barn, The Disney Store,** and **babyGAP,** then grabbing chocolates from **Godiva** before settling down to coffee and a book or CD at **Borders.** Also check out **The Sports Authority** for low-priced sporting goods, and hit **Williams-Sonoma** for a look at upscale cooking gear.

with home furnishings, books, shoes, and plenty of outdoor gear for camping, fishing, and hunting (a particularly good section). The staff is incredibly knowledgeable—Bean's encourages staff to take the gear home and try it out so as to better serve customers. 95 Main St. (at Bow St.). ✆ **877/755-2326.** www.llbean.com.

Mangy Moose A souvenir shop with a twist: Virtually everything in this place is moose-related. Really. There are moose wineglasses, moose trivets, moose cookie cutters, and (of course) moose T-shirts. Somehow this merchandise is a notch above what you'll find in most other souvenir shops around the state. 112 Main St. ✆ **800/606-6517** or 207/865-6414. www.themangymoose.com.

Thos. Moser Cabinetmakers ★★ Classic furniture reinterpreted in lustrous wood and leather is the focus at this shop, which—thanks to a steady parade of ads in the *New Yorker* and a Madison Avenue branch—has become nearly as representative of Maine as L.L.Bean has. Shaker, mission, and modern styles are wonderfully reinvented by Tom

Fun Facts All Bean's, All the Time

One of the big reasons that L.L.Bean's flagship shop is such a tourist draw is that it's open 365 days a year, 7 days a week, 24 hours a day—note the lack of any locks or latches on the front doors. As such, it's a popular spot even in the dead of night, especially during summer or around holidays. Folks have been known to set out from New Hampshire at 1 or 2 in the morning to enjoy the best deals (and empty aisles) on their middle-of-the-night arrival.

Moser and his designers and woodworkers, who produce heirloom-quality signed pieces. Nationwide delivery is easy to arrange. There's a good selection of knotted rugs made by an independent artisan, and a good gallery of rotating Maine-made art on-site. Finally, don't miss the Special Opportunity Room and its samples, prototypes, and refurbished pieces; you can save big bucks here. 149 Main St. ✆ **800/708-9041** or 207/865-4519. www.thomasmoser.com.

Where to Stay

Reservations are strongly recommended in Freeport during peak summer season; the opening of a clutch of mid-range chain hotels and motels just south of town on Route 1 (around the interstate exit, and then for the next few miles south of it) has helped alleviate the summer crush somewhat. Head there if you're stuck for a room.

Harraseeket Inn ★★ The Harraseeket is a large, modern hotel a short walk north of L.L.Bean on Freeport's main street. Despite its size, a traveler could drive right past and not even notice it—which a good thing. A 19th-century home is the soul of the hotel, though most rooms are in annexes added 1989 and 1997. Guests can relax in the dining room, read the paper in a common room while the baby grand player piano plays, or sip a cocktail in the homey Broad Arrow Tavern (with its wood-fired oven and grill, it serves lunch and dinner). Guest rooms are large and tastefully furnished, with quarter-canopy beds and a mix of contemporary and antique furnishings; some have gas or wood-burning fireplaces, more than half now have whirlpools, and some are even done up with wet bars and refrigerators. The big second-floor Thomas Moser Room is a nod to the local furniture craftsman, with a pencil-post bed, writing desk, dresser, and flatscreen TV in the bedroom, plus a sitting room with a modern sofa, lounge chair, coffee table, Bose stereo, and stone fireplace. And a soaking tub. This inn is especially pet-friendly, with doggy beds and treats for four-footed guests.

162 Main St., Freeport, ME 04032. ✆ **800/342-6423** or 207/865-9377. Fax 207/865-1684. www.harraseeketinn.com. 84 units. $120–$295 double; $245–$315 suite. All rates include full breakfast and afternoon tea. MAP rates available. AE, DC, DISC, MC, V. Take exit 22 off I-295 and turn left; continue to Main St. Pets welcome ($25 per pet per night). **Amenities:** 2 restaurants; bar; concierge; indoor pool; room service. *In room:* A/C, TV, fridge (some units), hair dryer (some units), Wi-Fi (free).

Maine Idyll Motor Court ★ Value Talk about a throwback to a happier time: This motel, 2 short miles north of Freeport's busy Main Street, doesn't take credit cards—but they *will* take your personal check. This 1930s "motor court" is a Maine classic, a cluster of 20 cottages scattered around a grove of oak and beech trees. It could have faded into oblivion, yet it hasn't: The place is still good enough for a simple night's sleep. Most cottages come with a tiny porch, wood-burning fireplace (birch logs are provided), television, modest kitchen facilities (no ovens), and dated furniture. These cabins aren't especially large, but they're comfortable enough and kept clean; some have showers, while others have bathtubs, and a good number of the cottages have two bedrooms (one even has three bedrooms). Ask for a cottage with air-conditioning if that's important—a few units have it. Kids like the swing set and play area, dog-walkers head for nature trails accessible from the property, while picnickers fire up grill sets. The only interruption is the occasional drone of traffic: I-295 is just through the trees to one side, and Route 1 is on the other side. Get past that traffic sandwich, though, and this place is a good value. They even have free Wi-Fi access.

1411 Rte. 1, Freeport, ME 04032. ✆ **207/865-4201.** www.maineidyll.com. 20 units. May–Oct $63–$110 double. Rates include continental breakfast. No credit cards. Closed Nov–Apr. Pets on leashes allowed ($4 per pet per night). *In room:* A/C (some units), TV, kitchenette, no phone, Wi-Fi (free).

Where to Dine

Gritty McDuff's ★ BREWPUB Spacious, informal, and air-conditioned in summer, Gritty's is an offshoot of Portland's original brewpub. It's a short drive south of Freeport's village center and is best known for a varied selection of house-brewed beers, like the unfiltered Black Fly Stout. The pub offers a wide-ranging bar menu of reliable salads, burgers, steaks, stone-oven pizzas, cheesesteak sandwiches, quesadillas, and pub classics such as shepherd's pie and fish and chips. There's a kids' menu as well.

187 Rte. 1 (Lower Main St.). ✆ **207/865-4321.** www.grittys.com. Reservations not accepted. Main courses $10–$17. AE, DISC, MC, V. Daily 11:30am–11pm.

Harraseeket Lunch & Lobster ★ Finds LOBSTER Next to a boatyard on the Harraseeket River, about a 10-minute drive from Freeport's busy shopping district, this lobster pound's picnic tables get crowded on sunny days—although, with its little heated dining room, it's a worthy destination anytime. Point and pick out a lobster, then take in river views from the dock as you wait for your number to be called. Advice? Come in late afternoon to avoid the lunch and dinner hordes—and don't wear your nicest clothes.

Tips Need an Outlet?

L.L.Bean's campus just keeps expanding and super-sizing and modernizing—though I'm not altogether sure Leon Leonwood himself would approve of the "1812 Cafe" and the huge new fishing and hunting store. That's right: In addition to the main store, L.L.Bean now maintains several new **satellite shops** stocking small, rapidly changing inventories of specialized goods, some of them used. **The Bike, Boat & Ski Store,** behind the flagship store, holds lots of canoes, kayaks, paddles, cycles, and helmets. Next to it, the **Hunting & Fishing Store** (marked by a huge Bean boot, naturally) is the place for fly-fishing gear, hunting boots, and tons of other undeniably cool stuff—from freeze-dried camp food to hand-crank-powered LED flashlights (no batteries required), folding Adirondack chairs, 13-foot game-hunting perches, and a zillion lures, fly ties, buck knives, tent lines, and watercraft. Also adjacent is a huge new **Home Store** selling hand-crafted beds, sofas, and other furniture, plus home accessories (doormat, anyone?). Finally, Bean's **outlet shop** is downhill off Main Street in the new Freeport Village Station complex.

 This is roll-up-your-sleeves eating. You can also order fried fish, burgers, chowder, or ice cream from the window.

36 Main St., South Freeport. ✆ **207/865-4888.** www.harraseeketlunchandlobster.com. Lobsters market price (typically $8–$15). No credit cards. Mid-June to Labor Day daily 11am–8:45pm; May to mid-June and early Sept to mid-Oct daily 11am–7:45pm. Closed mid-Oct to Apr. From Freeport, take South St. (off Bow St.) to South Freeport and turn left at stop sign.

Jameson Tavern ★ AMERICAN In a farmhouse right in the shadow of L.L.Bean (on the north side), Jameson Tavern touts itself as the birthplace of Maine. And it really is: In 1820 papers were signed here legally separating Maine from Massachusetts. Mainers still appreciate that pen stroke today. The historic Tap Room is to the left, a compact spot of beer and pubby food. The rest of the house contains the main dining room, decorated in a more formal, country-colonial style. Meals here are hearty: filet mignon wrapped in bacon, poached salmon, baked haddock, fresh pastas, and seafood salads. What's new in this old place? A nice porch, open about half of the year (not in winter, obviously) for dining semi-alfresco.

115 Main St. ✆ **207/865-4196.** www.jamesontavern.com. Reservations recommended. Main courses $7–$18 in taproom and dining room at lunch, $15–$26 in dining room at dinner. AE, DC, DISC, MC, V. Taproom daily 11am–11pm. Dining room Sun–Thurs 11:30am–9pm; Fri–Sat 11:30am–10pm.

PEMAQUID PENINSULA ★★

The Pemaquid (native tongue for "longest finger") Peninsula is an irregular, rocky wedge driven deep into the Gulf of Maine. It's extremely quiet, far less commercial than the Boothbay Peninsula across the Damariscotta River, and thus much more suited to relaxed exploration and nature appreciation than the Boothbays.

Rocky **Pemaquid Point,** at the extreme southern tip of the peninsula, is very scenic when the ocean surf pounds up against the shore and the requisite lighthouse.

Essentials

GETTING THERE The peninsula and point are accessible from the south and west by taking Route 1 to Damariscotta, then turning south down Route 130 and driving south; it's about 15 miles to land's end. Coming from the north or northeast, take Route 1 through Waldoboro, then turn south down Route 32 just south of town and continue about 20 miles to the point.

VISITOR INFORMATION The **Damariscotta Region Chamber of Commerce** (✆ **207/563-8340;** www.damariscottaregion.com) is a good source of local information and maintains a seasonal information booth just off Route 1 during the summer months. To get to its office at 15 Courtyard St. in Damariscotta, follow Route 27 south, branching off from Route 1 just east (across the bridge) of **Wiscasset.**

Exploring the Pemaquid Peninsula

The Pemaquid Peninsula invites slow driving and frequent stops. South on Route 129 toward Walpole is **Damariscotta,** a sleepy head-of-the-harbor village. On the left is the austerely handsome **Walpole Meeting House** ★, dating from 1772. Services are held here during the summer and the public is welcome.

Continue on Route 129 to picturesque **Christmas Cove** ★, so named because Capt. John Smith (of Pocahontas fame) anchored here on Christmas Day in 1614. Look for the rustic **Coveside Bar and Restaurant** (✆ **207/644-8282;** www.covesiderestaurant.com), a popular marina with a pennant-bedecked lounge and basic dining room. The food is okay, but the atmospheric views are outstanding. Reservations are a good idea on summer weekends—it gets crowded with visiting yachtsmen. Sometimes they're even famous.

About 5 miles north of **South Bristol,** turn right on Pemaquid Road, which will take you to Route 130, and that leads all the way south to **Pemaquid Point** ★★ (✆ **207/677-2494**), owned by the town of Bristol. The ocean views are superb, and the only distractions are the tenacious seagulls that might take a profound interest in your lunch. The lighthouse—no longer lit by whale oil—is especially worth viewing: The tower, built by a local stone mason, was finished in 1835. Entry to the beach at the point costs $4 per person, while entering the lighthouse park costs $2. (Kids 13 and under can enter both parks for free.)

Head back north along Route 32 from **New Harbor,** the most scenic way to leave the peninsula if you plan on continuing northeast along Route 1 to places like Camden and Rockland. Along the way, look for the sign pointing to the **Rachel Carson Salt Pond Preserve** ★★, a Nature Conservancy property. The noted naturalist Rachel Carson studied these roadside tide pools extensively while researching her 1956 bestseller *The Edge of the Sea,* and it's still a good spot for budding naturalists and experts alike. At low tide, you can see starfish, green crabs, periwinkles, and other creatures in the tidal pools and among the rocks.

Where to Stay

Bradley Inn ★ This quiet, thrown-back-in-time inn in a remote location is within hiking or biking distance of Pemaquid's point, but there are reasons to lag behind at the inn, as well. Wander the landscaped grounds, settle in for a game of cards in the pub, or sink into a massage in the seaside spa. Rooms are tastefully appointed with four-poster cherry beds (no televisions, though). Third-floor rooms are the best, despite the hike up the stairs, thanks to distant glimpses of John's Bay. A high-ceilinged second-floor suite occupying the entire floor is equipped with a full kitchen and dining room, while the separate Garden Cottage has a lofty ceiling, fieldstone fireplace, and Jacuzzi. Breakfasts are good. The inn is popular for summer weddings, so ask if it's booked with one if you're seeking solitude and quiet.

3063 Bristol Rd. (Rte. 130), New Harbor, ME 04554. ✆ **800/942-5560** or 207/677-2105. Fax 207/677-3367. www.bradleyinn.com. 17 units. Apr–Dec $155–$250 double; $175–$375 suite and cottage. Rates include full breakfast and afternoon tea. AE, MC, V. Closed Jan–Mar. **Amenities:** Dining room; pub; bikes; room service; spa. *In room:* Kitchen (1 unit), Wi-Fi (free).

Hotel Pemaquid Value This 1889 inn isn't directly on the water—but it's just a minute's walk from the Point. The main house has the flavor of an old-time boardinghouse, while outbuildings are (slightly) more modern. The place remains steadfastly old-fashioned: no credit cards accepted whatsoever, narrow hallways, some bathrooms are shared. And the halls and walls are filled with antiques, including a fine collection of old radios and phonographs. The two- and three-bedroom suites here—one with a sun porch, one with a kitchen—are decent choices for traveling families, and cottages and a carriage house are available by the week. But this is mostly simple sleeping, nothing fancy.

3098 Bristol Rd. (Rte. 130), New Harbor, ME 04554. ✆ **207/677-2312.** www.hotelpemaquid.com. 23 units, 4 with shared bathrooms. $85–$95 double with private bathroom; $70–$80 double with shared bathroom; $90–$205 suite and bungalow; cottages and carriage house $825–$1,400 weekly. 2-night minimum stay Sat–Sun. No credit cards. Closed mid-Oct to mid-Apr. *In room:* TV (some units), no phone.

For more casual dining while in the area, don't miss the **Cupboard Café ★**, 137 Huddle Rd. (✆ **207/677-3911;** www.thecupboardcafe.com), in New Harbor. It serves country breakfasts, great sticky buns, and soup-and-sandwich lunches Tuesday through Saturday (breakfast only Sun; closed Mon) year-round.

Shaw's Fish & Lobster Wharf ★ Finds LOBSTER Shaw's attracts hordes of tourists in summer, and it's not hard to see why: This is one of the very best-situated lobster pounds on the coast, with postcard-perfect views of a working harbor. (It's so scenic that Hollywood filmed scenes of the Kevin Costner film *Message in a Bottle* here.) Eat on the open deck upstairs or in the indoor dining room—I say, go for the deck—or even order beer and shooters from the raw bar downstairs. This is one of very few lobster joints in Maine with a full liquor license, and the simple but meaty lobster rolls are considered among Maine's best by eaters in the know. A great, scenic find.

129 Rte. 32, New Harbor. ✆ **207/677-2200.** Lobster priced to market, main courses $10–$25. MC, V. Mid-May to mid-Oct daily 11am–9pm. Closed mid-Oct to mid-May.

5 PENOBSCOT BAY

Camden: 230 miles NE of Boston; 8 miles N of Rockland; 18 miles S of Belfast

Traveling east along the Maine coast, you might suddenly discover (if you use a compass or GPS) that you're abruptly heading almost due north as you approach **Rockland.** The culprit behind this turn toward Canada is none other than **Penobscot Bay,** a big bite out of the coastline that forces you to make a lengthy northern detour to cross the head of the bay (where the Penobscot River flows in at **Bucksport**).

You'll find some of Maine's most distinctive coastal scenery in this bay's region, which is dotted with broad offshore islands and high hills rising above its mainland shores. Though the mouth of the bay is occupied by two large islands, its waters still churn up when the winds and tides are right.

The bay's western shore gets a heavy stream of tourist traffic, especially along the stretch of Route 1 passing through Rockland and lovely **Camden.** Nevertheless, it offers some of the best moments on the Maine coast wedged between the gourmet bakeries and T-shirt shops: moments like sitting on a grassy knoll in Camden watching tall ships in the harbor and waiting for a concert to begin, for instance.

Services for travelers are abundant here, though during peak season you need a small miracle to find a weekend bed at the last minute. This region's quiet beauty is no secret.

ROCKLAND & ENVIRONS

On the southwestern edge of Penobscot Bay, **Rockland** has long been proud of its blue-collar waterfront. Built around the fishing and shipbuilding industries, Rockland only dabbled in tourism for centuries, but with the decline of fisheries and the rise of Maine's tourist economy, the balance has begun shifting. Now the city is being swiftly colonized by creative restaurateurs, innkeepers, artisans, and other types slowly transforming the place from a one-trick pony (as in, fish processing) to a genuinely diverse place—and the arts capital of the Midcoast. Pretty amazing.

The city's waterfront has a small park from which windjammers come and go, but even more appealing is Rockland's downtown—basically, one long street lined with

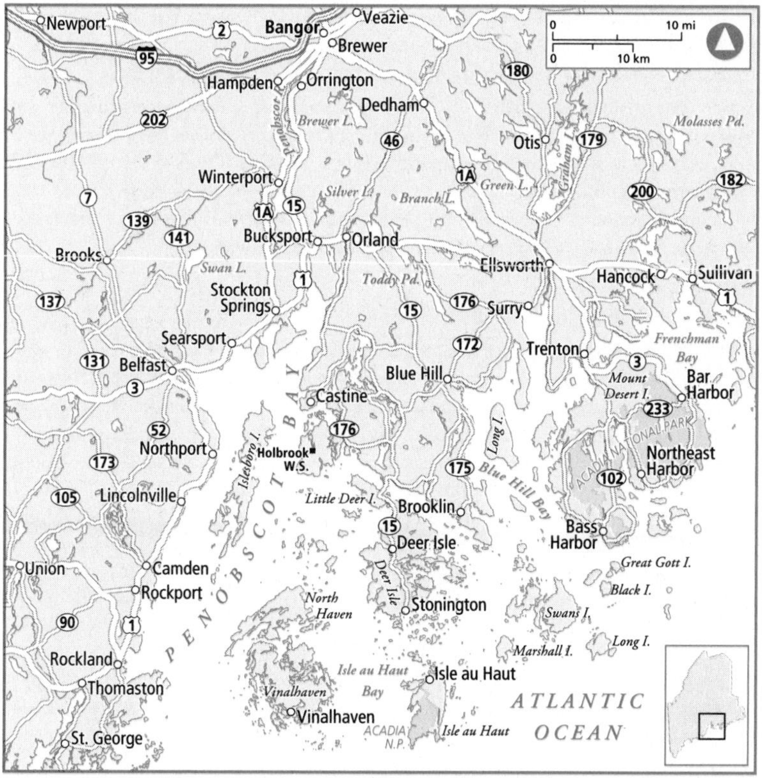

historic brick architecture. If you're seeking picturesque harbor towns, head instead for nearby **Camden, Rockport, Port Clyde,** or **Stonington.** Rockland itself is best as a local base for exploring a beautiful coastal region—especially if you like your towns to be a bit rough and salty around the edges—and luckily there are a few luxury B&Bs, inns, and resorts in town in which you can sequester yourself.

Essentials

GETTING THERE By car, Route 1 passes directly through the center of Rockland. It's about a 3½-hour drive here from Boston via I-95 and Route 1, nearly a 7-hour drive from New York City.

Concord Coach (✆ **800/639-3317** or 603/228-3300; www.concordcoachlines.com) runs two to three daily buses from Portland and Boston to Rockland; the ride takes 4½ hours from Boston and costs $57 to $62 round-trip.

From mid-May through late October, the **Maine Eastern Railroad** (✆ **866/637-2457;** www.maineeasternrailroad.com) runs excursion trains between Brunswick and Rockland. Round-trip fares are $40 per adult, $35 for seniors, and $20 for children ages 5 to 15.

VISITOR INFORMATION The **Penobscot Bay Regional Chamber of Commerce** (✆ **800/562-2529** or 207/596-0376; www.therealmaine.com) staffs an information desk in the city's Harbor Park. It's open daily from Memorial Day through Labor Day, on weekdays the rest of the year.

SPECIAL EVENTS The **Maine Lobster Festival** (✆ **800/562-2529** or 207/596-0376; www.mainelobsterfestival.com) takes place at Harbor Park during the first weekend in August (plus the preceding Thurs–Fri). Entertainers and vendors, plus all sorts of Maine products, fill the waterfront parking lot for thousands of festivalgoers who enjoy the steamy (sorry) atmosphere. Admission is $8 per day ($2 for children), or $32 for a 4-day pass (but there's a discount for buying online in advance). Food, of course, costs extra—as do reserved tickets for certain musical performances.

Museums

Farnsworth Art Museum ★★★ Rockland, for all its rough edges, has long and historic ties to the arts. Noted sculptor Louise Nevelson grew up in Rockland, and in 1935 philanthropist Lucy Farnsworth bequeathed a fortune to establish the Farnsworth Art Museum, which has since become one of the most respected little art museums in New England. Located right downtown, the Farnsworth has a superb collection of paintings and sculptures by renowned American artists with connections to Maine—not only Nevelson, but also three generations of Wyeths (N. C., Andrew, and Jamie), plus Rockwell Kent, Childe Hassam, and Maurice Prendergast. The exhibit halls are modern, spacious, and well designed, and shows are professionally prepared. Equally interesting is the museum-owned **Olson House ★**, a 25-minute drive away, in the village of Cushing; it's perhaps Maine's most well-known home, immortalized in Andrew Wyeth's famous painting *Christina's World.*

16 Museum St., Rockland. ✆ **207/596-6457.** www.farnsworthmuseum.org. Museum $10 adults, $8 seniors and students 18 and older, free for children 17 and under (includes admission to Olson House and Farnsworth Victorian Homestead); Olson House only $4 per person. MC, V. Memorial Day to Columbus Day daily 10am–5pm; rest of year Tues–Sun 10am–5pm.

Owls Head Transportation Museum ★ Finds You don't need to be a car or plane buff to enjoy this museum—though it helps. Founded in 1974 and located 3 miles south of Rockland on Route 73, the museum has an extraordinary collection of cars, motorcycles, bicycles, and planes, nicely displayed in a tidy, hangarlike building at the edge of the Knox County Airport. Look for an early Harley Davidson motorcycle and a sleek Rolls-Royce Phantom dating from the roaring '20s.

117 Museum St., Owls Head. ✆ **207/594-4418.** www.ohtm.org. Admission $8 adults, $7 seniors, $5 children 5–17, $20 families. Apr–Oct daily 10am–5pm; Nov–Mar daily 10am–4pm.

Windjammer Tours ★★★

During the transition from sail to steam, captains of fancy new steamships belittled old-fashioned sailing ships as "windjammers." The term stuck; through a curious metamorphosis, the name evolved into one of adventure and romance.

Today windjammer vacations combine adventure with limited creature comforts—like lodging at a backcountry cabin floating on the water. Guests typically bunk in small, two-person cabins with cold running water, a porthole to let in fresh air, and not much else. You know it's not going to be a luxe experience when a ship's brochure boasts its cabins are all "at least 6 feet by 8 feet."

Maine is the windjammer cruising capital of the U.S., and the two most active Maine harbors are here in **Rockland** and **Camden.** Cruises last from 3 days to a week, during which these handsome, creaky vessels poke around tidal inlets and small coves that ring the beautiful bay. It's a superb way to explore the coast the way it's historically always been explored—from out on the water, looking in. Rates might run between $120 and $150 per person per night (in other words, $300–$1,000 per person for the entire trip); you'll find that rates are most affordable early and late in the season.

More than a dozen windjammers cruise the bay region during summer (some migrate south to the Caribbean for the winter); the ships vary widely in size and vintage, and accommodations range from cramped and rustic to fairly spacious and well appointed. Schedules can vary, too, if the weather is tricky, although captains have become much more organized in recent years.

A "standard" cruise *usually* features a stop at one or more spruce-studded islands in the bay (perhaps with a lobster bake onshore, prepared by the captain); breakfasts served at tables below decks (or perched cross-legged on the deck); and a real sense of getting away from it all as the ship plows through frothy waters.

Ideally, you'll get a chance to look at a couple of ships in person on the harbor to find one that suits you. If you can't do that, contact the **Maine Windjammer Association** ★ (✆ **800/807-9463;** www.sailmainecoast.com) or check its good website for a listing of a dozen member ships—it's easy to comparison-shop, because prices, specifications, schedules, and even the captains' identities are clearly laid out on the site.

If you're trying to book a *last-minute* windjammer cruise, though, it's better to drop by the tourist office on the Rockland waterfront (see "Visitor Information," above) and inquire about open berths.

Where to Stay

Captain Lindsey House Inn ★ The three-story brick Captain Lindsey House is a couple minutes' walk from the Farnsworth Museum, a nice advantage over farther-out digs. It was built in 1835 by a sea captain and then went through several subsequent incarnations (including one as headquarters of the Rockland Water Co.). Guests enter through a doorway a few steps off Main Street into an opulent first-floor common area done up in rich tones, dark-wood paneling, and a mix of antique and contemporary furniture. Upstairs rooms are decorated in simple country style with old-style wooden beds, coffee tables, rocking chairs, and desks; rooms on the third floor have attractive exposed pine floors and Oriental carpets. All the beds are covered with feather duvets, though only a few rooms have tubs. This isn't the most luxurious inn in town (which is no knock on the place; it's plenty comfy enough), but it does have a good dose of throwback-Maine character and some of the friendliest inn owners on the entire Midcoast.

5 Lindsey St., Rockland, ME 04841. ✆ **800/523-2145** or 207/596-7950. Fax 207/596-2758. www.lindseyhouse.com. 9 units. $136–$211 double. Rates include breakfast. AE, DISC, MC, V. *In room:* A/C, TV, hair dryer, Wi-Fi (free).

LimeRock Inn ★★ This turreted, Queen Anne–style inn sits sleepily on a quiet side street just 2 blocks off Rockland's main drag, yet it's one of the best lodging options in town. Attention has been paid to detail throughout, from the kingly choices of country Victorian furniture to the Egyptian cotton bed sheets. All eight guest rooms are welcoming; among the best are the Island Cottage Room, a bright and airy south-of-France-like chamber wonderfully converted from an old shed (it has a private deck and a Jacuzzi); the Turret Room, with a canopy bed, cherry daybed, and French doors leading into a bathroom with a claw-foot tub and shower; and the elegant Grand Manan Room, with a big four-poster mahogany king bed, fireplace, and double Jacuzzi that puts one in mind of a Southern plantation home.

96 Limerock St., Rockland, ME 04841. ✆ **800/546-3762** or 207/594-2257. www.limerockinn.com. 8 units. $119–$239 double. Rates include full breakfast. DISC, MC, V. *In room:* Hair dryer, Wi-Fi (free).

Samoset Resort ★★ Established in 1889 on a scenic hill outside Rockland, the Samoset was meant as a grown-up summer camp for the wealthy. This is not the original building—the original was shuttered, auctioned off, and destroyed by fire decades ago. But the place has bounced back, big-time, as a noted golf resort and luxury property thanks to a number of exciting recent upgrades. Most recently, in 2009, a new heated pool and hot tub were added on the hill's highest point, with sweeping views of the bay, plus a tiki bar serving frozen drinks and light meals; it's a huge hit already. Rooms vary in position and view, but many have balconies or porches with grand Penobscot Bay views; all have rich wood-leather headboards, flatscreen TVs, and marble vanities. Bathrooms are extra-big, some with whirlpool tubs. The golf course remains one of the most scenic in New England, while the quiet local roads are perfect for strolling, and there's even a minilighthouse adjacent to the property. Check out the good health club before heading to dinner—your options include seasonal **Marcel's** (see "Where to Dine," below), serving excellent resort fare, and the Breakwater Grill, serving lighter fare year-round. All in all, a great luxury comeback.

220 Warrenton St., Rockport, ME 04856. ✆ **800/341-1650** or 207/594-2511. www.samoset.com. 178 units. Early July to late Aug $259–$289 double, $369 suite, $539–$769 cottage; May to early July and late Aug to Nov $179–$289 double, $259–$289 suite, $539–$769 cottage. MAP rates available. AE, DC, DISC, MC, V. **Amenities:** 3 restaurants; babysitting; children's programs; concierge; Jacuzzi; 2 pools (1 indoor, 1 heated outdoor); room service; sauna; 4 tennis courts. *In room:* A/C, TV, hair dryer, Wi-Fi (free).

Where to Dine

In addition to the choices listed below, locals often drop by the unpretentious **Brown Bag** (✆ **207/596-6372;** www.thebrownbagrockland.com), at 606 Main St. in Rockland, for lunch or breakfast. This place has occupied its simple no-frills storefront for decades; breakfasts are better than lunches, but it's still a decent quick sandwich or picnic option when you're on the road.

Cafe Miranda ★★ *Finds* CONTEMPORARY AMERICAN Even a 2007 fire couldn't stop this place, which offers one of the best values/craziest menus in New England. Hidden on a side street, it's a tiny, contemporary restaurant with a huge, ever-morphing menu of big flavors and hip attitude. "We do not serve the food of cowards," owner/chef Kerry Altiero says right on top of the menu, and he's right. I could write a whole book on the regularly changing menu here—and probably should—but suffice to say you never know what you'll get 'til you get there. Small plates and entrees could include things like grilled lamb patties with parsley and garlic; "50 MPH tomatoes" deep-fried and served with spicy ranch dressing; a "squash-o'-rama" (roasted squash with cheese); fire-roasted feta with sweet peppers, tomatoes, "really good" olives, and herbs; a Portuguese seafood combo of mussels, shrimp, clams, fish, and sausage steamed in wine and pummeled with parsley; or, of course, the immortal "Pitch a Tent"—sausage, gravy, onions, garlic, and mushrooms beneath a "tent" of pasta. Share everything with your fellow diner(s), because you'll never eat at a place this original again. Altiero, again: "It's comfort food for whatever planet you're from." Amen.

15 Oak St., Rockland. ✆ **207/594-2034.** www.cafemiranda.com. Reservations strongly recommended. Small plates $9–$14, main courses $19–$27. DISC, MC, V. Daily 5–9:30pm.

Cod End Cookhouse ★ Finds Kids SEAFOOD Half the allure of Cod End is its hidden, scenic location—it's as though you'd stumbled upon a secret place. Situated between the Town Landing and the East Wind Inn in little Tenants Harbor, this a classic lobster pound with fine views of a working harbor from its deck. To get to the cookhouse, you walk through a fish market first (where you can buy fish or lobster to go), then place your order at an outdoor shack. Steamed lobsters are the main draw, obviously, but there's actually a lot more to eat here, too—everything from chowders, stews, and lobster bisque to seafood pastas, char-broiled salmon, clam and haddock rolls, and a simple kids' menu of burgers, dogs, and sandwiches (including a classic PB&J). Yes, you probably do want to sample the sweetish blueberry cake for dessert.

Commercial St. (next to the town dock), Tenants Harbor. ✆ **207/372-6782.** www.codend.com. Main courses $5–$10 at lunch, $8–$15 at dinner. DISC, MC, V. Memorial Day to Sept daily 11am–8:30pm. Closed Sept to Memorial Day.

Marcel's ★★ AMERICAN This upper-crust (but never too stuffy) seasonal eatery on the ground level of the Samoset resort (see "Where to Stay," above) is a great place for a fancy bite in the Midcoast. In a room with big windows looking out on the water, chef Tim Pierce employs astounding creativity within the confines of his classic American resort fare (think steak Diane, lobster thermidor, filet mignon, and bisque). The menu changes annually, but you can always start with a Caesar salad prepared tableside (as it has been for decades); a lobster stew rich with cream and sherry; or inventive, summery salads such as one of grilled watermelon, spinach, and shallot "onion" rings. Pan-seared scallops in a knockout citrus cream are ever-popular, as are the annual permutation of lobster and steak. Pierce has even begun sneaking some Asian influences into the menu, such as tuna tataki and yuzu sauce. Desserts run to sundaes, cakes, and ice creams—no molecular experiments here, just summery classics. Great spot; be sure to dress up. (Gentlemen should wear a jacket.)

220 Warrenton St., Rockport. ✆ **800/341-1650** or 207/594-2511. www.samoset.com. Reservations required. Main courses $24–$36. AE, MC, V. June to mid-Sept Thurs–Tues 5:30–9pm.

Primo ★★★ MEDITERRANEAN/NEW AMERICAN Primo is one of northern New England's top eats. The restaurant occupies two nicely decorated floors of a century-old home located a short drive south of Rockland's downtown. Owner/chef Melissa Kelly graduated first in her class at the Culinary Institute of America and won a James Beard Foundation award for "best chef in the Northeast" in the 1990s. Her Italian-inflected menu reflects the seasons and draws from local products wherever available. Start with an appetizer such as wood-fired pizza with artisanal mushrooms, planked octopus with chickpea salad, antipasti, or fried and roasted local oysters paired with rémoulade sauce and house-cured Tasso ham. Entrees might run to seared diver scallops with fettuccine, local halibut over a white bean puree, monkfish medallions with peekytoe-crab-and-risotto cakes, grilled steak or duck, or chicken with lavender-and-honey-roasted figs and a sweet ricotta gnocchi. Finish with one of co-owner/pastry chef Price Kushner's inventive desserts: warm Belgian chocolate cake, an espresso float, a rhubarb-strawberry tartlet with vanilla gelato and strawberry sauce, or a bowl of hot *zeppole* (small Italian doughnuts) tossed in cinnamon and sugar. The wine list is outstanding. It's hard to get a last-minute table here during summer; failing that, order off the menu from the cozy upstairs bar.

 2 S. Main St. (Rte. 173), Rockland. ✆ **207/596-0770.** www.primorestaurant.com. Reservations highly recommended. Appetizers $9–$18, main courses $25–$42. AE, DC, DISC, MC, V. Summer daily 5:30–9pm; call for hours in off season.

CAMDEN ★★

A quintessential coastal Maine town at the foot of wooded Camden Hills, the affluent village of **Camden** sits on a picturesque harbor no Hollywood movie set could ever improve upon. The village has been attracting wealthy travelers from the East Coast for more than a century, and the mansions of the moneyed still dominate the shady side streets (though many have since been converted into B&Bs). Simply put, Camden is possessed of a grace and sophistication that eludes many other coastal towns.

The best way to enjoy this town is to park your car—and that might require driving a block or two off of busy Route 1, which runs right through the center of town. Camden is of a perfect scale to explore on foot, with plenty of boutiques and galleries. Don't miss the scenic, bowl-shaped **town park** ★★ on the hill behind the town library: It was designed by the firm of Frederick Law Olmsted, the famed landscape architect who designed New York City's Central Park.

Yes, there are T-shirt shops and throngs of tourists here now. Yes, prices have escalated. Yes, on a summer weekend, you'll need to elbow your way past the crowds to get anywhere. But so long as you don't expect it to be a pristine, undiscovered fishing village, Camden is pretty enjoyable.

Essentials

GETTING THERE Camden is on Route 1. Coming from the south, however, it's easier to get here by turning left onto Route 90 about 6 miles north of **Waldoboro,** thus bypassing the busy downtown streets of Rockland.

Concord Coach (✆ **800/639-3317** or 603/228-3300; www.concordcoachlines.com) runs two to three daily buses from Boston. See "Getting There" under "Rockland & Environs," earlier in this chapter, for more details.

VISITOR INFORMATION The **Camden-Rockport-Lincolnville Chamber of Commerce** (✆ **800/223-5459** or 207/236-4404; www.camdenme.org) dispenses helpful information from its tourist office down at Camden's **Public Landing** (by the harbor), where there's also free parking (although spaces are very scarce in summer). The office is open year-round Monday to Saturday; in summer it's also open Sunday.

Exploring Camden

Camden Hills State Park ★★ (✆ **207/236-3109**), one of the Midcoast's best parks, is about a mile north of the village center on Route 1. This 6,500-acre park has an oceanside picnic area, camping at more than 100 sites, a toll road winding up 800-foot **Mount Battie** with spectacular bay views from the summit, and a variety of well-marked hiking trails. The day-use fee is $4.50 for adults, $1 for children ages 5 to 11. It's open from mid-May to mid-October, sunrise to sunset.

If hikes and mild heights don't bother you, you might climb to the ledges of **Mount Megunticook** ★★, preferably early in the morning before the crowds have amassed (and while mists still linger in the valleys). Leave from near the state park's campground—the trail head is clearly marked—and follow the well-maintained path to open ledges, where you should step carefully. The hike takes only 30 to 45 minutes; spectacular views of the harbor await, plus glimpses of smaller hills and valleys. Depending on

DINING♦
Atlantica 12
Boynton-McKay 5
Francine Bistro 6
French & Brawn 10
Marriner's Restaurant 7

Camden

ACCOMMODATIONS■
Blue Harbor House Inn 9
Camden Harbour Inn 11
Camden Maine Stay Inn 3
Camden Windward House 4
The Hartstone Inn 8
Norumbega Inn 1
Whitehall Inn 2

COASTAL MAINE

9

PENOBSCOT BAY

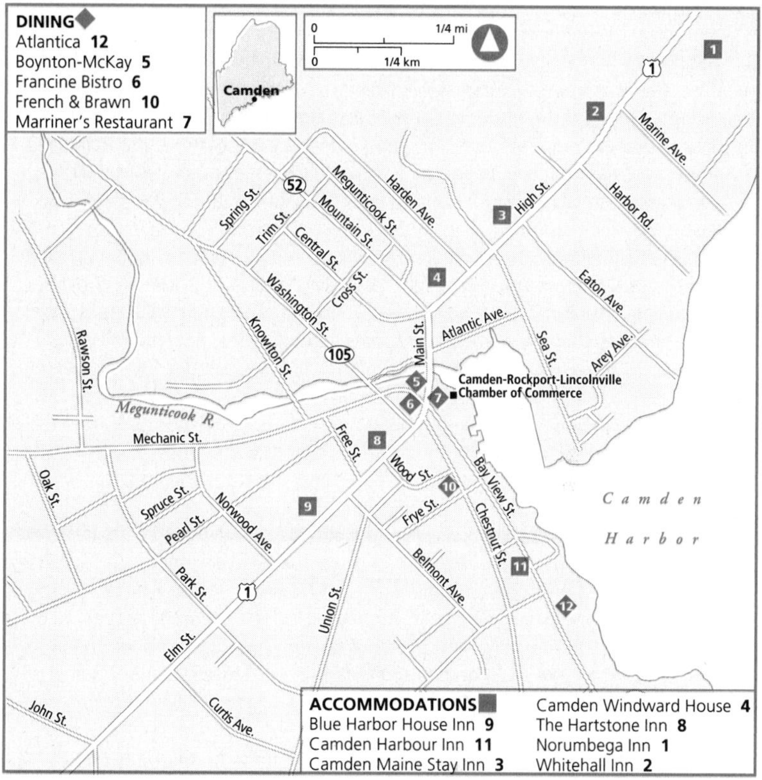

your stamina level, you can keep walking on the park's trail network to Mount Battie, or into lesser-traveled woodlands on the east side of the Camden Hills.

The Camden area is great to explore by bike. One nice loop several miles long takes you from Camden into the cute little village of **Rockport** ★, which has an equally scenic harbor and fewer tourists than Camden. There's a boat landing, park, cafe, and art galleries (see "Rocking It in Rockport," below). The Camden-Rockport Historical Society has drawn up a 9-mile bike (or car) tour, with brief descriptions of some of the historic properties along this route. The brochure is free; check for it at the chamber of commerce at the town's Public Landing (see "Visitor Information," above). The brochure also includes a 2-mile walking tour of downtown Camden.

If you want to cycle the area, bike rentals ($20 per day), repairs, maps, and local riding advice are available at **Bikesenjava** (© **207/596-1004;** www.haybikesenjava.com), located at 481 Main St. in Rockland. As you might have guessed, they also serve coffee.

Where to Stay

Camden vies mightily with Kennebunkport (p. 296), and Manchester, Vermont (p. 215), for the title of "bed-and-breakfast capital of northern New England." B&Bs are

Moments Rocking It in Rockport

Rockport ★★ is absolutely worth a few hours' time during any trip to Camden. Try this route, either by bike or by car: From the waterfront, follow Bayview Street away from the center of Camden and along the bay, passing by a number of opulent seaside estates en route. The road soon narrows and becomes quiet and pastoral, overarched by leafy trees. At the stop sign just past the cemetery, turn left and continue into Rockport. (Along the way, you might pass happily grazing cows.)

Once in Rockport, snoop around the historic harbor and stop by the **Center for Maine Contemporary Art** ★★, 162 Russell Ave. (✆ **207/236-2875;** www.artsmaine.org), a stately gallery with rotating exhibits of local painters, sculptors, and craftspeople. Admission is $5 per adult (free for children). The gallery is open Tuesday to Saturday from 10am until 4pm and Sunday from 1 to 4pm in summer; November through May it's closed Monday through Wednesday, with the same hours the rest of the week.

everywhere in this town. The two stretches of **Route 1** just north and south of the village center—called Elm Street and High Street, respectively—are virtual bed-and-breakfast alleys of handsome homes converted to lodgings. (Others are tucked away on side streets.)

Despite the preponderance of B&Bs, summer or fall weekends can still get tight. It's best to reserve well in advance. Failing to snag a room, you might try **Camden Accommodations** (✆ **800/344-4830** or 207/236-6090; www.camdenac.com), which provides assistance year-round with anything from booking a room at a local B&B to finding cottages for seasonal rentals or extended stays.

Also check out the village of **Lincolnville,** about 6 miles north of town on Route 1. You can find anything from a family-owned motel (rooms $50 a night in the off season) to a plush resort at ocean's edge with a balcony and a Jacuzzi.

And there's good camping at **Camden Hills State Park** (see "Exploring Camden," above), which is open from mid-May until mid-October. Sites cost $25 to $38 per night for non-Maine residents in summer ($10 discount for residents), depending on whether or not you need electric and water hookups; from mid-September until the park closes the price dips to just $18 per site.

Blue Harbor House Inn ★★ On busy Route 1 just south of town, this pale-blue 1810 farmhouse has been an inn since 1978 and is decorated throughout with a feminine country look. Rooms and suites vary in size; some are smallish, with slanting angles and low ceilings, but you can expect touches such as four-poster beds, claw-foot tubs, wicker furniture, Jacuzzis, writing desks, and slipper chairs. And the exposed wood floors are absolutely lovely. The best rooms are the carriage-house suites, with their private entrances and extra amenities—two of them, Captains Quarters and Bali Hai, share a private outdoor patio. The early evening hours feature a nice cocktail service, with cocktails made to order and lovely hors d'oeuvres for a small extra charge. (Fun fact: One of the owners used to work as a cocktail bartender on the real *Love Boat* cruise ship. Gopher, Isaac, and Julie would be proud.)

67 Elm St., Camden, ME 04843. ✆ **800/248-3196** or 207/236-3196. Fax 207/236-6523. www.blueharborhouse.com. 11 units. $95–$155 double; $145–$185 suite. Rates include full breakfast. AE, DISC, MC, V. Closed mid-Oct to mid-May. Pets allowed in some units with prior notice. **Amenities:** Dining room. *In room:* A/C, TV, fridge (some units), hair dryer.

Camden Harbour Inn ★★★ Finds This 1871 mansion sits in a quiet neighborhood on a rise with a view of the sea and mountains beyond, on the way to Rockport—think of it as Camden's quiet side. This had been just another fusty, Victorian-era hotel until 2007, when it got a complete makeover from the two Dutchmen who bought it. No longer a creaky place of floral wallpaper or simple antiques, it's now a luxury inn with a spa, gourmet restaurant, even a wine refrigerator in every room. The place is all about modern design. All rooms have private bathrooms and flatscreen TVs, of course, but most also sport water views, fireplaces, and/or terraces. The New Amsterdam Suite is one of the poshest in town, with its king-size featherbed and two private decks; other suites are designed in Taiwanese, Thai, and Mauritian themes. The inn is within walking distance of downtown, and there's an excellent French restaurant, **Natalie's ★**, as well.

83 Bayview St., Camden, ME 04843. ✆ **800/236-4266** or 207/236-4200. Fax 207/236-7063. www.camdenharbourinn.com. 22 units. $175–$375 double; $235–$700 suite. Rates include full breakfast. 2-night minimum stay in peak season. AE, DISC, MC, V. Pets allowed on ground floor only. Children 12 and over welcome. **Amenities:** Restaurant; bar; spa. *In room:* A/C, TV, hair dryer, Wi-Fi (free).

Camden Maine Stay Inn ★ The Maine Stay is one of Camden's friendliest bed-and-breakfasts. In a home dating from 1802 (expanded in Greek Revival style in 1840), it's your classic slate-roofed New England manse in a shady yard, within walking distance of both downtown *and* Camden Hills State Park. Guest rooms, spaced out over three floors, have ceiling fans (only a few have televisions); each is distinctively furnished in antiques; things are mostly frilly and floral, but the wooden floors are often exposed as a sort of counterpoint. Note that top-floor rooms have foreshortened ceilings with intriguing angles. The downstairs Carriage House Room unit, away from the buzz of Route 1, is popular; its French doors lead to a private stone patio, while a Vermont Castings stove keeps things toasty inside.

22 High St., Camden, ME 04843. ✆ **207/236-9636.** Fax 207/236-0621. www.mainestay.com. 8 units. $110–$240 double; $170–$270 suite. Rates include full breakfast. AE, MC, V. Children 12 and over welcome. **Amenities:** Dining room. *In room:* TV (some units), kitchenette (1 unit), Wi-Fi (free).

Camden Windward House ★★ One of the big complaints from travelers staying on Camden's High Street is the noise from passing traffic. The Windward's owners solved that problem by installing double windows on their historic 1854 home; as a result, when you close the door, the village feels miles away. Welcoming common rooms are decorated with a light Victorian hand and cranberry glass. Rooms vary in size and decor—some are quite frilly, some rather solid and plain—but all have flatscreen TVs, phones, and air-conditioning; some suites add gas fireplaces, Jacuzzis, claw-foot tubs, decks, or canopy beds. The Chart Room's white canopy bed is lovely and bridal-looking; the expansive Quarterdeck suite features exposed beamwork, skylights, and a Jacuzzi; and even the simple, elegant Brass Room has a private deck. Guests choose from plenty of hot breakfast entrees, served in a pleasant dining room of maple tables, and you can order an in-room massage—rare at a B&B. This place is better and friendlier than you might expect.

6 High St., Camden, ME 04843. ✆ **877/492-9656** or 207/236-9656. www.windwardhouse.com. 8 units. Peak season $190–$280 double; off season $99–$240 double. Rates include full breakfast and afternoon tea. AE, MC, V. Children 12 and over welcome. **Amenities:** Bar. *In room:* A/C, TV/DVD, hair dryer, Wi-Fi (some units; free).

The Hartstone Inn ★★★ Finds Among the many great inns in the Camden area, this one's just a little more special. Chef/innkeeper Michael Salmon draws raves for his cooking at this downtown inn, and the accommodations in the early-19th-century Victorian home owned by him and his wife are top-rate, too. The Hartstone's rooms are designed with grace, furnished in lovely antiques and some of the most beautiful decor in the Midcoast; all suites here include Jacuzzis, Wi-Fi access, fridges, fireplaces, and other luxe touches, but even the smaller rooms are plenty comfortable, with MP3 docking stations and flatscreen TVs (and some Jacuzzis and canopy beds). The full breakfasts here are wonderful, as are five-course **dinners** ★★ marrying local Maine seafood with Caribbean chilies, spices, and cooking techniques—lobster with vanilla beurre blanc, for instance. (The chef cooked at resorts in Aruba prior to coming to Maine.) It's a unique experience on a coastline already full of good inns, and the small spa and cooking school here are cappers to the experience.

41 Elm St., Camden, ME 04843. ✆ **800/788-4823** or 207/236-4259. www.hartstoneinn.com. 14 units, 1 with bathroom across hall. $135–$190 double; $175–$275 suite. Rates include full breakfast. MC, V. Closed late Nov to late Apr. **Amenities:** Dining room; spa. *In room:* A/C, TV/DVD, fridge (some units), MP3 docking station, Wi-Fi (some units; free).

Norumbega Inn ★★ You'll have no problem at all finding the Norumbega: Just head north out of town and look for the castle on the right. Well, it's actually a mansion (built of stone by telegraph-system inventor Joseph Stearns in 1886), but it *looks* like a castle. Wonderfully eccentric and full of curves, turrets, angles, and rich materials, this hotel is on the National Historic Registry. There's extravagant carved-oak woodwork in the lobby, a stunning oak-and-mahogany inlaid floor, and a kingly downstairs billiards room. New management is currently updating all furnishings, but some "king" beds still consist of two twin beds pushed together. Still, all units have robes, some have fireplaces, most have air-conditioning, and three ground-level units sport private decks. The two suites here rank among the finest in northern New England: the bright and airy Library suite, in the original two-story library (so big it has an *interior* balcony), and the sprawling Penthouse with its superlative bay views, king-size bed, and huge oval tub. And if you're the sort of traveler who goes gaga over Sherlock Holmes, Hercule Poirot, Angela Lansbury, or the board game Clue, don't miss **Norumbega's Murder Mystery** weekends—be the first to solve the mystery, and you win a free stay. No lie.

63 High St., Camden, ME 04843. ✆ **877/363-4646** or 207/236-4646. www.norumbegainn.com. 12 units. June–Oct $195–$525 double and suite; Nov to mid-Feb and mid-Apr to May $105–$345 double, $275-$525 suite. All rates include full breakfast. 2-night minimum stay in summer Sat–Sun, and holidays. AE, DISC, MC, V. Closed mid-Feb to mid-Apr. Children age 7 and over welcome. **Amenities:** Concierge. *In room:* A/C (most units), TV, fridge (1 unit), hair dryer, Wi-Fi (most units; free).

Whitehall Inn ★ Value Set at the edge of town on busy Route 1, the Whitehall is a venerable Camden institution thanks partly to its association with local poet Edna St. Vincent Millay, who was "discovered" here by a guest who went on to fund Edna's college education. The room where the discovery happened still has a 1904 Steinway piano that Edna played. As for the three-story inn, it's all columns, gables, a long roofline, and atmospherically winding staircases. The antique furnishings—including a handsome Seth Thomas clock, Oriental carpets, and cane-seated rockers on the front porch—are well cared for. Guest rooms are simple yet appealing, and have recently been updated with important additions like flatscreen TVs (previously, there were *no* TVs in many rooms), though the "economy" rooms still share hallway bathrooms just as they did in olden days. The only drawback? That traffic—try to get a room in back.

52 High St., Camden, ME 04843. ✆ **800/789-6565** or 207/236-3391. www.whitehall-inn.com. 45 units, some w/shared bathroom. July–Oct $129–$199 double; mid-May to June $99–$159 double. Rates include full breakfast. AE, MC, V. Closed Nov to mid-May. **Amenities:** 2 restaurants; babysitting; tennis court. *In room:* TV, no phone (some units).

Where to Dine

In addition to its fine-dining options, downtown Camden has a wealth of places to nosh, snack, lunch, and brunch.

Some great doughnuts, for instance, are fried up at **Boynton-McKay** ★ (✆ **207/236-2465;** www.boynton-mckay.com), at 30 Main St.—a former pharmacy that's now a prime spot for lunch, coffee, a quick sandwich, or a blue-plate special. Just up the street, pick up a bag of gourmet groceries at **French & Brawn** (✆ **207/236-3361**), on Main Street at the corner of Elm.

Atlantica ★★ SEAFOOD/BISTRO Atlantica gets high marks for its menu, always well prepared under the management of chef Ken Paquin, a graduate of the Culinary Institute of America (and former top dog at the Equinox in Vermont). On the waterfront with a small indoor seating area and an equally small deck, Paquin cooks subtly creative fare that leans toward seafood and takes in Asian and French influences: seared day boat scallops over lemon risotto with a steamed lobster, roasted breast of duck, porcini-dusted bass, local oysters baked with spinach and Pernod, Maine shrimp in an Asian egg-drop soup, tournedos of beef with a shallot confit and shiitake mushrooms, and grilled lamb chops. All good. Plus there's that great harbor view. At press time, the restaurant was for sale, so eat there while you can.

1 Bayview Landing. ✆ **888/507-8514** or 207/236-6011. www.atlanticarestaurant.com. Reservations recommended. Main courses $12–$24. AE, MC, V. Thurs–Mon 5–9pm. Closed Jan–Mar.

Francine Bistro ★★ FRENCH This place feels more like a French brasserie in Manhattan's Meatpacking District than a coastal seafood joint—and that's a good thing. A meal from chef/owner Brian Hill (long ago, of the seminal Boston alternative-rock band Heretix, but I digress) might begin with fish, onion, or lentil soup; a seviche of halibut, serrano chilies, and red onions; mussels in bordeaux and shallots; or skewers of grilled lamb with white pesto, orange, and endive—nice to see in a state dominated by fried fish and lobster. Entrees might run to roast chicken with a chèvre gratin or a cauliflower-cheese hash; Duck a l'Orange; a crispy skate wing with Jerusalem artichokes; roasted sea bass in caramelized garlic sauce; seared halibut with shrimp; haddock stuffed with scallops; or some reliable steak frites. Hill cut his teeth in some truly great kitchens around the country, and it shows.

55 Chestnut St., Camden. ✆ **207/230-0083.** www.francinebistro.com. Reservations recommended. Main courses $17–$25. MC, V. Tues–Sat 5:30–10pm.

Marriner's Restaurant DINER "The last local luncheonette" is how Marriner's sums itself up, and it has used a sign with the legend DOWN HOME, DOWN EAST, NO FERNS, NO QUICHE to also get its message across: namely, that this is a no-frills affair, so don't expect snootiness or fancy food. The space is done up in a nautical theme of pine booths and vinyl seats, and the kitchen has been spooning up filling breakfasts and lunches for locals since 1942. It's a good place for early risers to get a quick start on the day and check out some local characters. Go for pancakes, chowders, or the lobster and crab rolls—and don't miss the homemade pies, either.

35 Main St., Camden. ✆ **207/236-4949.** Most breakfast items $4–$6, lunch items $4–$12 (most under $7). MC, V. Daily 6am–2pm.

6 THE BLUE HILL PENINSULA ★★

Blue Hill: 136 miles NE of Portland; 23 miles N of Stonington; 14 miles SW of Ellsworth

Forming the eastern boundary of Penobscot Bay—though you must drive north and then *south* to get there, diverging from Route 1 by a good 15 miles or more—the **Blue Hill Peninsula** is a little piece of back-roads paradise. The roads are hilly, winding, and narrow, passing through sprucey forests, past old saltwater farms and over bridges, touching down at the edges of inlets and boatyards from time to time. And the light is nearly always a special, misty color of yellow.

The essayist E.B. White recognized a special quality here: He bought a farm and memorialized the experience in great little books like *One Man's Meat* and *Charlotte's Web.* (White's ashes are buried in a village cemetery on the peninsula.) While they may take a little extra time to find, the island of **Deer Isle** and villages like **Brooklin** and **Blue Hill** are well worth building into any Maine-coast itinerary.

There's also a strong countercultural streak running through the area; somehow, though, the boatbuilders, fishermen, artists, and ex-hippies all get along just fine. Together they've create a unique blend of quiet water views, hand-painted boats, small-town churches and general stores, tiny art galleries, organic produce, and grassroots radio: a place that could only happen in Maine.

DEER ISLE ★★

The island known as **Deer Isle** is well off the beaten path, yet worth the long detour from Route 1. Looping, winding roads cross through forest and farmland, and travelers are rewarded with sudden glimpses of hidden coves. An occasional settlement even crops up now and again. This island doesn't cater exclusively to tourists the way many coastal towns and islands do; it's still largely occupied by fifth- or sixth-generation fishermen, farmers, second-home owners, and artists who prize their seclusion here.

The main village—**Stonington,** on the island's southern tip—is still a rough-hewn sea town. This village does now have a handful of inns and galleries, but its primary focus is to serve locals and summer residents, not travelers. *Outside* magazine once named this one of America's 10 best towns to live in if you're an extreme/outdoorsy type.

Well, maybe if you don't mind living hours removed from the nearest significant population center and airport. I've yet to see a lobsterman kayaking on his downtime, either—they're too busy working—though I suppose it does happen.

Be that as it may, this is a great island on which to simply relax, smell the salt air, and watch the changing landscapes.

Essentials

GETTING THERE The island of Deer Isle is connected to the mainland via a high, narrow, **suspension bridge** built in 1938—still a bit scary to cross during high winds. You get to the bridge via one of several winding roads that split off of Route 1.

Coming from the south or west (Portland or Camden), turn onto Route 175 in Orland, then connect to Route 15 and continue to Deer Isle. From the east (Mount Desert Isle or Canada), head south on Route 172 to Blue Hill, where you can also pick up Route 15.

VISITOR INFORMATION The **Deer Isle–Stonington Chamber of Commerce** (✆ **207/348-6124;** www.deerislemaine.com) staffs a seasonal information booth just beyond the bridge on Little Deer Isle. This booth is normally open daily during summer, but its hours depend on the availability of volunteer staffers. Call or check the website first.

Exploring Deer Isle

With its network of narrow roads leading nowhere, Deer Isle is ideal for rambling around on—by car or bike. Especially tranquil is the narrow road between Deer Isle and the village of **Sunshine** to the east. Plan to stop and explore the various coves and inlets en route. To get here, follow Route 15—then, south of Deer Isle, turn east toward **Stinson Neck,** continuing about 10 scenic miles over bridges and causeways.

Stonington ★, at the southern end of the island, consists of one commercial street that wraps along harbor's edge. While B&Bs and boutiques have made inroads here in recent years, it's still a bit of a rough-and-tumble waterfront town—a good place for taking pictures and eating fish.

Where to Stay

Inn on the Harbor ★ **Value** This quirky waterfront inn has the best location in town, right on Stonington's main street. After a makeover, the guest rooms (more than half of which overlook the harbor) are now nicely appointed with antiques and carpets. The most inexpensive rooms are a real bargain, in or out of season (when rates plummet), especially so because every unit in the place has a phone, television, and Wi-Fi access. This is a good spot for resting up before or after a local kayaking expedition, or as a base for day trips out to Isle au Haut (which is part of Acadia National Park).

45 Main St. (P.O. Box 69), Stonington, ME 04681. ✆ **800/942-2420** or 207/367-2420. Fax 207/367-5165. www.innontheharbor.com. 14 units. Mid-May to mid-Oct $139–$225 double; mid-Oct to mid-May $65–$135 double. Rates include continental breakfast mid-May to mid-Oct only. AE, DISC, MC, V. Children 12 and over welcome. *In room:* TV, kitchenette (1 unit), no phone (1 unit), Wi-Fi (free).

Pilgrim's Inn ★★ Set between an open bay and a mill pond, the Pilgrim's is a historic, handsomely renovated inn with a few adjacent cottages. The home was built in 1793 by Ignatius Haskell, a prosperous sawmill owner; his granddaughter later opened the home to boarders, and it has housed summer guests ever since. The interior is tastefully decorated in a style that's informed by early Americana: Think exposed wooden floors, woody canopy beds, flowery bed prints, and rugs and quilts galore. The rooms are also appointed in antiques and painted in muted Colonial colors. (Especially intriguing are the units on the top floor, which show off the home's impressive diagonal beams.) Other accents include private staircases, antique tubs, woodstoves, and fireplaces. Breakfasts here are big and fancy: goat-cheese pancakes, eggs Benedict, smoked salmon, and the like. Three nearby cottages are also rented by the inn (and two of them stay open year-round, unlike the main inn), and allow pets inside. The inn maintains a tavern-style dining room with several intriguing spaces; expect typical American resort fare like steaks, fish, lobsters, and rack of lamb.

20 Main St. (P.O. Box 69), Deer Isle, ME 04627. ✆ **888/778-7505** or 207/348-6615. Fax 207/348-7769. www.pilgrimsinn.com. 15 units. $109–$209 double; $179–$249 cottage. Rates include full breakfast. MC, V. Closed mid-Oct to mid-May (2 cottages open year-round). Pets allowed in cottages only ($50 fee). Children 10 and over welcome in inn, all children welcome in cottages. **Amenities:** Restaurant; pub; bikes. *In room:* Kitchenette (1 room), Wi-Fi (free).

Where to Dine

Fish and shellfish completely dominate the menus of the restaurants on this island, just as you'd expect.

If you don't end up eating on the dock at the Fishermen's Friend (see below), you're probably eating at the **Maritime Café** ★ (✆ **207/367-2600**), a short block away on Main Street. The cafe serves a lunch menu of hearty sandwiches (organic sausage, turkey, lobster and crab rolls), and dinners of steamed lobsters, pan-seared scallops over linguine, crab cakes, crab-stuffed haddock filets, and grilled rib-eye steaks plus beer, wine, and espresso.

Fisherman's Friend ★ Value SEAFOOD Just one dock over from the Isle au Haut ferry and attached to a general store, this seasonal seafood eatery is a locals' sort of place: lively, crowded, completely unpretentious. The menu features home-cooked meals, including a range of broiled and fried fresh fish. But many people come for lobsters—the owners boast that they prepare it 30 different ways here, and those permutations include baked and stuffed, baked with spinach and cream, steamed, stir-fried, buttered, champagne-poached (!), cooked in a pie, thin-sliced and placed in crepes, or served with other sauces ranging from coconut curry to tomato. The popular lobster stew brims with meaty chunks. There's even a wine list, a selection of pastas, and a dessert menu of typical seasonal New England favorites like blueberry pie, strawberry-rhubarb pie, strawberry shortcake, raspberry crisp, and tollhouse pie.

5 Atlantic Ave. (off Main St., at end of dock), Stonington. ✆ **207/367-2442.** www.stoningtonharbor.com. Reservations recommended in summer. Lobster dishes market-priced; main courses $13–$20 at dinner. DISC, MC, V. Mid-May to mid-Oct daily 11am–9pm (Fri–Sat to 10pm); mid-Oct to mid-May call for hours.

BLUE HILL ★★

Blue Hill, population 2,400, is very easy to find—just look for the dome of Blue Hill itself, which lords over the northern end of Blue Hill Bay. You can see it from miles away, looming like a whaleback.

Set between the hill and the bay is a quiet and historic town, clustered compactly along the shore. There's not much going on here, a quality which curiously seems to attract repeat summer guests who love the place. The village center offers an old-fashioned general store, art galleries, boats on a harbor, a fried-seafood joint, and a couple of choices for both lodging and fine dining. It's a good place for a (very) quiet break.

Essentials

GETTING THERE Blue Hill is southeast of **Ellsworth,** at the junction of routes 15 and 172. From **Bar Harbor,** follow Route 3 through Ellsworth, cross the bridge and follow Route 172 about 14 miles to Blue Hill. Coming from the south (from **Rockland** or Belfast) on Route 1, turn south onto Route 15 about 5 miles east of **Bucksport** and continue about 12 miles to Blue Hill.

VISITOR INFORMATION It's tiny, so Blue Hill doesn't maintain a true visitor information office or kiosk. Instead, look for the town's brochure and map at state information centers, or contact the **Blue Hill Peninsula Chamber of Commerce** (✆ **207/374-3242;** www.bluehillpeninsula.org), located at 107 Main St. Locals are also often willing to answer strangers' questions.

Exploring Blue Hill

One good way to start your exploration of this area is to climb to the open summit of **Blue Hill** ★★, from which you can get good views of the bay and the bald mountaintops of nearby Mount Desert Island.

The trail is free. To reach the trail head from the center of the village, drive north on Route 172 about 1½ miles, then turn west (left) on Mountain Road at the Blue Hill Fairgrounds. Drive another ¾ mile and look for the well-marked trail on the right; park

Tips Tune in to Community Radio

When in the Blue Hill area, be sure to tune into the local community radio station, WERU, at 89.9 FM (and also at 102.9 FM). Started by partners including Noel "Paul" Stookey—the "Paul" in the folk trio Peter, Paul, and Mary—in a former chicken coop (only in Maine . . .), the idea was to spread good local and rootsy music while also encouraging provocative, countercultural thinking. It's become a little bit slicker and more professional in recent years, but WERU still retains a pleasantly homespun quality and plays some of the best true folk, roots, Americana, Celtic, and blues music of any station in New England. There's also some from-the-left news and commentary during the dinner hour each day, rock and electronic music late at night, and reggae and spoken-word poetry during other time slots.

on either shoulder of the road. The moderate ascent is about a mile long and takes about 45 minutes; there are no tricky, death-defying stretches along the way, and you'll know you've arrived when you spy the fire tower. Bring a picnic lunch, but don't dump your leftover food on the trail afterward—bears have occasionally been sighted around here.

Blue Hill has traditionally attracted lots of writers, artists, and potters; you can't throw a stone without hitting a gallery or studio here. Family-run **Rackliffe Pottery** ★ (✆ **888/631-3321** or 207/374-2297; www.rackliffepottery.com), on Route 172 (Ellsworth Rd.), uses native clay and lead-free glazes for its works, for instance. Visitors are welcome to watch the potters at work, and it's open year-round.

The best museum in town is the **Parson Fisher House** ★★ (✆ **207/374-2459;** www.jonathanfisherhouse.org), on routes 176 and 15, a half-mile west of the village. Fisher, Blue Hill's first permanent minister, was a small-town Renaissance man when he settled here in 1796. Educated at Harvard, Fisher not only delivered sermons in six different languages (including Aramaic), but was also a writer, painter, and inventor of boundless energy. On a tour of this home, which he built himself in 1814, you can view a clock with wooden works and a camera obscura that Fisher made, plus pictures he painted and books he wrote, published, and bound by hand. Outside, the property's owners are slowly recreating Fisher's original orchard.

The house is open from July to mid-October Thursday through Saturday from 1 to 4pm. Admission is by donation; $5 per person is suggested.

Where to Stay

Blue Hill Farm Country Inn Comfortably situated on 48 acres about 2 miles north of the Blue Hill's village center, this inn (not to be confused with its similar-named neighbor; see below) has some of the most relaxing and comfortable common areas in the region. The first floor of a big barn was converted into a spacious living room, with sitting areas arrayed so that you can opt for either privacy or the company of others. Guest rooms are small and lightly furnished, though—none come with anything larger than a double bed. The more modern rooms are upstairs in the barn loft and are decorated in a country farmhouse style, though they're a bit motel-like. The seven older rooms in the farmhouse have more character—but they share a single bathroom with a small tub and hand-held shower head.

Rte. 15 (P.O. Box 437), Blue Hill, ME 04614. ✆ **207/374-5126.** www.bluehillfarminn.com. 14 units, 7 with shared bathroom. $115 double with private bathroom; $95 double with shared bathroom. Rates include continental breakfast. AE, MC, V. *In room:* No phone.

Blue Hill Inn ★★ The Blue Hill Inn has been hosting travelers since 1840 on one of the village's main streets, within walking distance of everything. It's a Federal-style inn, decorated in a Colonial American motif; creaky wooden floors stamp it with authenticity. The innkeepers have pleasantly furnished all rooms with antiques and down comforters; a few units in the main house have wood-burning fireplaces (these rooms are open only from mid-May through Oct), while a large contemporary suite in an adjacent, free-standing building has a cathedral ceiling, fireplace, full kitchen, living room, and deck (and it's open year-round). Breakfasts here are very good.

40 Union St. (P.O. Box 403), Blue Hill, ME 04614. ✆ **800/826-7415** or 207/374-2844. Fax 207/374-2829. www.bluehillinn.com. 12 units. $155–$205 double; $175–$275 suite. Rates include full breakfast and afternoon pastries. 2-night minimum stay in summer. DISC, MC, V. Main inn closed Dec to mid-May, suite open year-round. Children 13 and over are welcome. **Amenities:** Dining room. *In room:* A/C, TV (1 unit), kitchenette (1 unit), no phone (most units).

Where to Dine

The **Fish Net** (✆ **207/374-5240**), at the north end of Main Street (near the junction of rtes. 172 and 177), is the place locals go for quick meals of fried fish, lobster rolls, clam baskets, and ice-cream cones. It's open seasonally. There's also a bakery, **Blue Hill Hearth** (✆ **207/610-9696**), at 58 Main St., serving sandwiches, pizzas, and soups.

Arborvine ★★ SEAFOOD/FUSION The Arborvine gives this sleepy town a top-flight eatery. In a beautifully renovated Cape Cod–style house, the restaurant's interior is warm and inviting—think rough-hewn timbers, polished wooden floors, and a cozy bar area. The owners are careful to use locally procured ingredients, such as Bagaduce River oysters on the half shell as an appetizer. The intriguing nightly main courses change but might run to haddock niçoise, broiled Stonington halibut with grilled polenta, coriander-crusted ahi with seaweed and Japanese flavorings, or seared local scallops in a garlicky saffron broth. The nonseafood choices are equally exciting: a rack of lamb in pine nuts and basil, beef medallions over a dollop of Vermont chèvre, crispy roast duckling with a quince glaze, or just a simple boneless rib-eye with duxelle sauce. Yummy desserts could include a Grand Marnier–spiked chocolate mousse; chocolate cake with raspberry ganache; a lemon mousse Napoleon; a gingery vanilla crème brûlée; or a Bartlett pear in puff pastry sided with macadamia-nut-flavored cream, pomegranate sauce, and a bit of cinnamon ice cream.

Main St. ✆ **207/374-2119.** www.arborvine.com. Main courses $27–$31. MC, V. Summer daily 5:30–8:30pm; off season Fri–Sun 5:30–8:30pm.

7 MOUNT DESERT ISLAND ★★★

Bar Harbor: 270 miles NE of Boston; 160 miles NE of Portland

Mount Desert Island is home to spectacular **Acadia National Park,** and for many visitors, these two places are one and the same. Yet the park's holdings are only *part* of the appeal of this wonderful island, which is connected to the mainland by a short causeway. Besides the

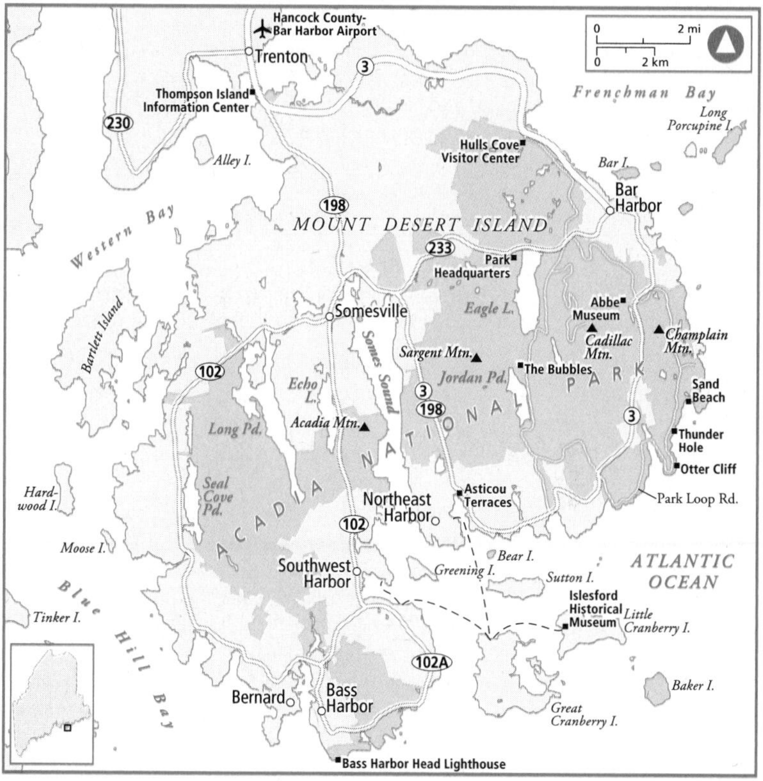

parklands, you'll find scenic harborside fishing villages and remote backcountry roads aplenty, lovely B&Bs and fine restaurants, oversize 19th-century summer "cottages," and the historic tourist town of **Bar Harbor.**

Mount Desert Island is split almost precisely in two by a deep inlet known as Somes Sound (see "Fjord Tough," below). Most of the parklands are on the eastern lobe of the island, though it does take in some large tracts, campgrounds, and mountains on the isle's western flank, too.

The eastern side is much more heavily developed. **Bar Harbor** is the center of commerce and entertainment, a once-charming resort now in danger of being swallowed whole by all its T-shirt and trinket shops. The western side has a quieter, more settled air and teems with more wildlife than tourists; the villages are mostly filled with fishermen and second-homers, rather than actual businesses.

This island isn't huge—it's only about 15 miles from the causeway to the southernmost tip at Bass Harbor Head—yet you can do an awful lot of adventuring within this compact space. And you can see many different kinds of villages and landscapes, too. The

Tips — See It, Say It

There is some debate about how to correctly pronounce the island to which I'm referring throughout this chapter. The name is of French origin; technically, it should be "Mount days-AIRT," but nobody says it that way anymore. Some locals say "Mount Des-SERT," like what you have after dinner, which is pretty close to the French way of saying things. (Notice the accent on the last syllable.) However, plenty of tourists, transplants, and locals *also* say DEZ-ert (like the Sahara), and that's not wrong. After all, that's how it's *spelled.* As for me, I go with "dessert."

best strategy is to take it slowly, exploring on foot, by bicycle, even by canoe or kayak. Give yourself a week if you have that much time to spare. You'll be glad you did.

ACADIA NATIONAL PARK ★★★

It's not hard to understand why Acadia is one of the crown jewels of the National Park system. (It draws the second-most visitors, annually, of any of the U.S. national parks.) The landscape here is a rich tapestry of rugged cliffs, pounding ocean surf, fishing and leisure boats lolling in harbors, and quiet forest paths.

Acadia's terrain, like so much of the rest of northern New England, was shaped by the cutting action of the last great glaciers moving into and then out of the region about 18,000 years ago. A mile-high ice sheet rumbled slowly over the land, scouring valleys into deep U shapes, rounding many once-jagged peaks, and depositing boulders at odd places in the landscape—including the famous 10-foot-tall Bubble Rock, which appears perched precariously on the side of South Bubble Mountain.

In the 1840s, Hudson River School painter Thomas Cole brought his sketchbooks and easels to remote Mount Desert Island, which was then home to a small number of fishermen and boatbuilders. His stunning renditions of the coast were displayed in New York City museums and galleries, triggering a tourism rush as urbanites flocked to the island to "discover" nature and "rusticate" in wood-beamed lodges and Victorian inns. By 1872 national magazines were touting Eden (the town of Bar Harbor's name before 1919) as a summer getaway. It attracted the attention of wealthy industrialists and soon became the summer home of Carnegies, Rockefellers, Astors, and Vanderbilts, who built massive "cottages" (mansions, really, in the shingle style of the time) with dozens of bedrooms.

By the early 1900s, the island's popularity and growing development began to concern people. Textile heir George Dorr and Harvard president Charles Eliot, aided by the largesse of John D. Rockefeller, Jr., began acquiring and protecting large tracts of the island for the public to enjoy. These parcels were eventually donated to the U.S. government, and in 1919 the land was designated Lafayette National Park—the first national park east of the Mississippi—after the French general.

Renamed Acadia National Park in 1929, the park has now grown to encompass nearly half the island in piecemeal holdings. It is a world-class destination for those who enjoy outdoors adventure. In parts, the park seems to share more in common with Alaska than New England: You can see bald eagles soaring overhead, whales breaching below, cliffs and fir-topped mountains at nearly every turn.

In between, you'll find remote coves perfect for beach picnics; lovely offshore islands accessible only by sea kayak; clear ponds and lakes with nary a boat in them; and uncrowded mountaintops with views of it all and outstanding foliage in fall.

Essentials

GETTING THERE Acadia National Park is near Ellsworth. Normally, travelers take Route 1 to Ellsworth from southern Maine, but you can avoid coastal congestion by taking the Maine Turnpike to Bangor, then picking up I-395 to Route 1A and continuing south into Ellsworth. Though this is longer in terms of miles, it's the quicker route in summer.

From Ellsworth, bear right onto Route 3 (Rte. 1 doesn't go there) and continue about 15 minutes to the island causeway in **Trenton.** Cross the bridge, and you're on the island. Consult a map carefully to determine which route to take from here; there are three possible choices, all leading to very different destinations—routes 3 and 233 go to Bar Harbor, Route 198 goes to Northeast Harbor, and Route 102 leads to Southwest Harbor.

Year-round there are several flights daily from Boston on small planes to the **Hancock County–Bar Harbor airport** (airport code BHB; www.bhbairport.com) in Trenton, just across the causeway from Mount Desert Island; for more information contact **U.S. Airways Express** (✆ **800/428-4322;** www.usairways.com). From here, call a taxi, rent a car, or—best of all—ride the **free shuttle bus** (see below) to downtown Bar Harbor from late June through mid-October.

GETTING AROUND A **free summer shuttle bus service ★★**, known as the *Island Explorer* (www.exploreacadia.com), was inaugurated in 1999 as part of an effort to reduce the number of cars on the island's roads. It's working: The propane-powered buses—equipped with racks for bikes—serve multiple routes covering nearly the entire island and will stop anywhere you request outside the village centers, including trail heads, ferries, small villages, and campgrounds. (Bring a book, though; there are lots of stops.)

All routes begin or end at the central **Village Green** in Bar Harbor, but you can and should pick up the bus almost anywhere else to avoid parking hassles in town. Route no. 3 runs from Bar Harbor along much of the Park Loop, offering easy, free access to some of the park's best hiking trails. The buses operate from late June through mid-October; ask for a schedule at island information centers, in shops, or at any hotel or campground.

GUIDED TOURS **Acadia National Park Tours** (✆ **207/288-0300;** www.acadiatours.com) offers 2½-hour park tours from mid-May through October, departing twice daily (10am and 2pm) from downtown Bar Harbor. The bus tour includes three stops (Sieur

Fun Facts Fjord Tough

Mount Desert Island is divided deeply right down the middle into two lobes (almost like a brain) by **Somes Sound,** a tidal inlet that is also the only true fjord—that is, a valley carved out by a glacier and then subsequently filled in with rising ocean water—in the entire lower 48 states. No, it's not nearly as scenic as the ones in Norway and Alaska, but when you drive over that little bridge from one side to the other, you can truthfully report to friends back home that you crossed a fjord this morning. Pretty cool.

Fun Facts How the Carriage Roads Came to Be

John D. Rockefeller, Jr., *alone* purchased and donated some 11,000 acres of Acadia National Park—about one-third of the entire park's area—and it was he who is almost singularly responsible for its extraordinary **carriage roads.**

It happened this way: Around 1905 a dispute erupted over whether to allow noisy new motorcars onto the island. Islanders wanted this new convenience, but Rockefeller (whose fortune had been made in the oil industry) strenuously objected, preferring the tranquillity of a car-free island for his summer vacations. The multimillionaire went down to defeat on the issue, though, and the island was opened to cars in 1913; in response Rockefeller set about building an elaborate 57-mile system of private carriage roads on his holdings in the park, complete with a dozen gracefully handcrafted stone bridges.

These roads, open today to pedestrians, bicyclists, horses, and carriages, are concentrated most densely around **Jordan Pond,** but they also wind through wooded valleys and ascend some of the park's most scenic peaks.

De Monts Springs, Thunder Hole, and Cadillac Mountain) and plenty of park trivia, courtesy of the driver. This is an easy way for first-time visitors to get a quick introduction to the park before setting out on their own side trips. Tickets are available at Testa's Restaurant (53 Main St.) in Bar Harbor; the cost is $28 for adults, $15 for children 12 and under.

ENTRY POINTS & FEES Entrance fees to the park are collected at several gates and points from May through October; the rest of the year, entrance is free—one of this nation's great outdoor bargains either way. A 1-week pass, which includes unlimited trips on the Park Loop Road (closed in winter), costs $20 per car from late June through early October and $10 per car in spring and fall; there's no additional charge per passenger once you've bought the pass. Hikers, cyclists, and anyone else traveling without a vehicle (that is, motorcyclists or boaters) must pay a $5-per-person fee.

You can enter the park at several points in the interwoven network of park and town roads—a glance at a park map, available free at the visitor center, will make these access points self-evident. The main point of entry to Park Loop Road, the park's most scenic byway, is near the official park visitor center at **Hulls Cove** (on Rte. 3 just north of Bar Harbor); the entry fee is collected at a tollbooth on the loop road, a half-mile north of Sand Beach.

VISITOR CENTERS & INFORMATION Acadia staffs two visitor centers. The **Thompson Island Information Center** (© **207/288-3411**), on Route 3, is the first you'll pass as you enter Mount Desert Island. This center is maintained by the local chambers of commerce, but park personnel are often on hand to answer inquiries. Open daily at 6am mid-May through mid-October (its closing hours vary depending on staff), it's a good first stop for general lodging and restaurant information.

If you're interested primarily in information about the park itself, continue on Route 3 to the National Park Service's **Hulls Cove Visitor Center,** about 7½ miles beyond Thompson Island. This attractive, stone-walled center has professionally prepared park-service displays, such as a large relief map of the island, natural history exhibits, and a short introductory film. You can also request free brochures about hiking trails and the carriage roads, or purchase postcards and more detailed guidebooks. The center is open daily from mid-April through the end of October.

And information is available year-round, by phone or in person, at the **park headquarters** (**© 207/288-3338**), on Route 233 between Bar Harbor and Somesville, open daily (but closed weekends in summer). You can also ask questions online at their website, **www.nps.gov/acad**.

SEASONS Spring is forgettable in Acadia, but summer is the peak season. The weather in July and August is perfect for just about any outdoor activity. Most days are warm (in the 70s or 80s Fahrenheit/low to mid-20s Celsius), with afternoons frequently cooler than mornings owing to the sea breezes. (Fog occasionally rolls in from the southeast on a hot day, which gives the landscape a magical quality.) While sun seems to be the norm, come prepared for rain; it's not uncommon at all. Once or twice every summer, a heat wave somehow settles onto the island, producing temperatures in the 90s Fahrenheit (30s Celsius), dense haze, and stifling humidity, but this rarely lasts more than a few days. Enjoy summer: Soon enough (sometimes even during late Aug), a brisk north wind will blow in from the Canadian Arctic, forcing visitors into sweaters at night. You'll smell the approach of autumn, with winter not far behind.

Fall here is wonderful. Between Labor Day and the foliage season in early October, days are often warm and clear, nights have a crisp tang, and you can avoid the congestion, crowds, and pesky insects of summer. It's not that the park is empty in September; bus tours seem to proliferate at this time, which can mean periodic crowds and backups at the most popular sites (such as Thunder Hole). Not to worry: If you walk a minute or two off the road, you can find solitude and an agreeably peaceful walk or perch. Hikers and bikers will have the trails and carriage roads to themselves.

Winter is an increasingly popular time to travel to Acadia, especially among those who enjoy cross-country skiing the carriage roads. Be aware, though, that snow along the coast is inconsistent, and services—including most restaurants and many inns—are often closed down in winter. Expect to stay in either a really cheap motel or an expensive resort, and to eat what locals do: pizza, burgers, and sandwiches.

RANGER PROGRAMS Frequent ranger programs are offered throughout the year at Acadia. These include talks at campground amphitheaters and tours of various island locales and attractions. Examples include an Otter Point nature hike, walks across the carriage roads' stone bridges, cruises on Frenchman Bay (rangers provide commentary on many trips), and discussions of the changes in Acadia's landscape. Ask for a schedule of park events and more information at any visitor center or campground.

Tips Cost-Effective Acadia

No daily pass to Acadia is available, so if you'll be here more than 2 weeks, purchase a $40 annual Acadia pass for your car instead of several $20 weekly passes. Or if you really travel a lot, consider buying an $80 **America the Beautiful** national parks pass (www.nps.gov/fees_passes.htm)—it gets you, your vehicle, and your passengers into *all* national parks for an entire calendar year.

The 20-mile **Park Loop Road** ★★ is to Acadia what Half Dome is to Yosemite—the park's premier attraction, but also a magnet for crowds. This remarkable road starts near the Hulls Cove Visitor Center and runs along ridges high above Bar Harbor before dropping down along the rocky coast. Here spires of spruce and fir cap dark granite ledges, making a sharp contrast with the white surf and blue-black sea. After following the picturesque coast and touching upon several coves, the road loops back inland along Jordan Pond and Eagle Lake, with a detour to the summit of the island's highest peak, Cadillac Mountain.

Ideally, visitors should try to make two circuits of the loop road. The first time, get the lay of the land. On the second circuit (one pass gets you all-day access), plan to stop frequently and poke around on foot, setting off on trails or scrambling along the coastline and taking photos. (Scenic pull-offs are strategically staggered at intervals.) The two-lane road is one-way along some of its coastal sections; in these cases, the right-hand lane is set aside for parking, so you can stop wherever you'd like, admire the vistas from the shoulder, and click away.

From about 10am until 4pm every good-weather day in July and August, anticipate big crowds along the loop road. Parking lots often fill up and close their gates early at the most popular destinations, such as Sand Beach, Thunder Hole, and the Cadillac Mountain summit—so try to visit these spots early or late in the day. Alternatively, on cloudy or drizzly days, you'll practically have the loop road to yourself.

From the Hulls Cove Visitor Center, the Park Loop initially runs atop:

❶ Paradise Hill

Our tour starts with sweeping views eastward over Frenchman Bay. You'll see the town of Bar Harbor far below, and just beyond it the Porcupines, a cluster of islands that look like, well, porcupines. Sort of.

Following the Park Loop Road clockwise, you'll dip into a wooded valley and come to:

❷ Sieur de Monts Spring

Here you'll find a rather uninteresting natural spring, unnaturally encased, along with a botanical garden with some 300 species showcased in 12 habitats. The

Tips Avoiding Crowds in the Park

Early fall is the best time to miss the mobs yet still enjoy the weather here. If you come midsummer, try to venture out in early morning or early evening to the most popular spots, such as Thunder Hole or the summit of Cadillac Mountain. Setting off into the woods at every opportunity is also a good strategy. Probably four out of every five visitors restrict their tours to the loop road and a handful of other major attractions, leaving most of the gorgeous backcountry to the more adventurous.

The best guarantee of solitude is to head to the most remote outposts managed by Acadia, such as **Isle au Haut** and **Schoodic Peninsula,** across the bay to the east. Ask for more information about these areas at the visitor centers.

Tips: Packing a Picnic for Acadia

Before you set out to explore, pack a lunch and keep it handy. Once you get inside the park, you'll find very few places (other than the Jordan Pond House; see "Where to Dine," below) to stop for lunch or snacks. Having drinks and snacks at hand will prevent you from having to backtrack into Bar Harbor or elsewhere midday to fend off hunger. The more food you bring, the more your options for a day expand, so hit one of the charming general stores in any of the island's villages first and stock up on sandwiches, sweets, camera batteries, and hydration.

original **Abbe Museum** (**© 207/288-3519**) is here, featuring a small but select collection of Native American artifacts. It's open daily late May to early October from 9am to 4pm; admission is $3 for adults, $1 for children ages 6 to 15. (A larger and more modern branch of the museum in Bar Harbor features more and better-curated displays; a ticket here gets you a discount there. See "Exploring Bar Harbor," below, for details.)

The Tarn is the main reason to stop here; a few hundred yards south of the springs via a footpath, it's a slightly medieval-looking and forsaken pond sandwiched between steep hills. Departing from the south end of the Tarn is the fine **Dorr Mountain Ladder Trail** (see "Hiking," below).

Continue the clockwise trip on the loop road; views eastward over the bay soon resume, almost uninterrupted, until you get to:

3 The Precipice Trail

The park's most dramatic walking track, the **Precipice Trail** ★★ ascends sheer rock faces on the eastern side of **Champlain Mountain.** Only about .75 mile to the summit, it's nevertheless a rigorous climb and involves scrambling up iron rungs and ladders in exposed places (those with a fear of heights and those under 5 ft. tall should *avoid* this trail). The trail is often closed midsummer to protect nesting peregrine falcons, and at these times rangers are often on hand at the trail-head parking lot to suggest alternative hikes.

Between the Precipice Trail and the next stop is a tollbooth where visitors pay the park's **entrance fee.**

Picturesquely set between the arms of a rocky cove is:

4 Sand Beach

Sand Beach ★★ is virtually the only sand beach on the island, although swimming these cold waters (about 50°F/10°C) is best enjoyed on extremely hot days or by those with hardy constitutions. When it's sunny out, the sandy strand is crowded midday with picnickers, tanners, tide-pool combers, and book readers.

Two worthwhile hikes begin near the beach. **The Beehive Trail** overlooks Sand Beach (see "Hiking," below); it starts from a trail head across the loop road. From the east end of Sand Beach, look for the start of the **Great Head Trail,** a loop of about 2 miles that follows on the bluff overlooking the beach, then circles back along the shimmering bay before cutting through the woods back to Sand Beach.

About a mile south of Sand Beach is:

5 Thunder Hole

Thunder Hole ★ is a shallow oceanside cave into which the ocean surges, compresses, and bursts out violently like a thick cannon shot of foam. (A roadside walking trail allows you to leave your car parked at the Sand Beach lot and hike to this point.)

If the sea is quiet—as it sometimes is on midsummer days—don't bother visiting this attraction; there'll be nothing to see. But on days when the seas are rough, and big swells are rolling in all the way from the Bay of Fundy, this is a must-see, three-star attraction; you can feel the ocean's power and force. The best viewing time is **3 hours before high tide;** check tide tables, available at local hotels, restaurants, and info kiosks, to figure out when that is.

Just before the road curves around Otter Point, you'll be driving atop:

6 Otter Cliffs

This set of 100-foot-high precipices is capped with dense stands of spruce trees. From the top, look for spouting whales in summer. In early fall, thousands of eider ducks can sometimes be seen floating in big, raftlike flocks just offshore. A footpath traces the edge of the crags.

At Seal Harbor, the loop road veers north and inland back toward Bar Harbor. On the route is:

7 Jordan Pond

Jordan Pond ★★ is a small but beautiful body of water encased by gentle, forested hills. A 3-mile hiking loop follows the pond's shoreline (see "Hiking," below), and a network of splendid carriage roads converges at the pond. After a hike or mountain-bike excursion, spend some time at a table on the lawn of the Jordan Pond House restaurant (see "Where to Dine," below).

Shortly before the loop road ends, you'll pass the entrance to:

8 Cadillac Mountain

Reach this **mountain** ★ by car, ascending an early carriage road. At 1,528 feet, it's the highest peak touching the Atlantic Ocean between Canada and Brazil. During much of the year, it's also the first place on U.S. soil touched by the rays of sunrise. But because this is the only mountaintop in the park accessible by car (and also because it's the island's highest point), the parking lot at the summit often gets jammed.

Views are undeniably great, even if the shopping-mall-at-Christmas crowds can put a serious crimp in your enjoyment of the place. Luckily, some lower peaks accessible only by foot—such as Acadia and Champlain mountains—have equally excellent views and far fewer crowds.

Getting Outside

CARRIAGE RIDES ★★ Several types of carriage rides are offered by the official concessionaire, **Carriages of Acadia** (✆ **877/276-3622;** www.carriagesofacadia.com), from the park's stables about a half-mile south of the Jordan Pond House (just north and inland from **Seal Harbor**). These 1- to 2-hour tours depart daily in season, and might take in sweeping ocean views from a local mountaintop, a ramble through the Rockefeller bridges, or a stop by the Jordan Pond House for tea and popovers. Check for current pricing; reservations are recommended. (You can also rent a stall at the stables and ride the trails yourself—*if* you've brought your own horse. Gives a new meaning to the term "horse power.")

GOLF Mount Desert Island has two good golf courses. The **Kebo Valley Golf Club** (✆ **207/288-3000;** www.kebovalleyclub.com) is one of the oldest in America, open since 1888. The **Northeast Harbor Golf Club** (✆ **207/276-5335;** www.nehgc.com) is another good choice. Greens fees at both are $85 per person for 18 holes during peak summer season (July through Labor Day); these rates dip considerably, however, during the shoulder seasons of spring and fall.

HIKING Hiking is the quintessential Acadia activity, and it should be experienced by everyone at least once. The park has perhaps 120 miles of hiking trails (which are well maintained *and* well marked), plus nearly 60 more miles of carriage roads, which are also good for easy strolling. Some of these trails traverse the sides or faces of the island's low "mountains," and almost all of their summits have good, unimpeded views of the Atlantic far below. Many of these pathways were crafted by stonemasons or others with aesthetic intentions, so the routes aren't always direct—instead, they're incredibly scenic, taking advantage of natural fractures in the rocks, picturesque ledges, and sudden vistas that open up as you round certain bends.

The Hulls Cove Visitor Center has a brief chart summarizing area hikes; combined with the park map, it's all you need to find a trail and start exploring. Try stringing together several hikes to make your walk more varied, and be sure to plan your hiking according to the weather: If it's damp or foggy, you'll stay drier and warmer strolling the carriage roads; if it's clear and dry, head for the high peaks (Cadillac Mountain, the **Bubbles**) with the best views.

MOUNTAIN BIKING The 57 miles of gravel **carriage roads** ★★★ built by Rockefeller are among this park's hidden treasures. These were maintained by Rockefeller until his death in 1960, after which they became somewhat shaggy and overgrown. A major restoration effort was launched in 1990, though, and today the roads are superbly restored and maintained—and wide open. With their hard-packed surfaces, gentle grades, and good signage, they make for excellent mountain biking. (Note that bikes are allowed onto the island's free shuttle buses; see "Getting Around," above.)

A useful map of the carriage roads is available free at any visitor center on the island; more detailed guides can be purchased at area bookshops, but they really aren't necessary. Remember that anywhere carriage roads cross private land (mostly btw. **Seal Harbor** and **Northeast Harbor**), they're *closed* to mountain bikes, which are also banned from hiking trails.

Mountain bikes can be rented along Cottage Street in Bar Harbor, with rates running around $20 for a full day, or $12 to $15 for a half-day (which is 4 hr. in the bike-rental universe). Most bike shops include locks and helmets as basic equipment, but ask what's included before you rent. Also ask about closing times, since you'll be able to squeeze in a couple of extra hours of biking in early summer (it stays light until 9pm) with a late-closing shop. The **Bar Harbor Bicycle Shop** (✆ **207/288-3886;** www.barharborbike.com), at 141 Cottage St., gets many people's vote for most convenient and friendliest. Or you could try **Acadia Bike** (✆ **800/526-8615;** www.acadiabike.com), at 48 Cottage St., also very good.

Camping

The National Park Service maintains two campgrounds within the park. Both are extremely popular; during July and August, expect both to fill up by early to mid-morning.

The more popular of the two is **Blackwoods** ★★ (✆ **207/288-3274**), on the island's eastern side, with about 300 sites. To get there, follow Route 3 about 5 miles south out of Bar Harbor; bikers and pedestrians have easy access to the loop road from the campground via a short trail, and the Island Explorer bus stops here as well. This campground has no public showers or electrical hookups, but an enterprising business just outside the campground entrance provides clean showers for a modest fee. Camping fees at Blackwoods are $20 per night from May through October, $10 per site in April and November. Advance **reservations** can be made to Blackwoods by calling ✆ **877/444-6777** between 10am and midnight (until 10pm in winter), or by using a new reservations system online at **www.recreation.gov**. An Acadia pass (see "Entry Points & Fees," above) is also required for campground entry.

The **Seawall** ★ (✆ **207/244-3600**) campground is located over on the quieter, western half of the island, near the tiny fishing village of Bass Harbor (one of the Island Explorer shuttle bus lines also stops here). Seawall has about 215 sites, and it's a good base for cyclists or those wishing to explore several short coastal hikes within easy striking distance. However, it's quite a ways from Bar Harbor and Sand Beach on the other side of the island; for families, it might not be the best choice. The campground is open mid-May through the end of September, but they *do not take reservations.* It's first come, first served all the way—and the lines form early. In general, if you get here by 9 or 10am, you're pretty much assured of a campsite, especially if you want a walk-in site.

Camping fees at Seawall are $14 to $20 per night, depending on whether you want to drive directly to your site, or can pack a tent in for a distance of up to 150 yards. There are also no electrical or water hookups here, and (as it is with Blackwoods) prior acquisition of an Acadia entrance pass is required to stay at the campground.

Where to Dine

Jordan Pond House ★★ **Moments** AMERICAN The secret to the Jordan Pond House? Location, location, location. The restaurant traces its roots from 1847, when a farm was established on this picturesque property at the southern tip of Jordan Pond looking north toward The Bubbles, a pair of glacially sculpted mounds. In 1979 the original structure and its birch-bark dining room were destroyed by fire. A more modern, two-level dining room was built in its place—less charm, but it still has one of the island's best dining locations, on a nice lawn spread out before the pond. Afternoon tea with popovers and jam is a hallowed tradition here. The lobster stew is expensive but very good. Dinners include classic entrees like prime rib, steamed lobster, pasta, and lobster stew; the prix-fixe meal special is a deal.

Park Loop Rd. (near Seal Harbor), Acadia National Park. ✆ **207/276-3316.** www.jordanpond.com. Advance reservations not accepted; call before arrival to hold a table. Main courses $12–$17 at lunch, $15–$23 at dinner. AE, DISC, MC, V. Mid-May to late Oct daily 11:30am–8pm (until 9pm July–Aug).

BAR HARBOR ★

Bar Harbor provides most of the meals and beds to travelers coming to Mount Desert Island, and it has done so since the grand resort era of the late 19th century, when wealthy vacationers first discovered this region. Sprawling hotels and boardinghouses once cluttered the shores and hillsides here, as a newly affluent middle class arrived by steamboat and rail car from the city in droves to find out what all the fuss was about.

The tourist trade continued to boom through the early 1900s—until it all but collapsed from the double hit of the Great Depression and the advent of car travel. The town was dealt yet another blow in 1947, when an accidental fire spread rapidly and leveled many of the opulent cottages in town (as well as a large portion of the rest of the island).

In recent years, however, Bar Harbor has bounced back with a vengeance, revived and rediscovered by visitors and entrepreneurs alike. Some see the place as a tacky place of T-shirt vendors, ice-cream cones, and souvenir shops, plus crowds spilling off the sidewalks into the street and appalling traffic. That is all true. Yet the town's history, distinguished

ATTRACTIONS●
Abbe Museum **14**
Agamont Park **9**
Bar Harbor Historical
 Society **13**
College of the Atlantic **1**
George B. Dorr Museum
 of Natural History **1**

ACCOMMODATIONS■
Acadia Hotel **15**
Bar Harbor Grand Hotel **19**
Bar Harbor Inn **10**
Black Friar Inn **5**
Bluenose Inn **2**
Mira Monte Inn **12**
Primrose Inn **11**

DINING◆
Alternative **17**
Cafe This Way **16**
Havana **20**
Jordan's Restaurant **4**
Lompoc Café **8**
Mâche Bistro **3**
Maggie's Restaurant **6**
Michelle's Fine Dining **18**
Rosalie's **7**

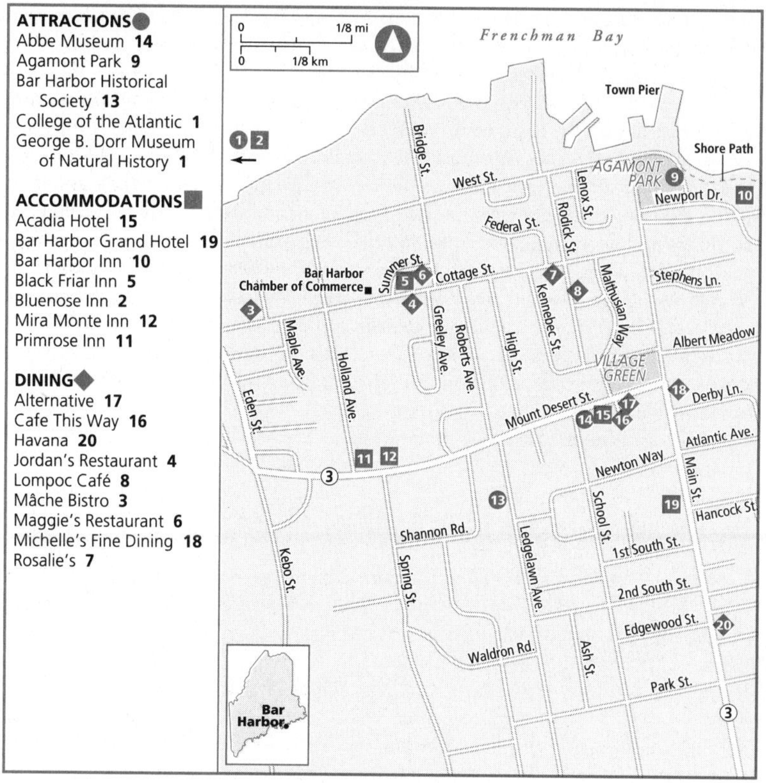

architecture, and beautiful location on Frenchman Bay still make it a desirable base for exploring the island, and it has by far the best selection of lodging, meals, supplies, and services on the isle. (If you want to shop, fine-dine, or go out at night, you've pretty much *got* to stay here.) Otherwise, if quiet is what you're seeking, consider bunking elsewhere on the island (see "Where to Stay," below).

Essentials

GETTING THERE Bar Harbor is on Route 3, about 10 miles southeast of the causeway leading onto Mount Desert Island.

VISITOR INFORMATION The **Bar Harbor Chamber of Commerce** (© **800/345-4617;** www.barharborinfo.com), stockpiles a huge arsenal of information about local attractions, both at its offices on 1 West St. (at the pier) and in a welcome center on Route 3 in Trenton, just before the bridge onto the island. Write, call, or e-mail in advance for a directory of area lodging and attractions. The chamber's website is chock-full of information and helpful links, too.

Exploring Bar Harbor

The best water views in town are from the foot of Main Street at grassy (and free) **Agamont Park ★★**, which overlooks the town pier and Frenchman Bay. From here, stroll past the Bar Harbor Inn on the **Shore Path ★★**, a wide, winding trail that follows the shoreline for half a mile along a public right of way. The pathway also passes in front of many elegant summer homes (some converted into inns), offering a superb vantage point from which to view the area's architecture.

The **Abbe Museum ★**, 26 Mount Desert St. (✆ **207/288-3519;** www.abbemuseum.org), opened in 2001 as an in-town extension of the smaller, simpler museum at the Sieur de Monts spring in the national park (see the driving tour, above), showcasing a top-rate collection of Native American artifacts. A 17,000-square-foot gallery, this downtown branch has an orientation center and a glass-walled lab where visitors can see archaeologists at work preserving recently recovered artifacts, along with changing exhibits and videos that focus largely on Maine and other New England tribes. From late May through October, it opens daily from 10am to 6pm; the rest of the year, it's open Thursday to Sunday only. Admission costs $6 for adults, $2 for children ages 6 to 15, and is free for younger children.

A short stroll around the corner from the new Abbe Museum is the **Bar Harbor Historical Society,** 33 Ledgelawn Ave. (✆ **207/288-0000** or 207/288-3807). Housed in a handsome 1918 former convent, the historical society showcases artifacts of life in the old days—dishware and photos from those grand old hotels that once dotted the town, exhibits on the noted landscape architect Beatrix Farrand, and so forth. Scrapbooks document the devastating 1947 fire, too. The museum is open from June through October Monday to Saturday from 1 to 4pm; admission is free. Even during the off season, entrance can sometimes be arranged.

Just at the northern edge of the town, on Route 3 with a spectacular bay view, is the campus of the **College of the Atlantic** (✆ **207/288-5015**), a school founded in 1969 with an emphasis on environmental education. The college's campus, a blend of old and new buildings, features the **George B. Dorr Museum of Natural History** (✆ **207/288-5395;** www.coamuseum.org) at 105 Eden St. It features exhibits that focus on interactions among island residents, from the two-legged to the four-legged, finny, and furry. It's open Tuesday through Saturday from 10am to 5pm; admission is by donation, though I'd toss in at least $3 per adult and $1 per child (more if you're deeply appreciative of the place).

Where to Stay

Bar Harbor is the bedroom community for Mount Desert Island, with hundreds of hotel, motel, and inn rooms. They're invariably filled during the busy days of summer, and even the most basic rooms can be quite expensive in July and August. It's essential to reserve as early in advance as possible.

Expensive

Bar Harbor Grand Hotel ★ Bar Harbor's newest big hotel (it opened in 2003) fills a gap between quaint, expensive inns and B&Bs and the island's family-owned motels, hotels, and cottages. The hotel's blocky, two-tower design faithfully copies the style of the Rodick House, a now-defunct 19th-century lodging in Bar Harbor that could once boast of being Maine's largest hotel. The Grand, however, does the former one better with spacious rooms and bathrooms and, of course, all-modern fixtures. Rooms and suites are decked out in the same floral bedspreads and curtains you'd expect in any upscale business hotel, and the access to downtown Bar Harbor and the nearby ocean are big pluses.

Concessions to business and tourist travelers include a guest laundry facility, gift shop, and high-speed Internet access (for a fee). Not surprisingly, they're getting a lot of tour groups here. Expect comfort, rather than island character.

269 Main St., Bar Harbor, ME 04609. ✆ **888/766-2529** or 207/288-5226. Fax 207/288-8548. www.barharborgrand.com. 70 units. May–Oct $119–$229 double, $209–$279 suite; Apr and mid-Oct to early Nov $89–$109 double, $139–$195 suite. Rates include continental breakfast. DISC, MC, V. Closed mid-Nov to Mar. **Amenities:** Exercise room; Jacuzzi; heated outdoor pool. *In room:* A/C, TV/DVD, fridge, Wi-Fi (free).

The Bar Harbor Inn ★★ The Bar Harbor Inn, just off Agamont Park, nicely mixes traditional style with contemporary touches. On shady grounds just a moment's stroll from Bar Harbor's downtown, this property offers both convenience and charm. The shingled main inn, which dates from the turn of the 19th century, has a settled, old-money feel with its semicircular dining room and buttoned-down lobby. Guest rooms, located in the main building and two outbuildings, are much more contemporary: Units in the Oceanfront Lodge and main inn both offer spectacular bay views, and many have private balconies. (The less expensive Newport Building lacks views but is still comfortable and up-to-date.) In 2006 the inn added a spa with Vichy showers, aromatherapy, heated-stone treatments, and facial treatments, while the somewhat formal **Reading Room** dining room serves resort meals with the best dining-room views in town.

Newport Dr., Bar Harbor, ME 04609. ✆ **800/248-3351** or 207/288-3351. www.barharborinn.com. 153 units. Mid-May to mid-Oct $119–$379 double; mid-Mar to mid-May and mid-Oct to Nov $79–$215 double. Rates include continental breakfast. AE, DISC, MC, V. Closed Dec to mid-Mar. **Amenities:** Dining room; exercise room; Jacuzzi; heated outdoor pool; limited room service; spa. *In room:* A/C, TV, hair dryer, Wi-Fi ($8.95 per day).

Bluenose Inn ★ This resort-style complex—situated in two buildings—offers stunning views of the surrounding terrain. Facilities here are more modern, too: Expect spacious carpeted rooms with huge bathrooms, small refrigerators, and balconies, as well as a good fitness center, indoor and outdoor pools, and one of the town's best hotel dining rooms, the **Rose Garden ★**. The two buildings are slightly different in character, but in either case upper-floor rooms with sea views are worth the extra cost, especially if the weather is good. The staff here is professional and friendly.

90 Eden St., Bar Harbor, ME 04609. ✆ **800/445-4077** or 207/288-3348. www.barharborhotel.com. 97 units. Mid-June to mid-Oct $179–$369 double, $349–$499 suite; spring and late fall $139–$219 double, $259–$279 suite. AE, DC, DISC, MC, V. Closed Nov–Apr. **Amenities:** Restaurant; exercise room; Jacuzzi; 2 pools (1 indoor, 1 outdoor); spa. *In room:* A/C, TV, fridge, hair dryer, Wi-Fi (free).

Moderate

Acadia Hotel ★ Value The simple, seasonal Acadia Hotel is nicely situated overlooking Bar Harbor's village green, easily accessible to in-town activities and the free shuttle buses running around the island. A handsome, simple home dating from the late 19th century, the hotel features a wraparound porch; guest rooms are plain but decorated in nice floral motifs. Units vary widely in size and amenities, however—some have simple whirlpool tubs, phones, or king beds; one has a kitchenette; and about half have small refrigerators. Others are as basic as it comes. It's a no-frills place, clean and well run—all things considered, a good value in an expensive town.

20 Mt. Desert St., Bar Harbor, ME 04609. ✆ **888/876-2463** or 207/288-5721. www.acadiahotel.com. 11 units. July to mid-Oct $129–$169 double; May–June $59–$109 double. Packages available. Closed late Oct to Apr. AE, MC, V. *In room:* A/C, TV, fridge (some units), no phone (some units), Wi-Fi (free).

Black Friar Inn ★ Value The seasonal Black Friar, tucked on a Bar Harbor side street overlooking a parking lot, is a yellow-shingled home with quirky pediments and an eccentric air. A former owner "collected" interiors and installed them throughout the home, including a replica of a pub in London with elaborate carved-wood paneling (it's now a common room); stamped-tin walls (look in the breakfast room); and a doctor's office (now one of the guest rooms). Rooms are carpeted and furnished in a mix of antiques; most are smallish, though the big suite features nice paneling, a sofa, wingback chair, private porch, and gas fireplace. Other rooms sport such touches as rose-tinted stained-glass windows and brass beds. The least expensive units are the two garret rooms on the third floor. The inn features a small restaurant and a pub when it's open.

10 Summer St., Bar Harbor, ME 04609. ✆ **207/288-5091.** Fax 207/288-4197. www.blackfriarinn.com. 6 units. $65–$175 double; $100–$175 suite. Rates include full breakfast. 2-night minimum stay required most of year. MC, V. Closed Dec–Apr. Children 12 and over welcome. **Amenities:** Restaurant; pub. *In room:* A/C, Wi-Fi (free).

Mira Monte Inn ★ A stay at this Italianate home (built in 1864), a few minutes' walk from Bar Harbor's restaurants and attractions and open year-round, used to feel like a trip to your grandmother's house. It's gotten a lot more contemporary lately (TVs, phones, and Wi-Fi are all fairly recent additions), even if the common rooms are still furnished in a country Victorian style. The grounds are nicely landscaped, and a nice brick terrace off the street is a good place to enjoy breakfast in warm weather. Most rooms have a balcony, fireplace, or both, and some now even have Jacuzzis. Others have the feel of a spare country farmhouse. If you're a light sleeper, avoid rooms facing Mount Desert Street; those facing the gardens in the rear are much quieter. Families should ask about booking a suite in the adjacent outbuilding: These have better amenities, and some have double Jacuzzis.

69 Mount Desert St., Bar Harbor, ME 04609. ✆ **800/553-5109.** www.miramonte.com. 12 units. $95–$244 double; $105–$290 suite. Rates include full breakfast. 2-night minimum stay in midsummer. AE, DISC, MC, V. Most units closed late Oct to mid-May. *In room:* A/C, TV, CD player, hair dryer, Wi-Fi (free).

Primrose Inn ★★ This handsome Victorian stick–style inn, originally built in 1878, is one of the most notable properties on the "mansion row" along Mount Desert Street. Its distinctive architecture has been preserved, and was perhaps even enhanced during a 1987 addition of rooms, private bathrooms, and balconies. This inn is comfortable, furnished with "functional antiques" and modern reproductions; many of the spacious rooms have a floral theme, thick carpets, marble vanities, canopy beds, sitting or reading rooms, and handsome daybeds. (Two newer "premium" rooms also have private entrances and are stocked with king beds, gas fireplaces, and such other amenities as a porch or whirlpool tub.) The owners have gone ahead and added flatscreen TVs and Wi-Fi access, too, while the 24/7 free soft drinks fridge remains. Breakfasts of eggs Florentine, Belgian waffles, blueberry pancakes, and the like are a hit, and the innkeepers can furnish you with a GPS unit if you'll be driving around the island and worry about getting lost.

73 Mt. Desert St., Bar Harbor, ME 04609. ✆ **877/846-3424** or 207/288-4031. www.primroseinn.com. 13 units. Late June to Aug $159–$229 double; late May to mid-June and Sept–Oct $99–$209 double. Rates include full breakfast and afternoon tea. 2-night minimum stay summer and fall. AE, DISC, MC, V. Closed Nov to mid-May. *In room:* A/C, TV/DVD, hair dryer, Wi-Fi (free).

Where to Dine

In addition to the selections listed below, you can get good local pizza at **Rosalie's** (✆ **207/288-5666;** www.rosaliespizza.com), on Cottage Street; eat upstairs or down, or take out a pie to go. There's also a superb natural foods market, **Alternative** ★ (✆ **207/288-8225**), on Mount Desert Street right across from the Village Green.

And the owners of the island's best vegetarian eatery, **Eden Vegetarian Café,** took a hiatus in 2009 but will likely re-open in 2010 in a new location. Ask at the tourist office if you're interested in dining there.

Cafe This Way ★★ CONTEMPORARY AMERICAN Cafe This Way is the kind of place where they know how to do wonderful Asian and Mediterranean things with simple ingredients. It has the feel of a hip coffeehouse, yet it's much more airy and creative than that. Bookshelves line one wall, and there's a small bar tucked into a nook; oddly, they serve breakfast and dinner but no lunch. Breakfasts are excellent though mildly sinful—it's more like brunch. Go for the burritos, corned beef hash with eggs, a range of omelets (build your own if you like), or the calorific Café Monte Cristo: a French toast sandwich stuffed with fried eggs, ham, and cheddar cheese, served with fries and syrup. Yikes. Dinners are equally appetizing, with tasty starters that might run to Maine crab cakes in tequila-lime sauce, grilled chunks of Cyprus cheese, or lobster spring rolls. The main-course offerings of the night could include anything from lobster cooked in sherry cream, or stewed in spinach and Gruyère cheese to sea scallops in vinaigrette, grilled lamb and steaks, peach-flavored pork chops, or the Korean stir-fry dish known as *bibimbap.* You'll always find a tasty vegetarian option, as well.

14½ Mt. Desert St. ✆ **207/288-4483.** www.cafethisway.com. Reservations recommended for dinner. Breakfast items $5–$8, main courses $15–$26. MC, V. Mid-Apr to Oct Mon–Sat 7–11am and 5:30–9pm; Sun 8am–1pm and 5:30–9pm.

Havana ★★ **Finds** LATIN AMERICAN/FUSION Havana excited foodies all over Maine when it opened in 1999 in what was then a town of fried fish and baked haddock. The spare decor in an old storefront is as classy as anything you'll find in Boston, and the menu can hold its own in the big city, too. Chef/owner Michael Boland's menu is inspired by Latino fare, which he melds nicely with New American ideas. Expect items like appetizers of crab cakes, duck empanadas, fig-and-blue-cheese tarts, or spicy beef and pork skewers dusted with cinnamon and vanilla. Entrees could include choices as adventurous as a lobster poached in butter served with a saffrony potato empanada; paella made with local lobsters and mussels; breast of duck with a blueberry glaze; broiled filet mignon with ancho gravy; pork tenderloin stuffed with cranberry and chorizo stuffing; seared black cod; or coconut-encrusted tuna steaks with a plum-red chili jam. Finish with an equally dazzling dessert, such as a chocolate lava cake with cinnamon churros; apple empanadas; caramel and cream; *dulce de leche* cheesecake with guava sauce; a maple carrot cake; or spicy pumpkin crème brûlée kicked up with jalapeño peppers.

318 Main St. ✆ **207/288-2822.** www.havanamaine.com. Reservations recommended. Main courses $24–$32. AE, DC, DISC, MC, V. Daily 5–10pm. Sometimes closed in late fall.

Jordan's Restaurant **Value** DINER This unpretentious breakfast-and-lunch joint has been dishing up filling fare since 1976 and offers a glimpse of the old Bar Harbor. It's a popular haunt of local working folks and retirees, but the staff is also friendly to tourists. Diners can settle into a pine booth or at a laminated table and order off the place-mat menu, choosing from basic fare such as grilled cheese sandwiches with tomato or slim burgers. The soups and chowders are all homemade, and there are some crab dishes (though no lobster). But breakfast is the star here, with a broad selection of three-egg omelets, muffins, and pancakes made with plenty of those great wild Maine blueberries (best when they're in season). With its atmosphere of seniors at coffee klatch and its rock-bottom prices, this is *not* a gourmet experience, but fans of big breakfasts, Americana-style cuisine, and diners will enjoy it.

80 Cottage St. ✆ **207/288-3586.** Breakfast and lunch items $3–$13. MC, V. Daily 4:30am–2pm. Closed Feb–Mar.

Lompoc Café ★ AMERICAN The Lompoc Café has a well-worn, neighborhood-bar feel to it—waiters and other workers from around Bar Harbor congregate here after-hours. The cafe consists of three sections: the original bar, a tidy beer garden just outside (try your hand at bocce), and a small and open barnlike structure at the garden's edge to handle the overflow. Most of the beers are local (ask for a sample before ordering a full glass of blueberry ale). Bar menus are normally yawn-inducing, but this one has some surprises—lamb meatballs in mint, good salads, Vietnamese-style *bahn mi* sandwiches, or a BLT using fried green tomatoes. There's also quite a little wine list and some house cocktails, like the lemony Blonde with an Attitude. The outdoor tables are fun, and live music acts often play here.

36 Rodick St. ✆ **207/288-9392.** www.lompoccafe.com. Reservations not accepted. Sandwiches and salads $7–$12. MC, V. Daily 11:30am–1am.

Mâche Bistro ★★ NEW AMERICAN Little Mâche Bistro has developed a devoted local following; its soothing, plain decor conceals a sophisticated kitchen—you wouldn't expect an imported-cheese course offered in a place with plywood floors, but there is one here. Chef Kyle Yarborough's menu changes monthly; appetizers could include local crab with aioli, fish chowder, excellent house antipasti, or a wine-poached pear with Maytag blue cheese. Main courses, now more New American than French bistro, might run to herb-encrusted haddock over garlic mashed potatoes, slow-roasted pork with chorizo and vegetables, grilled hanger steak with a blue-cheese butter, seared duck over white beans, or a grilled portobello stuffed with goat cheese and caramelized onions.

135 Cottage St. ✆ **207/288-0447.** www.machebistro.com. Reservations recommended. Main courses $16–$23. AE, MC, V. Tues–Sun 5:30–9pm (closed Sun in winter).

Maggie's Restaurant ★★ SEAFOOD The slogan for Maggie's is "Notably fresh seafood," and the place invariably delivers on that understated promise. (Only locally caught fish is used.) It's a casually elegant spot, good for a romantic evening while you enjoy the soothing music, attentive service, and excellent seafood. Appetizers could run to cheesy potatoes with lobster, grilled clams in wine sauce, a kid-sized pizza, or a simple salad; main courses might include "bronzed" cod with a lime-tartar sauce, lobster crepes, Gulf shrimp with feta and olives over rice, pan-seared scallops, or salmon seared in Indian spices and served with cucumber-mint salsa. They also do nice steaks and chicken, though that's not why you come here. Desserts are homemade, and it's also worth leaving room for them: blueberry pie, lemon curd, and dark chocolate pudding cakes, and a delicious rotating menu of gourmet ice-cream sundaes—the island's best.

6 Summer St. ✆ **207/288-9007.** www.maggiesbarharbor.com. Reservations recommended July–Aug. Main courses $16–$24. MC, V. Mon–Sat 5–9:30pm.

Michelle's Fine Dining ★★ FRENCH/SEAFOOD Michelle's, located inside the Ivy Manor Inn, supplies one of the island's best dinner experiences. The three dining rooms are elegant, plus there's outside seating when the weather's good. The extensive menu elaborates on traditional French cuisine with New England twists. Nightly appetizers might include lobster bisque, French onion soup, crab cakes, or steak tartare. Main courses—divided into seafood and nonseafood entrees—are even more elaborate, with dishes such as chateaubriand for two (carved tableside); roasted rack of lamb; seared salmon with a pine-nut crisp; two versions of duck; Cornish hen; and a big bouillabaisse for two of lobster, mussels, clams, and scallops. Finish with a cheese plate, one of several soufflés, the crème brûlée, or Michelle's unique "bag of chocolate": It comes with berries and is served in an edible chocolate bag. This place is expensive but worth it.

194 Main St. ✆ **888/670-1997** or 207/288-2138. www.michellesfinedining.com. Reservations required during peak season. Main courses $24–$54. AE, DISC, MC, V. Daily 6–9pm. Closed late Oct to early May.

Shopping

Bar Harbor is full of boutiques and souvenir shops, nearly all of them located along two commercial streets (Main and Cottage sts.); both intersect at the central Village Green. Most of these shops sell touristy knickknacks (lobster-shaped beer-bottle openers and refrigerator magnets), and you can safely pass them by. But a few places do offer originality and value.

Bar Harbor Hemporium The Hemporium is dedicated to all things hemp, including as paper, clothing, and more. 116 Main St. ✆ **207/288-3014.** www.barharborhemp.com.

Cadillac Mountain Sports Catering to the ragged-wool-and-fleece set, this place sells sleeping bags, backpacks, outdoor clothing, and hiking boots, as well as a selection of hiking guides to the island. 26 Cottage St. ✆ **207/288-4532.** www.cadillacmountain.com.

Island Artisans This is the place to browse for products made by local craftspeople, such as tiles, baskets, pottery, jewelry, and soaps. There's also a second location in Northeast Harbor, over on the western side of the island. 99 Main St. ✆ **207/288-4214.** www.islandartisans.com.

RainWise This Bar Harbor–based firm manufactures professional, compact weather stations for companies, agencies, and serious followers of the Weather Channel; at this facility off Cottage Street, you can view the stations plus browse a range of thermometers and barometers. 25 Federal St. ✆ **800/762-5723** or 207/288-5169. www.rainwise.com.

ELSEWHERE ON THE ISLAND

You'll find plenty to explore outside Acadia National Park and Bar Harbor, too. Quiet fishing villages, deep woodlands, and unexpected ocean views are among the jewels you can turn up once you get beyond Bar Harbor town limits.

Essentials

GETTING AROUND The eastern half of the island is best navigated using Route 3, which forms a rough loop from Bar Harbor through **Seal Harbor** and past **Northeast Harbor,** then runs up along the eastern shore of Somes Sound. Routes 102 and 102A provide access to the island's western half. If you don't have a car, use the free **Island Explorer shuttle** (p. 341).

VISITOR INFORMATION The Thompson Island Information Center as you enter the island is a great info source. Locally, the **Southwest Harbor–Tremont Chamber of Commerce** (✆ **800/423-9264** or 207/244-9264; www.acadiachamber.com) in Southwest Harbor and the **Mount Desert Chamber of Commerce** (✆ **207/276-5040;** www.mountdesertchamber.org) in Northeast Harbor can also help.

Exploring the Rest of the Island

Down one peninsula of the eastern lobe of the island is the staid, prosperous village of **Northeast Harbor** ★★, long a favorite retreat of well-heeled folks. You can see shingled palaces poking out from the forest and shore, but the village itself (which consists of just one short main street and a marina) is also worth investigating for its art galleries, restaurants, and general store.

One of the best, least-publicized places for enjoying views of the harbor is from the understated, wonderful **Asticou Terraces** ★★. Finding the parking lot can be tricky: Head a half-mile east (toward Seal Harbor) on Route 3 from the junction with Route 198, and look for the small gravel lot on the water side of the road with a sign reading ASTICOU TERRACES. Park here, cross the road on foot, and set off up a magnificent path made of local rock that ascends the sheer hillside, with expanding views of the harbor and the town.

When leaving Northeast Harbor, think about a quick detour out to Sargent Drive. This one-way route runs through Acadia National Park along the shore of Somes Sound, affording superb views of the glacially carved inlet. On the far side of Somes Sound, there's good hiking. The nearby towns of **Southwest Harbor** ★★ and **Bass Harbor** are both home to fishermen and boat-builders, and though the character of these towns is changing, they're still far more humble than Northeast and Seal harbors.

Where to Stay

In addition to the hotels and inns described below, there are also a number of excellent **campgrounds** on the island, including two (Seawall and Blackwoods) that are part of the national park—see p. 347 for more details on both sites. Also consider tenting at one of the many privately owned campgrounds dotting the island; you can obtain a complete listing and guide from any tourist office on Mount Desert Isle.

Just remember that some campgrounds fill up ahead of time or by midday; an advance booking, if possible, is always better.

The Claremont ★★ Early prints of the venerable Claremont show an austere, four-story wooden building overlooking Somes Sound from a grassy rise. It hasn't changed much since. The place offers classic New England grace. (It's somehow appropriate that the state's largest croquet tournament is held here each Aug.) Common areas are pleasantly appointed in country style—the library, with its fireplace, is popular. Most of the guest rooms are bright and airy, outfitted in antiques, old furniture, and modern bathrooms. There's also a set of 14 cottages of varied vintages and styles in the woods and on the water, all with fireplaces and kitchenettes; they sleep from two to seven people each. Outdoor amenities include the aforementioned croquet lawn, plus rowboats, a tennis court, and bicycles for guest use. The dining room, **Xanthus** ★, offers fabulous views of the fjord and an upscale menu of lobster, crab cakes, fish, scallops, pork, and steaks.

P.O. Box 137, Southwest Harbor, ME 04679. ✆ **800/244-5036** or 207/967-2321. www.theclaremonthotel.com. 44 units. July–Aug $170–$275 double, $200–$335 cottage; late May to June and Sept to mid-Oct $125–$190 double, $155–$235 cottage. Room (not cottage) rates include breakfast. 15% service fee for cottages. 3-night minimum stay in cottages. MC, V. Closed mid-Oct to late May. From center of Southwest Harbor, follow Clark Point Rd. almost to end and turn left on Claremont Rd. **Amenities:** Dining room; lounge; babysitting; bikes; tennis court. *In room:* Kitchenette (some units).

Inn at Southwest ★ There's a late-19th-century feel to this mansard-roofed Victorian home, which thankfully stays spare rather than frilly. All guest rooms, named for Maine lighthouses, are outfitted simply in contemporary and antique furniture, and all have ceiling fans and down comforters. Among the most pleasant rooms is Blue Hill Bay on the third floor, with its yellow-and-blue color scheme, big bathroom, sturdy oak bed and bureau, and glimpses of the harbor. The Pumpkin Island unit features a sleigh bed and rosewood sofa. The lone suite (Winter Harbor) has a pencil-poster canopy bed, French doors, and a gas-log fireplace. Breakfasts give you good incentive to rise early: The changing entrees could include Belgian waffles with raspberry sauce, poached pears, or blueberry French toast.

371 Main St. (P.O. Box 593), Southwest Harbor, ME 04679. ✆ **207/244-3835.** www.innatsouthwest.com. 7 units. $105–$185 double. Rates include full breakfast. DISC, MC, V. Closed Nov to late Apr. *In room:* No phone, Wi-Fi (free).

Kingsleigh Inn ★★ In a 1904 Queen Anne–style home on Southwest Harbor's bustling Main Street, the Kingsleigh has long been a reliable place to bunk down in the area. Its living room features a wood-burning fireplace and fine art, while sitting and breakfast rooms offer further refuge. All guest rooms are outfitted with sound machines (to drown out the ambient noise), wineglasses, and robes; some also have air conditioners. Prints and wallpapers are flowery in the rooms, most of which are small to moderate size, though a few have private decks. The huge third-floor penthouse suite—by far the most expensive room here—has outstanding views (plus a telescope to see them better with); the inn's only TV (with VCR and DVD players); a fireplace; and a king-size bed. Three-course breakfasts are filling and genuinely artistic—expect choices such as asparagus frittata, crepes, Belgian waffles, and French toast. Other nice touches include walking sticks for guests and all-day, self-service espresso.

373 Main St. (P.O. Box 1426), Southwest Harbor, ME 04679. ✆ **207/244-5302.** Fax 207/244-7691. www.kingsleighinn.com. 8 units. $110–$195 double; $225–$305 suite. Rates include full breakfast. AE, MC, V. Closed Nov–Mar. Children 13 and over welcome. *In room:* A/C (some units), TV/DVD (1 unit), hair dryer, no phone, Wi-Fi (free).

Lindenwood Inn ★★ Finds Australian innkeeper Jim King gave up cabinetmaking to open a string of successful B&Bs in Southwest Harbor, and his latest is his best; it feels like renting a home with friends. In a handsome Queen Anne–style captain's home built in 1904 over harbor's edge, King has modernized the rooms in simple, bold colors and accented them with items from his collections of African and aboriginal art—a strikingly unique interior and feel you can't find anywhere else in New England. Most units have balconies and plenty of windows; some have fireplaces, French doors, and/or private porches or decks; and all possess comfy beds. The public areas remain funky and appealing, and the heated in-ground pool and Jacuzzi are wonderful in summer. There's a small honor bar for fixing a late-night cocktail upstairs, plus a lounge in the basement with a pool table, darts, and a big-screen TV. The biggest draws, however, are the outstanding hospitality, great decor, yummy breakfasts, and laid-back vibe.

118 Clark Point Rd., Southwest Harbor, ME 04679. ✆ **800/307-5335** or 207/244-5335. www.lindenwoodinn.com. 8 units. $95–$215 double; $145–$295 suite. Rates include full breakfast. AE, MC, V. **Amenities:** Lounge; Jacuzzi; heated outdoor pool. *In room:* TV, fridge (2 units), kitchenette (1 unit), no phone.

Where to Dine

In addition to the choices listed here, you'll find ice-cream, pizza, sandwich, and takeout-seafood shops scattered about the island. Even most of the village grocery stores offer good prepared sandwiches or meals.

Beal's Lobster Pound ★ LOBSTER Some say Beal's is among the best lobster shacks in Maine, and it's certainly got the right atmosphere: Creaky picnic tables sit on a plain concrete pier overlooking a working-class harbor, right next to a Coast Guard base. (Don't wear a jacket and tie.) You go inside to pick out lobster from a tank, pay by the pound, choose some side dishes (corn on the cob, slaw, steamed clams), then pop coins in a soda machine outside while you wait for your number to be called. The food will arrive on Styrofoam and paper plates, but who cares? These lobsters are good. There's also a takeout window across the deck serving fries, fried clams, and fried fish (sensing a theme?), plus ice cream.

182 Clark Point Rd., Southwest Harbor. ✆ **207/244-7178** or 207/244-3202. www.bealslobster.com. Lobsters market priced. AE, DISC, MC, V. Summer daily 9am–8pm; after Labor Day 9am–5pm. Closed Columbus Day to Memorial Day.

The Burning Tree ★★ Finds SEAFOOD Located on a busy straightaway of Route 3 between Bar Harbor and Otter Creek, the Burning Tree is an easy restaurant to blow right past—but that would be a mistake. This low-key place, with its bright, open, and sometimes noisy dining room, is a find: It serves up some of the best and freshest seafood dinners on the island, with New American twists. Much of the produce and herbs comes from the restaurant's own gardens, while the rest of the ingredients are bought locally whenever possible. Everything's prepared with imagination and skill; expect unusual preparations like a New Orleans–style lobster, lobster fritters (great idea), and mixed seafood over noodles and cream, plus old standards like salmon and halibut (served with inventive and tasty sauces). The seafood stew is good, too, but desserts are middling at best. Don't miss the bartender's house cocktails, made with local fruits and berries when possible.

Rte. 3, Otter Creek. ✆ **207/288-9331.** Reservations recommended. Main courses $18–$23. DISC, MC, V. Wed–Mon 5–10pm. Closed Columbus Day to late May.

Fiddlers' Green ★★ NEW AMERICAN Island native Chef Derek Wilbur's bistro is a big hit in these seafaring parts. Begin with something from the cold seafood bar: oysters on the half shell or a trio of smoked fish and shellfish, for instance. Or start with one of Wilbur's small plates, like Thai-curried shrimp with coconut milk, fried catfish filet with a Cajun rémoulade, grilled merguez, or smoked baby back ribs. You'll always find steaks and pasta dishes (such as Maine Lobster Strozzapretti with a *vinho verde* cream sauce) on the menu, but seafood is the true star: tempura-fried scallops, lobster potpie, or a good old steamed lobster. There's an extensive wine list, too, and martini drinkers should take note: Wilbur's bar serves a long list of classic and obscure versions. Desserts run to chocolate cakes, a Mayan-style fruit-and-chocolate soup, ice creams, cheese with figs, and caramel crepes filled with mascarpone cream and local blueberries.

411 Main St., Southwest Harbor. ✆ **207/244-9416.** www.fiddlersgreenrestaurant.com. Reservations recommended. Main courses $16–$32. AE, DISC, MC, V. Tues–Sun 5:30–9pm. Closed Columbus Day to Memorial Day.

Redbird Provisions ★★ CONTINENTAL/SEAFOOD Redbird opened in 2007 in a renovated cottage right on Northeast Harbor's cute main street, and it has been an unqualified winner so far. The kitchen cooks up local seafood and other main courses with a talented hand, using Asian, French, and Italian accents in a no-pretenses dining room. Lunches run to harvest-style soups and extremely inventive flatbreads, sandwiches, and salads. (The smoked trout salade niçoise is especially good.) Dinnertime sees a broadening of the menu's scope to include appetizers like truffled cauliflower soup and ricotta-stuffed squash blossoms; pasta dishes such as risotto or a saffrony homemade orecchiette with clams and lemon confit; and main courses like organic Scottish salmon with white bean ragout and roasted figs, loin of lamb, or a strip streak served with a Yukon potato gratin. The small, porchside outdoor dining space is nice in warmer weather.

11 Sea St., Northeast Harbor. ✆ **207/276-3006.** www.redbirdprovisions.com. Reservations recommended. Main courses $9–$22 at lunch, $25–$34 at dinner. DISC, MC, V. Tues–Sat 11:30am–2pm and 6–9pm; Sun 6–9pm. Closed late Oct to late May.

8 DOWNEAST COAST

Machias: 200 miles NE of Portland; 310 miles NE of Boston

The term "Downeast" comes from old sailing-ship days. Ships heading east had the prevailing winds behind them, making it an easy "downhill" run to the most easterly ports. (Heading the other way took more skill and determination.) Today few tourists venture east of Ellsworth, but there's an authenticity here that's missing from much of the rest of coastal Maine. Many longtime visitors say this is what Maine *used* to look like, and they mean that in a good way.

ESSENTIALS

GETTING THERE Downeast Maine is best reached via Route 1 from Ellsworth; just keep heading north. You can also take a more direct, less congested route via Route 9 from Brewer (across the river from Bangor); get there via routes 192 or 193.

VISITOR INFORMATION For information on the Machias area and other parts of Downeast Maine, contact the **Machias Bay Area Chamber of Commerce** (✆ **207/255-4402;** www.machiaschamber.org), at 85 Main St. in Machias. It's open weekdays from 10am to 3pm.

EXPLORING DOWNEAST MAINE ★

Attractions and sites are strung out few and far between along this stretch of coast; the chief pleasure is simply driving from village to village. Here are some of the highlights.

Eastport Historic District ★ In the late 19th century, Eastport (3 miles from Lubec by water, but 50 min. by car) was home to nearly 5,000 residents and 18 sardine plants. The census now counts fewer than 2,000 residents here, and the sardine plants are gone, but much of the handsome brick architecture remains along Water Street—a compact thoroughfare that also gives you lovely views of Campobello Island and Passamaquoddy Bay while you're walking down it. Most of the buildings between the town post office and the library are on the National Register of Historic Places.

Water St., Eastport. From Rte. 1 in Perry, take Rte. 190 S. for 7 miles.

Roosevelt Campobello International Park ★★ Franklin Delano Roosevelt made an annual trek to the prosperous summer colony at Campobello Island, just across a bridge from Lubec (it's actually in Canada). You can learn much about Roosevelt and his early life at the visitor center of this park, and take a self-guided tour of the elaborate mansion. But be sure to save some time to explore the parklands, which offer scenic coastline and plenty of walking trails. The visitor center closes in late October, but the grounds remain open year-round. Maps and walk suggestions are available at the visitor center. You can easily spend a half-day here. (***Note:*** Because this is in Canada, be *sure* to bring your U.S. passport or other government-issued documentation, or you'll probably be denied entry.)

459 Rte. 774, Welshpool, NB (in Canada). ✆ **506/752-2922.** www.fdr.net. Free admission. Daily 10am–6pm (last tour at 5:45pm). Visitor center closed mid-Oct to mid-May; grounds open year-round. Reached via Rte. 1 to Whiting, and then Rte. 189 to Lubec; follow signs to bridge.

Schoodic Point ★★ This remote, scenic unit of Acadia National Park is just 7 miles from Mount Desert Island across Frenchman Bay, but it's a 50-mile drive to get here. It's worth it, though (and it's free, unlike some of Acadia's most scenic parts). A pleasing one-way loop road hooks around the point, along the water, and through forests of spruce and fir. Good views of the mountains of Acadia open up across Frenchman Bay; you can also see part of a historic naval station on the point. Park near the tip and explore the salmon-colored rocks that plunge into the ocean, which are especially dramatic when the seas are agitated—during those times, stay a bit back from the edge, as waves can get big.

Acadia National Park, Winter Harbor. ✆ **207/288-3338.** Free admission. Drive east from Ellsworth on Rte. 1 for 17 miles to W. Gouldsboro, then turn south on Rte. 186 to Winter Harbor and look for the brown-and-white national-park signs.

West Quoddy Head Light & Quoddy Head State Park ★★ This famed red-and-white lighthouse, which has been likened to a barbershop pole and a candy cane, marks the easternmost point of the United States and ushers boats into the Lubec Channel. (Interestingly, it's also the nearest geographical point in the U.S. to Africa.) The light, operated by the Coast Guard, isn't open to the public, but visitors can walk the grounds near the light and along headlands at the adjacent state park. A new visitor center opened in 2002 inside the light-keeper's house; it overlooks rocky shoals, pounding waves, and some of the most powerful tides in the world. Watch for fishing boats straining against the currents and seals playing in the waves or sunning on offshore rocks. The park also includes another 480 acres of coastline and bogs, with several trails winding through the forest and atop rocky cliffs. Some of the most dramatic views can be found just a short walk down the path at the far end of the parking lot.

West Quoddy Head Rd., Lubec. ✆ **207/733-0911** (state park) or 207/733-2180 (lighthouse). www.westquoddy.com. Lighthouse and visitor center free admission; state park $3 adults, $1 seniors and children 5–11. Lighthouse visitor center daily 10am–4pm; state-park grounds daily 9am–sunset. Lighthouse and park closed mid-Oct to mid-May.

WHERE TO STAY & DINE

Crocker House Country Inn Built in 1884, this handsome shingled inn is off the beaten track on picturesque Hancock Point, across Frenchman Bay from Mount Desert Island. It's a cozy retreat, good for rest, relaxation, and quiet walks. (It's a quick walk to water's edge.) Rooms are tastefully decorated in comfortable country decor and solid furniture; there's nothing lavish here, but they do have phones. The common areas are more relaxed than fussy. The inn has a few bikes for guests to explore the point. The **dining room ★** here is a highlight: Dinner is served in a fun atmosphere daily from May

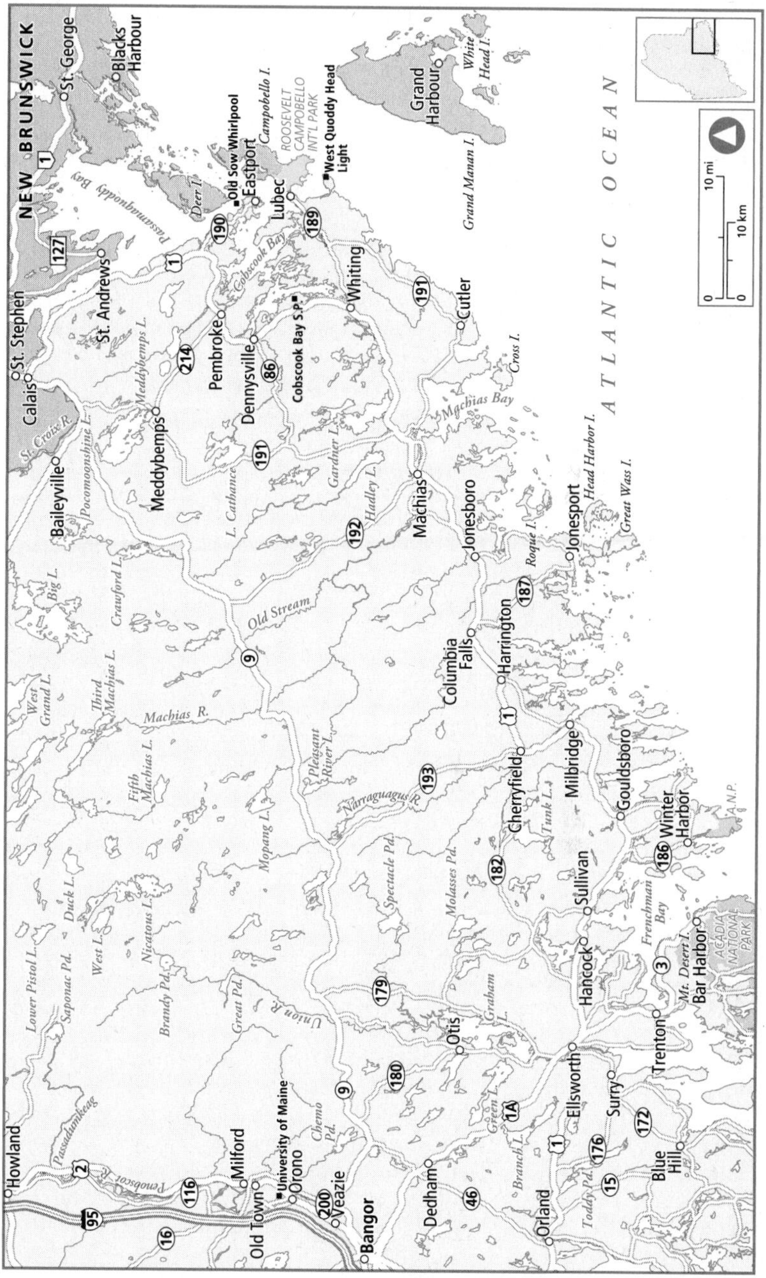

COASTAL MAINE 9 DOWNEAST COAST

through October. The menu consists of resort fare such as oysters Rockefeller, scallops, fish, pasta, steak au poivre, filet mignon, roast duckling, and rack of lamb.

967 Point Rd. (Box 171), Hancock Point, ME 04640. ✆ **877/715-6017** or 207/422-6806. Fax 207/422-3105. www.crockerhouse.com. 11 units. Mid-June to mid-Oct $110–$170 double; off season $85–$120 double. Rates include full breakfast. AE, DISC, MC, V. Closed Jan–Feb; open weekends only in Mar. **Amenities:** Dining room; bikes. *In room:* A/C.

Le Domaine ★ **Finds** Set on Route 1 about 10 minutes east of Ellsworth, this inn has the Continental flair of an impeccable French *auberge.* While the highway in front can be a bit noisy, the garden and woodland walks out back offer plenty of serenity. Five inn rooms are comfortable and tastefully appointed without being pretentious, with a truly southern-France feel to the furniture and decor. Two suites with private terraces face the gardens and 90 acres of forest (owned by the inn). But the *real* draw here is the excellent **dining room** ★★, serving French country cooking in a handsome space with pine floors and a big fireplace. Meals might run to brandied pâté, filet mignon in Bordelaise sauce, grilled halibut, or quail wrapped in bacon; finish with custard-filled tarts or bread pudding from the recipe of the inn's original owner, Marianne Dumas-Purslow, who emigrated from Provence to the U.S. during World War II. The wine list is great (and all French, of course).

1513 Rte. 1, Hancock, ME 04640. ✆ **800/554-8498** or 207/422-3395. Fax 207/422-3916. www.ledomaine.com. 5 units. $200–$285 double; $285–$370 suite. Rates include full breakfast and dinner. AE, MC, V. Closed Nov to mid-June. **Amenities:** Dining room. *In room:* A/C, Wi-Fi (free).

10

Northern & Western Maine

Maine's western mountains make up a rugged, brawny region that stretches northeast between the White Mountains and the Carrabassett Valley. Yes, the Whites are higher, and the Maine coast is a lot more picture-postcard and convenient for travelers. But you can find natural wonders here in northern and western Maine that those other places can't touch: huge azure lakes and sparkling little ponds; forests thick with spruce and fir; mossy, mossy woods (to borrow from Thoreau); and more mountains and foothills than you could tramp through in a lifetime.

And there's a *lot* to love here. Maine is roughly the size of the other five New England states combined, and about half of this big state still consists of northern woods without any formal governance (and barely any human population)—many areas are simply known as "unorganized townships." This makes Maine one of the wildest states in the lower 48, even if hardly anybody else in those 48 realizes it.

It was like this when Henry David Thoreau came through in 1846 to climb Mount Katahdin (he was one of the first Westerners to do so, in fact), and it still is today. In fact, Maine is still *90% covered with forest* as I write this, a truly staggering statistic considering it's on the densely populated eastern coast of the wealthiest nation in the world.

These woods touch an emotional nerve in lots of Mainers. Nature lovers want to see the woods left pristine, but that puts them at odds with the wishes of developers, small-town officials, local millworkers, and paper-company executives. So far, they've all managed to get along (more or less), but it hasn't been easy. A number of heartfelt appeals to save the Maine Woods by creating a vast state or national park have sprung up, and national groups have even become involved in the effort, but the ultimate fate of these woods still remains very much up in the air.

Moosehead Lake and Baxter State Park—which is dominated by, but not limited to, the massive stone peak of Mount Katahdin—are the two names to know in northern Maine. Both of these areas allow for serious wilderness outdoor pursuits; they're big, empty landscapes that are still mostly wild—wild enough to get lost in. Literally.

It's true that big timber firms still own, manage, tree-farm, spray, and log much of the rest of the land up here—a process that began long ago, when King George III laid claim to his "Crown Lands" and started cutting the tallest, choicest white pines for ship masts. But public access is allowed on some of the paper-company lands, and the state has protected a number of other important tracts as well.

Western Maine is more pastoral, consisting of foothills leading up to the big mountains. This area offers some of my favorite back-road driving and cycling in New England—you never know when you'll stumble across a deer, a moose, a silvery pond, a little mountain with a hiking trail to its summit, an apple orchard (or apple festival), a little main street, or boys fishing off a river bridge.

The upshot? There aren't a lot of services and sights here, but that's okay. Mother Nature *is* the sight.

1 ENJOYING THE GREAT OUTDOORS

CANOEING To many outdoor enthusiasts, Maine means canoeing. From thousands of acres of lakes and ponds to the tumbling white water of mountain rivers, Maine is very alluring to serious paddlers. The **Saco River** is one prime destination; see "Canoeing the Saco River," in section 2, "The Western Lakes & Mountains," below. But don't forget about the upper west branch of the **Penobscot River,** either, which winds through moose country and connects to one of Maine's more pristine lakes.

In fact, you can't travel very far in Maine without stumbling upon a great canoe trip. Two excellent sources of information are the *AMC River Guide: Maine* and *Quiet Water Canoe Guide: Maine,* both published by the Appalachian Mountain Club, 5 Joy St., Boston, MA 02108.

FISHING Anglers from all over the Northeast indulge their obsessions on some of Maine's 6,000 lakes and ponds and countless rivers and streams.

For options on rustic fishing camps statewide, request one of the attractive brochures that describe more than 50 sporting camps between the Rangeley Lakes and Eagle Lake (near Fort Kent) from **Maine Sporting Camp Association,** HC 76 Box 620, Greenville, ME 04441 (www.mainesportingcamps.com).

Licenses for adult nonresidents of Maine cost $72 for the season, or $23 for 3 days. (You can also buy 1-, 7-, and 15-day licenses; there are discounts for children 15 and under.) Purchase the licenses at outdoor shops or general stores. Remember that there are catch limits on some species of fish, and at this writing, fishing for Atlantic salmon or sturgeon in Maine is forbidden. For a booklet of complete fishing regulations, contact the **Maine Department of Inland Fisheries and Wildlife,** 284 State St. (State House Station #41), Augusta, ME 04333 (© **207/287-8000;** www.state.me.us/ifw).

HIKING Good hiking is abundant throughout western, central, and northern Maine. In western Maine, 50,000 acres of the White Mountains spill over New Hampshire's border and boast an excellent network of trails. Pathways in and around **Evans Notch** and **Grafton Notch** (both easily reached from Bethel) are for hikers of all levels. Finally, the **Bigelow Range,** near the Sugarloaf/USA ski resort, has challenging trails and stunning vistas from high, blustery ridges. The **Appalachian Trail** traverses the range on its way from Grafton Notch to the trail's terminus at **Mount Katahdin;** a good source of trail info is the Appalachian Trail guide. Also consult *50 Hikes in the Maine Mountains,* by Chloe Chunn (Backcountry Publications), one of the best guides to hikes in the Bigelow Range and Baxter State Park.

SKIING Maine has only two major destination downhill-ski resorts, plus 10 smaller areas. The big resorts, Sugarloaf and Sunday River, are under the same ownership but have distinct characteristics. **Sugarloaf** (© **800/843-5623** or 207/237-2000; www.sugarloaf.com), in the lovely spare Carrabassett Valley, is compactly arrayed on a single high peak and has the second-highest vertical drop in New England. The resort's base area is self-contained, like an established campus, and is a big hit with families. **Sunday River** (p. 370), near Bethel, has grown lengthwise along an undulating ridge—the local nickname for it used to be "Someday Bigger." Once a less-developed resort, it eventually caught up and offers diverse terrain and state-of-the-art snowmaking and grooming, plus an array of decent hotels and restaurants and a "we're cool" vibe you don't usually find in New England, except maybe at Mad River.

For more information about downhill skiing, contact the **Ski Maine Association** (© **207/773-7669;** www.skimaine.com). The association's website also has up-to-date reports on ski conditions during the winter.

Cross-country skiers have a glorious mix of terrain to choose from, too, though groomed cross-country ski areas aren't as extensive here as in New Hampshire or Vermont.

WHITE-WATER RAFTING Maine's three northern rivers are dam-controlled, so good rafting is available through the season. The **Dead River** has limited releases of water from the dam and is open only a half-dozen times a year for rafting in early summer and fall, but you can paddle the waters in inflatable kayaks during the summer. The **Kennebec River** has monstrous waves just below its dam, then tapers off into a gentle afternoon paddle as you float out of a scenic gorge. The West Branch of the **Penobscot River** has a challenging, technical section called the "cribworks" at the outset, several serious drops and falls after that, and dramatic views of Mount Katahdin en route.

Raft Maine (© **800/723-8633;** www.raftmaine.com) is a trade association of Maine's white-water outfitters, headquartered near a river (naturally) in West Forks. Call its toll-free line to connect to one of its member outfitters.

2 THE WESTERN LAKES & MOUNTAINS ★

Fryeburg: 55 miles NW of Portland; 85 miles NE of Concord; 140 miles N of Boston

Though cultural sites are pretty scarce in Maine's western mountains, the natural amenities in this region are impressive indeed. Here hikers can walk some of the loveliest stretches of the entire **Appalachian Trail,** which crosses into Maine in the Mahoosuc Mountains (near where Rte. 26 enters New Hampshire), then follows rivers and ridgelines northeast to **Bigelow Mountain** and beyond. Canoeists and anglers can head for the **Rangeley Lakes** area, a chain of deepwater ponds and lakes that has attracted sportsmen for more than a century. And in winter, skiers can choose from among several downhill ski areas, including big, busy, agreeable **Sunday River.**

This section focuses on two of the prettiest villages in western Maine, Fryeburg and Bethel, plus some attractive side trips from each town. Either one works well as a regional base: Both have prim brick and whitewashed homes, pretty lawns, and easy access to hills, mountains, and history.

FRYEBURG TO GILEAD ★

Travelers typically scurry through **Fryeburg** on their way from the Maine coast to the White Mountains or vice versa. They might buy a tank of gas or a sandwich, but they don't give much thought to this handsome little colonial town set in a region of rolling hills and placid lakes. Most of these drivers probably don't even realize that some 50,000 acres of the **White Mountain National Forest** spill across from New Hampshire into Maine just north of the town, or that those mountains' foothills offer some of the best hiking, canoeing, and fall foliage in all of Maine: **Evans Notch** offers granite peaks and tumbling cascades, and the meandering **Saco River** is full of sandbars that invite canoeists to pull over and laze away sunny afternoons.

The Fryeburg is also full of historical buildings and tales, and contains one of the most pristine, appealing lakes in Maine: **Kezar Lake,** which has the White Mountains as its backdrop. The lake is all the more appealing because public access is so difficult; very few roads encroach upon it.

Day-trippers from Portland and Boston have finally discovered this region's allure (at about 1½ hr. away, it's virtually in Portland's backyard), yet it still lacks the crowds or commercialism of the more developed valleys of New Hampshire's White Mountains—and it probably always will. For you, that's a good thing.

Essentials

GETTING THERE Fryeburg is on U.S. Route 302, about 1½ hours northwest of **Portland** and only 15 minutes east of **North Conway.** Route 113 departs from Fryeburg on the west side of town, headed for **Gilead.** From Boston, it's a 2½ to 3-hour drive.

VISITOR INFORMATION You'll find a **Maine State Information Center** (✆ **207/935-3639**) on Fryeburg's Main Street (Rte. 302) near the junction of Route 113 N. It's open year-round.

There's nothing much worth seeing in Bridgton, but you can pick up information at the **Greater Bridgton Lakes Region Chamber of Commerce** (✆ **207/647-3472**), open 9am to 5pm Monday to Saturday (closed Wed). It's on Route 302, a bit south of the main street stoplight.

You can also pick up info in Bethel at the Evans Notch Information Center (✆ **207/824-2134**) at 18 Mayville Rd., just off Route 2 north of the main village of Bethel (on the way to Sunday River).

SPECIAL EVENTS Maine's largest agricultural fair, the **Fryeburg Fair** (✆ **207/935-3268;** www.fryeburgfair.com) is held annually in early October, during the 10 days leading up to Columbus Day. Often coinciding with the near-peak of foliage season, this huge fair is even more colorful than its surroundings. It's a classic New England extravaganza of snorting pigs, horse-pulling matches, llamas, pumpkins the size of Rhode Island, and contests for the best-looking and best-tasting pies. Tickets are $10 Saturday, $8 any other day; entrance is free for children 11 and under. Parking on-site will cost you an additional $5 per vehicle; budget extra time to get in and out due to heavy traffic during afternoon and early-evening hours.

Canoeing the Saco River

The **Saco River** ★ is home to some of the most accessible, inviting canoeing in the entire state of Maine. The river forms in the White Mountains near New Hampshire's Crawford Notch, then wends its way to the sea just south of Portland, passing through flat, gentle farmlands around Fryeburg en route. The river is slow-moving but steady for much of its run, with relatively gentle rapids, which make it interesting yet almost never threatening. And thanks to its sandy glacial deposits, the river channel contains numerous sandbars that make for superb lounging spots. Bring a beach towel. (The river's banks are mostly privately owned, but a few landowners graciously allow quiet recreation and even overnight camping.)

The largest outfitter in the area is **Saco Bound** (✆ **603/447-2177;** www.sacobound.com), on Route 302 in Center Conway, New Hampshire, just across the state line (btw. Fryeburg and North Conway). From a busy shop across the highway from the river, the staff provides equipment, advice, shuttle service, and guided trips. For more personal, smaller-scale service, try **Saco River Canoe & Kayak** (✆ **888/772-6573** or 207/935-2369; www.sacorivercanoe.com), at 1009 Main St., in Fryeburg. Rentals run $24 to $45 per day for a canoe with all equipment, including river access and parking. (You can often find discounts during the week.)

Tips: Tackling the Saco: Tips for the Trip

Should you decide to accept the mission of **canoeing the Saco,** congratulations and good luck. But bear a few things in mind: First and foremost, early summer—especially after a damp spring—brings mosquitoes onto the river in numbers you can't believe. The solution? Lots of good 'skeeter repellent. Or if you're not into that, schedule your trip later in the season, when things have dried out. The bug population (usually) declines after July 4th, and by August, the pesky ones will almost certainly be all gone.

Also be aware that the Saco's popularity has soared in recent decades. You're not going to have a true wilderness experience here, especially on summer weekends, when armadas of lunkheads fueled by cheap beer sometimes descend on the river in big numbers and bring a frat-party atmosphere to the place. It became such a problem at one point that police set up "river blocks" to randomly check boaters and paddlers for sobriety. (The courts then told police to cut it out—I'm not sure why.) It's mostly a weekend phenomenon and has abated somewhat. Anyway, on weekdays the crowds tend to thin out and run more toward solo local nature lovers, quiet families, and couples enjoying a relaxing paddle.

Hiking

Superb hiking trails lace the rugged, low hills of **Evans Notch** ★★ on either side of Route 113, offering something for hikers of every stripe and inclination. Far more trails exist than can be covered here. Pick up a hiking brochure at the info center in Bethel (see "Visitor Information," above), or consult one of several trail guides covering the area. Among them are the *White Mountain Guide* and the *Maine Mountain Guide* (published by the Appalachian Mountain Club), and *Fifty Hikes in Southern Maine* by John Gibson (Backcountry Publications).

You won't need a guide, though, for the easy hike to the summit of **East Royce Mountain** ★. The trail leaves from a parking area on Route 113 north of the road's high point. A well-marked, 3-mile round-trip walk follows a small stream before it begins a steeper ascent. The summit is bald and rocky, with fine views of Kezar Lake and the mountains to the west. Return via the same path.

Other local hikes include the summit of **Caribou Mountain** in the heart of the Caribou Wilderness Area, and demanding **Baldface Mountain** ★★, with a ridge-top trail that follows the edge of a ragged glacial cirque carved out of the mountain eons ago. A loop up and over Baldface is a tough, all-day hike that rewards experienced hikers; check the trail guides or ask the Forest Service for details.

Skiing

Shawnee Peak ★ Value Kids Shawnee Peak is a good family destination, a solid intermediate-level ski area carved (and I do mean carved) out of the side of Pleasant Mountain near Fryeburg. It's a good low-cost, low-key alternative (they don't even have a toll-free number) to larger, more crowded resorts in the White Mountains or western Maine. I really appreciate the creative packages this resort has developed: There has traditionally been a men's night and a ladies' night (tickets included lunch), and there's now a "Saturday night special"—not a weapon, but a Saturday night/all-day Sunday combination deal. Night? That's right: Shawnee has some of northern New England's best night skiing, with fully half its trails lit until at least 9pm daily. Night tickets (good 4pm to closing) are a true steal (just $13 for adults) on weekdays. The lodge scene is sedate and family-oriented. For snowboarders, the hill maintains one of the largest park-and-pipe combinations in Maine—which is also lit nightly.

119 Mountain Rd. (at Rte. 302, approx. 5 miles west of Main St.), Bridgton, ME 04009. ✆ **207/647-8444.** www.shawneepeak.com. Adults $38–$53 day lift tickets, $13–$45 half-day; discounts for kids.

Where to Stay & Dine

Quisisana ★★ Finds This is New England vacationing the way it used to be. Quisisana's views across Kezar Lake to the White Mountains are spectacular, but the real ear-opener is the music: It's everywhere. Nearly the entire staff consists of students recruited from conservatories across the nation. You're never far from arias practiced in rehearsal halls and full production numbers in the lakeside lodge; the menu of musical theater, recitals, and one-act operas changes daily. Lodgings consist of one-, two-, or three-bedroom cabins with the rugged charm of an old summer camp; most have private bathrooms, but not all—some "family" cabins share them. Days are spent canoeing, hiking, playing tennis, water-skiing, or sitting at lake's edge; three creative, well-prepared meals a day are included in your rate. Note some quirks: First, it's very expensive (rates on the website are per *person*). Second, they *do not take credit cards.* Third, they'll ask for a required $600 pre-booking deposit. And you must stay an entire week in inn rooms and most of the cottages, though there are a few exceptions. No, it's not for everyone, but for New England–style relaxing in a quiet, lovely location with great music as accompaniment, it's wonderful.

Pleasant Point Rd. (turn west off Rte. 5 just south of village market), Center Lovell, ME 04016. ✆ **207/925-3500.** www.quisisanaresort.com. 54 units, some w/shared bathroom. Mid-June to Aug $320–$390 double; cottages $370–$470 double. Rates include 3 meals daily. 1-week stay required in most units; shorter stays possible in some cottages. No credit cards. Closed Sept to mid-June. **Amenities:** Dining hall; babysitting; 3 clay tennis courts; watersports equipment/rentals. *In room:* No phone.

BETHEL ★★

Until somewhat recently, **Bethel** was a sleepy resort town with one of those family-oriented ski areas that seemed destined for mothballs. But then the **Sunday River** ski area (7 miles north of town) changed hands; a brash entrepreneur dusted it off and polished it up, and it eventually became what it is today, which is one of New England's most vibrant and challenging ski destinations.

With the rise of Sunday River, the sturdy town of Bethel itself has been dragged into the modern era, yet without taking on the artificial, packaged flavor of many other ski towns. (There are no outlet malls here.) This village is still defined by the stoic buildings of the respected Gould Academy prep school; a broad, green village common; and the Bethel Inn, a sprawling, old-fashioned resort that's managed to stay ahead of the tide by adding condos without ever losing its pleasant, timeworn character or lovely appearance.

Essentials

GETTING THERE Downtown Bethel is a simple turnoff from the intersection of two busy roads, Route 26 and U.S. Route 2. Get there from Portland or Boston via the Maine Turnpike (I-95), taking exit 63 ("Gray") and heading west on Route 26 for about an hour. From New Hampshire, drive east of Gorham on U.S. Route 2 for 20 to 30 minutes.

In fall and winter, there's a helpful free shuttle called the **Mountain Explorer** ★ (✆ **207/784-9335**), which runs between downtown Bethel and one or the other of the ski resorts' base lodges about once per hour. The catch? The bus operates weekends only from Thanksgiving until mid-December, then daily from mid-December through mid-April (from around 6:30am until around midnight). When the snows melt, though, the bus disappears until the following winter.

VISITOR INFORMATION The **Bethel Area Chamber of Commerce** (✆ **800/442-5826** or 207/824-2282; www.bethelmaine.com) has offices at 30 Cross St. (also referred to as Station Place), behind the movie theater. It's open Monday to Saturday from 9am to 5pm and Sunday from noon to 5pm; during off season it sometimes closes weekends, so it's best to call ahead.

Exploring Local History

Stately, historic homes ring the **Bethel Common** ★★, a long, rectangular green space created in 1807 atop a low, gentle ridge. (It was originally laid out as a street, wide enough for training the local militia.) The town's **historic district** encompasses more than two dozen homes, most of them within a Frisbee toss of this green and all of them representing the various architectural styles that were popular during the mid-to-late 19th century. White clapboards predominate, as they should.

The oldest home here is the 1813 **Moses Mason House** ★ at 14 Broad St., now a museum housing the collections and offices of the **Bethel Historical Society** (✆ **800/824-2910** or 207/824-2908; www.bethelhistorical.org). Mason was a doctor and local civic leader who was willing to try anything once, including building his Federal-style house on a stone foundation. His neighbors argued the home would topple over in a strong wind, but it didn't, and all the other local houses were soon being built on similar foundations. Mason also commissioned an itinerant painter—possibly the renowned landscape artist Rufus Porter—to paint his foyer and stairwell. The result is an engagingly primitive panorama (still in pristine condition) of boats at anchor in a calm harbor flanked by a still forest of white pine—quite remarkable, really.

The museum opens to the public in July and August, Tuesday through Sunday from 1 to 4pm. (You can sometimes snag an appointment during other times of year.) Admission is $3 for adults, $1.50 for children 11 and under.

Right next to this museum is another historic home, the **O'Neil Robinson House** ★, built in 1821 and later updated in a somewhat Italianate style. Unlike the Mason House, it's open year-round Tuesday through Friday (and also weekends during July–Aug). Admission is by donation.

Grafton Notch State Park

Grafton Notch State Park ★★ straddles Route 26 as it angles northwest from Bethel into New Hampshire. This 33-mile drive, one of my favorites in the state, is both picturesque and dramatic, and unlike the Kancamangus Highway, it's never stop-and-go (there are no services along the way; gas up and buy food in Bethel). You begin by passing through fertile farmlands in a broad river valley before ascending through bristly forests to a glacial notch hemmed in by rough, gray cliffs on the hillsides above.

Foreboding **Old Speck Mountain** ★★ towers to the south; views of **Lake Umbagog** ★★ open to the north as you continue into New Hampshire. The foliage is excellent in early October most years. This route attracts few crowds, but it's popular with throughgoing Canadian tourists *and* Canadian logging rigs loaded up with Maine timber (drive carefully and yield the road if necessary) headed for the Maine coast or I-95.

Public access to the park consists of a handful of roadside parking lots near scenic areas. The best of the bunch is **Screw Auger Falls ★**, where the Bear River drops through several small cascades before tumbling dramatically into a narrow, corkscrewing gorge carved long ago by glacial runoff through granite bedrock. Picnic tables dot the forested banks upriver of the falls, and kids seem inexorably drawn to splash and swim in the smaller pools on warm days.

This is as good a state park as you'll find in northern New England, yet it's incredibly affordable. From mid-May through mid-October, access to the 3,000-acre parks costs $3 per nonresident ($1 for kids and seniors); get a pass at the self-pay station in any of the parking lots.

Downhill Skiing

Sunday River Ski Resort ★★★ Sunday River has grown at stunning speed, to swiftly become one of the best ski mountains in New England with great, well-maintained terrain. Unlike ski areas that developed around a single tall peak, Sunday River expanded along an undulating ridge 3 miles wide that encompasses *seven* peaks—so simply traversing the resort, stitching a run together via the various chairlift rides, can take an hour or more. As a result, you're rarely bored. The descents offer something for everyone, from deviously steep and bumpy runs to wide, wonderful intermediate trails. Sunday River is also blessed with plenty of river water for snowmaking and makes tons of the fluffy stuff. The superb skiing conditions are, alas, offset by an uninspiring base area; the lodges and condos here tend to be architecturally dull, and there's little nightlife save a brewpub (see "Where to Dine," below). Anyway, you won't care, because the trails here are usually so good that they're often crowded all weekend even though there isn't a town or city of significant size for many tens of miles. Come on a weekday, though, and you'll pretty much have the place to yourself. There's good night skiing, with good discounts to match, and they'll even *refund* your ticket if you don't like the day's snow conditions and ask for your money back by 10am.

Skiway Rd., Newry, ME 04261. ✆ **207/824-3000.** www.sundayriver.com. Adults $77–$79 day lift tickets; discounts for seniors, youths, and night skiing. Turn off rtes. 2/5/26 at brewpub onto Sunday River Rd.; after 2½ miles, bear left onto Skiway Rd.

Other Outdoor Pursuits

BIKING An easy, scenic route for touring cycles follows winding **Sunday River Road ★** several miles into the foothills of the Mahoosuc mountain range. Start at the Sunday River ski resort (see above); follow the same directions, but continue past the resort and west alongside the river through a tranquil scene marked by a little cemetery and a covered bridge. Eventually, you head into forested hills (the road turns to dirt). This dead-end road is lightly traveled beyond the resort, and views from the valley are rewarding throughout. Ask locally, or consult a local cyclists' hangout (such those listed just below) for a map.

Serious mountain bikers should head for the **Sunday River Mountain Bike Park ★★** (✆ **207/824-3000**) at the ski area, with 28 trails (of every skill level) covering more than 25 miles open during summer and fall weekends. Experienced riders will enjoy taking their bikes by chairlift to the summit, then careening back down on service roads and ski trails. Visit the South Ridge Lodge first for your rental, then hit the slopes. An adult trail pass costs $10 per day; an adult pass including all-day chairlift rides costs $27 (about half-price for children 12 and under). Cycle rentals—a bit pricey—are also available. The park is open from spring through mid-October, Friday through Sunday only.

Bethel Outdoor Adventure ★★ (✆ **800/533-3607** or 207/824-4224; www.bethel outdooradventure.com), on Route 2 in Bethel, rents off-road bikes for $25 per day, in addition to its steady business renting out canoes and kayaks and leading fishing tours locally. The center is located right where U.S. Route 2 crosses the Androscoggin River, on the way from Bethel to Sunday River.

BOATING Canoe rentals and shuttles for exploring the Androscoggin River can be arranged by **Bethel Outdoor Adventure** (see "Biking," above). You can also hire a guide here to take you out by canoe or kayak, or sign up for a 2-hour lesson to brush up on skills before heading out on your own.

GOLF Bethel has two excellent courses. Bethel Inn's **Country Club** ★ (✆ **207/824-6276;** www.bethelinn.com) is an unusually scenic 18-hole golf course right next to the inn; the course is somewhat flat but undeniably attractive. Greens fees for 18 holes are $50 per person; twilight rates are about half-price. Clubs and golf carts can be rented, and the club also has a driving range. Tee times are not mandatory, but they're strongly recommended in high season, which includes fall, when the setting borders on the spectacular. The course is open early May through late October, weather permitting.

Sunday River also maintains a **golf course** ★★ (www.sundayriver.com/golf), with its own obviously splendid views and some lovely mountainside golfing. It's expensive: Greens fees range from $95 to $120 per person (cart included and required). Twilight rates are 70% to 75% cheaper for a pair of golfers playing together, though.

HIKING The **Appalachian Trail** ★★★ crosses the Mahoosuc Range northwest of Bethel. Many who have hiked the entire 2,000-mile trail say this stretch is both the most demanding and the most strangely beautiful. The trail doesn't forgive here; it gives up switchbacks in favor of sheer, rocky ascents and descents. (It's also hard to find water along this part of the trail during the high summer months.) Still, it's worth the effort for serious hikers for the views and unrivaled sense of remoteness.

One stretch of the trail crosses **Old Speck Mountain** ★★, which at 4,170 feet, is (surprisingly) Maine's third-highest peak. Even weekend walkers can tackle this hike. Look for the well-signed parking lot where Route 26 intersects the trail to the state park; park, pay, strap on boots (some parts are muddy), and join the A.T. right from the parking lot. In just one-tenth of a mile, you'll intersect the Eyebrow Trail—this moderately difficult side trail ascends an 800-foot cliff called the Eyebrow, but don't walk it if you're afraid of heights. Otherwise, stay on the main trail and continue up past several great notch overlooks, over rushing streams and past mild cascades, and into increasing views of the valley foliage. The summit is wooded, so there are no views from the top, but you can keep walking down into a bowl containing **Old Speck Lake** and a very primitive campsite. (I don't usually recommend this, though, because the total walking time might leave you out on the trail after dark; stop at the summit unless you're camping overnight at the lake.)

You can also take a walk on the A.T. *east* up **Baldpate Mountain** ★, the cliff whose face and top show patches of open ledge right across Route 26 from Old Speck, on the way to distant Mount Katahdin (p. 386). The trail continues right across the highway. Baldpate is higher than you might think: Its summit is only about 400 feet lower than Old Speck's. Check trail books if you're trying to decide which trail to hike. The Appalachian Mountain Club's *Maine Mountain Guide* contains detailed information about these and other area walks; pick up a copy before arriving in the Notch—shops in Bethel should carry it—if you're a serious walker.

Just outside Grafton State Park's boundaries, there's camping at the **Grafton Notch Campground** (✆ **207/824-2292;** www.campgrafton.com) for $25 per night. It's not part of the park, but privately owned. Find it on the west (left) side of Route 26, a mile or two before the entrance to the park.

There's also a less-wild campground on Route 2 at the headquarters of **Bethel Outdoor Adventure** (✆ **800/533-3607** or 207/824-4224; www.betheloutdooradventure.com). RVs and tenters are both welcome; call for current site rates.

The Bethel Inn Resort A classic, old-fashioned resort set on 200 acres right in the village, Bethel's signature inn has a quiet and settled air—appropriate, since it was built to house the patients of one Dr. John Gehring, who put Bethel on the map by treating nervous disorders here through a regimen of healthy country living. (The town was once known as "the resting place of Harvard" for the legions of faculty who were treated here.) The rambling white inn's rooms are more quaint than spacious—tired, even. Rooms and suites added to an outbuilding in the late 1990s are more modern, with amenities such as DVD players, Jacuzzis, and air-conditioning (which the main inn still lacks). You might also be placed in the row of condo units down by the golf course, but again the condition is slipping. Some spa services are available; there's a fitness center on the grounds; and the **cross-country ski center** ★ and **golf course** (see above) are scenic—yet this property seems to have really lost its footing of late. Stay for the history if you must, but don't expect a luxurious experience in spite of the very high prices; if you want that, look elsewhere.

21 Broad St. (on the Common), Bethel, ME 04217. ✆ **800/654-0125** or 207/824-2175. www.bethelinn.com. 150 units. Summer $198–$418 double; winter $158–$454 double. Rates include breakfast and dinner. 2- to 3-night minimum stay summer weekends and ski season. AE, DISC, MC, V. Pets allowed ($10 per night). **Amenities:** 2 restaurants; bar; babysitting; golf course; health club; Jacuzzi; heated outdoor pool; sauna; tennis court; watersports equipment/rentals. *In room:* A/C (some units), TV, hair dryer, Wi-Fi (free).

Jordan Grand Resort Hotel ★★ (Kids) The anchor for expanded development in the far-flung Jordan Bowl area, this hotel feels miles away from the rest of the Sunday River resort of which it's part, mostly because it *is* far away—even staff joke about its remoteness. A modern, sprawling hotel, it manages to be family-friendly, clean, and shipshape enough, and is a positively great hotel for (experienced) skiers who want to ski out the door and be first on untracked slopes every morning. Owing to the quirky terrain, parking is inconvenient; you might have to walk quite a long distance to your room (opt for the valet parking). Rooms are simply furnished in a durable condo style, many quite spacious and most with balconies and/or washers and dryers; all now have custom-made Boyne beds, too. This hotel has become a popular destination for ski-happy families—possibly because it has day care and kitchenettes—so it wouldn't be the best choice in town for a couple seeking a quiet, romantic getaway. Otherwise, it's very good. The two hotel restaurants serve food that's a notch above ski-hill pub fare.

Sunday River Rd. (P.O. Box 450), Bethel, ME 04217. ✆ **800/543-2754** or 207/824-5300. Fax 207/824-2111. www.sundayriver.com. 195 units. Ski season $140–$210 double, $275–$460 suite; rest of year $119 double, $235 suite. AE, DC, DISC, MC, V. **Amenities:** 2 restaurants; babysitting; children's center; concierge; exercise room; Jacuzzi; outdoor pool; room service; sauna; spa; steam room; Wi-Fi (in public areas; free). *In room:* A/C, TV, kitchenette (some units).

The Victoria Inn ★★ Built in 1895 and damaged by lightning some years back, the homey Victoria was restored in 1998 with antique lighting fixtures, period furniture, and the original, formidable oak doors. It's a good sleeper pick when you want to get away from resortville. Guest rooms have a William Morris feel, with patterned, flowery wallpaper, canopy-like beds, and handmade duvet covers. (If you enjoy sleek, modern hotel rooms, though, skip this place.) Room no. 1 is a luxurious master suite with a turret window and sizable bathroom, but most intriguing are the four "loft" rooms in the attached carriage house, each with a gas fireplace, Jacuzzi, and soaring ceilings revealing some of the building's rugged original beams. These suites have small second-story sleeping lofts and sleep up to eight guests each. The dining room serves the best fancy meal in the area (see "Where to Dine," below).

32 Main St., Bethel, ME 04217. ✆ **888/774-1235** or 207/824-8060. www.thevictoria-inn.com. 15 units. $109–$179 double; $149–$309 suite. Rates include full breakfast. 2-night minimum stay Sat–Sun and holidays. AE, MC, V. Pets sometimes allowed ($30 per night). **Amenities:** Restaurant. *In room:* A/C, TV, hair dryer, Wi-Fi (free).

Where to Dine

Bethel is pretty short on good eats, even if most hotels and inns in the area serve dinners to the public as well as their own guests.

The **Sunday River** ski resort is your best bet for a casual meal: It offers a total of *nine* different dining experiences at last count, including a crepe shop, the Foggy Goggle (a nightspot), and several pubs. Of them all, those inside the resort's two hotels—the **Grand Summit Resort** and the **Jordan Grand Resort**—are best for a sit-down dinner.

There's also an excellent little natural-foods store, the **Good Food Store** ★★ (✆ **207/824-3754;** www.goodfoodbethel.com), on Route 2 west of downtown Bethel but before the turnoffs to Sunday River and Grafton Notch. It's very convenient for grabbing a bite pre-hike or post-ski; the local beers, baked goods, ice creams, produce, meats, and other items are excellent.

Sunday River Brewing Company BREWPUB This modern brewpub, on prime real estate at the corner of Route 2 and the Sunday River access road, is a good choice if your objective is to quaff locally brewed ales and porters. Its motto? "Eat Food. Drink Beer. Have Fun." That about says it. The beers are good; the food (burgers, nachos, wings, pork sandwiches) doesn't strive for culinary heights. Come early if you're looking for a quiet bite, as it gets louder when bands take the stage.

29 Sunday River Rd. (at Rte. 2), Bethel. ✆ **207/824-4253.** www.sundayriverbrewpub.com. Main courses $8–$16. AE, MC, V. Mon–Thurs 11:30am–9:30pm; Fri–Sun 11:30am–11:30pm.

Victoria Restaurant ★★ Finds CONTINENTAL One of Bethel's best inns, the Victoria (see "Where to Stay," above), also operates one of its best eateries 6 nights a week. The predictably Continental menu is prepared with skill. Start with chowder, crostini with goat cheese and eggplant, or some smoked Maine salmon tartine, then move on to main courses like lobster in a Champagne butter sauce (served over pappardelle), grilled rib-eyes, bacon-wrapped filet mignon, grilled rack of lamb, chicken piccata, pork tenderloin, shrimp fra diavola, or salmon. Not many surprises, but again, it's all quite well done. Desserts run to items like chocolate cake with a cappuccino filling, Key lime pie, and a maple-flavored take on that New England favorite, apple crisp. Much better than you'd expect in a small mountain town.

32 Main St., Bethel, ME 04217. ✆ **888/774-1235** or 207/824-8060. www.thevictoria-inn.com. Main courses $18–$28. MC, V. Mon–Sat 5:30–9:30pm.

3 THE NORTH WOODS

There are two versions of the Maine Woods. There's this huge stand of virgin trees, threaded with tumbling rivers and inhabited by bears and moose. And then there's the reality, which is a bit different.

The perception that this is the last big wilderness in the East, with thousands of acres of unbroken forest, miles of free-running streams, and more azure lakes than you can shake a canoe paddle at isn't quite right. True, only a few roads cut through the terrain—there are many more lakes than highways—but in this case "undeveloped" doesn't mean "untouched."

The reality is that this forest is not only a wilderness; it's also now a massive tree plantation, partly (largely) owned and managed by a handful of international paper and timber companies. An extensive network of timber roads has opened the region up to extensive clear-cutting, which is most visible not from the ground or the rivers but from the air. In the early 1980s, *New Yorker* nature writer John McPhee noted that much of northern Maine "looks like an old and badly tanned pelt. The hair is coming out in tufts." That's even truer today; timber harvesting has accelerated thanks to technological advances in logging and demands for faster production to pay down the large debts incurred during all the paper-industry buying, selling, merging, and acquisitioning that's taken place over the past few decades.

So the North Woods are *not* a vast, howling wilderness. So what? This region still has fabulously remote enclaves where moose and loon *do* predominate, and where the look of the land hasn't changed much at all since Thoreau paddled through here in the mid–19th century and found it "moosey and mossy" (his words). As long as you don't arrive expecting complete wilderness, you'll still be wowed in the right spots.

MOOSEHEAD LAKE REGION ★★

Thirty-two miles long and 5 miles across at its widest, **Moosehead Lake** is Maine's largest lake by far. It's a great—if hard-to-reach—destination for hikers, boaters, and canoeists alike. This lake was historically a center of Maine's logging activity, a history that preserved the lake and kept it largely unspoiled by development for years and years. Timber companies *still* own much of Moosehead's shores (though the state of Maine has since acquired a significant amount, too), and the 350-mile shoreline mostly consists of unbroken second- or third-growth forest. The second-home building frenzy of the 1980s had an impact on the southern shores of the lake, but Moosehead is so huge that it has absorbed the boom fairly gracefully—so far.

Greenville, scenically situated at the very southern tip, is the de facto capital of the lake. What was once a rugged outpost town is now slowly orienting itself toward the tourist trade, with boutiques and souvenir shops and outfitters popping up in increasing numbers. The shops here stock a few too many T-shirts featuring moose on the front, but the town is still a good enough base—heck, the *only* base—for excursions in the area of Moosehead.

Essentials

GETTING THERE Greenville is about 160 miles north and west of Portland, roughly a 3-hour drive. Take the Maine Turnpike to the Newport/Palmyra exit (exit 157), then head north on Route 7/11 to Route 23 in Dexter. Continue north from Dexter to Route 6/15 near Sangerville, then follow Route 6/15 to Greenville.

Inside the Debate over Maine's North Woods

Much of Maine's outdoor recreation takes place on private lands—and that's especially true in the North Woods, about 9 million acres of which are owned by fewer than two dozen **timber companies.** This sprawling, uninhabited land is increasingly at the heart of a simmering debate over land-use policies.

Hunters, fishermen, canoeists, rafters, bird-watchers, and hikers have long been accustomed to having the run of this forest with the tacit permission of those timber companies, many of which had long and historic ties to Maine's small towns because the companies were founded here and depended on locals to do the grunt work.

But a lot has changed in recent years. Lakefront property is much more valuable than it was a generation or two ago, so the North Woods are suddenly worth much more as second-home properties than as standing trees. A number of parcels have already been sold off, and some formerly open land has been closed to visitors in anticipation of future **housing developments** (and profits).

Recreational users—who range from noisy **snowmobilers** to moose-thirsty **hunters** to tree-hugging **hikers,** gentle **fly-fishermen,** and high school outing-club **canoeists**—all have different opinions on how to protect this land and what it should be used for. These groups all have their own coalitions and trade groups and lobbyists (well, except for the canoeists maybe), and they rarely agree with each other on anything. That will make a consensus difficult to impossible, because even potential allies are at odds with each other.

At the same time, **corporate turnovers** in the paper industry have led to increased debt loads and pressure from shareholders to produce more from existing woodlands; this, in turn, has led to accelerated timber harvesting and big land swaps and sales. **Environmentalists** say this is a disaster waiting to happen; they believe the forest won't sustain jobs in the timber industry or remain a recreational destination if the industry continues on its present course of tree-cutting and herbicide spraying, both of which are done with great zeal. (The timber companies deny this, naturally, insisting they're practicing responsible forestry.)

A number of proposals to restore and conserve the woods have circulated in recent years, ranging from sweeping steps (such as establishing a new 2.6-million-acre national park here) to more modest notions such as encouraging timber companies to practice **sustainable forestry** and keep access free and open for public recreation through tax incentives.

In the 1990s, statewide referendums calling for a clear-cutting ban and new timber-cutting laws were shot down not once but twice; still, the land-use issue hasn't fully sorted itself out yet. The debate over the future of Maine's forest lands isn't as volatile as it in the Pacific Northwest—nobody here is spiking trees or sitting up in them protesting (yet). But few people lack opinions on the matter, and things could still come to a head someday.

VISITOR INFORMATION The **Moosehead Lake Region Chamber of Commerce** (✆ **888/876-2778** or 207/695-2702; www.mooseheadlake.org) maintains a helpful information center in Greenville. In addition to a selection of the usual brochures, the center has files and bookshelves of maps, trail information, wildlife guidebooks, and videos. From Memorial Day through mid-October, it's open daily except Tuesday; it's on your right as you come into town, next to the Indian Hill Trading Post. Call for hours during the rest of the year.

Outdoor Pursuits

BOATING Open daily, **Northwoods Outfitters** ★ on Main Street in Greenville (✆ **866/223-1380;** www.maineoutfitter.com) can help plan a trip up the lake or into the woods and load you up with enough equipment to stay out for weeks. The shop rents complete adventure equipment sets—canoes, paddles, life jackets, a tent, sleeping bags, pads, camp stoves, axes, cook kits, and more—and they also run tours taking in everything from bass fishing to snowmobiling. Shuttle service and individual pieces of equipment are also available for rent.

For more boating outfitters and rental outfits, check out the town of **Rockwood** (on Rte. 6/15, partway up the lake's western shore), which maintains a helpful website with listings at **www.rockwoodonmoosehead.org**.

CANOEING Follow Thoreau's footsteps into the Maine woods on a canoe excursion down the **West Branch of the Penobscot River** ★. This 44-mile trip is typically done in 3 days. Here's how most folks do it: They put in at Roll Dam, north of Moosehead Lake and east of Pittston Farm, paddling north on the generally smooth waters of the Penobscot. After choosing one of several campsites along the river, they spend the night, watching for moose as evening descends; on the second day, they paddle to huge, wild Chesuncook Lake. Near where the river enters the lake is the **Chesuncook Lake House** (✆ **207/745-5330;** www.chesuncooklakehouse.com), a farmhouse dating from 1864 with a handful of rooms and three cabins for rent. Double rooms in the main inn cost about $220 per night, cabins $100 to $140 per night double occupancy (there are kitchens, bathrooms, and running water in these cabins in summer and fall only). The final day of the journey involves a paddle down Chesuncook Lake, with its views of Mount Katahdin to the east, and a final take-out near Ripogenus Dam.

To help arrange a canoe excursion, consult **Allagash Canoe Trips** (✆ **207/237-3077;** www.allagashcanoetrips.com), which has been leading guided canoe trips in the North Woods—including the Allagash, Moose, Penobscot and St. John's rivers—since 1953. A

Tips The Best Views? Whatever Floats Your Boat

The first thing one needs to know about Moosehead Lake is that it's not meant to be seen by car. Some great views can be had from a handful of roads—especially from Route 6/15 as you get close to **Rockwood,** and from high elevations on the way to **Lily Bay** in the lake's southeastern quadrant—but for the most part, roads are set at a distance from the shores, and the driving is mostly dull. Instead, see the lake from a steamship or a canoe. (If you really only want to sightsee by car, skip the lake and head instead for the mountains of western Maine or the fishing villages of the coast.)

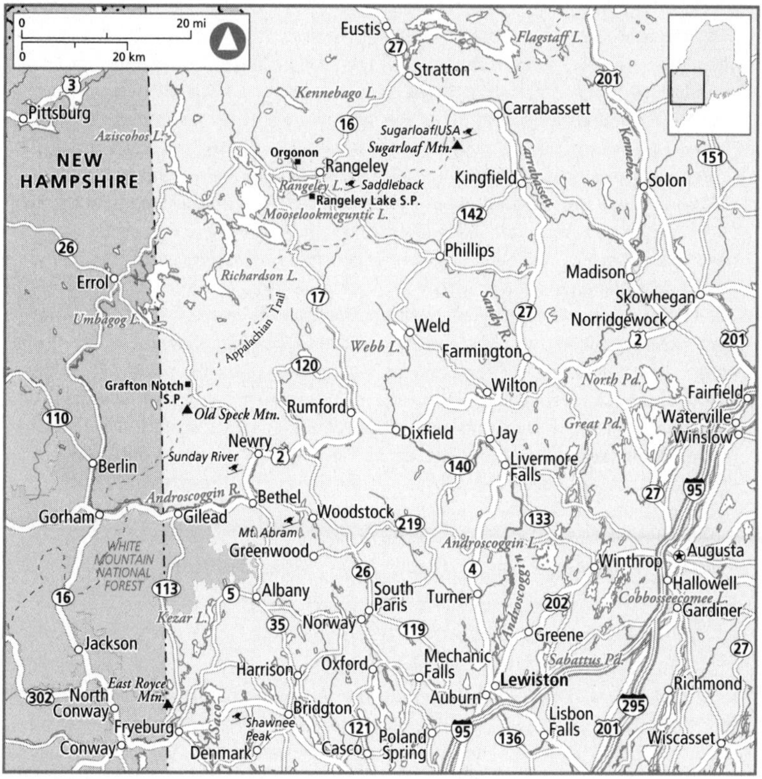

5-day guided camping trip down the West Branch—including all equipment, meals, and transportation—costs $660 per person for adults, 20% less for kids.

HIKING A good destination for a day hike, especially for families, is the **Borestone Mountain Audubon Sanctuary** ★ (✆ **207/631-4050** or 207/781-2330; www.maine audubon.org), south of Greenville and north of the town of Monson. The mountain, once a fox ranch (yes, really), hasn't been logged in more than a century and is now owned by the Maine Audubon Society as part of a 1,600-acre nature preserve. It's about 3 miles to the top of this gentle prominence; a booklet helps explain some of the natural attractions along the way. About halfway up is a staffed nature center at Sunrise Pond, with natural history exhibits and artifacts. You'll see and hear amazing varieties of songbirds and forest mammals.

To find the mountain, drive 10 miles north of Monson on Route 6/15 (en route to Greenville) and look for the sign for Eliotsville Road on your right; turn here and continue until you cross a bridge over a river, and then turn left and head uphill for ¾ mile until you see signs for the sanctuary. It's open dawn to dusk, from Memorial Day through the end of October. No pets are allowed on the property, and Maine Audubon asks a hiking fee of $4 per adult, $2 per child and senior.

Fun Facts The King's Pines: Maine's Trees Sent to Sea

Despite being 90% covered with forest, Maine doesn't have many truly big trees left. That's mostly thanks to the British Royal Navy (17th-century style), who needed the biggest, straightest trees to build tall wooden warships in England. Maine white pines were considered the ideal wood for the masts of those ships. In 1691 the Massachusetts Bay Charter was issued by British King William and Queen Mary—a document that established New Hampshire (which included Maine at the time) as a separate territory from Massachusetts, but also contained a "mast-preservation clause" allowing the Navy rights to any tree that measured 24 inches or more in diameter at a height of 1 foot growing on any piece of land that had not already been granted to a private person.

King-appointed forest runners swiftly moved through broad swaths of previously untouched forest land, marking the choicest trees with distinctively broad arrow-shaped axe slashes that meant, basically, "hands off, bro." The free-spirited colonists, who were actually living right at the edge of this wilderness, were furious at the long reach of London's arm into their backyards (a theme that would be heard again soon). But there was little they could do, and all the King's men soon began felling trees at a breakneck pace. Today just a handful of giant old-growth pines remain, none of them on public view (unless you know where to go), but they once stood proud and numerous. Just think what these woods would be like today if not for our old friend King George. Even the Beatles don't really make up for it.

Closer to Greenville, 3,196-foot **Big Moose Mountain** ★ offers superb views of Moosehead Lake and the surrounding area from its summit. A hike to the top requires about 4 hours; the trail begins about 5 miles northwest of Greenville on Route 6/15 (turn west on the gravel road and continue 1 mile to the trail head). Ask for more detailed information at the visitor center in Greenville.

One of the best hikes in the region is up **Mount Kineo** ★★, the massive, broad cliff that rises from the shores of Moosehead. Near the town of Rockwood, look for signs advertising shuttles across the lake to Kineo from the town landing. It's usually quite inexpensive for a lift. Once across to the other side, you can explore the grounds of the former Kineo Mountain House (alas, the huge 500-room hotel was demolished in 1938; the big building you see today was the *servants'* quarters). Cut across the golf course and follow the shoreline to a trail that leads to the 1,800-foot summit. Views from the cliffs are dazzling, but they might give you vertigo if you don't like heights.

If you *like* steep vertical drop-offs, though, continue along the trail to the old (ca. 1910) fire tower, which you can ascend for a hawk's-eye view that's even more spine-tingling—during peak foliage season, it's positively stunning.

A number of other hikes can be enjoyed in the area, too, but get good guidance since the trails aren't as well marked here as they are in the White Mountains or in Baxter State Park. Ask at the visitor information center, or pick up a copy of *50 Hikes in Northern Maine,* which contains good descriptions of several area hikes.

WHITE-WATER RAFTING Hard-core rafters love the heart-thumping run through **Kennebec Gorge** at the headwaters of the **Kennebec River,** southwest of Greenville.

Moments Going Deeper: A Hike to Gulf Hagas

The famed **"100-Mile Wilderness"** ★★ section of the Appalachian Trail begins in the town of **Monson** (south of Greenville) and runs northeast to **Abol Bridge,** near Baxter State Park (p. 382). This is a spectacularly remote section of the state, which allows for some of the best deep-woods hiking in the eastern U.S. This trip is for experienced backpackers—there are *no* points along the route to resupply yourself, so you've got to pack in food and have wilderness skills—though day trips in and out are a possibility if you've got a friend and a car. Check hiking and trail guides for more info.

One especially beautiful stretch of this trail passes along **Gulf Hagas** ★★, sometimes called "Maine's Grand Canyon" (though that name is a bit overblown). The Pleasant River has carved a canyon that cuts up to 400 feet deep into the bedrock; a trail runs along its lip, with side trails extending all the way down to the river's banks, where brave hikers sometimes swim (carefully) in the eddies and cascades. (I'd avoid that.)

To see the Gulf on a day hike, drive north from the town of **Milo** on Route 11 (east of Greenville) and follow signs to the **Katahdin Iron Works,** an intriguing historic site worth exploring in its own right. Pay the fee at the timber-company gate and ask for directions—basically, you'll drive about 3½ miles to a fork in the road, bear left, cross the river, and then continue to a parking lot and trail head about 3½ more miles beyond the fork. The 8-mile hike takes perhaps 6 hours; don't try unless you're in good shape.

If you're staying at the Appalachian Mountain Club's Little Lyford Lodge and Cabins (see "Where to Stay" below), you can reach the trail head for free on foot from the camps; it's about 8 miles round-trip from the lodge to the Gulf and back.

Dozens of rafters line up along the churning river below the dam, awaiting the siren that signals the release. (Your guide will tell you to hop in.) Once you're off, heading through huge, roiling waves and down precipitous drops with such names as Whitewasher and Magic Falls, buckle in. Most of the excitement is over in the first hour; after that, it's a more relaxing trip down the river, interrupted only by lunch and the occasional water fight with neighboring rafts. Nearby is the less thrilling, more technical **Dead River,** with a half-dozen dam release dates, mostly in early summer.

Commercial white-water outfitters have trips in summer at a cost of about $90 to $120 per person (more expensive on weekends). **Northern Outdoors** (✆ **800/765-7238;** www.northernoutdoors.com) is the oldest of the bunch and offers rock-climbing and fishing expeditions as well, plus snowmobiling in winter. Their base is in the tiny river village called **The Forks** (pop. 35, at last count), about 20 miles north of **Waterville** on U.S. Route 201.

Other reputable rafting companies include **Wilderness Expeditions** (✆ **800/825-9453;** www.wildernessrafting.com), which is affiliated with the rustic Birches Resort in Rockwood, and the **New England Outdoor Center** (✆ **800/766-7238** or 207/723-5438; www.neoc.com) in Millinocket.

Cross-Country Skiing

You can cross-country ski at **The Birches Resort** ★ (✆ **800/825-9453;** www.birches.com), a rustic resort on the shores of Moosehead north of Rockwood, which has more than a dozen log cabins along with limited lodge accommodations. About 25 miles of rolling backcountry trails here are groomed daily; a full-day adult trail pass costs $14 and gains you access to the resort's hot tub and sauna. Discounts are available for kids and seniors as well as half-day tickets; the resort also offers ski rentals and lessons.

Where to Stay & Dine

Some surprisingly luxe inns are tucked into these woods—trust me. Of course, for every one of those in this region, there are a hundred threadbare motels, sketchy campgrounds, blah pizza places, and small-town delis serving food that could charitably be called "fuel" rather than "food."

But the top-rated places I list below can hold their own with any luxury inns in New England, which is somewhat remarkable given the location. I imagine their owners figure if you've made the effort to get all the way up here, why not give you the best?

Blair Hill Inn ★★★ An eight-room gem that's not nearly as well known as it should be, this classy Queen Anne mansion (built in 1891) occupies a hilltop with unbelievable views of Moosehead Lake and the surrounding hills at its feet—the builder jacked the house up on 20 feet of stone walls, then cut the windows strategically to give the very best views. This is a truly luxe experience thanks to owners Dan and Ruth McLaughlin, Chicagoans who fell in love with the home, fixed it up, added their own collected antiques, and converted it into upscale accommodations. The interior is elegantly decorated in rustic and classic appointments like Oriental carpets and deer-antler lamps. The first-floor common rooms are bright, and the porch is gorgeous; handsome guest rooms are stocked with terrycloth robes, locally made soaps, and the like. Room no. 1, the original master bedroom, is most expensive and features panoramic sunset views, a fireplace, and a deep soaking tub with a knockout view through French windows, plus a TV, DVD and CD players, and Wi-Fi. (Several other rooms also have these modern conveniences.) Other

Fun Facts Question: So Where Are the Moose?

Answer: Everywhere around you. If you're staying at any of the accommodations around Moosehead Lake, you'll probably soon figure out how it got its name. The prime times to spot them are from around Memorial Day until the middle of September—which is prime time for you to visit the region, too, luckily. From fall until spring, the moose go into their winter routines (a lot less perambulating; a whole lot more sleeping), and they become much harder to spot. Some local outfitters might try to rope you into a "moose-spotting" tour, but I wouldn't pay for one of those. Instead, just set out on a drive outside Greenville (bring a map or GPS and your cellphone, just in case you have car trouble or get lost); it's quite possible you'll see one of the shaggy beasts. But don't get too near them, and don't search near dusk or dawn—and *absolutely* not after dark. Why? They're harder to see (and you're harder for them to see). Violent moose/car collisions are all too frequent in the North Woods, and the occupants of the cars sometimes suffer the same tragic fate as the unfortunate moose do.

units are furnished with cedar or marble baths, country cottage furniture, and similarly refined touches. The **dining room** ★★★ serves five-course *prix fixe* dinners ($55 per person)—some of northern New England's best. The chef often picks vegetables and greens for the evening meal himself. This is a one-of-a-kind lodging experience.

351 Lily Bay Rd., Greenville, ME 04441. ✆ **207/695-0224.** Fax 207/695-4324. www.blairhill.com. 8 units. $300–$495 double. Rates include full breakfast. 2-night minimum stay Sat–Sun. DISC, MC, V. Closed Nov and Apr. From center of town, about 3 miles north on the right. Children 10 and over welcome. **Amenities:** Restaurant; Jacuzzi. *In room:* TV/DVD (some units), CD player (some units), hair dryer, no phone, Wi-Fi (some units; free).

Greenville Inn ★★★ This lovely 1895 Queen Anne, formerly a lumber baron's home, sits regally on a side street above Greenville's commercial district, amid a small complex of outbuildings dotting its grounds. Inside everything's sumptuous, with wonderful cherry and mahogany woods and a lovely stained-glass window. Room no. 23 is representative: handsome blue-printed wallpapers and a fine view of the lake right from its king-size bed, plus a fireplace, its original English tiles, a big soaking tub, and a big plasma-screen TV. Six simple cottages sleep two to four each. But the two main-house suites are even more luxurious—the master suite almost feels like a private English country home, while the tower suite has a private porch and a telescope for scoping out lake views. A third, newer "suite" is actually a two-bedroom, two-bathroom home, while the lone carriage-house unit is country-simple. The half-dozen piney cottages are a bit less fancy, but every bit as clean and quiet (they feel like Maine). Nearly all units here come with plush robes, nonallergenic pillows, and TVs with DVD players. Don't miss the handsome **bar,** either, where you can sit in front of a fire or retreat to a front porch to watch the sun slip behind Squaw Mountain and the lake. The **dining room** ★★ is terrific, too: The chef has a philosophy of slow-cooking food carefully, and you might sup on poached Moosehead Lake trout in a licorice, maple, and vanilla butter; venison chops in a minty pâté; medallions of lamb; filet mignon with truffled potatoes; or the day's catch from the Maine coast.

Norris St., Greenville, ME 04441. ✆ **888/695-6000.** www.greenvilleinn.com. 14 units. $185–$265 double; $215–$450 suite; $195–$265 cottage. Rates include breakfast. 2-night minimum stay on holiday weekends. DISC, MC, V. From center of town, make 2nd right off Lily Bay Rd. Children 8 and over welcome. **Amenities:** Restaurant; bar. *In room:* A/C (some units), TV, hair dryer, no phone, Wi-Fi (in main inn; free).

Little Lyford Lodge and Cabins ★ Finds This AMC-owned logging camp is a great North Woods experience if you don't mind roughing it. Built in the 1870s, each cabin has a small woodstove, propane lantern, cold running water, and an outhouse. That's it. At mealtime, guests gather in a main lodge for dinner and board games; during the day, there's abundant fishing for brook trout, canoeing on two nearby ponds (canoes provided), and walks along the Appalachian Trail to the scenic Gulf Hagas gorge a few miles away. There are also communal bunks here. In winter cross-country skiing is superb—and the sauna helps guests forget about the cold. You'll need a four-wheel-drive vehicle to get here in summer: Access is via a rough logging road. In winter it's even tougher to reach the place—transport is either by an AMC shuttle, or you have to ski in (yes, ski in) yourself. Note that rates on the AMC website are per *person,* but they include all your meals: dinner and breakfast at the lodge, plus a "trail" (packed) lunch.

P.O. Box 310, Greenville, ME 04441. ✆ **207/280-0708** (lodge) or 603/466-2727 (reservations). www.outdoors.org. 8 units, plus bunkhouse of communal bunks (summer only). Advance reservations required. May–Oct $156–$238 double cabin or 2 bunks in bunkhouse; discounts for kids. Rates include breakfast, lunch, and dinner. $10 additional fee (summer only) to enter private land at KI/Jo-Mary Gate.

2- to 3-night minimum stay required. MC, V. Closed Apr to mid-May and Nov to late Dec. 17 miles from Greenville; from center of town, turn onto Pleasant St., following LLPC signs; in winter, must use AMC shuttle or ski in. **Amenities:** Sauna. *In room:* No phone.

The Lodge at Moosehead Lake ★★ It's pretty odd, but the second-biggest concentration of truly top-tier resorts in northern New England (just behind Stowe) is in little Greenville. This is yet *another* smashing home on a hillside just north of town (built "only" in 1917). Like the Blair Hill and Greenville inns, it's the polar opposite of a logging camp—this is luxury all the way. A mix of woodsy and modern decor sets the tone: Adirondack-style stick furnishings, wingback chairs, and antique English end tables, but also Jacuzzis in all the suites. Beds in the main lodge were all carved by a local artist, and each room pays homage to a different type of local wildlife: Bears, trout, and moose all get their props. Four amazingly luxurious suites in the carriage house have swinging beds—suspended from the ceiling by logging chains—plus chandeliers, French doors, sunken living rooms, and whirlpools fashioned from river stones. (One of these suites, the Katahdin, has a fireplace in the *bathroom;* the Mt. Kineo Suite, the newest, sleeps four in two bedrooms, and has a full working kitchen.) And the Allagash Suite has a private deck. Outdoorsy outings such as fly-fishing trips can be booked for an additional charge through the lodge, and the **restaurant** ★, open 3 nights per week in season, is very good.

368 Lily Bay Rd. (P.O. Box 1167), Greenville, ME 04441. ✆ **800/825-6977** or 207/695-4400. www.lodgeatmooseheadlake.com. 9 units. $250–$375 double; $395–$680 suite. Rates include full breakfast. 2- to 3-night minimum stay required. AE, MC, V. Located 2½ miles north of Greenville on Lily Bay Rd. (head north through blinker). Pets allowed ($40 per dog per night). Children 14 and over welcome. **Amenities:** Restaurant; pub; concierge. *In room:* A/C, TV, hair dryer, Wi-Fi (free).

Maynard's-in-Maine ★ This is the real Maine deal—not one iota of cute, faux, luxury, or "neo" about it. While logging-truck noises may occasionally jar you, you'll also hear wooden screen doors clacking shut and the amiable clank of horseshoes. In the main lodge, it seems nothing has even *moved,* never mind been replaced, in a half-century: The compound consists of a handful of rustic cabins edging a lawn, most furnished eclectically in classic camp furniture plus flea-market finds. The main house's long, rustic front porch is a highlight. The Wildwood cottage has three bedrooms sharing a bathroom, woodstove, and large screened porch; Birch Cottage is smaller and better for a couple, though less modernized. Remember, there are neither in-room phones nor even a pay phone here. The dining room—all meals are included—serves New England favorites like pot roast, soup, salad, beverages, and dessert. (There's no alcohol, but you can BYOB.) Yes, you can book hunting and fishing trips.

Maynard Rd., Rockwood, ME 04478. ✆ **866/699-0857** or 207/534-7703. www.maynardsinmaine.com. 14 units, some with shared bathrooms. $80–$130 double. Rates include continental breakfast (full breakfast May–June only), bag lunch, and full dinner. AE, DISC, MC, V. From Rte. 6/15 in center of Rockwood, turn onto Northern Rd. and cross bridge over Moose River; make immediate left onto Maynard Rd. Dogs allowed ($20 per dog). **Amenities:** Watersports equipment/rentals. *In room:* No phone.

BAXTER STATE PARK & ENVIRONS ★★★

Baxter State Park is one of Maine's crown jewels, even more spectacular in some ways than **Acadia National Park.** This 200,000-plus-acre park in the remote north-central part of the state is unlike any other state park in New England—don't look for fancy bathhouses or groomed picnic areas. When you enter Baxter State Park, you're entering near-wilderness.

Former Maine governor and philanthropist Percival Baxter single-handedly created this park, using his inheritance and investment profits to buy up the land and donate it

NORTHERN & WESTERN MAINE 10 THE NORTH WOODS

Tips Grinning and Bearing It in Baxter

A few dozen black bears dwell in Baxter State Park, and while they're not interested in eating you, they do get ornery when disturbed (it's a mama-bear protective thing). And they get *very* hungry at night. The park has published the following tips to help you keep a safe distance from the bears:

- Put food and anything else with an odor (toothpaste, repellant, soap, deodorant, perfume) **in a sealed bag or container** and keep it in your car.
- If you're camping in the backcountry without a car, put all your food, dinner leftovers, and other "smelly" things in a bag and **hang it between two trees** (far from your tent, not close to it) so that a bear can't reach it easily.
- *Never* keep food **inside your tent.**
- **Take all trash** with you from the campsite when you check out.
- **Don't toss food** on the trail.
- Finally, do I really need to say this? **Do not feed the bears,** or any other animals in the park, for that matter; they might bite the hands that feed them.

to the state in 1930. Baxter stipulated that it remain "forever wild," and caretakers have done a great job fulfilling his wishes: You won't find any paved roads or electrical hookups at the campgrounds, and strict vehicle-size restrictions keep all RVs out, too. You *will* find rugged backcountry and remote lakes. You'll also find **Mount Katahdin,** a granite monolith that rises above all the sparkling lakes and boreal forests around it.

To the north and west of the park lie several million acres of forestland, owned by timber companies and managed for timber production. If you drive on a local logging road outside the park very far, you'll soon run into a gate and be asked to **pay a fee** for using the paper company's roads or camping on its land.

But take a word of advice from me: *Don't* try to tour these woodlands by car. Industrial forestland is boring at best, downright depressing at its worst. A better strategy is to pick out one pond or river for your camping or fishing, then spend a couple of days getting to know the area around it. Just remember that, anywhere outside the state park, the whine of chainsaws and the thump of logging trucks' tires will never be far away, even in winter.

On the other hand, deep-woods creatures such as moose, black bears, eagles, bobcats, lynx, and minks still live here—in some cases, they even thrive, thanks to the state's ardent ongoing conservation efforts. Your park experience just might include an encounter with one of these creatures.

Essentials

GETTING THERE Baxter State Park is 85 miles farther north past the city of **Bangor,** and the local tourism office says it takes about 5½ hours to drive here from Boston, about 10 hours from New York. To find the park, take I-95 to **Medway** (exit 244), then head west 11 miles on Route 11/157 to the mill town of **Millinocket,** the last major stop for supplies. Go through town and follow signs to Baxter State Park.

Another, lesser-used entrance is in the park's northeast corner. Follow I-95 to exit 259, then take Route 11 north through **Patten** and west on Route 159 to the park. The speed limit throughout the park is 20 mph, and neither motorcycles nor ATVs are allowed inside its boundaries. (No pets are allowed inside, either.)

VISITOR INFORMATION Baxter State Park provides maps and information from a **park headquarters** at 64 Balsam Dr. in **Millinocket** (✆ **207/723-5140;** www.baxterstateparkauthority.com).

For information on canoeing and camping *outside* Baxter State Park, contact **North Maine Woods, Inc.,** 92 Main St. (P.O. Box 425), Ashland, ME 04732 (✆ **207/435-6213;** www.northmainewoods.org). This group is not an environmental group, but rather a consortium of the paper companies, logging companies, other North Woods landowners, and various concerned individuals who control and manage nearly all recreational access to private parcels of the Maine woods. They can answer all your questions about fees, campgrounds, access rights, rules, and the like.

For help in finding cottages, rentals, and tour outfitters in the region, contact the **Katahdin Area Chamber of Commerce,** 1029 Central St., Millinocket, ME 04462 (✆ **207/723-4443;** www.katahdinmaine.com), usually open for a half-day every weekday until early afternoon.

FEES Baxter State Park visitors driving cars with out-of-state license plates into the park are charged a flat fee of $13 per car per day. (It's *free* for Maine residents, as well as to any occupants of a rental car bearing Maine plates.) This fee is charged only once per stay if you're coming to camp; otherwise, you need to pay each day you enter the park. But you can cut your costs by buying a **seasonal pass** for $39 at the gate. Note that there's no running water inside the park during winter.

Outdoor Pursuits

BACKPACKING The park maintains about 180 miles of backcountry hiking trails and a few dozen backcountry campsites, some of them accessible only by canoe. Most hikers coming to the park are intent on ascending **Mount Katahdin** (see "Hiking," below), Maine's highest peak. But dozens of other peaks here are also worth scaling—heck, even simply walking through the deep woods here is a sublime (and sublimely quiet) experience. Reservations are required for backcountry camping; many of the best spots fill up quickly in early January, when reservations open for the calendar year (see "Camping," below).

En route to Mount Katahdin, the Appalachian Trail winds through the "100-Mile Wilderness," a remote and bosky stretch where the trail crosses few roads and passes no settlements. It's the quiet habitat of loons and moose. Trail descriptions are available from the **Appalachian Trail Conservancy,** 799 Washington St. (P.O. Box 807), Harpers Ferry, WV 25425 (✆ **304/535-6331;** www.appalachiantrail.org).

CAMPING Baxter State Park has a clutch of **campgrounds** accessible by car, plus a few backcountry camping areas that must be walked into; most are open summer only, from mid-May until mid-October. Some bunkhouses are open year-round.

But don't count on finding a spot if you show up without reservations in midsummer—the park starts processing requests on a first come, first served basis the first week in January, and dozens of die-hard campers traditionally spend a cold night outside headquarters to secure the best spots. **Call well in advance** (as in, during the previous year) for the forms you'll need to mail in.

Camping inside the park is charged per person (minimum charge $20), and the cabins and bunkhouses cost $11 to $27 per person. Reservations can be made by mail, in person at the headquarters in Millinocket (see "Visitor Information," above), and (sometimes) by phone—but *only* less than 14 days from arrival. Don't call them about any other dates.

North Maine Woods, Inc. (see "Visitor Information," above) also maintains a small network of **primitive campsites** on its 2-million-acre holdings. While you may have to drive through massive clear-cuts to reach them, some are positioned on secluded coves or picturesque points. A map showing logging-road access and campsite locations is available for a small fee plus postage from the North Maine Woods headquarters. Daily camping fees are minimal, though you must also pay an access fee to the lands.

CANOEING The state's premier canoe trip is the **Allagash River** ★★, starting west of Baxter State Park and running northward for nearly 100 miles, finishing at the village of Allagash. The **Allagash Wilderness Waterway** (✆ **207/941-4014**) was the first state-designated wild and scenic river in the country, protected from development since 1970. Most travelers spend between 7 and 10 days making the trip from Chamberlain Lake to Allagash. The trip begins on a chain of lakes involving light portaging. At Churchill Dam, a stretch of Class I to II white water runs for about 9 miles, then it's back to lakes and a mix of flat water and mild rapids. Toward the end, there's a longish portage (about 450 ft.) around picturesque Allagash Falls before finishing up above the village of Allagash.

About 80 simple campsites are scattered along the route; most have outhouses, fire rings, and picnic tables. There's a small nightly fee to use them.

HIKING With 180 miles of maintained backcountry trails and 46 peaks (including 18 that are higher than 3,000 ft.), Baxter State Park is a serious destination for serious hikers. The most imposing peak is 5,267-foot **Mount Katahdin** ★★★, the northern terminus of the **Appalachian Trail.** An ascent up this rugged, glacially scoured mountain is a trip you'll not soon forget. The raw drama and grandeur of the rocky, windswept summit is equal to anything you'll find in the White Mountains.

Allow at least 8 hours for the round-trip, and abandon your plans if the weather takes a turn for the worse while you're en route. The most popular route departs from **Roaring Brook Campground;** in fact, it's popular enough that it's often closed to day hikers—when the parking lot fills, hikers are shunted off to other trails. You ascend first to dramatic **Chimney Pond,** which is set like a jewel in a glacial cirque, then continue upward toward Katahdin's summit via one of two trails. (The **Saddle Trail** is the most forgiving, the **Cathedral Trail** ★ the most dramatic.) From here, descent begins along the aptly named **Knife Edge,** a narrow, rocky spine between Baxter Peak and Pamola Peak. *Do not take this trail if you are afraid of heights.* In spots the trail narrows to 2 or 3 feet with a drop of hundreds of feet on either side. Obviously, it's also not the spot to be if high winds move in or thunderstorms are threatening. From the Knife Edge, the trail follows a long and gentle ridge back down to Roaring Brook.

Katahdin draws the biggest crowds, but there are numerous other trails in the park where you'll find more solitude and wildlife than on the main peak. One pleasant day hike is to the summit of **South Turner Mountain,** which offers wonderful views across to Mount Katahdin and blueberries for picking (in late summer). This trail also departs from Roaring Brook Campground, and requires about 3 to 4 hours for a round-trip. To the north, more good hikes begin at the **South Branch Pond Campground.**

My advice for picking the best hike for yourself? Talk to rangers, and buy a trail map at park headquarters when you first enter Baxter.

WHITE-WATER RAFTING One unique way to view Mount Katahdin is by rafting the West Branch of the **Penobscot River.** Flowing along the park's southern border, this wild river has some of the most technically challenging white water in the East. At least a dozen rafting companies operate trips on the Penobscot, with prices in the neighborhood of $100 or $120 per person, including a lunch.

Among the outfitters in the area is the **New England Outdoor Center** (✆ **800/766-7238;** www.neoc.com), on a stretch of the river southeast of Millinocket. Its **River Drivers Restaurant** ★ (✆ **207/723-5438**) is among the best eateries in the vicinity of Baxter. The same owners also run nearby **Twin Pine Camps Cabins,** a rustic lodge on the shores of Millinocket Lake with stellar views of Katahdin (cabins for two start at around $120), as well as another facility near **Caratunk** on the **Kennebec River.**

11 Fast Facts, Toll-Free Numbers & Websites

1 FAST FACTS: NORTHERN NEW ENGLAND

AREA CODES Vermont's area code is 802, New Hampshire's area code is 603, and Maine's area code is 207.

AUTOMOBILE ORGANIZATIONS Auto clubs can supply useful maps, suggested routes, guidebooks, accident and bail-bond insurance, and emergency road service. The **American Automobile Association (AAA)** is the major auto club in the United States. If you belong to a motor club in your home country, inquire about AAA reciprocity before you leave. You may be able to join AAA even if you're not a member of a reciprocal club; to inquire, call AAA (✆ **800/222-4357;** www.aaa.com). Call the same number for AAA nationwide emergency road-service.

BUSINESS HOURS Banks are generally open Monday to Friday 9am to 3pm. Drive-through teller hours are longer. Shops are usually open Monday to Friday from 9am to 6pm, Saturday from 10am to 6 or 7pm, and Sunday from noon until 5 or 6pm. In bigger cities or in shopping-mall or outlet-shop areas, these hours will be somewhat extended, as late as 9pm during peak summer shopping season.

DRINKING LAWS The legal age for purchase and consumption of alcoholic beverages in all three states is 21; proof of age is required and often requested at bars, nightclubs, and restaurants, so it's always a good idea to bring ID when you go out.

In Maine, New Hampshire, and Vermont, liquor is sold at state-operated stores, grocers, and convenience stores. Restaurants without liquor licenses sometimes allow patrons to bring in their own. Ask first. Bars sell liquor until 2am in Vermont and until 1am in New Hampshire and Maine.

Don't carry open containers of alcohol in your car or any public area that isn't zoned for alcohol consumption. The police can fine you on the spot. And don't even think about driving while intoxicated.

ELECTRICITY The United States uses 110 to 120 volts AC (60 cycles), the same as in Canada and Japan but different from the 220 to 240 volts AC (50 cycles) used in most of Europe, Australia, and New Zealand. Downward converters that change 220–240 volts to 110–120 volts are difficult to find in the United States, so bring one with you.

EMBASSIES & CONSULATES All embassies are located in the nation's capital, Washington, D.C. Some consulates are located in major U.S. cities, and most nations have a mission to the United Nations in New York City. If your country isn't listed below, call for directory information in Washington, D.C. (✆ **202/555-1212**) or check **www.embassy.org/embassies.**

The embassy of **Australia** is at 1601 Massachusetts Ave. NW, Washington, DC 20036 (✆ **202/797-3000;** usa.embassy.gov/au).

The embassy of **Canada** is at 501 Pennsylvania Ave. NW, Washington, DC 20001 (✆ **202/682-1740;** www.canadainternational.gc.ca/washington). Other Canadian consulates are in Buffalo (New York), Detroit, Los Angeles, New York, and Seattle.

The embassy of **Ireland** is at 2234 Massachusetts Ave. NW, Washington, DC 20008 (✆ **202/462-3939;** www.embassyofireland.org). Irish consulates are in Boston, Chicago, New York, San Francisco, and other cities. See website for complete listing.

The embassy of **New Zealand** is at 37 Observatory Circle NW, Washington, DC 20008 (✆ **202/328-4800;** www.nzembassy.com). New Zealand consulates are in Los Angeles, Salt Lake City, San Francisco, and Seattle.

The embassy of the **United Kingdom** is at 3100 Massachusetts Ave. NW, Washington, DC 20008 (✆ **202/588-6500;** http://ukinusa.fco.gov.uk). Other British consulates are in Atlanta, Boston, Chicago, Cleveland, Houston, Los Angeles, New York, San Francisco, and Seattle.

EMERGENCIES For fire, police, and ambulance, find any phone and dial ✆ **911.** If this fails, dial ✆ **0** (zero) and report an emergency.

GASOLINE (PETROL) Northern New England's gas prices are a bit higher than the U.S. average; at press time, the price was somewhere around $2.70 per gallon. There are very few "full-service" gas stations in northern New England (for some reason, Bennington, Vermont, is an anomaly), and if you do find one, you'll often pay up to 10¢ extra per gallon for the privilege of letting someone else pump the gas and maybe clean your windshield. Taxes are always included in the listed per-gallon price of gas in the U.S. International travelers should note that 1 U.S. gallon equals 3.8 liters or .85 imperial gallons.

HOLIDAYS Banks, government offices, post offices, and many stores, restaurants, and museums are closed on the following legal national holidays: January 1 (New Year's Day), the third Monday in January (Martin Luther King, Jr., Day), the third Monday in February (Presidents' Day), the last Monday in May (Memorial Day), July 4 (Independence Day), the first Monday in September (Labor Day), the second Monday in October (Columbus Day), November 11 (Veterans' Day/Armistice Day), the fourth Thursday in November (Thanksgiving Day), and December 25 (Christmas). The Tuesday after the first Monday in November is Election Day, a federal government holiday in presidential-election years (held every 4 years, and next in 2012).

Some states have their own special state holidays, too. Maine celebrates **Patriot's Day** on a Monday in mid-April, while Vermont observes **Town Meeting Day** on the first Tuesday in March and also **Bennington Battle Day** in mid-August. All state offices are closed on these days. Most state offices in the states also close on the day after Thanksgiving.

For more information on holidays, see "Calendar of Events," in chapter 3.

HOSPITALS All large and small cities in northern New England maintain good hospital facilities, and some smaller towns have them, too. The quality of service is very good here. If health is a serious issue for you, check ahead with your accommodations (or consult the phone book when you arrive) about the nearest emergency-room service or 24-hour clinic.

In **Vermont,** major hospitals or medical centers are in Burlington, Barre, Brattleboro, Rutland, Springfield, St. Albans, and Newport (near the Canada border), and smaller clinics and health centers are dispersed throughout the state in places like Bennington, Windsor, Waterbury, and Morrisville. The biggest and best-equipped, by far, is Burlington's **Fletcher**

Allen Health Care facility (✆ **802/847-0000;** www.fletcherallen.org), with more than 560 beds.

In **New Hampshire,** there are plenty of hospitals and medical centers in places like Concord, Manchester, Nashua, Portsmouth, Keene (in the Monadnock region), Claremont, Exeter, New London, Laconia, and Plymouth, among other communities; you're rarely far from a good doctor. One of the best is the **Dartmouth-Hitchcock Medical Center** (✆ **603/650-5000;** www.hitchcock.org), in downtown Hanover, partly staffed by medical students and graduates from adjacent Dartmouth College. If you're going deep into the backcountry of the White Mountains, make sure you're fit enough—it can take time to get rescued and transported to a clinic in bad weather.

The largest hospital in **Maine** is the **Maine Medical Center** (✆ **207/662-0111;** www.mmc.org), a professional facility located on a hilltop in a residential neighborhood of Portland at 22 Bramhall St. There's also **Mercy Hospital** (✆ **207/879-3000;** www.mercyhospital.org), a Catholic-owned hospital nearby at 144 State St. in Portland. Both are excellent. Smaller admitting hospitals are located in communities such as York, Biddeford, Brunswick, Damariscotta, Ellsworth, and Bar Harbor. North of Camden, however, they thin out.

INSURANCE For information on traveler's insurance, trip-cancellation insurance, and medical insurance while traveling, please visit www.frommers.com/planning.

INTERNET ACCESS Internet cafes are scattered throughout northern New England, though they're getting less common; these days, most travelers find a coffee shop or hotel equipped for wireless (Wi-Fi) access instead. You'll need a card or antenna in your laptop to access Wi-Fi, plus a password for the local network. Some cafes and hotels charge a fee for this service, but others don't.

Many **public libraries** in the northern New England states—even those in small towns—offer free Internet access via free terminals. You'll probably need to surrender a piece of picture ID when you sign up, but you'll get it back when you sign out.

LEGAL AID If you are "pulled over" for a minor infraction (such as speeding), never attempt to pay the fine directly to a police officer; this could be construed as attempted bribery, a much more serious crime. Pay fines by mail, or directly into the hands of the clerk of the court. If accused of a more serious offense, say and do nothing before consulting a lawyer. Here the burden is on the state to prove a person's guilt beyond a reasonable doubt, and everyone has the right to remain silent, whether he or she is suspected of a crime or actually arrested. Once arrested, a person can make one telephone call to a party of his or her choice. International visitors should call their embassy or consulate.

MAIL At press time, domestic postage rates were 28¢ for a postcard and 44¢ for a letter. For international mail, a first-class letter of up to 1 ounce costs 98¢ (75¢ to Canada and 79¢ to Mexico); a first-class postcard costs the same as a letter. For more information, go to **www.usps.com**.

If you aren't sure what your address will be in the United States, mail can be sent to you, in your name, c/o General Delivery at the main post office of the city or region where you expect to be. (Call ✆ **800/275-8777** for information on the nearest post office.) The addressee must pick up mail in person and must produce proof of identity (driver's license, passport, and so on). Most post offices will hold your mail for up to 1 month, and are open Monday to Friday from 8am to 6pm, and Saturday from 9am to 3pm.

Always include zip codes when mailing items in the U.S. If you don't know your zip code, visit the post office website **www.usps.com/zip4**.

NEWSPAPERS & MAGAZINES Almost every small town in this region used to have a daily or weekly newspaper covering the events and happenings of the area. That is changing, but you can still find plenty of papers in northern New England; they're good sources of information for small-town events and specials at local restaurants—the day-to-day things that slip through the cracks at the tourist bureaus.

The largest **daily papers** in this region are the *Portland Press Herald* (Maine), *Manchester Union Leader* (New Hampshire), and *Burlington Free Press* (Vermont); all have websites. Burlington (*Seven Days*) and Portland (*The Portland Phoenix*) also have **free alternative weeklies** that are handy sources of information on concerts and shows at local clubs, also with websites.

The *Boston Globe, New York Times,* and *Wall Street Journal* are also often available daily in many shops around the region.

PASSPORTS See "Embassies & Consulates," above, for whom to contact if you lose yours while traveling in the U.S. For other information, please contact the following agencies:

For Residents of Australia Contact the **Australian Passport Information Service** at ✆ **131-232,** or visit the government website at www.passports.gov.au.

For Residents of Canada Contact the central **Passport Office,** Department of Foreign Affairs and International Trade, Ottawa, ON K1A 0G3 (✆ **800/567-6868;** www.ppt.gc.ca).

For Residents of Ireland Contact the **Passport Office,** Setanta Centre, Molesworth Street, Dublin 2 (✆ **01/671-1633;** www.dfa.ie).

For Residents of New Zealand Contact the **Passports Office** at ✆ **0800/225-050** in New Zealand or 04/474-8100, or log on to www.dia.govt.nz.

For Residents of the United Kingdom Visit your nearest passport office, major post office, or travel agency or contact the **United Kingdom Passport Service** at ✆ **0870/521-0410** or search its website at www.ips.gov.uk.

For Residents of the United States To find your regional passport office, either check the U.S. State Department website (http://travel.state.gov) or call the **National Passport Information Center** toll-free number (✆ **877/487-2778**) for automated information.

POLICE For police, dial ✆ **911.** If this fails, dial ✆ **0** (zero) and report the emergency.

SMOKING Smoking is banned in all public places (restaurants, bars, offices, hotel lobbies) in all three northern New England states.

TAXES The United States has no national sales tax or value-added tax (VAT). However, states, counties, and cities can add local taxes to purchases—including hotel bills, restaurant checks, and airline tickets. These taxes will *not* appear as part of the quoted prices; they'll be added when you pay.

The **sales, dining,** and **lodging taxes** in northern New England vary wildly according to which state you're in. **Maine** charges a 5% sales tax in stores, 7% at hotels and restaurants, and 10% for auto rentals. **New Hampshire** has *no* sales tax in stores, but charges an 8% tax on lodging and dining. And **Vermont** is the tax king of this region: There's a 6% sales tax on store purchases, a 9% tax on hotel rooms and restaurant meals, and a 10% tax on alcohol purchased in restaurants. On top of *that,* Vermont towns and cities can (and mostly do) add another 1% local tax to meals, lodgings, and purchases.

TELEPHONES Pay phones are becoming extinct in northern New England, but you do still sometimes find them on main streets and inside shopping malls. Local calls usually cost 50¢ for a few minutes of talk time; you need to deposit more coins for more time or longer-distance calls.

For additional information on using telephones, calling cards, and cellphones in this region, see section 11, "Staying Connected," in chapter 3.

TIME The continental United States is divided into **four time zones:** Eastern Standard Time (EST), Central Standard Time (CST), Mountain Standard Time (MST), and Pacific Standard Time (PST). Alaska and Hawaii have their own zones. For example, when it's 9am in Los Angeles (PST), it's 7am in Honolulu (HST), 10am in Denver (MST), 11am in Chicago (CST), noon in New York City (EST), 5pm in London (GMT), and 2am the next day in Sydney.

All three states in northern New England are in the **Eastern time zone** (the same zone as New York and Boston) and 5 to 6 hours "behind" the time in London. Why 5 to 6? Because **daylight saving time** is in effect from 1am on the second Sunday in March to 1am on the first Sunday in November, except in Arizona, Hawaii, the U.S. Virgin Islands, and Puerto Rico. Daylight saving time moves the clock 1 hour ahead of standard time.

TIPPING In hotels, tip **bellhops** at least $1 per bag ($2–$3 if you have a lot of luggage) and tip the **chamber staff** $1 to $2 per day (more if you've left a disaster area for him or her to clean up). Tip the **doorman** or **concierge** only if he or she has provided you with some specific service (for example, calling a cab for you or obtaining difficult-to-get theater tickets). Tip the **valet-parking attendant** $1 every time you get your car.

In restaurants, bars, and nightclubs, tip **service staff** and **bartenders** 15% to 20% of the check, tip **checkroom attendants** $1 per garment, and tip **valet-parking attendants** $1 per vehicle.

As for other service personnel, tip **cab drivers** 15% of the fare; tip **skycaps** at airports at least $1 per bag ($2–$3 if you have a lot of luggage); and tip **hairdressers** and **barbers** 15% to 20%.

TOILETS You won't find public toilets or "restrooms" on the streets in most U.S. cities, but they can be found in hotel lobbies, bars, restaurants, museums, department stores, railway and bus stations, and service stations. Large hotels and fast-food restaurants are often the best bet for clean facilities. Restaurants and bars in resorts or heavily visited areas may reserve their restrooms for patrons.

VISAS For information about U.S. visas, go to **http://travel.state.gov** and click on "Visas." Or go to one of the following websites:

Australian citizens can obtain up-to-date visa information from the **U.S. Embassy Canberra,** Moonah Place, Yarralumla, ACT 2600 (✆ **02/6214-5600**) or by checking the U.S. Diplomatic Mission's website at **http://canberra.usembassy.gov/visas**.

British subjects can obtain up-to-date visa information by calling the **U.S. Embassy Visa Information Line** (✆ **9042/450-100**) or by visiting the "Visas to the U.S." section of the American Embassy London's website at **www.usembassy.org.uk**.

Irish citizens can obtain up-to-date visa information through the **Embassy of the USA Dublin,** 42 Elgin Rd., Dublin 4 (✆ **353/1-668-8777**) or by checking the "Visas to the U.S." section of the website at **http://dublin.usembassy.gov**.

Citizens of **New Zealand** can obtain up-to-date visa information by contacting the **U.S. Embassy New Zealand,** 29 Fitzherbert Terrace, Thorndon, Wellington (✆ **644/462-6000**), or get the information directly from the website at **http://newzealand.usembassy.gov**.

VISITOR INFORMATION All three of the northern New England states maintain excellent tourism information offices and kiosks throughout their key areas. Call or e-mail these offices in advance and ask for information to be mailed to you before departure, or collect it online. I provide local tourism and chamber of commerce addresses and phone numbers in each of the destination chapters in this book.

Here's the contact information for each state's tourism authority:

- **Maine Office of Tourism,** 59 State House Station, Augusta, ME 04333 (✆ **888/624-6345** or 207/287-5711; www.visitmaine.com)
- **New Hampshire Division of Travel and Tourism Development,** 172 Pembroke Rd. (P.O. Box 1856), Concord, NH 03302 (✆ **800/386-4664** or 603/271-2665; www.visitnh.gov)
- **Vermont Department of Tourism and Marketing,** National Life Building, Sixth Floor, Montpelier, VT 05620 (✆ **800/837-6668** or 802/828-3237; www.travel-vermont.com)

If you're going back-roading or backcountry hiking, consider purchasing one or more of the **DeLorme atlases,** which depict every road and stream in these three states, plus many hiking trails and access points for canoes. DeLorme's headquarters and map store (✆ **800/561-5105** or 800/642-0970; www.delorme.com) are in Yarmouth, Maine, open daily, and their products are also available at many bookstores, gas stations, and convenience stores in the region.

Travel blogging hasn't really developed in this region yet—there are hundreds of microbloggers writing about local travel, news, or dining, but none is really considered authoritative or universally followed yet. It's best to follow the blogs of local newspaper reporters in the region (see "Newspapers & Magazines," above) or of the official tourism agencies listed above.

2 AIRLINE, HOTEL & CAR RENTAL WEBSITES

MAJOR AIRLINES

American Airlines
www.aa.com

Cape Air
www.flycapeair.com

Continental Airlines
www.continental.com

Delta Air Lines
www.delta.com

JetBlue Airways
www.jetblue.com

Northwest Airlines
www.delta.com

Southwest Airlines
www.southwest.com

United Air Lines
www.united.com

US Airways
www.usairways.com

MAJOR HOTEL & MOTEL CHAINS

Best Western International
www.bestwestern.com

Clarion Hotels
www.clarionhotel.com

Comfort Inn
www.comfortinn.com

Courtyard by Marriott
www.marriott.com/courtyard

Crowne Plaza Hotels & Resorts
www.ichotelsgroup.com

Days Inn
www.daysinn.com

Doubletree Hotels
www.doubletree.com

Econo Lodge
www.econolodge.com

Embassy Suites
www.embassysuites.com

Fairfield Inn & Suites by Marriott
www.marriott.com/fairfieldinn

Hampton Hotels & Suites
www.hamptoninn.com

Hilton Worldwide
www.hilton.com

Holiday Inn
www.holidayinn.com

Howard Johnson International
www.hojo.com

Hyatt
www.hyatt.com

La Quinta Inns & Suites
www.lq.com

Marriott International
www.marriott.com

Motel 6
www.motel6.com

Omni Hotels
www.omnihotels.com

Quality Inn
www.qualityinn.com

Radisson Hotels & Resorts
www.radisson.com

Ramada Worldwide
www.ramada.com

Red Roof Inn
www.redroof.com

Residence Inn by Marriott
www.marriott.com/residenceinn

Sheraton Hotels & Resorts
www.sheraton.com

Super 8
www.super8.com

Travelodge
www.travelodge.com

Wyndham Hotels & Resorts
www.wyndham.com

CAR RENTAL AGENCIES

Alamo
www.alamo.com

Avis
www.avis.com

Budget
www.budget.com

Dollar
www.dollar.com

Enterprise
www.enterprise.com

Hertz
www.hertz.com

National
www.nationalcar.com

Rent-A-Wreck
www.rentawreck.com

Thrifty
www.thrifty.com

INDEX

See also Accommodations Index, below.

Accommodations—Vermont

Accommodations—New Hampshire

Accommodations—Maine